LEGAL METHOD:
TEXT AND MATERIALS

C000156515

AUSTRALIA
LBC Information Services
Sydney

CANADA and USA
Carswell
Toronto

NEW ZEALAND
Brooker's
Auckland

SINGAPORE and MALAYSIA
Sweet & Maxwell Asia
Singapore and Kuala Lumpar

LEGAL METHOD: TEXT AND MATERIALS

by

CARL F. STYCHIN, B.A., LL.B., LL.M.
Professor of Law and Social Theory,
University of Reading

LONDON
SWEET & MAXWELL
1999

Published in 1999 by
Sweet & Maxwell Limited of
100 Avenue Road,
London NW3 3PF
Typeset by
Servis Filmsetting Ltd, Manchester
Printed and bound in Great Britain by
Clays Ltd, St Ives plc

A CIP catalogue record for this book
is available from the British Library

ISBN 0 421 634 707

All rights reserved. UK statutory material in this publication is acknowledged as Crown copyright. No part of this publication may be reproduced or transmitted in any form or by any means, or stored in any retrieval system of any nature without prior written permission, except for permitted fair dealing under the Copyright, Designs and Patents Act 1988, or in accordance with the terms of a licence issued by the Copyright Licensing Agency in respect of photocopying and/or reprographic reproduction. Application for permission for other use of copyright material including permission to reproduce extracts in other published works shall be made to the publishers. Full acknowledgment of author, publisher and source must be given. Application for permission for other use of copyright material controlled by the publisher shall be made to the publishers. Material is contained in this publication for which publishing permission has been sought, and for which copyright is acknowledged. Permission to reproduce such material cannot be granted by the publishers and application must be made to the copyright holder.

No natural forests were destroyed to make this product,
only farmed timber was used and re-planted.

©
CARL F. STYCHIN
1999

PREFACE

This text emerged out of course materials developed over several years for the Legal Method module at Keele University. The aim of that course, of which I was course director from 1993–98, was to introduce students, not only to the "traditional" foundations of legal reasoning—statutory interpretation and precedent, as well as a smattering of basic constitutional law and English legal system—but also to introduce them to more socio-legal and theoretical scholarship, including feminist and critical legal theories. This broader based approach to legal education is common to many modules in the Keele joint honours law programme. This text carries on that approach. I sought to create a sourcebook of materials and commentary, along with questions suitable for tutorials and essays, for introductory law courses, covering both "core" doctrinal material, as well as theoretical and empirical perspectives.

The title of the book is not intended to restrict its usage to "Legal Method" courses *per se*. The selection of topics includes material typically found in "English Legal System" and "Introduction to Law" courses. Obviously, the choice of topics and extracts for any casebook is eclectic, and, for an introductory casebook, even more so. While some may claim that the choice of material and the "spin" placed upon it lacks the "neutrality" expected of a casebook, one of the primary goals of this collection is to encourage students to question liberal ideals of "objectivity" and "neutrality", and to encourage critical thinking more generally. The aim is not to indoctrinate, but to stimulate lively debate and skepticism about legal authorities (including the casebook itself!). Too often, in my view, introductory materials fail to stimulate interest in the study of law, encouraging students to memorize facts rather than to think analytically and critically. I have tried to avoid that pitfall.

Because the text seeks to introduce students to theory at an early stage in their legal education, my expectation is that lecturers will "unpack" the material where necessary in lectures, tutorials, and seminars. The commentary is also intended as a "roadmap" through the materials, particularly the more theoretically challenging excerpts.

Finally, on a personal note, I would like to thank my former colleagues at Keele University, who provided an endless source of ideas for the teaching of Legal Method, and I particularly thank those who tutored on the course over the years. Special thanks to Tony Dugdale, who introduced me to teaching Legal Method, and who provided a great deal of assistance, support, and ideas, in the original design of the module. Thanks also to my research assistant, Millicent Hamilton-Hazeley, for her help in tracking down materials. My greatest debt, though, is owed to my Legal Method students who withstood my attempts at experimentation in the design of the course, and whose enthusiasm I will always appreciate and remember.

Carl F. Stychin
London
January 1999

ACKNOWLEDGMENTS

Grateful acknowledgement is made to the following authors and publishers for permission to quote from their works:

ABEL-SMITH, B. and STEVENS, R.: *In Search of Justice: Society and the Legal System* (1968), Penguin

ABRAMCZYK, J.: "The Tyranny of the Majority: Liberalism and Legal Education" (1992) 5 Canadian Journal of Women and the Law 442

ARMSTRONG, N.: "Making Tracks", in *Reform of Civil Procedure: Essays on 'Access to Justice'*, eds. A.A.S. Zuckerman and Ross Cranston (1995). Copyright © The Several Contributors and, in this collection, Adrian Zuckerman and Ross Cranston 1995. Reprinted by permission of Oxford University Press

ATIYAH, P.S.: *Law and Modern Society* (2nd ed., 1995). Copyright © P.S. Atiyah 1983, 1995. Reproduced by permission of Oxford University Press

BAKER, J.H.: "Statutory Interpretation and Parliamentary Intention" (1993) 52 C.L.J. 353

BALE, C.G.: "Parliamentary Debates and Statutory Interpretation: Switching on the Light or Rummaging in the Ashcans of the Legislative Process (1995) 74 Canadian Bar Review 1, Canadian Bar Association

BATES, T. St. J.N.: "The Contemporary Use of Legislative History in the UK" (1995) 54 C.L.J. 127

BELL, J. and ENGLE, Sir G.: *Cross on Statutory Interpretation* (3rd ed., 1995), Butterworths

BOGNADOR, V.: "Britain and the European Community", in *The Changing Constitution*, eds. Jeffrey Jowell and Dawn Oliver (3rd ed., 1994). Reprinted by permission of Oxford University Press

BRADLEY, A.W.: "The Sovereignty of Parliament—in Perpetuity?", in *The Changing Constitution*, eds. Jeffrey Jowell and Dawn Oliver (3rd ed., 1994). Copyright © Jeffrey Jowell and Dawn Oliver 1994. Reprinted by permission of Oxford University Press

BRAZIER, R.: "New Labour, New Constitution?" (1998) 49 N.I.L.Q. 1

BUTTERWORTHS LAW PUBLISHERS LTD: All England Law Reports; New Law Journal

CAPPELLETI, M.: "Alternative Dispute Resolution Processes within the Framework of the World-Wide Access-to-Justice Movement", (1993) 56 M.L.R. 282. Copyright © Modern Law Review Ltd

CARROLL, R.: "The document: Three linked bodies created and guidelines drawn up on decommissioning, release of prisoners and policing" *The Guardian*, April 11, 1998

COLLINS, H.: *Marxism and Law* (1982). Copyright © Hugh Collins 1982. Reprinted by permission of Oxford University Press

CONAGHAN, J.: "Feminist Perspectives on the Law of Tort", in *The Critical Lawyers' Handbook 2*, eds. Paddy Ireland and Per Laleng (1997), Pluto Press

COOTER, R. and ULEN, T.: *Law and Economics* (1998), HarperCollins

COTTERRELL, R.: *The Sociology of Law* (2nd ed., 1992), Butterworths
——: *The Politics of Jurisprudence* (1989), Butterworths

COWNIE, F. and BRADNEY, A.: *English Legal System in Context* (1996), Butterworths

CRAIG, P.: "Formal and Substantive Conceptions of the Rule of Law: An Analytical Framework" [1997] Public Law 467, Sweet & Maxwell Ltd

CRAIG, P. and DE BURCA, G.: *E.C Law: Text, Cases and Materials* (1995). Copyright © Paul Craig and Grainne de Burca 1995. Reprinted by permission of Oxford University Press

CROSS, R. and HARRIS, J.W.: *Precedent in English Law* (4th ed., 1991). Copyright © Lady Cross and Jim Harris 1991. Reprinted by permission of Oxford University Press

DARBYSHIRE, P.: *Eddey on the English Legal System* (6th ed., 1996), Sweet & Maxwell Ltd

DEHN Q.C., C.: "The Woolf Report: Against the Public Interest?", in *Reform of Civil Procedure: Essays on 'Access to Justice'*, eds. A.A.S. Zuckerman and Ross Cranston (1995). Copyright © The Several Contributors and, in this collection, Adrian Zuckerman and Ross Cranston 1995. Reprinted by permission of Oxford University Press

DICEY, A.V.: *An Introduction to the Law of the Constitution* (8th ed., 1915) Macmillan Press Ltd. Copyright © Albert Venn Dicey 1915.

DOWNES, T.A.: *Textbook on Contract* (5th ed., 1997), Blackstone Press Ltd

DWORKIN, R.: *Law's Empire* (1986), HarperCollins Publishers Ltd

ELLIOTT, C. and QUINN, F.: *English Legal System* (1996). Reprinted by permission of Addison Wesley Longman Ltd

FARRAR, J.D. and DUGDALE, A.M.: *Introduction to Legal Method* (3rd ed., 1990), Sweet & Maxwell Ltd

FISS, O.M.: "Against Settlement" (1984) 93 Yale Law Journal 1073. Reprinted by permission of The Yale Law Journal Company and Fred B. Rothman & Company from The Yale Law Journal, Vol. 93, pages 1073–1090

FLETCHER, G.P.: *The Basic Concepts of Legal Thought* (1996). Copyright © 1996 by George P. Fletcher. Used by permission of Oxford University Press, Inc.

FRANK, J.: *Law and the Modern Mind* (1970), Peter Smith

GELDART, W.: *Introduction to English Law* (11th ed., 1995). Reprinted by permission of Oxford University Press

GENN, H.: "Access to Just Settlements: The Case of Medical Negligence", in *Reform of Civil Procedure: Essays on 'Access to Justice'*, eds. A.A.S. Zuckerman and Ross Cranston (1995). Copyright © The Several Contributors and, in this collection, Adrian Zuckerman and Ross Cranston 1995. Reprinted by permission of Oxford University Press

——*Hard Bargaining: Out of Court Settlement in Personal Injury Actions* (1987). Copyright © Hazel Genn 1987. Reprinted by permission of Oxford University Press

——"Tribunals and Informal Justice" (1993) 56 M.L.R. 393. Copyright © Modern Law Review Ltd

GOODRICH, P.: *Reading the Law* (1986), Blackwell Publishers

GRAYCAR, R.: "The Gender of Judgments: An Introduction", in *Public and Private: Feminist Legal Debates*, ed. Margaret Thornton (Melbourne, 1995), Oxford University Press

GRIFFITHS, J.A.G.: *The Politics of the Judiciary* (4th ed., 1991), HarperCollins Publishers Ltd

GRILLO, T.: "The Mediation Alternative: Process Dangers for Women" (1991) 100 Yale Law Journal 1545. Reprinted by permission of The Yale Journal Company and Fred B. Rothman & Company from <u>The Yale Law Journal</u>, Vol. <u>100</u>, pages <u>1545–1610</u>

HARLOW, C.: *Understanding Tort Law* (1987), Sweet & Maxwell Ltd

HARRIS, P.: *An Introduction to Law* (5th ed., 1997), Butterworths

HARTLEY, T.C.: "Five Forms of Uncertainty in European Community Law" (1996) 55 C.L.J. 265

HER MAJESTY'S STATIONERY OFFICE: *Human Rights Bill*. Parliamentary copyright is reproduced with permission of the Controller of Her Majesty's Stationery Office

HEUSTON, R.F.V.: "*Donoghue v. Stevenson* in Retrospect" (1957) 20 M.L.R. 1. Copyright © Modern Law Review Ltd

HORWITZ, M.J.: "The Rule of Law: An Unqualified Human Good?" (1977) 86 Yale Law Journal 561. Reprinted by permission of The Yale Law Journal Company and Fred B. Rothman & Company from <u>The Yale Law Journal</u>, Vol. <u>86</u>, pages <u>561–566</u>

HOWARTH, D.: *Textbook on Tort* (1995), Butterworths

INDUSTRIAL RELATIONS SERVICES/ECLIPSE: *Dawkins v. Department of Environment* [1993] I.R.L.R. 284

INGLEBY, R.: "Court Sponsored Mediation: the Case Against Mandatory Participation" (1993) 56 M.L.R. 441. Copyright © Modern Law Review Ltd

IRVINE, The Lord Chancellor.: "And Justice for everyone" *The Guardian*, April 4, 1998

IRVINE OF LAIRG, Lord.: "The Development of Human Rights in Britain under an Incorporated Convention on Human Rights" [1998] Public Law 221, Sweet & Maxwell Ltd

JOHN HOWARD SOCIETY OF ALBERTA, INC.: *Briefing Paper on Alternative Dispute Resolution*, online publication: <http://www.acjnet.org/docs/alterjhs.html>

JOWELL, J.: "The Rule of Law Today", in *The Changing Constitution*, eds. Jeffrey Jowell and Dawn Oliver (3rd ed., 1994). Copyright © Jeffrey Jowell and Dawn Oliver 1994. Reprinted by permission of Oxford University Press

KWAW, E.M.A.: *The Guide to Legal Analysis, Legal Methodology and Legal Writing* (1992), Emond Montgomery Publications

LEGRAND, P.: "How to Compare Now" (1996) 16 Legal Studies 232, Butterworths

LESTER OF HERNE HILL Q.C., Lord.: "European Human Rights and the British Constitution", in *The Changing Constitution*, eds. Jeffrey Jowell and Dawn Oliver (3rd ed. 1994). Reprinted by permission of Oxford University Press

LORD CHANCELLOR'S DEPARTMENT: Press release: "Lord Chancellor Seeks More Woman Judges" (April 25, 1998); Lord Woolf, "Access to Justice: Final Report to the

Lord Chancellor on the Civil Justice System in England and Wales"; Press Release: "Lord Chancellor Set to Announce Reforms for Civil Appeal System" (July 22, 1998). Crown copyright is reproduced with the permission of the Controller of Her Majesty's Stationery Office

MacCormick, N.: *Legal Reasoning and Legal Theory* (1978). Reprinted by permission of Oxford University Press

McLeod, I.: *Legal Method* (2nd ed. 1996), Macmillan Press Ltd

Manchester, C., Salter, D., Moodie, P. and Lynch, B.: *Exploring the Law: The Dynamics of Precedent & Statutory Interpretation* (1996), Sweet & Maxwell Ltd

Mansell, W., Meteyard, B. and Thompson, A.: *A Critical Introduction to Law* (1995), London: Cavendish Publishing. Reproduced with kind permission of Cavendish Publishing

Markesinis, B.S.: "A Matter of Style" (1994) 110 Law Quarterly Review 607, Sweet & Maxwell Ltd

Marshall, G.: "Interpreting Interpretation in the Human Rights Bill" [1998] Public Law 167, Sweet & Maxwell Ltd

Menski, W.: "Race and Law", in *The Critical Lawyers' Handbook 2*, eds. Paddy Ireland and Per Laleng (1997), Pluto Press

Miers, D.: "Taxing Perks and Interpreting Statutes: *Pepper v. Hart*" (1993) 56 M.L.R. 695. Copyright © Modern Law Review Ltd

Mossman, M.J.: "Feminism and Legal Method: The Difference it Makes". Copyright © 1990. From *At the Boundaries of Law* by Martha Albertson Fineman and Nancy Sweet Thomadsen. Reproduced by permission of Routledge, Inc.

Nicholas, B.: *The French Law of Contract* (2nd ed., 1982). Copyright © J.K.B.M. Nicholas 1992. Reprinted by permission of Oxford University Press

Office for Official Publications of the European Communities: *The Queen v. Immigration Appeal Tribunal, ex parte Antonissen* [1991] E.C.R. 1–745

Paterson, A.: "The Racial, Ethnic and Cultural Values Underpinning Current Legal Education", in *The Critical Lawyers' Handbook 2*, eds. Paddy Ireland and Per Laleng (1997), Pluto Press

Rifkin, J.: "Mediation from a Feminist Perspective: Promise and Problems" (1984) 2 Law and Inequality 21

Sainsbury, R. and Genn, H.: "Access to Justice: Lessons from Tribunals" in *Reform of Civil Procedure: Essays on 'Access to Justice'*, eds. A.A.S. Zuckerman and Ross Cranston. Copyright © The Several Contributors and, in this collection, Adrian Zuckerman and Ross Cranston 1995. Reprinted by permission of Oxford University Press

Sayers, M. and Webb, A.: "Franks Revisited: A Model of the Ideal Tribunal" (1990) 9 Civil Justice Quarterly 36, Sweet & Maxwell Ltd

Scottish Office: *Scottish Office White Paper: Scotland's Parliament*. Crown copyright is reproduced with the permission of the Controller of Her Majesty's Stationery Office

Shaw, J.: *Law of the European Union* (2nd ed., 1996), Macmillan Press Ltd

Sheldon, S.: *Beyond Control: Medical Power and Abortion Law* (1997), Pluto Press

Slapper, G. and Kelly, D.: *Principles of the English Legal System* (3rd ed., 1997), London: Cavendish Publishing. Reproduced with kind permission of Cavendish Publishing

SMART, C.: *Feminism and the Power of Law* (1989), Routledge

STREET, H.: *Justice in the Welfare State* (1975), Sweet & Maxwell Ltd

SUGARMAN, D.: "A Hatred of Disorder: Legal Science, Liberalism and Imperialism", in *Dangerous Supplements*, ed. Peter Fitzpatrick (1991), Pluto Press

THE INCORPORATED COUNCIL OF LAW REPORTING FOR ENGLAND AND WALES: Weekly Law Reports; Queen's Bench Division; Appeal Cases; King's Bench Law Reports

THOMPSON, E.P.: *Whigs and Hunters* (1990), Penguin Books

UNITED STATES GOVERNMENT PRINTING OFFICE: *McBoyle v. USA* 293 US 25 (1930)

VAGO, S.: *Law and Society* (3rd ed., 1991), Prentice Hall

VANDEVELDE, K.J.: *Thinking Like a Lawyer* (1996). Copyright © 1996 by Westview Press, Inc. Reprinted by permission of Westview Press, a member of Perseus Books, L.L.C.

WALDRON, J.: *The Law* (1990), Routledge

WELSH OFFICE: *Welsh Office White Paper: National Assembly for Wales*. Crown copyright is reproduced with the permission of the Controller of Her Majesty's Stationery Office

WILLIAMS, P.J.: *The Alchemy of Race and Rights* (1991). Copyright © 1991 by the President and Fellows of Harvard College. Reprinted by permission of Harvard University Press

ZANDER, M.: *Cases and Materials on the English Legal System* (7th ed., 1996), Butterworths

——"The Government's Plans on Legal Aid and Conditional Fees" (1998) 61 M.L.R. 538. Copyright © Modern Law Review Ltd.

ZUCKERMAN, A.A.S.: "Lord Woolf's Access to Justice: Plus ça change" (1996) 59 M.L.R. 773. Copyright © Modern Law Review Ltd

While every care has been taken to establish and acknowledge copyright, and contact the copyright owners, the publishers tender their apologies for any accidental infringement. They would be pleased to come to a suitable arrangement with the rightful owners in each case.

CONTENTS

Contents

11. JUDGE MADE LAW: A CASE STUDY ON THE LAW OF NEGLIGENCE   255

12. PROCEDURAL ASPECTS OF LEGAL METHOD: INTRODUCTION TO THE CIVIL JUSTICE SYSTEM   293

13. PROCEDURAL ASPECTS OF LEGAL METHOD: THE ADVERSARIAL SYSTEM AND ALTERNATIVES   327

14. COMPARATIVE LEGAL METHOD: THE CIVILIAN TRADITION   364

TABLE OF CASES

TABLE OF STATUTES

TABLE OF STATUTORY INSTRUMENTS

1

INTRODUCTION TO LEGAL METHOD: APPROACHES TO LAW AND LEGAL REASONING

In this first chapter, we begin with an introduction to legal reasoning and analysis. The readings are designed to help you to think critically about the basic question "what is law", and to think about the varied meanings of that term. One of the famous debates over the character of law involves two divergent ways of thinking about law—positivism and natural law—and we consider those schools of thought in this chapter. The debate between positivists and natural lawyers is one of the most famous confrontations in legal theory.

Following on from that debate, this chapter includes a range of readings which inquire into the characteristics of law and legal reasoning from a variety of perspectives. Many of these readings apply ways of thinking developed in other academic disciplines—such as sociology and economics—to legal analysis. This type of academic work is known as "interdisciplinary", because it involves bringing the learning which has been developed in one field of inquiry to the discipline of law. This material is important because it can provide lawyers (and students of law) with a broader and deeper understanding of the way legal analysis operates.

Finally, in this chapter we consider legal education. Since most students studying this text will be introductory law students, the readings in this section may be useful for you to consider throughout your studies. These selections might be characterised as critical, because of the ways in which the authors interrogate how legal education is conducted. The authors argue that the way in which students are taught—and what they are taught—is highly political, but the politics of legal education is often disguised and made to appear politically neutral and objective. For example, beginning law students are taught that there is a "method" to legal reasoning—and that is the title of this book—but you should also ask yourself, even while you are learning this method, whether there are not other methods of analysing problems which might be preferable to legal reasoning. Thus, one of the aims of this chapter (and, indeed, this book) is to provoke you to think critically about law, legal reasoning, and the way in which law is taught to students in universities.

What is the law?

If you begin by asking yourself what we mean by the term "law", you will probably assume that it presupposes the existence of a society. Law is often conceived, by lawyers and others alike, as a set of rules which govern a society and create a structure of authority or government to run the social order. In the seventeenth century, the English writer Thomas Hobbes explained and justified the existence of rules and authority in terms of a "social contract". In our original state, Hobbes argued, we lived without rules, which ensured that life was (in his famous phrase) nasty, brutish, and short. In time, people came to realise that an alternative might be preferable, and they entered into agreements with each other; creating rules which governed their relationships. In social contract terms, law might be understood as the set of rules and regulations of the social contract, and those rules are enforced by political institutions, which we refer to as the state or government. In this theory, the idea of law also includes the notion of enforcement of the rules with punishments (or *sanctions*) which follow from the disobedience of rules. Thus, for proponents of social contract theory, law might be said to reflect the values of the population, and this value system, which the legal system advances, might also be called an *ideology*, made up of political, economic, moral and social values. As we will see throughout this book, most of us never *actually* agreed to the laws in force in this society, and the ideology which underpins the legal system may well reflect the interests and beliefs of only some people. But the idea that there is an ideology which underpins the legal order is one to which we shall frequently return. We will also see in this chapter that understanding law simply as a set of rules does not fully answer the question of what constitutes law. We begin with an historical consideration of the question.

Peter Goodrich, *Reading the Law* (Blackwell, Oxford, 1986), pp. 3–13:

"One of the most longstanding and intractable of the debates surrounding the study of law concerns the nature and definition of the term law itself. At different times and in different cultures the term law may be taken to refer to institutions as radically different as magic, song-contests, vendetta (feuding), trial by ordeal and the rules of war. Even within the relative homogeneity of the western legal tradition, law has taken very diverse forms and has been derived from very distinct sources. At different stages in the development of western law it has been said variously that law 'comes from' God, from nature or the 'natural order of things', from the monarch, from the various forms of commonwealth or sovereignty, from the 'spirit of the people' or from custom and social usage, to name but a few of the more acceptable or prevalent views. Obviously the way in which we define law will, in terms of the examples given, make a considerable difference to the requisite manner of its study; if law comes from God then it would be best to be theologians or priests for the purposes of studying it professionally, whereas if it is really self-help or vendetta then skill with an axe or a gun is more likely to be useful than any knowledge of rules or texts or any ability to argue. The question posed by the difficulty of defining law is a serious practical problem for students and practitioners of the law, and it raises directly important issues of how law is to be differentiated from other social phenomena. Such issues go to the very heart of the professional status of law as a discipline and indeed of lawyers as its interpreters. In the present chapter we shall outline the traditional modes of defining law by reference to its ideational (conceptual) and institutional (legal) sources and shall then comment more broadly upon the practical meaning of the status law. . . .

To claim that law is a distinct enterprise, that it is independent of other forms of social control and requires institutions and experts, indeed a science, for its proper organization and functioning, is a fairly constant claim within the western legal tradition. Despite the apparent diversity of both the form and the content of law during the course of its lengthy history and of the very different social, political and economic roles played by the law, the legal institution itself has maintained a virtually uninterrupted doctrinal belief in the distinctiveness of law, a belief in its unity and its separation from other phenomena of social control. The two claims, those of unity and of separation, have traditionally been closely linked in legal doctrine; law is kept separate and distinct from other institutions and forms of control precisely by virtue of being a unity, by virtue of having an 'essential' characteristic which distinguishes law from all else. That 'essence' or unifying feature of law has been variable in its content but relatively constant in its form: the formal unity of law has traditionally been based upon its derivation from an absolute source or origin; 'a unitary necessity or cause' is singled out as the basis and origin of all law. Although the content of the ideational source of law has varied within legal doctrine, as we shall see, from being the divine commandments, to the dictates of nature or 'natural law', justice, the commands of the sovereign or even the logical entailments of a basic rule or norm, the conceptual characteristics of the absolute source of law do not greatly alter. The divine origin of law becomes the secular sovereign, the State or even the 'will of the people', but as a source of law it retains its quality as an external and absolute justification for legal regulation, discipline and law. This external, non-legal, legitimation of the legal order provides the law with its ideational unity and renders the wide spectrum of substantive rules into a 'system' of rules. . . . The ideational source of law refers to the 'idea' or 'belief' that lies at the basis of the system of law and provides, either directly or indirectly, an answer to the question of why law is authoritative, the question of why it should be obeyed. The commands and the judgments traditionally obeyed as 'the law' within a given community must 'come from' somewhere or be derived from some acceptable—even if mythical or notional—conceptual source of law. The question of the ideational source of law here invokes the profound and extremely contentious issue of the role of law as the form of communal order: what is it that binds the community, that gives rise to the sense of belonging and the habit of obeying which seem, historically, to be inseparable social functions? We cannot here endeavour to answer directly such questions but we can point to the traditional doctrinal resolutions to the problem of the authority or ideational source and legitimacy of law, and we can also refer to the importance that this definition of law in terms of its source has for legal practice, for the interpretation and application of law. . . .

The assumptions that lawyers make as to the inevitability, the validity and the moral benefit of legal regulation are crucial to their practice and to the maintenance of legal rules, to the ideology of law within the industrialized western nations. Such assumptions as to the conceptual unity of law are, however, increasingly infrequently utilized as explicit sources of law, reference to moral, political and economic factors generally being seen as a function of interpretation and argumentation—of implicit or tacit sources of law—rather than of formally designated legal authority. At the same time as stressing the practical importance of the ideational source of law, we would also rapidly point out that the abstract and external, ideational source of law is neither the most obvious nor the most frequently stated meaning of source of law in contemporary legal cultures. The preferred view is currently one which stresses the institutional sources of law rather than directly or consciously elaborating the myth of an origin or essence of law or indeed the dogmatic status of legal science or legal reason as sources of law. The current legal wisdom views law as a tradition and as a process or practice of regulation. Rather than defining law, legal doctrine is now more content to see it as a series of traditionally established texts and similarly established techniques for the interpretation of those texts . . . The institutional source of law is here seen to be the established practice of the legal institution and of its officials—law is taken to be what lawyers 'recognize' as law."

Our focus in this chapter will be on conceptual or ideational sources for the definition of law. In later chapters, we will shift to institutional sources for understanding what counts as law. The difficulty of defining what "law" is should be readily apparent if we think, for a moment, of the different ways in which the term is used in the English language. It encompasses both scientific laws (such as the law of gravity), and laws created to govern human behaviour. The different ways in which the term is used also leads us to a consideration of the idea of *positivism* as an approach to understanding law.

George P. Fletcher, *Basic Concepts of Legal Thought* (Oxford University Press, New York, 1996), pp. 28–38:

"When a legislature enacts a proposed law, the law is called a statute or statutory law. When a scientist validates a hypothesis, he or she confirms a scientific law. This correlation in the use of the word 'law' holds across a large number of languages. This usage of the word 'law' (*Gesetz* in (German), *loi* (French), *zakon* (Russian), *ley* (Spanish) or *hok* (Hebrew)) should make us sit up and take notice. Wherever you go in Europe or the Middle East, you will hear lawyers referring to the work product of their parliaments in the same idiom as physics teachers use to describe the law of gravity or the second law of thermodynamics. This is true, we should note, only for the word used to refer to the law laid down by an authoritative legislature. The notion of 'higher law' as expressed in the terms like *Recht* and *droit* does not fit this pattern. There may, of course, be exceptions, but the correlation between the word for legislated law and scientific law is sufficiently strong that we must wonder about its implications.

Why should one think about human laws as though they were akin to scientific laws? Do we think that when Congress enacts a law, its action will be translated automatically into conforming behavior? Perhaps the question should be put the other way around: Do we expect falling objects to obey the law in the way that humans are expected to obey the criminal law? It seems that either there is some important point underlying the persistent use of the same word for human and scientific laws or, alternatively, we are dreadfully confused.

We are not confused. Nor are we fully conscious of the ways in which the popular model of scientific laws, lurking in the background, influences our thinking about law. The idea of law stands, more than anything, for inevitability. When a law applies, things cannot be otherwise; they conform necessarily to the law. Scientific laws represent more than just an observed correlation between cause and effect. As the eighteenth-century German philosopher Immanuel Kant put it in developing his theory of causation, the very fact that we perceive causal relationships means that we bring to our observations an innate notion of necessary connection. We see necessity in the spring sun's melting of winter's ice and therefore we describe the relationship as a causal law. To speak about laws, then, is to speak about necessity.

One thing we know for sure, however, is that human laws are not necessarily obeyed. Legislatures can pass laws telling people how to behave, but there is no necessary response from the public at large. Sometimes people conform to changes in the statutory law; sometimes they continue to do what they want to, despite new decrees from the powers that be. This is particularly the case if the law seeks to change pleasurable habits, such as those connected to smoking, drinking, using drugs, or sex. Yet there is an element of inevitability or necessity in human laws as well as scientific laws. The necessity arises not in the response of state officials to violations of the law. Representatives of the state assume that violations of the law necessitate a response. The most familiar of these responses is criminal condemnation and punishment. But the range of possible responses includes compensation for injury and judicial injunction to compel compliance with the law.

One assumption unites the phenomena of scientific law, as common people perceive law in nature, and laws by which society lives. The facts may diverge from the law. When a divergence of this sort occurs under scientific laws, the appropriate remedy is to reformulate the law. When, for example, the evidence became inescapable that the planets moved in elliptical orbits rather than in perfect circles, the response was to abandon Copernicus's model and adopt one that better fit the facts. When a similar divergence occurs in the realm of human conduct under human laws, we assume that the right thing to do is to change not the law, but rather to discipline the deviant conduct. This need to change conduct produces the practices of stigmatization, sanctioning, and punishment that some philosophers, call positivists, have taken to be the essence of the legal system. The positivist premise is that a legal system worth its name must use force to close the gap between norms and actual behavior. The nineteenth-century German philosopher G.W.F. Hegel wrote in metaphysical terms of the criminal's Wrong displacing Society's Right, with punishment of the criminal as the only means of reinstating Right over Wrong. We would not so readily engage in this assumption, were it not for the association in our thinking between scientific and human laws. The idea of law carries with it the ideal of full compliance. . . .

Antipositivists deny the proposition that 'all law is enacted law.' They claim that some principles of law simply exist and are perceived within a particular legal culture. As we have noted, this second, indwelling conception of law is expressed in the Continental European languages as *Recht* (German), *droit* (French), *pravo* (Russian), *derecho* (Spanish). English originally used the term 'Right' as the analogue to *Recht*. This comes through clearly in the seventeenth-century English decision, Dr Bonham's case, in which the great English judge Lord Coke (pronounced: Cook) declared a statute of Parliament void as a violation of 'common right and reason.' The assumption guiding Coke's reasoning was that the court could perceive, without a written source to back it up, what 'common right' requires. If the will of Parliament was at odds with the court's perception, then so much the worse for Parliament. . . .

It is hard to know why the term Right has atrophied in English usage. The idea survives in Continental European languages, but the proper terminology now eludes lawyers in the common law tradition. It may be that a long line of positivist legal thinkers, extending from Thomas Hobbes in the seventeenth century to H.L.A. Hart in the twentieth century, has influenced the language we use in discussing jurisprudence. Admittedly, the notion of Right survives in the idiom of individual and human rights. . . . Consider the debate between those who advocate a pregnant woman's right to an abortion and those who insist upon the fetus's right to life. Both sides of the debate treat these asserted rights as morally true. In this respect debates about personal or human rights fulfill the normative role of the abstract theory of Right in Continental European legal cultures. . . .

The debate between the positivists and the nonpositivists has recurred over the last three hundred years. The issues seem always to be the same—is all law enacted law?—but the political motives change. Positivism is usually associated with the defense of legislative as opposed to judicial authority. The English philosophers Thomas Hobbes (1588–1679) and Jeremy Bentham (1748–1832) sought to vindicate the authority of Parliament to legislate for the common good—without being curtailed by the supposedly given and unchangeable principles of the common law. At the outset of the debate, the antipositivist Sir Edward Coke (1552–1634) led the fight for the power of the courts to limit both legislative and executive authority.

In the mid-twentieth century, the debate took on new contours. Positivism provided a vehicle for de-politicizing legal analysis. Because positivism provides an account of the entire legal system rather than the justice of particular laws, regimes that were stable and predictable qualified as legal systems. It did not matter whether they lacked moral and democratic legitimacy. Nazi Germany, South Africa, and Communist governments in Eastern Europe could meet the supposedly neutral criteria of regular obedience to enacted rules. . . .

Of course, no one expected in the 1960s and 1970s that the most unjust regimes in the world —South Africa, the Soviet Union, the German Democratic Republic—would soon fall. Perhaps a positivist, non-moral approach toward law served the interests of peaceful co-operation in the hostile world of the cold war. After all, one could think that in South Africa under apartheid, all law was enacted law. This meant that regardless of the immorality of the legal system, it was still a legal system. The South African judges even prided themselves on deploying their wits to counteract the worst effects of apartheid. One might say the same for the functioning of the courts under the more or less reformed Communist systems of the 1980s. There is something fundamentally unsatisfying, however, about approaching law in a way that blurs the distinction between legal systems that survive and those that the people overthrow at the first opportunity."

For Fletcher, the definition of law offered by positivism—that any law which satisfies the appropriate technical criteria of enactment "counts" as law—is problematic because of the absence of reference to its *moral* quality. For the positivist, by contrast, the *validity* of a rule—whether it counts as law or not—is determined simply by reference to the question of whether it has been enacted in accordance with the formal requirements set down by the legal system. As we will see in Chapter 2, in the United

Kingdom, traditionally that has meant that whatever is enacted by the Queen in Parliament is law. By contrast, an anti-positivist—that is, a proponent of *natural law* —argues that in order to "count" as valid law, positive law must be measured success- fully against some standard found outside of the legal system. Under a natural law approach, there must exist some moral code of principles which exists irrespective of positive law, and against which it can be judged. For the proponent of natural law, the "unjust" law, as defined by the criteria of natural law, does not count as law properly called and, as a consequence, the individual may be under no moral duty to obey such a "law". This obviously raises interesting political questions about when people are entitled to disobey positive law.

The positivist tradition has dominated Anglo-American legal thought, despite the concerns raised by proponents of natural law. As we will see in Chapter 2, the emer- gence of the principle of Parliamentary supremacy (that Parliament may make or unmake any law no matter what its substantive content) is most easily understandable in terms of positivism. The basic tenets of the two approaches to legality have been summarised by Cotterrell. First, the positivist tradition.

Roger Cotterrell, *The Sociology of Law* (2nd ed., Butterworths, London, 1992), p. 9:

"In essence, positivism is a philosophical position which asserts that scientific knowledge derives from observation of the data of experience and not from speculation that seeks to 'look behind' observed facts for ultimate causes, meanings or essences. What we observe is, therefore, what really exists—and, scientifically speaking, all that exists. Hence judgments of value, of what is good or bad, political or policy questions, questions about the ultimate nature of things which cannot be determined by generalisations from observation—all of these are unscientific. Because these matters are subjective, existing only in the minds of indi- viduals, they are unanalysable by scientific means. In the strongest versions of positivism they do not constitute knowledge at all. Fact and value are thus rigidly separated. Science should be 'value free' in two senses. It should not, itself, make value judgments about what it observes. And it should not seek to inquire into the meaning or ultimate significance of the values held by those it observes. This is not to say that values cannot be studied but they can be studied only as the observable preferences and commitments of actual individuals, not as having sig- nificance or reality in their own right.

    In the Anglo-American legal world, and indeed to a greater or lesser extent in most modern highly-developed legal systems, a positivist outlook on law is the typical outlook of lawyers and informs much legal scholarship and teaching. Law consists of data—primarily rules—which can be recognised as such by relatively simple tests or 'rules of recognition'. A familiar such simple test is that the rules have passed through certain formal stages of a legislative process, or (less simple) that they can be derived from the *ratio decidendi*—the essential grounds of decision—of a case decided by a court having the jurisdiction and authority to lay down new rules in such a case. According to a positivist conception, these rules of law—possibly with some subsidiary legal phenomena—constitute the law, the data which it is the lawyer's task to analyse and order. In this sense, law is a 'given'—part of the data of experience. If it can be recognised as existing according to certain observational tests it can be analysed. The tests by which legal positivism recognises the existence of law or particular laws are thus analogous to those by which a scientist might recognise the presence of a particular chemical."

Roger Cotterrell, *The Politics of Jurisprudence* (Butterworths, London, 1989), p. 120:

"In contrast to legal positivism stands a tradition of thought adopting an apparently diamet- rically opposed position—that law cannot be properly understood except in moral terms;

that it is fundamentally a moral phenomenon; that questions of law's nature and existence cannot be isolated from questions about its moral worth. This tradition is usually termed *natural law theory*. Its history extends through at least 2,500 years of Western philosophy. One of its most powerful themes (though an ambiguous one, as will appear) is expressed in the declaration that *lex iniusta non est lex*—an unjust law is no law at all. It may well be that statements like this in this history of natural law theory have never meant what they seem, at face value, to mean. Nevertheless, they do suggest the persistent claim that questions about the nature of law and the conditions of its existence as an authoritative normative order cannot be treated in isolation from questions about its moral foundations. Thus typically, in many different ways throughout its long history, natural law theory has postulated the existence of moral principles having a validity and authority independent of human enactment, and which can be thought of as a 'higher' or more fundamental law against which the worth or authority of human law can be judged. This fundamental 'natural law' is variously seen as derived from human nature, the natural conditions of existence of humanity, the natural order of the universe, or the eternal law of God. The method of discovering it is usually claimed to be human reason. Natural law thus requires no human legislator. Yet it stands in judgment on the law created by human legislators."

The strength of the positivist tradition as a means of understanding law and the *legitimacy* of law within the English legal tradition has been explored by Atiyah. Of particular interest for us is the way in which positivism sought to answer claims about the legitimacy of law which were grounded in the idea of a social contract and the consent of the governed to the law.

P.S. Atiyah, *Law and Modern Society* (2nd ed., Oxford University Press, Oxford, 1995), pp. 148–151:

"This kind of analytical jurisprudence [the positivist approach] had its origins in the work of Jeremy Bentham (1748–1832) and John Austin (1790–1859). Bentham was a great law reformer and critic of legal and social institutions, and one of the things which he was reacting against was the tendency of lawyers, as he saw it, to assume that law had some legitimacy over and above that given to it by its own creation or observance. Eighteenth-century lawyers often justified particular laws and legal institutions by talking the language of 'natural law' and 'natural rights'. For example, rights of property were seen as 'natural' and the function of property law (and hence the law of trespass, theft, and so on) was therefore to preserve the natural rights of the property owner. Much of this in turn derived from the works of John Locke, whose (second) *Treatise on Civil Government* came to be regarded as an apologia for the Revolution of 1688 and was treated as a sort of political bible by the Whig landowners through most of the eighteenth century. To Locke the only function of government was to preserve and protect the natural rights which men had 'in the state of nature'; it had to be assumed that men in the state of nature had voluntarily consented to the establishment of the State by a 'social contract'; it was this which gave legitimacy to laws and the State, and once the ruler neglected to do his job properly (as of course James II had done) it was right and justifiable for the people to overthrow him by revolution.

But to Bentham, all this talk of natural law and natural rights was just nonsense—'nonsense upon stilts' he called it. The 'state of nature' and the 'social contract' were pure fictions. Property rights did not antedate the existence of society and law; on the contrary, it was only in a society and through law that the very idea of ownership of property had any meaning. So it was impossible to insist that societies existed in order to protect pre-existing property rights. Laws were a human creation, made by humans, for humans; there was nothing sacred or mysterious about them, and bad laws could be and ought to be changed. In propagating this message Bentham was, in the long run, completely successful. None of Bentham's ideas has more powerfully taken root than the notion that laws are mere human creations which can be made and unmade at man's mere pleasure. Indeed, it is permissible to wonder (as previously suggested) whether we are today not too prone to think that modern societies can get along happily without the elements of mystery and majesty and sacredness about law. But to recognize Bentham's triumph in these respects is not to say that the Lockean tradition is completely dead; there is still powerful support for the idea that the State and the laws derive their legitimacy from the consent of the people; and the notion that the function of society and law is to protect pre-existing moral rights is still vigorously defended by some modern theorists.

One of the curious by-products of Bentham's work was the positivist tradition which has had such a profound influence on the development of English law and legal thinking since his time. 'Positivism' is a label which has been used somewhat imprecisely for a variety of theories and ideologies, but, for present purposes, the principal beliefs associated with the positivist tradition can be said to be these: first, laws are commands of human beings addressed to other human beings; secondly, there is no necessary connection between law and morals; thirdly, the analysis of law and legal concepts is a true 'scientific' inquiry which is concerned with the formal requirements of valid law, and not with its content; and fourthly, judges, when deciding new points of law, must confine themselves to 'legal' arguments and not rely upon moral or policy arguments."

QUESTIONS

- Compare "legal positivism" and "natural law". Which do you find more persuasive as a legal theory?

- Do you think that a morally bad law still "counts" as law?

- Give a contemporary example where an attempt was made to justify the disobedience of the law by claiming that a "higher" natural law ran counter to positive law.

Many of the legal problems we will focus on in this text should make you skeptical about whether legal reasoning can be separated from moral or political arguments, and whether legal method is, in any sense, a scientific or *objective* inquiry which is "value free". Despite the criticisms, the underlying beliefs of the positivist tradition have had an enormous impact upon the way in which legal reasoning and decision making is understood in this country and, for that reason, a working familiarity with its basic tenets is important.

A COURT-CENTRED APPROACH TO LAW AND ALTERNATIVES

Up to this point, our focus has been on understanding what law is through an examination of the positivist/natural law debate. That debate concerns the question what "counts" as a valid law. However, for most people—lawyers, non-lawyers, and law students alike—an answer to the question "what is law?" would centre on the work of the courts. This "court-oriented view of law", as Atiyah describes, is widespread within the English legal tradition but, as we shall see shortly, it might also create a rather incomplete definition of the term "law".

P.S. Atiyah, _Law and Modern Society_ (2nd ed., Oxford University Press, Oxford, 1995), pp. 1–7:

"This association between the law and the legal process, between the rules of law and the courts, is one which lawyers are particularly prone to make. To a lawyer, the courts are the very heart and centre of the law. A modern lawyer would find it impossible to conceive of a legal system which contained rules of law, but no courts. In fact he would probably find it less difficult to imagine a society which contained courts but no rules of law.

Why should this be so? It might seem that logically speaking laws come first, and that courts are merely secondary. After all, in modern society it is the primary function of the courts to apply and enforce the law which actually exists. And anyhow courts and judges are themselves creatures which owe their status, their authority, and in a sense their very existence to the law. It is the law itself which tells us that this elderly gentleman sitting on the dais in that Victorian building in the Strand known as the Royal Courts of Justice, is a judge of the High Court, and that while he sits there he actually _is_ the court.

Moreover, anyone who looks at the whole machinery of government in the broadest sense might find it odd that lawyers should place the courts at the centre of their legal universe. Isn't that a bit like pre-Copernican astronomy? Isn't Parliament the real sun round which the law revolves? Acts of Parliament after all are very real laws, as lawyers would unhesitatingly agree. And Acts of Parliament have a very tangible 'existence'. They are often quite solid documents running to a hundred pages or more. You can buy them, and bind them into volumes, as lawyers do. In them you will find all sorts of rules which often say very little or nothing about the courts or judges who are to enforce them.

Then again, it must be admitted that there are some laws—sometimes extensive and complex bodies of law—which are rarely handled by ordinary courts and judges at all. This is particularly true of modern welfare state legislation, such as the law relating to social security. This enormous mass of law defines the conditions under which people are entitled to a wide variety of welfare benefits, and how these benefits are to be calculated in particular cases. There is a great deal of this law and it is complex and difficult to find. But the point is that it is not generally administered or applied by ordinary courts, judges, or magistrates. For the most part it is administered by civil servants working in the Department of Social Security—the DSS. People who want to claim benefits go to their local DSS office and fill in a form. The form is processed by officials. It is true that a special system of tribunals exists to which the citizen can appeal if he is not satisfied by the initial decisions of the officials. And these tribunals hear cases and decide them according to the law, in much the same way (though with far less formality) as ordinary courts. But lawyers rarely penetrate into these tribunals, and they certainly would not think of them, as they think of the ordinary courts, as being at the very centre of the legal system.

So it may seem curious that lawyers tend to identify 'the law' so heavily with courts and judges. But there are reasons for it, some historical, some practical, and others perhaps less easy to classify.

Among the historical reasons for the modern lawyer's pre-Copernican perception of the legal universe we can identify two factors in particular. The first is that it is not true, in a historical sense, to say that laws came before courts. The central court of the modern English legal system—the High Court of Justice—is the direct descendant of a number of old courts, some of them dating back to the twelfth century, which were never created by a deliberate act of law-making. These courts grew up gradually as offshoots of the authority of the King and, as the very word 'court' indicates, these courts of justice were originally a part of the royal court. They were not created by law in order to administer pre-existing laws. They were created, or grew up, in order to solve pressing practical questions—to dispose of arguments, to solve disputes, and to suppress violence and theft. As they developed into what we would today recognize as courts of law, they actually created the law as they went along. Eventually their decisions began to fall into regular and predictable patterns, people began to take notes of what the judges were deciding, and in due course there emerged the modern 'law reports'. A substantial body of English law was created in this way, and much of it remains in force to this day, modified and modernized in all sorts of respects both by more recent judicial decisions and by Acts of Parliament. This part of the law, usually known as the 'common law', was thus created by the courts in the very process of deciding cases before them.

So when the modern lawyer thinks of the common law it is not surprising if he still tends to think of the courts as in some sense primary, and the law as secondary, rather than the other way around. What is more, the old common law remains in a sense the more fundamental part even of modern English law. In sheer bulk modern legislation is no doubt outstripping the common law, but naturally enough the common law tended to deal with more essential and basic legal issues than much modern legislation. The common law was the *first* part of the law to be created, and the first part of the law in any society must necessarily deal with essentials. Naturally the common law evolved the basic principles of the criminal law—it was the common law which first prohibited murder, violence, theft, and rape. Similarly, much of our basic property law was first laid down by common law courts, and so was the law of civil liability. The law of contract and the law of torts (or civil wrongs) were very largely created by the courts out of the simplest of ideas—that it is wrong to harm or injure others. Although much of this law has been amended and qualified in all manner of ways in modern times, there is a sense in which the modern lawyer tends still to see the common law as the central repository of legal ideas and principles. Given the very basic values and interests recognized by the common law, this is hardly surprising, and this also helps to explain why courts are still so very central to the way lawyers think about law.

The second historical factor which helps to explain the lawyer's perspective on these matters is that until quite recent times the courts were, relatively speaking, a far more important part of the whole machinery of government than they are today. In modern times the day-to-day administration of government lies in the hands of vast armies of officials in central and local government, including in particular the police; and at the central level, the authority of Parliament is generally undisputed and can readily be used to overturn rules of law laid down by the courts which do not find favour with the government. So in one sense the courts are today a small, though important, part of a very extensive machine. But in historical terms this is all a fairly recent development. Until the eighteenth century the machinery of government was very weak, at both central and local levels. Parliament's law-making activities were confined within fairly narrow limits in practice, and so the role of the courts was then relatively far more important than it is today. Indeed, it is widely thought by historians that the early common law courts were deliberately used as one of the main instruments by which royal authority was extended over the whole country in the twelfth century and onwards. It is from these, and perhaps even earlier, days that the custom began of sending judges out on assize, travelling from town to town, hearing cases, helping to create a body of uniform law across the country, and at the same time, showing the people that the authority of the King extended to every corner of his realm. . . .

There are, in addition, other very practical reasons why lawyers tend to have such a court-oriented view of law. One of them is the simple fact that the courts are where the lawyer goes, on behalf of his clients, when disputes arise which cannot be settled amicably. Just as the civil servant doubtless tends to have a government-oriented vision of law and regulation, because most problems that he deals with tend to get settled within or by governments and government departments, so, for similar reasons, the lawyer sees the courts as the focus of the system of dispute settlement in which he is involved.

A related factor is that when disputes arise it is frequently the case that both the facts and the law applicable to those facts may be unclear. When this happens, a lawyer tends to take a severely practical approach to the question of legal rights and duties: he asks himself what a court is likely to decide if the case comes before it. Indeed, this can quite often be a necessary exercise even where the facts appear clear enough to the client and the lawyer, but there is great difficulty about proving them. To the lawyer, a fact is really a provable fact or it is nothing. Similarly, where the law is uncertain, or where its application is uncertain in particular cases, the lawyer's main concern is with the available lines of argument—he knows that some forms of legal argument are acceptable and others less so—and with the probable outcomes. He is in fact interested in *predicting* what a court is likely to do. This does not, of course, mean that all law is nothing more than a series of predictions about how judges and other officials of the legal system are likely to behave in certain circumstances. It is absurd to suggest that the law prohibiting murder is really just a prediction that anybody who commits murder and is brought before the courts will be sent to gaol for life, or until the Home Secretary chooses to release him. But it is nevertheless a fact of life that practising lawyers, when faced with legal problems, habitually ask themselves: If I had to argue this in court, how would I present the case? How would the judge be likely to react? It is also a fact that making predictions of this kind is not always something that can easily be done by merely looking the law up in books. The lawyer needs a 'feel' for how a judge is likely to react to his case, and this is something which can normally be acquired only by actually practising in the courts and appearing regularly before the judges.

It is this which gives some truth to the aphorism, 'the law is what the court says it is'. Snappy sayings like this can be misleading if pressed too far (for instance, judges themselves do not think the law is merely what they say it is), but there is undoubtedly some truth in them. In this last analysis it doesn't matter what is in the books, the law reports, even Acts of Parliament. If a judge sentences someone to gaol, then to gaol he will assuredly go. The judge may have got it wrong, he may even be perverse, but the immediate result is the same. Of course there may be the possibility of an appeal. But the decision of the appeal court may be equally wrong or perverse. Then what *that* court decides is what matters. Perhaps it is wrong to suggest that this is what counts 'in the last analysis', because obviously if judges habitually flouted Acts of Parliament or established precedents, they would be removed from office. But that is to enter the realms of fantasy. It is because judges don't behave in these extreme ways that one can safely assert that in the last analysis what they decide is the law.

Finally, there are other factors of a less readily identifiable nature which tend to make the lawyer think of courts as the centre of the law. In particular, the leaders of the legal profession tend to be seen, both by the public and also by the profession, as the judges, particularly the high court and appeal court judges. Most able barristers see judicial appointment as the apex of a successful career at the Bar. Judges actually decide cases over which lawyers have pondered and argued. So naturally lawyers are encouraged in their tendency to think of the law as something almost wholly associated with, or even dependent upon, the courts."

In focusing upon the courts as the centre of the legal universe, the implicit assumption is that law can be understood as a means for the resolution of disputes through the machinery of the state. After all, the common law courts, as Atiyah describes, were created by the King as a means to solve disputes, prevent violence, and to consolidate his authority throughout the realm. Courts today continue to be an important part of the machinery of modern government, although they are *relatively* less important given the rise of other elements of the state, such as the administrative agencies and dispute resolution tribunals described by Atiyah. However, Cownie and Bradney argue that this focus on the institutions of the state as the centre of dispute resolution creates a distorted picture of the meaning of law and legal system. Their analysis, which draws on the work of the Portugese legal anthropologist de Sousa Santos, is an attempt to understand law in a broader, social context.

Fiona Cownie and Anthony Bradney, *English Legal System in Context*
(Butterworths, London, 1996), pp. 8–9:

"There are two possible problems with the state-rule-centred approach. The first is that this approach asserts rather than proves that there is an important difference between what is happening in state agencies concerned with dispute resolution and non-state agencies. The provenance of the authority of the agency, the fact that it comes from the state, is deemed to be significant. This significance has not been obvious to everyone.

De Sousa Santos, a Portugese legal anthropologist, studied the activities of an institution, the Residents' Association, in a favela or shanty town, Pasargada, in Rio de Janeiro. The land upon which Pasargada was built belonged to the state. The residents were, so far as the Brazilian legal system was concerned, no more than squatters. They had no legal title to the land upon which they had built their houses. However, the Residents' Association was willing to register such sales. Written agreements were drawn up by the association. Standard phrases were used in these agreements. Copies were exchanged, one being kept by the Residents' Association, others by the parties to the sale. Residents of the favela were thus able to pass property amongst each other in a similar way to that in which they would have been able to had they been title-holders under Brazilian state law. When there were disputes about matters relating to housing the Residents' Association were willing to determine which party was in the right. The Residents' Association had no power to do this under Brazilian state law. Its power came from the fact that those who lived in Pasargada regarded it as having a judicial function.

De Sousa Santos concluded that the activities of the Residents' Association could be described as 'Pasargada law' which was 'an example of an informal and unofficial legal system'. According to de Sousa Santos, Pasargada was an example of legal pluralism; a situation where two legal systems, Brazilian state law and Pasargada law, coexisted alongside each other. In deciding which was law there was, for de Sousa Santos, no special significance in the fact that the rules of one legal system, Brazilian state law, emanated from the state. Using the approach which typifies 'English legal system' texts a description of the work of the Residents' Association would form no part of a book on the Brazilian legal system. Yet, for de Sousa Santos, that institution was central to the way in which the inhabitants of the favela brought law into their lives."

NOTES AND QUESTIONS

• What is meant by the term "legal pluralism"? Give an example of an unofficial legal system which exists in this country.

• Legal pluralism, as exemplified by the research of de Sousa Santos, underscores that in defining what is law, we may need to be careful to avoid privileging the institutions of the state. Dispute resolution and the rules which govern social relations can exist, as they did in the favela, outside of the institutions and rules propagated by government. The law of the state thus might be viewed as one amongst a plurality of legal orders which govern social groups.

SOCIOLOGICAL AND ECONOMIC APPROACHES TO LAW

The excerpt from Cownie and Bradney also hints at another issue central to defining law; namely, what are the *functions* which law serves? De Sousa Santos emphasizes the dispute resolution function as central to the purpose of law; but that, arguably, is only one of a number of functions which law and legality might be said to serve.

Steven Vago, *Law and Society* (3rd ed., Prentice Hall, Englewood Cliffs, NJ, 1991), pp. 12–16:

Functions of law

"Why do we need law, and what does it do for society? More specifically, what functions does law perform? As with the definitions of law, there is no agreement among scholars of law and

society on the precise functions, nor is there consensus on their relative weight and importance. . . .

Social Control

In a small, homogeneous society, behavioral conformity is insured by the fact that socializing
experiences are very much the same for all members. Social norms tend to be consistent with
each other and are strongly supported by tradition. Social control in such a society is primarily dependent upon self-sanctioning. Even on those occasions when external sanctions are
required, they seldom involve formal punishment. Deviants are subjected to informal mechanisms of social control, such as gossip, ridicule, or humiliation. . . .

In modern societies there are many methods of social control, both formal and informal.
Law is considered one of the forms of formal social control. In the words of Roscoe Pound:
'I think of law as in one sense a highly specialized form of social control in developed politically organized society—a social control through the systematic and orderly application of
the force of such a society.'

Lawrence M. Friedman calls attention to two ways in which law plays an important role in
social control:

'In the first place, legal institutions are responsible for the making, care and preservation of
those rules and norms which define deviant behavior; they announce (in a penal code, for
example) which acts may be officially punished and how and which ones may not be punished at all. In the second place, the legal system carries out many rules of social control.
Police arrest burglars, prosecutors prosecute them, juries convict them, judges sentence
them, prison guards watch them, and parole boards release them.'

Of course, as we shall see, law does not have a monopoly on formal mechanisms of social
control. Other types of formal mechanisms (such as firing, promotion, demotion, and so
forth) are found in industry, academe, government, business, and in various private groups.

Dispute Settlement

As Karl N. Llewellyn so aptly put it:

'What, then, is this law business about? It is about the fact that our society is honeycombed
with disputes. Disputes actual and potential, disputes to be settled and disputes to be prevented; both appealing to law, both making up the business of law. . . . This doing of something about disputes, this doing of it reasonably, is the business of law.'

By settling disputes through an authoritative allocation of legal rights and obligations, the
law provides an alternative to other methods of dispute resolution. Increasingly, people in all
walks of life let the courts settle matters that were once resolved by informal and nonlegal
mechanisms, such as negotiation, mediation, or forcible self-help measures. . . .

Social Engineering

Many scholars contend that a major function of law in modern society is social engineering.
It refers to purposive, planned, and directed social change initiated, guided, and supported by
the law. Roscoe Pound captures the essence of this function of law in stating:

'For the purpose of understanding the law of today, I am content to think of law as a social
institution to satisfy social wants—the claims and demands involved in the existence of civilized society—by giving effect to as much as we need with the least sacrifice, so far as such
wants may be satisfied or such claims given effect by an ordering of human conduct through
politically organized society. For present purposes I am content to see in legal history the
record of a continually wider recognizing and satisfying of human wants or claims
or desires through social control; a more embracing and more effective securing of social
interests; a continually more complete and effective elimination of waste and precluding of

friction in human enjoyment of the goods of existence—in short, a continally more effica-cious social engineering.'

In many instances law is considered a 'desirable and necessary, if not a highly efficient means of inducing change, and that, wherever possible, its institutions and procedures are prefer-able to others of which we are aware'. Although some sociologists disagree with this conten-tion, law is often used as a method of social engineering, a way of bringing about planned social change by the government. Social engineering is a prominent feature of modern welfare states.

Dysfunctions of law

Although law is an indispensible and ubiquitous institution of social life, it possesses—like most institutions—certain dysfunctions that may evolve into serious operational difficulties if they are not seriously considered. . . .

By establishing a social policy of a particular time and place in constitutional and statutory precepts, or by making the precedents of the past binding, the law exhibits a tendency towards conservatism. Once a scheme of rights and duties has been created by a legal system, contin-uous revisions and disruptions of the system are generally avoided in the interests of predict-ability and continuity. Social changes often precede changes in the law. In times of crisis, the law can break down, providing an opportunity for discontinuous and sometimes cataclysmic adjustments. . . .

Related to these conservative tendencies of the law is a type of rigidity inherent in its nor-mative framework. Since legal rules are couched in general, abstract, and universal terms, they sometimes operate as straightjackets in particular situations. An illustration of this would be the failure of law to consider certain extenuating circumstances for a particular illegal act; for example, stealing because one is hungry or stealing for profit.

A third dysfunction of the law stems from the restrictive aspects of normative control. Norms are shared convictions about the patterns of behavior that are appropriate or inappro-priate for the members of a group. Norms serve to combat and forestall anomie (a state of normlessness) and social disorganization. Law can overstep its bounds, and regulation can turn into over-regulation, in which situation control may become transformed into repression. . . .

Donald Black's contention that certain kinds of discrimination are inherent in law itself can also be construed as a fourth dysfunction. Rules, in principle, may apply to everyone, but legal authority falls unevenly across social place. . . . For example, when a black person is convicted of killing a white person in America, the risk of capital punishment far exceeds every other racial combination. . . .

One may add to this list a variety of procedural inefficiencies, administrative delays, and archaic legal technologies. One may also include the cost of justice to the middle class and its unavailability to the poor, to the consumer, and to minority group members."

In outlining some of law's functions and dysfunctions, Vago is analysing law from a sociological perspective; that is, he seeks to understand the relationship between law and society. Another of law's functions, Smart argues, is to make claims as to the "Truth" of things. Law is a form of knowledge which sometimes disqualifies other ways of thinking—namely, those in which someone is not "thinking like a lawyer". According to Smart, legal method (the subject of this book!) is the means through which law (and practitioners of the law) construct law and legal *discourse* as a privi-leged way of understanding. Smart's analysis should be remembered in those moments in your legal education when you may feel that you are being "indoctrinated" into a particular way of thinking; a way of thinking which seems to run counter to other ways of analyzing problems and of viewing society.

Carol Smart, *Feminism and the Power of Law* (Routledge, London, 1989), pp. 10–13:

"[L]aw sets itself above other knowledges like psychology, sociology, or common sense. It claims to have the method to establish the truth of events. The main vehicle for this claim is the legal method which is taught in law schools. . . . A more 'public' version of this claim, however, is the criminal trial which, through the adversarial system, is thought to be a secure basis for findings of guilt and innocence. Judges and juries can come to correct legal decisions; the fact that other judges in higher courts may overrule some decisions only goes to prove that the system ultimately divines the correct view.

Law's claim to truth is not manifested so much in its practice, however, but rather in the ideal of law. In this sense it does not matter that practitioners may fall short of the ideal. If we take the analogy of science, the claim to scientificity is a claim to exercise power, it does not matter that experiments do not work or that medicine cannot find a cure for all ills. The point is that we accord so much status to scientific work that its truth outweighs other truths, indeed it denies the possibility of others. We do not give quite such a status to law, although we operate as if the legal system does dispense justice (*i.e.* correct decisions), and we certainly give greater weight to a judge's pronouncement of guilt than a defendant's proclamation of innocence. Indeed there are those who would say that 'law is what the judges say it is'. The judge is held to be a man of wisdom, a man of knowledge, not a mere technician who can ply his trade.

If we accept that law, like science, makes a claim to truth and that this is indivisible from the exercise of power, we can see that law exercises power not simply in its material effects (judgements) but also in its ability to disqualify other knowledges and experiences. Non-legal knowledge is therefore suspect and/or secondary. Everyday experiences are of little interest in terms of their meaning for individuals. Rather these experiences must be translated into another form in order to become 'legal' issues and before they can be processed through the legal system. For the system to run smoothly, whether it is criminal or civil, the ideal is that all parties are legally represented and that the parties say as little as possible (*i.e.* they are mute). The problem for the lawyer is that the litigant may bring in issues which are not, in legal terms, pertinent to the case, or s/he might inadvertently say something that has a legal significance unknown to her/him. So the legal process translates everyday experience into legal relevances, it excludes a great deal that might be relevant to the parties, and it makes its judgements on the scripted or tailored account. . . .

Law sets itself outside the social order, as if through the application of legal method and rigour, it becomes a thing apart which can in turn reflect upon the world from which it is divorced. Consider the following quotation from Lord Denning, written when he was Master of the Rolls (*i.e.* head of the Court of Appeal).

'By a series of Acts of Parliament, however, starting in 1870, all the disabilities of wives in regard to property have been swept away. A married woman is now entitled to her own property and earnings, just as her husband is entitled to his. Her stocks and shares remain hers. Her wedding presents are hers. Her earnings are hers. She can deal with all property as fully as any man. . . . No longer is she dependent on her husband. She can, and does, go out to work and earn her own living. Her equality is complete.'

In this conceptualisation it is law that has given women equality (accepting for the moment that they do have formal equality). In this way law is taken to be outside the social body, it transcends it and acts upon it. Indeed the more it is seen as a unified discipline that responds only to its own coherent, internal logic, the more powerful it becomes. It is not simply that in this passage Denning omits to point out how many women chained themselves to railings, demonstrated and lobbied in Parliament to change the law, nor that he ignores the dramatic changes to women's economic position which occurred quite independently of law, it is rather that he constructs law as a kind of sovereign with the power to give or withhold rights. . . . Linked to this idea, law is constructed as a force of linear progress, a beacon to lead us out of darkness. . . .

Lastly in this section on truth and knowledge, I want to consider how law extends itself beyond uttering the truth of law, to making such claims about other areas of social life. What is important about this tendency is that the framework for such utterances remains legal—and hence retains the mantle of legal power. To put it figuratively, the judge does not remove his wig when he passes comment on, for example, issues of sexual morality in rape cases. He retains the authority drawn from legal scholarship and the 'truth' of law, but he applies it to non-legal issues. This is a form of legal imperialism in which the legitimacy law claims in the field of law extends to every issue in social life. Hence Lord Denning states,

> 'No matter how you may dispute and argue, you cannot alter the fact that women are quite different from men. The principal task in the life of women is to bear and rear children: . . . He is physically the stronger and she the weaker. He is temperamentally the more aggressive and she the more submissive. It is he who takes the initiative and she who responds. These diversities of function and temperament lead to differences of outlook which cannot be ignored. But they are, none of them, any reason for putting women under the subjection of men.'

Here Denning is articulating a Truth about the natural differences between women and men. He combines the Truth claimed by socio-biology (*i.e.* a 'scientific' truth) with the Truth claimed by law. He makes it clear that there is no point in argument; anyone who disagrees is, by definition, a fool. Hence the feminist position is constructed as a form of 'disqualified knowledge', whilst the naturalistic stance on innate gender differences acquires the status of a legal Truth. In this passage both law and biological determinism are affirmed, whilst law accredits itself with doing good."

Question

What can sociological perspectives tell us about law and the legal system?

Both Vago and Smart seek to analyse the functions of law from a sociological perspective. Others have sought to understand law's functions from an economic perspective, concluding that the primary role for law is to further the value of economic *efficiency*. This way of thinking about law, which is highly controversial, is known as "law and economics".

Robert Cooter and Thomas Ulen, *Law and Economics* (Harper Collins, New York, 1988), pp. 1–3:

"*Example:* An oil company signs a contract to deliver oil by a certain date from the Middle East to a European manufacturer. Before the oil is delivered, war breaks out in the exporting country, so that the oil company cannot perform the contract as promised. The lack of oil causes the European manufacturer to forego profitable business investments. The manufacturer brings an action against the oil company for breach of contract and asks the court to award damages equal to the amount of profits the manufacturer would have realized if the oil had been delivered as promised. Unfortunately, the contract is silent about the risk of nonperformance in the event of war so that the court cannot simply read the contract and resolve the dispute on the contract's own terms. In resolving the suit, the court must decide whether to excuse the oil company from performance on the grounds that the war made the performance 'impossible' or to find the oil company in breach of contract and to require the oil company to compensate the manufacturer for lost profits.

For an economist analyzing this case, the crucial point is that the parties failed to allocate between themselves the risk of a certain contingency—in this instance, war—that has arisen to frustrate performance of the contract. War is a risk of doing business in the Middle East, a risk that must be borne by one of the parties to the contract. Because the contract is silent about the allocation of this risk, the court must allocate it, and, depending on how the court decides the case, one party or the other will have to bear the costs of that risk. What are the *consequences* of different court rulings on how to allocate the loss?

If the court excuses the oil company from responsibility for performing the contract, then the manufacturer is going to bear the losses that arise from the non-delivery of oil. On the other hand, suppose that the court holds the oil company responsible for compensating the European manufacturer for the profits lost because of the failure to deliver the oil. In that case, the oil company bears the losses that arise from non-delivery of the oil. Therefore, the way the court decides the case accomplishes an apportionment of losses between the two parties.

Can economics provide a method for the court to decide which apportionment is better? From the standpoint of economic efficiency, the court should assign the loss from non-delivery so as to make future contractual behavior more efficient. And a rule for doing this is *to assign the losses to the party who can bear the risk of such a loss at least cost*. In this case it seems that a company doing business in the Middle East is in a better position than a European manufacturer to assess the risk of war in that region and to take steps to mitigate its effects. For example, the oil company might be able to purchase insurance against non-performance because of war much more cheaply than could the European manufacturer. The oil company could more cheaply arrange for alternative shipping routes that might not be blocked by a Middle Eastern war. That company could make arrangements with other oil companies in other, less sensitive parts of the world to make emergency purchases of oil in the event of war in the Middle East.

In so far as it is true that the oil company is better able to bear the risk of non-performance because of war, a court whose objective was to promote economic efficiency would hold the oil company liable for breach of contract. This conclusion is consistent with the outcome of some actual cases that arose as a consequence of the 1967 war in the Middle East."

NOTES AND QUESTIONS

- Summarise the analysis offered by the school of law and economics. Do you find the argument convincing?

- While the promotion of economic efficiency may seem a reasonable function of the law in the area of contractual agreements between sophisticated commercial parties, we ought to be skeptical as to whether efficiency is the *primary* objective which the law should serve. This is particularly true outside of the commercial law context. Economists of law often prioritise the promotion of economically efficient outcomes over other values, but many would argue that efficiency is only one of many values which the law should promote.

LEGAL EDUCATION AND THE LEARNING OF LEGAL METHOD

Most students who are using this book are beginning university law studies, and many will have ambitions to practice law either as a barrister or solicitor. It is sometimes claimed that legal education is a process of indoctrination; of teaching students to think in a particular way, namely, as "lawyers". Legal Method as a course in the university curriculum might be seen as a primary location for this process of indoctrination. One of the aims of this text is to encourage you to think critically about the ways that legal reasoning and legal method "works", and, at times, to be skeptical of this method of solving problems. You might also begin to think about how legal reasoning tends to assume that other methods of analysis are somehow inferior to its own method. This is what Smart referred to as law's claim to "Truth". These claims, as they are taught in university legal education, will sometimes seem strange and counterintuitive and, for that reason (along with many others), legal education is sometimes an exasperating and frustrating experience. As Cownie and Bradney argue, university law schools have a particular culture and hierarchy to which students are expected to adjust. In this selection, the authors refer frequently to the "black-letter tradition". This phrase refers to the frequent focus of legal education on abstract legal rules, which are presented without consideration of the social, political, and economic context in which the legal rules operate. Another critique of legal reasoning, as it is taught in law schools, by Abramczyk, follows. She describes legal method as representative of a particular political standpoint: liberal objectivity.

Fiona Cownie and Anthony Bradney, *English Legal System in Context* (Butterworths, London, 1996), pp. 126–130:

"Law schools normally assume that 'although law may appear to be irrational, chaotic and particularistic, if one digs deep enough and knows what one is looking for, then it will become evident that law is an internally coherent and unified body of rules.' This is part of the historical tradition of university law schools in Britain. One of the earliest Professors of Law in Britain, A.V. Dicey, began his academic career by arguing that '[i]t is for law professors to set forth the law as a coherent whole—to analyse and define legal conceptions—to reduce the mass of legal rules to an orderly series of principles . . .'. This has become translated into the more modern proposition that, for example, 'the English law of real property rests on the logical development of clear principles, and it is these principles that throughout we have sought to emphasise [in writing our textbook]'. Following this idea, the university law school's function is to identify legal principles. These are to be found in law reports and statutes and are written up in textbooks and legal periodicals. Students are present in law schools to inculcate both these principles and that which is the method of understanding these principles, English legal reasoning. This approach is not necessarily something which is unwelcome and imposed on law students. There is some evidence to suggest that it is in accord with their expectations and desires. Sherr and Webb's study of students in Warwick University law school, an avowedly non-traditional law school, found that '[t]he students thought most emphasis is and should be placed on thinking like a lawyer and on substantive legal doctrine and rules'.

Training for a hierarchy

To say that English university law schools are dominated by a black-letter tradition does not seem to say anything about the values that law students will imbibe or the kinds of communities they will form or wish to enter because of the nature of this education. It might appear to be merely descriptive. One might want to argue that a diet of material limited to cases, statutes and textbooks is too restricted; that law should involve a wider study which includes materials taken from the social sciences. This, however, is a separate point.

During the last fifteen years many academics have argued that to concentrate on the form of the material used in black-letter law teaching is to miss its social effect and political impact: 'Law school can be an intense, powerful experience.' For most students it involves largely unfamiliar materials in a wholly unfamiliar atmosphere: 'We cope with law school by reducing the chaos to manageable terms.' But, it is argued, this ordering of chaos is more than simply an intellectual process of taking on new knowledge.

In an early, very influential article Kennedy argued that '[l]aw schools are intensely political places despite the fact that the modern law school seems intellectually unpretentious, barren of theoretical ambition or practical vision of what social life might be.'

Kennedy's argument pointed to a number of features which he thought were important in the ideological impact of the university law school. First, the law school was hierarchical, with the nature of the relationship between lecturer and student being determined by the lecturer. Second, the study of law involved the study of a new language. Third, law was put forward as a matter of rules. Fourth, in applying these rules one's emotions or sympathies were deemed to be irrelevant. Finally, the law school provided no overt theory in its teaching which could act as a source of critique. . . .

Using these methods black-letter law presents itself, through the cases, statutes and textbooks, as a form of objective knowledge; there is a legally correct outcome to a particular dispute which, with proper training, the student will discern. A failure to see the objectively right answer by the student is characterised by the lecturer (and frequently the student) as a failure to learn the language of law or a failure in knowing the correct rules or an inability to disentangle one's emotional or political sympathies from one's intellectual understanding of the law. However, in Kennedy's view, in fact all there is in law is a distinctive argumentative technique. This technique does not determine any particular outcome; does not produce a closure which will require a predestined answer. Legal technique is simply a form of argument that literally will sound right to another lawyer.

One of the results of the black-letter approach to law teaching is that there appears to be a strict separation of the question of what law is and what law should be. In learning the former questions about the latter do not need to be raised. Outcomes of cases do not need justifying from either an ethical or a political standpoint. They simply are the law. . . .

Stanley has applied Kennedy's argument to the British context. Most law in the curriculum, he argues, is private law rather than public law; contract law or the law of tort rather than social security law or planning law. 'This dominance of rule based, procedural subjects which are of relevance only to certain sections of society ensures the continued individualist, free-market ethos.' The subjects which command the curriculum are of relevance only to the lives of a small section of the population. The disputes they concern are largely disputes about property which are settled on an individual basis. Large sections of the population have relatively little property. What is of greatest importance to them is not individual dispute resolution but, rather, collective decisions about general resource allocation. Quite simply, on this argument, the lives of the majority of the population are written out of the law school curriculum in favour of the needs of the economic system. This teaches the student that the important areas of law are the areas which involve large amounts of money, major companies or significant economic actors. Law for other purposes is of little account.

If the arguments above are accepted university law schools teach not just particular facts but also particular values. They inculcate into students the ideas that law is fixed and that law is neutral. Moreover, they do this not by proving either of these two points but by assuming that they are so and then by repeating that assertion until the majority of the audience, students, believe them. Equally important is what university law schools do not teach. By not giving the same prominence to theoretical courses as they do to black-letter courses university law schools fail to give law students any method by which they might criticise the material that they are being presented with."

Jill Abramczyk, "The Tyranny of the Majority: Liberalism in Legal Education" (1992) 5 Canadian Journal of Women and the Law 442 at 451:

". . . One of the results of the primacy of liberal objectivity is that one dominant but narrow perspective becomes the most (or only) acceptable approach in the law school classroom, and in legal discourse in general. To the extent that this perspective encodes a particular view of the world, and a particular vision of the way in which the world should be ordered, liberalism can be both 'dominant' and a vehicle for entrenching systemic domination. Ignorance of the experience of others, and disrespect for those who are 'different' from the dominant culture, is thereby legitimized. Those who are different become 'outsiders', the oddities at whom we laugh or shake our heads. Any structural forces are systematically ignored.

Legal reasoning is taught 'as though enduring principles of social organization [are] imbedded in the logic of the doctrines themselves,' rather than as though the doctrines have political and ethical meanings. That law students study rules, which do not take into account backgrounds, socialization, or political beliefs, illustrates that legal reasoning treats people and conflicts as atomistically as liberalism does. When the gender, class, race, age, and gender orientation of the people involved are excluded systematically from discussion, the underlying principles of doctrines and their political and ethical meanings are disregarded. . . . [I]t encourages students to accept at face value what they are told is 'reality' without being encouraged or taught to question it, or to analyze it from any number of critical/analytical perspectives. . . .

Liberal theory directs that the application of 'legal reasoning' leads to 'sound law', which conforms to 'legal conventions concerning interpretation, precedent, rights and so forth, rather than by conformity to political goodness'. Legal reasoning 'says it can take us from legal premises (precedents, notions of rights) to determine answers without resort to political or ethical choice.' The law student is taught that legal reasoning leads us to the 'correct' legal result, and indeed, that there is *one* correct legal result.

This result, and the reasoning produced, is presented as being logical, objective, and neutral. Events are presented 'as they are', in full confidence that the presentation is free from any particular perspective or ideology. But it bears repeating that (legal) reasoning necessarily reflects the perspectives of its participants, and that those perspectives are not neutral. As has been noted, 'most professors, just as most legislators, and judges, and lawyers are white and male and middle-class and heterosexual.' "

Legal education in the United Kingdom has been frequently criticised for its failure to recognise a diversity of racial and ethnic perspectives. This is but one example of Abramczyk's point that a dominant (in this case, "white") perspective is presented as the "universal", thereby erasing the diversity of perspectives which participants in legal education and the practice of law bring to the discipline. University legal education has been slow to recognise the importance of broadening its perspective in this regard.

Aimee Paterson, "The Racial, Ethnic and Cultural Values Underpinning Current Legal Education", in *The Critical Lawyers' Handbook 2* (Paddy Ireland and Per Laleng, eds., Pluto Press, London, 1997), pp. 77–81:

"An exploration of the courses taught within UK law schools reveals the persisting conservative traditions of the British legal profession. Very few law schools have expanded their curriculum beyond the narrow confines of traditional law courses. It is, surely, important to recognise that 'straight' law courses alone are no longer (if ever they were) sufficient to meet the needs of a multicultural society. Law schools need to adopt a more progressive stance. There is an urgent need for greater academic appreciation of the value of multiculturalism in legal education. Legal education needs to embrace a wider range of disciplines in order to properly inform and serve its new consumers. Equally important, law schools, responsible for producing future lawyers, need to ensure they have the ability to relate to clients of diverse ethnic, cultural and religious backgrounds.

Multiculturalism in legal education would provide a platform for informing and educating students about key race relations issues where ignorance and misconception currently prevail. Training in race relations would help lawyers respond to the needs of contemporary British society. Indeed, this is vitally important if persistent allegations of injustice are seriously to be addressed and eradicated. The value of this policy has been recently emphasised by the Judicial Studies Board, when it noted that it is 'essential to equip all judges and magistrates with a basic amount of knowledge and understanding if they are to be seen to be administering justice fairly to people with whom they have little in common in terms of upbringing, culture and experience'. . . .

Given the cultural and ethnic diversity of both British society and law students, is there not a case for 'a wholesale permeation of virtually the entire curriculum with multiracial, multicultural themes'?. . .

Legal education appears to be structured to create and produce a stereotyped ideal lawyer. Both the content and delivery of courses, consciously or otherwise, seem designed to persuade its consumers to adopt a certain image. As noted by the Barrow Report, 'anyone who does not conform and has no wish to, or is unable to, may feel uncomfortable. This is equally so of pupillage, tenancy and further eminence at the Bar . . .' although '. . . it is less noticeable then because those who have reached the later stages will already have successfully conformed'."

A major element in the construction of the "ideal lawyer" through legal education is indoctrination in the form of legal method which has been analysed in the excerpts in this section. Williams has illustrated this method of reasoning through the telling of a story, which highlights the pitfalls of "thinking like a lawyer".

Patricia J. Williams, *The Alchemy of Race and Rights* (Cambridge, MA: Harvard University Press, 1991), pp. 12–13:

"Walking down Fifth Avenue in New York not long ago, I came up behind a couple and their young son. The child, about four or five years old, had evidently been complaining about big dogs. The mother was saying, 'But why are you afraid of big dogs?' 'Because they're big,' he responded with eminent good sense. 'But what's the difference between a big dog and a little dog?' the father persisted. 'They're *big*,' said the child. 'But there's really no difference,' said the mother, pointing to a large slathering wolfhound with narrow eyes and the calculated amble of a gangster, and then to a beribboned Pekinese the size of a roller skate, who was founcing along just ahead of us all, in that little fox-trotty step that keep Pekinese from ever being taken seriously. 'See?' said the father. 'If you look really closely you'll see there's no difference at all. They're all just dogs.'

And I thought: 'Talk about your iron-clad canon. Talk about a static, unyielding, totally uncompromising point of reference. These people must be lawyers. Where else do people learn so well the idiocies of High Objectivity? How else do people learn to capitulate so uncritically to a norm that refuses to allow for difference? How else do grown-ups sink so deeply into the authoritarianism of their own world view that they can universalize their relative bigness so completely that they obliterate the subject positioning of their child's relative smallness? (To say nothing of the position of the slathering wolfhound, from whose own narrow perspective I dare say the little boy must have looked exactly like a lamb chop.)' "

Notes and questions

- You may want to keep Williams' story in mind as you proceed through your study of Legal Method. It provides a useful reminder of the dangers of uncritically accepting legal reasoning as a means of discovering the "truth" of things, erasing individual perspectives and differences in social positioning in the process.

- How might the critics of legal education (*e.g.* Kennedy, Stanley, Williams) respond to the claims of the "law and economics" school of legal reasoning?

- What is your perspective on legal education as a participant? How do you react to the criticisms of legal reasoning and of "thinking like a lawyer"?

- Define "legal method" (you may want to revise your answer at the end of the text and in three years time).

2

CONSTITUTIONAL ASPECTS OF LEGAL METHOD: THE RULE OF LAW AND THE SUPREMACY OF PARLIAMENT

In this chapter, we begin examining those key constitutional concepts and doctrines which are relevant to the way in which legal reasoning in this country is carried out. Our primary focus is on two concepts which historically were seen as foundational to legal analysis: the "rule of law" and the supremacy of Parliament. These concepts will be dealt with in far more detail in law courses dealing specifically with constitutional and administrative law. However, an understanding of them is also important to an understanding of legal method and reasoning.

THE RULE OF LAW

If you were to conduct a poll on any street in the United Kingdom, and ask the so-called "average person" if he or she was subject to the "rule of law", you would probably get an affirmative response. However, if you also asked what is meant by the phrase "rule of law", you would likely get a great variety of responses. On one level, to claim that a society is subject to the rule of law is simply to make the claim that it is governed by fixed rules set down in law, rather than by the arbitrary force of a despot. But, of course, a society governed by rules will also be governed by individuals who make, amend, and enforce the law. Moreover, the simple fact that a society is governed by rules—even lots of rules—may mean that it is subject to the rule of law, but it certainly does not in itself ensure that the society qualifies as a "just" or fair regime.

Wade Mansell, Belinda Meteyard and Alan Thompson, *A Critical Introduction to Law* (Cavendish, London, 1995), p. 136:

"There is, of course, no necessary causal link between the rule of law and the restraint of the powerful. Apartheid South Africa always claimed to be a rule of law state even while 4.5 million white people ruled 28 million disenfranchised black people and also owned 87% of the land. Apartheid South Africa also executed more people than any comparable state (in fact no other state was comparable) and yet, because of the appearance of safeguards for defendants, was able to claim that this practice too was consistent with the rule of law. Certainly in some ways it was the rule of law ideology which provided the clothes with which the state attempted to hide the nakedness of government aggression."

The example of apartheid in South Africa suggests that the rule of law may be a rather empty concept, capable of being deployed to justify the most egregious violations of individual and group dignity and self-determination. In fact, some might argue that given the *types* of laws which characterised apartheid, it is inappropriate to describe that regime as governed by the rule of law. At this point, we can make another observation about the rule of law: it means different things to different people, and the concept is a difficult one to pin down with an easy definition.

George P. Fletcher, *Basic Concepts of Legal Thought* (Oxford University Press, New York, 1996), pp. 11–13:

"Of all the dreams that drive men and women into the streets, from Buenos Aires to Budapest, the 'rule of law' is the most puzzling. We have a pretty good idea what we mean by 'free markets' and 'democratic elections'. But legality and the 'rule of law' are ideals that present themselves as opaque even to legal philosophers. Many American jurists treat the rule of law as though it were no more than governance by rules. Thus we find Justice Scalia arguing explicitly that the rule of law is no more than the law of rules. And philosophers, such as Friedrich Hayek and Joseph Raz, make the same assumption that the rule of law means that the government 'is bound by rules fixed and announced beforehand.' Playing by the rules is, in some dubious contexts, a great achievement, but once societies have minimized graft and arbitrary rule, the 'rule of law' seems to promise more than blindly playing the game. After all, the rules of the game might be horribly unjust.

There are in fact two versions of the rule of law, a modest version of adhering to the rules and a more lofty ideal that incorporates criteria of justice. We shuffle back and forth between them because we are unsure of the import of the term 'law' in the expression 'rule of law.' . . . Do we mean rule by the laws laid down—whether the legal rules are good or bad? Or do we mean 'rule by Law,' by the right rules, by the rules that meet the tests of morality and justice? Because we have only one word for law in place of the two commonly found in other legal systems, we suffer and perhaps cultivate this ambiguity."

Paul Craig, "Formal and Substantive Conceptions of the Rule of Law: An Analytical Framework" [1997] P.L. 467 at 467:

"Formal conceptions of the rule of law address the manner in which the law was promulgated (was it by a properly authorised person, in a properly authorised manner, etc.); the clarity of the ensuing norm (was it sufficiently clear to guide an individual's conduct so as to enable a person to plan his or her life, etc.); and the temporal dimension of the enacted norm (was it prospective or retrospective, etc.). Formal conceptions of the rule of law do not however seek to pass judgment upon the actual content of the law itself. They are not concerned with whether the law was in that sense a good law or a bad law, provided that the formal precepts of the rule of law were themselves met. Those who espouse substantive conceptions of the rule of law seek to go beyond this. They accept that the rule of law has the formal attributes mentioned above, but they wish to take the doctrine further. Certain substantive rights are said to be based on, or derived from, the rule of law. The concept is used as the foundation for these rights, which are then used to distinguish between 'good' laws, which comply with such rights, and 'bad' laws which do not."

QUESTION

Explain what is meant by the claim that there are two versions of the rule of law.

The tension between formal and substantive conceptions of the rule of law is central to the confusion over its meaning. Nevertheless, it has longed been claimed that the English legal system is characterised by the rule of law, most famously in the late nineteenth century by the law professor Albert Venn Dicey. According to Dicey, the rule of law was a key feature which distinguished the English *constitution* (or fundamental structure of government) from those of continental Europe. While "foreigners" might be subject to the exercise of *arbitrary* power, the English, by contrast, were protected by the rule of law. It is hardly surprising that Dicey is chracterised as a thoroughly chauvinistic "anti-European"!

Albert Venn Dicey, *An Introduction to the Law of the Constitution* (8th ed., Macmillan, London, 1915), pp. 183–197:

"When we say that the supremacy of the rule of law is a characteristic of the English constitution, we generally include under one expression at least three distinct though kindred conceptions.

We mean, in the first place, that no man is punishable or can be lawfully made to suffer in body or goods except for a distinct breach of law established in the ordinary legal manner before the ordinary Courts of the land. In this sense the rule of law is contrasted with every system of government based on the exercise by persons in authority of wide, arbitrary, or discretionary powers of constraint.

Modern Englishmen may at first feel some surprise that the 'rule of law' (in the sense in which we are now using the term) should be considered as in any way a peculiarity of English institutions, since, at the present day, it may seem to be not so much the property of any one nation as a trait common to every civilised and orderly state. Yet, even if we confine our observation to the existing condition of Europe, we shall soon be convinced that the 'rule of law' even in this narrow sense is peculiar to England, or to those countries which, like the United States of America, have inherited English traditions. In almost every continental community the executive exercises far wider discretionary authority in the manner of arrest, of temporary imprisonment, of expulsion from its territory, and the like, than is either legally claimed or in fact exerted by the government in England; and a study of European politics now and again reminds English readers that wherever there is discretion there is room for arbitrariness, and that in a republic no less than under a monarchy discretionary authority on the part of the government must mean insecurity for legal freedom on the part of its subjects. . . .

We mean in the second place, when we speak of the 'rule of law' as a characteristic of our country, not only that with us no man is above the law, but (what is a different thing) that here every man, whatever be his rank or condition, is subject to the ordinary law of the realm and amenable to the jurisdiction of ordinary tribunals.

In England the idea of legal equality, or of the universal subjection of all classes to one law administered by the ordinary Courts, has been pushed to its utmost limit. With us every official, from the Prime Minister down to a constable or a collector of taxes, is under the same responsibility for every act done without legal justification as any other citizen. The Reports abound with cases in which officials have been brought before the Courts, and made, in their personal capacity, liable to punishment, or to the payment of damages, for acts done in their official character but in excess of their lawful authority. A colonial governor, a secretary of state, a military officer, and all subordinates, though carrying out the commands of their official superiors, are as responsible for any acts which the law does not authorise as is any private and unofficial person. Officials, such for example as soldiers or clergymen of the Established Church, are, it is true, in England as elsewhere, subject to laws which do not affect the rest of the nation, and are in some instances amenable to tribunals which have no jurisdiction over their fellow countrymen; officials, that is to say, are to a certain extent governed under what may be termed official law. But this fact is in no way inconsistent with the principle that all men are in England subject to the law of the realm; for though a soldier or a clergyman incurs from his position legal liabilities from which other men are exempt, he does not (speaking generally) escape thereby from the duties of an ordinary citizen. . . .

There remains yet a third and a different sense in which the 'rule of law' or the predominance of the legal spirit may be described as a special attribute of English institutions. We may say that the constitution is pervaded by the rule of law on the ground that the general principles of the constitution (as for example the right to personal liberty, or the right of public meeting) are with us the result of judicial decisions determining the rights of private persons in particular cases brought before the Courts; whereas under many foreign constitutions the security (such as it is) given to the rights of individuals results, or appears to result, from the general principles of the constitution. . . .

There is in the English constitution an absence of those declarations or definitions of rights so dear to foreign constitutionalists. Such principles, moreover, as you can discover in the English constitution are, like all maxims established by judicial legislation, mere generalisations drawn either from the decisions or dicta of judges, or from statutes which, being passed to meet special grievances, bear a close resemblance to judicial decisions, and are in effect judgments pronounced by the High Court of Parliament. To put what is really the same thing in a somewhat different shape, the relation of the rights of individuals to the principles of the constitution is not quite the same in countries like Belgium, where the constitution is the result of a legislative act, as it is in England, where the constitution itself is based upon legal decisions. In Belgium, which may be taken as a type of countries possessing a constitution formed by a deliberate act of legislation, you may say with truth that the rights of individuals to personal liberty flow from or are secured by the constitution. In England the right to individual liberty is part of the constitution, because it is secured by the decisions of the Courts . . . [I]n Belgium individual rights are deductions drawn from the principles of the constitution, whilst in England the so-called principles of the constitution are inductions or generalisations based upon particular decisions pronounced by the Courts as to the rights of given individuals. . . .

The fact, again, that in many foreign countries the rights of individuals, *e.g.* to personal freedom, depend upon the constitution, whilst in England the law of the constitution is little else than a generalisation of the rights which the Courts secure to individuals, has this important result. The general rights guaranteed by the constitution may be, and in foreign countries constantly are, suspended. They are something extraneous to and independent of the ordinary course of the law. . . . [W]here the right to individual freedom is a result deduced from the principles of the constitution, the idea readily occurs that the right is capable of being suspended or taken away. Where, on the other hand, the right to individual freedom is part of the constitution because it is inherent in the ordinary law of the land, the right is one which can hardly be destroyed without a thorough revolution in the institutions and manners of the nation."

It is essential to recognise that Dicey was writing at a particular historical period, and more importantly, he was writing from a political perspective that saw the maintenance of individual property and freedom to use that property as the paramount value to be protected. He was opposed to any increase in activity by the state. He clearly thought that law should ignore differences that existed between people in terms of wealth and power, and should treat them all the same (*formally* equal), rather than the state taking steps to make people more *substantively* equal. Yet he was also opposed to the movement for women's suffrage (a demand for *formal* equality).

Since Dicey's time, most lawyers have come to realise many inadequacies in his limited concept of the rule of law. Today, governments do have fairly wide discretionary powers, and most people would agree that governments do need *discretion* to operate effectively. That is, ensuring that officials of government only act in accordance with strict *rules* may prove too inflexible in the implementation of public policies. Instead, officials need flexibility and discretion in tailoring law and policy to fit individual circumstances. However, while we increasingly have come to recognise the importance of discretion on the part of officials of the state, there are also situations in which clear rules and guidelines—the rule of law—may seem important as a way to limit the power of officials to act in ways which are perceived as *arbitrary* or unfair. Thus, it might be argued that although discretion is not inconsistent with the rule of law, discretion should also be exercised in accordance with general principles of law. The actions of state officials thereby should be constrained by the law so that they do not act arbitrarily. This historical tension between clear rules and administrative discretion has been described by Jowell, along with other criticisms of Dicey's rule of law vision.

Jeffrey Jowell, "The Rule of Law Today", in *The Changing Constitution*
(3rd ed., Jeffrey Jowell and Dawn Oliver, eds., Clarendon Press, Oxford, 1994),
pp. 59–66:

"The second and third of Dicey's meanings of the Rule of Law display a concern not to allow the British to go the way of other countries, where a separate system of public law is administered by separate courts dealing with cases between the State and the individual. In 1928 William Robson wrote his celebrated book *Justice and Administrative Law*, in which he roundly criticized Dicey for his misinterpretation of both the English and French systems on that ground. He pointed out there there were in England 'colossal distinctions' between the rights and duties of private individuals and those of the administrative organs of government even in Dicey's time. Public authorities possessed special rights and special exemptions and immunities, to the extent that the citizen was deprived of a remedy against the State 'in many cases where he most requires it'. Robson also convincingly showed how Dicey has misinterpreted French law, where the *droit administratif* was not intended to exempt public officials from the rigour of private law, but to allow experts in public administration to work out the extent of official liability. Robson also noted the extent of Dicey's misrepresentation that disputes between officials and private individuals in Britain were dealt with by the ordinary courts. He pointed to the growth of special tribunals and inquiries that had grown up to decide these disputes outside the courts, and was in no doubt that a 'vast body of administrative law' existed in England.

The attack on Dicey continued a few years later with W. Ivor Jennings's *The Law and the Constitution*, which appeared in 1933. Repeating many of Robson's criticisms of Dicey's second and third meanings of the Rule of Law, Jennings delivered a withering, and almost fatal, attack upon Dicey's first meaning—his claim that wide discretionary power had no place under the Rule of Law. It should be remembered here that Dicey was a trenchant critic of notions of 'collectivism'. . . . Jennings felt that the Rule of Law implicitly promoted Dicey's political views. He equated Dicey's opposition to State regulation with that of the 'manufacturers who formed the backbone of the Whig Party', who 'wanted nothing which interfered with profits, even if profits involved child labour, wholesale factory accidents, the pollution of rivers, of the air, and of the water supply, jerry-built houses, low wages, and other incidents of nineteenth-century industrialism'. . . .

The Second World War then provided compelling reasons to centralize power, an opportunity further built upon by the Labour Government of 1945. As Robson wrote in the second edition of his book in 1947, increasingly Parliament had given decision-making powers not to the courts—to Dicey's 'ordinary law'—but to specialized organs of adjudication. This was not 'due to a fit of absentmindedness' but because these bodies would be speedier and cheaper, and would possess greater technical knowledge and have 'fewer prejudices against government' than the courts. Here he may have been echoing the words of Aneurin Bevan, Minister of Health in the 1945 Labour Government and architect of the National Health Service, who caused a stir in the House of Commons by establishing tribunals in the Health Service, divorced from 'ordinary courts', because he greatly feared 'judicial sabotage' of socialist legislation.

Despite this onslaught on Dicey's revision of the Rule of Law, its epitaph refused to be written. Two particularly strong supporters wrote in its favour in the 1940s. F.A. Hayek's *The Road to Serfdom* in 1943 graphically described that road as being paved with governmental regulations. C.A. Allen, with less ideological fervour, pleaded for the legal control of executive action. Not much heed was paid however until the late 1950's when the Franks Committee revived interest in Diceyan notions by suggesting judicial protections over the multiplying tribunals and inquiries of the growing State. It was in the 1960s, however, that disparate groups once again started arguing in favour of legal values. Some of these groups were themselves committed to a strong governmental role in providing social welfare, but objected to the manner in which public services were carried out. Recipients of Supplementary Benefit, for example, objected to the fact that benefits were administered by officials in accordance with a secret code (known as the 'A Code') and asked instead for publication of a set of welfare 'rights'. They also objected to the wide discretion allowed their case-workers to determine the level of their benefits. The heirs of Jennings and his followers, such as Professor Richard Titmus, opposed this challenge to the free exercise of official discretion and objected strongly to a 'pathology of legalism' developing in this area.

Just one other example of a plea for the Rule of Law came at about the same time from individuals and groups who were being displaced from their homes by programmes of urban redevelopment. While not asking for a catalogue of 'rights', the claim here was for participation in decisions by which they were affected. The plea of these groups (and others like them) did not primarily concern the substance of the law. The welfare recipients were not simply arguing for higher benefits, but for fair procedures to determine the benefits. They and the local amenity groups directed their demands for the Rule of Law less at the content of the decisions ultimately taken than at the procedures by which they were reached. They were by no means adopting the undiluted Diceyan view that all discretionary power is bad. Nevertheless, they recognized the value of legal techniques to control the exercise of official power. . . .

An official possessed of discretion frequently has a choice about how it should be operated: whether to keep it open-textured, maintaining the option of a variety of responses to a given situation, or to confine it by a rule of standard—a process of legalisation. For example, officials administering welfare benefits could provide them on a case-by-case basis according to their conception of need, or they could announce precise levels of benefit for given situations. Similarly, laws against pollution could be enforced by a variable standard whereby the official must be satisfied that the polluter is achieving the 'best practicable means' of abatement. Alternatively, levels of pollution could be specified in advance, based on the colour of smoke emission, or the precise quantities of sulphur dioxide. A policy of promoting safe driving could, similarly, be legalised by a rule specifying speeds of no more than 30 miles per hour on given streets.

Now for Dicey, and particularly for Hewart and Hayek, who mistrusted the grant of virtually any official discretion, the virtue of rule-bound conduct was principally that it allowed affected persons to know the rules before being subjected to them *ex post facto*. As a principle of justice, it was felt that no person should be condemned without a presumed knowledge of the rule alleged to have been breached. This assumes a penal law or criminal regulation of one form or another, and is understandable in that context where the lack of rules would involve risky guesses with serious consequences for non-compliance. It is fairer to a person prosecuted for a tax offence to have been made aware of the precise tax required than for the levels to be determined at the discretion of an official.

This argument, however, has a somewhat different compulsion when dealing not with penalties but with regulation involving the allocation of scarce resources. Should an applicant for a university place be entitled, out of fairness, to know the precise grades required for entrance? Should the applicant for welfare benefits be entitled to know the rules about allocations of winter coats? In cases such as these the argument in favour of rules over discretion is an argument less from certainty than from *accountability*. This argument has two facets, the first being a concern to provide a published standard against which to measure the legality of official action and thus to allow *individual redress* against official action that does not accord with the rule or standard. Thus, an announced level of resources to qualify for welfare assistance ought to allow redress to a person who qualifies but is refused assistance. The second facet of accountability refers to the fact that the actual process of making rules and their publication generates *public assessment* of the fidelity of the rule to legislative purpose. Many statutes confer powers on officials to further the policy of the Act in accordance with wide discretion. The power may be to allocate council housing, or to provide for the needy, or to diminish unacceptable pollution of the air or water. The process of devising a points system for housing allocation, benefits for the needy, and acceptable emission levels of pollution thus forces the official into producing a formal operational definition of purpose. . . .

The virtues of rules, as we have seen, include their qualities of legality, certainty, consistency, uniformity, congruence to purpose, and accountability loosely so called, all of which play an important part in the control of official discretion and may be seen as concrete manifestations of the Rule of Law. . . .

Officials are well aware of the benefit of rules to their own efficiency. Rules announce or clarify official policies to affected parties, and thus facilitate obedience. They may also allow routine treatment of cases, thus increasing the speed of decision-making. A zoning system in planning, a list of features of 'substandard' housing, and a list of grades for university admission allow decisions to be taken more quickly than a system that requires constant reappraisal of each case on its merits. Rules therefore reduce the anxiety and conserve the energy needed to reach decisions on a case-by-case basis. . . . Despite the fact that rules may promote criticism, they also, in the short run at least, provide a shield behind which officials may hide, pleading consistent and uniform justice in response to criticism that the individual's case is unique.

So here we have the tension: the virtues of rules—their objective, even-handed features— are opposed to other administrative benefits, especially those of flexibility, individual treatment, and responsiveness. The virtue of rules to the administrator (routine treatment) may be a defect to the client with a special case (such as the brilliant applicant for a university place who failed to obtain the required grades because of a family upset or illness just before the examination). The administrator's shield may be seen as an unjustified protection from the client's sword. Officials themselves may consider that the job itself requires flexibility, or genuinely want to help a particular client, but feel unable to do so: hence the classic bureaucratic response, 'I'd like to help you—but there is this rule.' . . .

Before leaving the relative merits of rule-based official action, we should note that rules in themselves do not ensure their implementation. The existence of a rule outlawing a speed of over 30 miles per hour, for example, will not necessarily mean that people who speed are automatically prosecuted. Sometimes the prosecuting official will lack the resources to prosecute some offenders, or lack the will. Occasions may exist, however, when non-enforcement has the express purpose of avoiding legalism. Legalistic enforcement would, for example, prosecute a doctor narrowly exceeding the limit of 30 miles per hour on a deserted street late at night while speeding to the scene of an accident. The prosecution makes no sense in furthering the goal of preventing unsafe driving. Full enforcement would in this case play no part in the achievement of fidelity to purpose. On other occasions laws may not be enforced in order to further other values in society. For example, studies have shown that assault laws may not be enforced in a situation of marital violence as police will not wish to exacerbate poor relations or cause deprivation for children. The objective of the law prohibiting violence is in these situations considered secondary to a value which seeks to preserve the well-being of the family unit.

This last example shows that even the most clear-cut rule may not be enforced, or may be relaxed. Most law-enforcers assessing prosecution weigh the cost in damages of the prohibited act against the cost of abating the act. An example is the regulation of pollution, where the damage of the polluter to the environment is, according to recent studies, measured against the costs of abatement: the firm may be forced out of business, or may locate elsewhere, causing damage to the local economy and unemployment. Or the cost of abatement may be passed on to the ultimate consumer of a needed product."

QUESTIONS

- To what extent is the rule of law compatible with the exercise of discretion by officials and agencies of the state? Give examples.

- Should a lecturer's decision whether to grant someone an extension on his or her essay deadline be governed by clear rules or the exercise of a broad discretion tailored to the particular circumstances?

Besides the question of the merits of rules versus discretion on the part of officials in the implementation of policy, there are a number of other meanings associated with the rule of law. For example, "equality before the law" was a central element of Dicey's vision understood, as noted above, in *formal* terms. By this Dicey meant, in part, that officials of the state should be subject to the same rules (and courts) as everyone else. Although Jowell examines how Dicey's assertions about equality under law in the English legal system were somewhat erroneous, the idea nevertheless has some contemporary relevance, as Waldron demonstrates.

Jeremy Waldron, *The Law* (Routledge, London, 1990) pp. 29–42:

PEDRO v. DISS

"Late one night in 1979, a man called Ya Ya Pedro was standing by the door of his brother's house in London. Another man, Martin Diss, came up to him, identified himself as a police officer, and asked Pedro what he was doing there. Pedro walked away without answering. When Constable Diss repeated his question, Pedro told him to 'fuck off'. Eventually he allowed himself to be searched, but when the policeman began to question him about some keys that he found in his pockets, Pedro walked away again. Constable Diss grabbed him by the arm and said, 'Do you live here?' Pedro replied with another obscenity and swung backwards, striking the constable in his chest with an elbow. As he did this, the constable took hold of his clothing, and Pedro punched him. He was eventually restrained with the assistance of two other officers, and they arrested Pedro and charged him with assaulting a constable in the execution of his duty.
When Pedro appeared before the Highbury magistrates, he was convicted and fined £50. But he appealed to the High Court, and the Chief Justice, Lord Lane, with one other judge, overturned the conviction and sentence. They said that when Pedro punched Constable Diss, the officer was *not* acting in the lawful execution of his duty. The police, said Lord Lane, do not have an unlimited power to detain people for questioning: their powers of legitimate detention and arrest are set down and governed by law. If they go beyond those powers, the person they have got hold of is entitled to strike back in self defence, just as he may resist *any* other person who attacks him. Lord Lane went on:

'It is a matter of importance, therefore, to a person at the moment when he is first physically detained by a police officer, to know whether that physical detention is or is not regarded by that officer as a formal arrest or detention. That is one of the reasons why it is a matter of importance that the arresting or detaining officer should make known to the person in question the fact that, and the grounds on which, he is being arrested or detained.'

Constable Diss claimed that he had thought Pedro was a burglar, and that he was authorized by Section 66 of the Metropolitan Police Act 1839 to 'stop, search and detain any person who may be reasonably suspected of having or conveying in any manner anything stolen or unlawfully obtained'. The problem was he didn't tell Pedro that that was what he was doing; he didn't say this was the power he was exercising and these were the grounds of his suspicion. So Pedro had no way of distinguishing the situation from one in which he was being unlawfully attacked. That was why Lord Lane held that he was entitled to defend himself, even against a police officer.

It is tempting to say that Pedro got off on a 'technicality'. In some countries, you are not allowed to resist a police officer even if his attempt to detain you is unjustified; moreover the officer has no obligation to say why you are being detained and you certainly have no entitlement to resist him if he does not. I don't want to argue that the rule in *Pedro v Diss* is necessarily better. But the case illustrates a couple of broader points of principle.

First, it involves a determination to subject members of the police force, as far as possible, to the same basic rules of law as every other citizen. Ordinary members of the public are not normally allowed to detain one another forcibly and they are entitled to resist anyone who tries to do that to them. The police are subject to that basic framework of rules along with everyone else.

Second, it embodies a particular attitude towards any *special* powers that may be thought necessary for the police to be able to do their job. The special powers of the police are to be limited and governed by rules—not just any rules, but rules which are known and publicized rather than hidden away in the Police Training Manual. Indeed, the striking thing about the case is the judges' insistence that Diss ought to have told Pedro the particular rule on which he was relying. Members of the public shouldn't have to submit to a general sense that the police are simply 'special' and can interfere with their lives in ways in which they may not interfere with one another. They are entitled to know what's going on, and to know by what authority the constable is acting in what would otherwise be an objectionable (and resistable) way. Otherwise they will be at the mercy of unpredictable arbitrary power. . . .

One law for all

Think back for a moment to Ya Ya Pedro and Constable Diss. Diss grabs hold of Pedro, and Pedro punches him in the struggle to free himself. The magistrates say he is guilty of assault. On appeal, the High Court says (in effect): 'No. Unless the arrest is lawful, Pedro is entitled to defend himself against Martin Diss just as if he were any other citizen who tried to grab hold of him. Once they go beyond their specified powers, the police have no special privileges. The ordinary rules of self-defence apply. If it's wrong for me to attack Pedro, it's also wrong for Constable Diss to attack Pedro. The law is the same for everyone.'

This requirement of universality—the idea of 'one law for all'—is a prominent feature of the normative ideal of the rule of law. But why is universality a good thing? Why is it desirable that there should be one law for everyone, irrespective of who they are, or what their official status?

One obvious application of universality is that we don't, on the whole, allow personalized laws; we don't have laws that make exceptions for particular people. In medieval England, there used to be things called 'Bills of Attainder', announcing that someone in particular (the Earl of Warwick, or the king's brother for example) was thereby banished from the realm and his estates confiscated. The idea of the rule of law is that the state should not use personalized mechanisms of that sort.

Moral philosophers link this requirement of universality with morality and with rationality. They say that if you make a moral judgement about someone or something, your judgement can't be based simply on that person or that incident in particular, or if it is, it's arbitrary. It must be based on some feature of the person or action—something *about* what they did, something that might in principle be true of another person or another situation as well. In other words it must be based on something that can be expressed as a universal proposition. For example, if I want to say, 'It is all right for Diss to defend himself', I must say that because I think self defence is all right in general in that sort of case, not merely because I want to get at Pedro or say something special about Diss. So I must also be prepared to say that it would be all right for Pedro to defend himself in a similar circumstance. Unless I can point to some clearly relevant difference between the two cases, then I must accept that the same reasoning applies to both.

Another way of putting it is that universalizability expresses an important principle of justice: it means dealing even-handedly with people and treating like cases alike. If I am committed to treating like cases alike, then I ought to be able to state my principles in a universal form. If I cannot—that is, if I can't find a way to eliminate references to particular people from my legislation—that is probably a good indication that I am drawing arbitrary distinctions based on bias or self-interest or something of that sort.

As well as these philosophical reasons, there are also pragmatic arguments in favour of universality. We are less likely to get bad laws or oppressive laws, if the burden of any law falls as much on those who make it as on the rest of the population. The king might think twice about banning tobacco, if it means that he can't have a cigarette. An MP may be reluctant to impose heavy penalties on adultery when he remembers what he was doing last week. If our legislators are human in their inclinations and temptations, they may be less likely to enact laws that are inhumanly demanding if they know that the legislation may be applied to their conduct as well.

Now I say you are *less* likely to get oppressive laws. There are no guarantees. An ascetic sovereign may be perfectly willing to subject his own conduct to the same harsh discipline he imposes on his subjects. When the Iranian parliament enacted amputation as a penalty for repeated offences of theft, its members presumably welcomed the possibility that they too should have their hands cut off if they offend against Allah in that way. The idea of the rule of law usefully prohibits legislation which singles somebody out for special treatment. But being singled out is only one way of being oppressed. People may be oppressed as members of a group or because they possess some general characteristic, such as being a black or being a woman, and it is much more difficult to rule out this sort of legislation on the basis of the ideal of the rule of law. As soon as we recognize that, then we recognize that the idea of universality—the idea of 'one law for all'—is not nearly as straightforward as it looks. It rules out one type of discrimination: discrimination against (or in favour of) named individuals. But it doesn't rule out discrimination against (or in favour of) certain *types* of people. It doesn't, for example, rule out the sort of discrimination that we find in the [former] South African Group Areas Act, since that discrimination is stated in terms that make no reference whatever to particular individuals. It is true of course that the Group Areas Act treats different people differently: apartheid applies one set of standards to blacks and another set of standards to whites. But if that *by itself* were enough to rule out apartheid legislation, it would also rule out an awful lot of legislation which we regard as desirable and necessary.

The trouble with the purely formal idea of 'one law for all' is that, if it is interpreted absolutely literally, it becomes really far too simple to capture the requirements of good legislation in a modern state. When you think about it, it seems crazy to say we should apply literally the *same* legal rules to everyone in all circumstances. Do we want to enforce the same standards of cleanliness in a paint-shop as in a restaurant? Is there to be one law to govern children and adults? Must ambulance drivers observe the same speed limits as the rest of us? No-one thinks that ought to be the case. . . . We don't want our commitment to universality to blind us to those distinctions and discriminations that are morally or pragmatically justified.

Special rules for officials?

As a matter of fact, this point has important implications for the way law applies to politics. The simple idea with which we began was that the same rules should apply to officials like Constable Diss as apply to citizens like Ya Ya Pedro. There should be one law for all, and no special law for officials of the state. But now if it is reasonable to apply different standards of hygiene to paint-shops and restaurants, if it is reasonable to allow a higher speed limit for ambulances than for private motorists, why isn't it also reasonable to apply rules of behaviour to police officers that are different from the ones we apply to ordinary citizens? After all, don't the police—like ambulance drivers—have a *special* job to do?

It is amazing what a grip the simple idea of 'one law for all' has had in British law and legal theory. For a long time, it was fashionable to pretend that a police officer was nothing but 'a citizen in uniform'—that his powers to question suspects and arrest felons were no greater than that of the ordinary 'man in the street'. It was simply that he did this for a living, and was trained at it, whereas the ordinary citizen had better things to do. This has long since become a fiction. The police have a whole array of powers to arrest people, to detain them for questioning, to break, enter and search their homes, and so on, which are conferred on them specifically by legislation. And the same is true of many other state officials—from the VAT-man to the social worker. They have a job to do, and Parliament has given them special powers to do it. These special powers may or may not be excessive; the issue is politically controversial. But few deny that state officials need *some* special powers (and also *some* special protections) if they are to be able to do their job.

Equally important, we may also want to say that state officials need to have special *restrictions* on their conduct (that are different from, and additional to, the ones that apply to the rest of us), as well as special powers. I will use a case to illustrate this point.

In a 1979 case, *Malone v. Metropolitan Police Commissioner*, an antiques dealer, James Malone, who was suspected of handling stolen property, sued for an injunction [an order to stop someone from doing something] to restrain the London police from tapping his telephone. The judge refused to give an injunction. He held that the police had a perfect right to do it, not because there was any specific legal authorization, but simply because telephone-tapping did not involve any trespass or other unlawful act.

> 'The subscriber speaks into his telephone, and the process of tapping appears to be carried out by Post Office officials making recordings, with Post Office apparatus on Post Office premises, of the electrical impulses on Post Office wires provided by Post Office electricity. There is no question of there being any trespass on [Malone's] premises for the purpose of attaching anything either to the premises themselves or to anything on them: all that is done is done within the Post Office's own domain.'

In other words, since the ordinary law of trespass has not been violated here, the action of the officials does not require any specific authorization. Malone's case, the judge said, rested on the assumption 'that nothing is lawful that is not positively authorized by law'. But England has always been a country where anything not expressly forbidden by the law is permitted: that is the basis of our liberty. It seems to follow that, since there is no law on the matter, the police have the right to tap telephones.

We have already seen the absurdity of holding that the police should have no more powers than the ordinary citizen. Now we are seeing the absurdity of the converse proposition—that the police should not be subject to any special restrictions that don't apply to other people. They should have as much freedom as the rest of us. That proposition is absurd, because the power (both legal and physical) that the police have makes them especially dangerous *as well as* especially useful. Acting within the state apparatus, officials can do things to citizens which are quite different in character from the sort of things citizens can do to one another. It is a mistake for us to think that the laws we use to deal with one another will necessarily be adequate for our dealings with the officials of the state. . . .

In other words, we might talk in terms of a *modified* 'rule of law' doctrine to be applied to the conduct of officials. The simple principle of 'one law for all' holds that state officials should be bound by exactly the same rules as everyone else. That's the version we have to give up. The modified version, however, insists that official conduct should be governed by *the same sort* of legal rules, even if they are not literally the same rules, as the rest of us. We may take the simple version as our default position. State officials (police officers etc) are to be governed by the ordinary law of the land, unless there is a specific legal provision to the contrary. If, however, there is a need for a special provision (because the police, for example, have a special job to do), we should not simply make an exception in the ordinary law of the land; we should lay down *rules* to govern the conduct of the officials."

QUESTIONS

- What is meant by the claim that the rule of law includes a requirement of universality? Does that mean that the law should not be used to draw distinctions between people? When, if ever, are such distinctions justifiable?

- How does the rule of law apply to the conduct of officials? Are state officials governed by the same rules as everyone else?

The rule of law is capable of encompassing a range of ideas. For example, it has been argued that the rule of law requires that laws generally should be prospective and not retrospective. That is, Parliament should not enact laws which seek to regulate (and make illegal) events which have already occurred, and which were permitted at that time. Furthermore, the rule of law sometimes is said to include the idea that laws should be open, published, and reasonably intelligible to those who are required to regulate their conduct in accordance with them. In other words, people need to be able to understand the law. A judiciary which is independent of the other branches of government is also sometimes described as central to the rule of law, as is the accessibility of the courts to the general public. Further elements of the rule of law might be said to include: the fact that new laws should be enacted only after publicity, opportunity for debate and consultation; and that warning should be given to the public before the law is changed (so that behaviour can be changed to meet the altered legal situation).

For some commentators, the range of constraints on the exercise of the power of the state, which are contained within the concept of the rule of law, make it an inherently positive and important ideal. Despite its limitations, such as the way in which equality is defined in a formal rather than substantive way, the rule of law, for them, remains a valuable concept in our constitutional rhetoric.

E.P. Thompson, *Whigs and Hunters* (Penguin Books, London, 1990), p. 266:

"I am insisting only upon the obvious point, which some modern Marxists have overlooked, that there is a difference between arbitrary power and the rule of law. We ought to expose the shams and inequities which may be concealed beneath this law. But the rule of law itself, the imposing of effective inhibitions upon power and the defence of the citizen from power's all-intrusive claims, seems to me to be an unqualified human good. To deny or belittle this good is, in this dangerous century when the resources and pretentions of power continue to enlarge, a desperate error of intellectual abstraction."

Other commentators, especially on the political left, argue that the rule of law is not an "unqualified human good", because its limited scope does not advance the cause of social justice or substantive equality. Moreover, the underlying philosophy of the rule of law, especially in the form articulated by Dicey, positively discourages progressive social change because of its conservative focus on rules, formal equality, and rights under law. That is, while the rule of law may constrain the exercise of state power, it does not recognise how the power of the state might be used to create a more just, equal society. Horwitz has made this point in a direct response to Thompson.

Morton Horwitz, "The Rule of Law: An Unqualified Human Good?" (1977) 86 Yale Law Journal 561 at 566:

"I do not see how a man of the left can describe the rule of law as an 'unqualified human good'! It undoubtedly restrains power, but it also prevents power's benevolent exercise. It creates formal equality—a not inconsiderable virtue—but it *promotes* substantive inequality by creating a consciousness that radically separates law from politics, means from ends, processes from outcomes. By promoting procedural justice it enables the shrewd, the calculating, and the wealthy to manipulate its forms to their own advantage. And it ratifies and legitimates an adversarial, competitive and atomistic conception of human relations."

Finally, the rule of law is based upon an assumption about the character of human relationships; namely, that law (and its "rule") is necessary to the maintenance of civilized society. The assumption here is that without the rule of law, society would degenerate into a chaotic and/or authoritarian state. Marxists criticise this idea because, they argue, it accords too much power to law, and it ignores the way in which the rule of law actually serves to legitimate the political and economic status quo.

Hugh Collins, *Marxism and Law* (Clarendon Press, Oxford, 1982), pp. 12–13:

"Few would doubt the important role of law in preventing the disintegration of social order or restricting authoritarian governments. Yet Marxists claim that legal fetishism embodies a distorted image of reality which must be unmasked. To begin with, the notion that society rests on law is too simplistic. It is implausible to think that without law everyone would be at each other's throat, or would use superior physical force to take another's possessions. It is much more likely that informal standards of behaviour based on reciprocity would permit an elementary form of stable community to exist. Clearly there is a subtle relationship between the function of laws and informal customs in constituting the normative basis for a peaceful and prosperous society which will not be revealed if an assumption about the necessity and priority of law is adopted. Growing from that insight, Marxists portray the heavy dependence of organizations of power in modern society upon law as the result of a specific historic conjuncture of circumstances, and argue that the important role of law today in maintaining social order is not an immutable feature of human civilization in the future."

We thus have seen how the rule of law for some is an ideal, for others, an illusion which justifies the existing social and political order (and its hierarchies). The concept of the rule of law, then, is not a neutral one, but rather, is politically charged. Your view of the rule of law will depend upon your assessment of its political and ideological underpinnings. Your social, political, and ideological positioning inevitably will impact upon your views of the politics of the rule of law. As a student, the most important point is to think *critically* about any claim to speak the "truth" about the rule of law (or anything else!).

THE SUPREMACY OF PARLIAMENT

Returning again to Dicey's analysis of the English constitution, the rule of law was only one of two fundamental elements; the other was the supremacy of Parliament. The tension between the rule of law and Parliamentary supremacy is particular to the

British Parliamentary system of government. According to Dicey, the essence of the law of the constitution was that Parliament has the right to make or unmake any law whatever. Thus, no person or body is recognised as having a right to override or set aside legislation. Parliament is the supreme law making body, its legislative power is substantively unrestricted, and the laws it passes cannot be invalidated by the courts. The role of judges, in relation to statutes enacted by Parliament, is to interpret and apply them, rather than to pass judgment on their merits. This fact distinguishes the British constitutional structure from that found in many other jurisdictions, in which a written constitutional document—such as a Bill of Rights—is the fundamental law which provides the basis for courts to invalidate legislation on constitutional grounds, should it contradict, for example, the rights and freedoms guaranteed in the constitution. In Chapter 4, we will see that this historic principle of British constitutionalism is now altered by virtue of membership in the legal order of the European Union.

Parliamentary supremacy also includes the idea that no Parliament can bind itself or a future Parliament to retain any particular law now on the books, for to do so would mean that the Parliament in the future was not supreme. Thus, any law, no matter how fundamental, in theory can be repealed by ordinary Parliamentary procedure at any time in the future. Parliamentary supremacy, as a constitutional principle, intuitively would seem to have the potential to easily undermine the ideal of the rule of law, which we have already examined. The fact that Parliament conceivably can do just about anything would seem extremely dangerous to the idea of a society governed by law. Dicey sought to answer such concerns, and claimed that the rule of law and Parliamentary supremacy (or sovereignty, as he referred to it) in fact were complementary.

Albert Venn Dicey, *An Introduction to the Law of the Constitution* (8th ed., Macmillan, London, 1915), pp. 402–409:

"The sovereignty of Parliament and the supremacy of the law of the land—the two principles which pervade the whole of the English constitution—may appear to stand in opposition to each other, or to be at best only counterbalancing forces. But this appearance is delusive; the sovereignty of Parliament, as contrasted with other forms of sovereign power, favours the supremacy of the law, whilst the predominance of rigid legality throughout our institutions evokes the exercise, and thus increases the authority, of Parliamentary sovereignty.

The sovereignty of Parliament favours the supremacy of the law of the land.

That this should be so arises in the main from two characteristics or peculiarities which distinguish the English Parliament from other sovereign powers.

The first of these characteristics is that the commands of Parliament (consisting as it does of the Crown, the House of Lords, and the House of Commons) can be uttered only through the combined action of its three constituent parts, and must, therefore always take the shape of formal and deliberate legislation. The will of Parliament can be expressed only through an Act of Parliament.

This is no mere matter of form; it has most important practical effects. It prevents those inroads upon the law of the land which a despotic monarch, such as Louis XIV., Napolean I., or Napolean III., might effect by ordinances or decrees, or which the different constituent assemblies of France, and above all the famous Convention, carried out by sudden resolutions. The principle that Parliament speaks only through an Act of Parliament greatly increases the authority of the judges. A Bill which has passed into a statute immediately becomes subject to judicial interpretation, and the English Bench have always refused, in principle at least, to interpret an Act of Parliament otherwise than by reference to the words of the enactment. . . .

The second of these characteristics is that the English Parliament as such has never, except at periods of revolution, exercised direct executive power or appointed the officials of the executive government.

No doubt in modern times the House of Commons has in substance obtained the right to designate for appointment the Prime Minister and the other members of the Cabinet. But this right is, historically speaking, of recent acquisition, and is exercised in a very roundabout manner; its existence does not affect the truth of the assertion that the Houses of Parliament do not directly appoint or dismiss the servants of the State; neither the House of Lords nor the House of Commons, nor both Houses combined, could even now issue a direct order to a military officer, a constable, or a tax-collector; the servants of the State are still in name what they once were in reality — 'servants of the Crown'; and, what is worth careful notice, the attitude of Parliament towards government officials was determined originally, and is still regulated, by considerations and feelings belonging to a time when the 'servants of the Crown' were dependent upon the King, that is, upon a power which naturally excited the jealousy and vigilance of Parliament.

Hence several results all indirectly tending to support the supremacy of the law. Parliament, though sovereign, unlike a sovereign monarch who is not only a legislator but a ruler, that is, head of the executive government, has never hitherto been able to use the powers of the government as a means of interfering with the regular course of law; and what is even more important, Parliament has looked with disfavour and jealousy on all exemptions of officials from the ordinary liabilities of citizens or from the jurisdiction of the ordinary Courts; Parliamentary sovereignty has been fatal to the growth of 'administrative law.' The action, lastly, of Parliament has tended as naturally to protect the independence of the judges, as that of other sovereigns to protect the conduct of officials. It is worth notice that Parliamentary care for judicial independence has, in fact, stopped just at that point where on *a priori* grounds it might be expected to end. The judges are not in strictness irremovable; they can be removed from office on an address of the two Houses; they have been made by Parliament independent of every power in the State except the Houses of Parliament. . . .

The fact that the most arbitrary powers of the English executive must always be exercised under Act of Parliament places the government, even when armed with the widest authority, under the supervision, so to speak, of the Courts. Powers, however, extraordinary, which are conferred or sanctioned by statute, are never really unlimited, for they are confined by the words of the Act itself, and, what is more, by the interpretation put upon the statute by the judges. Parliament is supreme legislator, but from the moment Parliament has uttered its will as lawgiver, that will becomes subject to the interpretation put upon it by the judges of the land, and the judges, who are influenced by the feelings of magistrates no less than by the general spirit of the common law, are disposed to construe statutory exceptions to common law principles in a mode which would not commend itself either to a body of officials, or to the Houses of Parliament, if the Houses were called upon to interpret their own enactments. In foreign countries, and especially in France, administrative ideas — notions derived from the traditions of a despotic monarchy — have restricted the authority and to a certain extent influenced the ideas of the judges. In England judicial notions have modified the action and influenced the ideas of the executive government. By every path we come round to the same conclusion, that Parliamentary sovereignty has favoured the rule of law, and that the supremacy of the law of the land both calls forth the exertion of Parliamentary sovereignty, and leads to its being exercised in a spirit of legality."

According to Dicey, then, the concepts of rule of law and Parliamentary supremacy were actually complementary. Both acted as a control mechanism on officials of the state (the "executive" branch of government). The government of the day always needs the support of Parliament to act, and judges, in their role as interpreters of statutory law, can ensure that the powers of government, as granted by Parliament, have not been exceeded. Finally, the ultimate political supremacy, according to Dicey, rested with the electorate. Once again, Dicey's constitutional vision is informed by a political ideology; one in which government should have a *limited* role, and where individualism and individual rights to private property are central.

Despite being grounded in a particularly nineteenth century Diceyan view of the world, the idea of Parliamentary supremacy as central to the British constitutional structure has continued to be of central importance.

A.W. Bradley, "The Sovereignty of Parliament—in Perpetuity?", in *The Changing Constitution* (3rd ed., Jeffrey Jowell and Dawn Oliver, eds., Clarendon Press, Oxford, 1994), pp. 81–85:

"The sovereignty of Parliament describes in formal terms the relationship which exists between the legislature and the courts. As analysed by Dicey, the Queen in Parliament (the legislature) has 'the right to make or unmake any law whatever' and no person or body outside the legislature 'is recognised by the law of England as having a right to override or set aside the legislation of Parliament'. In other words, there are no legal limits to the legislative authority of Parliament. When that authority is exercised in the form of an Act of Parliament, no court or other body has power to hold such an Act to be void or invalid or in any respect lacking in legal effect. As Sir Robert Megarry V-C said in a case which challenged the validity of the Canada Act 1982, 'from first to last I have heard nothing in this case to make me doubt the simple rule that the duty of the court is to obey and apply every Act of Parliament, and that the court cannot hold any such Act to be ultra vires [beyond the power of Parliament]'. . . .

Comparison with other constitutions

These statements of the fundamental relationship between the courts and the legislature present a strong contrast with those countries in which a written constitution imposes limitations upon the powers of the legislature, and where such limitations may be enforced by the courts. In 1803 this power of judicial review of legislation was declared to be a fundamental rule of the United States constitution by the Supreme Court in a famous and influential decision, *Marbury v. Madison*. As Chief Justice Marshall said then:

'The constitution is either a superior paramount law, unchallengeable by ordinary means, or it is on a level with ordinary legislative acts, and, like other acts, is alterable when the legislature is pleased to alter it. If the former part of the alternative is true, then a legislative act contrary to the constitution is not law; if the latter part be true, then written constitutions are absurd attempts, on the part of the people, to limit a power in its own nature illimitable.'

It was, Marshall continued, 'emphatically the province and duty of the judicial department to say what the law is'. Therefore, it was for the court where necessary to hold that an Act of Congress was void should it conflict with the terms of the constitution. . . .

We have seen that where there is a written constitution, its terms may prevail over acts of the legislature. In the absence of a written constitution, it is theoretically possible that the judges could exercise a power to review legislation, based for example on principles of natural justice and fundamental human rights. But the practice of British judges for several centuries has been to deny that they have any such role. Their duties extend to the application and interpretation of legislation, but stop short of a power to review Acts of Parliament. As Lord Reid said in a case arising out of the unilateral declaration of independence by the government of Rhodesia in 1965:

'It is often said that it would be unconstitutional for the United Kingdom Parliament to do certain things, meaning that the moral, political and other reasons against doing them are so strong that most people would regard it as highly improper if Parliament did these things. But that does not mean that it is beyond the power of Parliament to do such things. If Parliament chose to do any of them the courts would not hold the Act of Parliament invalid. . . .'

The authority of the courts

It is often said that the willingness of British judges to accept without question the authority of a controversial Act of Parliament, means that the judges are subordinate to Parliament. In one sense this is plainly true, since (for example) it is for Parliament, not the courts, to approve a government decision that the railways should be privatized or, in issues on which the government prefers to leave the decision to Parliament, to decide whether abortion or capital punishment should be permitted. But once the political decision has been taken to make a change in social or economic policy, and this decision has been expressed in legislation, it is for the judges to decide authoritatively on the extent of the new rights and duties which that legislation creates. In this respect, the courts have an essential part to play in ensuring that government is conducted according to law. Indeed, Dicey emphasized that the 'rule of law' was a fundamental principle of constitutional law, along with the sovereignty of Parliament. The sovereignty of Parliament, in Dicey's view, did not mean that Parliament could exercise arbitrary authority over the law, since such authority could be exercised only through an Act of Parliament. . . . [S]tatutory interpretation is not a mechanical process and can be a means for the expression of important constitutional values. But today judicial interpretation of Acts of Parliament is not in itself sufficient to guard against arbitrary executive decisions, since statutes are often deliberately framed to give wide scope for discretionary action. This is one reason why in recent years there have been demands for the courts to have a broader jurisdiction, which would inevitably make inroads into the sovereignty of Parliament."[1]

This relationship between Parliament and the courts, in which Parliament is supposedly supreme, and the courts apply laws enacted by Parliament, is demonstrated by a case decided by the House of Lords (the highest court in the United Kingdom). Decisions of the Law Lords generally include five judgments, and portions of three of those judgments (all of which agreed in the result) illustrate how the Lords in this case sought to respect the principle of Parliamentary supremacy.

British Railways Board and another v. Pickin [1974] 1 All E.R. 609, HL.

The Bristol and Exeter Railway Co. was incorporated (created) by statute in 1836 to make a railway from Bristol to Exeter with branch lines to Bridgwater and Tiverton. The Act provided that if the line was abandoned, the lands acquired by the company to build the railways would return to the owners of the land on either side of the railway. In the 1960s, the line fell into disuse. The land adjacent was sold to George Pickin. Meanwhile, Parliament, at the behest of the British Railway Board (the successor to the Bristol and Exeter Railway Co), enacted the British Railways Act 1968, which provided that provisions such as the one governing the reversion of the land on either side of the Bristol and Exeter railway, would not apply to land vested in the British Railway Board. Pickin commenced action against the Board claiming, amongst other things, that the Board had misled Parliament in its promotion of the bill and that the court should declare him owner of the adjacent land. The portions of the judgments in the House of Lords of interest to us concern the claim that Parliament was misled into enacting the statute.

Lord Reid [Lord Reid recited the facts of the case and the issues raised]:
". . . The respondent's [Pickin's] alternative ground of action is not easy to state concisely. He appears to allege that in obtaining the enactment of s 18 of the 1968 Act in their favour the board fraudulently concealed certain matters from Parliament and its officers and thereby misled Parliament into granting this right to them. . . .

The function of the court is to construe and apply the enactments of Parliament. The court has no concern with the manner in which Parliament or its officers carrying out its standing orders perform these functions. Any attempt to prove that they were misled by fraud or other-

---

[1] We will examine these inroads in Chapter 3.

wise would necessarily involve an enquiry into the manner in which they had performed their functions in dealing with the bill which became the British Railways Act 1968.

In whatever form the respondent's case is pleaded he must prove not only that the board acted fraudulently but also that their fraud caused damage to him by causing the enactment of s 18. He could not prove that without an examination of the manner in which the officers of Parliament dealt with the matter. So the court would, or at least might, have to adjudicate on that.

For a century or more both Parliament and the courts have been careful not to act so as to cause conflict between them. Any such investigations as the respondent seeks could easily lead to such a conflict, and I would only support it if compelled to do so by clear authority. But it appears to me that the whole trend of authority for over a century is clearly against permitting any such investigation.

The respondent is entitled to argue that s 18 should be construed in a way favourable to him and for that reason I have refrained from pronouncing on that matter. But he is not entitled to go behind the Act to shew that s 18 should not be enforced. Nor is he entitled to examine proceedings in Parliament in order to shew that the board by fraudulently misleading Parliament caused him loss. . . ."

Lord Morris of Borth-y-Gest:

". . . The question of fundamental importance which arises is whether the court should entertain the proposition that an Act of Parliament can so be assailed in the courts that matters should proceed as though the Act or some part of it had never been passed. I consider that such doctrine would be dangerous and impermissible. It is the function of the courts to administer the laws which Parliament has enacted. In the processes of Parliament there will be much consideration whether a bill should or should not in one form or another become an enactment. When an enactment is passed there is finality unless and until it is amended or repealed by Parliament. In the courts there may be argument as to the correct interpretation of the enactment: there must be none as to whether it should be on the statute book at all. . . ."

Lord Simon of Glaisdale:

". . . The system by which, in this country, those liable to be affected by general political decisions have some control over the decision-making is parliamentary democracy. Its peculiar feature in constitutional law is the sovereignty of Parliament. This involves that, contrary to what was sometimes asserted before the 18th century, and in contradistinction to some other democratic systems, the courts in this country have no power to declare enacted law to be invalid. . . ."

QUESTION

Why is the principle of the supremacy of Parliament difficult to reconcile with a substantive version of the rule of law?

A NOTE ON THE CONSTITUTION

The Law Lords in several places in their judgments in *Pickin* refer to the constitution and constitutional law. Although law students take at least one course in constitutional and administrative law, a few notes on the constitution are needed now in order for you to understand its implications for legal reasoning and legal method. The term constitution refers to the fundamental rules and limitations under which the power of the state is exercised. The constitution establishes institutions of government and divides powers between them; it limits the power of the state; and sometimes, it sets out rights held by citizens. The constitution is the fundamental framework of the legal and political system. In some countries, such as the United States, that constitutional framework is easy to identify. It is written down in a document called the "Constitution", and it includes a "Bill of Rights". But, in the United Kingdom, the constitution is more elusive. It is sometimes referred to as an "unwritten" constitution, because it is not set down in a single, comprehensive document. Rather, the British constitution consists of a variety of rules, customs, and understandings which empower and limit government. We would say, for example, that the idea of Parliamentary supremacy and the rule of law are elements of our constitution.

The constitutional framework can be "found" in a variety of places: in ordinary statutory law enacted by Parliament, which deals with matters which are considered to be fundamental to the structure of governance; in laws created by judges in the course of deciding cases before them (which is known as the "common law"); and the rules which Parliament has set down to govern its own internal procedures ("the law and custom of Parliament").

It is also of constitutional significance that the United Kingdom is a constitutional monarchy. This means that government is still conducted in the name of the Queen, which signifies the ultimate governing authority. Our governing structure is also characterised by a bicameral Parliament. This means that Parliament is composed of two "houses": a lower house (the House of Commons) chosen through popular election, and an upper house (the House of Lords), which is hereditary and now partly appointed. We also characterize our system as an example of "responsible government", in that the government of the day (the executive) is accountable to the House of Commons (the legislature) and can be defeated on the floor of the House in a vote. We also would describe the United Kingdom as a unitary, rather than a federal state, in that ultimate power rests with a central government in London (although this might be characterised somewhat differently given decentralisation of power to Scotland, Wales, and Northern Ireland through the policy of the devolution of power). Finally, the British constitution might be described as exemplifying the principle of "limited government", to the extent that government can only do what it is empowered under law to perform. This idea was central to Dicey's ideal of the rule of law.

Also of constitutional significance is what Dicey referred to as "conventions of the constitution", which he acknowledged were sometimes more important in constitutional terms than the law itself. These are simply practices or customs which have become so fundamental to our governing structure as to be considered of constitutional significance. They include the fact that the Queen assents to all laws passed by both Houses of Parliament (this is called the "Royal Assent"); the Queen acts only on the advice of her ministers, and ministers exercise the prerogatives (rights) which have been retained by the Crown; ministers are responsible to Parliament; members of the government are collectively responsible to Parliament; and the Prime Minister must be a member of the House of Commons rather than the House of Lords.

These conventions are not written down. They are simply practices of constitutional government which have grown up over time. Most importantly, disobedience of a convention means that it ceases to exist. If the Prime Minister was chosen from the House of Lords (and he or she chose to stay a member of the Lords) then the convention would no longer be a convention. This is what distinguishes convention from law: disobedience of a law does not signal its demise. Moreover, unlike law, there is no *sanction*, other than potentially a political one at the ballot box, for violating a convention. Thus, a convention may be recognised as part of the constitution, but it is not *enforceable* by the courts. It is *politically*, rather than *legally*, binding.

For Dicey, writing at the end of the nineteenth century, Britain's constitutional structure—the rule of law, supremacy of Parliament, and conventions of the constitution—was a *model* of constitutional government, superior to anything offered in other countries with written constitutions contained in a single document. Central to that balanced constitutional structure was the role of the courts. For Dicey, the courts' job was to uphold the intention of Parliament in the interpretation of legislation, but the role of the courts also was to review the actions of the executive branch of government (the cabinet and civil service) to ensure that its actions were within the lawful authority granted by Parliament. In this way, the courts upheld the rule of law, because they protected the individual against the potential for the arbitrary exercise of power by the executive.

However, in the twentieth century, that model of a balanced and harmonious constitution (if it ever really existed) increasingly has come unstuck. The House of Commons has become dominant, while the role of the House of Lords has been constricted both by legislation and the political environment in which an unelected body is seen an illegitimate. In this way, the upper house becomes less of a "check" on the actions of the Commons. Nor does the Royal Assent act as a "check" on legislation, because of the convention that the Queen acts only on the advice of ministers and does not withhold her consent (which also was the case in Dicey's time). Moreover, because of the development and entrenchment of the system of political parties, the individual Member of Parliament has less and less a role in independently scrutinising legislation proposed by the government (although there are still instances where this effectively occurs).

As a result of these developments, the government of the day dominates the legislative and executive functions of government. Moreover, the principle of Parliamentary supremacy limited the power of the courts to act as a "check" on government in that, as we have seen, they could not invalidate legislation on its merits. This relationship between Parliament, the executive branch of government, and the courts is often referred to as the doctrine of *separation of powers*. This term refers to the three primary functions of government: legislative (the making of laws); executive (the execution of laws, or putting laws into operation); and judicial (the interpretation of laws), and the degree to which those functions are distributed amongst different people. The classic example of a pure separation of powers is found in the United States, where the legislative function is the task of Congress; the executive function is the job of the President and his or her cabinet, who are not members of Congress; and the judicial function is the task of judges. That degree of separation of powers is absent in the United Kingdom. In part, this is because the Prime Minister and his or her cabinet are Members of Parliament; they are part of the legislature as well as being the head of the executive branch. Consequently, we say that the legislative and executive branches are largely fused together.

However, there is a partial separation of powers in the United Kingdom. While the legislative and executive functions are fused, the courts are more or less separate, with some exceptions. The most obvious exception is the House of Lords. The House of

Lords is the highest court of appeal in the United Kingdom and, although the Law Lords are not members of the government, they do sit in the House of Lords in its legislative capacity. However, constitutional convention dictates that the Law Lords should not offer opinions to the government on political matters, at least until retirement from the bench. The judiciary has an important function with respect to the executive, in that judges act as a "check" on executive actions. That is, judges can and do assert their power, derived from the rule of law, to *review* actions taken by the executive. We look at the relationship between Parliamentary supremacy, judicial review, and the rule of law in Chapter 3.

ESSAY QUESTION

"The rule of law is neither a simple ideal nor an easy one to live up to. It expresses a number of principles and requirements, based on various grounds. They look attractive enough when they are expressed as slogans, but they prove to be strikingly difficult to apply in any straightforward way to the governing apparatus of modern society" (Jeremy Waldron, *The Law* (Routledge, London, 1990), p. 52).
Discuss with examples.

3

CONSTITUTIONAL ASPECTS OF LEGAL METHOD: JUDICIAL REVIEW

In this chapter, we continue to look at fundamental constitutional doctrines which are of importance to a study of legal method. Our focus now turns to *judicial review*, one of the principal ways in which the judiciary is supposed to "check" (or control) the actions of the executive branch of government, to ensure that the executive acts in accordance with the principle of legality. Judicial review is not concerned with the wisdom or merits of executive action. Rather, it is the judicial function of determining whether the executive has acted under legal authority and has followed proper procedure in its actions. The sorts of questions judges ask in judicial review are: did the government have the power granted to it under law to take this action? Did it follow the procedure set down in legislation? Has it acted unreasonably and, therefore, outside of its powers? This inherent power of the courts to review the executive exemplifies Dicey's rule of law vision; that under our constitutional structure, judges will ensure that executive power is not exercised in an arbitrary fashion. Rather, it must be exercised under lawful authority. In this way, the judiciary is supposed to keep the government in "check". Judicial review raises important questions about the relationship between the judiciary and the executive and legislative branches of government and, in addition, it has given rise to difficult questions about the legitimacy of judges appearing to "override" the intention of Parliament as expressed in legislation.

JUDICIAL REVIEW AND THE RULE OF LAW

The basis for judicial review of executive action can be found in the fundamental tenets of the rule of law, which we examined in Chapter 2. For Dicey, the role of the judiciary was to ensure that power was not exercised by governments in an arbitrary, "lawless" fashion. Judicial review, it is argued, is the means by which judges ensure that power is exercised in conformity with the authority granted by Parliament under statute.

Jeffrey Jowell, "The Rule of Law Today" in *The Changing Constitution* (3rd ed., Jeffrey Jowell and Dawn Oliver, eds., Clarendon Press, Oxford, 1994), pp. 73–75:

"How does the Rule of Law operate in practice in the United Kingdom? Let us first note that our courts have not, outside of directly effective European Law, felt themselves able to review the validity of primary legislation. This means that a principle like the Rule of Law *can* be expressly overridden by Parliament. As Dicey required, the principle of Parliamentary Sovereignty prevails. But the absence of judicial review of primary legislation is by no means fatal to the Rule of Law. As a constitutional principle it still serves as a basis for evaluation of laws and a critical focus for public debate. A British government may succeed in introducing detention without trial, or retroactive legislation, but strong justification is needed for such a law to withstand the Rule of Law's moral strictures.

In addition, the Rule of Law is upheld by the courts to this extent: in interpreting the scope of a statutory power, the courts make the implication that Parliament intended to conform to the Rule of Law. If the scope of the power is ambiguous, the principle applies. It is only excluded where clearly stated to the contrary.

Beyond Parliamentary legislation the practical application of the Rule of Law is more obvious. It is applied through judicial review of the actions and decisions of all officials performing public functions. It is enforced through our Administrative Law. In large part, Administrative Law is the implementation of the constitutional principle of the Rule of Law. There are three principal 'grounds' of judicial review: review for 'illegality', for 'procedural impropriety', and for 'irrationality' (or unreasonableness). The implementation of each of these grounds involves the courts in applying different aspects of the Rule of Law.

Under the ground of illegality the courts act as guardian of Parliament's purpose, and may strike down official decisions which violate that purpose. Even when wide discretionary power is conferred upon an official the courts are not willing to permit decisions which go outside its 'four corners'. Under the ground of procedural propriety the courts may, even where the statute is silent, supply the 'omission of the legislature' in order to insist that the decision-maker grant a fair hearing to the applicant before depriving him or her of a right, interest or legitimate expectation. (The doctrine of legitimate expectation is itself rooted in the notion of legal certainty; the courts require a decision-maker at least to provide the affected person with a hearing before disappointing him of an expectation reasonably induced. At times the promised benefit itself may be required. In either case certainty triumphs over administrative convenience.)

It is perhaps more difficult to countenance the application of the Rule of Law in the third ground of judicial review, that of irrationality or unreasonableness, because it raises the question whether the principle governs the substance and not merely the procedure of official action.

To what extent does the Rule of Law touch on the substance, as well as the procedure, of official action? We have seen that laws in practice are not always enforced rigorously, but rather selectively, allowing for personal and other mitigating factors (as with the doctor speeding to the scene of an accident in the early hours of the morning). But suppose the police decide to charge only bearded male drivers with traffic offences and leave the clean-shaven and women drivers alone? Or to charge only drivers of a particular race? Suppose an education authority chose to dismiss all teachers with red hair? Would these decisions infringe the Rule of Law on the ground of their substance? Courts in this country interfere with this kind of decision on the ground of its being an abuse of discretion, the term used being 'unreasonableness' in the sense set out in the celebrated *Wednesbury* case. Is this judicial interference ultimately justified on the ground that the offending decision was a breach of substantive Rule of Law? If so justified, judges lay themselves open to accusations of improper interference with the substance of administration, about which they are reputed to know very little.

Denials of substantive interference are made on the ground that what the courts are doing when interfering with arbitrary, capricious, or oppressive decisions is ensuring that the official action is faithful to the law's purpose, thus achieving the containment of the administration in accordance with an implied legislative scheme. Even if a minister has power to act 'as he thinks fit', it is assumed that the statute conferring that power requires standards that are rationally related to purpose, and that the charging of only bearded drivers could not be related to the purpose of preventing unsafe driving. In practice, however, the legislation frequently has no clear 'purpose' itself, and to pretend otherwise is to adopt a fiction. Parliament often delegates enforcement to ministers, other authorities, or officials precisely in order to allow *them* to define and elaborate purpose. Implementation is often a process from the bottom up, rather than from the top down. When the Rule of Law allows judicial interference on grounds of 'unreasonableness', 'irrationality', or 'oppressiveness', it does become a sub-stantive doctrine—one that is less easily accepted than the procedural, particularly in a society without a written constitution. Courts therefore tread warily on substantive Rule of Law and seek to exclude (or disguise) policy considerations from the decision. The 'unreason-ableness' doctrine itself carefully avoids judicial second-guessing of the administration on the grounds of mere disagreement, and only permits interference if the official decision verges on the outlandish.

Nevertheless, in certain cases the 'unreasonableness' doctrine does not even attempt to pretend that judicial interference with administrative action is based on lack of fidelity to stat-utory purpose. Take, for example, the case where a condition attached to a planning permis-sion was held 'unreasonable' because it required the owner to dedicate some of his land to the local authority for a public right of way. The condition here is by no means unrelated to the purpose of the planning legislation (the right of way was necessary for good planning), but it violates the owner's legitimate expectation not to be deprived of his property without com-pensation. Here the Rule of Law as substantive principle justifies judicial intervention. A local authority which withdrew the licence of a rugby football club because some of their members had visited South Africa also fell foul of the principle in the form of the doctrine that there should be no punishment where there was no law (prohibiting contact with South Africa).

The Rule of Law does, therefore, possess substantive content. It is a principle that promotes the virtues of regularity, rationality, and integrity on the part of officials, and thus protects the legitimate expectations (to both fair procedures and substance) of affected individuals."

QUESTION

How does judicial review forward both a procedural and a substantive conception of the rule of law?

Jowell hints at the possibility that judicial review, at times, may appear to involve the judiciary substituting its view of appropriate public policy for that which has been implemented by officials of government. In those situations, the judiciary appears to be exercising a highly *political* function. Moreover, the politics of the judiciary, as we will see in Chapter 6, has often appeared to be very conservative. A "classic" example of judical review which seemed to tread very close to party politics occurred in the early 1980s:

Bromley London Borough Council v. Greater London Council and another [1982] 1 All E.R. 129, CA.

[This case was a judicial review of the action of the Greater London Council (GLC) in attempting to reduce fares on London Transport by 25 per cent. Bromley London Borough Council brought the proceedings, asking the courts to stop the implementa-tion of the policy (which required substantial increases in rates) on the grounds that it was beyond the powers of the GLC as defined by the relevant statutes of Parliament or, alternatively, that the policy implementation was an invalid exercise of the GLC's dis-cretion provided under statute. The Divisional Court refused the application, but the Borough Council appealed to the Court of Appeal.]

Lord Denning M.R.:

Introduction in outline

"On 7 May 1981 there was an election for the Greater London Council (the GLC). In advance of the election, the Labour Party issued a manifesto. In it they promised that, if they won, they would within six months cut the fares on London's buses and tubes by 25%. They did win the election. They kept their promise. They told the London Transport Executive (the LTE) to cut the fares by 25%. The travelling public were well pleased with the gift. It meant millions of pounds in their pockets instead of in the ticket machines. But not the ratepayers of London. They were required to contribute £69m to pay for it. In order to enforce payment, the GLC made a supplementary precept. This was an order directed to all the 35 London boroughs commanding them to raise the necessary funds. They were to do it by making a supplementary rate on all the ratepayers. The London boroughs have most reluctantly obeyed. They have made the supplementary rate and have required their ratepayers to pay it. But meanwhile one London borough, Bromley, has challenged the validity of the whole procedure. They apply to the courts for an order of certiorari to quash the supplementary precept.

At the outset I would say that all three members of this court are interested on all sides. We are all fare-paying passengers on the tubes and buses and benefit from the 25% cut in fares. My wife and I also have the benefit of senior citizens to travel free. We are all ratepayers in the area of Greater London and have to pay the increase in rates imposed by the supplementary precept. No objection is taken by any party to our hearing the case. Any Court of Appeal would be likewise placed.

Now for the detail

The manifesto

In March 1981 the Greater London Labour Party issued a manifesto headed 'Socialist Policy for the G.L.C.' It filled a printed book of some 180 pages containing detailed proposals and promises. At the same time they issued a summarised version headed 'Vote Labour in London May 7th'. It was priced at 30p. It filled a printed booklet of 14 pages of close print. It said in the foreward: 'All candidates are committed to the proposals and pledges contained in the manifesto.' It set out proposals for action on jobs, on housing, on transport, on the environment, on safety and on recreation. On transport it made this pledge:

'*Fares*. Within six months of winning the election, Labour will cut fares on London Transport buses and tubes by an average of 25%. At the same time a much simpler system of fares will be introduced, one which will be easy to understand, will allow faster boarding and will ease the burden on transport workers. There will then be a freeze on fares for four years. The existing system of free travel for senior citizens on London's buses will be extended to the tubes and British rail services within London.'

There was a paragraph dealing with the cost of all the proposals, taken together. It was headed '*Paying for the Programme*':

'Labour presents this programme in the full knowledge of its financial implications. As more than half of the G.L.C.'s rate revenue comes from the commercial sector, individual householders will only be paying about £1 a week more by 1983/4 for cheaper fares, better public transport services, less congestion, better housing, more jobs, and a safer, cleaner environment. For example, regular users of London Transport will benefit by £1.50 a week.'

The effect of the election

At the election of 7 May 1981 the Labour Party won by a small majority of seats. This was interpreted by their spokesmen on many occasions as giving them a 'clear mandate' from the people of London to cut the fares by 25%. Not only as giving them a mandate but also as a 'promise' and also a 'commitment' by which they promised and committed themselves to implementing a reduction in fares by 25% overall.

The leader of the council gives instructions

The election was on Thursday, 7 May. They lost no time. On Tuesday, 12 May 1981 there was a meeting between Mr Kenneth Livingstone, the leader of the council, and Sir Peter Masefield, the chairman of the LTE. There is no record of what took place, but Dunn LJ inferred, and certainly reasonably inferred, that 'the leader told Sir Peter that the GLC intended to put into immediate effect the policy of overall reduction of fares of 25% and asked him to produce proposals for a new fare structure to implement the policy and a revised budget for 1981'.

This inference is supported by a report of 2 June which recorded that:

'The Leader of the Council has *instructed* London Transport to submit to the Transport Committee at their meeting on 1 July 1981 fares proposals which incorporate a proposal for an *immediate* reduction in London Transport fares of 25%.

That is the very word, 'instructed': 'The Leader of the Council has *instructed* London Transport . . .'

Those instructions were duly carried out. On 9 June 1981 London Transport submitted a memorandum and issued a press release saying that the GLC had made a '*requirement* of a 25 per cent overall cut' and put forward alternative methods of implementing that requirement. I stress again the words 'requirement of the GLC'.

The block grant

Whilst the LTE was arranging for the 25% cut, the officers of the GLC were looking into the effect on the rates. They then drew to the attention of the GLC that the ratepayers would suffer a heavy penalty. It would lose the block grant which the government gave it. So they would have to pay not only for the cut in fares but also for the loss of the grant. That was pointed out on 23 June 1981 by the comptroller of finance. In a report of that date he said:

'. . . The Council faces a loss of block grant of £91 million under the block grant system for a decision to finance £110 million revenue costs from rates instead of fares. Therefore, the Council has to decide not only how to finance the operating shortfall in 1981–82 but whether rate payers should pay a heavy penalty . . . the Council is faced with the fact that . . . the rate payers will pay heavily . . .'

This was nothing more nor less than a plea by the officers that the ratepayers should be considered. But it fell on deaf ears. Notwithstanding the clear warning, the GLC decided at a meeting on 7 July 1981 to implement the cut in full regardless of the heavy penalty on the ratepayers. It had before it a report saying that it was necessary to 'implement the *commitment* to reduce fares by an overall 25 per cent'. This meant the levy of a supplementary rate precept. The whole was to take effect by 4 October 1981. That recommendation was approved by a majority of 43 to 33.

The final steps are taken

On 21 July 1981 the GLC did all that was necessary to complete the cut and to issue a supplementary precept. In advance of it, it issued a press release which is most illuminating. It put all the blame on the government. I will quote two sentences from it:

'The bill to ratepayers for the GLC's cutting of bus and Tube fares by 25 per cent and keeping London Transport out of the red will be a 6.1p rate—"as predicted during the GLC election campaign", announced Dr. Tony Hart, Chairman of the Council's Finance and General Purposes Committee, today. But "vindictive" Government policies over local council grants will double the cost to ratepayers without any benefit to Londoners.'

The press release is worth reading in full. All I would say is that it shows that the Labour Party in their manifesto had reckoned only on a 6.1p increase in the rates; but also that in point of fact it would have to be 11.9p in the rates. So their calculations during the course of the election have all been falsified by events since the election in regard to the block grant. Nevertheless they determined to press on with their cut and the precept, regardless of the penal blow it would inflict on the ratepayers. It was carried by 42 to 38 on 21 July 1981.

The supplementary precept is issued

On 22 July 1981 the GLC issued to all the London boroughs a supplementary precept for 1981–82. It said:

> 'The Greater London Council hereby require you to levy in respect of the current year the rates specified below:
> General London Purposes at 6.1 new pence in the pound (chargeable on the whole of Greater London).'

Then there is this significant addition about the loss of the block grant:

> 'The supplementary precepts issued are gross precepts and therefore take no account of the GLC or ILEA block grant losses consequent on the issue of the supplementary precepts. Authorities are therefore recommended to levy an additional rate for grant loss . . . .'

The London borough of Bromley received that precept on 28 July. They took legal advice and decided to challenge it. They telephoned the GLC on 10 August and told it so. Then on 11 September they issued proceedings in the courts.

The law

This brings me to the law. It was divided in the argument in two parts. First, the statutory powers of the GLC. Second, the way it exercised its powers.

The statutory powers of the GLC

We have studied in detail the provisions of the Transport (London) Act 1969. I will state the result. The LTE is a statutory corporation, a body corporate. It is entrusted with the task of running the buses and tubes of London. It is its duty to run it on business lines. It must manage its income and expenditure so as to break even so far as practicable. If it cannot pay its way, the GLC can make grants to it to keep it going. The GLC have a degree of control over it, but it is of a limited character. The GLC can give it general directions on matters of policy (see s 11(1)) but it cannot interfere with the day-to-day running of its affairs. But even those matters of policy are not open-ended. They are confined to policies which will 'promote the process of integrated, efficient and economic transport facilities and services for Greater London' (see s 1(1)). This includes the objectives of quick, frequent, reliable services, and reasonable fares. But it does not include the promotion of social or philanthropic or political objectives. It does not include free travel for all. It does not include a reduction in fares which is completely uneconomic. The word 'economic' is significant. It means what we all mean when we say of a financial proposal, 'That is not an economic proposition,' meaning that under it expenditure will exceed the income. It certainly does not warrant the instruction given here to cut fares by 25%.

Apart from this fundamental point, the statute contains specific provisions about fares. The LTE is the charging authority, not the GLC. The LTE has in the first instance to settle the general level and structure of the fares to be charged. These are subject to the approval of the GLC. If the GLC approve, they are to be published. If the GLC disapprove, then there is this important provision in s 11(3):

> '. . . the Council may direct the Executive to submit proposals for an alteration in the Executive's fare arrangements to achieve any object of general policy specified by the Council in the direction.'

Any such direction has by s 41(3) to be in writing. No such direction was given in this case.

Furthermore, when the LTE is settling the general level and structure of fares, it must consider the position of those parts of its undertaking which fall outside the London area. It must consult the county councils concerned and see if they are prepared to make any contribution to the cost. No such consultation was held in this case.

In view of these considerations, I am of opinion that the GLC had no power whatever to give instructions to the LTE as it purported to do. The leader had no right whatever to go to Sir Peter Masefield and tell him to cut the fares by an overall 25%; nor had Sir Peter any business to accede to it. The GLC itself had no power to make resolutions to enforce a 25% cut. That was a completely uneconomic proposition done for political motives, for which there is no warrant; including the supplementary precept. It was beyond its powers. It is *ultra vires* and void. It cannot be allowed to stand.

The way it exercised its powers

In case I am wrong on that point, I go on to consider whether the GLC exercised its powers properly.

It appears to me that the GLC owed a duty both to the travelling public and to the ratepayers. Its duty to the travelling public is to provide an integrated, efficient and economic service at reasonable fares. Its duty to the ratepayers is to charge them as much as is reasonable and no more. In carrying out those duties, the members of the GLC have to balance the two conflicting interests: the interest of the travelling public in cheap fares and the interest of the ratepayers in not being overcharged. The members of the GLC have to hold the balance between these conflicting interests. They have to take all relevant considerations into account on either side. They must not be influenced by irrelevant considerations. They must not give undue weight to one consideration over another, lest they upset the balance. They must hold the balance fairly and reasonably. If they come to a decision which is, in all the circumstances, unjust and unreasonable, then the courts can and should interfere. . . .

[T]he majority of the GLC gave altogether undue weight to the following consideration. They had issued a manifesto in which they had promised to cut the fares on London Transport by 25%. They regarded the election result as giving them a *mandate* to fulfil that promise. They regarded themselves as *committed* to the implementation of that promise. They were determined to 'honour' that commitment, come what may. They afterwards discovered that it would injure the ratepayers severely, far more severely than they had realised when they made the promise. It would injure the ratepayers because of the loss of the block grant. This loss has doubled the burden on the ratepayers. But nevertheless the majority of the GLC determined to go ahead with the cut of 25% irrespective of the penalising hardship on the ratepayers.

In giving such weight to the manifesto, I think the majority of the GLC were under a complete misconception. A manifesto issued by a political party, in order to get votes, is not to be taken as gospel. It is not to be regarded as a bond, signed, sealed and delivered. It may contain, and often does contain, promises or proposals that are quite unworkable or impossible of attainment. Very few of the electorate read the manifesto in full. A goodly number only know of it from what they read in the newspapers or hear on television. Many know nothing whatever of what it contains. When they come to the polling booth, none of them vote for the manifesto. Certainly not for every promise or proposal in it. Some may be influenced by one proposal. Others by another. Many are not influenced by it at all. They vote for a party and not for a manifesto. I have no doubt that in this case many ratepayers voted for the Labour Party even though, on this item alone, it was against their interests. And vice versa. It seems to me that no party can or should claim a mandate and commitment for any one item in a long manifesto. When the party gets into power, it should consider any proposal or promise afresh, on its merits, without any feeling of being obliged to honour it or being committed to it. It should then consider what is best to do in the circumstances of the case and to do it if it is practicable and fair.

Another thing is that the figure of 25% was not explained in any way whatever. No councillor has given evidence or has made an affidavit before the courts at all. It is acknowledged by the GLC that the statute does not empower it to abolish fares altogether, or to give free travel for all. But in principle I see no difference between abolishing fares altogether and cutting them by one-half or one-quarter. It is a gift to the travelling public at the expense of the general body of ratepayers. There seems to be no financial reason for choosing 25%. Why not 20% or 30% or even 50%? It seems to me that the figure of 25% was an arbitrary figure clutched from the air in order to be attractive to the electorate.

In the result I hold the GLC did not hold the balance fair. The 25% was more than fair to the travelling public and less than fair to the ratepayers. Millions of passengers on the buses and tubes come from far outside the London area. They come every day. They get the benefit of the 25% cut in fares without paying a penny on their rates at home. That is more than fair to them. It is a gift indeed to them, given without paying a penny for it. Whereas thousands of ratepayers in London who pay the rates never use the buses or tubes at all. Bromley, for instance, has no tubes. It is less than fair to them. It is positively penal. It is not fair to make these ratepayers pay for these gifts to people who come from far afield. The employees of London Transport see the 'cut' as equivalent to a money gift. They get free travel anyway. They each claimed, and got, an extra £50 because the free travel was worth less after the 'cut'. It cost £3m, all to be paid by the ratepayers.

Conclusion

My conclusion is that the actions here of the GLC went beyond its statutory powers and are null and void. Even if they were within their statutory powers, they were distorted by giving undue weight to the manifesto and by the arbitrary and unfair nature of the decision. The supplementary precept must be quashed, and a declaration made accordingly.

I realise that this must cause much consternation to the GLC and the LTE. They will be at their wits end to know what to do. But it is their own fault. They were very foolish not to take legal advice before they embarked on this sequel to their election. Even after legal proceedings were intimated to them in August, they went ahead with their plans and put them into operation on 4 October 1981. They must unscramble the affair as best they can. At any rate, they cannot burden the ratepayers of London with this supplementary precept.

I would allow the appeal accordingly."

[Oliver L.J. and Watkins L.J. delivered separate reasons, concurring in the result reached by Lord Denning M.R. The case was appealed by the GLC to the House of Lords, which affirmed, on varied grounds, the result reached by the Court of Appeal.]

The *Bromley* decision was subject to harsh criticism, as an example both of judicial intervention in matters properly left to elected representatives, as well as for the alleged failure of the judiciary to properly recognise either the purpose of the legislation which empowered the GLC in this matter, or the legitimacy of the concerns which gave rise to the fare policy.

J.A.G. Griffith, *The Politics of the Judiciary* (4th ed., Harper Collins, London, 1991), pp. 130–131:

"In this case, the Law Lords chose to say that the GLC had not adequately taken into account the interests of the ratepayers and that the interests of the users of public transport had been unduly preferred. Such an argument can logically be applied whenever public authorities spend the ratepayers' (or the taxpayers') money to further some statutory purpose. Particular public expenditure can always be criticized on the ground that it is excessive or wrongly directed, whether on defence or education or the building of motorways or any other public service. The constitutional reply is that public authorities, being directly or indirectly elected, are the representatives of the public interest and that their function is precisely that of making such decisions. The criticism is then seen as being political and if the electors of Greater London disapprove of what is being done in their name by their representatives, the remedy lies in their hands at the next election. Nor is this merely constitutional or political theory, divorced from reality, for without doubt the election in 1985 for the GLC would have turned very largely on this issue and on the view taken of the controversial Labour administration at County Hall during its four years in office. It is surely no more the function of the judiciary to tell the GLC where the public interest lay in its spending of public money than it is the function of the judiciary to make similar arguments about spending by the Departments of the central government."

J.A.G. Griffith, *The Politics of the Judiciary* (4th ed., Harper Collins, London, 1991), pp. 302–304:

"The judgments delivered in the Court of Appeal and the House of Lords in *Bromley v GLC* demonstrate how ill-suited is judicial review to the examination of administrative policies. They show how the narrow approach of the courts to the interpretation of statutes leads to a misunderstanding of the purpose of legislation. . . .

The crisis in urban transport received popular recognition in the publication in 1963 of Colin Buchanan's *Traffic in Towns*. This was followed in 1966 by the white paper on *Transport Policy*. This emphasized the 'severe discomforts' brought by the growth of road traffic: congestion, the misery of commuter travel, noise, fumes, danger, casualties and the threat to the environment; and the need to plan, as a whole, for the related needs of industry, housing and transport. The paper drew attention to the mutually contradictory objectives of providing adequate services and self-financing.

In January 1968, the London Transport Joint Review was published and was followed in July by the white paper *Transport in London*. The Review found that the major factor underlying London Transport's recurrent financial deficit was the imbalance between peak and off-peak demand. The Review was somewhat ambiguous about the need for financial viability, but it certainly envisaged some form of grant and emphasized the social benefits of controlling the level of fares while providing proper services. *Transport in London* went further in emphasizing the need of the transport system to take account of 'the social as well as the economic needs of the country'. Subsidization through the local rates was one of the means adopted by the Transport Act 1968 for conurbations outside London and this was intended to enable the transport authorities to achieve, in part, the purpose of developing transport as a social service.

The Transport (London) Act 1969 was seen by ministers as taking this approach further. For the first time in London, the responsibility for transport was given to a directly elected local authority acting through an Executive appointed by itself. Comparison has been made with a nationalized industry operating the day-to-day management under the general directions of a minister. But the control by the GLC over the LTE was much tighter than that of a minister over the coal, gas or electricity authorities. The GLC was not merely empowered but required by section 1 'to develop policies, and to encourage, organize and, where appropriate, carry out measures'. The LTE existed to implement policies of the GLC (section 4(1)) and to act 'in accordance with principles laid down or approved by the GLC' (section 5(1)). Additionally, the GLC might give the LTE general directions in relation to functions which the GLC was under a duty to perform (section 11(1)). There were also other more detailed provisions emphasizing the powers of the GLC. Above all, the GLC's primary duty was to promote 'the provision of integrated, efficient and economic transport facilities and services for Greater London'. Finally, the LTE was required to submit to the GLC for their approval the general level and structure of the fares to be charged and the GLC might 'direct the Executive to submit proposals for an alteration in the Executive's fare arrangements to achieve any object of general policy specified by the Council in the direction' (section 11(3)). . . .

Bromley v GLC raises all the questions about the nature, the function, and the limits of judicial review. The whole method of adjudication as presently adopted by the courts is inappropriate to the consideration of political decisions affecting the distribution of costs between the tax and rate-paying public, on the one hand, and the users of public services, on the other."

Following the decision of the House of Lords in *Bromley v. GLC*, fares doubled, and the GLC produced a new scheme, in which it directed the LTE to cut fares by 25 per cent, with an accompanying grant from the Council to the LTE to make up the lost revenues. The LTE objected, and the case was heard by the Divisional Court, which upheld the validity of the scheme, on the ground that the grant allowed the LTE to balance its revenue account, and because the GLC had now considered its statutory duties. Griffith commented:

> "The new scheme, upheld by the Divisional Court in the later case, was made under the same statute and did not appreciably hold a different balance between ratepayers and transport users. The decision of the Divisional Court bears the marks of a rescue operation, seeking to save some sanity for transport policy in London and for the right of statutory authorities to exercise statutory powers within the statutory terms given to them."[1]

NOTES AND QUESTIONS

- To the extent that judicial review adopts a substantive conception, can it be constitutionally justified? Use the judgment of Lord Denning M.R. in *Bromley v. GLC* as evidence for your argument.

- The judgment of Denning M.R. in *Bromley v. GLC* contains numerous assertions about the political process, as well as a number of ideological assumptions about the self-interest of individuals with regard to tax and transport policy. Summarise those assertions and assumptions. Would you describe the judgment as more "political" than "legal"? Could a judgment be written in this case which did not appear to be "political"?

- In 1984 the Conservative government announced its intention to introduce legislation to abolish the GLC, and under the Local Government Act 1985 the abolition took effect on April 1, 1986.

In some cases, by contrast, the judiciary has been highly deferential to the actions of the executive, particularly in those cases where executive action is justified on the basis of "national security".

Council of Civil Service Unions and others v. Minister for the Civil Service [1984] 3 All E.R. 935, HL.

Lord Fraser of Tullybelton:
"My Lords, Government Communications Headquarters (GCHQ) is a branch of the public service under the Foreign and Commonwealth Office, the main functions of which are to ensure the security of the United Kingdom military and official communications, and to provide signals intelligence for the government. These functions are of great national importance and they involve handling secret information which is vital to the national security. The

---

[1] J.A.G. Griffith, *The Politics of the Judiciary* (4th ed., Harper Collins, London, 1991), pp. 135–136.

main establishment of GCHQ is at Cheltenham, where over 4,000 people are employed. There are also a number of smaller out-stations, one of which is at Bude in Cornwall.

Since 1947, when GCHQ was established in its present form, all the staff employed there have been permitted, and indeed encouraged, to belong to national trade unions, and most of them did so. Six unions were represented at GCHQ. They were all members, though not the only members, of the Council of Civil Service Unions (CCSU), the first appellant. The second appellant is the secretary of CCSU. The other appellants are individuals who are employed at GCHQ and who were members of one or other of the unions represented there. A departmental Whitley Council was set up in 1947 and, until the events with which this appeal is concerned, there was a well-established practice of consultation between the official side and the trade union side about all important alterations in the terms and conditions of employment of the staff.

On 25 January 1984 all that was abruptly changed. The Secretary of State for Foreign and Commonwealth Affairs announced in the House of Commons that the government had decided to introduce with immediate effect new conditions of service for all staff at GCHQ, the effect of which was that they would no longer be permitted to belong to national trade unions but would be permitted to belong only to a departmental staff association approved by the director. The announcement came as a complete surprise to the trade unions and to the employees at GCHQ, as there had been no prior consultation with them. The principal question raised in this appeal is whether the instruction by which the decision received effect, and which was issued orally on 22 December 1983 by the respondent (who is also the Prime Minister), is valid and effective in accordance with art 4 of the Civil Service Order in Council 1982. The respondent maintains that it is. The appellants maintain that it is invalid because there was a procedural obligation on the respondent to act fairly by consulting the persons concerned before exercising her power under art 4 of the Order in Council, and she had failed to do so. Underlying that question, and logically preceding it, is the question whether the courts, and your Lordships' House in its judicial capacity, have power to review the instruction on the ground of a procedural irregularity, having regard peculiarly to the facts (a) that it was made in the exercise of a power conferred under the royal prerogative and not by statute and (b) that it concerned national security.

It is necessary to refer briefly to the events which led up to the decision of 22 December 1983. Between February 1979 and April 1981 industrial action was taken at GCHQ on seven occasions. The action took various forms: one-day strikes, work to rule and overtime bans. The most serious disruption occurred on 9 March 1981, when about 25% of the staff went on one-day strike and, according to Sir Robert Armstrong, the Secretary to the Cabinet, who made an affidavit in these proceedings, parts of the operations at GCHQ were virtually shut down. The appellants do not accept the respondent's view of the seriousness of the effects of industrial action on the work at GCHQ. But clearly it must have had some adverse effect, especially by causing some interruption of the constant day and night monitoring of foreign signals communications. The industrial action was taken mainly in support of national trade unions, when they were in dispute with the government about conditions of service of civil servants generally, and not about local problems at GCHQ. In 1981 especially it was part of a campaign by the national trade unions, designed to do as much damage as possible to government agencies including GCHQ. Sir Robert Armstrong in his affidavit refers to several circular letters and 'campaign reports' issued by CCSU and some of its constituent unions, which show the objectives of the campaign. . . ."

[The first and second appellants obtained leave from Glidewell J. to bring proceedings for judicial review on the basis that the instruction of December 22, 1983 was invalid. Glidewell J. found it to be invalid on the basis of a procedural irregularity in failing to consult before issuing the instruction. The Court of Appeal reversed the judge's decision and dismissed the application for judicial review. Lord Fraser considered the first issue—the reviewability of the exercise of prerogative powers, leaving the question open. He then considered the national security issue, but only after finding that in the absence of a pressing matter of national security, a duty to consult the trade unions would be found on the basis of a legitimate expectation based on prior practice.]

> "The question is one of evidence. The decision on whether the requirements of national security outweigh the duty of fairness in any particular case is for the government and not for the courts; the government alone has access to the necessary information, and in any event the judicial process is unsuitable for reaching decisions on national security. . . .
>
>   The evidence in support of this part of the respondent's case came from Sir Robert Armstrong in his first affidavit . . . . [I]t does set out the respondent's view that to have entered into prior consultation would have served to bring out the vulnerability of areas of operation to those who had shown themselves ready to organise disruption. That must be read along with the earlier parts of the affidavit in which Sir Robert had dealt in some detail with the attitude of the trade unions which I have referred to earlier in this speech. The affidavit, read as a whole, does in my opinion undoubtedly constitute evidence that the minister did indeed consider that prior consultation would have involved a risk of precipitating disruption at GCHQ. I am accordingly of the opinion that the respondent has shown that her decision was one which not only could reasonably have been based, but was in fact based, on considerations of national security, which outweighed what would otherwise have been the reasonable expectation on the part of the appellants for prior consultation."

[All of the Law Lords dismissed the appeal. Lords Scarman, Diplock and Roskill found that powers exercised directly under the prerogative are not automatically immune from judicial review. Rather, the issue was the justiciability of its subject matter. But the Lords agreed that once a minister produced evidence that her decision was taken for reasons of national security, the question became non-justiciable because the executive alone was sole judge of what national security required.]

QUESTIONS

- In light of the decision of the House of Lords in *CCSU v. Minister for the Civil Service*, what advice would you give a government minister as to how to ensure that his or her decisions are immune from judicial review?

- Compare the level of *deference* given to the executive in *Bromley* and *CCSU* by the judiciary. How would you explain the difference?

PARLIAMENTARY SUPREMACY AND JUDICIAL REVIEW

The *Bromley v. GLC* case did not directly raise the issue of Parliamentary supremacy. The Greater London Council had limited powers which it had been granted pursuant to statutes enacted by Parliament. The issue was whether, in its attempt to implement the fare policy, it had exceeded those powers or had exercised its discretion unreasonably. In that sense, the judges saw the case as one directly raising "rule of law" issues about the importance of ensuring that officials of the state exercise only those powers granted to them under statute, and do so in a reasonable, rather than arbitrary, fashion.

However, the principle of Parliamentary supremacy, as we saw in Chapter 2, demands that Parliament, provided its procedural rules are followed, has unlimited scope in terms of the substance of the laws it wishes to enact. Parliament thus could have specifically and explicitly empowered the GLC to cut fares, had it so wanted. Moreover, Parliament has frequently attempted to prevent the courts from judicially reviewing the exercise of discretionary powers by officials of the state, by including provisions within the empowering statutes, known as *ouster clauses* (designed to "oust" the judiciary from reviewing government actions). An ouster clause is an attempt by the legislature to explicitly exclude review of a decision by judicial review, within the terms of the relevant statute. Given the principle of Parliamentary supremacy, we might think that such clauses—if they are clear and unambiguous in their language—should ensure that judges do not review the decisions made by officials. However, courts in general have interpreted ouster clauses narrowly, and have jealously guarded their ability to judicially review, on the basis of the importance of this supervisory role for the judiciary in ensuring the legality of executive actions. The "classic" case on ouster clauses is *Anisminic*.

Anisminic Ltd v. Foreign Compensation Commission and another [1969] 2 A.C. 147, HL.

Lord Reid:
"My Lords, in 1956 the appellants owned a mining property in Egypt which they claim was worth over £4,000,000. On the outbreak of hostilities in the autumn of that year it was occupied by Israeli forces and damaged to the extent of some £500,000. On November 1, 1956, property in Egypt belonging to British subjects was sequestrated by the Egyptian Government and on April 29, 1957, after the Israeli forces had withdrawn, the Egyptian Government authorised a sale of the appellants' property and it was sold to an Egyptian organisation referred to in this case as T.E.D.O.

The appellants' property had included a large quantity of manganese ore and steps were taken by them to dissuade their customers from buying ore from T.E.D.O. This seems to have embarrassed the Egyptian authorities, and on November 23, 1957, an agreement was made between the appellants, T.E.D.O. and the Sequestrator General whereby the appellants purported to sell to T.E.D.O. for a price of £500,000 their whole business in Egypt, but this was not to include any claim which the appellants might 'be entitled to assert against any government authority other than the Egyptian government, as a result of loss suffered by, or of damage to or reduction in the value of' their business or assets during the events of October and November, 1956. . ."

[Lord Reid then described a treaty between the Governments of the United Kingdom and the United Arab Republic whereby £27,500,000 was paid in full and final settlement of any claims arising from properties such as Sinai Mining (the name of which was changed to Anisminic). The Foreign Compensation Commission, which had been established in the United Kingdom with powers contained in the Foreign Compensation Act, 1950, was responsible for the payment of compensation arising out of agreements with foreign governments. The primary claim made by Anisminic was dismissed by the commissioner, on the basis that it had sold its interest to T.E.D.O., which was its "successor in title". Anisminic brought an action in the courts against the commission, seeking a declaration to the effect that this determination was a "nullity" and that they were entitled to participate in the compensation fund, on the basis that the commission had misconstrued the statutory order which defined their jurisdiction (which was the basis for the determination that Anisminic was not eligible for compensation). Of relevance to us is the language of the 1950 legislation.]

"The next argument was that, by reason of the provisions of section 4(4) of the 1950 Act, the courts are precluded from considering whether the respondent's determination was a nullity, and therefore it must be treated as valid whether or not inquiry would disclose that it was a nullity. Section 4 (4) is in these terms:

'The determination by the commission of any application made to them under this Act shall not be called in question in any court of law.'

The respondent maintains that these are plain words only capable of having one meaning. Here is a determination which is apparently valid: there is nothing on the face of the document to cast any doubt on its validity. If it is a nullity, that could only be established by raising some kind of proceedings in court. But that would be calling the determination in question, and that is expressly prohibited by the statute. The appellants maintain that that is not the meaning of the words of this provision. They say that 'determination' means a real determination and does not include an apparent or purported determination which in the eyes of the law has no existence because it is a nullity. Or, putting it in another way, if you seek to show that a deter-mination is a nullity you are not questioning the purported determination—you are maintain-ing that it does not exist as a determination. It is one thing to question a determination which does exist: it is quite another thing to say that there is nothing to be questioned. . . .

But there are many cases where, although the tribunal had jurisdiction to enter on the inquiry, it has done or failed to do something in the course of the inquiry which is of such a nature that its decision is a nullity. It may have given its decision in bad faith. It may have made a decision which it had no power to make. It may have failed in the course of the inquiry to comply with the requirements of natural justice. It may in perfect good faith have miscon-strued the provisions giving it power to act so that it failed to deal with the question remitted to it and decided some question which was not remitted to it. It may have refused to take into account something which it was required to take into account. Or it may have based its deci-sion on some matter which, under the provisions setting it up, it had no right to take into account. I do not intend this list to be exhaustive. But if it decides a question remitted to it for decision without committing any of these errors it is as much entitled to decide that question wrongly as it is to decide it rightly."

[Lord Reid then construed the relevant statutory order empowering the commission as not empowering them to inquire into the existence of a "successor in title" (T.E.D.O.) in this case. As a consequence, he found the decision of the Commission to be a nullity, despite the existence of the ouster clause.]

Notes and Questions

- Lord Reid's analysis exemplifies what we might call *legalese*—the use of com-plicated legal language, difficult to understand, in part to disguise the impact of the decision. What Lord Reid has done, in substance, is to review the decision of the Commission, despite the existence of the ouster clause; and that clause was explicitly designed to keep the courts from reviewing decisions of the Commission! Lord Reid's point is that the kind of mistake made by the Commission in this case—which he argues goes to its very *jurisdiction* (or powers granted under the statute) could not have been the kind of review which Parliament intended to oust the courts from conducting. Thus, Lord Reid *inter-prets* the ouster clause narrowly, reading it as not covering this situation. We might ask how such reasoning can be reconciled with the fundamental constitu-tional concept of Parliament supremacy; that is, that Parliament's wisdom, as enacted into statutory law, should be applied, rather than overridden, by the courts.

- Does the language of the ouster clause seem clear? What does it appear to mean? Does Lord Reid's reasoning persuade you of his interpretation?

- Consider Lord Reid's statement that, subject to the provisos he sets out, an agency of the state is entitled to decide an issue rightly or wrongly. Implicitly, from whose perspective is the "rightness" of a decision to be interpreted? Does this statement confirm the argument that judges assume themselves to be in a position from which they alone can determine "Truth"?

A recent case demonstrates the continuing impact of judicial review on *ministerial* action, in the context of the obligations of the state to give *reasons* in respect of decisions made in the exercise of discretion. It is an example of one of the many cases in which judicial review was successfully taken against ministerial actions in the latter years of the Conservative administration.

R. v. Secretary of State for the Home Department, ex p. *Fayed* [1998] 1 W.L.R. 763, CA.

Lord Woolf M.R.:
"This appeal raises issues which concern the relationship between the legislature, the executive and the courts. This is because of the terms of section 44(2) of the British Nationality Act 1981. Section 44(2) lays down that in the case of decisions to which the section applies the Home Secretary is not 'required to assign any reason for the grant or refusal of any application under' the Act of 1981 and the decisions 'shall not be subject to appeal to, or review in, any court.'

Normally any decision taken by a minister under a discretion conferred on him by Parliament which affects a member of the public is required to be exercised in a manner which is fair or, as used to be said, in accordance with the rules of natural justice. This is a long established principle confirmed in a series of cases in the House of Lords. . . .

It is also a principle of our administrative law that when a decision is taken in a manner which breaches the requirement that it should be taken fairly, in the absence of any alternative satisfactory remedy, the member of the public who has been unfairly treated is entitled to a remedy from the High Court on an application for judicial review. In providing a remedy the court is ensuring that decisions of the executive are taken in the manner required by Parliament. . . .

The language of section 44(2) obviously could alter the usual position and in order to determine this appeal it is necessary to decide the extent to which the section relieves the minister from the normal obligation to act fairly and interferes with the ability of the court to play its usual role of protecting members of the public who have been unfairly treated.

The facts

Although these appeals raise issue of principle the facts are not unimportant in determining the issues. . . . The applicants are two brothers, Mr Mohamed Fayed ('Mohamed') and Mr Ali Fayed ('Ali'). Both were born in Egypt, Mohamed in 1933 and Ali in 1943. Mohamed has lived permanently in this country since 1964. He was granted leave to remain indefinitely. Ali started to live permanently in this country in the late 1960s and was granted indefinite leave to remain in 1977. Mohamed is married to a citizen of Finland, but he has dependent children who are British citizens. Ali is married to a British citizen and his three children are also British citizens. As well as making their homes here the Fayeds have substantial business interests in the United Kingdom.

Both are resident here for tax purposes and are fulfilling their fiscal obligations. Their financial contributions to the commercial life of this country are significant. In addition both brothers have made generous contributions to United Kingdom charities. Their careers both before and after they arrived in this country have, however, been the subject of controversy and considerable media interest.

On 29 January 1993, Ali submitted an application for naturalisation as a British citizen under the Act and this was followed by an application by Mohamed on 15 February 1994. The applications were made on forms provided for this purpose which request very limited information. On 23 February 1995 in separate letters, both applications were refused.

During the lengthy period when the applications were under consideration they were merely two out of the 42,000 outstanding applications for British citizenship. The judge therefore was right in stating in his judgment:

'As well as raising questions of moment to the applicants personally, the present case involves consideration of issues of general significance in relation to procedures currently adopted by the Secretary of State to enforce and implement the Act of 1981 and the very large number of applications by citizens of other countries for naturalization here.'

Because Ali was married to a British citizen, his application was governed by section 6(2) of the Act while Mohamed's was made under section 6(1) of the Act. I will refer to section 6 later but the difference in the two brothers' positions are of no significance to the outcome of their appeals.

Ali's application showed that he had been absent from the United Kingdom for a few more than the maximum 90 days allowed in the year prior to submission of his application. However by a letter of 10 May 1995 it is confirmed on behalf of the Home Office that Ali's failure to meet the residence requirement was not the reason for refusal of his application.

In March 1993 the then Home Secretary informed one of Ali's referees that inquiries (the nature of which have not been revealed) were under way and in August 1993 the Home Office requested further documentation including his marriage certificate and confirmation of his tax position.

On 6 December 1993 the head of the Nationality Division confirmed to those representing Ali the receipt of all documentation requested and gave what proved to be an optimistic forecast that a decision would be made in 'up to two months' and that a report was going shortly to the Secretary of State. After consideration by officials Ali's application was passed to a junior minister at the Home Office, Mr Charles Wardle. Subsequently, Mohamed's application was also considered by Mr Wardle. In April 1994 the Home Secretary himself suggested that further inquiries should be made and following a ministerial reshuffle in July 1994 Mr Nicholas Baker replaced Mr Wardle as minister responsible for making the decisions. This appeared in a news release on 24 October 1994 made by the Secretary of State in which he set out his own involvement with the applications. The release also indicated that the applications by the brothers were regarded as being 'especially difficult or sensitive.' No further inquiries or investigations were made of or directed to either of the applicants.

After questions in the House of Commons during the autumn of 1994, in November 1994 Ali's solicitors offered to meet the minister to discuss the application because they were concerned about the delay. They were also concerned that his application might, in some unspecified way, be adversely affected unless it was treated on its own merits. An assurance was given with regard to Ali's concerns but the offer of a meeting was rejected. Discussions were described as 'unnecessary.'

Neither of the brothers has ever been informed what were the aspects of their applications which have given rise to the difficulties or reservations about their applications. Without information as to this it would in practice be impossible for them to try and volunteer information which would support the applications which they have made or any fresh applications which they might want to make in the future.

The letters communicating the decision to refuse the applications were dated 23 February 1995 and were, as the judge said, 'terse in the extreme.' They merely informed each of the Fayeds that 'after careful consideration your application has been refused.' No reasons were given for the decisions so applications were made to the Home Office for reasons for the refusals but they were declined. In March 1995 applications for leave to apply for judicial review were made. Leave was granted by Popplewell J. Judge J. dismissed the applications for judicial review on 26 February 1996. . . .

The fairness issue

It is obvious that the refusal of their application has damaging implications for the Fayeds. This is a matter which is for them, because of their high public profile, of particular significance. The damage is the greater because it is not in dispute that they comply with the formal requirements other than that of good character the relevance of which to the refusal is not known.

Apart from the damaging effect on their reputations of having their applications refused the refusals have deprived them of the benefits of citizenship. The benefits are substantial. Besides the intangible benefit of being a citizen of a country which is their and their families' home, there are the tangible benefits which include freedom from immigration control, citizenship of the European Union and the rights which accompany that citizenship—the right to vote and the right to stand in parliamentary elections. The decisions of the minister are therefore classically ones which but for section 44(2) would involve an obligation on the minister making the decision to give the Fayeds an opportunity to be heard before that decision was reached.

The fact that the Secretary of State may refuse an application because he is not satisfied that the applicant fulfills the rather nebulous reuqirement of good character or 'if he thinks fit' underlines the need for an obligation of fairness. Except where non-compliance with a formal requirement, other than that of good character, is relied on, unless the applicant knows the areas of concern which could result in the application being refused in many cases, and especially this case, it will be impossible for him to make out his case. The result could be grossly unfair. The decision-maker may rely on matters as to which the applicant would have been able to persuade him to take a different view. . . .

This is therefore a case where, ignoring section 44(2), the courts would intervene to achieve fairness for the Fayeds by requiring the minister to identify the areas which were causing them such difficulty in reaching their decision. . . .

The section 44 issue

I have already explained that the fact that section 44 provides that the decision is not to be subject to appeal or review does not affect the obligation of the Secretary of State to be fair or to interfere with the power of the court to ensure that requirements of fairness are met. That this power has no application in this case depends alone on the argument that to comply with what would be the normal requirement to inform the Fayeds of the case which they had to meet would be inconsistent with the express prohibition contained in section 44(2) on the Secretary of State being *required to assign any reason for the grant or refusal of any application under this Act*. This prohibition it is submitted impliedly excludes the requirement to give the Fayeds and other applicants in the same position the notice which fairness dictates they need to make an application. It is contended that unless this is the situation the intention of Parliament expressed in section 44(2) would be frustrated. I cannot accept that this can possibly be the position. It is wholly inconsistent with the principles of administrative law to which I have referred. . . .

It [the approach adopted by Woolf L.J.] does not require the Secretary of State to do more than to identify the subject of his concern in such terms as to enable the applicant to make such submissions as he can. In some situations even to do this could involve disclosing matters which it is not in the public interest to disclose, for example, for national security or diplomatic reasons. If this is the position then the Secretary of State would be relieved from disclosure and it would suffice if he merely indicated that this was the position to the applicant who if he wished to do so could challenge the justification for the refusal before the courts. The courts are well capable of determining public intererst issues of this sort in a way which balances the interests of the individual against the public interests of the state.

I appreciate there is also anxiety as to the administrative burden involved in giving notice of areas of concern. Administrative convenience cannot justify unfairness but I would emphasise that my remarks are limited to cases where an applicant would be in real difficulty in doing himself justice unless the area of concern is identified by notice. In many cases which are less complex than that of the Fayeds the issue may be obvious. If this is the position notice may well be superfluous because what the applicant needs to establish will be clear. If this is the position notice may well not be required. However, in the case of the Fayeds this is not the position because the extensive range of circumstances which could cause the Secretary of State concern mean that it is impractical for them to identify the target at which their representations should be aimed.

The reasons issue

Mr Beloff argued that this is a case which despite section 44(2) the minister is required to give reasons. As I have indicated the minister is not prohibited by the section from giving reasons. On the contrary he has a clear discretion to give reasons. So Mr Beloff argues in a case like this which cries out for reasons the discretion can only lawfully be exercised by giving reasons.

I have already indicated that at common law there is no universal obligation to give reasons but despite this I would certainly regard this as a case where reasons should be given but for section 44(2). However in the light of the *express* prohibition on requiring the Secretary of State to give reasons I would not myself regard this as a case where the need for reasons is so essential that fairness cannot be achieved without reasons as long as an applicant has been given sufficient information as to the subject matter of the decision to enable him to make such submissions as he wishes. I therefore reject Mr Beloff's argument.

The result

The Home Office wrote to the Fayeds' solicitors on 16 March 1995 giving an assurance:

'that very careful consideration was given to all the representations put forward . . . and that further dialogue or opportunity to make further comments was not considered necessary for the purposes of reaching a properly informed decision.'

This is not however an answer to these applications. The problem with the assurance, though no doubt sincerely given, is that it was given without knowing what information could have been provided if there had been compliance with the requirements of fairness so the Fayeds were aware of the targets they had to address.

It is true that until the areas of concern are identified so that it can be ascertained whether the Fayeds would be in a position to make further representations it will not be possible to say whether an injustice has occurred. However justice must not only be done but be seen to be done and it has not been seen to be done in relation to the application of the Fayeds. They have not had the fairness to which they were entitled and the rule of law must be upheld. This being so the Secretary of State is not entitled to take advantage of his own error and contend that the Fayeds have failed to show they have been prejudiced. It follows that the Secretary of State's decisions must be quashed so they can be retaken in a manner which is fair. This is the concern of the courts, Parliament not having excluded the obligation to be fair. They are not concerned with the merits of the decision which should then be made. That is the concern of the Secretary of State.

This decision does not involve any criticism of the Secretary of State or his department. Until this court decided otherwise it was perfectly reasonable to take a different view of the procedural requirements on an application for naturalisation being made."

Kennedy L.J. [Kennedy L.J. delivered dissenting reasons, concluding:]
"How can this court properly give effect to the words of section 44(2) of the Act of 1981? In order to give effect to those words it seems to me that the Secretary of State when called upon to exercise his discretion must be relieved not only of any obligation to give reasons at the

time of or immediately after he makes his decision, but also of any duty to indicate to an applicant at any earlier stage why he is minded to refuse. . . ."

[Phillips L.J. delivered reasons concurring in the judgment of Lord Woolf M.R.]

QUESTION

Are you convinced by Lord Woolf's distinction between a requirement to give reasons (which is explicitly not required under the statute enacted by Parliament), and a requirement to give an indication of the nature of the matter weighing against the granting of citizenship? In ruling that the latter requirement exists, is Lord Woolf undermining the policy which Parliament clearly adopted of excluding a requirement for the Minister to give reasons? Is this compatible with Parliamentary supremacy?

4

CONSTITUTIONAL ASPECTS OF LEGAL METHOD: THE IMPACT OF MEMBERSHIP IN THE EUROPEAN UNION

In this chapter, we examine the most significant change to English legal method in recent years, which continues to unfold: the impact of our membership in the European Union (the E.U.). Although you will study the E.U. in much greater depth in law school courses devoted exclusively to it, a rudimentary knowledge of the impact of membership in the E.U. is essential for a complete picture of the constitutional context within which our legal method operates. We begin with a brief overview of the institutional framework of the E.U., followed by a consideration of its impact on the supremacy of Parliament and, finally, we examine the increasing role and impact of European individual rights on our constitutional structure.

THE INSTITUTIONAL STRUCTURE OF THE E.U.

When the United Kingdom joined the E.U. in 1972, it signed up to a political and economic union of nation states, with a wide ranging institutional structure by which this community (and now "union") was governed.

Phil Harris, *An Introduction to Law* (5th ed., Butterworths, London, 1997), pp. 205–210:

"The European Economic Community was established by the Treaty of Rome in 1957, with the purpose of creating closer relationships between the countries of Europe. The original members of the Community were Germany, France, Italy, Belgium, the Netherlands and Luxembourg. Britain, Denmark, and the Republic of Ireland joined in 1973, followed by Greece in 1979, Spain and Portugal in 1986, and Sweden, Finland and Austria in 1995. It seems likely that membership will increase still further in the future, with a number of east European countries, including Hungary, the Czech Republic, and Romania, expressing an interest in joining.

The Treaty of Rome, together with the Single European Act 1986, made provision, inter alia, for the harmonisation of the legal codes of member states to the extent required for the proper functioning of the common market. What was originally an *economic* community, however, has increasingly moved towards both monetary and political union: the Treaty on European Union (the Maastricht Treaty) of 1992 established the European Union, and contains provision for closer ties on matters including foreign policy, national security, and defence. Two particularly controversial matters in the Treaty are the single European currency, and the 'social chapter', providing for, among other things, expanded legal protection of workers' rights. These developments have been the cause of substantial debate and disagreement between and within all political parties in Britain, with firmly held views ranging from those advocating Britain's full integration into the European Community, to those insisting that Britain should pull out of Europe altogether. Many are fearful of Britain's loss of sovereignty, as EC policies seem increasingly to shift policy-making and political power from Westminster to Brussels. There is little doubt that Britain's membership of the still-developing EC will generate political upheavals for some time to come, especially as the union expands to take in countries of increasingly disparate economic and social backgrounds.

The effect of the European Communities Act 1972 is that the legal provisions contained in the Treaties are part of the law of the United Kingdom, and there is also provision for the output of the European legislative bodies to be incorporated into English law. There are various kinds of EC legislation in addition to the Treaties themselves, the most important of which are the Regulation and the Directive.

Principal institutions of the European Community

Before we discuss in more detail the forms which EC law-making may take, and the implications for domestic law in Britain, it is important to appreciate the principal institutions of the European Community. It is by means of these institutions that the political representatives of member states are able to register the positions taken and views adopted by the governments of EC countries.

The Council of the European Union, created by Article 147 of the EEC Treaty, comprises one representative of the government of each member state. The Council is essentially a co-ordinating body with regard to general EC economic policies. It should not be thought that Britain's representative on the Council is always the same person: exactly which government minister represents Britain's interests will depend on the issue under discussion—if it is transport policy, for example, then it will be the British Minister for Transport who represents the country. The Council is presided over by the representative of member states, each taking a six-month stint, and rotating in a strict cycle. This Council is distinguishable from the *European Council*, which refers to the meetings of the heads of government of all the member states—in fact, what we would normally understand by the term 'summit meetings'. . . .

Although the Council can initiate EC legislation, it is common for such initiatives to originate with the *Commission*. This body comprises 20 Commissioners who, though citizens of member states, are chosen for their known competence and independence. It is not their function simply to represent the interests of their own country; and member states must respect their independence and not try to influence them. A member state must have one Commissioner, but may not have more than two, and at present the larger states—France, the United Kingdom, Germany, Spain and Italy—have two Commissioners (in practice one from the party in government and one from the opposition parties) while the remaining states have one. . . .

The functions of the Commission, in essence, are to initiate and coordinate EC policy and to act as the executive body of the Community. In the process of initiating and formulating policies, the Commission engages in consultation with interested parties from across the whole Community, including industry, trade unions and the civil service equivalents of each member state: it is clear that such consultation should ensure that the positions taken on any given matter by member states' governments are brought to the Commission's attention. The Commission's role includes the specification of detailed practical aspects of policy, and the final policy statements of the Commission go to the Council for deliberation.

The executive powers of the Commission include both the making and the enforcement of rules of EC law, these powers deriving either from the general terms of the Treaty, or in some instances through specific delegation by the Council to the Commission of law-making powers with regard to specific areas, such as the common agricultural policy. The Single European Act 1986 has strengthened this law-making role as delegate of the Council. As to general law-making powers, Article 189 of the EC Treaty provides that:

'In order to carry out their task the Council and the Commission shall, in accordance with the provisions of this Treaty, make regulations, issue directives, take decisions, make recommendations or deliver opinions.'

We will examine this provision in more detail below. With regard to the enforcement of EC rules, the Commission has a major role in investigating alleged breaches of EC law, and notifying the defaulting member state of the breach. In practice, it is usually the case that the member state concerned takes steps to remedy the problem well before the completion of an investigation. . . .

At this point it will be clear that a considerable amount of output from the Commission must be referred for further deliberation and/or action to the Council. Given the fluctuating composition of the latter body, and its relatively infrequent meetings, there was established a body sitting, so to speak, between the Council and the Commission: this is a Committee of Permanent Representatives of the member states, normally known as 'COREPER' (an acronym derived from the French term for this committee). COREPER is a permanent, full-time committee whose function is to sift and filter proposals coming from the Commission to the Council. Through this filtering process, only issues involving major problems or controversies actually come before the Council: the unproblematic and uncontentious proposals are effectively dealt with by COREPER, though the Council always has the final say.

Originally known as the European Assembly, an unelected body with few powers and certainly never meant to be a law-making body, the *European Parliament* (so called since the Single European Act 1986) has undergone significant change and is now (since 1979) composed of members democratically elected by the electorate of each member state.

Over the years, the role and powers of the European Parliament have been considerably extended, and those powers have been extended further by the provisions of the Maastricht Treaty (the Treaty on European Union) which came into force in 1993. There are 626 Members of the European Parliament (MEPs) elected from the member states and each serving for five years. Germany, France, the United Kingdom and Italy each elect 87, Spain 64, the Netherlands 31, Belgium, Portugal and Greece 25, Sweden 21, Austria 20, Denmark and Finland 16, Ireland 15 and Luxembourg 6. MEPs are not mandated by their home governments, but rather operate on a personally independent basis. Not surprisingly for a political body, however, MEPs do make political alliances, though these are political groupings which reflect European, as opposed to domestic, political stances. The essential and original function of the European Parliament is to act as a consultative body; however, since the introduction of elections for MEPs in 1979, the Parliament has sought and won wider powers with regard to the legislative functions of the EC. On some issues, the European Parliament must be consulted as part of the EC's specific procedural requirements, and it has been known for legal rules made by the Council to be annulled on the grounds that the latter failed to consult with the European Parliament on the matter. . . .

One of the most important powers of the European Parliament is that of political control over the Commission. It discusses the reports of the Commission; it may question individual Commissioners, who must answer either orally or by a written response; and it has power, ultimately, to dismiss the entire Commission by a vote of censure. This power, though threatened on occasion, has never been used. The European Parliament has no direct powers of control over the Council, although it has been held by the European Court that the European Parliament may bring an action against either the Council or the Commission if either of these bodies fails to act in circumstances where it should have done so.

The *European Court of Justice*, comprising 15 judges (one from each member state and the President) has as its main task the responsibility of 'ensuring that in the interpretation and application of this Treaty the law is observed' (Article 164). The role and functions of the Court have been concisely summarised thus:

'It is the supreme authority on all matters of Community Law, and in this capacity may be required to decide matters of constitutional law, administrative law, social law and economic law in matters brought directly before it or on application from national courts. In its practices and procedures it draws on Continental models; in developing the substantive law it draws on principles and traditions from all the member states. . . .'

Article 177 (i) provides that:

> 'The Court of Justice shall have jurisdiction to give preliminary rulings concerning:
> (a) the interpretation of this Treaty;
> (b) the validity and interpretation of acts of the institutions of the Community;
> (c) the interpretation of the statutes of bodies established by an act of the council, where those statutes so provide.'

Article 177 also provides that, where such a question arises in any case before a court or tribunal within any member state, that court or tribunal may refer the question to the European Court for a ruling. This jurisdiction is essentially one of preliminary rulings on matters of interpretation of European law (not the domestic law of member states). The European Court hears and decides disputes concerning matters of EC law arising from Article 177 references from domestic courts, and so has an important function regarding matters of interpretation of the Articles of the Treaty."

QUESTION

List the principal institutions of the European Union and their functions.

The mission of the European Union, which is important to an understanding of the way in which the E.U. legal order is evolving, has been described by Shaw.

Jo Shaw, *Law of the European Union* (2nd ed., Macmillan, Basingstoke, 1996), pp. 9–10:

"Broad statements of the aims of the European Community and the more recently created European Union are to be found in the Preambles and introductory sections of the basic Treaties. Article A TEU [Treaty on European Union] recalls the long standing commitment in the Preamble to the EEC Treaty to the creation of an ever closer union among the peoples of Europe, and identifies the creation of the Union as a new stage in this process. A reference to the federal mission of the Union was eradicated from the final version at the insistence of the UK delegation at the meeting of the European Council at Maastricht which finalised the Treaty on European Union. The Union has the following objectives (Article B TEU):

- 'to promote economic and social progress which is balanced and sustainable, in particular through the creation of an area without internal frontiers, through the strengthening of economic and social cohesion and through the establishment of economic and monetary union, ultimately including a single currency in accordance with the provisions of this Treaty;

- to assert its identity on the international scene, in particular through the implementation of a common foreign and security policy including the eventual framing of a common defence policy, which might in time lead to a common defence;

- to strengthen the protection of the rights and interests of the nationals of its Member States through the introduction of a citizenship of the Union;

- to develop closer cooperation on justice and home affairs;

- to maintain in full the *acquis communautaire* and build on it with a view to considering, through the procedure referred to in Article N(2), to what extent the policies and forms of cooperation introduced by this Treaty may need to be revised with the aim of ensuring the effectiveness of the mechanisms and the institutions of the Treaty.'

The specifically socio-economic aspects of these aims are further elaborated in Articles 2, 3 and 3A EC. These identify the task of the European Community as being the promotion of harmonious and balanced economic development, of sustainable and non-inflationary growth respecting the environment, of a high degree of convergence of economic performance, of high levels of employment and social protection, of the raising of the standard of living and quality of life of citizens, and of economic and social cohesion and solidarity among Member States. The twin means for attaining this task are the creation of a common market and an economic and monetary union, and these are themselves to be achieved through the pursuit of the activities set out in Article 3 (common market and common policies) and 3A (monetary union and single currency). So far, the law of the European Community has been, above all, the law of the common market (including the customs union) which has been developing steadily since 1958. For present purposes, we can take the common market referred to in Article 2 as practically identical to the 'internal market' defined in Article 7A EC, the achievement of which was the official central objective of the old European Economic Community between 1986 and the end of 1992. This provides that:

> 'The internal market shall comprise an area without internal frontiers in which the free movement of goods, persons, services and capital is ensured in accordance with the provisions of this Treaty.'

The goal appears, therefore, to be a free market ideal that, as far as possible, the territory of the fifteen member States should resemble a single national market, wheire there is a level competitive playing field for all economic actors and where distortions of competition based on artificial legal barriers such as differences in consumer protection or environmental regulation will be eliminated.

Article 3 EC in turn gives more details on the activities which are to be pursued with a view to attaining this goal. These include the creation of a customs union, involving the abolition of internal customs duties on trade in goods and the erection of a common external tariff and a complementary common policy on external trade, the abolition of other obstacles to trade in goods, and the free movement of services, persons and capital between the Member States. These are essentially negative measures, in that they promote integration by removing existing barriers. Positive integration measures include the establishment of common policies, in fields such as agriculture and transport; the creation of these policies also reveals a certain *dirigiste* element in the thinking of the founders of the Treaty, alongside the commitment to the free market principles of the four freedoms. The commitment to a policy on the harmonisation of national legislation also demonstrates a recognition that deregulated markets alone will not bring about the creation of a single internal market which respects the interests of consumers and the environment, to name but two interests which may be sacrificed in unfettered free market competition. In addition, although subsequent amendments to the original Treaty have brought regional policy goals of social and economic cohesion and solidarity within the remit of the EU's prescribed activities, there is no clear commitment in Article 3 to a general social policy, as a complement to the economic policies described above. However, particularly with the effective conclusion of the lengthy legislative programme to complete the internal market by the end of 1992, the focus of lawmaking has shifted more into the fields of social policy, consumer policy and environmental policy."

QUESTION

Describe the objectives of the European Union.

THE EUROPEAN UNION AND PARLIAMENTARY SUPREMACY

Harris states the issue succinctly:

"Now, given that European law takes precedence over the domestic law of the member states, it can happen that a legal rule of the EC is in direct conflict with a rule of domestic law. What is the consequence of this for English law, and the constitutional doctrine of the supremacy of Parliament? Can we still, in Britain, speak of the constitutional 'sovereignty' of our own Parliament, given the relationships between our law and legislation and those of the European Community?"[1]

That question—the impact of membership in the European Union on the supremacy of Parliament—has been explored by Bradley.

A.W. Bradley, "The Sovereignty of Parliament—in Perpetuity" in *The Changing Constitution* (3rd ed., Jeffrey Jowell and Dawn Oliver, eds., Clarendon Press, Oxford, 1994), pp. 90–95:

"The Union is a novel, supranational grouping of states which was created in 1993 when the Maastricht Treaty took effect. It is directly founded upon the European Communities, in particular the European Economic Community, created by the Treaty of Rome 1957. The United Kingdom acceded to the EEC by the Treaty of Brussels 1972, which took effect in the United Kingdom by means of the European Communities Act 1972. What is distinctive about the Community compared with many international organizations is that broad executive, legislative, and fiscal powers are vested in organs of the Community. Moreover, the European Court of Justice exercises extensive judicial powers in applying and enforcing Community law. Regulations made by the Council of Ministers are directly applicable in all Member States as soon as they have been promulgated by the Council. Treaty provisions and other Community measures may have direct effect in Member States, *i.e.* they may create rights which are directly enforceable by individuals in national courts. As was said by the European Court of Justice in 1963, ' . . . the Community constitutes a new legal order of international law, for the benefit of which the states have limited their sovereign rights, albeit within limited fields, and the subjects of which comprise not only Member States but also their nationals.'

The Court has often emphasized the importance of Community law being uniformly applicable throughout Member States, without the need to wait for separate legislative action by individual states: 'The law stemming from the treaty, an independent source of law, could not, because of its special and original nature, be overridden by domestic legal provisions, however framed, without being deprived of its character as Community law and without the legal basis of the Community itself being called into question.' Community law thus creates specific obligations which bind Member States, and also individual rights which are enforceable in national courts. Member States through their governments participate in the complex procedures which take place before the Community decisions are made.

It is evident that the Community legal order is inconsistent with the traditional doctrine of the sovereignty of Parliament. Thus, Dicey asserted that 'no person or body is recognised by the law of England as having a right to override or set aside the legislation of Parliament.' In fact, United Kingdom law now recognizes that Community organs have the right to make decisions and issue regulations, which may have the effect of overriding legislation by Parliament. The supremacy or primacy of Community law within the economic or social

---

[1] Phil Harris, *An Introduction to Law* (5th ed., Butterworths, London, 1997), p. 210.

areas with which it deals cannot stand comfortably alongside a simple version of national leg-islative supremacy. While the problem takes a special form in the United Kingdom, other Member States have experienced comparable difficulties in adjusting their own systems of constitutional law to take account of the requirements of Community law. . . .

In the case of Denmark and Ireland formal constitutional amendments were necessary. This course of action was not open to the United Kingdom, but it was essential that Parliament should authorize the reception of Community law and should empower British courts to administer Community law. The force of law within the United Kingdom had to be given not only to existing but also to future rules of Community law.

Given these objectives, the sovereignty of Parliament was 'at once an advantage and a source of difficulty'. The advantage was that no formal constitutional amendment was necessary. It took only a few lines in an Act of Parliament to receive within the United Kingdom a massive body of Community law and to equip the British government with additional powers to handle Community affairs. In vain did anti-Marketeers in Parliament complain that the pro-visions of the European Communities Act 1972 were an unjustifiable and illegitimate depar-ture from British constitutional tradition.

The difficulty came in so far as the future was concerned: could any constitutional guaran-tee be given or an undertaking entrenched that Parliament would not at some future date either legislate to leave the Community or (whether inadvertently or intentionally) legislate in a manner which conflicted with Community law? . . .

On 19 January 1972 the EC Commission gave its formal opinion on Britain's application for membership. It must be assumed that the Commission had already seen and approved the text of what was to become the European Communities Act 1972.

Section 2(1) of that Act gave effect within the United Kingdom to all rules of Community law which have direct application or direct effect within Member States. This applied both to exist-ing and to future Community rules. By section 2(4) it was, *inter alia*, provided that 'any enact-ment passed or to be passed, other than one contained in this part of the Act, shall be construed and shall have effect subject to the foregoing provisions of this section'—subject, in other words, to the comprehensive reception of Community law made by section 2 (1). Further, by section 3, questions of Community law were to be decided by the European Court of Justice or in accordance with the decision of that Court, and all courts in the United Kingdom were required in future to take judicial notice of decisions made by the European Court.

When these provisions were debated in Parliament, it was widely agreed that they did not exclude the possibility that the United Kingdom Parliament might one day wish to repeal the Act and thus effectively prevent the continued operation of Community law within the United Kingdom. In this sense the ultimate sovereignty of Westminster was not affected, as ministers admitted, even though they refused to allow a statement to this effect to be included in the Act. But there was for many years uncertainty about a less extreme situation, should an Act passed after 1972 be found to contain a provision inconsistent with an established rule of Community law. In this situation, we have already seen that the European Court will insist that Community law must prevail. But should the British courts take up the same position (as section 3 of the 1972 Act would indicate is their duty) or does the later Act of Parliament over-ride the 1972 Act, including sections 2 and 3, to the extent of requiring the conflict to be resolved from a British standpoint?. . .

The case-law under the 1972 Act did not at first speak with a certain voice. Initially British judges were inclined to avoid finding clashes and inconsistencies between domestic law and Community law. In 1974, Lord Denning M.R. said that the incoming tide of Community law could not be held back. 'Parliament has decreed that the Treaty is henceforward to be part of our law. It is equal in force to any statute.' The crucial question, however, was not whether Community law has the same force as a statute, but whether it has greater force than a statute by prevailing over subsequent Acts which may be in conflict with it.

Some light on the problem was cast by cases concerning equal pay for men and women, an area in which Community law went further than national law in imposing a duty on employ-ers to treat men and women equally. Westminster legislated on this subject in the Equal Pay Act 1970 and the Sex Discrimination Act 1975. But by Article 119 of the EEC Treaty, Member States must maintain the principle that men and women receive equal pay for equal work. The

European Court held that this Article creates rights directly enforceable by an individual against the employer, even though these rights go beyond those arising out of national legislation on equal pay. Ordinarily courts and tribunals in Britain apply national legislation, but it is now established that they must recognize and protect the rights of employees under directly effective provisions of Community law."

As Bradley suggests, British courts have faced a number of claims by female workers seeking to enforce their rights to equal pay under European law. These cases underscore how the principle of Parliamentary supremacy by necessity has had to be modified by the judiciary to reflect the new European legal order.

Garland v. British Rail Engineering Ltd [1982] 2 All E.R. 402, ECJ and HL.

[The appellant, a married woman, complained to an industrial tribunal that her employer, British Rail, was discriminating against her because of sex contrary to section 6(2) of the Sex Discrimination Act 1975 by continuing to provide male employees after they retired with non-contractual concessionary travel facilities for themselves and their wives and dependent children. When female employees retired the provision of such facilities for their families was withdrawn. The industrial tribunal dismissed the complaint on the ground that section 6(4) of the Act exempts "a provision in relation to . . . retirement" (*i.e.* such provisions are outside of the purview of the Sex Discrimination Act) and, therefore, the discrimination was not unlawful. An appeal to the Employment Appeal Tribunal was upheld on the basis that the continuation of the privilege after retirement was not "a provision in relation to . . . retirement". The Court of Appeal then restored the decision of the industrial tribunal on the grounds that the statutory phrase "a provision in relation to . . . retirement" included any provision about retirement. The appellant then appealed to the House of Lords, which referred to the European Court of Justice the question whether the discrimination was contrary to article 119 of the EEC (now E.C.) Treaty (which reads "each Member State shall . . . maintain the application of the principle that men and women should receive equal pay for equal work"), and if so, whether the article conferred enforceable Community rights on individuals.]

European Court of Justice [After reviewing the facts and questions raised, the Court ruled]:

"It follows from those considerations that rail travel facilities such as those referred to by the House of Lords fulfil the criteria enabling them to be treated as pay within the meaning of article 119 of the EEC Treaty.
The argument that the facilities are not related to a contractual obligation is immaterial. The legal nature of the facilities is not important for the purposes of the application of article 119 provided that they are granted in respect of the employment.
It follows that where an employer (although not bound to do so by contract) provides special travel facilities for former male employees to enjoy after their retirement this constitutes discrimination within the meaning of article 119 against former female employees who do not receive the same facilities. . . ."

[Following receipt by the House of Lords of the judgment of the European Court of Justice, the matter was reconsidered:]

Lord Diplock [Lord Diplock reviewed the facts, legislation, and the ruling of the Court of Justice]:

". . . My Lords, even if the obligation to observe the provisions of article 119 were an obligation assumed by the United Kingdom under an ordinary international treaty or convention and there were no question of the treaty obligation being directly applicable as part of the law to be applied by the courts in this country without need for any further enactment, it is a principle of construction of United Kingdom statutes, now too well established to call for citation of authority, that the words of a statute passed after the treaty has been signed and dealing with the subject matter of the international obligation of the United Kingdom, are to be construed, if they are reasonably capable of bearing such a meaning, as intended to carry out the obligation and not to be inconsistent with it. A fortiori is this the case where the treaty obligation arises under one of the Community treaties to which s 2 of the European Communities Act 1972 applies."

[The other Law Lords concurred, and the appeal was allowed.]

The *Garland* case stands for the proposition that the judiciary should interpret, if possible, domestic legislation in such a way as to be consistent with obligations entered into by the United Kingdom government under international treaties. This is especially true with respect to the treaties of the European Union, which are part of United Kingdom law. Given that this principle deals only with the *interpretation* of domestic legislation, (*i.e.* how broadly or narrowly it is read), it can be argued that it does not directly undermine the principle of Parliamentary supremacy. Lord Diplock undoubtedly would say that we must *assume* that Parliament intended to abide by its international obligations, and judges must interpret legislation accordingly. This has proven to be an important principle in widening the scope of sex discrimination provisions in British law.

Although E.U. law has been important in widening the scope of employment protection, particularly for women, it was not perceived as directly challenging the historic, constitutional precept of the supremacy of Parliament. Rather, the impact of the European legal order on Parliamentary supremacy was demonstrated by a different legal struggle, known simply as the *Factortame* decisions. Atiyah sets the scene.

P.S. Atiyah, *Law and Modern Society* (2nd ed., Oxford University Press, Oxford, 1995), pp. 96–97:

"The profound effects of membership of the Community on the sovereignty of Parliament were not fully demonstrated until the dramatic *Factortame* case, when it first became apparent that English courts now had the power to declare Acts of Parliament to be void or invalid because they contravened European Community law. In this case the Community had allocated fishery quotas to its members, but a number of Spanish fishermen attempted to evade the effect of the quotas by registering companies in England, and then transferring their trawlers into the names of these companies, which were thus English companies. Their trawlers fished in British waters, but continued to land their catch in Spain. Not surprisingly, the British government thought that this was an evasion of the whole system of quotas and they introduced into Parliament a bill which was in due course enacted as the Merchant Shipping Act 1988. Under this Act the companies, though registered in England, were to be treated as Spanish companies because their owners were Spanish. This Act of Parliament was then challenged as invalid on the ground that it contravened one of the basic corner-stones of European Community law, namely, that member states were not allowed to *discriminate* against nationals of other states. In this particular case the non-discrimination principle was invoked in a highly technical way, and because the fishery quotas had actually been agreed by the

Community, it was obviously somewhat unfair that the Spanish fishermen were able to invoke it. But that is not really relevant to the crucial importance of the case. What happened when the case first reached the House of Lords was that it was held that as a matter of English law it was impossible to challenge the validity of the Merchant Shipping Act, and it was not even possible to suspend the operation of the Act while the case was referred to the European Court. But the matter *was* referred to the European Court, which decided that since European Community rights were at stake (the right not to be discriminated against) the English courts *had* to have the power to suspend the operation of the Act pending a full hearing of the issue at the European Court."

Factortame Ltd and others v. Secretary of State for Transport (No. 2) [1991] 1 All E.R. 70, ECJ and HL.

European Court of Justice:

". . . In accordance with the case law of the court, it is for the national courts, in application of the principle of co-operation laid down in article 5 of the EEC Treaty, to ensure the legal protection which persons derive from the direct effect of provisions of Community law. . . .

The court has also held that any provision of a national legal system and any legislative, administrative or judicial practice which might impair the effectiveness of Community law by withholding from the national court having jurisdiction to apply such law the power to do everything necessary at the moment of its application to set aside national legislative provisions which might prevent, even temporarily, Community rules from having full force and effect are incompatible with those requirements, which are the very essence of Community law . . . .

It must be added that the full effectiveness of Community law would be just as much impaired if a rule of national law could prevent a court seised of a dispute governed by Community law from granting interim relief in order to ensure the full effectiveness of the judgment to be given on the existence of the rights claimed under Community law. It follows that a court which in those circumstances would grant interim relief, if it were not for a rule of national law, is obliged to set aside that rule. . . .

Consequently, the reply to the question raised should be that Community law must be interpreted as meaning that a national court which, in a case before it concerning Community law, considers that the sole obstacle which precludes it from granting interim relief is a rule of national law must set aside that rule."

[Upon receipt of the opinion of the Court of Justice, the House of Lords granted an interim injunction restraining the enforcement of legislation pending a decision in the case. In so doing, Lord Bridge commented on the relationship between E.C. law and Parliamentary supremacy:]

Lord Bridge of Harwich:
". . . Some public comments on the decision of the Court of Justice, affirming the jurisdiction of the courts of member states to override national legislation if necessary to enable interim relief to be granted in protection of rights under Community law, have suggested that this was a novel and dangerous invasion by a Community institution of the sovereignty of the United Kingdom Parliament. But such comments are based on a misconception. If the supremacy within the European Community of Community law over the national law of member states was not always inherent in the EEC Treaty it was certainly well established in the jurisprudence of the Court of Justice long before the United Kingdom joined the Community. Thus, whatever limitation of its sovereignty Parliament accepted when it enacted the European Communities Act 1972 was entirely voluntary. Under the terms of the 1972 Act it has always been clear that it was the duty of a United Kingdom court, when delivering final judgment, to override any rule of national law found to be in conflict with any directly enforceable rule of Community law. Similarly, when decisions of the Court of Justice have exposed areas of

United Kingdom statute law which failed to implement Council directives, Parliament has always loyally accepted the obligation to make appropriate and prompt amendments. Thus there is nothing in any way novel in according supremacy to rules of Community law in those areas to which they apply and to insist that, in the protection of rights under Community law, national courts must not be inhibited by rules of national law from granting interim relief in appropriate cases is no more than a logical recognition of that supremacy."

A full hearing of the European Court of Justice subsequently declared that the Merchant Shipping Act did indeed violate Community law, and it was eventually invalidated by the High Court. The offending sections were removed by Parliament through amending legislation. The significance of the decision is considered by Atiyah.

P.S. Atiyah, *Law and Modern Society* (2nd ed., Oxford University Press, Oxford, 1995), pp. 97–100:

"In one sense this decision was little more than a practical necessity. If national courts could not declare their own national law to be invalid when it conflicted with European Community law, the practical working of the European Community legal system would be immensely cumbersome. It would mean that any conflict of this kind would have to be decided in defiance of Community law, the government would then be obliged to introduce amending legislation, and in the meantime, anyone whose rights had been adversely affected would be entitled to compensation, but there would be no machinery by which that compensation could be secured in an English court. So it would take years to enforce rights accorded by Community law, and if governments dragged their heels, the whole system would collapse into chaos. In this connection, it must be appreciated that conflicts between our national law and Community law are potentially very common, far more common than conflicts with international law or ordinary treaties. Even though the UK government has one of the best records among members of the Community in giving effect to Community Directives and other decisions, it has become increasingly apparent that many conflicts arise because our ministers and their advisers have not fully appreciated the way in which the European Court was likely to interpret Community law. So, in a practical sense it is really imperative that national courts should recognize the precedence of Community law over national laws, and the courts of all other member states in the Community in fact do recognize this. It must also be said that this is an absolute prerequisite of a federal state, and although the Community is not yet a federal state, it may eventually evolve into one. Without the *Factortame* decision it is doubtful if that could be done.

So the *Factortame* decision was a practical necessity. But at the same time it was, in a legal sense, a revolutionary decision. It was the first time for more than 300 years that an English Court had declared an Act of Parliament to be unenforceable in law. What this means, therefore, is that English law is now subject to European Community law. If there is a conflict between them, the English law may, and sometimes *must*, be declared invalid by English courts. In a sense, therefore, we have now acquired a written constitution—consisting of the various European Treaties—and laws contrary to the constitution will in future be invalid. So the sovereignty of Parliament seems to have been dethroned from its pivotal point at the centre of English constitutional law with very little appreciation of that fact by Parliament, politicians, or the public.

How has this happened? Many lawyers thought that the sovereignty of Parliament was the centre-piece of our unwritten constitution, and was something which simply could not be surrendered or abandoned. Every Parliament was traditionally thought to be legally sovereign and so capable of altering any previous law simply by passing a new Act. Why therefore was the Merchant Shipping Act of 1988 not treated simply as altering all previous law and, if necessary, the European Communities Act itself? If this had been done, the UK government would have been in breach of the Treaties and would have been under an obligation to amend or repeal the Merchant Shipping Act, but at least the traditional doctrine of Parliamentary sovereignty would have been preserved. In fact, the judges in the House of Lords did not deny that this *could have been done*. Parliament could have phrased the Merchant Shipping Act to make it quite clear that it was to be applied whether or not it was in conformity with European law. In that case, said the judges in the House of Lords, they would have obeyed the Act, and so the sovereignty of Parliament would have been respected. But of course the government and Parliament did not *want* to pass an Act which violated European law. They thought that the Act they passed was good in law, but it turned out that they were mistaken. So the judges in the House of Lords thought that they should look at the Merchant Shipping Act as though Parliament had said at the beginning of the Act:

'The following Act is passed on the assumption that it is not in violation of European Community law; if it is contrary to Community law, do not enforce it.'

In this way the traditional respect for Parliamentary sovereignty was to some degree reconciled with the practical need to recognize the supremacy of European Community law.

In one sense this reconciliation may seem pretty empty. It now seems quite clear that we shall see many Acts of Parliament challenged in future as contrary to European law, and some of these challenges will be upheld. Moreover, it will not, of course, be open to Parliament to overrule these decisions by passing another Act, unless Parliament chooses openly to defy the Community Treaties—which could only provoke a political crisis of the first order. So, to a limited extent, we shall have what many politicians (and perhaps the public and the press) intensely dislike, 'government by judges'. On the other hand, there is also reality in the way the House of Lords approached this problem, because it is very unlikely that Parliament will ever pass an Act which is clearly and plainly invalid as contrary to European law. Where it happens at all, it will nearly always happen by accident or mistake, and it may well accord with Parliament's intent that if the Act is found to conflict with Community law, it should not be enforced.

It must not be thought that all this means that English law can be challenged as invalid because (for instance) it is contrary to French or German law. It is only invalid if it is contrary to European Community law, which is the central law of the Community. In this respect the Community increasingly resembles a federal system of law, like that of the USA or Canada or Australia, where there is a federal government and a federal legislature, on the one hand, and state governments and state legislatures on the other. There are two sets of laws, each perfectly valid within its own sphere, but state laws which conflict with (valid) federal laws are invalid. In a strict legal sense, the situation in the European Community is thus similar to that of a federal state."

THE EUROPEAN UNION AND THE RELATIONSHIP OF NATIONAL AND LOCAL GOVERNMENT

We saw in Chapter 3 that local authorities are the creation of Parliamentary legislation and their powers are limited by statute. The exercise of their powers therefore was subject to judicial review to ensure that authorities remained within their *jurisdiction*. Local authorities thus also could be constitutionally abolished by Parliament. It has been argued that membership in the European Union—a *supranational* level of government—may have an impact upon this constitutional relationship between national and local government.

Vernon Bogdanor, "Britain and the European Community" in *The Changing Constitution* (3rd ed., Jeffrey Jowell and Dawn Oliver, eds., Clarendon Press, Oxford, 1994), pp. 20–25:

"The European Community, as well as requiring fundamental alterations in the procedures of Parliament, is likely also to require a redefinition of the relationships between central and local government. For local authorities have been developing links with the Community which will have important implications for their constitutional position. This is so for two main reasons.

The first is that Community legislation is bound to impinge upon local government responsibilities. Even before the Maastricht Treaty, the Community has competence over such matters as economic development, transport, energy, and environmental health, all of which are in Britain in part the responsibility of local authorities. Maastricht considerably widens the scope of the competences of the Community, adding to this list education, culture, consumer protection, and tourism. Moreover, the Treaty gives the Community for the first time authority to approve measures relating to town and country planning, land use, and management of water resources (Art 130s).

Secondly, Community law makes the member states, not local authorities, legally responsible for ensuring compliance with its provisions, even where the actual responsibility for carrying out the policies lies with local government. Local authorities, however, are responsible for *implementing* Community legislation on such matters as, for example, trading standards and consumer protection, and if they do not, they can, so it appears, be liable in civil proceedings.

Thus, in addition to the traditional central-local relationship, and the relationship between member states and Brussels, there is a third intergovernmental relationship, that between local authorities and the Community. Indeed, one authority has argued that, with regard to 'the 1992 process' alone, the completion of the internal market, 'no area of local government activity will be unaffected by this major shift towards closer European integration'.

At first sight, however, because it is member states and not local authorities which are responsible for compliance with Community legislation, it would seem that the extension of Community competences will exert a constraining effect upon local government through a process of creeping centralization.

The Community, however, is naturally concerned with the distribution of power between central government and local authorities within the Member States, even though it has no authority over the structure of government in any Member State. The Community's concern arises because it has a responsibility to ensure that its policy instruments, such as for example, its structural funds, are distributed in an effective and equitable way. But, more fundamentally, the Community has come into existence because, in the modern world, some governmental functions are best exercised at a level larger than that of the member state; as a corollary, it follows that some governmental functions may best be exercised at a level smaller than that of the Member State. If power can shift away from the level of the State in one direction, so also it can shift away from the State in another. The project of European Union needs to embrace both contingencies.

The Maastricht Treaty undoubtedly centralizes power through extending the competences of the Community in areas such as energy and the environment, as well as in its proposals for economic and monetary union. But, at the same time, the Treaty signifies a first attempt to counteract the trend towards creeping centralization and to seek a new equilibrium capable of balancing power between the Community, member states, and local authorities. This is to be achieved in two ways—first through the principle of subsidiarity, and second through the establishment of a new consultative Committee of the Regions.

The principle of subsidiarity is introduced in the preamble to the Maastricht Treaty, and enacted by a newly inserted Article 3b of the Treaty. The preamble to Maastricht declares that the signatories are:

'. . . resolved to continue the process of creating an ever closer union among the peoples of Europe, in which decisions are taken as closely as possible to the citizen in accordance with the principle of subsidiarity.'

Article 3b declares that:

'The Community shall act within the limits of the powers conferred upon it by the Treaty and of the objectives assigned to it therein.
In areas which do not fall within its exclusive competence, the Community shall take action, in accordance with the principle of subsidiarity, only if and in so far as the objectives of the

proposed action cannot be sufficiently achieved by the Member States and can therefore, by reason of the scale or effects of the proposed action, be better achieved by the Community.
Any action by the Community shall not go beyond what is necessary to achieve the objectives of this Treaty. . . .'

The principle of subsidiarity takes its place in the constitution of the European Community as a principle of judicial interpretation, a guide for the European Court of Justice. It is legally binding upon the institutions of the Community, and imposes a three-fold test upon putative Community legislation. The first is whether there is a legal basis for a Community action. That was, of course, already part of Community law before the Maastricht Treaty, and Article 164 required the Court of Justice to ensure it. The second is whether, even if there is a legal basis, the Community should activate it, or whether instead the objective of the proposal might not be sufficiently achieved by the Member States. Moreover, even if the objective in question cannot be sufficiently achieved by the Member States, the question has to be asked whether the objective can be *better* achieved by the Community. The third test relates to the intensity rather than the scope of Community legislation, and asks whether the Community is leaving enough discretion to the member states. Is it, for example, using a regulation that is directly applicable in a situation where a directive that would leave implementation to a member state would suffice? . . .

Although the principle of subsidiarity will not directly affect central-local relations, it may well give rise to a new mood in which decentralization is seen as a necessary complement to the transfer of competences to the Community. In such circumstances it is difficult to believe that Britain will or can remain unaffected. For, if the question: 'Has the Community made the case that this competence cannot be carried out at Member State level?' comes to be asked, so also might the question: 'Has the case been made that this competence cannot be carried out at local level?'. If that happens, the principle of subsidiarity will have helped to create a new atmosphere in central-local relations, and one which is far more favourable to local government.

The principle is, moreover, complemented by Articles 198a-c of the Maastricht Treaty, establishing a Committee of the Regions. The establishment of this Committee may be regarded as an institutional means of ensuring that subsidiarity leads to the devolution of powers to sub-national levels of government, as well as from the Community to Member States.

The Committee of the Regions comprises 189 members from regional and local government, and has advisory status. Britain, together with France, Germany, and Italy, has 24 members on it. Members of the Committee, although appointed by the Council of Ministers, acting unanimously on proposals from the respective Member States, may not be bound by any mandatory instructions. They must be completely independent in the performance of their duties. The British members are required to be elected local government representatives.

The Council and the Commission are *required* to consult the Committee where so provided by the Treaty, and *may* consult it on other occasions. The Committee may also submit an opinion whenever its specific regional interests are involved in any Community action.

Although the Committee has solely advisory powers, its significance should not be underestimated. The Committee cannot force the Council of Ministers to come to a decision, but, since it is required to give its opinion, it has a delaying power. This power can, however, be limited by Article 198a which allows the Commission to set a time limit of one month for the Committee to give its opinion.

Nevertheless, the setting up of the Committee constitutes a clear institutional recognition on the part of the Community that the construction of European Union requires the contribution of regional and local bodies, as well as national governments. Since the regions and localities are responsible for the implementation of some Community legislation, and often have to enforce it, logic requires that they should be given a voice in helping to determine what that legislation should be. The Maastricht Treaty transforms the regional problem from a merely economic one to a political and institutional one. It recognizes the role of sub-national bodies, and seeks to organize their participation in the decision-making process of the Community."

- We will consider further the impact of the sub-national level of governmental authority on the principle of the supremacy of Parliament in the next chapter, when we examine the *devolution* of powers in Scotland, Wales, and Northern Ireland.

- How does membership in the European Union directly impact upon the constitutional principle of the supremacy of Parliament?

- Given our membership in the European Union, is Parliament supreme as either a political or legal matter? Does a "legal" versus a "political" perspective lead to a different answer?

- Explain the legal and political significance of the *Factortame* case.

THE IMPACT OF EUROPE ON THE PROTECTION OF INDIVIDUAL RIGHTS

The constitutional structure of the United Kingdom, with its historical focus on the supremacy of Parliament, has often been contrasted against those systems of government in which a fundamental, constitutional bill of rights serves as a means for the judiciary to limit the exercise of power by the state. The merits and demerits of constitutionally entrenched rights is a complex subject, and one which you will undoubtedly consider in more detail in your constitutional law course. For our purposes, of particular interest is the way in which political and legal developments have altered the principle of Parliamentary supremacy with respect to the judicial recognition (and enforcement) of rights, particularly those of *individuals*.

The first example of the judicial recognition of rights in the United Kingdom is in Britain's adoption of the European Convention on Human Rights. This document should not be confused with those obligations which arise by virtue of our membership in the European Community and European Union. Rather, it was the product of the Council of Europe, and is a reflection of the political climate of the post-War period. Its impact, as Lord Lester explains, has been more limited and narrow than the interpretation of a judicially entrenched constitutional bill of rights. Nonetheless, it has been a significant document.

Lord Lester of Herne Hill Q.C., "European Human Rights and the British Constitution" in *The Changing Constitution* (3rd ed., Jeffrey Jowell and Dawn Oliver, eds., Clarendon Press, Oxford, 1994), pp. 33–46:

"The European Convention on Human Rights is the jewel in the crown of the Council of Europe. It is widely recognized in this country as an important means of protecting civil rights and liberties against the misuse of the powers of the State. . . .

The Convention guarantees basic civil and political rights to everyone within the jurisdiction of the Contracting States. The rights and freedoms which the Contracting States undertake to secure to everyone within their jurisdiction include the rights, without discrimination, to life, liberty, and security of the person, not to be required to perform forced or compulsory labour, not to be subjected to torture, inhuman and degrading treatment or punishment, the right to a fair trial and to the presumption of innocence, not to be held guilty of retrospective criminal offences, to respect for private life, home, and correspondence, to freedom of expression, to freedom of thought, conscience, and religion, to freedom of assembly and association, including the right to form and join trade unions, to marry and to found a family, and to effective national remedies for alleged violations of Convention rights and freedoms. . . .

The Cabinet reluctantly accepted Foreign Secretary Ernest Bevin's advice to sign the Convention for diplomatic reasons, while maintaining their firm opposition to allowing individuals to take their complaints to the European Commission or Court.

The Attlee Cabinet had well understood what a momentous step the government's acceptance of the right of individual petition would be for our legal system. By contrast, when the first Wilson Government decided, some fifteen years later, in December 1965, to permit individuals to complain to the European Commission of Human Rights, the Cabinet did not even meet to discuss the implications of this change in policy; not even a Cabinet Committee did so. It took a year for the decision to be made, but it was not regarded as a sufficiently important matter to be discussed in Cabinet, or in a Cabinet Committee. There was merely an exchange of correspondence between the relevant ministers. Their only concern was that acceptance of the right of petition might create difficulties in some of the remaining dependent territories to which the Convention had been extended, and in Hong Kong to which the Convention was not extended. It does not appear to have occurred to ministers and their advisers in 1965, as it had to their predecessors fifteen years earlier, that the right of petition would in practice mean the transfer of sovereignty, where some fundamental human rights are at stake, from the theoretically omnipotent Queen in Parliament to the European Commission and Court in Strasbourg. The Convention case-law was still sparse, and no-one appreciated what a major impact the right of individual complaint would have upon the British Constitution, Parliamentary sovereignty, British law and public administration. . . .

Judgments of the European Court on Human Rights may involve findings that any of the three branches of government have breached the Convention: not only the actions of administrators, but also of national legislatures, or national supreme courts. These judgments often involve highly controversial political, social, or moral issues, and issues touching national security. They are binding in international law upon the state concerned. If it flouts them it risks expulsion from the Council of Europe and even from the European Union. To obey them may mean having to enact legislation to repeal an offending statute or to overrule a judgment of the House of Lords.

Some examples of important cases in which the United Kingdom has been held in breach of the Convention show the very wide range of serious issues which have arisen. In *Campbell and Cosans*, the European Court of Human Rights held that the suspension of children from schools in Scotland for refusing to submit to the disciplinary punishment of birching breached the parents' right to respect for their philosophical convictions. The government had to take the unpopular step of persuading Parliament to legislate to abolish corporal punishment in State-maintained schools.

In the *Dudgeon* case, the European Court held that the United Kingdom was in breach of the right to respect for private life, because Victorian criminal law prohibited homosexual conduct between consenting adult males in Northern Ireland. The central issue was whether the maintenance in force of the legislation was necessary in a democratic society either for the protection of the rights and freedoms of others or for the protection of others. The Court decided that, although members of the public who regard homosexuality as immoral might be shocked or disturbed by the commission by others of private homosexual acts, this did not warrant the application of penal sanctions when it was consenting adults alone who were involved. The decision was highly controversial in Northern Ireland, but it had to be implemented there, just as a later case compelled an equally unpopular change in the criminal law of the Irish Republic.

In another emotive and divisive area of social policy—immigration, race relations, and citizenship—the European Commission of Human Rights decided that the Westminster Parliament, in enacting the Commonwealth Immigrants Act 1968 to exclude British-Asian-passport holders from East Africa from entering and settling in the United Kingdom, had subjected this group of British citizens to racial discrimination and hence to degrading treatment. . . .

The *Brogan* case challenged the validity of the arrest and detention, executed under Section 12 of the Prevention of Terrorism (Temporary Provisions) Act 1984, of persons suspected of involvement in acts of terrorism in Northern Ireland. . . . The European Court reviewed the facts against the strict requirements of the Convention. It agreed with the Government that the special context of terrorism in Northern Ireland has the effect of prolonging the period during which persons suspected of serious terrorist offences can be kept in custody before being brought before a judge or other judicial officer, subject to adequate procedural safeguards. The applicants had been detained for periods ranging from four days six hours to seven days without being brought before a judge or other judicial officer. The Court considered that this amounted to an unjustifiable delay wihich denied the applicants their right to prompt judicial control of their detention. This was a rare case in which the government did not accept the Court's judgment, derogating instead from the Convention in this respect, and their derogation was subsequently upheld by the Court. . . .

The first *Sunday Times* case involved the conflict between the right to free speech and the right to a fair trial. The House of Lords unanimously granted an injunction restraining the *Sunday Times* newspaper from publishing an article about the drug thalidomide which had caused birth deformities. The injunction was granted on the ground that publication would interfere with the administration of justice in pending proceedings concerning alleged negligence in the manufacture and distribution of the drug and so could constitute criminal contempt.

The European Court held that the House of Lords' decision violated Article 10 because it was not 'necessary' to restrain publication in that there was no 'pressing social need'. The Court emphasized that it was incumbent on the mass media to keep the public informed on judicial proceedings as a matter of public interest, and that the public had a right to receive such information. This landmark decision compelled the government and Parliament to enact the Contempt of Court Act 1981.

The *Spycatcher* case became a cause *célèbre* when Mrs Thatcher's Government obtained injunctions in Australia, New Zealand, and Hong Kong, as well as in the United Kingdom, to prevent the publication of Peter Wright's *Spycatcher: The Candid Autobiography of a Secret Intelligence Officer.*

The use of Article 10 of the Convention, and its case-law was central to the argument for the newspapers in seeking recognition of a constitutional right to freedom of expression, subject only to narrow exceptions to be construed strictly on the basis of objective necessity. The newspapers failed to persuade a majority of the House of Lords, pending the trial of the Attorney-General's claim for alleged breach of confidence, to permit publication of extracts from the book in the United Kingdom. This was despite the fact that the book was freely available in the rest of the world. The newspapers, did, however, convince the House of Lords that Article 10 of the Convention provided the appropriate legal test as to whether an injunction should be granted, even though the Convention is not part of UK law.

In its *Spycatcher* judgment, the European Court reaffirmed the major principles of interpretation of Article 10. . . . The Court added that:

'the dangers inherent in prior restraints [on free expression] are such that they call for the most careful scrutiny on the part of the Court. This is especially so far as the press is concerned, for news is a perishable commodity and to delay its publicaiton, even for a short period, may well deprive it of all its value and interest.'

The twenty-four members of the European Court applied these principles to the facts of the *Spycatcher* case, and unanimously decided that the majority of the House of Lords had unnecessarily interfered with freedom of speech when they restrained the British press from publishing extracts from Peter Wright's book, pending the trial of an action for breach of confidence, at a time when the book was on sale in the United States of America."

The impact of the European Convention on domestic law may be strengthened by the decision of the government to *incorporate* the Convention into British law by statute, an issue which we consider in more detail in Chapter 9, in the context of statutory interpretation.

In addition to the European Convention, the law of the European Union legal order also increasingly is proving a source of legally enforceable rights for individuals. The *Garland* case, which we have already examined, exemplifies how European rights of equal pay and equal treatment in employment and social security, on the basis of sex, will be enforced by the judiciary. The *Factortame* case exemplifies the enforcement of rights of free movement of nationals within the European Union, which again was enforced by the courts directly against the British government. Moreover, the European Court of Justice has recognized that European law confers rights on individuals which can be enforced against other *individuals*, rather than the state. This is a complex area of European law, and one which you will look at in much greater detail in courses on the law of the European Union. For our purposes, these developments highlight the extent to which important social and economic rights are no longer solely the prerogative of Parliament to grant. Instead, the sources of these rights are the Treaties, regulations, and directives of the European Union, and will be enforced by the European Court of Justice and, ultimately, domestic courts.

The recognition of rights cannot be separated from broader social and political questions; issues with which Parliament might not be prepared to deal. Thus, it might be argued that the recognition of European rights (and the derogation of the principle of Parliamentary supremacy) is an important means for the furtherance of social change—for altering the norms and values of society as a whole. The relationship between legal and social change is complex, but a recent case illustrates that there are presently limits on the extent to which the European Court of Justice is prepared to go in its furtherance of the "equal pay" principle.

Grant v. South-West Trains Ltd [1998] All E.R. 193, ECJ.

European Court of Justice:

"1. By decision of 19 July 1996, received at the Court of Justice of the European Communities on 22 July 1996, the Industrial Tribunal, Southampton, referred to the Court of Justice for a preliminary ruling under art 177 of the EC Treaty six questions on the interpretation of art 119 of that Treaty, Council Directive (EEC) 75/117 on the approximation of the laws of the member states relating to the application of the principle of equal pay for men and women (OJ 1975 L45 p 19), and Council Directive (EEC) 76/207 on the implementation of the principle of equal treatment for men and women as regards access to employment, vocational training and promotion, and working conditions (OJ 1976 L39 p 40).

2. Those questions were raised in proceedings between Ms Grant and her employer South-West Trains Ltd (SWT) concerning the refusal by SWT of travel concessions for Ms Grant's female partner.

3. Ms Grant is employed by SWT, a company which operates railways in the Southampton region.

4. Clause 18 of her contract of employment, entitled 'Travel facilities', states:

'You will be granted such free and reduced rate travel concessions as are applicable to a member of your grade. Your spouse and depend[a]nts will also be granted travel concessions. Travel concessions are granted at the discretion of [the employer] and will be withdrawn in the event of their misuse.'

5. At the material time, the regulations adopted by the employer for the application of those provisions, the Staff Travel Facilities Privilege Ticket Regulations, provided in cl 8 ('Spouses') that:

'Privilege tickets are granted to a married member of staff . . . for one legal spouse but not for a spouse legally separated from the employee . . . Privilege tickets are granted for one common law opposite sex spouse of staff . . . subject to a statutory declaration being made that a meaningful relationship has existed for a period of two years or more.'

6. The regulations also defined the conditions under which travel concessions could be granted to current employees (cls 1 to 4), employees having provisionally or definitively ceased working (cls 5 to 7), surviving spouses of employees (cl 9), children of employees (cls 10 and 11) and dependent members of employees' families (cl 12).

7. On the basis of those provisions Ms Grant applied on 9 January 1995 for travel concessions for her female partner, with whom she declared she had had a 'meaningful relationship' for over two years.

8. SWT refused to allow the benefit sought, on the ground that for unmarried persons travel concessions could be granted only for a partner of the opposite sex.

9. Ms Grant thereupon made an application against SWT to the Industrial Tribunal, Southampton, arguing that that refusal constituted discrimination based on sex, contrary to the Equal Pay Act 1970, art 119 of the EC Treaty and/or Directive 76/207. She submitted in particular that her predecessor in the post, a man who had declared that he had had a meaningful relationship with a woman for over two years, had enjoyed the benefit which had been refused her. . . .

13. As a preliminary point, it should be observed that the court has already held that travel concessions granted by an employer to former employees, their spouses and dependents, in respect of their employment are pay within the meaning of art 119 of the Treaty (see, to that effect the judgment in *Garland v. British Rail Engineering Ltd* 12/81 [1982] 2 All ER 402). . . .

15. In view of the wording of the other questions and the grounds of the decision making the reference, the essential point raised by the national tribunal is whether an employer's refusal to grant travel concessions to the person of the same sex with whom an employee has a stable relationship constitutes discrimination prohibited by art 119 of the Treaty and Directive 75/117, where such concessions are granted to an employee's spouse or the person of the opposite sex with whom an employee has a stable relationship outside marriage.

16. Ms Grant submits, first, that such a refusal constitutes discrimination directly based on sex. She submits that her employer's decision would have been different if the benefits in issue in the main proceedings had been claimed by a man living with a woman, and not by a woman living with a woman.

17. Ms Grant argues that the mere fact that the male worker who previously occupied her post had obtained travel concessions for his female partner, without being married to her, is enough to identify direct discrimination based on sex. In her submission, if a female worker does not receive the same benefits as a male worker, all other things being equal, she is the victim of discrimination based on sex (the 'but for' test).

18. Ms Grant contends, next, that such a refusal constitutes discrimination based on sexual orientation, which is included in the concept of 'discrimination based on sex' in art 119 of the Treaty. In her opinion, differences in treatment based on sexual orientation originate in prejudices regarding the sexual and emotional behaviour of persons of a particular sex, and are in fact based on those persons' sex. . . .

19. Ms Grant claims, finally, that the refusal to allow her the benefit is not objectively justified. . . .

26. The refusal to allow Ms Grant the concessions is based on the fact that she does not satisfy the conditions prescribed in those regulations, more particularly on the fact that she does not live with a 'spouse' or a person of the opposite sex with whom she has had a 'meaningful' relationship for at least two years.

27. That condition, the effect of which is that the worker must live in a stable relationship with a person of the opposite sex in order to benefit from the travel concessions, is, like the other alternative conditions prescribed in the undertaking's regulations, applied regardless of the sex of the worker concerned. Thus travel concessions are refused to a

male worker if he is living with a person of the same sex, just as they are to a female worker if she is living with a person of the same sex.

28. Since the condition imposed by the undertaking's regulations applies in the same way to female and male workers, it cannot be regarded as constituting discrimination directly based on sex.

29. Second, the court must consider whether, with respect to the application of a condition such as that in issue in the main proceedings, persons who have a stable relationship with a partner of the same sex are in the same situation as those who are married or have a stable relationship outside marriage with a partner of the opposite sex.

30. Ms Grant submits in particular that the laws of the member states, as well as those of the Community and other international organisations, increasingly treat the two situations as equivalent.

31. While the European Parliament, as Ms Grant observes, has indeed declared that it deplores all forms of discrimination based on an individual's sexual orientation, it is nevertheless the case that the Community has not as yet adopted rules providing for such equivalence.

32. As for the laws of the member states, while in some of them cohabitation by two persons of the same sex is treated as equivalent to marriage, although not completely, in most of them it is treated as equivalent to a stable heterosexual relationship outside marriage only with respect to a limited number of rights, or else is not recognised in any particular way. . . .

35. It follows that, in the present state of the law within the Community, stable relationships between two persons of the same sex are not regarded as equivalent to marriages or stable relationships outside marriage between persons of opposite sex. Consequently, an employer is not required by Community law to treat the situation of a person who has a stable relationship with a partner of the same sex as equivalent to that of a person who is married to or has a stable relationship outside marriage with a partner of the opposite sex.

36. In those circumstances, it is for the legislature alone to adopt, if appropriate, measures which may affect that position. . . .

50. Accordingly, the answer to the national tribunal must be that the refusal by an employer to allow travel concessions to the person of the same sex with whom a worker has a stable relationship, where such concessions are allowed to a worker's spouse or to the person of the opposite sex with whom a worker has a stable relationship outside marriage, does not constitute discrimination prohibited by art 119 of the Treaty or Directive 75/117."

Notes and questions

- The ECJ in *Grant* adopts a posture which might be described as judicial *restraint*, in that it explicitly throws the issue over to the legislatures, and the political institutions of the European Union. Do you think that such an approach to rights is justifiable? Why do you think the Court did not adopt a more *activist* stance, as it had done in other cases, such as *Garland*?

- Should "spouses" of employees (or "partners" or *whatever*) be entitled to benefits such as these? Why?

- Do you think that the ECJ might have been worried that a result in favour of Lisa Grant would have been out of step with current thinking in some E.U. countries? Is that concern justifiable? How should the judiciary approach the relationship between progressive law reform through claims to individual rights, and more socially conservative attitudes which may be present in the general population? Is there only one perspective on these issues across the E.U.?

ESSAY QUESTION

"There is little reason to trust judges as arbiters of controversial political issues. They will generally interpret law and facts from the standpoint of dominant groups in society".

Discuss, with particular reference to the decisions in *Grant v. South West Trains*, *Garland*, *CCSU*, and *GLC v. Bromley*.

5

CONSTITUTIONAL ASPECTS OF LEGAL METHOD: THE DEVOLUTION OF POWERS

In this chapter, our focus turns briefly to new constitutional arrangements in the United Kingdom and Northern Ireland which will result in a substantial *devolution* of governmental powers. That is, power currently is in the process of being turned over from direct exercise by Parliament to newly created assemblies in Scotland, Wales, and Northern Ireland. These assemblies will be responsible for areas of particular relevance to each jurisdiction. The devolution of powers raises issues of constitutional importance, and thus we examine these arrangements as a new aspect of our legal method. The relationship between the devolution of powers and the supremacy of Parliament is an important issue but, as we will see, Parliamentary supremacy perhaps is less affected by the way in which power is being devolved at the moment, than it is by membership in the European Union. As the devolution of power is now very much in its early stages, questions about how the assemblies will operate in practice cannot yet be answered.

THE BACKGROUND TO DEVOLUTION

The current moves towards the devolution of power are a direct result of the election of the Labour government on May 1, 1997. The Labour Party came to embrace constitutional reform in the late 1980s, and, as Brazier explains, when it was elected the Labour government quickly took steps to implement its promises of devolution of power to Scotland and Wales, with the support of the Liberal Democratic Party, which had long advocated reform in this area.

Rodney Brazier, "New Labour, New Constitution?" (1998) 49 N.I.L.Q. 1 at 17:

"To demonstrate its commitment to devolution, the Labour Government introduced the Referendums (Scotland and Wales) Bill into the House of Commons as its very first Bill. Under the Bill the people of Scotland and Wales would be invited to vote at referendums on the Government's proposals for a Scottish Parliament and a Welsh Assembly; the Bill was subsequently amended at the Government's request to set the dates as 11 and 18 September 1997. In Scotland each voter would receive two ballot papers, asking him or her (on the first paper) to agree, or to disagree, that there should be a Scottish Parliament, and (on the second) to agree, or to disagree, that such a Parliament should have tax-varying powers. In Wales there would be one ballot paper only, asking voters whether they agreed or disagreed that there should be a Welsh Assembly. . . . The Bill passed the Commons speedily, assisted on its way through the Committee of the Whole House by the use of the guillotine; it subsequently passed the Lords, though with amendments which the Commons was to reverse, and in which action the peers were to acquiesce. The two White Papers on the Government's devolution plans, *Scotland's Parliament* and *A Voice for Wales*, followed closely the general plans which had been set out both by the Scottish Constitutional Convention and in the Joint Report of the Labour and Liberal Democrat Parties. Enough detail was given to allow the two electorates to make an informed choice in the referendums."

TOWARDS A SCOTTISH PARLIAMENT

The Scottish White Paper outlined the Government's devolution plans.

Scottish Office, White Paper: *Scotland's Parliament* [available at: <http://www.scottish-devolution.org.uk/white%20paper>]:

A summary of proposals

"What the Scottish Parliament can do
    The Scottish Parliament will have law-making powers over a wide range of matters which affect Scotland. There will be a Scottish Executive headed by a First Minister which will operate in a way similar to the UK Government and will be held to account by the Scottish Parliament. The Scottish Parliament and Executive will be responsible for:
    Health including the National Health Service in Scotland and public and mental health;
    Education and training including pre-5, primary, secondary, further and higher education; and training policy and programmes;
    Local government, social work and housing including local government structure and finance; social work; the voluntary sector; housing policy; area regeneration; building control; and the statutory planning framework;
    Economic development and transport including responsibility for the economic development of Scotland; financial and other assistance and support for Scottish business and industry; promotion of trade and exports; inward investment; tourism; functions in relation to the energy sector; the administration of the European Structural Funds; and a range of road, rail, air, sea transport and inland waterways matters;
    The law and home affairs including most civil and criminal law and the criminal justice and prosecution system including police and prisons; fire services; legal aid; parole, the release of life-sentence prisoners and alleged miscarriages of justice; certain Crown, church, ceremonial and local government electoral matters; and civil defence and emergency planning;
    The environment including environmental protection policy and matters relating to air, land and water pollution; the natural and built heritage; and water supplies, sewerage, flood prevention and coastal protection;
    Agriculture, fisheries and forestry including The Scottish Office's existing responsibilities for promoting agriculture and fisheries in Scotland and those of the Forestry Commission in Scotland;
    Sport and the arts including the Scottish Sports Council, the Scottish Arts Council and the national institutions;
    Research and statistics in relation to devolved matters.

Scotland in the United Kingdom

The legislation setting up the Scottish Parliament will specify those powers which are reserved to the UK Parliament. These matters include the constitution of the United Kingdom; UK foreign policy including relations with Europe; UK defence and national security; the stability of the UK's fiscal, economic and monetary system; common markets for UK goods and services; employment legislation; social security; and most aspects of transport safety and regulation.

The new consitutional arrangements

Scotland will remain an integral part of the United Kingdom, and The Queen will continue to be Head of State of the United Kingdom. The UK Parliament is and will remain sovereign.

Scotland's MPs will continue to play a full and constructive part at Westminster. The number of Scottish seats will be reviewed.

The Secretary of State for Scotland will work with the new Scottish Parliament and represent Scottish interests within the UK Government.

The Scottish Executive and the UK Government will work closely together at both Ministerial and official level.

There will be arrangements for resolving disagreements about whether legislation is within the powers of the Scottish Parliament.

Relations with the European Union

Relations with the EU will remain the responsibility of the UK Government, but the Scottish Executive will be involved as closely as possible in the UK decision-making on Europe.

Ministers of the Scottish Executive will participate in relevant meetings of the Council of Ministers and in appropriate cases could speak for the United Kingdom.

The Scottish Parliament will be able to scrutinise EU legislative proposals.

There will be a Scottish representative office in Brussels to further Scotland's interests and complement the role of the UKREP.

The Scottish Executive will have an obligation to implement EU legislation on devolved matters. The UK Parliament will continue to have the ability to legislate to give effect to EU obligations in Scotland.

Relations with local government and other bodies

The Scottish Parliament will set the framework within which other Scottish public bodies — local government, non-departmental public bodies and health bodies — operate. The detailed arrangements will be for the Scottish Parliament and Scottish Executive to develop.

Financial arrangements

The financial framework for the Scottish Parliament will be closely based on existing arrangements for financing The Scottish Office, and will allow the Scottish Parliament to approve spending decisions in accordance with Scottish needs and priorities.

The control of local authority expenditure, non-domestic rates and other local taxation will be devolved to the Scottish Parliament.

Subject to the outcome of the referendum, the Scottish Parliament will be given power to increase or decrease the basic rate of income tax set by the UK Parliament by up to 3p. Liability will be determined by residence in Scotland. Income from savings and dividends will not be affected.

The Inland Revenue will administer any tax variation, with the Scottish Parliament meeting the administrative costs.

Electoral arrangements

The Scottish Parliament will consist of 129 members, 73 directly elected on a constituency basis, plus 56 additional members (7 from each of the 8 current European Parliament constituencies) allocated to ensure the overall result more directly reflects the share of votes cast for each party.

Eligibility to vote will be based on residency.

Parliamentary arrangements

Each Scottish Parliament will have a 4 year fixed term.

The Scottish Parliament is expected to adopt modern methods of working; and to be accessible and responsive to the needs of the public. Detailed arrangements will be left to the Scottish Parliament itself.

Making it happen

The Government are looking at options available in Edinburgh for the Scottish Parliament building.

The staff of the Scottish Executive will continue to be part of a unified Home Civil Service.

The annual running costs are estimated to be between £20 and £30 million a year i.e. about £5 per year per head of Scottish population.

Next steps

Scotland will be asked to vote on 11 September in a referendum on the proposals set out in this White Paper.

Following a positive referendum result, legislation to establish a Scottish Parliament will be brought forward as soon as possible.

Once the legislation has been enacted, elections to the Scottish Parliament will be held in the first half of 1999, and the Parliament will become fully operational in the year 2000."

NOTES AND QUESTIONS

- The Referendum result on September 11, 1997 was decisive, despite opposition to devolution from the Conservative Party. On the first question, whether there should be a Scottish Parliament, 74.3 per cent voted in favour; 25.7 per cent against. On the second question, whether that Parliament should have tax varying powers, 63.5 per cent voted in favour, 36.5 per cent against. Consequently, the Scotland Act 1998 was enacted to bring into effect the process outlined in the White Paper.

- The Scotland Act makes provision in s. 32 for the determination of any question concerning whether a Scottish bill is within the legislative competence of the Scottish Parliament. Such questions can be referred to the Judicial Committee of the Privy Council—a judicial body made up of members of the House of Lords —for decision. The decision to refer can be made by the Advocate General for Scotland (a new law officer for Scotland), the Lord Advocate (the principal law officer to the Scottish administration), or the Attorney General for the United Kingdom. Thus, there is the potential for a new field of *judicial review* of legislation, so as to ensure that the jurisdiction of the devolved Parliament has not been exceeded. This is clearly of constitutional significance.

- To what extent is the devolution of power to a Scottish Parliament compatible with a system of Parliamentary supremacy? What sorts of disputes between Parliaments can you envision arising?

- Should Scottish members of the United Kingdom Parliament be allowed to vote on matters solely affecting England? Explain your position.

• For further reading, see Rodney Brazier, "The Scottish Government" [1998] P.L. 212; Timothy H. Jones, "Scottish Devolution and Demarcation Disputes" [1997] P.L. 283.

TOWARDS A WELSH ASSEMBLY

The other strand of the government's devolution plan was the creation of an assembly for Wales. This assembly would have more limited powers, particularly in that there was no intention that it would be able to vary taxes. The proposals once again were set out in a White Paper:

Welsh Office, *White Paper: National Assembly for Wales* [available at: <http://www.assembly.wales.gov.uk/wp/002.html>]:

White Paper: Chapter 1. An Assembly for Wales

An Assembly for Wales: An Overview

"The Government proposes that a directly-elected Assembly will assume responsibilities for policies and public services currently exercised by the Secretary of State for Wales. The Assembly will have at its disposal the £7 billion budget currently assigned to the Welsh Office, and will allocate resources from it to public services in Wales for which it is responsible. The Assembly will also set policies and standards for those services; reform and oversee the work of unelected public bodies; and make detailed rules and regulations, through secondary legislation, within the framework laid down in Acts of Parliament.

The Assembly will be able to debate all issues of concern in Wales, and will be required to observe the highest standards of behaviour, and proper respect for equal opportunities. It will give equal status to the English and Welsh languages. The Secretary of State's powers will be transferred to the Assembly by Order. . . .

The Assembly

The Government proposes that the Assembly will have 60 members, directly elected by the Welsh people every four years. Its headquarters will be in Cardiff, and it will be staffed by existing Welsh Office staff who will remain members of the Home Civil Service.

The Assembly's overall political leadership will be provided by an Executive Committee, made up of the leaders of each of its subject committees. It would operate in a similar way to the UK Cabinet, and would normally be formed by members of the majority party within the Assembly. . . .

What the Assembly will do

The Assembly will take over responsibilities that the Secretary of State exercises in Wales. These are shown briefly here and will be listed in the Bill that establishes the Assembly.

The Secretary of State for Wales has responsibilities for: economic development; agriculture, forestry, fisheries and food; industry and training; education; local government; health and personal social services; housing; environment; planning; transport and roads; arts, culture, the Welsh language; the built heritage; sport and recreation. . . .

The Bill will contain the power to transfer the Secretary of State's responsibilities to the Assembly by Order, subject to the approval of the House of Commons and of the House of Lords. The Government's intention is that the Transfer Order will pass to the Assembly virtually all the functions of the Secretary of State for Wales. It would come into force soon after the Assembly is established in May 1999.

The Government does not propose to transfer to the Assembly responsibility for functions which currently operate on a common basis throughout the United Kingdom. These include foreign affairs, defence, taxation, macro-economic policy, policy on fiscal and common markets, social security and broadcasting.

The Assembly's powers

The Assembly will be able to set policies which can drive the Welsh economy forward and make a difference to the quality of life in Wales. It will have powers to reduce the number of Welsh quangos, establish their priorities and hold them to account. It will be able to examine proposals for UK legislation, advising on whether they are appropriate for Wales.

The Assembly will help to create the body of law which governs Wales. The basic framework of the law is set in Acts of Parliament — primary legislation — within which Secretaries of State make rules and regulations in secondary legislation. For example, the detail of the school curriculum or the designation of environmentally sensitive areas are currently decided by the Secretary of State for Wales within the framework laid down in Acts of Parliament. The Government proposes that in Wales the Assembly will assume these powers to make secondary legislation. . . .

The Secretary of State for Wales

The establishment of an Assembly will create a new relationship between Wales and Westminster. But Wales will remain firmly a part of the United Kingdom. Wales and England will continue to share a common legal system and much else besides. In the making of legislation and in the debates on UK policy, Wales's voice and influence must be felt in Cabinet and Parliament. There will therefore be a continuing role for a separate Secretary of State for Wales, with a seat in the Cabinet, to safeguard Welsh interests.

The Secretary of State will need to work closely with the Assembly and be informed, though not bound, by its views. The Secretary of State will represent Wales — with the benefit of having heard the democratic voice of the Assembly in policy formation and resource decisions.

The Secretary of State will be able in his own right to attend meetings of the Assembly to participate in its debates but will not be able to vote. The Government expects that the Secretary of State will meet the Assembly's Executive Committee regularly to exchange views and information about Government policy.

The Secretary of State will retain a small team of civil servants to support his work. They will work in partnership with the Assembly and other government departments on policy matters covering Wales and other parts of the UK.

Royal matters

The Assembly will be a Crown body. The Government envisages that Her Majesty The Queen or Her representative would formally open the Assembly after each election.

The Secretary of State for Wales will continue to advise Her Majesty on Welsh matters that are considered by the Privy Council, such as appointments that are made by Her. The Secretary of State will also be responsible for other dealings with Her Majesty and other members of the Royal Family, including Royal Visits. He will be responsible for submitting to the Prime Minister recommendations for honours in Wales and for appointments to Royal Commissions in Wales."

NOTES AND QUESTIONS

• Once again, the proposals outlined in the White Paper were confirmed by referendum in Wales on September 19, 1997. However, unlike in Scotland, the result was very close. With an overall turnout of 50.3 per cent of voters, a total of 559,419 (or 50.3 per cent) voted in favour of the Welsh Assembly; while 552,698 (or 49.7 per cent) voted against. As a result, the Government introduced and Parliament has enacted the Government of Wales Act 1998, pursuant to which the National Assembly for Wales will be created following elections in 1999.

• Schedule 8 of the Government of Wales Act makes provision for the resolution of devolution issues, such as whether a function is exercisable by the Assembly, in the U.K. courts. Pursuant to section 10 of Schedule 8, the Court of Appeal may refer any devolution issue which arises in proceedings before it to the Judicial Committee of the Privy Council.

• In what ways can the more limited devolution of powers to Wales, as compared with Scotland, be justified? Can there be a principled basis for the difference?

THE NORTHERN IRELAND ASSEMBLY

We conclude this chapter with a consideration of the third new legislative body recently brought into existence by Parliament: the Northern Ireland Assembly. Although not part of the government's devolution programme *per se*, the success of the Assembly obviously will be of the utmost importance in the years to come. In fact, the Assembly is one of three new, linked bodies which are a product of the multi-party Good Friday agreement reached in 1998, as explained by a newspaper report at the time.

Rory Carroll, "The document: Three linked bodies created and guidelines drawn up on decommissioning, release of prisoners and policing", *The Guardian*, April 11, 1998, p. 4:

"STRAND ONE: DEMOCRATIC INSTITUTIONS IN NORTHERN IRELAND

A democratically elected assembly in Northern Ireland capable of exercising executive and legislative authority. It will be subject to checks and balances to ensure unionists cannot dominate nationalists, as they did in the previous Stormont parliament until it was abolished in 1972.

A 108-member assembly will be elected by PR[1] from existing Westminster constituencies. The assembly will exercise full legislative and executive authority in those matters currently under the remit of the six departments of the Northern Ireland Office.

Operating where appropriate on a cross-community basis, it will be the prime source of authority in respect of all devolved responsibilities. There will be safeguards to ensure that all sections of the community share power.

Key decisions requiring cross-community support will be designated in advance, including election of the chair of the assembly, the First Minister and Deputy First Minister, standing orders and budget allocations.

The chair and deputy chair of the assembly will be elected on a cross-community basis. There will be a committee for each of the main executive functions of the Northern Ireland Administration. The chairs and deputy chairs of the assembly committees will be allocated proportionally. Membership of the committees will be in broad proportion to party strengths.

---

[1] Proportional representation.

Executive authority to be discharged on behalf of the assembly by a First Minister and Deputy First Minister and up to 10 ministers with departmental responsibilities.

The First Minister and Deputy First Minister shall be jointly elected into office by the assembly voting on a cross-community basis. The ministers will constitute an executive committee, which will be convened, and presided over, by the First Minister and Deputy First Minister. The executive committee will discuss executive and legislative proposals for recommending a common position in external relations.

Disputes between the committee and assembly over legislative competence will be decided by the courts.

The assembly will meet first to decide its standing orders and working practices and prepare for the effective functioning of the assembly, the British-Irish Council and the North/South Ministerial Council.

STRAND TWO: NORTH/SOUTH MINISTERIAL COUNCIL

A forum for ministers from Dublin and Belfast to promote joint policy-making with the assembly. It will develop consultation, co-operation and action within the island of Ireland—including through implementation on an all-island and cross-border basis—on matters of mutual interest.

All Council decisions to be by agreement between the two sides. Northern Ireland to be represented by the First Minister, Deputy First Minister and any relevant ministers, the Irish Government by the Taoiseach and relevant ministers.

The Council to meet in different formats: (i) in plenary format twice a year, with Northern Ireland representation led by the First Minister and Deputy First Minister and the Irish Government led by the Taoiseach; (ii) in specific sectoral formats on a regular and frequent basis with each side represented by the appropriate minister; (iii) in an appropriate format to consider institutional or cross-sectoral matters.

As soon as practically possible after elections to the assembly, inaugural meetings will take place of the three strands' new institutions. All three will meet regularly and frequently during the period between the elections to the assembly, and the transfer of powers to the assembly.

STRAND THREE: BRITISH–IRISH COUNCIL

Lawmakers from the Republic will meet regularly with members of the British Parliament, the Northern Ireland assembly, and with representatives of the new assemblies for Scotland and Wales, the Isle of Man and the Channel Islands. It will promote the harmonious and mutually beneficial development of the totality of relationships among the peoples of these islands.

The BIC will meet in different formats: at summit levels, twice per year; in specific sectoral formats on a regular basis, with each side represented by the appropriate minister. The BIC will exchange information, discuss, consult and try to reach agreement on co-operation on matters of mutual interest. Suitable issues for early discussion could include transport links, agriculture, environmental issues, cultural issues, health, education and EU issues.

It will be open to the BIC to agree common policies or common actions. Individual members may opt not to participate in such common policies and common action.

BRITISH–IRISH INTERGOVERNMENTAL CONFERENCE

There will be a new British-Irish Agreement dealing with the totality of relationships. It will establish a standing British-Irish Intergovernmental Conference, which will subsume both the Anglo-Irish Intergovernmental Council and the Intergovernmental Conference established under the 1985 Agreement.

The Conference also will address the areas of rights, justice, prisons and policing in Northern Ireland (unless and until responsibility is devolved to a Northern Ireland administration) and will intensify co-operation between the two governments on the all-island or cross-border aspects of these matters."

NOTES AND QUESTIONS

- The Good Friday agreement also includes provisions, sometimes controversial, dealing with the decommissioning of arms, the early release of prisoners, and security. A referendum on the Good Friday agreement was held in Northern Ireland on May 22, 1998. A high turnout (81 per cent) was achieved, in which 71 per cent of voters supported the Agreement. In a referendum in the Republic of Ireland, 94 per cent of voters endorsed changes to the Irish Constitution required to implement the Agreement. Consequently, the Northern Ireland Secretary signed an Order bringing into effect all provisions of the Northern Ireland (Elections) Act 1998, pursuant to which election to the new Northern Ireland Assembly took place on June 25, 1998. The implementation of the Good Friday agreement continues.

- The Agreement, of course, is of historical significance. From a constitutional perspective, it is of interest how an ongoing relationship between two national governments—of the United Kingdom and the Republic of Ireland—has become somewhat constitutionalised. To what extent do traditional notions of Parliamentary supremacy make sense in an era of increasingly entrenched international relationships—such as the Good Friday agreement or, indeed, membership of the European Union?

- Should further steps towards the devolution of powers be taken *within* England? Should assemblies be established within the regions, with a devolution of power to them?

- What is the impact of the new constitutional arrangements discussed in this chapter on (i) Parliamentary supremacy; and (ii) judicial review?

6

JUDGES, COURTS AND THE RESOLUTION OF DISPUTES

To this point, we have discussed those fundamental constitutional components of our legal system, which are important for an understanding of our legal method. In this chapter, we begin to look in more depth at an aspect of legal method which will occupy us for much of this text: the role of the judiciary and courts in the resolution of legal disputes. We have already touched upon courts in the chapters dealing with constitutional aspects of legal method. We have also looked at the European Court of Justice and its role in our legal system. In this chapter, our focus is on the domestic courts. We review the court structure, examine the membership of the judiciary, explore the fundamental rule of *stare decisis* in a "common law" legal system and, finally, we consider the "politics" of judicial resolution of disputes.

FUNDAMENTALS OF THE LEGAL SYSTEM

We begin with some fundamental ideas that are central to our legal method.

Jeremy Waldron, *The Law* (Routledge, London, 1990), pp. 3–6:

"Technically, there is not one legal system in the United Kingdom but two or (depending how you count) several. The Acts of Union, bringing England and Scotland together under one Parliament in 1707, guaranteed the independence of the Scottish courts and the preservation of Scots law, particularly in areas like tort, contracts or delict: areas in which people sue one another for damages. At the time, the legal system in Scotland differed from its English counterpart not only in substance but in ethos and tradition (it was much more heavily influenced by the tradition of Roman law), and many of these differences remain. There has also been a separate system for the administration of justice in Northern Ireland; indeed from 1921 till the introduction of 'direct rule' from Westminster in 1972, the Northern Ireland Parliament made laws for the Province under the auspices of its own constitution. From a political point of view, however, the legal system in the United Kingdom is unitary and the Parliament at Westminster remains the most powerful source of law, with authority to legislate for the whole realm or for Scotland and Northern Ireland separately if that is thought desirable. Britain as a whole is now subject also to European Community law, and that takes precedence over all British legislation.

Almost every aspect of law in Britain is governed both by statute and by judge-made law. Statutes are Acts of Parliament, passed by the House of Commons and the House of Lords and assented to by the Queen. Unlike their counterparts in the United States, the courts in

Britain have no authority to hold a statute 'unconstitutional'. Acts of Parliament prevail over all other sources of law, and (subject to the force of European Community law) where they conflict, the earlier statute gives way to the later. This is what people mean (among other things) when they say Parliament is 'sovereign'. Readers should not need to be told that for the most part Parliament is controlled in effect by the Cabinet, and most legislative proposals originate there. A collection of *Statutes in Force* can be found in any good library, usually ordered by subject matter. Statutes are organized into sections and sub-sections which lay down particular rules and definitions, and they are usually cited by what is called their short title and date, for example, the Tumultuous Petitioning Act 1661, followed by the number of the section in question.

Specific statutes may authorize the making of regulations—sometimes referred to as sub-ordinate legislation—by Ministers of the Crown, local councils, or other public bodies. These have the force of law, but they are governed strictly by the requirement that they must fall within the terms of reference which Parliament has laid down. If they go beyond this, they are *ultra vires* and have no legal validity. The Crown (in effect the Cabinet) also has authority to issue orders which have the force of law in areas governed by the royal prerogative (examples include the dissolution of a parliament or the declaration of war).

It is customary to say that the law is applied and interpreted by the courts. For the most part that is false. Law is interpreted and applied to particular situations by ordinary people and ordinary officials doing roughly what they think it says and ordering their relations in some kind of accordance with its provisions. The courts are involved only in the compara-tively rare case where an official or a private individual wants to make an issue of someone else's behaviour so far as the law is concerned.

When someone raises such an issue, the courts will attempt to interpret and apply not only statute law but also earlier reported decisions of other courts in similar cases. The practice of following decisions in earlier cases is known as 'the doctrine of precedent' . . . . There is a hier-archy of courts; those lower in the hierarchy are expected slavishly to follow the decisions of those above them, and in most cases they are also expected to follow the decisions of other courts at the same level. Obviously, though, a certain amount of flexibility derives from the fact that no two cases are ever *exactly* alike and, even when they are, no two people will give exactly the same account of *how* they are alike.

In the judicial hierarchy the courts above hear appeals from the courts immediately beneath them. There is not always an automatic right of appeal: sometimes the aggrieved party has to have the approval of the court she is appealing from or the one she is appealing to before she can proceed. Though occasionally serious issues of law are raised in Magistrates' Courts, and though serious criminal cases always originate in the Crown Courts, most of the *influential* cases in our law begin life in one of the divisions (Family, Chancery, or Queen's Bench) of what is called 'the High Court'. From a political point of view, the Queen's Bench Division of the High Court is the most interesting, for it has responsibility for reviewing the legality of governmental and administrative action. Appeals from the High Court are taken to the Court of Appeal. Above the Court of Appeal, the highest court in the land is Parliament, in the guise of the House of Lords. Appeals there are heard not by the whole House (earls, bishops, and all), but by a committee of senior judges called Lords of Appeal or Law Lords. They sit usually five at a time on each case and they decide by a majority.

Court decisions that are thought noteworthy are published in the *Law Reports*. A reported decision will begin with a summary of the facts and of what was decided, and it will then set out the full text of the judge's decision (often running to many pages) saying why this partic-ular finding was given in this particular case. If there is more than one judge, then all the deci-sions will be printed. If they disagree, the side with the greater support wins (though the majority decision may still comprise several distinct speeches). Cases are referred to by the (often abbreviated) names of the parties—for example, *Swallow and Pearson v. Middlesex C.C.*—and the year and abbreviated title of the volume in which they appear.

The official Law Reports are published every month or so, and bound into one or more volumes corresponding to each year. When they first come out, they are called *The Weekly Law Reports* (WLR), but they are eventually organized into separate volumes corresponding to the different levels and areas of judicial decision-making. Thus, for example, *Christie v.*

Leachinsky [1947] AC 573 refers to the report of a decision of the House of Lords taken in the case of Christie against Leachinsky (or, as we say in the trade, *Christie and Leachinsky*), published in the 1947 volume of the official Law Reports devoted to 'Appeal Cases', beginning on page 573. And '*R. v. Kulynycz* [1971] 1 QB 367' refers to a report of a criminal case—the Queen ('R.' or 'Regina') against Kulynycz—decided by a court a little lower down in the hierarchy and reported in the first volume of the 'Queen's Bench' reports for 1971, beginning at page 367. You get the idea. In a law library, you will find the volumes organized chronologically for each series: all the ACs are together from the earliest reported cases till the present, all the QBs (or, before 1953, KBs) are together in order, and so on. (As well as these official reports, most law libraries also stock an excellent series of semi-official reports known as the *All England Reports* (All ER). These are published quite quickly, and they accumulate into two or three volumes for each year. Unlike the official reports, they do not divide the cases up by level of court or subject-matter.)

It is important to realize that, when they decide the cases and the appeals that come before them, judges are not only interpreting Acts of Parliament (saying what the various sections and sub-sections mean), nor are they merely following others judges' interpretations. They are also often following and developing principles of law which have no statutory basis at all, and which have grown up entirely in the courts. Thus, for example, the principle that if you are injured in a road accident you can sue the careless driver for negligence, and the various elaborations and qualifications to that, have been developed entirely in the courts, though it interlaces with and is modified by statute law in various respects. Much of our law is judge-made and not made by Parliament. Judge-made law, to the extent that it can be separated from the rest is referred to as 'common law', and a system like the English one in which this sort of law plays a significant role is called a 'common law' system.

For the most part, the common law systems of the world represent a residue of English influence: apart from the United States of America, they are mainly the legal systems of the British Commonwealth (some of which still preserve a right of appeal to the House of Lords, known for that purpose as 'the Judicial Committee of the Privy Council'). Common law systems may be contrasted with 'civil law' systems. The difference is one of ethos and tradition: in civil law systems, such as France or Germany, the law tends to have been developed in a more systematic and abstract way. Nothing like the same emphasis is put on the role of the judge; the emphasis is on the logical structure of a code of laws developed from first principles. (As a matter of fact, judges do have to decide hard questions of interpretation just as their common law counterparts do, but in a civil law system this is not *advertised* as the primary vehicle for the development of the law, in the way that it is in England or America.) The inspiration for the civil law systems was, of course, the great Roman Law code of Justinian and more recently the Code Napolean. The differences between English and Scots law are to be explained in part by the much greater influence of civil law in Scotland."

The common law, as the basis of the English legal system, has a long history. Prior to the Norman Conquest of 1066, there was no unitary legal system. The emergence of the common law was an attempt to create that system under the control of the sovereign king. The common law was developed by judges travelling throughout the country establishing the "King's peace". They settled disputes and adopted local legal customs, which became the basis of a unitary, national legal order. This judicial appropriation and development of law became a means of exerting central political authority, and the law that emerged was "common", in that it applied to everyone. Today, the term common law refers to the substantive law and procedural rules that have been created by judges through decisions on specific disputes which they have heard. Thus, it is a body of *general* case law, which is the product of resolutions to *specific* disputes. Statute law, by contrast, refers to the law created by Parliament in the form of legislation. The courts also play an important role, as we shall see, in the interpretation of legislation.

Another set of terms frequently referred to is public and private law. Private law refers to the body of law which regulates the relationship between individual citizens and the state. To this point, our focus has been on the public law aspects of legal method. Private law, by contrast, involves relationships between individual citizens. The division between public and private law is a rather artificial one, for the power of the state is central to the creation and maintenance of legal relationships between citizens. For example, although we refer to property law as private (because it involves relationships between individuals over the ownership of things), property, as we know it, would not exist without the power of the state ensuring its protection. In that respect, property law is just as "public" as constitutional law, and just as "political" in the way in which the state *chooses* to recognize rights which it calls "property".

The resolution of disputes in both public and private law ultimately is the domain of courts, and it is the constitutional position of courts, and the structure of courts in the English legal system, to which we now turn.

Phil Harris, *An Introduction to Law* (5th ed., Butterworths, London, 1997), pp. 163–170:

"[A]lthough the court may be regarded as the clearest instance of official means of dispute-settlement in modern society, in fact only a tiny proportion of disputes are ever aired before the courts. In fact, the total number of cases coming before courts of law is extremely small when compared to the frequency with which disputes—many of which may involve legal aspects—occur and are settled without recourse to legal proceedings.

The court is, nevertheless, perhaps the central institution within the English legal system; the pronouncements of the higher courts, in particular, have great significance for, among other things, the substance of the law itself; dominant social and political attitudes and values are communicated through judicial utterances in the courts; and the courts of law are the ultimate arenas where disputes which cannot be settled in any other way may be taken. The courts are also a feature of the state, connected with, but in certain important ways independent of, other agencies of state and government. For these reasons, it is important to consider in more detail the present position of the courts of law within the legal system and within the social structure.

Constitutional lawyers used to regard as fundamental the doctrine of the 'separation of powers', whereby the courts, the legislature (Parliament) and the executive (government) are constitutionally separate, thus serving democratic ideals by ensuring that no one of these 'arms of the state' becomes all-powerful, through complex 'checks and balances' of each arm by the other two. Thus in theory the judges operate independently of party politics, and in a manner untainted by political bias. . . .

The doctrine involves three propositions, each of which, it is argued, is open to question. First, the doctrine requires that the same persons should not occupy positions in more than one of the three arms of the state—judiciary, legislature and executive. In practice, however, as is well known, members of the Cabinet (executive) are invariably members of one or other House of Parliament (legislature). Cabinet government as we know it in the UK could not possibly work without this convention, and this is one example of departure from the strict doctrine; as is the case of the Lord Chancellor, who is not only a Cabinet Minister, but is also a judge, is president of the House of Lords in both its legislative and judicial capacities, and is involved in the appointment of other judges. The mixture, in one appointment, of judicial, legislative and executive functions is striking.

Second, the doctrine requires that each arm of the state exercises its functions independently of any control or interference from the others. Again, this requirement is not fulfilled. The House of Commons (part of the legislature) in theory controls the executive, but with a majority government the House can be effectively controlled, in fact, by the executive. Either way, the requirement is breached, though there appears to be little or no attempt to influence the judicial function, at least regarding court hearings, today. . . .

Third, the doctrine of the separation of powers requires that one organ of the state should not exercise the functions of either of the others. In practice, the distinction between functions may be seriously blurred. To take the outstanding illustration, an Act of Parliament may empower a minister of the government to make rules having legal effect; this is known as *delegated legislation*, and it is arguable that in some cases this device amounts to a minister having law-making power (as opposed to mere power to make regulations *in furtherance of* Parliamentary enactments). Important examples of delegated legislative powers are the powers given to ministers under the European Communities Act 1972, to make regulations implementing European Community policies which do not have automatic direct effect; the wide powers given to the Lord Chancellor to amend or repeal rules relating to the provision of legal services under the Courts and Legal Services Act 1990; and the rule-making powers delegated to the Secretary of State for Education and Employment under the Education Reform Act 1988. As we have seen, it is one of the functions of the courts to ensure, through their supervisory jurisdiction, that powers entrusted to ministers, tribunals or other executive or administrative agencies are not abused or exceeded.

Apart from the case of delegated legislative powers, which may be seen as a legislative function being exercised by a member of the executive, there is virtually no situation in which one arm of the state exercises the powers of either of the others, though we must note that the House of Lords does have both a legislative and a judicial capacity: in practice, the judicial members of the House are judges, not politicians, whose role is to sit when the House operates in its judicial capacity. They rarely sit in legislative debates, and by the same token, the political members of the Lords do not participate in judicial hearings. There is, then, a separation of judicial and legislative functions in this particular institution. . . .

The English Court structure

English courts are arranged in a structure according to three sets of criteria. First, does the court deal with *civil* or *criminal* matters? This division is central to English law, though it is not easy to explain with any precision. Criminal law rules cover offences such as murder, theft and assaults, offences against the consumer . . ., offences involving firearms and other weapons, crimes against public order and state security and of course the many road traffic offences. These cases may be seen as disputes between the alleged offender and the state, representing the community at large.

Civil law comprises all legal rules which are not part of the criminal legal code, but the dividing line is difficult to draw. It is sometimes said that whilst criminal proceedings are brought by the state, civil proceedings are brought by private individuals against other individuals. Thus, a *plaintiff* sues a *defendant*. Criminal proceedings are often said to be public, and civil proceedings private, but this 'public-private' distinction is by no means watertight. Certainly, we speak of 'private law' remedies being available in civil actions for, say, breach of contract, and of criminal proceedings being brought on behalf of the public; but there are many occasions when *public* bodies may be party to civil actions, and *private* individuals may initiate criminal prosecutions. . . .

A second distinguishing feature is often said to lie in the different aims of the two branches of the law. The traditional aims of the criminal law are the apprehension and disposition of wrongdoers, whilst the aims of civil law are usually stated to be those of restitution, or compensation. The problem with this distinction appears when we consider that there are some cases in which civil awards may be intended by the court to be punitive. Such cases are rare, but may arise for example when a defendant may make a profit from wrongful conduct, over and above the amount of compensation which he or she must pay to the plaintiff. . . . And there are instances in criminal law where compensation may be payable by a convicted person to the victim: the Powers of Criminal Courts Act 1973, for example, provides that compensation orders may be made by any criminal court against any person convicted of damaging other people's property or causing some other type of loss.

Despite these difficulties, there does remain, for practical purposes, a broad distinction between civil and criminal law along the lines of their respective aims and remedies, and this distinction is firmly embedded in the court structure. The civil courts, with one or two exceptions, deal exclusively with civil matters; the most important exception is probably the Queen's Bench Division of the High Court, which has some criminal jurisdiction by way of appeals from magistrates' courts and Crown courts through the 'case stated' procedure. Here, the appeal is made by either defendant or prosecution (the only instance where the latter can appeal from an acquittal) over a point of law raised by, say, the interpretation of a statute where a decision of a higher court is required to clarify the matter. On the criminal side, magistrates' courts have some civil jurisdiction, mainly involving liquor, gaming and betting licences, and actions for certain debts, as well as some family law matters, notably separation orders upon marriage breakdown and questions of custody and adoption of children.

The second criterion affecting the position of a given court in the overall structure is that concerning the *extent* of the court's jurisdiction. The county court, for instance, at the lowest rung of the civil court ladder, deals with actions in contract and tort, proceedings involving mortgages, estates of deceased persons, and other equity matters. Though there is now no financial restriction on the jurisdiction of the county court (that is to say, cases involving any amount of claim values may be heard there) there is a statutory presumption that any action involving claims for less than £25,000 will be heard in the county court, whereas claims involving more than £50,000 will be heard in the High Court. The High Court hears civil cases involving more than £50,000, though may hear cases involving lower claims if circumstances (such as issues of general public importance, or matters involving complex facts or legal issues) make it appropriate. The magistrates' court, dealing in the main with minor criminal offences, has a limited jurisdiction regarding sanctions for cases heard in that court. The Criminal Law Act 1977 and the Criminal Justice Act 1991 contain provisions for sentences for various crimes which may attract imprisonment or fines. Such provisions, it must be stressed, relate to the court's *summary* jurisdiction, and the vast majority of criminal cases, being of a relatively minor or trivial nature, are dealt with by these courts. For offences of a more serious nature, however, and in those cases where the accused elects to be tried *on indictment* (that is, with a jury), the case must go before the higher Crown Court. We may note here that magistrates' courts also hold *preliminary examinations* in *all* criminal cases. This is a procedure to ascertain whether, on the face of all the evidence, there is a case against the accused. If so, then the case will be dealt with either summarily or on indictment, depending on the offence and upon the circumstances.

The third criterion affecting the position of a court in the hierarchy is the question whether the court is one of *first instance* (where the original trial takes place) or whether it is a court of *appeal*. Magistrates' courts and county courts are both courts of first instance; and the Court of Appeal and the House of Lords are both appellate courts only. The courts which lie in between these levels of the structure may, depending on the case before them, be either of first instance or appellate jurisdiction. The three Divisions of the High Court—Chancery, Queen's Bench, and Family—are civil courts (excepting the criminal jurisdiction of the Queen's Bench as noted above) which deal, in the main, with first instance trials. In the Chancery Court, disputes over property, trusts, wills, revenue, bankruptcy and company matters are heard, and this court includes the Company Court and Patents Court; in the Queen's Bench are heard contract and tort cases which cannot be dealt with in the county courts below, and this division includes the Admiralty Court and the Commercial Court; and the Family Division hears divorce cases and other matrimonial matters. But the Family Division may also hear appeals from magistrates' courts acting in their civil capacity over matrimonial and other family affairs; and the Queen's Bench may hear appeals by way of case stated and also, in the limited circumstances where they are permitted by statute, appeals from tribunal decisions."

QUESTIONS

- Describe the basic functions of courts within a "common law" legal system.

- To what does the term "common law" refer?

- What (if anything) is the difference between "public" and "private" law?

- Explain what is meant by the "separation of powers". To what extent do we have a separation of powers in the United Kingdom?

- What is the difference between "civil" and "criminal" law?

- What is the difference between a "court of first instance" and one with "appellate jurisdiction"?

An understanding of the English legal system also demands an awareness of the ways in which judges are appointed.

J.A.G. Griffith, *The Politics of the Judiciary* (4th ed., Harper Collins, London, 1991), pp. 20–30:

"The most remarkable fact about the appointment of judges is that it is wholly in the hands of politicians. High Court and Circuit judges, Recorders, stipendary and lay magistrates are appointed by the Lord Chancellor who is a member of the Government. Appointments to the Court of Appeal, to the Appellate Committee of the House of Lords, and to the offices of Lord Chief Justice and President of the Family Division are made by the Prime Minister after consultation with the Lord Chancellor, who himself consults with senior members of the judiciary before making his choice or consulting with the Prime Minister. The Lord Chancellor has his own department headed, since the 1880s, by a permanent secretary. The department is the centre for the collection of information about the activity, the legal practice, and the reputation of members of the bar including those more senior, almost always Queen's Counsel (the conferment of which status is in the gift of the Lord Chancellor), from whom senior judicial appointments will be made. Inevitably the officials in the department exercise some influence but the extent of this varies and is difficult to assess. . . .

How far the Prime Minister uses his or her power of appointment or, to put this another way, merely accepts the Lord Chancellor's advice varies with different Prime Ministers and differing circumstances. It seems to be unusual for the Prime Minister or the Lord Chancellor to consult other ministers (except that the Lord Chancellor may discuss the matter with the Attorney-General and the Solicitor-General) unless any such minister happens to be also a distinguished member of the bar. . . . But it would be a mistake to assume that Prime Ministers are necessarily mouth-pieces of their Lord Chancellors when making the most senior appointments. . . .

Today being an active member of a political party seems to be neither a qualification nor a disqualification for appointment. But those barristers retained to represent the Government —called Treasury Counsel—are very likely to be offered High Court judgeships in due course.

It must be remembered that Lord Chancellors in making their appointments to the High Court have a relatively small group to select from. Effectively, the group consists of experienced barristers between the ages of forty-five and sixty and the number of genuine possibilities—the short list—may be as small as half a dozen.

Personal characteristics must be taken into account. A man or woman whose social or personal habits are unconventional or uncertain is not likely to be risked. Homosexuality is likely to be a bar or, if discovered later, to result in resignation. On the other hand, it is obvious from the appointments made that the strength of a candidate's convictions, including his political opinions, is not considered a disadvantage. But those opinions should fall within the ordinary range represented in the House of Commons, excluding the more extreme.

Politically the most important judicial appointment is the Master of the Rolls. As president of the Court of Appeal his view on the proper relationship between the Executive government and the individual, including powerful private organizations, is crucial. When Sir John Donaldson was appointed to succeed Lord Denning in July 1982, this was seen as a strongly political appointment and one which the Prime Minister favoured. Sir John had been a Conservative councillor and had presided over the National Industrial Relations Court for the two and a half years of its existence during the Heath administration. On its demise he reverted to his position as a judge of the High Court and was not promoted during the years of the Labour Government 1974–9. From the beginning of 1984 when it seemed probable that Lord Halisham would soon resign as Lord Chancellor, Sir John was widely discussed as his probable successor in the Thatcher cabinet. This highlighted his political characteristics and qualifications and may have led to his decision not to preside over the Court of Appeal when it considered the appeal by the Government against the decision of Glidewell J. rejecting the decision to ban trade union membership at GCHQ."[1]

THE DOCTRINE OF PRECEDENT

The starting point for a consideration of the role of judges in the common law system is the concept of *precedent*. Precedent refers to the idea that judges make law in the course of resolving disputes in common law *litigation*. One of the basic characteristics of our law can be summed up in the idea that "like cases should be treated alike". All things being equal, it seems fair that cases with similar facts and issues in dispute should be disposed of consistently by courts. But within a common law system, precedent means something more than the idea that consistency is a virtue. The obligation on a common law judge is that, in certain circumstances, precedents (previous judicial decisions) must be "followed", whether the second court agrees with the reasoning or not.

We say that a precedent is either "binding" on a judge, or it is merely "persuasive" authority. Judges are under a duty to follow binding precedents, but not persuasive ones. An example of a persuasive authority is a decision from another jurisdiction. For example, a judgment of the High Court of Australia (the highest court in that country) is a persuasive precedent in that English judges might adopt and apply the reasoning of the High Court if they think that the Australian judges have come up with a good solution to a legal problem. However, they are not *obligated* to apply that reasoning, and may resolve the dispute by a different legal route.

When judges follow binding precedents, they observe the principle known as *stare decisis*, or the doctrine of binding precedent. Once an issue of law is decided by the courts, it will normally be binding on courts lower down the hierarchy and, in many circumstances, on courts at the same level in the hierarchy. *Stare decisis* means more than simply that precedents are "followed" because judges think either that they provide "good" solutions which should be imitated, or that judges feel that deciding similar cases similarly advances the value of fairness between individuals. Rather, *stare decisis* signifies that decisions are followed because judges feel an *obligation* to do so, no matter what their view of the merits of the precedent. Yet, as Vandevelde argues, the principle of *stare decisis* is paradoxical:

"The doctrine of stare decisis rests on a paradox. On the one hand, a court has the power to decide only the dispute before it, and the rules that it announces are binding only in like cases. On the other hand, it is left to the courts deciding future

---

[1] You will recall that we examined this dispute in Chapter 3.

cases to determine whether those cases are like the prior case and, therefore, whether the prior case must be followed. The paradox is thus that a prior case binds a court, but only if the court decides that the prior case is binding.

Most lawyers, noting this paradox, eventually come to the understanding that the common law is not a set of fixed rules, but rather a process. It is a process whereby later cases are decided in a way that seems consistent with prior cases, although it is only when the later cases have been decided that the true meaning of the prior cases becomes known. By continually deciding which cases are similar or dissimilar to prior cases, courts in effect are shaping the content of the previously announced rules. The rules are defined as they are applied, and the law is in a constant state of evolution, explication, and elaboration."[2]

The principle of *stare decisis* is fundamental to the common law system, which is based on "judge made" law. We can think of it as the "glue" which holds the legal system together, and this is what distinguishes a common law system from the civil law system found in continental European countries (which we shall examine in Chapter 14). In a civilian system, the fundamental law is the product of the legislature and is called a *code*, and the obligation on judges is to faithfully interpret the code, rather than to follow precedent. Thus, in civil law countries, such as France and Germany, the code is the basis of the substantive law. In the common law system, by contrast, it is judge made law (in addition to statutes enacted by the legislature) which is fundamental, and the obligation on judges is to *follow* decisions made by (some) courts in the past.

We have already seen how one of the prerequisites for a system of precedent is a hierarchy of courts, and a set of rules which indicate the relationship between the courts; *i.e.* which decisions are binding upon which courts.

At the top of the legal structure in the United Kingdom today, arguably, is the European Court of Justice, and we have looked at its relationship to domestic courts in Chapter 4. Within the system of domestic courts, the highest court, as we have seen, is the House of Lords. Most importantly, the decisions of the House of Lords are binding on all lower courts. Moreover, for most of this century, the decisions of the House of Lords were also binding on itself. But on July 26, 1966, the Lord Chancellor read a statement, on behalf of himself and the other Lords.

Practice Statement [1966] 3 All E.R. 77, HL.

Before judgments were given in the House of Lords on July 26, 1966, Lord Gardiner, L.C., made the following statement on behalf of himself and the Lords of Appeal in Ordinary:

"Their lordships regard the use of precedent (1) as an indispensable foundation upon which to decide what is the law and its application to individual cases. It provides at least some degree of certainty upon which individuals can rely in the conduct of their affairs, as well as a basis for orderly development of legal rules.

Their lordships nevertheless recognise that too rigid adherence to precedent may lead to injustice in a particular case and also unduly restrict the proper development of the law. They

---

[2] Kenneth J. Vandevelde, *Thinking Like a Lawyer* (Westview Press, Boulder, 1996), p. 35.

propose therefore to modify their present practice and, while treating former decisions of this House as normally binding, to depart from a previous decision when it appears right to do so.

In this connexion they will bear in mind the danger of disturbing retrospectively the basis on which contracts, settlements of property and fiscal arrangements have been entered into and also the especial need for certainty as to the criminal law.

This announcement is not intended to affect the use of precedent elsewhere than in this House."

The Law Lords explained, in a press statement, that the sort of cases where precedent might be departed from included those in which it was felt that social conditions had changed, such that the law ought to be altered. The ability of the House of Lords to "overrule" its own prior decisions also gives the Law Lords the opportunity to review the impact of its decisions and, should they deem it necessary and desirable, they can alter or "overrule" the precedent if the impact is found to be negative. This is a rare occurrence, but it has been known to happen, as can be seen in the decisions of the House of Lords in the *Zamir* and *Khawaja* cases.

Zamir v. Secretary of State for the Home Department [1980] 2 All E.R. 768, HL.

[In 1973, an application was made on behalf of Zamir, a Pakistani national, by his family for an entry certificate into the United Kingdom, to which he was entitled under the immigration rules, for his immediate family had already settled in the U.K. The entry certificate was not issued until November 1975 (Zamir was now 18 years old), and his passport was stamped with a visa which stated "settlement to join father". In February 1976, Zamir married and in March arrived in the U.K. alone. He was granted leave to enter for an indefinite period, was asked no questions by the immigration officer, and divulged no information about his marriage. When it was later discovered that he was married, he was detained as an illegal immigrant pending removal from the U.K. He claimed that his failure to disclose his change of status did not affect the lawfulness of his entry and make him an illegal entrant, and he brought an application for a writ of *habeus corpus* (a type of judicial review on the basis of a denial of natural justice). That application was refused by the Divisional Court, and his appeal was dismissed by the Court of Appeal. It was then appealed further to the House of Lords, which dismissed the appeal. In so doing, Lord Wilberforce considered both the extent to which the decision of an immigration officer, acting under powers granted the Secretary of State, to remove an alien were open to judicial review, and second, the extent of the duty on an individual to volunteer information to an immigration officer about changed circumstances which affected his immigration status.]

Lord Wilberforce:
". . . The immigration officer, whether at the stage of entry or at that of removal, has to consider a complex of statutory rules and non-statutory guidelines. He has to act on documentary evidence and such other evidence as inquiries may provide. Often there will be documents whose genuineness is doubtful, statements which cannot be verified, misunderstandings as to what was said, practices and attitude in a foreign state which has to be estimated. There is room for appreciation, even for discretion . . . .

I conclude therefore that the decision to remove the applicant, and his consequent detention, can only be attacked if it can be shown that there were no grounds on which the Secretary of State, through his officers, could have acted, or that no reasonable person could have decided as he did.

I approach then the second legal question: what is the standard of the duty owed by persons arriving in the United Kingdom and seeking leave to enter? . . . In my opinion an alien seeking entry to the United Kingdom owes a positive duty of candour on all material facts which denote a change of circumstances since the issue of the entry clearance. He is seeking a privilege; he alone is, as to most such matters, aware of the facts; the decision to allow him to enter, and he knows this, is based on a broad appreciation by immigration officers of a complex of considerations, and this appreciation can only be made fairly and humanely if, on his side, the entrant acts with openness and frankness. It is insufficient, in my opinion, to set as the standard of disclosure that which applies in the law of contract; the relation of an intending entrant and the authorities is quite different in nature from that of persons negotiating in business. The former requires a higher and more exacting standard. To set it any lower than as I have described is to invite, as unhappily so many of the reported cases show, a bureaucratic and anti-bureaucratic contest with increasing astuteness, manoeuvring and ingenuity on one side, and increasingly cautious technicality and procrastination on the other. This cannot be in the interest of sensitive administration."

[Viscount Dilhorne, Lord Salmon, Lord Fraser of Tullybelton, and Lord Russell of Killowen concurred with Lord Wilberforce's reasons].

Khawaja v. Secretary of State for the Home Department and another appeal
[1983] 1 All E.R. 765, HL.

[This case involved two appeals by allegedly "illegal entrants", both of which (again) involved undisclosed marriages which, the immigration authorities concluded, amounted to deception. They detained the individuals pending deportation. Judicial review was sought of these decisions by the individuals, which was dismissed by the lower courts, and appealed to the House of Lords. In this case, the Lords reconsidered their reasoning in *Zamir*, and held that, while in some instances silence as to a material fact could amount to deception or fraud, the statute in question did not impose a positive duty on an applicant seeking leave to enter, so that non-disclosure of relevant facts did not itself constitute deception. Moreover, the Lords explicitly overruled *Zamir* on the degree of scrutiny to which the courts should subject a decision of an immigration officer. They held that a statement by an immigration officer that he or she had reasonable grounds to conclude that a person was an illegal entrant, should be subject to review, not just to determine whether it was a reasonable decision, but also whether it was the "correct" decision based on a high degree of probability.]

Lord Scarman:
". . . Two questions of law fall to be considered in the two appeals. Both arise under the Immigration Act 1971. One is as to the construction to be put on the definition of 'illegal entrant' which is contained in s 33 (1) of that Act. The other is as to the proper scope of judicial review where the immigration authority has decided to exercise its statutory power to remove an illegal entrant from the United Kingdom and detains him, or permits his temporary admission into the country subject to restrictions pending removal.

Both questions were considered and answered by the House in the recent case of *Zamir v. Secretary of State for the Home Dept*. The House in these two appeals is being invited to reconsider that decision and to depart from it, using the power to depart from precedent which the House declared by its practice statement of 1966 it was prepared to use in certain circumstances.

The practice statement is an affirmation of the importance of precedent 'as an indispensable foundation upon which to decide what is the law and its application to individual cases'. However, it recognises that 'too rigid adherence to precedent may lead to injustice in a particular case and also unduly restrict the proper development of the law'. The House will depart in the exceptional case from the precedent of a previous decision 'when it appears right to do so'. This formula indicates that the House must be satisfied not only that adherence to the precedent would involve the risk of injustice and obstruct the proper development of the law, but also that a judicial departure by the House from the precedent is the safe and appropriate way of remedying the injustice and developing the law. The possibility that legislation may be the better course is one which, though not mentioned in the statement, the House will not overlook. . . . Provided, however, that due attention is paid to the dangers of uncertainty in certain branches of the law (especially the criminal law) the House, as it has already in a number of cases made clear, will, if it thinks it right, depart from a previous decision whether the decision be ancient or modern and whether the point of law arises on the construction of a statute or in the judge-made common law or equity. . . .

My Lords, in most cases I would defer to a recent decision of your Lordships' House on a question of construction, even if I thought it wrong. I do not do so in this context because for reasons which I shall develop I am convinced that the *Zamir* reasoning gave insufficient weight to the important (I would say fundamental) consideration that we are here concerned with, the scope of judicial review of a power which inevitably infringes the liberty of those subjected to it. This consideration, if it be good, outweighs, in my judgment, any difficulties in the administration of immigration control to which the application of the principle might give rise.

The *Zamir* construction of para 9 deprives those subjected to the power of that degree of judicial protection which I think can be shown to have been the policy of our law to afford to persons with whose liberty the executive is seeking to interfere. It does therefore, in my view, tend to obstruct the proper development and application of the safeguards our law provides for the liberty of those within its jurisdiction. . . .

Accordingly, it is enough to say that, where the burden lies on the executive to justify the exercise of a power of detention, the facts relied on as justification must be proved to the satisfaction of the court. A preponderance of probability suffices; but the degree of probability must be such that the court is satisfied. . . .

For these reasons I conclude that in these two appeals, once the applicant had shown, as each did, that he had entered the United Kingdom with the leave of the immigration officer, the burden of proving that he had obtained leave by deception was on the executive and the standard of proof was the balance of probabilities. In Khera's case, the executive failed to prove that he was guilty of deception. In Khawaja's case the evidence that he deceived the immigration authority was overwhelming. Accordingly, I would allow the appeal of Khera and dismiss that of Khawaja."

[Lords Fraser of Tullybelton, Wilberforce, Bridge of Harwich, and Templeman reached the same results, each delivering concurring reasons.]

Below the House of Lords in the hierarchy of courts comes the Court of Appeal. Throughout most of the modern history of our legal system, it was assumed that the Court of Appeal was bound by decisions of the House of Lords. The question, however, has been considered explicitly.

Broome v. Cassell & Co. Ltd and another [1971] 2 All E.R. 187, CA.

Lord Denning M.R.:
"The jury gave £40,000 damages. It is a large sum. How did they get to it? What were the facts known to them? These I will tell.

1 Introduction

Early in July 1942 a large convoy of 35 merchant ships—it had the code number PQ17—was sailing in the Arctic seas laden with materials of war for Russia. They were between North Cape and Spitzbergen, near the icefields. At that time of the year there was no nightfall. It was light all the time. The convoy was approaching the most dangerous part of the voyage. The German battle fleet had come up swiftly and secretly. It was lying in wait in Alten fjord, just by North Cape. It consisted of the most powerful warship afloat—the Tirpitz—with the cruisers Hipper and Scheer, and six destroyers. Nearby, at Banak, was an airbase whence the German aircraft could make sorties of 400 miles to bomb the convoy. Under the sea there were German submarines watching through their periscopes for a chance to strike. The convoy would seem an easy target. It could only make eight knots. It had to steam at the pace of the slowest. But it was in good hands; it was guarded by the Royal Navy. The close escort was under the Command of Commander Broome, RN, the plaintiff, in the destroyer Keppel. It consisted of six destroyers, which were very fast, and several converted merchantmen as naval escorts, which were much slower. In support was a cruiser covering force under Rear-Admiral Hamilton in the London. It consisted of four cruisers and three destroyers. Further behind, ready to do battle, was the Home Fleet under Admiral Tovey in the Duke of York.

4th July 1942 saw the climax. Enemy air attack was imminent. Rear-Admiral Hamilton thought it best to play for safety. He 'instructed' the plaintiff to route the convoy to the northward so that it should be 400 miles from the enemy aerodrome. But the plaintiff was bolder. He did as Nelson did. After all, 'instructions' were not orders. They were more in the nature of recommendations, as every naval officer knows. He kept an easterly course, even though it did bring him nearer the enemy. The plaintiff was right. He was the man on the spot. He had an independent command and was entitled to exercise his own judgment. He had to take advantage of low cloud when it gave cover. And he had been advised by the Admiralty that the convoy should be kept 'moving to the eastward even though it was suffering damage'. So the plaintiff did not route it so much northward as Rear-Admiral Hamilton suggested. He kept it moving eastwards as well. His decision was afterwards approved by Admiral Tovey. Later that day the expected attack came. Suddenly at 8.22 pm 25 enemy aircraft appeared flying fast and low at the convoy. They were torpedo bombers and pressed home their attack with great determination. They sank two of the merchantmen. But the convoy and escort gave a good account of themselves. They shot down four of the attackers and went on in perfect formation. They were brave men. The plaintiff said to those nearby: 'Provided the ammunition lasts, Convoy PQ17 can get anywhere.'

Soon after beating off this attack, there came a warning of fresh danger. This time it was the onset of enemy surface ships. The Admiralty sent out three signals which arrived one after the other on the bridge of the Keppel, and of the other ships. The signals were, of course, in cipher:

'9 11 pm Secret. Most Immediate. Cruiser force withdraw to westwards at high speed.'
'9 23 pm Secret. Immediate. Owing to threat from surface ships convoy is to disperse and proceed to Russian ports.'
'9 36 pm Secret. Most Immediate. My 9 23 pm. Convoy is to scatter.'

The last message arrived so close on the heels of the one before that, when deciphered, the signalman handed them both together to the plaintiff. They spelt only one thing. The German battle fleet was about to attack. Everyone expected to see masts appearing on the horizon. The order to 'disperse' meant that the convoy was to split up into smaller formations, which were still under escort able to defend them. The next order to 'scatter' was more urgent still. It had never been given before, except once by the captain of the Jervis Bay, and he gave it only when the enemy cruisers were opening fire. It meant that the ships of the convoy were to scatter fanwise, each by himself, in every direction without escort. Leaving the escorting force to engage the enemy.

The plaintiff did as he was told. He took the Keppel into the middle of the convoy and told the commodore that the convoy was to scatter. He knew that his destroyers could not tackle the enemy fleet by themselves. So he proposed to Rear-Admiral Hamilton that they should join up with the cruiser force. Rear-Admiral Hamilton at once agreed. So the plaintiff with his escorting destroyers joined the cruisers and came under the direct command of Rear-Admiral Hamilton. The naval escorts (the converted merchantmen) were slow and could do little to protect the scattering convoy. So the plaintiff ordered them to proceed independently to Archangel. He, with his destroyers, prepared to meet the enemy.

But the threatened attack never came. The enemy fleet never appeared over the horizon. The order from the Admiralty was a mistake. The First Sea Lord, Admiral of the Fleet Sir Dudley Pound, had convinced himself that the Tirpitz must have put to sea, whereas the intelligence reports indicated that she had not. But the order was given. The convoy scattered to the four winds. Without protection, they were attacked by enemy from the air and from beneath the sea. Many were sunk. Out of the 35, only 11 reached Russian ports. 153 merchant sailors were lost and vast quantities of war material went to the bottom. It was a tragedy. A severe blow to the allied cause.

The officers made their reports. The plaintiff was not blamed by those superior to him. Nor by his brother officers. Admiral Tovey reported:

'I do not consider that the [plaintiff] was in any way to blame for the subsequent heavy losses. From the signals which he had received, he deduced, quite reasonably, that surface attack was imminent; and was correct in his decision to concentrate his destroyers and join the Rear-Admiral Commanding First Cruiser squadron.'

Proof positive of the confidence in the plaintiff was that he was kept in sea-going commands and finished the war in command of the battleship Ramillies. Many persons afterwards wrote about the disaster. The official historian of the war wrote about it. He did not condemn the plaintiff. Nor did Sir Winston Churchill. The condemnation was made 20 years later by an author who knew nothing about the war, because he was a babe in arms at the time. David Irving, the second defendant, was determined to write 'an authentic account'. His regular publishers, William Kimber, refused to publish it. They thought it was too dangerous. So he got Cassell & Co Ltd, the first defendants, to publish it.

2 The libels

The book was called 'The Destruction of Convoy PQ17'. The first defendants advertised it in words which defamed the Royal Navy. They described it as 'the true story of the biggest-ever Russian convoy that the Royal Navy left to annihilation'. They issued a dust-cover on which they stated: 'Many people were convinced' that the merchantmen 'had been shamefully deserted by a Navy which lost only a fleet oiler in the convoy's passage'. 'The massacre of PQ17' was due, they said, to 'blunders, miscalculations and misunderstandings' which many wanted to 'remain hidden like so much dirty linen', and that 'elaborate deceptions have been practised to ensure this'. Then they went on to say that the second defendant's five years of intensive research 'have provided the answers'. Thus they underwrote all that he said.

Inside the book the plaintiff was singled out for attack as if he was the naval officer mainly responsible for this shameful conduct. I will not read all the passages. Suffice it to say that they fell into two groups. The first group related to the 'instructions' given by Rear-Admiral Hamilton. The plaintiff was accused of downright disobedience. In breach of orders, it was said, he had taken the convoy 30 miles closer to the German airbases in Norway and exposed it to the enemy air attack. These passages spoke of 'Hamilton's dismay at [the plaintiff's] disobedience' and of his 'icy signal to [the plaintiff]', and of his 'stern reminder' to him. It was all quite unfounded because the plaintiff was entitled to exercise his own judgment, and did so. And Admiral Tovey approved. In the second group the plaintiff was accused of cowardly deserting the convoy. He had taken his destroyers and the naval escorts away from protecting the convoy, thus leaving the merchantmen to their fate. It was suggested that he had lost his head. It was said in terms that in his 'agitation' he had not understood the Admiralty signals aright; that, when the order came for the convoy to scatter, he 'needed no second bidding'; and that his 'first reaction' ws to tell his destroyers to 'join me'; that 'on his own initiative, with no instructions to this effect' he issued a signal withdrawing the escorts, thus 'stripping the scattering merchant ships of their last protection'. Afterwards, when the plaintiff offered to go back to help the convoy, the book said that all he wanted to do was 'to go back and *collect his escorts*—no mention of the merchant ships'; thus implying that he was not interested in what happened to them. The accusing finger was pointed unmistakably at the plaintiff. . . .

The imputations were quite unfounded; and proved at the trial to be so. Men who were there at the time came and said what happened. Young officers then, they had since become captains and admirals. The leading signalman on the bridge of the Keppel was now a police constable. He read of this case in the newspapers; and of his own accord came and spoke of the plaintiff's brave conduct. Every single witness supported the plaintiff. He had not disobeyed orders but had exercised his right discretion in his independent command. He had not left the merchantmen to their fate but had taken up station himself to face the enemy. He was not a broken man but at all times in full command of the situation. . . .

During the trial counsel for the plaintiff made it clear that he was claiming exemplary damages. A question was raised whether this should be pleaded. The judge held that it should be. . . . At the end of the case the jury found that the words were defamatory and were untrue. In respect of the hard-back edition, they awarded the plaintiff £14,000 compensatory damages. In respect of the proof copies, they awarded him £1,000 compensatory damages. The plaintiff asked for exemplary damages in respect of the hard-back edition. [The jury awarded £25,000 exemplary damages].

The law before Rookes v. Barnard

Prior to *Rookes v. Barnard*, the law as to exemplary damages was settled. It was well settled in 1961 in Mayne and McGregor on Damages:

> 'Such damages are variously called punitive damages, vindictive damages, exemplary damages, and even retributory damages. They can apply only when the conduct of the defendant merits punishment, which is only considered to be so where his conduct is wanton, as when it discloses fraud, malice, violence, cruelty, insolence, or the like, or as it is sometimes put, when he acts in contumelious disregard of the plaintiff's rights . . . Such damages are recognised to be recoverable in appropriate cases of defamation.' . . .

If the present case is tested according to the law as it stood before *Rookes v. Barnard*, I see no reason whatever for interfering with the jury's verdict. . . . It was a large sum; but not in any view excessive. The jury were entitled to regard the conduct of the defendants as completely shocking; and to mark their disapproval of it by their verdict.

Rookes v. Barnard itself

It is important to notice that both sides in *Rookes v. Barnard* accepted that the jury could award exemplary damages in libel actions. . . . Yet, when the House came to deliver their speeches, Lord Devlin threw over all that we ever knew about exemplary damages. He knocked down the common law as it had existed for centuries. He laid down a new doctrine about exemplary damages. He said that they could only be awarded in two very limited categories, but in no other category; and all the other Lords agreed with him. [Lord Denning reviewed how *Rookes v. Barnard* had not been approved and followed in other jurisdictions].

This wholesale condemnation justifies us, I think, in examining this new doctrine for ourselves; and I make so bold as to say that it should not be followed any longer in this country. I say this primarily because the common law of England on this subject was so well settled before 1964—and on such sound and secure foundations—that it was not open to the House of Lords to overthrow it. It could only be done by the legislature. I say it also because the counsel who argued *Rookes v. Barnard* accepted the common law as it had been understood for centuries and did not suggest any alteration of it. Yet the House, without argument, laid down this new doctrine. If the House were going to lay down this new doctrine—so as to be binding on all our courts—it ought at least to have required it to be argued. They might then have been told of the difficulties which it might bring in its wake, particularly when there are two defendants, as in this case. Next, I say that there were two previous cases in which the House of Lords clearly approved the award of exemplary damages in accordance with the settled doctrine of common law. They were *Hulton v. Jones* and *Ley v. Hamilton*. It was not open to the House in 1964 to go against those decisions. Lord Devlin must have overlooked them or misunderstood them, for he said that: 'There is not any decision of this House approving an award of exemplary damages'; and yet there were those two. Finally, I say that the new doctrine is hopelessly illogical and inconsistent. Take the first category. According to it, exemplary damages can be awarded in the case of 'oppressive, arbitrary or unconstitutional action by servants of the government'; but not by anyone else. Why limit it to 'servants of the government'. Other people can be just as oppressive and arbitrary as the servants of the government. . . . Take the next category. According to it, exemplary damages can be awarded when 'the defendant's conduct has been calculated by him to make a profit for himself which may well exceed the compensation payable to the plaintiff'. Why this emphasis on cold cynical calculation for profit? It makes me ask this question: which of these two men is worse? The man who says to himself: 'I reckon I will sell enough copies of this publication to pay any damages for libel'; or the man who says: 'I will smash this professional man whatever it costs me.' If exemplary damages for libel can be awarded against the greedy seeker of profit, surely they should be able to be awarded against the wicked inventor of calumnies.

All this leads me to the conclusion that, if ever there was a decision of the House of Lords given *per incuriam*, this was it. The explanation is that the House, as a matter of legal theory, thought that exemplary damages had no place in the civil code, and ought to be eliminated from it: but, as they could not be eliminated altogether, they ought to be confined within the strictest possible limits, no matter how illogical those limits. Yet I am conscious that, in all that I have said I may myself be at fault. Some will say that it is our duty to follow the House of Lords and not to question their decision. We are not to reason why. Ours is but to do and die."

[Lord Denning then explained, in the alternative, why *Rookes v. Barnard* could be interpreted broadly to uphold the award of exemplary damages in this case. Salmon L.J. and Phillimore L.J. each delivered concurring reasons.]

It was hardly surprising that the decision of the Court of Appeal was appealed to the House of Lords. The Lord Chancellor responded directly to the criticisms which had been put forward by Lord Denning M.R.

Cassell & Co. Ltd v. Broome and another [1972] 1 All E.R. 801, HL.

Lord Hailsham of St Marylebone L.C.:
". . . [I]t is necessary to say something of the direction to judges of first instance to ignore *Rookes v. Barnard* as 'unworkable'. As will be seen when I come to examine *Rookes v. Barnard* in the latter part of this opinion, I am driven to the conclusion that when the Court of Appeal described the decision in *Rookes v. Barnard* as decided '*per incuriam*' or 'unworkable' they really only meant that they did not agree with it. But, in my view, even if this were not so, it is not open to the Court of Appeal to give gratuitous advice to judges of first instance to ignore decisions of the House of Lords in this way and, if it were open to the Court of Appeal to do so, it would be highly undesirable. The course taken would have put judges of first instance in an embarrassing position, as driving them to take sides in an unedifying dispute between the Court of Appeal or three members of it (for there is no guarantee that other Lords Justice would have followed them and no particular reason why they should) and the House of Lords. But, much worse than this, litigants would not have known where they stood. None could have reached finality short of the House of Lords, and, in the meantime, the task of their professional advisers of advising them either as to their rights, or as to the probable cost of obtaining or defending them, would have been, quite literally, impossible. Whatever the merits, chaos would have reigned until the dispute was settled, and, in legal matters, some degree of certainty is at least as valuable a part of justice as perfection.

The fact is, and I hope it will never be necessary to say so again, that, in the hierarchical system of courts which exists in this country, it is necessary for each lower tier, including the Court of Appeal, to accept loyally the decisions of the higher tiers."

The Lord Chancellor's judgment illustrates the principle of the *vertical effect* of precedent; that judgments of superior courts bind inferior courts. The decisions of the

House of Lords bind all other courts, and the decisions of second tier courts (such as the Court of Appeal) normally bind courts of "first instance", (*i.e.* trial courts).

The *horizontal effect* of precedent, by contrast, means that precedents set at a particular level bind future courts at the same level. As we have seen, the House of Lords no longer considers itself bound by its own previous decisions, and therefore (formally) there is no horizontal effect, although the House only rarely departs from precedent. At the Court of Appeal, precedent historically has had a strong horizontal effect, with limited exceptions.

Young v. Bristol Aeroplane Co. Ltd [1944] 2 All E.R. 293, CA.

[The facts of the case concerned the right of an injured worker to sue his employer for breach of a statutory duty, in light of the fact that he was receiving payments pursuant to the Workmen's Compensation Act, 1925. The interesting legal question turned on the fact that it was contended by the appellant Young that while the court of first instance found itself bound by two Court of Appeal decisions, those decisions were inconsistent with a decision of the House of Lords. The issue thus was under what circumstances could the Court of Appeal depart from its own previous decisions, (*i.e.* the doctrine of horizontal binding precedent)? Lord Greene M.R. found no inconsistency between the decisions, and went on to consider the applicability of horizontal binding precedent at the Court of Appeal].

Lord Greene M.R.:
". . . In considering the question whether or not this court is bound by its previous decisions and those of courts of co-ordinate jurisdiction, it is necessary to distinguish four classes of case. The first is that with which we are now concerned, namely, cases where this court finds itself confronted with one or more decisions of its own or of a court of co-ordinate jurisdiction which cover the question before it, and there is no conflicting decision of this court or of a court of co-ordinate jurisdiction. The second is where there is such a conflicting decision. The third is where this court comes to the conclusion that a previous decision, although not expressly overruled, cannot stand with a subsequent decision of the House of Lords. The fourth (a special case) is where this court comes to the conclusion that a previous decision was given *per incuriam*. In the second and third classes of case it is beyond question that the previous decision is open to examination. In the second class, the court is unquestionably entitled to choose between the two conflicting decisions. In the third class of case the court is merely giving effect to what it considers to have been a decision of the House of Lords by which it is bound. The fourth class requires more detailed examination . . .

It remains to consider *Lancaster Motor Co. (London), Ltd v. Bremith Ltd*, in which a court consisting of Sir Wilfrid Greene, M.R., Clauson and Goddard L.JJ., declined to follow an earlier decision of a court consisting of Slesser and Romer L.JJ. This was clearly a case where the earlier decision was given *per incuriam*. It depended upon the true meaning (which in the later decision was regarded as clear beyond argument) of a rule of the Supreme Court to which the court was apparently not referred and which it obviously had not in mind. The Rules of the Supreme Court have statutory force and the court is bound to give effect to them as a statute. Where the court has construed a statute or a rule having the force of a statute, its decision stands on the same footing as any other decision on a question of law. But where the court is satisfied that an earlier decision was given in ignorance of the terms of a statute or a rule having the force of a statute the position is very different. It cannot, in our opinion, be right to say that in such a case the court is entitled to disregard the statutory provision and is bound to follow a decision of its own given when that provision was not present to its mind. Cases of this description are examples of decisions given *per incuriam*. We do not think that it would be right to say that there may not be other cases of decisions given *per incuriam* in which this court might properly consider itself entitled not to follow an earlier decision of its own. Such cases would obviously be of the rarest occurrence and must be dealt with in accordance with their special facts. Two classes of decisions *per incuriam* fall outside the scope of our enquiry, namely (i) those where the court has acted in ignorance of a previous decision of its own or of a court of co-ordinate jurisdiction which covers the case before it—in such a case a subsequent court must decide which of the two decisions it ought to follow; and (ii) those where it has acted in ignorance of a decision of the House of Lords which covers the point—in such a case a subsequent court is bound by the decision of the House of Lords.

On a careful examination of the whole matter we have come to the clear conclusion that this court is bound to follow previous decisions of its own as well as those of courts of co-ordinate jurisdiction. The only exceptions to this rule (two of them apparent only) are those already mentioned which for convenience we here summarise: (i) The court is entitled and bound to decide which of two conflicting decisions of its own it will follow. (ii) The court is bound to refuse to follow a decision of its own which, though not expressly overruled, cannot in its opinion stand with a decision of the House of Lords. (iii) The court is not bound to follow a decision of its own if it is satisfied that the decision was given *per incuriam*."

With the relaxation of horizontal precedent at the House of Lords in 1966, the question of the continuing effect of horizontal precedent at the Court of Appeal became a live issue. Not surprisingly, Lord Denning M.R. led the charge.

Davis v. Johnson [1978] 1 All E.R. 841, CA.

[The case concerned the Domestic Violence and Matrimonial Proceedings Act 1976, which gave county court judges the power to exclude an individual from a "matrimonial home" because of domestic abuse. The parties were joint tenants of a council flat. Although not married, they lived together and were parents of a child. Their relationship was very violent, and the woman, Davis, applied to the county court for an injunction ordering Johnson to vacate the flat and to stop assaulting and molesting her and their child. The injunction was granted, but another county court judge rescinded that part of the order which required Johnson to leave the flat. Davis appealed to the Court of Appeal. Lord Denning's judgment is of particular interest for its consideration of the horizontal effect of precedent on the Court of Appeal].

Lord Denning M.R.:
". . . On principle, it seems to me that, whilst this court should regard itself as normally bound by a previous decision of the court, nevertheless it should be at liberty to depart from it if it is convinced that the previous decision was wrong. What is the argument to the contrary?

It is said that, if an error has been made, this court has no option but to continue the error and leave it to be corrected by the House of Lords.

The answer is this: the House of Lords may never have an opportunity to correct the error; and thus it may be perpetuated indefinitely, perhaps for ever. That often happened in the old days when there was no legal aid. A poor person had to accept the decision of this court because he had not the means to take it to the House of Lords. . . . Apart from monetary considerations, there have been many instances where cases have been settled pending an appeal to the House of Lords; or, for one reason or another, not taken there, especially with claims against insurance companies or big employers. When such a body has obtained a decision of this court in its favour, it will buy off an appeal to the House of Lords by paying ample compensation to the appellant. By so doing, it will have a legal precedent on its side which it can use with effect in later cases. . . . By such means an erroneous decision on a point of law can again be perpetuated forever. Even if all those objections are put on one side and there is an appeal to the House of Lords, it usually takes 12 months or more for the House to reach its decision. What then is the position of the lower courts meanwhile? They are in a dilemma.

Either they have to apply the erroneous decision of the Court of Appeal, or they have to adjourn all fresh cases to await the decision of the House of Lords. That has often happened. So justice is delayed, and often denied, by the lapse of time before the error is corrected.

The present case is a crying instance. If it took the ordinary course of appeals to the House, it would take some months before it was decided. Meanwhile many women would be denied the protection which Parliament intended they should have. They would be subjected to violence without redress; because the county court judges would have to say to them: 'We are sorry but the Court of Appeal says we have no jurisdiction to help you.' We were told that, in this very case, because of the urgency, the House might take special measures to hear it before Christmas. But, even so, I doubt whether they would be able to give their decision until well on in the New Year. In order to avoid all the delay, and the injustice consequent on it, it seems to me that this court, being convinced that the two previous decisions were wrong, should have the power to correct them and give these women the protection which Parliament intended they should have.

It was suggested that, if we did this, the county court judges would be in a dilemma. They would not know whether to follow the two previous decisions or the later decision of this court. There would be no such dilemma. They should follow this later decision. Such a position always arises whenever the House of Lords corrects an error made by a previous decision. The lower courts, of course, follow the latest decision. The general rule is that, where there are conflicting decisions of courts of co-ordinate jurisdiction, the later decision is to be preferred, if it is reached after full consideration of the earlier decision. . . .

The new Guidelines

So we suggest that new guidelines are entitled to be laid down. To my mind, this court should apply similar guidelines to those adopted by the House of Lords in 1966. Whenever it appears to this court that a previous decision was wrong, we should be at liberty to depart from it if we think it right to do so. Normally, in nearly every case of course, we would adhere to it. But in an exceptional case we are at liberty to depart from it.

Alternatively, in my opinion, we should extend the exceptions in *Young v. Bristol Aeroplane Co. Ltd* when it appears to be a proper case to do so."

[The Court of Appeal sat in a panel of five to hear the case. Sir George Baker and Shaw L.J. concurred that the Court of Appeal was not bound by the precedents, although their reasons differed. Goff and Cumming-Bruce L.JJ. dissented.]

Not surprisingly, *Davis v. Johnson* was appealed to the House of Lords and, on appeal, the House of Lords expressed strong disapproval of the Court of Appeal's disregard for precedent.

Davis v. Johnson [1978] 1 All E.R. 1132, HL.

Lord Diplock:
" . . . In an appellate court of last resort a balance must be struck between the need on the one side for the legal certainty resulting from the binding effect of previous decisions and on the other side the avoidance of undue restriction on the proper development of the law. In the case of an intermediate appellate court, however, the second desideratum can be taken care of by appeal to a superior appellate court, if reasonable means of access to it are available; while the risk to the first desideratum, legal certainty, if the court is not bound by its own previous decisions grows ever greater with increasing membership and the number of three-judge divisions in which it sits . . . . So the balance does not lie in the same place as in the case of a court of last resort. . . .

In my opinion, this House should take this occasion to re-affirm expressly, unequivocally and unanimously that the rule laid down in the *Bristol Aeroplane* case as to *stare decisis* is still binding on the Court of Appeal."

Lord Salmon:

" . . . I sympathise with the views expressed on this topic by Lord Denning M.R., but until such time, if ever, as all his colleagues in the Court of Appeal agree with those views, *stare decisis* must still hold the field. I think that this may be no bad thing. There are now as many as 17 Lords Justices in the Court of Appeal, and I fear that if *stare decisis* disappears from that court there is a real risk that there might be a plethora of conflicting decisions which would create a state of irremediable confusion and uncertainty in the law. This would do far more harm than the occasional unjust result which *stare decisis* sometimes produces but which can be remedied by an appeal to your Lordships' House. I recognise, as Cumming-Bruce L.J. points out, that only those who qualify for legal aid or the very rich can afford to bring such an appeal. This difficulty could however be surmounted if when the Court of Appeal gave leave to appeal from a decision it has felt bound to make by an authority with which it disagreed, it had a power conferred on it by Parliament to order the appellants and/or the respondents' costs of the appeal to be paid out of public funds. This would be a very rare occurrence and the consequent expenditure of public funds would be minimal."

As for the substantive issue of the appeal, the Law Lords held that the Matrimonial Proceedings Act 1976 should be interpreted to protect a party to a marriage or a relationship akin to a marriage from domestic violence by investing county court judges with the power to grant an applicant an injunction excluding the individual from the premises irrespective of the applicant's proprietary rights in the premises.

Thus, from *Davis v. Johnson* it is clear that the House of Lords has the ultimate responsibility for ensuring that the law is "on the right track". The Lords made clear to the Court of Appeal that the latter is bound to follow its own decisions under the principle of *stare decisis*, except for the narrow range of circumstances enunciated in *Bristol Aeroplane*. However, as we will see throughout this text, judges have many techniques for avoiding or deflecting the impact of precedent through *distinguishing* cases (showing how they are materially different from the precedents).

Davis v. Johnson was a case in the Civil Division of the Court of Appeal. By contrast, the Court of Appeal Criminal Division possesses somewhat greater flexibility as to the doctrine of *stare decisis* and there are cases where the court has refused to follow its own previous decisions.

The High Court, the next court down the hierarchy of courts, sometimes possesses *appellate* jurisdiction. In those cases, two or more High Court judges will sit on a panel and constitute a *Divisional Court*. In those circumstances, the same rule of *stare decisis* applies as if it was a panel of the Court of Appeal.

More generally, the High Court functions as a *court of first instance* (a court where cases begin). The decisions of courts of first instance are not generally horizontally binding. Thus a legal ruling by a High Court judge is not binding on other High Court judges, nor are decisions of county court judges or magistrates normally binding on other judges at those lower levels. But magistrates and county court judges would be bound by decisions of High Court judges and, obviously, by judgments from higher up the judicial hierarchy. Moreover, although High Court judges' decisions are not normally binding on other High Court judges, they are strongly persuasive and usually will be followed.

The crucial point is that the decisions of lower courts are *never* binding on higher courts although a non-binding precedent might well be of great persuasive authority. If a decision is not binding on a court, ultimately it is free to accept or reject the rule for which the case stands.

We conclude this section on *stare decisis* by asking exactly what is meant when we say that a previous statement of the law by a court is binding on subsequent courts. In answer, a decision is to be treated as binding if: (i) it is analogous to the immediate dispute; and (ii) if the precedent was decided by a court which has the status to create a binding precedent on the immediate court; and (iii) the decision has not been over-turned by a statute of the legislature or by a court higher up the judicial hierarchy. Of most interest to us will be the first condition: whether a precedent is directly analogous and "on point" in a case, or, alternatively, whether it can be distinguished (differen-tiated) from the immediate case. We shall see that this inquiry is not a mechanical one, and it can involve complex legal, as well as social and political, inquiries.

QUESTION

Define *stare decisis* and explain its significance within the common law system. Specific reference should be made to its effect on the House of Lords and the Court of Appeal.

THE POLITICS OF THE JUDICIARY

To this point, we have examined the *rules* which govern judicial decision making in our legal system. Our attention now turns to the *politics* of the judiciary and judicial deci-sion making. Our starting point is Griffith's analysis of the backgrounds of members of the judiciary in the United Kingdom. His conclusions concern what those back-grounds suggest about their decision making. His findings have proven controversial.

J.A.G. Griffith, *The Politics of the Judiciary* (4th ed., Harper Collins, London, 1991), pp. 34–36:

"All these figures show that, in broad terms, four out of five full-time professional judges are products of public schools, and of Oxford or Cambridge. Occasionally the brilliant lower-middle-class or working-class boy or girl has won their place in this distinguished gathering. With very few exceptions, judges are required to be selected from amongst practising barris-ters and it is difficult for anyone without a private income to survive the first years of prac-tice. To become a successful barrister, therefore, it is necessary to have financial support and so the background has to be that of the reasonably well-to-do family which, as a matter of course, sends its sons or daughters to public schools and then to Oxford or Cambridge.

Nevertheless, some men and women have, since the middle 1960s, benefited from the expansion of university education, from the growth of law faculties in universities, and from the wider availability of this education and, with little private income, have been able (largely because of the increase in publicly financed legal aid) to make a living at the bar. In the 1990s some of these will move into the ranks of successful barristers from whom judicial appoint-ments are made. Only then shall we be able to assess how far the dominance of the public schools and (what is of much less significance) of Oxford and Cambridge has begun to lessen. And not until the late 1990s shall we know whether (as seems most unlikely) judicial attitudes have changed as a result.

In March 1991, of the judges from the Law Lords to the Circuit bench (some 550 in all) only one was black. Two Lords Justice, two High Court judges and nineteen Circuit judges were women.

Judicial independence means that judges are not dependent on governments in ways which might influence them in coming to decisions in individual cases, though their promotion, like their appointment, is effectively in the hands of the Lord Chancellor with, nowadays, a measure of Prime Ministerial intervention. As we have seen, in financial terms, such promotion is not of much significance. But life in the Court of Appeal and, even more, in the House of Lords is not so strenuous as in the High Court (or below), personal prestige and status are higher among the fewer, with a life peerage at the top. These are not inconsiderable rewards for promotion, and the question is whether there are pressures on, particularly, High Court judges to act and to speak in court in certain ways rather than others. Are there decisions which could be classified as popular or unpopular in the eyes of the most important senior judges or the Lord Chancellor? Is a judge ever conscious that his reputation as a judge is likely to be adversely affected in their eyes if he decides one way, and favourably affected if he decides another way?

The answer is that such pressures do exist. For example, a judge who acquires a reputation among his seniors for being 'soft' in certain types of cases where the Lord Chancellor, the Lord Chief Justice, the Master of the Rolls and other senior judges favour a hard line is as likely to damage his promotion prospects as he would if his appointment were found to be unfortunate on other more obvious grounds. But this does not amount to dependence on the political wishes of governments or ministers as such. In no real sense does such direct dependence or influence exist. How far judges consciously or unconsciously subserve the wide interests of governments is another and more important question."

It is a question which has been brought to the forefront in recent years, both by Griffith, and by judicial decisions which have resulted in the now famous "miscarriage of justice" cases.

Phil Harris, *An Introduction to Law* (5th ed., Butterworths, London, 1997), pp. 430–434:

"In recent years the English judiciary too, has been 'battered and bruised' by a series of cases in which there was a clear and most serious miscarriage of justice. First came the release from prison of the Guildford Four and the Maguire Seven, and followed by the Birmingham Six— all of whom had been convicted of terrorist activity including the bombing of public houses in Guildford and Birmingham. Later came the release of the men convicted of the murder of the newspaper-boy Karl Bridgewater. It eventually transpired that all of the defendants in these cases had served long periods of imprisonment for crimes they did not commit, though all of the cases had previously been re-examined and duly rejected by the Court of Appeal. Not surprisingly, among the questions asked in the media at the time was simply, why had the court not recognised earlier the weaknesses in the Crown's case against these defendants (and in particular the police and scientific forensic evidence in some cases)? The Birmingham Six case is interesting for, among other things, Lord Denning's previous refusal to grant legal aid to the defendants in 1975 to allow them to bring an action against the West Midlands police:

'If the six men win it will mean that the police were guilty of perjury, that they were guilty of violence and threats, that the confessions were involuntary and were improperly admitted in evidence and that the convictions were erroneous. That would mean the Home Secretary would either have to recommend they be pardoned or he would have to remit the case to the Court of Appeal. This is such an appalling vista that every sensible person in the land would say: "It cannot be right that these actions should go any further"'.

In other words, it seemed to his Lordship more important that public confidence in the criminal justice system should not be undermined, than that six innocent men should be freed.

This series of events did little to bolster public confidence in the higher judiciary and there are more cases of people in prison in respect of whose convictions there may be serious doubt. In the wake of the release of the Birmingham Six came the establishment of a Royal

Commission on Criminal Justice, chaired by Lord Runciman, whose terms of reference included issues arising after trial and in particular arrangements for considering allegations of miscarriages of justice. The recommendations of the Commission on this point were implemented in the Criminal Appeal Act 1995, which set up the Criminal Cases Review Commission, which has the power to refer cases of convicted persons to the Court of Appeal if it considers that 'there is a real possibility that the conviction, verdict, finding or sentence would not be upheld [in the Court of Appeal] because of an argument, or evidence, not raised in the proceedings which led to it or on any appeal or application for leave to appeal against it'. It is to be hoped that this new body will play an important part in effectively preventing miscarriages of justice in the future.

In a more general context, and drawing on many cases from various areas of social activity as illustrations, Griffith has catalogued and discussed the extent to which the role of the judiciary (in particular the judges of the higher courts) can be seen to overlap into the sphere of political decision-making. In particular, Griffith discusses the broad areas of industrial relations, personal rights and freedoms, property rights and squatters, judicial control on ministerial discretion, the uses of conspiracy, and cases involving students and trade union members. He argues that 'judges are part of the machinery of authority within the State and as such cannot avoid the making of political decisions'; and that the senior judges in particular have, by reason of their legal education and their working life as practising barristers, 'acquired a strikingly homogeneous collection of attitudes, beliefs, and principles, which to them represents the public interest'. For Griffith, the idea of an impartial and neutral judiciary, especially in cases involving a political element, is mythical:

> '. . .judges in the United Kingdom cannot be politically neutral because they are placed in positions where they are required to make political choices which are sometimes presented to them, and often presented by them, as determinations of where the public interest lies; . . . that interpretation of what is in the public interest and therefore politically desirable is determined by the kind of people they are and the position they hold in our society; . . . this position is part of established authority and so is necessarily conservative and illiberal.'

When first published, Griffith's book met with considerable criticism, particularly, as one might expect, from members and ex-members of the judiciary. Lord Devlin, once a judge in the House of Lords, responded to some of Griffith's assertions and arguments. To a large extent, Devlin's reply may be summarised as a resounding 'so what?' To begin with, he explains, there is no denying the homogeneity of political and other outlooks on the part of the judges, but then the same is true of most other institutions in our society, or at least, those of them which 'like the law are not of a nature to attract the crusading or rebellious spirit'.

Further, argues Devlin, the question posed by Griffith, which is 'do the judges allow their devotion to law and order to distort their application of the law when they apply it to those who do not think as they do?' is beset by the twin difficulties of lack of unanimity among the senior judges whom Griffith, according to Devlin, seeks to present as 'a small group of senior judges who are policy makers': 'The law lords are sometimes divided: more frequently they quarrel with the Court of Appeal.' And the constraints imposed by the length of Griffith's book do not, argues Devlin, allow any rigorous analysis of the cases under discussion. Devlin accepts that Griffith's perspective may be seen as the view from the left, and explains that criticisms of the judiciary might also be made by those taking a different ideological stance: 'Professor Griffith cites cases on the use of police powers which he finds to be 'alarming'; someone right of centre could probably produce a list of cases which would alarm him by their tenderness towards crime.' In short, Devlin is inclined to the view that too much is made by Griffith of the 'politics of the judiciary', for 'their politics are hardly more significant than those of the army, the navy and the airforce; they are as predictable as those of any institution where maturity is in command'. . . . [Harris goes on to note one key factor which limits the 'politics' of judicial decision making:]

[A]n important constraining factor is the necessity, noted by Weber, Frank and others, for judicial decisions to be presented not as the outcome of subjective, arbitrary or capricious reasoning by the judge, but as the result of the application of *objective* criteria. This is the difference between the statement 'in my opinion, you are guilty' and the statement 'according to the law, you are guilty'. The former statement we would regard as somewhat suspect, as being unfair or biased. The issue of public credibility and confidence in the judiciary is once again relevant here: we would not place much faith in a legal system which allowed judges to decide cases according to their whim or their personal views about the parties to a dispute. We expect judges to decide cases in accordance with existing law, without personal views or prejudices colouring their judgment."

The politics of the judiciary frequently becomes more explicit and recognisable when judges are asked to consider the "public interest". In these situations, *ideological* assumptions about society often come to the surface of judicial decisions. Moreover, judicial decision making in this context often appears to *assume* that there is a shared system of values throughout society, and that judges are equipped to identify them, and to maintain them through the power of law. It is here that the relationship between "law" and "morality" becomes explicit.

Phil Harris, *An Introduction to Law* (5th ed., Butterworths, London, 1997), pp. 445–448:

"[T]he judicial protection of moral standards extends beyond the range of criminal law. Such concerns are the basis of much judicial comment and decisions in family law, and in the law of contract we find cases such as that of *Pearce v. Brooks* in 1866, where the judges refused to accept the legality of an agreement between the plaintiffs and the defendant whereby the former had hired out a carriage to the latter, to be used for the purposes of prostitution. In *Glynn v. Keele University* in 1971, a student who was excluded from residence on the campus for nude sunbathing failed in his attempt to challenge this disciplinary action. Although the court accepted that, in denying him a chance to put his side of the case, the university official had acted in breach of natural justice, the court none the less felt that the offence was such as to 'merit a severe penalty according to any standards current even today'. And in 1971, in *Ward v. Bradford Corpn*, the Court of Appeal denied a remedy to a student teacher who had broken the rules of her hall of residence by permitting her boy-friend to remain in her room overnight for a period of about two months. She had been expelled by the college and, despite irregularities in the manner in which the disciplinary procedure had been carried out, Lord Denning stated firmly his belief that her behaviour was not suitable for a trainee teacher: 'she would never make a teacher. No parent would knowingly entrust their child to her care.'

In such matters of morality, the tension between judicial conservatism and an increased social tolerance of moral behaviour which is not to everyone's taste, is manifest. It is worth asking the question whether, in today's climate in which sexual and other moral matters are relatively freely discussed and practices once regarded as beyond the pale are fairly openly indulged in, the attitude of the judges may in some cases be too far removed from the 'real social world', so to speak, to protect the interests of all involved. Having said this, however, one outstanding case in which the judges showed themselves well aware of modern public attitudes towards sexual morality was *R. v. R.* in 1991—the case which overturned the common law rule that a husband could not be criminally liable for committing rape upon his wife. In the Court of Appeal, Lord Lane stated that the old common law rule had become 'anachronistic and offensive and we consider that it is our duty having reached that conclusion to act upon it'—a view with which the House of Lords unanimously agreed. There can be no doubt that this decision was both welcome and long overdue.

Other notable areas where the courts have referred, in the various cases before them, to the 'public interest', or equivalent terms, include the law of property, where the judges have consistently upheld the protection of traditional rights to private property as against, for example, private tenants (through restrictive interpretation of rent legislation) and squatters; the law relating to conspiracy where, until the Criminal Law Act 1977 clarified and somewhat restricted the range of the offence, the judges had been quite prepared to uphold convictions for the offence even though the activity allegedly planned by the conspirators had not been carried out; and the law relating to public order and industrial disputes.

The problems underlying these assumptions and views on the part of the judiciary revolve around the difficulty of identifying exactly what constitutes the 'public interest' in a given area —even if such a monolithic entity exists at all. By what criteria do the judges, who wield considerable power in such cases, discover which particular body of attitudes or standards in our society constitute *the* public interest? Perhaps Lord Devlin, once again, expressed the view of most judges:

> 'English law has evolved and regularly uses a standard which does not depend on the counting of heads. It is that of the reasonable man. . . . It is the viewpoint of the man in the street. . . . He might also be called the right-minded man. For my purpose I should like to call him the man in the jury-box, for the moral judgment of society must be something about which any twelve men or women drawn at random might after discussion be expected to be unanimous.'

But how likely *is* such a consensus? Society is by no means homogeneous: it is composed of many groups and individuals differing in terms of sex, age, ethnic and cultural background, social class and political power. Would it be possible to obtain a unanimous judgment from any group of randomly selected people on the issues of industrial relations, prostitution or any of the other areas where the assumptions held by the judges, particularly in the appellate courts, have come to the fore? Surely *any* interest group might convincingly register a belief that *their* policies, beliefs or attitudes were an accurate reflection of a 'public morality' or a 'public interest'? Unless we are, literally, to embark upon a national referendum on all such matters, there would seem to be no clear way of ascertaining what the majority of people believe to be right or acceptable behaviour, with any degree of accuracy.

Furthermore, Lord Devlin and other judges using similar terminology commit a serious analytical error in using phrases such as 'society believes this' or 'society has decided that'. Such loose phrases obscure the fact of pluralistic interests and differential access to policy-making channels within the social structure. What is, therefore, presented as being in the 'public interest' may in fact serve limited, sectional interests. As Coulson and Riddell put it:

> '. . . to say that a decision is in the national interest usually means to identify the interests of one group of the population as the National Interest, while conveniently forgetting the interests of those members of the nation who are not benefited by the decision. By the appeal to nationalism, sectional decisions may appear more palatable to people they don't benefit.' "

The ideological underpinnings of judicial decision making are particularly apparent in the way in which the judiciary frequently constructs "common sense" in their reasons. Graycar argues that an underlying gendered perspective is at work in these judicial pronouncements.

Regina Graycar, "The Gender of Judgments: An Introduction" in *Public and Private: Feminist Legal Debates* (Margaret Thornton, ed., Oxford University Press, Melbourne, 1995), p. 266–272:

"I have suggested that the role of judging is gendered and implicitly male, and I think this follows inexorably from a history of social, political and legal practices, and beliefs now deeply entrenched in the substantive body of law with which judges work. Given the fact that women were not even permitted to practise law until well into this century, there is no question that the substantive legal doctrines we use on a day-to-day basis were developed by men, with their problems and concerns in mind, and reflecting their perspectives on the world. Despite the relatively recent entry of women into the profession, and their increasing numbers (though less so on the bench in Australia), legal doctrines and legal reasoning appear to have remained almost completely impervious to perspectives other than those of the (dominant) White, middle-class male. . . .

If law was developed by men in accordance with their needs and experiences and has neither dealt well with women, nor reflected their lives or experiences, then perhaps everything would change if there were some more women in there. But I am not very confident that, simply by adding some women to the bench and stirring, we will automatically change the male-centredness of law and legal reasoning. For a number of reasons—such as the ways in which legal education has been conducted to date and the ways in which certain forms of utterance are privileged by law in the construction of what is authoritative, and by corollary, what (or who) lacks credibility—I am somewhat sceptical of the view that simply as a result of women being there, everything will be different. We may just be adding more women to the bench—nothing more, nothing less. After all, the 'institution' of law remains and its '[i]nstitutional design is a way of allocating authority across different sets of actors', while ensuring that the 'legal texts always operate from a particular strategy of framing facts'. But if we could further our understanding of what judges know, how they know it, how this shapes the construction of reality in judgments—that is, how judges 'orient' their narratives—and how this is all affected by gender, then maybe things *could* change. While there are any number of barriers to women's stories being heard in courts and, even if heard, being given credibility and authority, judges' speech is quintessentially authoritative. Judges are speakers whose verdicts count, both generally, in that they have considerable social status and, most particularly for these purposes, in their power to construct realities in the domain of law.

Consider the following seven examples:

1. A negligence action was brought by a woman who had four children, did not want any more, but became pregnant after having a negligently performed tubal ligation. She sued and sought damages, *inter alia*, for the cost of upkeep of the child. The judge described the plaintiff as 'a motherly sort of woman, nice looking but rather overweight . . . She is not only an experienced mother but, so far as I am able to judge, a good mother, who has all the proper maternal instincts'.

2. A custody dispute in the Family Court of Australia involved two professional parents, both doctors. The judge said, 'the major question mark hanging over the wife . . . is whether she would be prepared to sacrifice her career for the sake of the children'. She was recently remarried and had given evidence that she and her husband planned to have a child, but the judge was not satisfied that she would give up her job and said, 'she wants her cake and eat it too: unremarkable in these days of equality of opportunity'. In a decision (subsequently overturned on appeal), the judge awarded the wife (in her late thirties) custody on a conditional basis: 'if she resigned her job and came back to court pregnant two months later, she would be awarded custody; otherwise, custody would be given to the father who was working full time'.

3. Discussing domestic work in the context of a damages claim, the judge said, 'regard must be had to public mores in Australia and, where a husband [and] wife are both working . . . the sharing of domestic burdens with the wife is expected of the husband, even where his wife is perfectly healthy'. The same judge, in another case of an injured woman, commented, 'The appellant and her husband both worked, despite the fact that she had two quite young children . . . The husband will have to do more in the domestic field than he would otherwise have had to. Most Australian males are expected to give domestic assistance to their wives.' And, before leaving this case, another judge remarked, 'Like many migrant women, she had been constantly in work . . . [I]n these days of changed practices of women working, but particularly so in the case of migrant settlers . . .'

4. Explaining why juries in rape cases had to be warned about the dangers of convicting on the uncorroborated evidence of the woman, a judge commented that 'Human experience has shown that in these courts girls and women do sometimes tell an entirely false story which is very easy to fabricate, but extremely difficult to refute. Such stories are fabricated for all sorts of reasons, which I need not now enumerate, and sometimes for no reason at all.' Even after the abolition by statute of the corroboration requirement, we are told: 'Experience has taught the judges that there have been cases where women have manufactured or invented false allegations of rape and sexual attack. It is a very easy allegation to make. It is often very hard to contradict.'

5. The case in which this last remark was made received some public attention in Australia. It involved a prosecution for six counts of rape by a man of his wife: 'There is, of course, nothing wrong with a husband, faced with his wife's initial refusal to engage in intercourse, in attempting, in an acceptable way, to persuade her to change her mind, and that may involve a measure of rougher than usual handling. It may be, in the end, that handling and persuasion will persuade the wife to agree.'

6. Or, 'it does happen, in the common experience of those who have been in the law as long as I have anyway, that no often subsequently means yes.'

7. And in yet another case, Justice O'Bryan in the Victoria Supreme Court, in the case of sentencing a man to eleven years' jail, commented that a seventeen-year-old girl who was bashed, raped, and had her throat slit was 'not traumatised' by the rape because she was 'probably comatose at the time', having been knocked unconscious by the offender.

It might be tempting to think that these are instances drawn from darkest history; but not one of these examples is more than fifteen years old and, significantly, not all of them are by men. While there are many other quotable quotes that would illustrate the point, merely reproducing them may take us only to an analytical dead end. But perhaps we can learn something from 'the stories judges tell' if we think about the epistemological content of each of them. What are the judges doing? What are they telling us about the things they know about the world? The examples quoted above are deeply politically coloured statements, (as well as being overwhelmingly 'personal'). The knowledge content of these examples goes something like this: in the first, appearance equals character, and a good mother can never be harmed by motherhood; the second is simple—never trust working mothers; the third, the one about domestic work, says that men help with women's work (it also looks like wishful thinking, or perhaps law's famous is/ought distinction). The remaining examples tell us both that we do not even need a stated rationale for our belief in women's mendacity and that rape is simply not a serious form of harm. Further, phrases such as 'as far as I am able to judge' (example 1), 'most Australian males are expected to give domestic assistance' and 'in these days of changed practices' (both from example 3), 'human experience has shown' and 'experience has taught the judges' (both from example 4), 'There is, of course, nothing wrong with a husband' (example 5), and, perhaps the clearest example, 'in the common experience of those who have been in the law as long as I have' (example 6) all illustrate the belief of judges in a pre-existing body of 'knowledge' on which they can, at least in part, base their judgments. Yet, while it may be relatively easy to identify and illustrate a clear problem with at least some judges' common sense understandings of the world and the dissonance between these and how women might experience these events, finding solutions may not be as simple."

We will return throughout this text to the different ways in which judicial "common sense" reflects, not sense which is "common" to everyone, but a *particular* perspective on the world, grounded, frequently, in assumptions about gender, race, sexuality, class, and other relations of power. The question whether a more *diverse* judiciary *alone*, composed of more women and members of ethnic minorities (many of whom would also be women!) could make a "difference" to the outcome of judicial decision making is questioned by Graycar. It is very much a live issue at the moment, and is on the agenda of the Lord Chancellor, who makes judicial appointments.

Press Release: Lord Chancellor's Department, "Lord Chancellor Seeks More Woman Judges" (April 25, 1998):

"Addressing the 1998 Woman Lawyer Conference in London today, the Lord Chancellor, Lord Irvine, again urged more women to seek judicial appointment.

The Lord Chancellor took the opportunity to explain the judicial appointments system which he believes is 'basically sound'. However, he said that 'any system can be improved. I intend to improve it. I want to oversee a judicial appointments system which is open, fair, effective, and—just as importantly—accessible. Everyone who is eligible for appointment and who wants appointment should have a fair chance to win appointment.'

Lord Irvine announced a transfer of resources within his Department to facilitate the modernising of the judicial appointments system. He told the Conference he had 'instructed that a senior official—Judith Lennard—should devote the majority of her time—not just a small part, as at present—to equal opportunity issues in judicial appointments. Her duties will include developing the many initiatives I have already announced, for example, block sittings; work shadowing; and appraisal of part-timers. This demonstrates that promoting equality of opportunity has become a core activity in the judicial appointments process.'

Identifying four guiding principles to ensure that the best people were chosen, he said: 'First, candidates who are interested in becoming judges should apply for appointment. I repeat my soundbite: 'don't be shy; apply.' Second, the appointments process must be founded on real equality of opportunity. Third, everyone should have access to information about the qualities and skills sought in a potential judge. And, fourth, appointments must be made on merit.'

Lord Irvine emphasised that he can only appoint the judiciary from those who are, ready and willing to do the job' and urged suitably qualified candidates to apply. He said that 'in some quarters, there is a culture of reticence. For example, I have come across many women who are far harsher judges of their own worth and suitability than others are of them. Some will only try for appointment if they feel they are almost bound to succeed.' He fears 'this lack of confidence is robbing me of good candidates.'

The Lord Chancellor also spelt out what he meant by 'merit'. He explained that there were potentially three parts to the assessment of candidates: the application form; the views provided through consultations; and performance at interview. He said he appoints, or recommends for appointment, those candidates who have best demonstrated that they meet criteria for appointment during the process. 'That is what I mean by appointment on merit.' "

ESSAY QUESTION

You have now read a number of judicial decisions. What are your considered views on the politics and ideology of judicial decision making? Give examples drawn from the cases which you have read.

7

STATUTORY INTERPRETATION: INTRODUCTION TO LEGISLATION

In this chapter, our focus shifts to the interpretation of legislation—statute law—by the judiciary. We begin with an examination of the historical relationship between the common law and legislation and then proceed to a brief introduction to the legislative process itself. Next, we look at the role of judges in interpreting legislation through some examples. We then turn to the "rules" of interpretation and the extent to which they constrain judicial decision making. Finally, we examine a case study on interpretation, involving the Race Relations Act.

THE RELATIONSHIP BETWEEN LEGISLATION AND COMMON LAW

Although our legal system is referred to as based on judge made "common law", we will see in this chapter that it is statutory law—the law enacted by Parliament—which is increasingly at the centre of our legal world. The historical relationship between these two pillars of the legal order provides a starting point for understanding the way in which statutes are dealt with by the judiciary.

Peter Goodrich, *Reading the Law* (Blackwell, Oxford, 1986), pp. 40–44:

"In historical terms the primary source of law within the English legal system is unwritten law. Whilst in this respect it does not differ significantly from the early history of vernacular local legal systems in the rest of Europe, it does differ from those legal systems in that the unwritten law has retained its position as a significant source of law. Unwritten law (common law) is defined as custom derived from time immemorial. Written law is seen as a subsequent development. It has since medieval times been seen as a technique used to strengthen, interpret, regulate or amend the common law. This image of the relationship between written and unwritten law has persisted even through the economic transformations of the eighteenth and nineteenth centuries, and Blackstone in the mid-eighteenth century refers to legislation as fulfilling a variety of roles, 'either declaratory of the common law, or remedial of some defects therein'. Remnants of this position can still be seen in operation contemporarily in that many of the presumptions brought to bear upon the interpretation of legislation have their basis in presuppositions as to the historical relationship between the common law and legislation. For example, there is the presumption against the alteration of the law, that Parliament knows the law and only consciously changes the law. More substantively, we would cite the presumption that, following the common law principles of culpability, liability may not be imposed without fault. The presumptions, too numerous to be here detailed, collectively suggest that there already exists a seamless web of law, the common law, which may be changed but only as a result of a conscious act which will be interpreted accordingly as an interference with pre-existing law and principle and will be interpreted restrictively in its effects. . . .

In effect, legislation is frequently ascribed a secondary role not only because it is seen to post-date the common law but also because it is not infrequently seen by the judiciary as a substantively inferior source of law. The common law is historically often represented as a statement of human reason that has been refined and perfected to such a degree that it is superior to other forms of law in its content, a view classically expressed by Lord Coke in *Dr Bonham's Case* (1610) 8 Co Rep 106. Blackstone, to take a later example, considered the common law to be the concentrated wisdom of the various peoples who had invaded and settled in Britain. They had brought with them their own legal system, imposing certain features upon the native system and refining parts of it. The resulting common law represented a body of law of superior quality. Legislation was therefore to be treated as a technique for the improvement of this body of law and confined to the extent that it improved the wisdom of ages rather than abrogating or ignoring that time-hallowed legal wisdom. . . .

The history of the English State machine is important in so far as it represents one of the oldest and most stable institutional orders in the western world. Its embryonic base is found to be in operation at least as early as the Norman Conquest of 1066. The administrative skill of the later Norman and Angevin monarchs created an administrative and adjudicative structure which effectively pervaded all parts of the kingdom and was controlled by a small elite of centrally based royal administrators. The court system itself was composed of central courts located at Westminster together with travelling judges who regularly visited the rest of the kingdom which was for legal purposes divided into assize circuits. This system was fully operational by the end of the thirteenth century and remained largely intact until the middle of the nineteenth century. It provided an effective bureaucratic structure which was capable of producing a coherent body of law based upon the custom of the realm—common law. Secondly, it provided a system whereby that law could be brought to effect upon the kingdom as a whole. The small number of royal judges who presided over both the central courts and the assize courts could effectively control the development of the substantive law, generally claiming to foster the doctrinal values of consistency and coherence which contributed significantly to the status of the common law. Common law was seen to represent a rational ordering of the rules governing human behaviour and it was the claim of the developing class of lawyers to provide a seamless web of regulation. All of these factors contributed to the ability of the common law to withstand the threat of codification and to provide an effective resistance to the incursion of piecemeal legislation.

A second important feature of the institutional history is the development of the dichotomy between the legislative and the judicial functions of the sovereign power. The separation of these two functions is a relatively modern and sophisticated development. Originally the king was the ultimate source of law, be it divine law, the custom of the realm or the creation of new law. The scale of the operation in practice demanded the delegation of tasks. In addition, changes in the structure of political power led to the transfer of power to a variety of administrative institutions. The capacity of the sovereign to declare what the law was represented the embryonic development of legislation. When the monarch was the sole source of knowledge as to both common law and new law (legislation), the likelihood of conflict between the two was minimal. Nor did the early delegation of the adjudicative function and the development of the role of the judiciary as the source of knowledge about the content of common law lead to problems, in so far as the judiciary was often intimately involved in the drafting of the new law and retained a close connection with the monarch which facilitated the relationship between legislation and the common law. A final factor in the early relationship was the infrequency of the use of legislation.

With the separation of the judicial and legislative roles of the sovereign the problem of the relative status of the two sources arises. From the time of the Tudor monarchs legislation begins to develop as a major source of new law. For example, in the reign of Henry VIII over 600 statutes were enacted, a number which probably exceeds the total number of statutes passed from the time of the Magna Carta of 1215. The importance of legislation and its incursion upon the field of interest of the common law and the activities of the judiciary at this time is also reflected in case law. For example, in *Dr Bonham's Case* (1610), Lord Coke provides one of the earliest reflections upon the nature of the distinction between the common law and legislation and it is also from this period that one of the earliest rules of statutory interpretation was formulated, the rule in *Heydon's Case* (1584), suggesting the growing importance of statutory law. The importance of legislation and the development of the power of the House of Commons continues throughout the Restoration until the crisis which culminated with the 'Glorious Revolution' of 1688 and led to the enactment of the Bill of Rights which provides a formal statement of the new balance of power within the State, establishing the supremacy of the two Houses of Parliament over the monarch.

The importance of Parliament and the primary status of its legislative statements was consolidated in the political and jurisprudential traditions arising from the seventeenth century through to the nineteenth century in the work of Hobbes, Bentham, Austin and Dicey, works which may generally be characterized as emphasizing the written law of the sovereign institution, Parliament, as the supreme source of law. The impact of the concept of the 'supremacy' of Parliament is to be found increasingly acknowledged in the contemporary decisions of the common-law courts, as for example, in *Edinburgh and Dalkeith Railway v. Wauchope* [1842] 8 Cl & F 710, and in *Lee v. Bude and Torrington Railway* [1971] LR CP 577, 582, where it was acknowledged that although natural equity represented the 'law of laws' or the 'immutable law of nature', the substantive principles of such law stand 'as a warning, rather than [as] authority to be followed. We sit here as servants of the Queen and the legislature. Are we to act as regents over what is done by Parliament with the consent of the Queen, Lords and Commons? I deny that any such authority exists . . . The proceedings here are judicial not autocratic'; and the judiciary are correspondingly the servants and not the judges of the content of legislation. The effect of this ideological tradition is that in the last instance legislation must supersede all previous law, be it previous enactments or the established common law."

The excerpt from Goodrich illustrates the development of the principle of Parliamentary supremacy, as legislation enacted by Parliament came to have priority both over the common law and earlier inconsistent statutes. The role of the judges, in relation to legislation, thus became *interpretive*, as they applied statute law to cases brought before them. Before we further consider the precise role of judges in relation to statutes, however, it may be useful to review the legislative process itself.

THE LEGISLATIVE PROCESS

Gary Slapper and David Kelly, *Principles of the English Legal System* (3rd ed., Cavendish, London, 1997), pp. 24–33:

The pre-Parliamentary process

"Any consideration of the legislative process must be placed in the context of the political nature of Parliament. Most statutes are the outcome of the policy decisions taken by government and the actual policies pursued will of course depend upon the political persuasion and imperatives of the government of the day. Thus a great deal of law creation and reform can be seen as the implementation of party political policies. . . .

As, by convention, the government is drawn from the party controlling a majority in the House of Commons, it can effectively decide what policies it wishes to implement and trust to its majority to ensure that its proposals become law. . . . The government generates most of the legislation that finds its way into the statute book but individual Members of Parliament may also propose legislation in the form of *private members' bills*. . . . Examples of this can be cited the Abortion Act 1967 which was introduced as a private members' bill to liberalise the provision of abortion; and the various attempts that have subsequently been made by private members' bills to restrict the original provision. . . .

The decision as to which bills are to be placed before Parliament in any session is under the effective control of two cabinet committees:

- the *Future Legislation Committee* determines which bills will be presented to Parliament in the *following* parliamentary session;

- the *Legislation Committee* is responsible for the legislative programme conducted in the *immediate* parliamentary session. It is the responsibility of this committee to draw up the legislative programme announced in the Queen's Speech delivered at the opening of the parliamentary session.

Green Papers are consultation documents issued by the government which set out and invite comments from interested parties on particular proposals for legislation. After considering any response, the government may publish a second document in the form of a *White Paper* in which it sets out its firm proposals for legislation.

The legislative process

Parliament consists of three distinct elements; the House of Commons, the House of Lords and the Monarch. Before any legislative proposal, known at that stage as a bill, can become an Act of Parliament it must proceed through and be approved by both Houses of Parliament and must receive the Royal Assent. The ultimate location of power, however, is the House of Commons which has the authority of being a democratically elected institution.

A bill must be given three readings in both the House of Commons and the House of Lords before it can be presented for the Royal Assent. It is possible to commence the procedure in either House although money bills must be placed before the Commons in the first instance.

When a bill is introduced in the Commons, it undergoes *five distinct procedures*:

- *First reading.* This is purely a formal procedure in which its title is read and a date set for its second reading.

- *Second reading.* At this stage the general principles of the bill are subject to extensive debate. The second reading is the critical point in the process of a bill. At the end a vote may be taken on its merits and if it is approved it is likely that it will eventually find a place in the statute book.

- *Committee stage.* After its second reading the bill is passed to a standing committee whose job is to consider the provisions of the bill in detail, clause by clause. The committee has the power to amend it in such a way as to ensure that it conforms with the general approval given by the House at its second reading.

- *Report stage.* At this point the standing committee reports the bill back to the House for consideration of any amendments made during the committee stage.

- *Third reading.* Further debate may take place during this stage but it is restricted to matters relating to the content of the bill and questions relating to the general principles of the bill cannot be raised.

When a bill has passed all these stages, it is passed to the *House of Lords* for its consideration. After consideration by the Lords, the bill is passed back to the Commons which must then consider any amendments to the bill that might have been introduced by the Lords. Where one House refuses to agree to the amendments made by the other, bills can be repeatedly passed between them but, as bills must complete their process within the life of a particular parliamentary session, a failure to reach agreement within that period might lead to the total loss of the bill.

Since the Parliament Acts of 1911 and 1949, the blocking power of the House of Lords has been restricted as follows:

- a *'money bill'*, *i.e.* one containing only financial provisions, can be enacted without the approval of the House of Lords after a delay of one month;
- any other bill can be delayed by one year by the House of Lords.

The Royal Assent is required before any bill can become law. There is no constitutional rule requiring the monarch to assent to any Act passed by Parliament. There is, however, a convention to that effect; and refusal to grant the Royal Assent to legislation passed by Parliament would place the constitutional position of the monarchy in jeopardy. The procedural nature of the Royal Assent was highlighted by the Royal Assent Act 1967 which reduced the process of acquiring Royal Assent to a formal reading out of the short title of any Act in both Houses of Parliament.

An Act of Parliament comes into effect on the date of the Royal Assent, unless there is any provision to the contrary in the Act itself. . . .

Types of legislation

Legislation can be categorised in a number of ways. For example, distinctions can be drawn between:

Public Acts which relate to matters affecting the general public. These can be further subdivided into either government bills or private members' bills.

Private Acts, on the other hand, relate to the powers and interests of particular individuals or institutions, although the provision of statutory powers to particular institutions can have a major effect on the general public. For example, companies may be given the power to appropriate private property through compulsory purchase orders.

Acts of Parliament can also be distinguished on the basis of the function they are designed to carry out. Some are unprecedented and cover new areas of activity previously not governed by legal rules but other Acts are aimed at rationalising or amending existing legislative provisions.

Consolidating legislation is designed to bring together provisions previously contained in a number of different Acts, without actually altering them. The Companies Act of 1985 is an example of a consolidation Act. It brought together provisions contained in numerous amending Acts which had been introduced since the previous Consolidation Act of 1948.

Codifying legislation seeks not just to bring existing statutory provisions under one Act but also looks to give statutory expression to common law rules. The classic examples of such legislation are the Partnership Act of 1890 and the Sale of Goods Act 1893, now 1979.

Amending legislation is designed to alter some existing legal provision. . . .

Delegated legislation

Delegated legislation is of particular importance. Generally speaking, delegated legislation is law made by some person or body to whom Parliament has delegated its general law-making power. A validly enacted piece of delegated legislation has the same legal force and effect as the Act of Parliament under which it is enacted; but equally it only has effect to the extent that its enabling Act authorises it. . . .

The output of delegated legislation in any year greatly exceeds the output of Acts of Parliament as may be seen from the 1996 statistics which reveal that although just over 60 general public acts were passed, no less than 3,200 statutory instruments were made.

In statistical terms, therefore, it is at least arguable that delegated legislation is actually more significant than primary Acts of Parliament.

There are various types of delegated legislation:

- *Orders in Council* permit the government through the Privy Council to make law. The Privy Council is nominally a non-party-political body of eminent parliamentarians but in effect it is simply a means through which the government, in the form of a committee of ministers, can introduce legislation without the need to go through the full parliamentary process. . . .

- *Statutory Instruments* are the means through which government ministers introduce particular regulations under powers delegated to them by Parliament in enabling legislation. . . .

- *Bye-laws* are the means through which local authorities and other public bodies can make legally binding rules. Bye-laws may be made by local authorities under such enabling legislation as the Local Government Act 1972; and public corporations . . . are empowered to make regulations relating to their specific sphere of operation.

- *Court Rule Committees* are empowered to make the rules which govern procedure in the particular courts over which they have delegated authority under such Acts as the Supreme Court Act 1981, the County Courts Act 1984, and the Magistrates' Courts Act 1980.

- *Professional regulations* governing particular occupations may be given the force of law under provisions delegating legislative authority to certain professional bodies who are empowered to regulate the conduct of their members. An example is the power given to the Law Society under the Solicitors' Act 1974 to control the conduct of practising solicitors. . . .

It is possible for delegated legislation to be challenged, through the procedure of judicial review, on the basis that the person or body to whom Parliament has delegated its authority has acted in a way that exceeds the limited powers delegated to them. Any provision outside this authority is *ultra vires* and is void. Additionally, there is a presumption that any power delegated by Parliament is to be used in a reasonable manner and the courts may on occasion hold particular delegated legislation to be void on the basis that it is unreasonable."

AN INTRODUCTION TO INTERPRETATION

Our primary focus in this chapter is on the *interpretation* of legislation by judges. After a statute successfully completes the Parliamentary process, it enters the statute book and will be implemented by the machinery of the state. However, questions about the scope, meaning, and applicability of legislation to particular factual situations may arise. This is where the judiciary may be called upon, within a legal dispute, to *interpret* the meaning of a statute. This is what we mean by the phrase statutory interpretation. We will see that while it is commonplace to say that the creation of law is the role of Parliament, the function of interpretation leaves the judiciary, in some cases, with a considerable degree of latitude in determining what that legislation *means*. This task often involves highly controversial *choices* which the judiciary is forced to make. Good examples of the problems faced by judges in interpretation are provided by Dworkin.

Ronald Dworkin, *Law's Empire* (Harper Collins, London, 1986), pp. 15–23:

Elmer's case

"Elmer murdered his grandfather—he poisoned him—in New York in 1882. He knew that his grandfather's existing will left him the bulk of the estate, and he suspected that the old man, who had recently remarried, would change the will and leave him nothing. Elmer's crime was discovered; he was convicted and sentenced to a term of years in jail. Was he legally entitled to the inheritance his grandfather's last will provided? The residuary legatees under the will, those entitled to inherit if Elmer had died before his grandfather, were the grandfather's daughters. Their first names are not reported, so I will call them Goneril and Regan. They sued the administrator of the will, demanding that the property now go to them instead of Elmer. They argued that since Elmer had murdered the testator, their father, the law entitled Elmer to nothing.

The law pertaining to wills is for the most part set out in special statutes, often called statutes of wills, which stipulate the form a will must take to be considered valid in law: how many and what kinds of witnesses must sign, what the mental state of the testator must be, how a valid will, once executed, may be revoked or changed by the testator, and so forth. The New York statute of wills, like most others in force at that time, said nothing explicit about whether someone named in a will could inherit according to its terms if he had murdered the testator. Elmer's lawyer argued that since the will violated none of the explicit provisions of the statute it was valid, and since Elmer was named in a valid will he must inherit. He said that if the court held for Goneril and Regan, it would be changing the will and substituting its own moral convictions for the law. The judges of the highest court of New York all agreed that their decision must be in accordance with the law. None denied that if the statute of wills, properly interpreted, gave the inheritance to Elmer, they must order the administrator to give it to him. None said that in that case the law must be reformed in the interests of justice. They disagreed about the correct result in the case, but their disagreement—or so it seems from reading the opinions they wrote—was about what the law actually was, about what the statute required when properly read.

How can people who have read the text of a statute in front of them disagree about what it actually means, about what law it has made? We must draw a distinction between two senses of the word 'statute.' It can describe a physical entity of a certain type, a document with words printed on it, the very words congressmen or members of Parliament had in front of them when they voted to enact that document. But it can also be used to describe the law created by enacting that document, which may be a much more complex matter. Consider the difference between a poem conceived as a series of words that can be spoken or written and a poem conceived as the expression of a particular metaphysical theory or point of view. Literary critics all agree about what poem 'Sailing to Byzantium' is in the first sense. They agree it is the series of words designated as that poem by W.B. Yeats. But they nevertheless disagree about what the poem is in the second sense, about what the poem really says or means. They disagree about how to construct the 'real' poem, the poem in the second sense, from the text, the poem in the first sense.

In much the same way, judges before whom a statute is laid need to construct the 'real' statute—a statement of what difference the statute makes to the legal rights of various people —from the text in the statute book. Just as literary critics need a working theory, or at least a style of interpretation, in order to construct the poem behind the text, so judges need something like a theory of legislation to do this for statutes. This may seem evident when the words in the statute book suffer from some semantic defect; when they are ambiguous or vague, for example. But a theory of legislation is also necessary when these words are, from the linguistic point of view, impeccable. The words of the statute of wills that figured in Elmer's case were neither vague nor ambiguous. The judges disagreed about the impact of these words on the legal rights of Elmer, Goneril, and Regan because they disagreed about how to construct the real statute in the special circumstances of that case.

The dissenting opinion, written by Judge Gray, argued for a theory of legislation more popular then than it is now. This is sometimes called a theory of 'literal' interpretation, though that is not a particularly illuminating description. It proposes that the words of a statute be given what we might better call their acontextual meaning, that is, the meaning we would assign them if we had no special information about the context of their use or the intentions of their author. This method of interpretation requires that no context-dependent and unexpressed qualifications be made to general language, so Judge Gray insisted that the real statute, constructed in the proper way, contained no exceptions for murderers. He voted for Elmer.

Law students reading his opinion now are mostly contemptuous of that way of constructing a statute from a text; they say it is an example of mechanical jurisprudence. But there was nothing mechanical about Judge Gray's argument. There is much to be said (some of which he did say) for his method of constructing a statute, at least in the case of a statute of wills. Testators should know how their wills will be treated when they are no longer alive to offer fresh instructions. Perhaps Elmer's grandfather would have preferred his property to go to Goneril and Regan in the event that Elmer poisoned him. But perhaps not: he might have thought that Elmer, even with murder on his hands, was still a better object for his generosity than his daughters. It might be wiser in the long run for judges to assure testators that the statute of wills will be interpreted in the so-called literal way, so that testators can make any arrangements they wish, confident that their dispositions, however amusing, will be respected. Besides, if Elmer loses his inheritance just because he is a murderer, then that is a further punishment, beyond his term in jail, for his crime. It is an important principle of justice that the punishment for a particular crime must be set out in advance by the legislature and not increased by judges after the crime has been committed. All this (and more) can be said on behalf of Judge Gray's theory about how to read a statute of wills.

Judge Earl, however, writing for the majority, used a very different theory of legislation, which gives the legislators' *intentions* an important influence over the real statute. 'It is a familiar canon of construction,' Earl wrote, 'that a thing which is within the intention of the makers of a statute is as much within the statute as if it were within the letter; and a thing which is within the letter of the statute is not within the statute, unless it be within the intention of the makers.' (Notice how he relies on the distinction between the text, which he calls the 'letter' of the statute, and the real statute, which he calls the 'statute' itself.) It would be absurd, he thought, to suppose that the New York legislators who originally enacted the statute of wills intended murderers to inherit, and for that reason the real statute they enacted did not have that consequence.

We must take some care in stating what Judge Earl meant about the role intention should play in constructing statutes. He did not mean that a statute can have no consequence the legislators did not have in mind. This is plainly too strong as a general rule: no legislator can have in mind all the consequences of any statute he votes for. The New York legislators could not have contemplated that people might bequeath computers, but it would be absurd to conclude that the statute does not cover such bequests. Nor did he mean only that a statute can contain nothing that the legislators intended that it not contain. This seems more plausible, but it is too weak to be of any use in Elmer's case. For it seems likely that the New York legislators did not have the case of murderers in mind at all. They did not intend that murderers inherit, but neither did they intend that they should not. They had no active intention either way. Earl meant to rely on a principle we might call intermediate between these excessively strong and weak principles: he meant that a statute does not have any consequence the legislators would have rejected if they had contemplated it.

Judge Earl did not rely only on this principle about legislative intention; his theory of legislation contained another relevant principle. He said that statutes should be constructed from texts not in historical isolation but against the background of what he called general principles of law: he meant that judges should construct a statute so as to make it conform as closely as possible to principles of justice assumed elsewhere in the law. He offered two reasons. First, it is sensible to assume that legislators have a general and diffuse intention to respect traditional principles of justice unless they clearly indicate the contrary. Second, since a statute forms part of a larger intellectual system, the law as a whole, it should be constructed so as to make that larger system coherent in principle. Earl argued that the law elsewhere respects the principle that no one should profit from his own wrong, so the statute of wills should be read to deny inheritance to someone who has murdered to obtain it.

Judge Earl's views prevailed. They attracted four other judges to his side, while Judge Gray was able to find only one ally. So Elmer did not receive his inheritance. . . .[T]he dispute about Elmer was not about whether judges should follow the law or adjust it in the interests of justice. At least it was not if we take the opinions I described at face value and (as I shall argue later) we have no justification for taking them any other way. It was a dispute about what the law was, about what the real statute the legislators enacted really said.

The Snail Darter case

I now describe a much more recent case, though more briefly, in order to show that this kind of dispute continues to occupy judges. In 1973, during a period of great national concern about conservation, the Untied States Congress enacted the Endangered Species Act. It empowers the secretary of the interior to designate species that would be endangered, in his opinion, by the destruction of some habitat he considers crucial to its survival and then requires all agencies and departments of the government to take 'such action necessary to insure that actions authorized, funded, or carried out by them do not jeopardize the continued existence of such endangered species.'

A group of conservationists based in Tennessee had been opposing dam construction projects of the Tennessee Valley Authority, not because of any threat to species but because these projects were altering the geography of the area by converting free-flowing streams into narrow, ugly ditches to produce an unneeded increase (or so the conservationists believed) in hydroelectric power. The conservationists discovered that one almost finished TVA dam, costing over one hundred million dollars, would be likely to destroy the only habitat of the snail darter, a three-inch fish of no particular beauty or biological interest or general ecological importance. They persuaded the secretary to designate the snail darter as endangered and brought proceedings to stop the dam from being completed and used.

The authority argued that the statute should not be construed to prevent the completion or operation of any project substantially completed when the secretary made his order. It said the phrase 'actions authorized, funded, or carried out' should be taken to refer to beginning a project, not completing projects begun earlier. It supported its claim by pointing to various acts of Congress, all taken after the secretary had declared that completing the dam would destroy the snail darter, which suggested that Congress wished the dam to be completed notwithstanding that declaration. Congress had specifically authorized funds for continuing the project after the secretary's designation, and various of its committees had specifically and repeatedly declared that they disagreed with the secretary, accepted the authority's interpretation of the statute, and wished the project to continue.

The Supreme Court nevertheless ordered that the dam be halted, in spite of the great waste of public funds. (Congress then enacted a further statute establishing a general procedure for exemption from the act, based on findings by a review board). Chief Justice Warren Burger wrote an opinion for the majority of the justices. He said, in words that recall Judge Gray's opinion in Elmer's case, that when the text is clear the Court has no right to refuse to apply it just because it believes the results silly. Times change, however, and the chief justice's opinion was in one respect very different from Judge Gray's. Burger recognized the relevance of congressional intention to the decision what statute Congress had made. But he did not accept Earl's principle about the *way* in which congressional intention is relevant. He refused to consider the counterfactual test that Earl's analysis made decisive. 'It is not for us,' he said, 'to speculate, much less act, on whether Congress would have altered its stance had the specific events of this case been anticipated.'

Instead he adopted what I called, in discussing Earl's opinion, the excessively weak version of the idea that judges constructing a statute must respect the legislature's intentions. That version comes to this: if the acontextual meaning of the words in the text is clear — if the words 'carry out' would normally include continuing as well as beginning a project — then the Court must assign those words that meaning unless it can be shown that the legislature actually intended the opposite result. The legislative history leading up to the enactment of the Endangered Species Act did not warrant that conclusion, he said, because Congress plainly wanted to give endangered species a high order of protection even at great cost to other social goals, and it is certainly possible, even if not probable, that legislators with that general aim would want the snail darter saved even at the amazing expense of a wasted dam. He rejected the evidence of the later committee reports and the actions of Congress in approving funding for the continuation of the dam, which might have been thought to indicate an actual intention not to sacrifice the dam to this particular species. The committees that had reported in favor of the dam were not the same as the committees that had sponsored the act in the first place, he said, and congressmen often vote on appropriations without fully considering whether the proposed expenditures are legal under past congressional decisions.

Justice Lewis Powell wrote a dissent for himself and one other justice. He said that the majority's decision constructed an absurd real statute from the text of the Endangered Species Act. 'It is not our province,' he said, 'to rectify policy or political judgments by the Legislative Branch, however egregiously they may disserve the public interest. But where the statutory and legislative history, as in this case, need not be construed to reach such a result, I view it as the duty of this Court to adopt a permissible construction that accords with some modicum of common sense and the public weal.' This states yet another theory of legislation, another theory of how the legislature's intentions affect the statute behind the text, and it is very different from Burger's theory. Burger said that the acontextual meaning of the text should be enforced, no matter how odd or absurd the consequences, unless the court discovered strong evidence that Congress actually intended the opposite. Powell said that the courts should accept an absurd result only if they find compelling evidence that *it* was intended. Burger's theory is Gray's, though in a less rigid form that gives some role to legislative intention. Powell's theory is like Earl's, though in this case it substitutes common sense for the principles of justice found elsewhere in the law.

Once again, if we take the opinions of these two justices at face value, they did not disagree about any historical matters of fact. They did not disagree about the state of mind of the various congressmen who joined in enacting the Endangered Species Act. Both justices assumed that most congressmen had never considered whether the act might be used to halt an expensive dam almost completed. Nor did they disagree over the question of fidelity. Both accepted that the Court should follow the law. They disagreed about the question of law; they disagreed about how judges should decide what law is made by a particular text enacted by Congress when the congressmen had the kind of beliefs and intentions both justices agreed they had in this instance."[1]

The examples outlined by Dworkin raise issues central to statutory interpretation, including whether words can have a "literal" meaning, how the purpose of a statute should be determined, and how the intention of the legislature in enacting statutory language should be discovered. These inquiries are important, for students, lawyers, legal academics and judges spend a good deal of their time determining what statutes mean in particular factual settings. And the first rule for engaging in that task is a simple one: START WITH THE WORDS OF THE STATUTE! After all, statutes operate in a *mandatory* fashion. That is, if the words of a statute clearly do apply to a factual situation, then courts cannot disregard the operation of a statute, given the fundamental principle of the supremacy of Parliament. So too, if the facts do not fall within the terms of the statute, then the statute does not apply. Otherwise, the will of Parliament would again be undermined by an overbroad application by the judiciary. The problem of statutory interpretation arises in the case where the facts are neither clearly within or outside the parameters of the statute. Generally speaking, that uncertainty is a product of the language of the statute—either it is found to be uncertain or vague in its scope and impact.

However, sometimes statutory language may give rise to contested issues of interpretation even when that language *appears* to be perfectly clear. For example, we might well think that we know what the phrase "in a street" means. But this phrase, it was argued, was ambiguous in its scope:

---

[1] For further reading on *Riggs v. Palmer*, see Kenneth S. Abraham, "Statutory Interpretation and Literary Theory: Some Common Concerns of an Unlikely Pair" (1979) 32 Rutgers Law Review 676.

Smith v. Hughes [1960] 1 W.L.R. 830, QBD.

Lord Parker C.J.:
"These are six appeals by way of case stated by one of the stipendiary magistrates sitting at Bow Street, before whom informations were preferred by police officers against the defendants, in each case that she 'being a common prostitute, did solicit in a street for the purposes of prostitution, contrary to section 1 (1) of the Street Offences Act, 1959.' The magistrate in each case found that the defendant was a common prostitute, that she had solicited and that the solicitation was in a street, and in each case fined the defendant.

The facts, to all intents and purposes, raise the same point in each case; there are minute differences. The defendants in each case were not themselves physically in the street but were in a house adjoining the street. In one case the defendant was on a balcony and she attracted the attention of men in the street by tapping and calling down to them. In other cases the defendants were in ground-floor windows, either closed or half open, and in another case in a first-floor window.

The sole question here is whether in those circumstances each defendant was soliciting in a street or public place. The words of section 1 (1) of the Act of 1959 are in this form: 'It shall be an offence for a common prostitute to loiter or solicit in a street or public place for the purpose of prostitution.' Observe that it does not say there specifically that the person who is doing the soliciting must be in the street. Equally, it does not say that it is enough if the person who receives the solicitation or to whom it is addressed is in the street. For my part, I approach the matter by considering what is the mischief aimed at by this Act. Everybody knows that this was an Act intended to clean up the streets, to enable people to walk along the streets without being molested or solicited by common prostitutes. Viewed in that way, it can matter little whether the prostitute is soliciting while in the street or is standing in a doorway or on a balcony, or at a window, or whether the window is shut or open or half open; in each case her solicitation is projected to and addressed to somebody walking in the street. For my part, I am content to base my decision on that ground and that ground alone. I think the magistrate came to a correct conclusion in each case, and that these appeals should be dismissed."

[Hilbery J. and Donovan J. agreed].

In *Smith v. Hughes,* Lord Parker, having found the language of the statute to be ambiguous, turned to a consideration of the statute's purpose in order to determine whether it applied to the conduct of the defendants. But can one criticise Lord Parker on the basis that, even though that may have been the intention of the legislature, it is not what the legislature actually wrote in the statutory provision. Should a defendant be found guilty of a criminal offence on the basis that an ambiguity in a statute is resolved against her? As we will see shortly, the judiciary often claims that "penal statutes" (those which punish the individual for his or her acts) should be construed "narrowly". This means that ambiguities are resolved in favour of the individual. Why do you think that "rule" of interpretation was not applied in *Smith v. Hughes*?

The issue of prostitution in the criminal law has given rise to other questions of statutory interpretation, one of which involved the meaning of "common prostitute".

R. v. McFarlane [1994] 2 All E.R. 283, CA.

Lord Taylor of Gosforth C.J.:
"Delivered the following judgment of the court. On 16 December 1991 in the Crown Court at Knightsbridge, the appellant was convicted of living on the earnings of prostitution. He was sentenced to four months' imprisonment. This appeal involves a point of law as to the meaning of prostitution which surprisingly has not been the subject of judicial decision with any finality prior to this.

The appellant lived as man and wife with Miss Josephs who, on the judge's ruling, was a prostitute. She maintained she was not a prostitute but a clipper—one who offers sexual services for reward and pockets the reward in advance never intending to provide the service. She said that she engaged in this occupation four or five nights a month, earning up to £400 on a good night. There was evidence, and it was accepted by the appellant and Miss Josephs, that he lived at least partly on her earnings in that they shared their living expenses. The main issue in the case was whether he was thus living on the earnings of prostitution knowingly. The prosecution pointed to the fact that he had lived with her for eleven years, the past five of which she had on her own account been engaged on this business. It was pointed out that he must have been aware of the pattern of her life, the fact that she had more money than could be accounted for by the £50 a week job as a cloakroom attendant which she said she told him she did.

Further, on 16 January 1990 the appellant was seen taking Miss Josephs and her sister into the court at Bow Street where they both appeared on charges of loitering for the purposes of prostitution. There was also evidence from two police officers who kept observation on the appellant between 29 January and 6 February 1991. Those observations tended to show that he assisted her in her occupation. At 10 pm on 30 January he drove Miss Josephs in his car to the West End of London. Later that night, in the same area, Miss Josephs offered one of the police officers sexual intercourse for £40 (which of course was not accepted). On 4 February the appellant drove Miss Josephs to Rupert Street and left her there. In Wardour Street she offered the other officer in the case sexual intercourse for £40. He too did not accept it. At 11.30 pm on 5 February the appellant drove Miss Josephs to the top end of Rupert Street and left her there. He met her an hour later in Shaftesbury Avenue. She took something from her shoe which she gave to the appellant. At 10.15 pm on 6 February the appellant again drove Miss Josephs to the same area and waited in the car in Rupert Street. At 10.40 pm she went off with someone in a taxi, returning to the appellant an hour later. Whether or not that was an occasion of 'clipping' or the real thing is a matter which we need not consider in any depth.

The defence case was that the appellant knew nothing of Miss Joseph's activities. She gave evidence that she told him she worked as a cloakroom girl and also behind the bar at a club. She kept her real occupation secret from him. She used to go out to make it look as if she was at the job which she told him she did. She told him the money for items she bought for the home came from her mother. As regards the attendance at Bow Street Magistrates' Court, the appellant said that he had not stayed for the hearing, and Miss Josephs told him that it concerned a deception charge of which she was acquitted. As regards the observation evidence, essentially the appellant and Miss Josephs, together with her sister, challenged the evidence of observations, maintaining that it was all lies.

A submission was made to the learned judge that acting as a clipper did not amount to acting as a prostitute. Although at that stage counsel both for the prosecution and the defence supported that view, the learned judge rejected it. When the appeal came on before another constitution of this court, counsel then appearing for the Crown (not counsel who has appeared for the Crown today) again supported the appellant's submission that the learned judge's ruling was wrong. However, the court itself took the view that the matter should be fully argued, saying: 'There was a substantial argument in favour of the view taken by the trial judge.' It is most convenient therefore to deal first with what the learned judge said both in giving his ruling and in directing the jury. In his ruling he said:

'The question of whether someone offering themselves, but intending—and it has to be intending—firmly never, ever to make good that offer—it has to go that far—it has never, so far as I can see, been adjudicated upon. My view is that the indications in the textbooks —and I have looked at *Blackstone's Criminal Practice* and it is not so obvious, but again it speaks of offering—the dictionary, and decided cases say that as soon as you are offering yourself for lewdness for reward, you are indulging in prostitution and that is how I propose to direct the jury.'

When it came to the summing up, the learned judge said this to the jury:

'She has told you she is not a prostitute, she is a clipper. But, a prostitute is a person who offers her body for lewdness for reward. Put in slightly more "with it" words, such as Sarah Tuckey [that is the sister] used, "offers sexual services". I am bound to say that I prefer the directness of the old Anglo-Saxon, but there it is. Miss Josephs said, "Yes, I do offer sexual services, but I do not mean to make that offer good." And she suggests to you that for that reason she is not a prostitute. But, members of the jury, she has made the offer. It is at that point that she is a prostitute. The fact that the offer is bogus, rather than genuine, if it was, is neither here nor there. There are not two categories—a clipper and a prostitute. There are prostitutes who are honest and prostitutes who are dishonest. Miss Josephs tells you that she is a dishonest prostitute. But she is a prostitute, members of the jury.'

The issue on this appeal is whether, as a matter of law, the judge was correct to rule and direct the jury that a woman who offers herself for sexual services, takes the money and fails to provide the services, is engaging in prostitution within the meaning of s 30 of the Sexual Offences Act 1956. Section 30, so far as is relevant, provides as follows:

'(1) It is an offence for a man knowingly to live wholly or in part on the earnings of prostitution . . .'

Mr Carne for the appellant submits that to be a prostitute a woman must not only offer sexual services, but must provide them, or be prepared to do so. For the Crown, Mr Carter-Manning Q.C. submits the essence of the offence is the offer of the sexual services in return for reward.

The word 'prostitute' and 'prostitution' are not defined in any statute. Our attention was drawn to dictionary definitions and to three decided cases. *The Concise Oxford Dictionary* defines a prostitute as: 'A woman who offers her body to promiscuous sexual intercourse esp. For payment . . .'. *The Shorter Oxford English Dictionary* defines a prostitute as: 'A woman who is devoted, or (usu.) [who] offers her body to indiscriminate sexual intercourse, esp. for hire; a common harlot . . .'. Mr Carne points to the definition of 'offer' in *The Shorter Oxford English Dictionary*, and to one meaning given there: 'To give, make presentation of . . . To tender for acceptance or refusal . . .'. However, another meaning within the same dictionary is: 'To make the proposal, suggest . . . To propose, or express one's willingness (to do something), conditionally on the assent of the person addressed.' . . .

[Lord Taylor then considered the relevant case law on the definition of prostitution, and concluded:]

In our judgment both the dictionary definitions and the cases show that the crucial feature in defining prostitution is the making of an offer of sexual services for reward. Mr Carne submits that the true offence here was not one of living off immoral earnings, and that the woman in question, Miss Josephs, was not acting by way of prostitution. She was acting dishonestly and she could have been proceeded against, he submits, for obtaining money by false pretences. It may be that the appellant could have been proceeded against for conspiring with her to do so, or of aiding and abetting her. But it is submitted that the offence of living off immoral earnings is not made out. Mr Carne also submits that the mischief against which s 30 of the Sexual Offences Act 1956 is directed is the exploitation of women. Here, the appellant was not exploiting Miss Josephs sexually, only dishonestly. . . .

We have no doubt that the ruling of the learned judge was both robust and correct (to adopt the phrase used by Mr Carter-Manning in his submission). For a man to live off the earnings of a woman who offers sexual services, takes the money and then reneges on the offer, if she does, is in our view to live off the earnings of prostitution, or, as it used to be termed, immoral earnings. Indeed, most people would consider such earnings doubly immoral. This appeal is dismissed."

NOTES AND QUESTIONS

- Does the Court of Appeal's definition of prostitution accord with a "common sense" understanding of the term? Would most people agree that the *essence* of prostitution is the offer of sexual services for compensation? The accused was convicted of the offence which is commonly known as being a "pimp". What evidence was there that he was a pimp? Is living with someone who sells sexual services sufficient to constitute living off the earnings of prostitution?

- The appellant in this case argued that he should have been charged with a different offence, namely, aiding and abetting the offence of obtaining money by false pretences, or conspiracy to do so. Why do you think the appellant was not charged with that offence? Finally, this case also involves a "penal statute", again raising the question why an apparent ambiguity was not resolved in favour of an accused, in accordance with the "rule" that penal statutes should be strictly construed.

- There are numerous cases which have considered the statutory language of the Street Offences Act 1959. For a good overview and discussion of the way in which the judiciary has developed a gendered interpretation of the law, see Alison Diduck and William Wilson, "Prostitutes and Persons" (1997) 24 Journal of Law and Society 504.

- Can a man be a "common prostitute"? For the answer, see *DPP v. Bull* [1994] 4 All E.R. 411 (Q.B.).

Although judges will rarely admit that the process of statutory interpretation is "political", in the sense of involving important *choices* concerning social issues of widespread concern, judges are sometimes required to make such decisions. Moreover, the *language* which judges use is often itself highly politically charged. A "classic" example is the judgment of Lord Denning M.R. in *Royal College of Nursing v. DHSS*. The case concerned the interpretation of the Abortion Act 1967. Pay close attention to the language which Lord Denning uses to describe the termination of a pregnancy.

Royal College of Nursing of the United Kingdom v. Department of Health and Social Security [1981] 1 All ER 545, QBD, CA & HL.

Lord Denning M.R.:
"Abortion is a controversial subject. The question for us today is this: when a pregnancy is terminated by medical induction, who should do the actual act of termination? Should it be done by a doctor? Or can he leave it to the nurses? The Royal College of Nursing say that the doctor should do the actual act himself and not leave it to the nurses. The Department of Health take a different view. They say that a doctor can initiate the process and then go off and do other things, so long as he is 'on call'. The controversy is so acute that it has come before us for decision.

Throughout the discussion I am going to speak of the unborn child. The old common lawyers spoke of a child *en ventre sa mère*. Doctors speak of it as the fetus. In simple English it is an unborn child inside the mother's womb. Such a child was protected by the criminal law almost to the same extent as a new-born baby. If anyone terminated the pregnancy, and thus destroyed the unborn child, he or she was guilty of a felony and was liable to be kept in penal servitude for life (see the Offences against the Person Act 1861), unless it was done to save the life of the mother. Likewise anyone who assisted or participated in the abortion was guilty, including the mother herself. I have tried several cases of 'backstreet abortions', where the mother died or was made seriously ill. I have passed severe sentences of imprisonment for the offence.

The Abortion Act 1967

The approach to the subject was revolutionised by the Abortion Act 1967. It legalised abortion if it was done so as to avoid risk to the mother's health, physical or mental. This has been interpreted by some medical practitioners so loosely that abortion has become obtainable virtually on demand. Whenever a woman has an unwanted pregnancy, there are doctors who will say it involves a risk to her mental health. But the Act contains some safeguards. It provided that, in order for the abortion to be lawful, it was subject to three conditions. (1) The woman had to get two doctors to give a certificate. (2) The abortion had to be done in hospital. (3) The pregnancy had to be 'terminated by a registered medical practitioner'. It is this last condition which comes up for consideration today. It arises because of the advance in medical science.

The material words of the 1967 Act, in s 1(1), are that '. . . a person shall not be guilty of an offence under the law relating to abortion when a pregnancy is terminated by a registered medical practitioner . . .'

At the time that the Act was passed, and for five years afterwards, there was no difficulty of interpretation. All abortions then, at any rate when the mother was three months pregnant or more, were done by surgical methods. The knife with the cutting edge was operated by a registered medical practitioner. He used it to remove the unborn child. The knife was never handled by a nurse. She was not a registered medical practitioner.

Medical induction

Since 1972 a new method has been used. It is called medical induction. It does not involve a knife. It started quite simply in ordinary full-time births, so as to induce labour a few hours early, to save the mother the stress of waiting, or for the convenience of doctors and staff. But it is now becoming much used to effect abortions, when the mother is pregnant for three months or more. It is done by pumping a chemical fluid into the mother's womb. It is called prostaglandin. This fluid so affects the muscles and shape of the mother's inside that it forces her into labour prematurely, so that the unborn child is expelled from the body, usually dead, but sometimes at the point of death.

There are two distinct stages in this process. The first stage is done by a doctor, a registered medical practitioner. The mother is taken from the ward to the operating theatre. She is given a general anaesthetic. The doctor inserts a fine catheter into her body so as to reach a particular part of her womb. But no fluid is pumped into her at that stage. She is then taken back to the ward. She is left there until she recovers from the anaesthetic. The doctor writes out a few notes telling the nurse what to do. He then goes off, saying, 'Give me a call if there is any difficulty'.

The second stage is done by the nurses. When the mother comes round from the anaesthetic, they get a flexible tube and connect up the catheter to a pump which is electrically driven; or to a dripping device. They then get the special fluid called prostaglandin. They have to see that it is of the right concentration. They have it in a bottle, and pump the fluid into the woman's body. They have to regulate the dose and control the intake, by speed and amount, as occasion requires. If need be, they have to get another bottle. They have to watch the woman and note her reactions; and take such steps as occasion requires. Labour is induced. The unborn child is expelled from the woman's body. The process make take 18 hours, or even up to 30 hours. If the unborn child is not expelled by that time, the process is stopped. The child is allowed to live on, to await normal delivery later.

Here I would stop for a moment to point out that the first stage (done by the doctor) does nothing to terminate the pregnancy. The insertion of the catheter is only a preparatory act. It is the second stage (done by the nurses) which terminates the pregnancy. There is an agreed statement of facts which shows that the causative factor is the administration of prostaglandin. . . .

The Royal College's objection

I can quite understand that many nurses dislike having anything to do with these abortions. It is a soul-destroying task. The nurses are young women who are dedicated by their profession and training to do all they can to preserve life. Yet here they are called on to destroy it. It is true that the statute gives them an escape clause. They can refuse to participate in any treatment to which they have a 'conscientious objection': see s 4 of the 1967 Act. But the report of Dame Elizabeth Lane and her colleagues (Report of the Committee on the Working of the Abortion Act) shows that many nurses do not take advantage of this 'escape clause': because it means that other nurses will have to do this heart-rending task; and they feel it may be held against them by their superiors. So they take part in it, much against their will.

It is against this background that the Royal College of Nursing ask the question: is it lawful for nurses to be called on to terminate pregnancy in this way? The Royal College say No, it is not lawful; it is not a nurse's job to terminate a pregnancy. The Department of Health and Social Security say Yes, it is lawful. They have issued a circular in which they presume to lay down the law for the whole of the medical profession. They say that it is no offence if the pregnancy is terminated by a suitably qualified person in accordance with the written instructions of a registered medical practitioner. This is the wording of the circular:

> 'However, the Secretary of State is advised that the termination can properly be said to have been terminated by the registered medical practitioner provided it is decided upon by him, initiated by him, and that he remains throughout responsible for its overall conduct and control in the sense that any actions needed to bring it to conclusion are done by appropriately skilled staff acting on his specific instructions but *not necessarily in his presence.*'

Note those words 'not necessarily in his presence'. They are crucial.

The interpretation of the 1967 Act

The lawfulness depends on the true interpretation of the statute; but, before going into it, I would say a word or two about the approach to it.

(i) Abortion is a subject on which many people feel strongly. In both directions. Many are for it. Many against it. Some object to it as the destruction of life. Others favour it as the right of the woman. Emotions run so high on both sides that I feel that we as judges must go by the very words of the statute, without stretching it one way or the other, and writing nothing in which is not there.

(ii) Another thing to remember is that the statute is directed to the medical profession, to the doctors and nurses who have to implement it. It is they who have to read it and to act on it. They will read it, not as lawyers, but as laymen. So we should interpret it as they would.

(iii) If there should ever be a case in the courts, the decision would ultimately be that of a jury. Suppose that during the process the mother died or became seriously ill, owing to the nurse's negligence in administering the wrong chemical fluid, and the nurse was prosecuted under the 1861 Act for unlawfully administering to her a noxious thing or using other means with intent to procure her miscarriage. The nurse would have no defence unless the pregnancy was 'terminated by a registered medical practitioner'. Those are simple English words which should be left to a jury to apply, without the judge attempting to put his own gloss on them. I should expect the jury to say that the pregnancy was not terminated by a registered medical practitioner but by a nurse.

(iv) If in such a case there were a claim for damages, the nurse might not be covered by insurance because she would not be engaged in 'nursing professional services acceptable to the Royal College of Nursing'.

(v) Statutes can be divided into two categories. In the first category Parliament has expressly said 'by a registered medical practitioner or by a person acting in accordance with the directions of any such practitioner', or words to that effect. In the second category Parliament has deliberately confined it: '*by* a fully registered medical practitioner' omitting any such words as 'or by his direction'. This statute is in the second category.

(vi) Woolf J. tested the statute by supposing that a registered medical practitioner performed an abortion operated on a woman whom he believed to be pregnant but who was not so in fact. The 1967 Act would give him no defence to a charge under the 1861 Act.[2] That is such a fanciful instance that I do not think it throws any light on the true construction of this statute.

(vii) The Solicitor General emphasised the word 'treatment' in ss 1(3), 3(1)(a) and (c) and 4(1). He suggested that s 1(1) should be read as if it said that a person should not be guilty of an offence 'when the treatment (for termination of a pregnancy) is by a registered medical practitioner'. He submitted that, whenever the registered medical practitioner did what the Department of Health advised, it satisfied the statute, because the treatment, being initiated by him and done under his instructions, was 'by' him. I cannot accept this interpretation. I think the word 'treatment' in those sections means 'the actual act of terminating the pregnancy'. When the medical induction method is used, this means the continuous act of administering prostaglandin from the moment it is started until the unborn child is expelled from the mother's body. This continuous act must be done by the doctor personally. It is not sufficient that it is done by a nurse when he is not present.

Conclusion

Stress was laid by the Solicitor General on the effect of this ruling. The process of medical induction can take from 18 to 30 hours. No doctor can be expected to be present all that time. He must leave it to the nurses: or not use the method at all. If he is not allowed to leave it to the nurses, the result will be *either* that there will be fewer abortions *or* that the doctor will have to use the surgical method with its extra hazards. This may be so. But I do not think this warrants us departing from the statute. The Royal College of Nursing have advised their nurses that under the statute they should not themselves terminate a pregnancy. If the doctor advises it, he should do it himself, and not call on the nurses to do it.

I think that the Royal College are quite right. If the Department of Health want the nurses to terminate a pregnancy, the Minister should go to Parliament and get the statute altered. He should ask them to amend it by adding the words 'or by a suitably qualified person in accordance with the written instructions of a registered medical practitioner'. I doubt whether Parliament would accept the amendment. It is too controversial. At any rate, that is the way to amend the law and not by means of a departmental circular.

I would allow the appeal accordingly."

[Brightman L.J. and Sir George Baker delivered separate reasons, allowing the appeal].

The case was then appealed to the House of Lords. The Law Lords divided 3:2, and the majority allowed the appeal from the Court of Appeal, restoring the original judgment of Woolf J. The analysis offered by Lord Diplock is in sharp contrast with that of Lord Denning.

Lord Diplock:

"... Subsection (1) although it is expressed to apply only 'when a pregnancy is terminated by a registered medical practitioner' ... also appears to contemplate treatment that is in the nature of a team effort and to extend its protection to all those who play a part in it. The exoneration from guilt is not confined to the registered medical practitioner by whom a pregnancy is terminated, it extends to any person who takes part in the treatment for its termination.

What limitation on this exoneration is imposed by the qualifying phrase, 'when a pregnancy is terminated by a registered medical practitioner'? In my opinion, in the context of the Act, what it requires is that a registered medical practitioner, whom I will refer to as a doctor, should accept responsibility for all stages of the treatment for the termination of the pregnancy. The particular method to be used should be decided by the doctor in charge of the treatment for termination of the pregnancy; he should carry out any physical acts, forming part of the treat-

---

[2] Woolf J., the trial judge in this case, was making the point that this anomaly would result from a narrow interpretation of the 1967 Act, from which he concluded that overly narrow interpretations should be eschewed.

ment, that in accordance with accepted medical practice are done only by qualified medical practitioners, and should give specific instructions as to the carrying out of such parts of the treatment as in accordance with accepted medical practice are carried out by nurses or other members of the hospital staff without medical qualifications. To each of them, the doctor, or his substitute, should be available to be consulted or called on for assistance from beginning to end of the treatment. In other words, the doctor need not do everything with his own hands; the requirements of the subsection are satisfied when the treatment for termination of a pregnancy is one prescribed by a registered medical practitioner carried out in accordance with his directions and of which a registered medical practitioner remains in charge throughout."

NOTES AND QUESTIONS

- Give examples, drawn from Lord Denning's judgment, where the language which he uses to describe abortion mirrors that which is often used by anti-abortion campaigners. What alternative phrases and sentences could have been employed to convey the ideas which he expressed, but which would be less inflammatory?

- What evidence does Lord Denning provide for his assertion that abortion "on demand" is now available in the United Kingdom because of the willingness of doctors to certify that a woman's health is endangered by the continuation of her pregnancy? Is this part of the judgment relevant to the issue before the Court?

- In his judgment at trial, Woolf J. made clear that the position of the Royal College of Nursing was "neutral" towards the issue in this case, but that they merely sought clarification of the law. Does Lord Denning portray their position in that way?

- Is Lord Diplock's analysis of the termination procedure as the work of a team of medical personnel more convincing than Lord Denning's analysis of the potential liability of nurses for carrying out their duties?

The decision of the House of Lords in *Royal College of Nursing v. DHSS* might seem a victory for the right of women to have safe, medical abortions. However, the decision can be read as more complex in its political meanings.

Sally Sheldon, *Beyond Control: Medical Power and Abortion Law* (Pluto Press, London, 1997), pp. 97–98:

"This case is notable for several reasons. Perhaps its most striking feature is the extent to which those judges who found for the DHSS are prepared to stretch an interpretation of the terms of the Abortion Act in order to reach an acceptable decision. The decision which the House of Lords eventually comes to is the common-sense verdict and no doubt accords with 'the obvious intention of the Act', yet it is one that is squared with the actual wording of the statute only with great difficulty. When the doctor's actual involvement in the termination is limited to the insertion of the catheter—an act preparatory to the administration of the postaglandins which cause the uterus to contract and expel the foetus—it involves a rather creative interpretation to see the doctor as terminating the pregnancy rather than the nursing staff who do everything else. Explicitly underlying this decision is a refusal to interfere with 'good medical practice'.

. . . Whilst nurses are hereby authorised to carry out certain actions in this kind of termination, they can still do so only under the control of the doctor who retains the ultimate responsibility for the operation. This strict hierarchy of the relationship between doctors and nurses is thus reproduced in the legal assessment and the doctors' monopoly over the performance of abortions is reasserted. . . .

The *RCN* case demonstrates again how the reluctance of law to interfere with medical discretion and good medical practice can benefit women by protecting the provision of abortion services. It also emphasises, however, how this goes hand in hand with an entrenchment of doctors' control over such services."

FURTHER READING

For further reading on the *DHSS v. Royal College of Nursing* case, see Elizabeth Kingdom, *What's Wrong with Rights?* (Edinburgh University Press, Edinburgh, 1991), Chapter 3; Jonathan Montgomery, "Doctors' Handmaidens: the Legal Contribution", in *Law, Health and Medical Regulation* (Sally Wheeler and Shaun McVeigh, eds., Dartmouth, Aldershot, 1992).

METHODS OF STATUTORY INTERPRETATION

No consideration of statutory analysis would be complete without some mention of the so-called "rules" of statutory interpretation: the literal rule; the golden rule; and the mischief rule. Most lawyers today would readily concede that these approaches to interpretation have been misnamed as "rules", for they provide at best guidance to different judicial approaches. Alternatively, they are merely justifications for decisions which have been reached by judges on other, unarticulated grounds. As Goodrich explains, the rules of interpretation also reflect different approaches to the judicial process itself.

Peter Goodrich, *Reading the Law* (Blackwell, Oxford, 1986), pp. 54–57:

"On numerous occasions judges, during the course of giving judgment in a dispute, have taken the opportunity to make statements as to how they approach the task of interpretation, not only to justify their own conclusions as to the meaning of statutory provisions under consideration, but also to provide models of behaviour for others to follow. The content and the taxonomy of the techniques is a reflection of many of the matters relating to the relationship between the legislature and the judiciary and the distinction between the written law and unwritten law discussed earlier. The methods of interpretation embody a vast collection of frequently overlapping and on occasion conflicting rules, principles and presumptions which have accumulated over several centuries.

The general approach which is said to be the primary method of common-law statutory interpretation is usually referred to as the *literal approach*. The classic statement of this technique is found in *The Queen v. Judge of the City of London Court* [1892] 1 QB 273: 'If the words of an Act are clear, you must follow them, even though they lead to a manifest absurdity. The Court has nothing to do with the question whether the legislature has committed an absurdity.' The literal approach demands that the court apply the ordinary, natural meaning of the words used . . . .

An adaptation of this first approach is often referred to as the Golden Rule. Its concern is to provide an alternative approach in the face of an absurdity resulting from the literal interpretation. The rule, however, is inadequate in that it provides little guidance as to how interpretation is to proceed beyond the conclusion of absurdity. The classic exposition of the rule is to be found in *River Wear Commissioners v. Adamson* [1877] 2 AC 743, where Lord Blackburn stated:

'But it is to be borne in mind that the office of the Judge is not to legislate, but to declare the expressed intention of the legislature even if that expressed intention appeared to the court to be injudicious; and I believe that it is not disputed that what Lord Wensleydale used to call the Golden rule is right viz. That we are to take the whole statute together and construe it all together, giving the words their ordinary significance unless when so applied they produce an inconsistency or an absurdity or inconvenience so great as to convince the court that the intention could not have been to use them in their ordinary signification and to justify the court in putting on them some other significance which though less proper is one which the court thinks the words will bear.' (763)

The third and oldest statement relating to techniques of interpretation is found in the rule known as the Mischief Rule or the Rule in *Heydon's Case* [1584] 3 Co Rep 7. This rule emphasizes the interrelationship between the status quo prior to the legislation and the objectives of the new law: 'four things are to be discussed and considered: 1. What was the common law before the making of the Act; 2. What was the mischief and defect for which the common law did not provide; 3. What remedy the Parliament hath resolved and appointed to cure the disease of the commonwealth; and 4. The true reason for the remedy.' In following this line of approach the ultimate objective is to interpret the law in such a fashion that the objectives of the enactment are realized.

Finally, a technique which is reminiscent of the rule in *Heydon's Case* is referred to as the *purposive approach*. It embodies the general ethos of the previous method in that it stresses the need to interpret the enactment in such a way that the objectives (purposes) of the statute are realized. It differs from Heydon's formulation in that it does not locate the approach purely in the context of the common law, nor does it confine objectives to their historical origin though this may be one source of information about the objectives. In *Royal College of Nursing v. DHSS* [1981] AC 800, Lord Diplock discusses the interrelationship of approaches with respect to the interpretation of the Abortion Act 1967: 'whatever may be the technical imperfections of its draftsmanship, however, its purpose in my view becomes clear if one starts by considering what was the state of the law relating to abortion before the passing of the Act, what was the mischief that required amendment, and in what respect was the existing law unclear'. The historical, social and economic aspects to abortion were then examined as well as the more obvious features of its moral and legal history to the conclusion that 'the wording and the structure of the section are far from elegant, but the policy of the Act, it seems to me, is clear. There are two aspects to it: the first is to broaden the grounds upon which abortions may be lawfully obtained; the second is to ensure that the abortion is carried out with all proper skill and in hygenic conditions.'

The relative importance of these styles of interpretation is itself a source of considerable controversy which raises the theoretical and substantive issues about the role of the judge, the law-making dimension of interpretation and the threat this poses to the abstract supremacy of written law. The controversy can be reduced, for present purposes, to two positions which have both a descriptive and a prescriptive quality. The first represents the judge as a passive actor in the process of interpretation, merely giving the words of the Act their natural meaning and applying that meaning to the situation in the dispute. It stresses a mechanical representation of interpretation, emphasizing the impartiality involved in adjudication. The model is most sympathetic to the adoption of the literalist style of interpretation. The second model rejects the notion that this can be the only role-model for a judge. This model represents the judge as a party who necessarily undertakes an active role in the task of interpretation. Whilst the judge is not a completely free agent, this model stresses the role of the judge as an active participant in the process of creating legal meaning and the need for the judge to resort to the whole range of resources within the legal culture which may lead variously to references to social policy, economics, and other broad-ranging administrative and political considerations of the 'consequences' of the rules to be applied. This model suggests a dynamic role for the judiciary. It is most sympathetic to those techniques of interpretation which seek to realize the purpose and objectives of legislation, the Mischief Rule and the purposive style of interpretation in particular. The first model, on the other hand, provides no threat to the law-making role of the legislature, as the judge is the passive servant merely reading the written law and applying it. The second model potentially threatens the superiority of the written law in that the judge may be seen as a law-maker with the capacity to change or even to undermine the supremacy of the written law by resorting to sources and materials outside the statutory provision, and thereby threatening its status.

Judicial observations on the merits and demerits of the various styles of role-model are numerous. One of the most quoted examples is found in a confrontation between Lord Denning when in the Court of Appeal and Viscount Simonds in the House of Lords in the case of *Magor and St Mellons Rural District Council v. Newport District Council* [1952] AC 189. A more recent example of the controversy, and one which provides a clearer expression of the political considerations which underpin the debate is to be found in the judgment of Lord Diplock in *Duport Steels Ltd v. Sirs and Others* [1980] 1 WLR 142:

> 'When Parliament legislates to remedy what the majority of its members at the time per-
> ceive to be a defect or a lacuna in the law (whether it be written law enacted by existing stat-
> utes or the unwritten common law as it has been expounded by the judges in decided cases),
> the role of the judiciary is confined to ascertaining from the words that Parliament has
> approved as expressing its intention, what the intention was, and to giving effect to it.
> Where the meaning of the statutory words is plain and unambiguous it is not for the judge
> to invent fancied ambiguities as an excuse for failing to give effect to its plain meaning
> because they themselves consider that the consequences of doing so would be inexpedient
> or even unjust or immoral.
>
> A statute passed to remedy what is perceived by Parliament to be a defect in the existing
> law may in actual operation turn out to have injurious consequences that Parliament did
> not anticipate at the time the statute was passed. . . . [I]t is for Parliament, not for the judi-
> ciary, to decide whether any changes should be made to the law as stated in the Acts . . .
>
> It endangers continued public confidence in the political impartiality of the judiciary,
> which is essential to the continuance of the rule of law, if judges, under the guise of inter-
> pretation, provide their own preferred amendments to statutes which experience of their
> operation has shown to have had consequences that members of the court before whom the
> matter comes consider to be injurious to the public interest.' "

First year law students frequently assume that the three "rules" of statutory interpre-
tation are just that; and that courts mechanically choose between them to resolve issues of statutory interpretation. This is not the way in which courts approach their task. As Lord Reid explained: "They are not rules in the ordinary sense of having some binding force. They are our servants not our masters. They are aids to construction, presumptions or pointers. Not infrequently one 'rule' points in one direction, another in a dif-
ferent direction. In each case we must look at all relevant circumstances and decide as a matter of judgment what weight to attach to any particular 'rule.'"[3] In that same case, Lord Simon of Glaisdale outlined an approach to interpretation which sought to synthesise the various rules, and which provides a useful description of the way in which courts go about the task of statutory interpretation:

> "It is sometimes put that, in statutes dealing with ordinary people in their everyday
> lives, the language is presumed to be used in its primary ordinary sense, unless this
> stultifies the purpose of the statute, or otherwise produces some injustice, absurdity,
> anomaly or contradiction, in which case some secondary ordinary sense may be pre-

---

[3] *Maunsell v. Olins* [1975] 1 All E.R. 16 at 18, HL.

ferred, so as to obviate the injustice, absurdity, anomaly or contradiction, or fulfil the purpose of the statute: while, in statutes dealing with technical matters, words which are capable of both bearing an ordinary meaning and being terms of art in the technical matter of the legislation will presumptively bear their primary meaning as such terms of art (or, if they must necessarily be modified, some secondary meaning as terms of art). . . .

But, in fact, these two statutory situations—dealing with ordinary people in their everyday lives, on the one hand, and dealing with technical branches of the law, on the other—are only two extreme situations. Statutory language, like all language, is capable of an almost infinite gradation of "register"—*i.e.* it will be used at the semantic level appropriate to the subject-matter and to the audience addressed (the man in the street, lawyers, merchants, etc). It is the duty of a court of construction to tune in to such register and so to interpret the statutory language as to give to it the primary meaning which is appropriate in that register (unless it is clear that some other meaning must be given in order to carry out the statutory purpose or to avoid injustice, anomaly, absurdity or contradiction). In other words, statutory language must always be given presumptively the most natural and ordinary meaning which is appropriate in the circumstances.

It is essential that this 'golden' rule is adhered to. An English court of construction must put itself in the place of the draftsman, and ascertain the meaning of the words used in the light of all the circumstances known by the draftsman—especially the 'mischief' which is the subject-matter of the statutory remedy."[4]

The determination of the "natural and ordinary meaning" of legislation may be a controversial task.[5] Note, for example, the contrasting views with respect to what constitutes "using" personal data.

R. v. Brown [1996] 1 All E.R. 545, HL.

Lord Goff of Chieveley:
"My Lords, the defendant, Gregory Michael Brown, was charged with offences under the Data Protection Act 1984, *viz.* that on two occasions he used personal data held within the memory of the police national computer for a purpose other than the purpose described in the relevant entry in the register, contrary to s 5(2)(b), (3) and (5) of the Act. In the case of the first offence (count 1) he was convicted of an attempt. In the case of the second (count 2) he was convicted of the full offence. His convictions were quashed on appeal, and the prosecution now appeal to your Lordships' House. The appeals raises the question of the meaning of the word 'use' in s 5(2)(b). To explain how the question has arisen, it is necessary first to set out briefly the simple facts of the case, and the outcome of the trial; and then to examine the relevant provisions of the Act in order to ascertain the meaning of the word 'use' in its statutory context.

The facts of the cases

The defendant was formerly a police constable in the Kent Constabulary. The Chief Constable of Kent is a registered data user for the purposes of the Act. His agents, of which the defendant

---

[4] *ibid.* at 25–26.
[5] For further reading on "ordinary meaning", see Robert S. Summers and Geoffrey Marshall, "The Argument from Ordinary Meaning in Statutory Interpretation" (1992) 43 N.I.L.Q. 213.

was one, were entitled to make use of the data stored in the database of the police national computer for the registered purpose of policing.

The defendant was friendly with a Mr English, who set up a debt collection business under the name of Capital Investigations Ltd. On two occasions the defendant made use of the police national computer to check the registration numbers of vehicles owned by debtors of clients of Capital Investigations. These checks were effected by him through other officers who operated the computer on his behalf.

In the case of the first vehicle (the subject of count 1) the search did not reveal any personal data as defined by the Act, because the vehicle was owned by a company. In the case of the second vehicle (the subject of count 2) the search did reveal personal data; but there was no evidence that the defendant, or indeed any person, subsequently made any use of the information so obtained. The judge directed the jury that, in the case of count 1, the defendant could only be guilty of an attempt. The essence of the defendant's defence was that he made his inquiries legitimately for the purposes of policing, and that it was a coincidence that the vehicles were also of interest to Capital Investigations. The jury convicted the defendant of an attempt under count 1, and of the full offence under count 2. It is therefore plain that they rejected his defence. The defendant was fined £500 on each count, and ordered to pay £1,750 towards the prosecution costs.

The 1984 Act

The Act is a substantial and elaborate statute, but for present purposes the essential provisions are the following. At the centre of the Act is Pt II, which provides for the registration and supervision of data users. A data user is a person who holds data (s 1(5)). 'Data' is defined in s 1(2) as—

'information recorded in a form in which it can be processed by equipment operating automatically in response to instructions given for that purpose.'

In other words, data may be broadly described as information recorded in computer readable form. 'Personal data' is 'data consisting of information which relates to a living individual who can be identified from that information' (s 1(3)). A data user must not hold personal data unless there is an entry in respect of him in the register (s 5(1)). Certain restrictions are placed upon such a person; these are set out in s 5(2). By s 5(3), a servant or agent of a person so registered is subject to the same restrictions as that person. By s 5(5) any person who knowingly or recklessly contravenes any of the provisions of s 5(2) shall be guilty of an offence.

The restrictions under s 5(2) are:

'A person in respect of whom such an entry is contained in the register shall not—(a) hold personal data of any description other than that specified in the entry; (b) hold any such data, or use any such data held by him, for any purpose other than the purpose or purposes described in the entry; (c) obtain such data, or information to be contained in such data, to be held by him from any source which is not described in the entry; (d) disclose such data held by him to any person who is not described in the entry; or (e) directly or indirectly transfer such data held by him in any country or territory outside the United Kingdom other than one named or described in the entry.'

The defendant, as the servant or agent of the Chief Constable of Kent (who was a data user so registered), was charged with two offences of *using* personal data for an improper purpose contrary to s 5(2)(b).

The question in the case

Now the only action taken by the defendant in relation to the relevant data was that he caused another police officer to operate the computer and so caused the information which constituted the data to be displayed on a screen. The defendant then read the information so displayed, and observed what it consisted of, but took no other action in relation to it. The question is whether by so acting he *used* the data, contrary to s 5(2)(b). . . .

The true construction of the Act

I approach the matter as follows. I accept that, since the word 'use' is not defined in the Act, it must be given its natural and ordinary meaning. Synonyms of the verb 'use' are to 'make use of' or to 'employ for a purpose'. Here the word is used in relation to 'data', and data means information recorded in a computer-readable form. I must confess that at first sight I would not have thought that simply retrieving such information from the database in which it is stored, so that it appeared on a screen or a print out and could therefore be read by a human being, could properly be described as 'using' the information so recorded. Of course, the computer would be used to retrieve it; but the retrieval of the information would not of itself be 'using' the information so retrieved. It would simply be transferring the information into a different form. This to my mind underlines the fact that the definition of data as information in a computer-readable form does not mean that such information is only data while it is so recorded. It means rather that, if information is so recorded, it becomes data for the purposes of the Act; and if such information from that source is thereafter made use of it is used within the meaning of the Act. So if for example a police constable with the Kent Constabulary operates the police computer to retrieve personal data from the database so that he becomes aware of its contents, and then proceeds to make use of that information, he uses the personal data within the meaning of the statute. In such a case, the retrieval is not the use; it is simply a prerequisite of the use. Moreover, if the police officer, who is the servant or agent of the data user (the chief constable) knowingly or recklessly puts the information to an improper use, he will be guilty of an offence under the Act. This may occur not only where the police officer retrieves the personal data from the database and then puts the information to an improper use, but also where, for example, he improperly makes use of personal data which has come to his knowledge when he operated the police computer innocently on a previous occasion, or where the data has been communicated to him by a colleague who had innocently operated the computer. . . .

It seems to me that the above reading of the statute accords not only with the natural and ordinary meaning of the word 'use' in its statutory context, but also with the statutory purpose of protecting personal data from improper use (or disclosure). It is a startling fact that, if the construction urged upon your Lordships by the prosecution were correct, a police officer who idly operated the police computer, retrieving personal data onto the screen without putting it to any use, would not merely be subject to disciplinary action (where appropriate) but would be guilty of a criminal offence; whereas another police officer who learned from a colleague of certain information constituting personal data stored in the database of the police computer and then, knowing of its source, used the information for business purposes, would not. This surely cannot be the statutory intention; indeed if it were so, it could give rise to justifiable concern on the part of individuals who are the subject of personal data. Strange results such as these would, in my opinion, be avoided if the relevant words in the statute were given their natural and ordinary meaning. If that had been done in the present case, the defendant would have been charged not with the full offence of using personal data, but with an attempt to do so. If the defendant had been so charged, the jury would have had to consider whether, on the evidence before them, the defendant's actions coupled with his state of mind showed that he was committing no more than acts preparatory for the commission of an offence, for example if he was just finding out whether there was information available which might be of use to him in assisting Capital Investigations in their debt-collecting business; or whether he had embarked on the commission of the offence of using personal data for an improper purpose because, when he caused his colleague to operate the computer to reveal the information about the owners of the two vehicles in question, he had a firm intention to put that information to an improper use if it proved to be useful for that purpose. In the latter circumstances the case would, as I see it, have been little different from that of a man who puts his hand in another man's pocket with an intention to steal anything he finds inside; even if he finds nothing, he will nevertheless be guilty of an attempt to steal. . . ."

Lord Griffiths (dissenting):

". . . Whilst I have found this to be a difficult question I have come to the conclusion that 'use' should be given a broad construction as otherwise the purpose of the Act will not be achieved, there will be a serious lacuna in the protection it provides, and there will be difficulties in its enforcement. . . .

It is not straining the meaning of language to say that a person is using the information stored in a computer if he informs himself of its contents. Whether or not he then goes on to apply the information for a particular purpose, and to use it in that sense, will depend on the value of the information to him: but whether or not he applies the information does not alter the fact that he has wrongly invaded the privacy of the individual, and now has the information available to apply at any time in the future.

Once information has entered the public domain it is impractical to attempt to place any restraints on its use or further dissemination. The Act therefore concentrates its protective provisions in s 5 upon the conduct of those who hold or have access to personal data, in an attempt to ensure that they do not abuse the data, and confine it to the proper purpose for which it is required.

The purpose of the offences created by s 5 of the Act is clearly to protect the integrity and security of the data. A servant or agent of the holder of data is guilty of an offence if he uses data for any purpose not described in the register, if he discloses it to any person not described in the register, if he obtains it from a source not described in the register, and if he transfers it to a territory outside the United Kingdom not described in the register. So what would be the position of a police officer who deliberately falsified personal data held in the computer? He undoubtedly processed the data within the meaning of s 1(7); but if he was not 'using' the data by processing it he committed no offence. I cannot believe that in the Data Protection Act it was intended that wrongful interference with the data by those with access to it should not be an offence. But such is the result if 'use' is given the limited meaning adopted by the Court of Appeal.

This police officer had no business to be reading the personal data on the police computer for debt-collecting purposes, and I see no hardship in adopting a construction of the section that creates an offence if he does so. If on the other hand an obligation is laid on the prosecution to prove not only that illegitimate access to the information in the computer was obtained, but also how that information was subsequently applied I can see great practical difficulties in the enforcement of the Act and the protection of personal data that the convention and the Act intended to achieve."

[Lord Hoffmann delivered separate reasons which were substantially in agreement with those of Lord Goff. Lord Browne-Wilkinson concurred with Lord Hoffmann. Lord Jauncey of Tullichettle concurred with Lord Griffiths in dissent.]

QUESTIONS

- How would you classify the judgments in *R v. Brown* in terms of Goodrich's two models of judicial interpretation?

- Do you think there is an "ordinary and natural meaning" to the word "use" which is of assistance in interpreting this statute?

If judges approach the task of interpretation through a determination of the "ordinary" meaning of words, then the question remains where that ordinary meaning is to be found. Parliament has enacted the Interpretation Act, which provides very limited assistance in the interpretation of a narrow range of terms. But, in most cases, the judiciary is left to turn to more mundane sources in order to determine meaning. An obvious place to turn is the dictionary and, for better or worse, it is a source which is sometimes relied upon.

R. v. Fulling [1987] Q.B. 426, CA.

Lord Lane C.J.:

"On 6 August 1986 in the Crown Court at Leeds before his Honour Judge Hurwitz and a jury the appellant was convicted by a majority verdict of ten to two of obtaining property by deception. She faced a further similar count, the trial of which was adjourned. No sentence has yet been passed. She appeals against conviction by leave of the single judge.

The facts which gave rise to the charge were these. In September 1981 the appellant claimed some £5,665 from her insurers in respect of what she claimed was a burglary at her flat in Leeds. The insurance company in July 1982 paid her £5,212 in settlement of the claim.

Many months later a man called Turnpenny, an acknowledged criminal, gave to the police a mass of information about the activities of other criminals, which resulted in a large number of people being arrested, among them being the appellant. Turnpenny gave evidence that the appellant had told him that her 'burglary' was bogus, that a man called Maddon had committed it and that she knew the whereabouts of the stolen property. She gave him to understand that the idea of the bogus burglary had been initiated by one Drewery, with whom the appellant had been living and with whom she was infatuated. Turnpenny conceded that he had good reasons for wishing to harm Drewery.

As a result of this information the appellant was arrested in the early hours of Friday, 12 July 1985. Drewery was arrested at the same time. She was interviewed twice on that day, but exercised her right to say nothing despite persistent questioning by the police. She was interviewed again on the following day, Saturday. The interview was split into two, with a break in between, according to the police of 50 minutes, according to her of about 5 or 10 minutes.

The police witnesses described how, after initially refusing to answer questions, her attitude started to change. One of the officers, Det Sgt Beech, said:

'Q. You've obviously got a lot on your mind, are you finding it difficult?
A. Yes.
Q. Would I be right in saying that you want to talk about this but every bone in your body is telling you you shouldn't?
A. Something like that.'

Then came the break already described.

When the interview was resumed, in answer to questions from the officer she admitted a number of offences. Amongst them was the setting up of the bogus burglary: 'I approached a man in a pub because I was short of money and asked him if he would break in for me.' She admitted obtaining money from her insurers. She said that she had spent some of it on a holiday for herself and Drewery. She expressed her sorrow at having committed the offences and said she felt relieved that she had confessed. She sought, it should be added, to exculpate Drewery.

Thus there were two legs to the prosecution case. Turnpenny's evidence and the police account of her confession. The only corroboration of the former was the latter. The prosecution concede that if the confession goes, then the appeal should be allowed. They would not seek to rely on Turnpenny's uncorroborated evidence.

The only issue in the appeal is whether or not the confession was properly admitted. A submission was made to the judge that the confession should be ruled inadmissible by virtue of the provisions of s 76 of the Police and Criminal Evidence Act 1984, which provides as follows:

'(1) In any proceedings a confession made by an accused person may be given in evidence against him in so far as it is relevant to any matter in issue in the proceedings and is not excluded by the court in pursuance of this section.

(2) If, in any proceedings where the prosecution proposes to give in evidence a confession made by an accused person, it is represented to the court that the confession was or may have been obtained—(a) by oppression of the person who made it; or (b) in consequence of anything said or done which was likely, in the circumstances existing at the time, to render unreliable any confession which might be made by him in consequence thereof, the court shall not allow the confession to be given in evidence against him except in so far as the prosecution proves to the court beyond reasonable doubt that the confession (notwithstanding that it may be true) was not obtained as aforesaid.'

It was represented to the judge that the confession was or might have been obtained by oppression of the appellant within the meaning of sub-s (2)(a).

The appellant's evidence on the voir dire as to her reason for making the confession was this. After the break in the final interview one of the police officers, Det Con Holliday, told her that Drewery, her lover, had been having for the last three years or so an affair with a woman called Christine Judge. Now Christine Judge was one of the many people who had been arrested as a result of Turnpenny's disclosures. She was in the next cell to the appellant and, said the appellant, Det Con Holliday told her so. These revelations, said the appellant, so distressed her that she 'just couldn't stand being in the cells any longer'. Then later in her evidence she said: 'As soon as the matter about Christine came out, Det Con Holliday left the room and my head was swimming. I felt numb and after a while I said to Det Sgt Beech, "Is it true?" and he said, "Ronnie shouldn't have said that, he gets a bit carried away. Look Ruth, why don't you make a statement?"'.

She said that she knew Drewery had in 1982 had an affair with a woman called Christine. She had before the interview noticed that the cell next door to hers had the name Christine Judge on its door, but said she did not realise that this was the same Christine until the police told her. After she had made her confession she had shouted to Christine to ask her if what the police told her was true. Up to that point she said she was not particularly expressing her distress, but once she had spoken to Christine she just cried and cried. Later in cross-examination she said, 'I agreed to a statement being taken, it was the only way I was going to be released from the cells', but she conceded that she was not suggesting that she had been offered bail in return for a statement. The officers denied that they had made to her any such revelation as she suggested.

The basis of the submission to the judge was that the information given to her by the police about Christine amounted to oppression, and that the confession was, or might have been, obtained thereby, and that the prosecution had failed to discharge the burden of proving beyond a reasonable doubt that the confession was not so obtained.

In his ruling on the matter the judge declined to make any express finding of fact as to whether the appellant or the police were correct in their account of events. He was prepared to assume for the purposes of argument that the appellant's version of events was the true one and to judge the matter on that basis. That is the subject of criticism by counsel for the appellant, but we think he has no proper ground for complaint on that score.

The material part of the ruling runs as follows:

'Bearing in mind that whatever happens to a person who is arrested and questioned is by its very nature oppressive, I am quite satisfied that in s 76(2)(a) of the Police and Criminal Evidence Act 1984, the word oppression means something above and beyond that which is inherently oppressive in police custody and must import some impropriety, some oppression actively applied in an improper manner by the police. I do not find that what was done in this case can be so defined and, in those circumstances, I am satisfied that oppression cannot be made out on the evidence I have heard in the context required by the statutory provision. I go on to add simply this, that I have not addressed my mind as to whether or not I believe the police or the defendant on this issue because my ruling is based exclusively on the basis that, even if I wholly believed the defendant, I do not regard oppression as having been made out. In those circumstances, her confession (if that is the proper term for it), the interview in which she confessed, I rule to be admissible.'

Counsel for the appellant has drawn our attention to a number of authorities on the meaning of 'oppression'. Sachs L.J. in *R. v. Priestly* (1967) 51 Cr App R 1 said:

'. . . to my mind this word [oppression] in the context of the principles under consideration imports something which tends to sap, and has sapped, that free will which must exist before a confession is voluntary . . . the courts are not concerned with ascertaining the precise motive of a particular statement. The question before them is whether the prosecution have shown the statement to be voluntary, whatever the motive may be, and that is always the point to which all arguments must return. To solve it, the court has to look to the questions which I have already mentioned. First, was there in fact something which could properly be styled or might well be oppression? Secondly, did whatever happened in the way of oppression or likely oppression induce the statement in question?'

R. v. Prager [1972] 1 All ER 1114, [1972] 1 WLR 260 was another decision on para (e) of the introduction to the Judges' Rules 1964 (see *Practice Note* [1964] 1 All ER 237, [1964] 1 WLR 152), which required that a statement by the defendant before being admitted in evidence must be proved to be 'voluntary' in the sense that it has not been obtained by fear of prejudice or hope of advantage or by oppression. In the judgment of the court, delivered by Edmund Davies L.J., appears the following passage ([1972] 1 All ER 1114 at 1119, [1972] 1 WLR 260 at 266):

'As we have already indicated, the criticism directed in the present case against the police is that their interrogation constituted "oppression". This word appeared for the first time in the Judges' Rules 1964, and it closely followed the observation of Lord Parker CJ in *Callis v Gunn* [1963] 3 All ER 677 at 680, [1964] 1 QB 495 at 501 condemning confessions "obtained in an oppressive manner" . . . In an address to the Bentham Club in 1968 (see 21 CLP 10), Lord MacDermott described "oppressive questioning" as—"questioning which by its nature, duration or other attendant circumstances (including the fact of custody) excites hopes (such as the hope of release) or fears, or so affects the mind of the subject that his will crumbles and he speaks when otherwise he would have stayed silent." We adopt these definitions or descriptions . . .'

DPP v. Ping Lin [1975] 3 All ER 175, [1976] AC 574 was again a case in which the question was whether a statement by the defendant was shown to be voluntary. It was held that a trial judge faced by the problem should approach the task in a commonsense way and should ask himself whether the prosecution had proved that the contested statement was voluntary in the sense that it was not obtained by fear of prejudice or hope of advantage excited or held out by a person in authority. Lord Wilberforce, Lord Morris and Lord Hailsham expressed the opinion that it is not necessary, before a statement is held to be inadmissible because not shown to have been voluntary, that it should be thought or held that there was impropriety in the conduct of the person to whom the statement was made. What has to be considered is whether a statement is shown to have been voluntary rather than one brought about in one of the ways referred to.

Finally counsel for the appellant referred us to a judgment of this court in *R. v. Rennie* [1982] 1 All ER 385, [1982] 1 WLR 64.

Counsel for the appellant submits to us that on the strength of those decisions the basis of the judge's ruling was wrong, in particular when he held that the word 'oppression' means something above and beyond that which is inherently oppressive in police custody and must import some impropriety, some oppression actively applied in an improper manner by the police. It is submitted that that flies in the face of the opinions of their Lordships in *DPP v. Ping Lin*.

The point is one of statutory construction. The wording of the 1984 Act does not follow the wording of earlier rules or decisions, nor is it expressed to be a consolidating Act, nor yet to be declaratory of the common law. The title runs as follows:

'An Act to make further provision in relation to the powers and duties of the police, persons in police detention, criminal evidence, police discipline and complaints against the police; to provide for arrangements for obtaining the views of the community on policing and for a rank of deputy chief constable; to amend the law relating to the Police Federations and Police Forces and Police Cadets in Scotland; and for connected purposes.'

It is a codifying Act, and therefore the principles set out in *Bank of England v. Vagliano Bros* [1891] AC 107 at 144–145, [1891–4] All ER Rep 93 at 113 apply. Lord Herschell, having pointed out that the Bills of Exchange Act 1882 which was under consideration was intended to be a codifying Act, said:

> 'I think that the proper course is in the first instance to examine the language of the statute and to ask what is its natural meaning, uninfluenced by any considerations derived from the previous state of the law, and not to start with inquiring how the law previously stood, and then, assuming that it was probably intended to leave it unaltered, to see if the words of the enactment will bear an interpretation in conformity with this view. If a statute, intended to embody in a code a particular branch of the law, is to be treated in this fashion, it appears to me that its utility will be almost entirely destroyed, and the very object with which it was enacted will be frustrated. The purpose of such a statute surely was that on any point specifically dealt with by it, the law should be ascertained by interpreting the language used instead of, as before, by roaming over a vast number of authorities in order to discover what the law was, extracting it by a minute examination of the prior decisions, dependent upon a knowledge of the exact effect even of an obsolete proceeding such as a demurrer to evidence.'

Such observations are to be found in *Bristol Tramways Carriage Co. Ltd v. Fiat Motors Ltd* [1910] 2 KB 831 at 836 *per* Cozens-Hardy M.R..

Section 76(2) of the 1984 Act distinguishes between two different ways in which a confession may be rendered inadmissible: first, where it has been obtained by oppression (para (a)); second, where it has been made in consequence of anything said or done which was likely in the circumstances to render unreliable any confession which might be made by the defendant in consequence thereof (para (b)). Paragraph (b) is wider than the old formulation, namely that the confession must be shown to be voluntary in the sense that it was not obtained by fear of prejudice or hope of advantage, excited or held out by a person in authority. It is wide enough to cover some of the circumstances which under the earlier rule were embraced by what seems to us to be the artificially wide definition of oppression approved in *R. v. Prager* [1972] 1 All ER 1114, [1972] 1 WLR 260.

This in turn leads us to believe that 'oppression' in s 76(2)(a) should be given its ordinary dictionary meaning. *The Oxford English Dictionary* as its third definition of the word runs as follows: 'Exercise of authority or power in a burdensome, harsh, or wrongful manner; unjust or cruel treatment of subjects, inferiors, etc.; the imposition of unreasonable or unjust burdens.' One of the quotations given under that paragraph runs as follows: 'There is not a word in our language which expresses more detestable wickedness than *oppression*.'

We find it hard to envisage any circumstances in which such oppression would not entail some impropriety on the part of the interrogator. We do not think that the judge was wrong in using that test. What however is abundantly clear is that a confession may be invalidated under s 76(2)(b) where there is no suspicion of impropriety. No reliance was placed on the words of s 76(2)(b) either before the judge at trial or before this court. Even if there had been such reliance, we do not consider that the policeman's remark was likely to make unreliable any confession of the appellant's own criminal activities, and she expressly exonerated (or tried to exonerate) her unfaithful lover.

In those circumstances, in the judgment of this court, the judge was correct to reject the submission made to him under s 76 of the 1984 Act. The appeal is accordingly dismissed."

NOTES AND QUESTIONS

• Although it provides a good illustration of how judges sometimes turn to dictionaries in order to discern the ordinary meaning of words, the *Fulling* case is now rather dated in terms of its relevance to policing. By virtue of section 34 of the Criminal Justice and Public Order Act 1994, if a defendant, during questioning, fails to mention a fact which he wishes to rely on in his defence and it is a fact which he could reasonably have been expected to mention, then a court or jury may draw "such inferences from the failure as appear proper". By virtue of section 35, an accused must be told that if he or she refuses to be sworn at trial, or to answer questions, then an adverse inference may be drawn from silence by a jury. See Fiona Cownie and Anthony Bradney, *English Legal System in Context* (Butterworths, London, 1996), pp. 275–279.

- Why did the problem of statutory interpretation arise in the case?

- What choices of interpretation were open to the Court?

- What arguments did the Court use to justify the interpretation it adopted?

- What arguments could have been used to support other possible interpretations?

- Did you agree with the interpretation adopted by the Court?

- Redraft the statutory provision so as to avoid the problem which arose in the case.

- What are your views on the policy merits of the statutory provision?

CASE BRIEFING EXERCISE

- Making a case brief is an essential legal skill. It is not the quantity of cases or the length of judgments that you read that matters, but rather the quality of your reading and note taking. It is important to read cases *actively*, noting key material facts, the principles on which the case was decided, and important policy considerations.

- Write a case brief of *R. v. Fulling* in no more than 250 words. In your summary you should set out (with headings) the material facts, the legal issue in dispute, the reasoning of the judge, the result reached, and your view on the significance of the case. The *Fulling* case has not been edited from its original form, so as to give you experience with reading a case exactly as it was written by the judge.

THE DISTINCTION BETWEEN FACT AND LAW

The distinction between questions of fact and law has been described as "one of the most vexed questions in the whole topic of legal classification".[6] It is an issue of particular importance in administrative law because a decision of an administrative body is more easily challengeable on judicial review if it is characterised as an issue of law rather than fact. The assumption is that the tribunal is in the best position to make determinations on questions of fact, but that the role of courts is to ensure that

---

[6] Ian McLeod, *Legal Method* (2nd ed., Macmillan, Basingstoke, 1996), p. 37.

questions of law have been properly decided by the original decision maker. The classic statement of the distinction between "fact" and "law" was provided by Denning L.J.:

> "It is important to distinguish between primary facts and the conclusions from them. Primary facts are facts which are observed by witnesses and proved by oral testimony or facts proved by the production of a thing itself, such as original documents. Their determination is essentially a question of fact for the tribunal of fact, and the only question of law that can arise on them is whether there was any evidence to support the finding. The conclusions from primary facts are, however, inferences deduced by a process of reasoning from them. If, and in so far as, those conclusions can as well be drawn by a layman (properly instructed on the law) as a lawyer, they are conclusions of fact for the tribunal of fact: and the only questions of law which can arise on them are whether there was a proper direction in point of law; and whether the conclusion is one which could reasonably be drawn from the primary facts. . . . If, and in so far, however, as the correct conclusion to be drawn from primary facts requires, for its correctness, determination by a trained lawyer —as, for instance, because it involves the interpretation of documents or because the law on the point cannot properly be understood or applied except by a trained lawyer—the conclusion is a conclusion of law."[7]

The distinction between questions of fact and law has proven important in the context of the interpretation of statutes. Is the interpretation of a word or phrase in a statute a question of fact (and therefore a matter primarily for the determination of the original decision maker) or a question of law (and, as a consequence, readily open to review by a judicial body on appeal or judicial review)? The law in this area is far from clear, but a succinct explanation of the law/fact distinction has been provided by Vandevelde.

Kenneth J. Vandevelde, *Thinking Like a Lawyer* (Westview Press, Boulder, 1996), pp. 11–12:

> "Because there are only three things to be decided in a dispute, there are only three types of issues that can arise in legal reasoning. These are issues of fact, issues of law, and issues requiring application of law to fact.
>
> Issues of fact all pose essentially the same basic question: What is the situation to which the law must be applied? In other words, what events have occurred to create the dispute?
>
> Issues of law also pose essentially one basic question: What are the rules of law governing this situation?
>
> Issues requiring the application of law to fact similarly pose one general question: What rights or duties exist between the parties under the governing law in this situation? These issues are sometimes called mixed questions of law and fact.
>
> A single dispute may present all three types of issues or any combination of them. For example, assume that a man sues a physician claiming that she was negligent in failing to administer a particular diagnostic test to him and that, as a result, he sustained injuries three years later that would have been preventable had his disease been diagnosed earlier.
>
> The physician may put at issue some of the plaintiff's factual allegations. She may raise as issues of fact two questions: Would the diagnostic test actually have revealed that the patient

---

[7] *British Launderers' Research Association v. Central Middlesex Assessment Committee and Hendon Rating Authority* [1949] 1 All E.R. 21 at 25–26.

was suffering from the disease? Would the disease have been less injurious had it been discovered earlier?

The parties may also disagree on the applicable law. For example, the physician may raise this question as an issue of law: Does the statute of limitations for negligence claims against a medical practitioner require the claims to be filed within two years of the time the negligence *occurred* or within two years of the time the negligence was *discovered*? If the law requires the claim to be filed within two years of the time the negligence occurred, then the patient would have no right to compensation from the physician.

In addition, the parties may disagree about the application of the law to the facts. For example, the parties may present another question to the court as a mixed issue of law and fact: In this situation, did the physician's failure to administer the test constitute negligence? This is a mixed question of law and fact because it requires the court to apply the legal definition of negligence to the facts to determine whether the physician's conduct constitutes negligence. If the physician was not negligent, then the patient has no right to compensation."

The Courts in this country have grappled with the law/fact distinction, and the results at times have been far from clear.

Brutus v. Cozens [1972] 2 All E.R. 1297, HL.

Lord Reid:
"My Lords, the charge against the appellant is that on 28 June 1971, during the annual tournament at the All England Lawn Tennis Club, Wimbledon, he used insulting behaviour whereby a breach of the peace was likely to be occasioned, contrary to section 5 of the Public Order Act 1936, as amended.

While a match was in progress on no 2 court he went on to the court, blew a whistle and threw leaflets around. On the whistle being blown nine or ten others invaded the court with banners and placards. I shall assume that they did this at the instigation of the appellant although that is not made very clear in the case stated by the justices. Then the appellant sat down and had to be forcibly removed by the police. The incident lasted for two or three minutes. This is said to have been insulting behaviour.

It appears that the object of this demonstration was to protest against the apartheid policy of the government of South Africa. But it is not said that that government was insulted. The insult is said to have been offered to or directed at the spectators. The spectators at no 2 court were upset; they made loud shouts, gesticulated and shook their fists and while the appellant was being removed some showed hostility and attempted to strike him. The justices came to the conclusion that the appellant's behaviour was not insulting within the terms of the offence alleged. They did not consider the other points raised in argument but dismissed the information without calling on the appellant.

On a case stated a Divisional Court set aside the judgment of the justices and remitted the case to them to continue the hearing of the case. They certified as a point of law of general public importance:

'Whether conduct which evidences a disrespect for the rights of others so that it is likely to cause their resentment or give rise to protests from them is insulting behaviour within the meaning of s 5 of the Public Order Act 1936.'

Section 5 is in these terms:

'Any person who in any public place or at any public meeting—(a) uses threatening, abusive or insulting words or behaviour . . . with intent to provoke a breach of the peace or whereby a breach of the peace is likely to be occasioned, shall be guilty of an offence.'

Subsequent amendments do not affect the question which we have to consider.

It is not clear to me what precisely is the point of law which we have to decide. The question in the case stated for the opinion of the court is 'Whether, on the above statements of facts, we came to a correct determination and decision in point of law'. This seems to assume that the meaning of the word 'insulting' in s 5 is a matter of law. And the Divisional Court appear to have proceeded on that footing.

In my judgment that is not right. The meaning of an ordinary word of the English language is not a question of law. The proper construction of a statute is a question of law. If the context shows that a word is used in an unusual sense the court will determine in other words what that unusual sense is. But here there is in my opinion no question of the word 'insulting' being used in any unusual sense. It appears to me . . . to be intended to have its ordinary meaning. It is for the tribunal which decides the case to consider, not as law but as fact, whether in the whole circumstances the words of the statute do or do not as a matter of ordinary usage of the English language cover or apply to the facts which have been proved. If it is alleged that the tribunal has reached a wrong decision then there can be a question of law but only of a limited character. The question would normally be whether their decision was unreasonable in the sense that no tribunal acquainted with the ordinary use of language could reach that decision. . . .

We were referred to a number of dictionary meanings of 'insult' such as treating with insolence or contempt or indignity or derision or dishonour or offensive disrespect. Many things otherwise unobjectionable may be said or done in an insulting way. There can be no definition. But an ordinary sensible man knows an insult when he sees or hears it. . . . If the view of the Divisional Court was that in this section the word 'insulting' has some special or unusually wide meaning, then I do not agree. Parliament has given no indication that the word is to be given any unusual meaning. Insulting means insulting and nothing else.

If I had to decide, which I do not, whether the appellant's conduct insulted the spectators in this case, I would agree with the justices. The spectators may have been very angry and justly so. The appellant's conduct was deplorable. Probably it ought to be punishable. But I cannot see how it insulted the spectators.

I would allow the appeal with costs."

[Lord Morris of Borth-y-Gest, Viscount Dilhorne, Lord Diplock, and Lord Kilbrandon agreed that the appeal should be allowed].

Notes and questions

- Why does Lord Reid state that he does not have to decide whether the appellant's conduct was "insulting"?

- Do you think that the appellant's strategy of drawing attention to the apartheid regime in South Africa was successful? Why or why not? Remember that these events occurred in 1971.

- It is interesting that no mention is made in the judgments of the South African regime against which the protest was aimed. It is perhaps ironic that the appellant's behaviour is described as deplorable, when its impact was simply to interrupt a tennis game for a few minutes in an attempt to gain international publicity regarding a government widely viewed as deplorable.

- The distinction between fact and law in the context of statutory interpretation is not as settled as the judgments in *Brutus v. Cozens* might suggest. See, *e.g.*, *Energy Conversion Devices Incorporated's Applications* [1982] F.S.R. 544, HL; *R. v. Spens* [1991] 4 All E.R. 421, CA; *Edwards v. Bairstow* [1955] 3 All E.R. 48, HL. For a thorough discussion of the distinction, see Ian McLeod, *Legal Method* (2nd ed., Macmillan, Basingstoke, 1996), pp. 37–45.

CASE STUDY ON STATUTORY INTERPRETATION: THE RACE RELATIONS ACT

The best way of understanding how courts approach statutory interpretation is through examples. In this section, we will examine one controversial instance of statutory interpretation in which the courts were sharply divided on the application of a statute: the Race Relations Act. We begin with what is now a "classic" case, *Mandla v. Dowell Lee*, in which the Court of Appeal and House of Lords differed sharply on the interpretation of the word "ethnic" in the context of Sikhs in Britain. We will then compare the way in which the Court of Appeal subsequently applied the reasoning of the House of Lords in *Mandla* to what appears to be a very similar set of facts in *Dawkins v. Department of the Environment*. A commentary on the cases which explores the relationship between "law" and "race" then follows.

Mandla v. Dowell Lea and another [1982] 3 All E.R. 118, CA.

Lord Denning M.R.:
"How far can Sikhs in England insist on wearing their turbans? A turban is their distinctive headgear. They do not cut their hair but plait it under their turbans. Some of them feel so strongly about it that, when they are motorcyclists, they do not wear crash helmets; and when they are barristers they do not wear wigs.

Sewa Singh Mandla is a Sikh and rightly proud of it. He is a solicitor of the Supreme Court, practising in Birmingham. In 1978 he applied to send his son Gurinder to a private school in Birmingham called the Park Grove School. Gurinder was then aged 13. The school was very suitable for him. It had a high reputation. It took boys of all races. There were 305 boys altogether. Over 200 were English, but there were many others. Five were Sikhs, 34 Hindus, 16 Persians, six Negroes, seven Chinese and about 15 from European countries.

Mr Mandla took his son to see the headmaster. Both he and his son were wearing their turbans. The headmaster felt that it might give rise to difficulties if Gurinder wore his turban in school. He asked the father: 'Will you consent to his removing his turban and cutting his hair?' The father said: 'No. That is completely out of the question.' The headmaster said that he would think about it. Then on 24 July 1978 he wrote:

> 'Thank you for bringing your son to see me. As I promised, I have given much thought to the problem and I have reluctantly come to the conclusion that on balance it would be unwise to relax the School Rules with regard to uniform at the moment. I do not see any way in which it would be possible to reconcile the two conflicting requirements. May I wish you well in your efforts to promote harmony and peace, and I hope you find a suitable school for Gurinder without difficulty.'

Mr Mandla did find another school for Gurinder where he is allowed to wear his turban. So all is now well with them. But Mr Mandla reported the headmaster to the Commission for Racial Equality. They took the matter up with the headmaster. On 19 September 1978 the headmaster wrote this letter:

> 'To make my position quite clear, the boy was not rejected because he was a Sikh since we do not make racial distinctions and we have several Sikhs in the School. It was the turban that was rejected, and I believe your Acts cover people, not clothes.'

The commission, however, did not let the matter rest. They pursued the headmaster relentlessly. They interviewed him. They demanded information from him. Eventually they decided to assist Mr Mandla in legal proceedings against him. With their assistance in money and advice Mr Mandla issued proceedings against the headmaster of the school in the Birmingham County Court. He claimed damages limited to £500 and a declaration that the defendants had committed an act of unlawful discrimination. The county court judge heard the case for five days in February and June 1980, with many witnesses and much argument. The judge dismissed the claim. The Commission for Racial Equality, in Mr Mandla's name, appeal to this court.

The headmaster appeared before us in person. He has not the means to instruct counsel and solicitors. He put his case moderately and with restraint. He has himself done much research in the India Office library and elsewhere. It must have taken him many hours and many days. Now we have to consider what it all comes to.

The Law

The case raises this point of great interest: what is a 'racial group' within the Race Relations Act 1976? If the Sikhs are a 'racial group' no one is allowed to discriminate against any of their members in the important fields of education and employment and so forth. No matter whether the discrimination is direct or indirect, it is unlawful. But, if they are not a 'racial group' discrimination is perfectly lawful. So everything depends on whether they are a 'racial group' or not.

The statute in s 3 (1) of the 1976 Act contains a definition of 'racial group'. It means a 'group of persons defined by reference to colour, race, nationality or ethnic or national origins'. That definition is very carefully framed. Most interesting is that it does not include religion or politics or culture. You can discriminate for or against Roman Catholics as much as you like without being in breach of the law. You can discriminate for or against Communists as much as you please, without being in breach of the law. You can discriminate for or against the 'hippies' as much as you like, without being in breach of the law. But you must not discriminate against a man because of his colour or of his race or of his nationality, or of 'his ethnic or national origins'. It is not suggested that the Sikhs are a group defined by reference to colour or race or nationality. Nor was much stress laid on national origins. But it is said most persuasively by counsel for the plaintiffs that the Sikhs are a group of persons 'defined by reference to ethnic origins'. It is so important that I will consider each word of that phrase.

'Ethnic'

The word 'ethnic' is derived from the Greek word 'ἔθνδς' which meant simply 'nation'. It was used by the 72 Palestinian Jews who translated the Old Testament from Hebrew into Greek (in the Septuagint). They used it to denote the non-Israelitish nations, that is, the Gentiles. When the word 'ethnic' was first used in England, it was used to denote peoples who were not Christian or Jewish. This was the meaning attached to it in the great *Oxford English Dictionary* itself in 1890.

But in 1934 in the *Concise Oxford Dictionary* it was given an entirely different meaning. It was given as: 'pertaining to race, ethnological'. And 'ethnological' was given as meaning: 'corresponding to a division of races'. That is the meaning which I, acquiring my vocabulary in 1934, have always myself attached to the word 'ethnic'. It is, to my mind, the correct meaning. It means 'pertaining to race'.

But then in 1972 there was appended a second supplement of the *Oxford English Dictionary*. It gives a very much wider meaning than that which I am used to. It was relied on by counsel for the plaintiffs:

'Also, pertaining to or having common racial, cultural, religious or linguistic characteristics, especially designating a racial *or other group* within a larger system; hence (U.S. colloquial), foreign, exotic.'

As an example of this new meaning, the second supplement refers to a book by Huxley and Haddon called *We Europeans* (1935). It mentions 'the non-committal terms *ethnic group*' and refers to the 'special type of *ethnic* grouping of which the Jews form the best-known example' (my emphasis). This reference to the Jews gives us a clue to the meaning of ethnic.

Why are 'the Jews' given as the best-known example of 'ethnic grouping'? What is their special characteristic which distinguishes them from non-Jews? To my mind it is a racial characteristic. *The Shorter Oxford Dictionary* describes a Jew as 'a person of Hebrew race'. Some help too can be found in our law books. . . . If a man desires that his daughter should only marry 'a Jew' and cuts her out of his will if she should marry a man who is not 'a Jew', he will find that the court will hold the condition void for uncertainty. The reason is because 'a Jew' may mean a dozen different things. It may mean a man of the Jewish faith. Even if he was a convert from Christianity, he would be of the Jewish faith. Or it may mean a man of Jewish parentage, even though he may be a convert to Christianity. It may suffice if his grandfather was a Jew and his grandmother was not. The Jewish blood may have become very thin by intermarriage with Christians, but still many would call him 'a Jew'. All this leads me to think that, when it is said of the Jews that they are an 'ethnic group', it means that the group as a whole share a common characteristic which is a racial characteristic. It is that they are descended, however remotely, from a Jewish ancestor. When we spoke of the 'Jewish regiments' which were formed and fought so well during the war, we had in mind those who were of Jewish descent or parentage. When Hitler and the Nazis so fiendishly exterminated 'the Jews', it was because of their racial characteristics and not because of their religion.

There is nothing in their culture of language or literature to mark out Jews in England from others. The Jews in England share all of these characteristics equally with the rest of us. Apart from religion, the one characteristic which is different is a racial characteristic.

'Origins'

The statute uses the word 'ethnic' in the context of 'origins'. This carries the same thought. I turn once again to the *Shorter Oxford Dictionary*. When the word 'origin' is used of a person it means 'descent, parentage'. I turn also to the speech of Lord Cross in *Ealing London Borough v. Race Relations Board* [1972] 1 All ER 15 at 117, [1972] AC 342 at 365:

> 'To me it suggests a connection subsisting at the time of birth . . . The connection will normally arise because the parents or one of the parents of the individual in question are or is identified by descent . . .'

So the word 'origins' connotes a group which has a common racial characteristic.

'Ethnic Origins'

If I am right in thinking that the phrase 'ethnic origins' denotes a group with a common racial characteristic, the question arises: why is it used at all? The answer is given by Lord Cross in the *Ealing London Borough* case ([1972] 1 All ER 15 at 117–118, [1972] AC 342 at 366):

> 'The reason why the word "ethnic or national origins" were added to the words "racial grounds" which alone appear in the long title was, I imagine, to prevent argument over the exact meaning of the word "race."'

In other words, there might be much argument whether one group or other was of the same 'race' as another, but there was thought to be less whether it was a different 'ethnic group'.

'Racial Group'

This brings me back to the definition in the statute of a 'racial group'. It means 'a group of persons defined by reference to colour, race, nationality or ethnic or national origins'.

The word 'defined' shows that the group must be distinguished from another group by some definable characteristic. English, Scots or Welsh football teams are to be distinguished by their national origins. The Scottish clans are not distinguishable from one another either by their ethnic or national origins, but only by their clannish or tribal differences. French Canadians are distinguished from other Canadians by their ethnic or national origins. Jews are not to be distinguished by their national origins. The wandering Jew has no nation. He is a wanderer over the face of the earth. The only definable characteristic of the Jews is a racial characteristic. I have no doubt that, in using the words 'ethnic origins', Parliament had in mind primarily the Jews. There must be no discrimination against the Jews in England. Anti-Semitism must not be allowed. It has produced great evils elsewhere. It must not be allowed here.

But the words 'ethnic origins' have a wider significance than the Jews. The question before us today is whether they include the Sikhs.

The Sikhs

The word 'Sikh' is derived from the Sanskrit 'Shishya', which means 'disciple'. Sikhs are the disciples or followers of Guru Nanak, who was born on 5 April 1469. There are about 14 m Sikhs, most of whom live in the part of the Punjab which is in India. Before the partition of the province in 1947 half of them lived in that portion which is now Pakistan; but on the partition most of them moved into India. There was tragic loss of life.

There is no difference in language which distinguishes the Sikhs from the other peoples in India. They speak Punjabi or Hindi or Urdu, or whatever the vernacular may be. There is no difference in blood which distinguishes them either. The people of India are largely the product of successive invasions that have swept into the country. They have intermingled to such an extent that it is impossible now to separate one strain from the other. The Sikhs do not recognise any distinction of race between them and the other peoples of India. They freely receive converts from Hinduism, or vice versa. Not only from outside, but even within the same family. The outstanding distinction between the Sikhs and the other peoples of India is in their religion, Sikhism, and its accompanying culture.

This is so marked that Dr Ballard, who is a lecturer in race relations in the University of Leeds, thought it was an ethnic difference. But, if you study his evidence, it is plain that he was using the word 'ethnic' in a special sense of his own. For him it did not signify any racial characteristic at all. These are some illuminating passages from his evidence:

> 'Sikhs, most obviously, are not a race in biological terms. Their origins are extremely diverse, probably more diverse than us English . . . I think they are a classic example of an ethnic group because of their distinctive cultural traditions . . . We are busy coining lots of new words here. I think ethnicity is the proper word to coin . . .'

The evidence shows that Sikhs as a community originate from the teaching of Guru Nanak. About the fifteenth century he founded the religious sect. There were a series of Gurus who followed Nanak, but the tenth and last is most important. Early in the nineteenth century he instituted major social and cultural reforms and turned the Sikhs into a community. He laid down the rules by which the hair was not to be cut and it was to be covered by a turban. By adopting this uniform Sikhs made their communal affiliation very clear, both to each other and to outsiders. But they remained at bottom a religious sect.

It is sometimes suggested that the Sikhs are physically a different people. But that is not so. In an important book on *The People of Asia* (1977) p. 327 Professor Bowles of Syracuse University, New York, says:

> 'The difference [between Muslims, Sikhs and Hindus] are mainly cultural, not biological. Much has been written about the tallness . . . and excellent physique of the Sikh, qualities often attributed to their well-balanced vegetarian diet. In part this may be true, but the Sikhs are matched in physique by several other Punjab populations—meat-eating as well as vegetarian. Muslims as well as Hindus. Some of the neighbouring Pathan tribesmen are even taller. The Sikh physique is probably due to the fact that many have entered professions that have given them an economic advantage over their compatriots, Indians or Pakistanis. A correlation between nutrition and physique holds throughout the entire sub-continent, but it may be more noticeable in the Punjab, where there is such a variety of merchants and traders . . .'

On all this evidence, it is plain to me that the Sikhs, as a group, cannot be distinguished from others in the Punjab by reference to any racial characteristic whatever. They are only to be distinguished by their religion and culture. That is not an ethnic difference at all.

Conclusion

I have dealt with the evidence at length because of the differences on the point in the lower courts and tribunals. In our present case the evidence has been more fully canvassed than ever before. It has been most well and carefully considered by His Honour Judge Gosling here. I agree with his conclusion that Sikhs are not a racial group. They cannot be defined by reference to their ethnic or national origins. No doubt they are a distinct community, just as many other religious and cultural communities. But that is not good enough. It does not enable them to complain of discrimination against them.

You must remember that it is perfectly lawful to discriminate against groups of people to whom you object, so long as they are not a racial group. You can discriminate against the Moonies or the skinheads or any other group which you dislike or to which you take objection. No matter whether your objection to them is reasonable or unreasonable, you can discriminate against them, without being in breach of the law.

No doubt the Sikhs are very different from some of those groups. They are a fine community upholding the highest standards, but they are not a 'racial group'. So it is not unlawful to discriminate against them. Even though the discrimination may be unfair or unreasonable, there is nothing unlawful in it.

In our present case the headmaster did not discriminate against the Sikhs at all. He has five Sikh boys in his school already. All he has done is to say that, when the boy attends school, he must wear the school uniform and not wear a turban. The other Sikh boys in the school conform to this requirement. They make no objection. Mr Mandla is, I expect, strictly orthodox. He feels so strongly that he insists on his son wearing his turban at all times. But that feeling does not mean that the headmaster was at fault in any way. He was not unfair or unreasonable. It is for him to run his school in the way he feels best. He was not guilty of any discrimination against the Sikhs, direct or indirect.

I cannot pass from this case without expressing some regret that the Commission for Racial Equality thought it right to take up this case against the headmaster. It must be very difficult for educational establishments in this country to keep a proper balance between the various pupils who seek entry. The statutes relating to race discrimination and sex discrimination are difficult enough to understand and apply anyway. They should not be used so as to interfere with the discretion of schools and colleges in the proper management of their affairs.

In the circumstances I need say nothing as to the contentions about the word 'can' or 'justifiable' in the statutes. They do not arise.

I would dismiss the appeal."

Oliver L.J. [Oliver L.J. delivered separate concurring reasons, and concluded with some comments on the actions of the Commission for Racial Equality in this case]:

"... In the result, I agree that the appeal fails. I would add only this. Without in any way minimising the great assistance which counsel for the plaintiffs have given the court in this difficult case, it is right that some tribute should be paid to the courtesy, skill and patience with which Mr Dowell Lee has conducted in person a case which must have caused him immense personal distress and anxiety. I cannot help observing that the events of which complaint have been made took place as long ago as the summer of 1978, four years ago. Throughout Mr Dowell Lee appears to have behaved with the greatest courtesy and restraint. After an entirely courteous correspondence with the first plaintiff, he found himself the subject of a visitation from a representative of the Commission for Racial Equality and the papers before us contain the notes of an interview with him at which he appears to have been deliberately interrogated with a view to extracting admissions of racial bias and at which barely concealed threats of 'investigation' were made unless he modified the stance which he had adopted. Thereafter he, whose proper business was running his school in a way which to him seemed most suited to the needs of his students, found himself involved in an action fostered and supported by the commission. The proceedings were commenced two years later and have throughout been maintained by the commission in the name of better race relations, although it emerged, ironically, at the trial that the first plaintiff would not, if the matter of his son's entry had been pursued, have been willing in any event for him to go to a school where he would have been expected to attend religious classes of the Christian faith as part of the normal curriculum. There is, and this should be made, I think, entirely clear, absolutely no foundation, in my judgment, for the suggestion that Mr Dowell Lee is seeking or has sought to exclude children from the school either on racial or religious grounds. . . . Mr Dowell Lee's objection to the wearing of the turban at school is precisely, as I understand it, because he feels that it would tend to accentuate those very religious and social distinctions which it is his desire to minimise in trying to effect a homogenous school community. Whether that is an objection which all or any of the members of this court would equally feel is immaterial. It is, in my judgment, a perfectly respectable viewpoint and is the sincerely held and responsible opinion of a man who is running a multiracial school in a difficult area. I have to say that, speaking entirely for myself, I regard it as lamentable that Mr Dowell Lee's entire livelihood and the future of his school should have been put at risk at the instance of a publicly financed body designed to foster better racial relations. Anything less likely to achieve that result than this case I find it difficult to imagine. As it is Mr Dowell Lee has been compelled to waste a great deal of his time and the resources of the school in defending himself against charges which could hardly have been levelled at any target less deserving of them. He has been dragged through two courts at enormous expense in order, apparently, to establish a point which no doubt is a difficult and important one, but is now entirely academic for both plaintiffs. It seems to me a great pity that it should have been thought necessary to test it at the expense of an entirely blameless individual who has done no more than to seek in the best way that he knows how to run his own business in his own way. What makes it, perhaps, particularly ironic is the evidence of the plaintiffs' expert Mr Indarijit Singh:

'Tolerance is the willingness, and a Sikh should be willing, to fight in every way including, if need be, eventually to give his life, to upholding the next person's right to determine his own particular way of life.'

For my part, I find it regrettable that this unimpeachable sentiment should not have been applied here and that machinery designed specifically for the protection of the weak and disadvantaged should have operated as, it seems to me, it has in this case, albeit no doubt with the loftiest of motives, as an engine of oppression.

I should only add that, in saying this, I am making no criticism whatever of counsel for the plaintiffs or those instructing him, who have conducted the appeal in accordance with their clients' instructions with the most punctilious fairness and propriety.

I too would dismiss the appeal."

Kerr L.J. [Kerr L.J. delivered concurring reasons, concluding with the following comment]:
". . . I would add my disquiet to what Lord Denning M.R. and Oliver L.J. have already said about the events which have led up to these proceedings. The Commission for Racial Equality is clearly highly motivated and does useful work in cases where there is clear evidence, or real ground for suspicion, that racial discrimination exists and is practised. But this is not such a case. This school was demonstrably conducted harmoniously on a multiracial basis. I have read in this evidence the notes of the interview of the headmaster by an official of the commission. In parts this reads more like an inquisition than an interview, and I can see no basis whatever for what I can only describe as harassment of this headmaster. All that the commission has achieved in this case, as it seems to me, is to create racial discord where there was none before."

QUESTIONS

- Consider Lord Denning's description of the ethnic mix of the school. Is there anything problematic about his description? What does he mean by "English" students?

- Is Lord Denning's explanation of why "ethnic" was included in the statutory language convincing? Can you come up with an alternative explanation?

- In Lord Denning's reasons, a substantial amount of expert evidence (that is, evidence given by experts in the area under consideration) is presented. On what basis is this evidence accepted or rejected? Specifically, on what basis does Lord Denning reject Dr Ballard's definition of Sikhs as an ethnic group?

- All of the judges are loathe to interfere with the "discretion" of the headmaster in running his school as he sees fit. Is that attitude potentially problematic in the face of the application of the Race Relations Act to education? Is not the point of the legislation to constrain the exercise of discretion when its impact is discriminatory?

- Lord Oliver mentions that Mr Mandla would not have sent his son to this school in any event because it conducted Christian religious education. Could you argue that such services are themselves in contravention of the Race Relations Act? Note here that Lord Denning stated that Jews definitely do constitute an "ethnic group" for the purposes of the legislation.

ESSAY QUESTION

Describe and evaluate the attitude of the members of this Court of Appeal to "race relations" and, in particular, the work of the Commission for Racial Equality.

The case was then appealed to the House of Lords.

Mandla v. Dowell Lee [1983] 1 All E.R. 162, HL.

Lord Fraser of Tullybelton [Lord Fraser described the facts and the issue of statutory interpretation, before considering whether Sikhs constituted an ethnic group]:
". . . My Lords, I recognise that 'ethnic' conveys a flavour of race but it cannot, in my opinion, have been used in the 1976 Act in a strict racial or biological sense. For one thing it would be absurd to suppose that Parliament can have intended that membership of a particular racial group should depend on scientific proof that a person possessed the relevant distinctive biological characteristics (assuming that such characteristics exist). The practical difficulties of such proof would be prohibitive, and it is clear that Parliament must have used the word in some more popular sense. For another thing, the briefest glance at the evidence in this case is enough to show that, within the human race, there are very few, if any, distinctions which are scientifically recognised as racial. . . .
    I turn, therefore, to the third and wider meaning which is given in the *Supplement to the Oxford English Dictionary* vol I (A-G) (1972). It is as follows: 'pertaining to or having common racial, cultural, religious, or linguistic characteristics, esp. designating a racial or other group within a larger system . . .' Counsel for the appellants, while not accepting the third (1972) meaning as directly applicable for the present purpose, relied on it to this extent, that it introduces a reference to cultural and other characteristics, and is not limited to racial characteristics. The 1972 meaning is, in my opinion, too loose and vague to be accepted as it stands. It is capable of being read as implying that any one of the adjectives, 'racial, cultural, religious *or* linguistic' would be enough to constitute an ethnic group. That cannot be the sense in which 'ethnic' is used in the 1976 Act, as that Act is not concerned at all with

discrimination on religious grounds. Similarly, it cannot have been used to mean simply any 'racial *or other* group'. If that were the meaning of 'ethnic', it would add nothing to the word group, and would lead to a result which would be unacceptably wide. But in seeking for the true meaning of 'ethnic' in the statute, we are not tied to the precise definition in any dictionary. The value of the 1972 definition is, in my view, that it shows that ethnic has come to be commonly used in a sense appreciably wider than the strictly racial or biological. That appears to me to be consistent with the ordinary experience of those who read newspapers at the present day. In my opinion, the word 'ethnic' still retains a racial flavour but it is used nowadays in an extended sense to include other characteristics which may be commonly thought of as being associated with common racial origin.

For a group to constitute an ethnic group in the sense of the 1976 Act, it must, in my opinion, regard itself, and be regarded by others, as a distinct community by virtue of certain characteristics. Some of these characteristics are essential; others are not essential but one or more of them will commonly be found and will help to distinguish the group from the surrounding community. The conditions which appear to me to be essential are these: (1) a long shared history, of which the group is conscious as distinguishing it from other groups, and the memory of which it keeps alive; (2) a cultural tradition of its own, including family and social customs and manners, often but not necessarily associated with religious observance. In addition to those two essential characteristics the following characteristics are, in my opinion, relevant: (3) either a common geographical origin, or descent from a small number of common ancestors; (4) a common language, not necessarily peculiar to the group; (5) a common literature peculiar to the group; (6) a common religion different from that of neighbouring groups or from the general community surrounding it; (7) being a minority or being an oppressed or a dominant group within a larger community, for example a conquered people (say, the inhabitants of England shortly after the Norman conquest) and their conquerors might both be ethnic groups. . . .

The result is, in my opinion, that Sikhs are a group defined by a reference to ethnic origins for the purpose of the 1976 Act, although they are not biologically distinguishable from the other people living in the Punjab. That is true whether one is considering the position before the partition of 1947, when the Sikhs lived mainly in that part of the Punjab which is now Pakistan, or after 1947, since when most of them have moved into India. It is, therefore, necessary to consider whether the respondent has indirectly discriminated against the appellants in the sense of s 1(1)(b) of the 1976 Act. That raises the two subsidiary questions. . . .

'Can comply'

It is obvious that Sikhs, like anyone else, 'can' refrain from wearing a turban, if 'can' is construed literally. But if the broad cultural/historic meaning of ethnic is the appropriate meaning of the word in the 1976 Act, then a literal reading of the word 'can' would deprive Sikhs and members of other groups defined by reference to their ethnic origins of much of the protection which Parliament evidently intended the 1976 Act to afford to them. They 'can' comply with almost any requirement or condition if they are willing to give up their distinctive customs and cultural rules. On the other hand, if ethnic means inherited and unalterable, as the Court of Appeal thought it did, then 'can' ought logically to be read literally. The word 'can' is used with many shades of meaning. In the context of s 1 (1)(b)(i) of the 1976 Act it must, in my opinion, have been intended by Parliament to be read not as meaning 'can physically', so as to indicate a theoretical possibility, but as meaning 'can in practice' or 'can consistently with the customs and cultural conditions of the racial group'. . . . Accordingly I am of opinion that the 'no turban' rule was not one with which the second appellant could, in the relevant sense, comply.

'Justifiable'

The word 'justifiable' occurs in s 1(1)(b)(ii). It raises a problem which is, in my opinion, more difficult than the problem of the word 'can'. But in the end I have reached a firm opinion that the respondent has not been able to show that the 'no turban' rule was justifiable in the relevant sense. Regarded purely from the point of view of the respondent, it was no doubt perfectly justifiable. He explained that he had no intention of discriminating against Sikhs. . . .

The reasons for having a school uniform were largely reasons of practical convenience, to minimise external differences between races and social classes, to discourage the 'competitive fashions' which he said tend to exist in a teenage community, and to present a Christian image of the school to outsiders, including prospective parents. The respondent explained the difficulty for a headmaster of explaining to a non-Sikh pupil why the rules about wearing correct school uniform were enforced against him if they were relaxed in favour of a Sikh. In my view these reasons could not, either individually or collectively, provide a sufficient justification for the respondent to apply a condition that is prima facie discriminatory under the 1976 Act.

An attempted justification of the 'no turban' rule, which requires more serious consideration, was that the respondent sought to run a Christian school, accepting pupils of all religions and races, and that he objected to the turban on the ground that it was an outward manifestation of a non-Christian faith. Indeed, he regarded it as amounting to a challenge to that faith. I have much sympathy with the respondent on this part of the case and I would have been glad to find that the rule was justifiable within the meaning of the statute, if I could have done so. But in my opinion that is impossible. The onus under para (b)(ii) is on the respondent to show that the condition which he seeks to apply is not indeed a necessary condition, but that it is in all circumstances justifiable 'irrespective of the colour, race, nationality or ethnic or national origins of the person to whom it is applied', that is to say that it is justifiable without regard to the ethnic origins of that person. But in this case the principal justification on which the respondent relies is that the turban is objectionable just because it is a manifestation of the second appellant's ethnic origins. That is not, in my view, a justification which is admissible under para (b)(ii). . . .

Final considerations

Before parting with the case I must refer to some observations by the Court of Appeal which suggest that the conduct of the Commission for Racial Equality in this case has been in some way unreasonable or oppressive. . . .

My Lords, I must say that I regard these strictures on the commission and its officials as entirely unjustified. The commission has had a difficult task, and no doubt its inquiries will be resented by some and are liable to be regarded as objectionable and inquisitive. But the respondent in this case, who conducted his appeal with restraint and skill, made no complaint of his treatment at the hands of the commission. He was specifically asked by some of my noble and learned friends to point out any part of the notes of his interview with the commission's official to which he objected, and he said there were none and that an objection of that sort formed no part of his case. The lady who conducted the interview on behalf of the commission gave evidence in the county court, and no suggestion was put to her in cross-examination that she had not conducted it properly. Opinions may legitimately differ as to the usefulness of the commission's activities, but its functions have been laid down by Parliament and, in my view, the actions of the commission itself in this case and of its official who interviewed the respondent on 3 November 1978 were perfectly proper and in accordance with its statutory duty.

I would allow this appeal. The appellants have agreed to pay the costs of the respondent in this House and they do not seek to disturb the order for costs in the lower courts in favour of the present respondent made by the Court of Appeal."

[Lord Templeman delivered separate concurring reasons. Lord Edmund-Davies, Lord Roskill, and Lord Brandon of Oakbrook concurred in the reasons of Lord Fraser and Lord Templeman].

QUESTIONS

• Lord Fraser expressed his sympathy with the respondent's desire to run a "Christian" school. Could such a desire be legally problematic in terms of the way in which the House of Lords defines "ethnic origins" in the Race Relations Act? Are there other "outward manifestations" of non-Christian faiths, the prohibition of which could lead to action under the legislation? Would it be more "just" if outward manifestations of Christianity were also prohibited?

• Note how Lord Fraser chastises the Court of Appeal for its criticism of the Commission for Racial Equality. How does he employ the doctrine of the supremacy of Parliament to ground his criticism of the Court of Appeal?

Compare the following judgment which seeks to apply the reasoning in *Mandla v. Dowell Lee* to what appear to be very similar facts:

Dawkins v. Department of the Environment [1993] I.R.L.R. 284, CA.

Neill L.J.:
"This is an appeal by leave of the single Lord Justice by Mr Trevor Dawkins from the order of the Employment Appeal Tribunal dated 24 April 1991 allowing the appeal of Crown Suppliers (SA) Ltd from the decision of the Industrial Tribunal dated 28 March 1989. I shall call Mr Dawkins 'the appellant' and the Crown Suppliers (PSA) Ltd 'the PSA'. . . . The respondent to the appeal is now the Department of the Environment.

The facts

The PSA, which is part of the Home Civil Service, is responsible for *inter alia* providing transport for the government Interdepartmental Despatch Service (IDS). In June 1988 the PSA inserted an advertisement in the *South London Press* seeking experienced drivers for the IDS. The advertisement stipulated that the applicants should be aged between 25 and 45 with a clean driving licence. The appellant responded to the advertisement and attended at the PSA's premises for interview at 10 am on 28 June 1988.

Before the Industrial Tribunal there was a conflict of evidence as to the appearance of the appellant at the interview. It is sufficient to say that the appellant, who is a Rastafarian, attended wearing a hat and that underneath the hat he had long hair arranged in the form of dreadlocks. Miss Barbara Herbert, who conducted the interview with the appellant, explained to him that the SA expected their drivers to have short hair. The appellant indicated that he was not willing to cut his hair and the interview was then concluded amicably.

On 26 September 1988 the applicant applied to the Industrial Tribunal for a finding whether he had been discriminated against contrary to the Race Relations Act 1976. The appellant's complaint was heard on 16 and 17 January 1989 at London South. By the decision of the Industrial Tribunal which was sent to the parties on 28 March 1989 the tribunal found by a majority that the appellant's claim succeeded. The question of remedies was left over for a later occasion. By their majority decision the Industrial Tribunal held that the PSA had been guilty of both direct and indirect discrimination. They held that the appellant had been refused employment not because he was black but because of the opinion which Miss Herbert formed as to his unsuitability by reason of the length of his hair. The central question at issue before the Industrial Tribunal was whether or not Rastafarians constituted a racial group within the meaning of the 1976 Act. By a majority the Industrial Tribunal decided that Rastafarians did constitute such a group. In reaching this conclusion the Industrial Tribunal made a number of findings of fact which have not been challenged. The difference of opinion between the members of the Industrial Tribunal was as to the application of the law to these facts.

I should set out the findings of fact made by the Industrial Tribunal in paragraph 10 of their reasons. These findings were as follows:

'(I) The Rastafarian movement as such began about 1930. We do not think it is possible to trace it back any further than this. It seems to us that it was in the decade between 1920 and 1930 that the ideas of Marcus Garvey began to crystallise, and that it cannot be said that the movement had any separate existence before 1930.

(II) That there is a distinct culture which although in some respects is vague and difficult to grasp seems to us nevertheless to exist. The fact that the Rastafarians do not, as most have, distinct centres of worship does not seem to us to be very material. We find that they do, as Dr Cashmore says, meet in groups in order to discuss matters of common interest as outlined in his evidence and that they do observe distinct customs such as a refusal to cut hair or to shave, and observe dietary laws and prohibitions on homosexuality and contraception. They also have, we find, a common language *i.e.* English and the Jamaican patois.

(III) They have a common geographical origin in that the majority of them come from Jamaica at least in origin, although by now a large number of Rastafarians in this country will have been born here.

(IV) That there is some literature and some cultural tradition, that is that there is some poetry which is distinctive to the group and there is also reggae music. We feel that if a group shows a musical tradition then this must also be taken into account as well as a written or oral literary tradition.

(V) That they do have a sense of being a minority and of being oppressed in that their distinctive appearance is likely to single them out for criticism by other members of the community thus causing them to have a feeling that they are a peculiar minority among other people.

(VI) We also find that there has been continuity, albeit tenuous, from 1930. We think the answer here is that until about 1970 Rastafarians, at least in this country, were few and far between. This is probably why not many were noticed between the 1950s, when immigration from the West Indies to this country started, and 1970 when the movement seems to have been noticed. We think, however, that it can be shown that the movement has either here or in Jamaica or in other parts of the world been continuous since 1930.'

I shall have to return later to consider how the Industrial Tribunal applied the relevant law to these facts.

The Law

The complaint by the appellant was brought before the Industrial Tribunal in accordance with s 54(1) of the Race Relations Acts 1976 which provides that a complaint that another person has committed an act of discrimination against the complainant which is unlawful by virtue of art II of the Act may be presented to an Industrial Tribunal. [Neill L.J. then explained the content and structure of the statutory regime]. . . .

In the present case the appellant claims that he was subjected to both direct and indirect racial discrimination in that he was refused employment by the PSA by reason of his membership of a particular racial group, namely the Rastafarians. It is contended on his behalf that Rastafarians constitute a group of persons who are defined by reference to their ethnic origins.

On behalf of the PSA it is accepted that the appellant was refused employment because he was a Rastafarian, but it is denied that Rastafarians constitute a group of persons defined by reference to their ethnic origins. It will be seen therefore that the crucial question to be decided by the Industrial Tribunal was whether or not Rastafarians were a group defined by reference to their ethnic origins. . . .

The decision of the Industrial Tribunal

In their full and careful reasons the Industrial Tribunal referred to the decisions in *Mandla* and in *King-Ansell*.[8] In addition they referred to the decision of the Court of Appeal in

---

[8] *King-Ansell v. Police* [1979] 2 N.Z.L.R. 531, a decision of the New Zealand Court of Appeal.

England in *Commission for Racial Equality v. Dutton* [1989] IRLR 8 (CA) where the question for decision was whether gypsies constituted an ethnic group within the meaning of the 1976 Act.

In paragraph 12 of their reasons the Industrial Tribunal considered whether Rastafarians satisfied the first of the 'essential' conditions set out in Lord Fraser's speech [*i.e.* whether the group can show a shared history]. . . .

The Industrial Tribunal were divided on the question whether a shared tradition of just under 60 years was long enough. Two members of the Tribunal were of the opinion that in the circumstances the test of a long shared history was satisfied because the test had to be examined not only in relation to its actual length but also by reference to its continuity and persistence. The third member disagreed on the basis that a far longer period of time than 60 years was required before it could be said that a group possessed a long shared history.

In paragraph 13 of the reasons the Industrial Tribunal considered the other conditions set out in Lord Fraser's speech. The majority considered that the condition of a cultural tradition was satisfied. In addition there was a unanimous finding that Rastafarians had a common geographical origin in that their ancestors came from Jamaica. The reasons continued:

'There is some sort of common literature, there is not a common religion, they do have a sense of being a minority or being an oppressed group because of their peculiar customs.'

In the light of their findings the Industrial Tribunal decided by a majority of two to one that Rastafarians constituted a racial group within the definition in s 3(1) of the 1976 Act.

The PSA appealed.

The decision of The Employment Appeal Tribunal

The judgment of the Employment Appeal Tribunal was delivered by Tucker J. By a majority the appeal by the PSA was allowed. In their judgment the Employment Appeal Tribunal referred to the *Mandla* case and the *Dutton* case . . . . At [1991] ICR 583, 594 Tucker J. said:

'Applying those tests to Rastafarians, we ask whether they possess any of the characteristics of a race? We very much doubt whether the majority of Rastafarians can claim that they are of group descent, though some of them may be. Their geographical origin is Jamaica. We doubt whether they can be said to have a group history. . . . There is in our view insufficient to distinguish them from the rest of the Afro-Caribbean community so as to render them a separate group defined by reference to ethnic origins. They are a religious sect and no more.

In any event returning to Lord Fraser's test, we are unable to agree with the majority of the Industrial Tribunal that Rastafarians have a long shared history. It cannot reasonably be said that a movement which goes back for only 60 years, *i.e.* within the living memory of many people, can claim to be long in existence. Its history, in the judgment of the majority, is insufficiently sustained. The fact that the movement has maintained itself and still exists is insufficient. We have no hesitation in disagreeing with the conclusion of the majority of the Tribunal on this point, because first we do not regard it as a finding of fact, and secondly, even if it were we would regard it as a finding which no reasonable Tribunal could make, and therefore perverse.

So far as Lord Fraser's second essential test is concerned, that of a cultural tradition of its own, our view is that Rastafarians are a group with very little structure, no apparent organisation and having customs and practices which have evolved in a somewhat haphazard way. Nevertheless, notwithstanding these reservations and placing them in the context of a formerly enslaved people striving for an identity, there may be a sufficient cultural tradition to satisfy the test, and we are not prepared to disagree with the finding of the Tribunal on this point.

These are the views of the majority of the members of the Tribunal. One member dissents from them. On the basis of a book *One Love Rastafari: History, Doctrine and Livity* by Jah Bones (not referred to in argument before us) he is of the view that Rastafarians have a sufficiently long shared history to fulfil the test. In addition he would hold that they are more than a religious sect. However, by a majority, we allow the appeal for the reasons which we have expressed.' . . .

Do the Rastafarians constitute a racial group?

. . . I am unable to accept that the Industrial Tribunal's decision by a majority that Rastafarians had a sufficiently long shared history to satisfy Lord Fraser's first condition was merely a finding of fact with which an appellate court cannot interfere. The finding that a group originated in 1930 was indeed a finding of fact, but a decision as to the length of a shared history, which is necessary for the purpose of satisfying a statutory test, is a very different matter. In any event it is important to remember that the relevant words in the statute are 'ethnic origins'. . . .

It is clear that Rastafarians have certain identifiable characteristics. They have a strong cultural tradition which includes a distinctive form of music known as reggae music. They adopt a distinctive form of hairstyle by wearing dreadlocks. They have other shared characteristics of which both the Industrial Tribunal and the Employment Appeal Tribunal were satisfied. But the crucial question is whether they have established some separate identity by reference to their ethnic origins. In speaking about Rastafarians in this context I am referring to the core group, because I am satisfied that a core group can exist even though not all the adherents of the group could, if considered separately, satisfy any of the relevant tests.

It is at this stage that one has to take account of both the racial flavour of the word 'ethnic' and Lord Fraser's requirement of a long shared history. Lord Meston submitted that if one compared Rastafarians with the rest of the Afro-Caribbean community in this country, there was nothing to set them aside as a separate ethnic group. They are a separate group but not a separate group defined by reference to their ethnic origins. I see no answer to this submission.

Mr Whitmore quite rightly stressed that this case is concerned with identity. The question is: have the Rastafarians a separate ethnic identity? Do they stand apart by reason of their history from other Jamaicans?

In my judgment it is not enough for Rastafarians now to look back to a past when their ancestors, in common with other peoples in the Caribbean, were taken there from Africa. They were not a separate group then. The shared history of Rastafarians goes back only 60 years or so. One can understand and admire the deep affection which Rastafarians feel for Africa and their longing for it as their real home. But, as Mr Riza recognises, the court is concerned with the language of the statute. In the light of the guidance given by the House of Lords in *Mandla*, I am unable to say that they are a separate racial group.

I would dismiss the appeal.

Beldam L.J. I agree.

Sir John Megaw. I also agree.

Appeal dismissed with costs. Application for leave to appeal to the House of Lords refused."

QUESTIONS

- After reading *Dawkins*, do you have a clear sense of when a "shared history" becomes long?

- The majority of the Employment Appeal Tribunal described Rastafarian culture as "haphazard" and as lacking in structure and organisation. Are those relevant considerations? Is the development of a culture not always somewhat haphazard given that it depends upon historical circumstance? Why is the degree of structure and organisation relevant to a statute which deals with discrimination?

- Note how the Employment Appeal Tribunal and the Court of Appeal employ the fact- law distinction to overturn the Industrial Tribunal's finding that Rastafarians have a long shared history. Both the Employment Appeal Tribunal and the Court of Appeal held that this was a legal inference rather than a finding of fact. Is the fact-law distinction any clearer in your mind after reading this case (hint: it shouldn't be!)?

- Remember that nowhere in the statute is there a definition of ethnicity which depends upon the existence of a long shared history. Reread Lord Fraser's judgment in *Mandla v. Dowell Lee*. Is the existence of a long shared history a *necessary* requirement for the finding of an ethnic group in Lord Fraser's analysis?

Consider the following analysis of "race" in legal discourse:

Werner Menski, "Race and Law" in *The Critical Lawyers' Handbook 2* (Paddy Ireland and Per Laleng, eds., Pluto Press, London, 1997), pp. 67–69:

"Western legal systems have long operated a pattern of selective toleration and recognition of 'ethnic' needs and claims. This approach is problematic, since recognition of diversity has tended to be viewed as a favour which may be withheld by those in authority, not as an integral structural element. Such strategies of selective recognition inevitably produce conflicts. In fact, they end up discriminating: not only in Britain does 'ethnic' recognition by the official law clearly discriminate between different claimant groups. Although we cannot explore this in detail here, while various forms of Asian ethnicity are widely accepted in English law, those of African and Afro-Caribbean groups have tended to be dismissed, probably because they were assumed to be racial rather than cultural.

The underlying argument against the recognition of racial diversities, that colour is only socially but not legally relevant, and that at any rate uniformity is best, so that diversities and pluralisms should be ignored as far as possible, has landed English race relations law in a conceptual mess: while the purpose of the law would appear to be protection against discrimination, the case-law shows that even when racial discrimination admittedly took place, the law as it stands now will not protect victims of discrimination unless they can bring themselves under the increasingly arbitrary judicial definition of 'racial group' in s 3 of the Race Relations Act 1976. The case-law confirms this: Trevor Dawkins, a Rastafarian driver told to cut his hair if he wanted a job, found that the decision in his case contrasted somewhat illogically with the leading case of *Mandla*, in which a Sikh schoolboy had been told to cut his hair if he wanted admission to a particular school. The Sikh boy achieved the full protection of English law, but not the Rastafarian appellant. Thus, in virtually identical factual situations, English law today protected only members of certain 'racial groups', and on the basis of heavily contested criteria.

While principled arguments against the recognition of diversity appear rather too defensive at the end of the twentieth century, they do not take into account the apparent fact that even codified Western legal systems have been making all kinds of allowances for various forms of diversity. Presumably guided by sociolegal and 'race relations' expertise, the historical development of English law in this regard has relied on extra-legal expertise and political pressure rather than legal analysis. The law has been reactive, rather than proactive. The results seem deeply unsatisfactory in terms of intellectual clarity and cohesiveness. They are also politically insensitive, to say the least: the very legal framework which is supposed to improve 'race relations' actually does the reverse. Curiously, the general public in Britain as well as many lawyers remain unaware that the law has been protecting only certain 'racial groups', so that it remains perfectly possible to discriminate against the majority of non-white citizens and co-residents. Leading judges, in critical moments, have been looking for general dictionaries rather than specialist legal analysis. Such simplistic techniques of law-making, almost inevitably, lead to strange mistakes which then have to be rectified.

Lack of research and of clarity about 'race' and 'ethnicity' have been coupled with an aversion to address religious issues in legal contexts, especially in Parliament, granting privileged status to the Sikhs as a 'racial group' under the Race Relations Act. But the Court of Appeal in 1993, faced with a claim by Rastafarians to the same effect, and in almost identical circumstances, refused them recognition as a 'racial group', sidelining the questions of religion and ethnic identity. Yet what distinguished the Sikhs from other Punjabis other than their religion? Clearly, the liberal dreams of a progressive, protective evolution of the relevant definitions in the 1976 Act have been shattered."

Essay question

"The canon of literal interpretation enjoys an exaggerated authority and is believed to be far more productive of automatic solutions than it really is. As already stated, the judge's view of meaning is always coloured by his view of the particular facts before him, and he often makes a meaning for those facts without realizing it. So he frequently legislates unconsciously and therefore necessarily in accordance with his own private view of policy. This, of course, is undesirable and it is, to a great extent, unnecessary. The democratic method requires that policy should be determined by discussion and vote. And on the whole, the policy of legislation is largely determined by public pressure upon the legislature by means of public opinion and periodic elections. Though the intention of the legislature is a fiction, the purpose or object of the legislation is very real. No enactment is ever passed for the sake of its details; it is passed in an attempt to realize a social purpose. It is what is variously called the aim and object of the enactment, the spirit of the legislation, the mischief and the remedy. Though real, it is not always easily discoverable, even if the rules of interpretation permitted a proper search to be made for it. . . . The statute must be treated as a means to an end; the end should be determined by the social forces which brought it about and not by private choices of the judge. On the highroad of plain meaning, he follows the signposts as they appear. In the deep —and widespread—forests of ambiguity, the details in the foreground merely adds to the confusion. He should follow the compass—the object and purpose of the legislation. Where that fails, as it sometimes will, he can only trust himself."

[J.A. Corry, "Administrative Law and the Interpretation of Statutes" (1935) 1 University of Toronto Law Journal 286 at 292–293.]

Although Corry was writing in 1935, are his sentiments still relevant to the task of judicial interpretation of statutes? Use examples drawn from this chapter to support your argument.

8

STATUTORY INTERPRETATION: THE SEARCH FOR LEGISLATIVE INTENTION

In this chapter, we continue our focus on statutory interpretation. The emphasis, however, changes. In Chapter 7, we looked primarily to the meaning of statutory language itself. By contrast, in this chapter, we will turn to what judges often see as their primary role in statutory interpretation: determining the intention of the legislature which enacted the statute. We begin with an examination of the meaning of legislative "intent" and the idea of purposive interpretation. Then, we look at ways in which the courts engage in the pursuit of intention, both through "internal aids" to interpretation and "external aids" such as Hansard (the record of Parliamentary debates). We then focus on a central tension in statutory interpretation between the desire to interpret statutes in accordance with the intention of the legislature, and the need for interpretation to reflect (and help consolidate) social *change*. Following on from this, we look at what are commonly known as the rules or "canons" of interpretation.

THE ROLE OF INTENTION AND PURPOSE IN STATUTORY INTERPRETATION

Judges frequently justify the statutory interpretations which they adopt through the claim that they are advancing the "intention" of Parliament. This justification is wedded to the idea of Parliamentary supremacy: that judges simply apply the law which Parliament has enacted. However, the idea of legislative intention is a more slippery concept than one would think by reading the cases.

John Bell and Sir George Engle, *Cross on Statutory Interpretation* (3rd ed., Butterworths, London, 1995), pp. 24–27:

"The 'intention of Parliament' with regard to a particular statute cannot mean the intention of all those who were members of either House when the royal assent was given, for many of them might have been out of the country at all material times and never have heard of the statute. Equally plainly the phrase cannot mean the intention of the majority who voted for the statute as this will almost certainly have been constituted by different persons at the different stages of the passage of the Bill and, in any event, it would be rash to assume that all those who vote for it have the same intentions with regard to a particular piece of legislation. For example, it has been pointed out that, in a debate on what became the Statute of Westminster 1931, Winston Churchill and the Solicitor-General agreed that there was no obscurity in the provisions concerning the Irish Free State, although they took diametrically opposite views concerning their effect.

Someone bent on identifying the intention of specific human beings as that to which reference is made when people speak of the intention of Parliament might resort to the notion of agency. It could be said that the promoters of a Bill must have some consequences in mind as its general and particular effects, but promoters, whoever they may be, are initiators who place proposals before Parliament rather than act as its agents; and many Bills contain amendments which are not the work of the promoters. . . .

The court may justify the meaning it ultimately attaches to statutory words by suggesting that this is the meaning which, it believes, members of the legislature would have attached to them had the situation before the court been present to their minds. But, . . . the following words of a South African judge surely hold good for English law:

> 'Evidence that every member who voted for a measure put a certain construction upon it cannot affect the meaning which the court must place upon the statute, for it is the product, not of a number of individuals, but of an impersonal Parliament.'

This last quotation helps to make clear . . . that the question of legislative intention is not about the historical or hypothetical views of legislators, but rather concerns the meaning of words used in a particular context. The objective is not to reconstruct a psychological model of Parliament or the promoters of a Bill, or even of the drafter, and then to use it to determine what was meant by them when they used certain words, or what would have been provided had a particular eventuality been envisaged at the time of drafting or enactment. . . . Judges are concerned instead with using the conventions of ordinary language and of statutory interpretation to determine the meaning of words in their context. . . .

In the context of the interpretation of statutes there are three principal situations in which people in general and judges in particular speak of the intention of Parliament. In the first place, whenever the meaning of specific words is under consideration, the idea that a particular meaning is that which would or would not have been attached to a word or phrase by the average member of Parliament, sitting at the time when the statute was passed, may be expressed or refuted by some such statement as 'that is (or is not) what Parliament intended by those words'. Second, when the consequences of a particular construction are under consideration, the idea that a particular consequence might well have been in the mind of the average member of Parliament is often expressed by some such statement as 'that was likely (or unlikely) to have been the intention of Parliament'. Finally, although it is impossible to identify the individual members whose purpose it was, it is common to speak of the purpose, aim or object of a statute as the intention of Parliament. The third situation is the most important if only because reflection upon it shows that those who feel uncomfortable about the use of the expression 'intention of Parliament' ought not to feel any more at ease if they abandon the phrase for some other one such as 'the intention of the statute', 'legislative purpose' or 'the object of the statute'. Only human beings can really have intentions, purposes or objects, but, in the situation under consideration, the intentions, purposes or objects are not those of identifiable human beings. The words are used by close analogy to the intentions of a single legislator. The analogy is more remote when the 'intention of Parliament' is used as a synonym for what the average member of Parliament of a particular epoch would have meant by certain words or expected as the consequences of a statutory provision."

In addition, although we have suggested that judges frequently turn to the "ordinary meaning" of statutory language in interpretation, this approach also is closely connected to the idea of legislative *purpose*.

John Bell and Sir George Engle, *Cross on Statutory Interpretation* (3rd ed., Butterworths, London, 1995), p. 32:

" '[T]he context of ordinary language' already involves a certain number of assumptions. Even in ordinary language, words have more than one meaning, *e.g.* a 'chair' can be something to sit on, the president of a meeting, or a job as a professor. The ordinary user of language selects the appropriate 'ordinary meaning' according to the context in which a communication takes place. Certain assumptions are made about the most likely use of the words in this context. Those assumptions relate, in part, to the purpose of the speaker or writer—if the word 'chair' is used by a university in an advertisement on the jobs page of a newspaper, it is unlikely to intend to refer to furniture. We still refer to this as an interpretation by reference to 'ordinary meaning' because the reader is able to rely on an immediate understanding of the purpose behind the use of the words without engaging in any further research. If this interpretation of the writer's words proves to be wrong, the reader can rightly complain that a warning should have been given that it was necessary to read the words in a different, less immediate context. Thus, an 'ordinary meaning' or 'grammatical meaning' does not imply that the judge attributes a meaning to the words of a statute independently of their context or of the purpose of the statute, but rather that he adopts a meaning which is appropriate in relation to the immediately obvious and unresearched context and purpose in and for which they are used. By enabling citizens (and their advisers) to rely on ordinary meanings unless notice is given to the contrary, the legislature contributes to legal certainty and predictability for citizens and to greater transparency in its own decisions, both of which are important values in a democratic society".

The judicial role in relation to purpose of the statute and intention of the legislature sometimes has been explicitly considered by the judiciary.

Duport Steels Ltd and others v. Sirs and others [1980] 1 All E.R. 529, HL.

[The appeal concerned the interpretation of the Trade Union and Labour Relations Act 1974 and, in particular, whether the decision of a union in dispute with (the publicly owned) British Steel Corporation to extend a strike to the private steel sector was an action "in . . . furtherance of a trade dispute" and therefore not subject to a potential prosecution in tort. The House of Lords unanimously reversed the decision of the Court of Appeal (which included Lord Denning M.R.) which had found against the union.][1]

Lord Scarman:
". . . [I]n the field of statute law the judge must be obedient to the will of Parliament as expressed in its enactments. In this field Parliament makes and unmakes the law, the judge's duty is to interpret and to apply the law, not to change it to meet the judge's idea of what justice requires. Interpretation does, of course, imply in the interpreter a power of choice where differing constructions are possible. But our law requires the judge to choose the construction which in his judgment best meets the legislative purpose of the enactment. If the result be unjust but inevitable, the judge may say so and invite Parliament to reconsider its provision. But he must not deny the statute. Unpalatable statute law may not be disregarded or rejected, merely because it is unpalatable. Only if a just result can be achieved without violating the legislative purpose of the statute may the judge select the construction which best suits his idea of what justice requires. Further, in our system the *stare decisis* rule applies as firmly to statute law as it does to the formulation of common law and equitable principles. And the keystone of *stare decisis* is loyalty throughout the system to the decisions of the Court of Appeal and this House. The Court of Appeal may not overrule a House of Lords decision; and only in the exceptional circumstances set out in the practice statement of 26 July 1966 will this House refuse to follow its own previous decisions.

Within these limits, which cannot be said in a free society possessing elective legislative institutions to be narrow or constrained, judges, as the remarkable judicial career of Lord

[1] For a discussion of this and related cases, see J.A.G. Griffith, *The Politics of the Judiciary* (4th ed., Harper Collins, London, 1991), pp. 93–99.

Denning M.R. himself shows, have a genuine creative role. Greater judges are in their different ways judicial activists. But the Constitution's separation of powers, or more accurately functions, must be observed if judicial independence is not to be put at risk. For, if people and Parliament come to think that the judicial power is to be confined by nothing other than the judge's sense of what is right (or, as Selden put it, by the length of the Chancellor's foot), confidence in the judicial system will be replaced by fear of it becoming uncertain and arbitrary in its application. Society will then be ready for Parliament to cut the power of the judges. Their power to do justice will become more restricted by law than it need be, or is today. . . ."

FURTHER READING

On statutory interpretation and legislative intention, the following provide interesting background material: William N. Eskridge Junior, *Dynamic Statutory Interpretation* (Harvard University Press, Cambridge, MA, 1994); Stanley Fish, *Doing What Comes Naturally: Change, Rhetoric, and the Practice of Theory in Literary and Legal Studies* (Clarendon Press, Oxford, 1989); A. Raymond Randolph, "Dictionaries, Plain Meaning, and Context in Statutory Interpretation" (1994) 17 Harvard Journal of Law and Public Policy 71; David Miers, "Legal Theory and the Interpretation of Statutes" in *Legal Theory and Common Law* (William Twining, ed., Blackwell, Oxford, 1986), p. 115.

INTERNAL AIDS TO DISCERNING INTENTION

To this point, our analysis of statutory interpretation has focused primarily upon the particular words which give rise to interpretive questions. But judges often find guidance to interpretation in *other* words within the context of the statute as a whole.[2] Thus, for example, it is commonly stated that "an act should be read as a whole". Thus, in order to understand the meaning of a word or phrase, it may well be helpful to look at the broader *context* of the statute as a whole, which may shed light on the particular interpretive question.

As well, there are a number of "rules" regarding the *admissibility* and *weight* of what are referred to as "internal aids" to the construction of statutes; that is, parts of a statute other than the enacted clauses themselves. These "rules" may seem quite arbitrary, but you should at least be aware that they exist.

Ian McLeod, *Legal Method* (2nd ed., Macmillan, Basingstoke, 1996), pp. 285–290:

The anatomy of a statute

Preambles

"Where there is a preamble to a statute it will recite the reasons why the statute was passed. However, modern drafting practice in relation to Public Bills has almost entirely dispensed

---

[2] See, *e.g. Courtauld v. Legh* (1869) L.R. 4 Exch. 126; *R. v. Allen* (1872) L.R. 1 C.C.R. 367; *R. v. Millward* [1985] 1 All E.R. 859.

with the use of preambles, although they still appear in Private Bills, and therefore in Private Acts. It follows that their status for the purposes of interpretation is relatively insignificant in quantitative terms. Nevertheless, preambles are encountered from time to time, and their status is quite clear. According to Lord Normand in *Attorney-General v. Prince Ernest Augustus of Hanover* [1957] 1 All ER 49: 'It is only when it conveys a clear and definite meaning in comparison with relatively obscure or indefinite enacting words that the preamble may legitimately prevail.' . . .

Long titles

Long titles have the same status as preambles, but they are much more important in practice because all statutes have them. In *R. v. Galvin* [1987] 2 All ER 851, Lord Lane C.J., speaking of the Official Secrets Act 1911, and its predecessor of 1889, said:

'One can have regard to the title of a statute to help resolve an ambiguity in the body of it, but it is not, we consider, open to a court to use the title to restrict what is otherwise the plain meaning of the words of the statute simply because they seem to be unduly wide.' . . .

Short titles

The short title is almost always found towards the end of the statute. The leading case is *R. v. Boaler* [1915] 1 KB 21, where it was acknowledged that the short title is part of the Act, and as such the court can and should consider it. However, it is by definition a *short* title and therefore, as Scrutton L.J. said, 'accuracy may be sacrificed to brevity'. Moreover, particular care should be taken when dealing with the short titles of old Acts. Before 1896 it was not the practice for Acts to have short titles, but the Short Titles Act of that year conferred short titles on many older Acts. However, all the short titles were not necessarily appropriate, so that, for example, the short title of the Criminal Procedure Act was given to one statute passed in 1865 which dealt with both criminal and civil procedure.

Headings, marginal notes and punctuation

A glance at any substantial statute will reveal a collection of *headings* (also known as *cross-headings*) between groups of sections, and *marginal notes* (also known as *side-notes* or *shoulder notes*) in the margin. These are both inserted by the drafter and are never subject to debate by Parliament. Where the text of a Bill is amended during its passage through Parliament, it is a matter for the drafter to amend these headings and notes appropriately. The best drafting practice, where this would cause problems, is to replace the original text with a whole new section, complete with a new heading or marginal note, as appropriate. It follows that where this has not been done, the original marginal notes and headings should be treated with a great deal of caution. However, leaving aside such special cases and returning to the mainstream, there is a reasonably clear judicial consensus that marginal notes and headings are relevant to the process of interpretation, 'provided that we realise that they cannot have equal weight with the words of the Act' (Lord Reid in *Director of Public Prosecutions v. Schildkamp* [1969] 3 All ER 1640).

Schedules

Bennion explains the nature of schedules:

'It is often convenient to incorporate part of the operative provisions of an Act in the form of a schedule. The schedule is often used to hive off provisions which are too long or detailed to be put in the body of the Act. This does not mean they are unimportant.'

As Brett L.J. said in *Attorney-General v. Lamplough* (1878) 3 ExD 214: 'A schedule in an Act is a mere question of drafting, a mere question of words. The schedule is as much a part of the statute, and is as much an enactment, as any other part.'

In *Re Baines* (1840) 41 ER 401 Lord Cottenham L.C. held that where there is inconsistency between the body of the Act and a schedule, the body of the Act should prevail. . . . Issues of this type are best resolved by recalling the fundamental principle that an Act should be construed as a whole, and attempting to give the best possible meaning to the words which have been used, having regard to the statutory purpose. . . .

Definition sections

Definition sections, which are commonly found towards the end of statutes but towards the beginning of statutory instruments, contain provisions of two types. First there are those which simply state that the defined terms shall 'mean' whatever the provision states them to mean. Second, there are those which state that the defined terms shall 'include' whatever the provision states them to include. In cases falling within the latter category the words will have not only their special statutory meaning but, according to Lord Selborne L.C. in *Robinson v. Barton-Eccles Local Board* (1883) 8 App. Cas. 798, they will also possess their 'ordinary, popular and natural sense whenever that would be applicable'. In other words, this category does not enact definitions in the strict sense of the term, since it is in the nature of a definition to restrict, rather than simply to illustrate, the meaning of a word. . . .

Commencement sections

Commencement sections are commonly found towards the end of statutes. Section 4 of the Interpretation Act 1978, whose ancestry can be traced to the Acts of Parliament (Commencement) Act 1793, states that, where provision is made for an Act or part of an Act to come into force on a particular day, it comes into force at the beginning of that day; and that, where no such provision is made, an Act comes into force at the beginning of the day on which it receives the Royal Assent. The limited degree of retrospectivity inherent in this provision appears to cause no injustice in practice, and is in any event a marked improvement over the pre-1793 position, when Acts took effect from the beginning of the Parliamentary session in which they were passed. . . .

In practice it is common for statutes to state that they will come into force either on a particular future date, or on the expiry of a stated period (commonly two months) after they receive the Royal Assent, but a degree of flexibility is often preserved by enacting a provision to the effect that the Act will come into force on whatever day may be appointed by the appropriate Secretary of State, who will usually be empowered to make a commencement order by way of a statutory instrument. . . .

It is common for different parts of the same Act to come into force on different days, and it is not unknown for provisions which are not yet in force to be amended, or even repealed."

ASSIGNMENT

Go to your law library and take a look at the statute books. Try and find the various parts of statutes which McLeod has outlined.

EXTERNAL AIDS TO DISCERNING INTENTION

If the task of the judiciary in interpreting legislation is to seek out the intention of the legislature, then intuitively it would seem reasonable that judges turn to those materials produced by Parliament which might well describe what Parliament had in mind when it was enacting new law. Although a variety of documents are produced by

Parliament which might provide some insight into its intention regarding a statutory word or phrase, the most obvious source undoubtedly is *Hansard*: the record of the debates in the two Houses of Parliament. It will perhaps come as a surprise to you that until recently these debates were not *admissible* in courts, (*i.e.* counsel was not allowed to introduce them as evidence into court) in order to assist in determining the meaning of a statute. As Lord Simonds explained:

> "The part which is played in the judicial interpretation of a statute by reference to the circumstances of its passing is too well known to need re-statement. It is suffi-cient to say that the general proposition that it is the duty of the court to find out the intention of Parliament—and not only of Parliament but of Ministers also—cannot by any means be supported. The duty of the court is to interpret the words that the legislature has used. Those words may be ambiguous, but, even if they are, the power and duty of the court to travel outside them on a voyage of discovery are strictly limited."[3]

The relationship between what may have been intended by the legislature, and what was actually enacted, was described by the Earl of Halsbury L.C. As Lord Chancellor (a member of the government), he had been responsible for legislation. Yet, as a member of the House of Lords, he was charged with the ultimate judicial function. In *Hilder v. Dexter* [1902] A.C. 474, the Earl of Halsbury discussed this anomalous situ-ation, and decided to remove himself from the task of statutory interpretation in that case:

> "My Lords, I have more than once had occasion to say that in construing a statute I believe the worst person to construe it is the person who is responsible for its draft-ing. He is very much disposed to confuse what he intended to do with the effect of the language which in fact has been employed. At the time he drafted the statute, at all events, he may have been under the impression that he had given full effect to what was intended, but he may be mistaken in construing it afterwards just because what was in his mind was what was intended, though, perhaps, it was not done. For that reason I abstain from giving any judgment in this case myself; but at the same time I desire to say, having read the judgments proposed to be delivered by my noble and learned friends, that I entirely concur with every word of them. I believe that the construction at which they have arrived was the intention of the statute. I do not say my intention, but the intention of the Legislature. I was largely responsible for the language in which the enactment is conveyed, and for that reason, and for that reason only, I have not written a judgment myself, but I heartily concur in the judg-ment which my noble and learned friends have arrived at (pp. 477–478)."

Note especially how the Earl of Halsbury differentiates between the intention of the individual responsible for the drafting of a piece of legislation, and the intention of the legislature as a whole. This distinction remains an important one, which we will explore in this chapter. The traditional approach to *Hansard* was substantially modified in 1992, when the House of Lords took the opportunity to change the rule.

---

[3] *Magor and St Mellons Rural District Council v. Newport Corporation* [1951] 2 All E.R. 839 at 841, HL.

Pepper (Inspector of Taxes) v. Hart and related appeals [1993] 1 All E.R. 42, HL.

[The background to the case has been summarized by Bale]:

"*Pepper v. Hart* was initially a run of the mill tax case involving the valuation of a fringe benefit. The taxpayers were nine teachers and the bursar of Malvern College who took advantage of a scheme which permitted staff members to have their children educated at the school for only 2% of the fees payable by the public. As higher-paid employees they were required to include in their income, as a benefit of employment, the cash equivalent of the benefit which s 63(1) of the Finance Act 1976 defined as 'an amount equal to the cost of benefit less so much (if any) of it as is made good by the employee to those providing the benefit.' The taxpayers contended that the cost of the benefit was the additional or marginal cost of educating an additional student in a school that had surplus capacity and, since this was less than the concessionary fees paid by them, the cash equivalent of the benefit was nil. The Revenue contended the cost of the benefit was the same for all pupils, namely, the average cost of educating each pupil. The taxpayers won before the special commissioner but the decision was reversed by Vinelott J., and that decision was affirmed by the Court of Appeal. The taxpayers then appealed to the House of Lords. After the first hearing before a panel of five Law Lords, three supported the assessment made by the Revenue and two would have held for the taxpayers. However, before the Lords rendered their decision, the debate in the House of Commons in 1976 concerning the Finance Bill came to their attention. The Financial Secretary in reply to a specific question about the tax treatment of concessionary fees for children of school staff stated that 'the benefit will be assessed on the cost to the employer, which would be very small indeed in this case.' Hansard clearly indicated that in determining the benefit to the employee the marginal cost and not the average cost was intended under the Finance Act 1976."[4]

Lord Mackay of Clashfern L.C., dissenting [Lord Mackay's discussion of the factual background to the case has been omitted]:

"... But much wider issues than the construction of the Finance Act 1976 have been raised in these appeals and for the first time this House has been asked to consider a detailed argument on the extent to which reference can properly be made before a court of law in the United Kingdom to proceedings in Parliament recorded in Hansard....

The principal difficulty I have on this aspect of the case is that in Mr Lester's submission reference to parliamentary material as an aid to interpretation of a statutory provision should be allowed only with leave of the court and where the court is satisfied that such a reference is justifiable (a) to confirm the meaning of a provision as conveyed by the text, its object and purpose, (b) to determine a meaning where the provision is ambiguous or obscure or (c) to determine the meaning where the ordinary meaning is manifestly absurd or unreasonable.

I believe that practically every question of statutory construction that comes before the courts will involve an argument that the case falls under one or more of these three heads. It follows that the parties' legal advisers will require to study Hansard in practically every such case to see whether or not there is any help to be gained from it. I believe this is an objection of real substance. It is a practical objection, not one of principle....

Your Lordships are well aware that the costs of litigation are a subject of general public concern and I personally would not wish to be a party to changing a well-established rule which could have a substantial effect in increasing these costs against the advice of the Law Commission and the Renton Committee unless and until a new inquiry demonstrated that that advice was no longer valid.

I do not for my part find the objections in principle to be strong and I would certainly be prepared to agree the rule should no longer be adhered to were it not for the practical consideration to which I have referred and which my noble and learned friend agrees to be of real

[4] Gordon Bale, "Parliamentary Debates and Statutory Interpretation: Switching on the Light or Rummaging in the Ashcans of the Legislative Process" (1995) 74 Canadian Bar Review 1 at 13.

substance. . . . If reference to parliamentary material is permitted as an aid to the construction of legislation which is ambiguous, or obscure or the literal meaning of which leads to an absurdity, I believe as I have said that in practically every case it will be incumbent on those preparing the argument to examine the whole proceedings on the Bill in question in both Houses of Parliament. Questions of construction may be involved on what is said in Parliament and I cannot see how if the rule is modified in this way the parties' legal advisers could properly come to court without having looked to see whether there was anything in the Hansard report on the Bill which could assist their case. If they found a passage which they thought had a bearing on the issue in this case, that passage would have to be construed in the light of the proceedings as a whole.

I fully appreciate, and feel the force of the narrowness of the distinctions which are taken between what is admissible and what is not admissible, but the exception presently proposed is so extensive that I do not feel able to support it in the present state of our knowledge of its practical results in this jurisdiction. For these reasons, I agree that these appeals should be allowed, although I cannot agree on the main issue for the discussion of which this further hearing was arranged."

Lord Browne-Wilkinson [The discussion of the factual and legislative background has been omitted]:

Should the rule prohibiting reference to parliamentary privilege be relaxed?

"Under present law, there is a general rule that references to parliamentary material as an aid to statutory construction is not permissible (the exclusionary rule) (see *Davis v. Johnson* [1978] 1 All ER 1132, [1979] AC 264 and *Hadmor Productions Ltd v. Hamilton* [1981] 2 All ER 724, [1983] 1 AC 191). This rule did not always apply but was judge-made. Thus, in *Ash v. Abdy* (1678) 3 Swan 664, 36 ER 114 Lord Nottingham L.C. took judicial notice of his own experience when introducing the Bill in the House of Lords. The exclusionary rule was probably first stated by Willes J. in *Millar v. Taylor* (1769) 4 Burr 233 at 2332, 98 ER 21 at 217. However, *Re Mew and Throne* (1862) 31 L.J. Bcy 87 shows that even in the middle of the last century the rule was not absolute: in that case Lord Westbury L.C. in construing an Act had regard to its parliamentary history and drew an inference as to Parliament's intention in passing the legislation from the making of amendment striking out certain words.

The exclusionary rule was later extended so as to prohibit the court from looking even at reports made by commissioners on which legislation was based (see *Salkeld v. Johnson* (1848) 2 Exch 256 at 273, 154 ER 487 at 495). This rule has now been relaxed so as to permit reports of commissioners, including Law Commissioners, and white papers to be looked at for the purpose solely of ascertaining the mischief which the statute is intended to cure but not for the purpose of discovering the meaning of the words used by Parliament to effect such cure. . . . Indeed, in *Factortame Ltd v. Secretary of State for Transport* [1989] 2 All ER 692, [1990] 2 AC 85 your Lordships' House went further than this and had regard to a Law Commission report not only for the purpose of ascertaining the mischief but also for the purpose of drawing an inference as to parliamentary intention from the fact that Parliament had not expressly implemented one of the Law Commission's recommendations. . . .

[T]he reasons put forward for the present rule are, first, that it preserves the constitutional proprieties, leaving Parliament to legislate in words and the courts (not parliamentary speakers) to construe the meaning of the words finally enacted, second, the practical difficulty of the expense of researching parliamentary material which would arise if the material could be looked at, third, the need for the citizen to have access to a known defined text which regulates his legal rights and, fourth, the improbability of finding helpful guidance from Hansard.

The Law Commissions of England and Scotland in their joint report on *Interpretation of Statutes* and the Renton Committee on *Preparation of Legislation* both recognised that there was much to be said in principle for relaxing the rule but advised against a relaxation at present on the same practical grounds as are reflected in the authorities. However, both bodies recommended changes in the form of legislation which would, if implemented, have assisted the court in its search for the true parliamentary intention in using the statutory words. . . .

My Lords, I have come to the conclusion that, as a matter of law, there are sound reasons for making a limited modification to the existing rule (subject to strict safeguards) unless there are constitutional or practical reasons which outweigh them. In my judgment, subject to the questions of the privileges of the House of Commons, reference to parliamentary material should be permitted as an aid to the construction of legislation which is ambiguous or obscure or the literal meaning of which leads to an absurdity. Even in such cases references in court to parliamentary material should only be permitted where such material clearly discloses the mischief aimed at or the legislative intention lying behind the ambiguous or obscure words. In the case of statements made in Parliament, as at present advised I cannot foresee that any statement other than the statement of the minister or other promoter of the Bill is likely to meet these criteria.

I accept Mr Lester's submissions, but my main reason for reaching this conclusion is based on principle. Statute law consists of the words that Parliament has enacted. It is for the courts to construe those words and it is the court's duty in so doing to give effect to the intention of Parliament in using those words. It is an inescapable fact that, despite all the care taken in passing legislation, some statutory provisions when applied to the circumstances under consideration in any specific case are found to be ambiguous. One of the reasons for such ambiguity is that the members of the legislature in enacting the statutory provision may have been told what result those words are intended to achieve. Faced with a given set of words which are capable of conveying that meaning it is not surprising if the words are accepted as having that meaning. Parliament never intends to enact any ambiguity. Contrast with that the position of the courts. The courts are faced simply with a set of words which are in fact capable of bearing two meanings. The courts are ignorant of the underlying parliamentary purpose. Unless something in other parts of the legislation discloses such purpose, the courts are forced to adopt one of the two possible meanings using highly technical rules of construction. In many, I suspect most, cases references to parliamentary materials will not throw any light on the matter. But in a few cases it may emerge that the very question was considered by Parliament in passing the legislation. Why in such a case should the courts blind themselves to a clear indication of what Parliament intended in using those words? The court cannot attach a meaning to words which they cannot bear, but if the words are capable of bearing more than one meaning why should not Parliament's true intention be enforced rather than thwarted?

A number of other factors support this view. As I have said, the courts can now look at white papers and official reports for the purpose of finding the 'mischief' sought to be corrected, although not at draft clauses or proposals for the remedying of such mischief. A ministerial statement made in Parliament is an equally authoritative source of such information; why should the courts be cut off from this source of information as to the mischief aimed at? In any event, the distinction between looking at reports to identify the mischief aimed at but not to find the intention of Parliament in enacting the legislation is highly artificial. Take the normal Law Commission report which analyses the problem and then annexes a draft Bill to remedy it. It is now permissible to look at the report to find the mischief and at the draft Bill to see that a provision in the draft was *not* included in the legislation enacted (see *Factortame v. Secretary of State for Transport* [1989] 2 ALL ER 692, [1990] 2 AC 85). There can be no logical distinction between that case and looking at the draft Bill to see that the statute as enacted reproduced, often in the same words, the provision in the Law Commission's draft. Given the purposive approach to construction now adopted by the courts in order to give effect to the true intentions of the legislature, the fine distinctions between looking for the mischief and looking for the intention in using words to provide the remedy are technical and inappropriate. Clear and unambiguous statements made by ministers in Parliament are as much the background to the enactment of legislation as white papers and parliamentary reports. . . .

It is said that parliamentary materials are not readily available to, and understandable by, the citizen and his lawyers, who should be entitled to rely on the words of Parliament alone to discover his position. It is undoubtedly true that Hansard and particularly records of committee debates are not widely held by libraries outside London and that the lack of satisfactory indexing of committee stages makes it difficult to trace the passage of a clause after it is redrafted or renumbered. But such practical difficulties can easily be overstated. It is possible to obtain parliamentary materials and it is possible to trace the history. The problem is one of expense and effort in doing so, not the availability of the material. In considering the right of the individual to know the law by simply looking at legislation, it is a fallacy to start from the position that all legislation is available in a readily understandable form in any event: the very large number of statutory instruments made every year are not available in an indexed form for well over a year after they have been passed. Yet, the practitioner manages to deal with the problem, albeit at considerable expense. Moreover, experience in New Zealand and Australia (where the strict rule has been relaxed for some years) has not shown that the non-availability of materials has raised these practical problems.

Next, it is said that lawyers and judges are not familiar with parliamentary procedures and will therefore have difficulty in giving proper weight to the parliamentary materials. Although, of course, lawyers do not have the same experience of these matters as members of the legislature, they are not wholly ignorant of them. If, as I think, significance should only be attached to the clear statements made by a minister or other promoter of the Bill, the difficulty of knowing what weight to attach to such statements is not overwhelming. In the present case, there were numerous statements of view by members in the course of the debate which plainly do not throw any light on the true construction of s 63. What is persuasive in this case is a consistent series of answers given by the minister, after opportunities for taking advice from his officials, all of which point the same way and which were not withdrawn or varied prior to the enactment of the Bill.

Then it is said that court time will be taken up by considering a mass of parliamentary material and long arguments about its significance, thereby increasing the expense of litigation. In my judgment, though the introduction of further admissible material will inevitably involve some increase in the use of time, this will not be significant as long as courts insist that parliamentary material should only be introduced in the limited cases I have mentioned and where such material contains a clear indication from the minister of the mischief aimed at, or the nature of the cure intended, by the legislation. Attempts to introduce material which does not satisfy those tests should be met by orders for costs made against those who have improperly introduced the material. Experience in the United States of America, where legislative history has for many years been much more generally admissible than I am now suggesting, shows how important it is to maintain strict control over the use of such material. That position is to be contrasted with what has happened in New Zealand and Australia (which have relaxed the rule to approximately the extent that I favour): there is no evidence of any complaints of this nature coming from those countries.

There is one further practical objection which, in my view, has real substance. If the rule is relaxed legal advisors faced with an ambiguous statutory provision may feel that they have to research the materials to see whether they yield the crock of gold, *i.e.* a clear indication of Parliament's intentions. In very many cases the crock of gold will not be discovered and the expenditure on the research wasted. This is a real objection to changing the rule. However, again it is easy to overestimate the cost of such research: if a reading of Hansard shows that there is nothing of significance said by the minister in relation to the clause in question, further research will become pointless.

In sum, I do not think that the practical difficulties arising from a limited relaxation of the rule are sufficient to outweigh the basic need for the courts to give effect to the words enacted by Parliament in the sense that they were intended by Parliament to bear. Courts are frequently criticised for their failure to do that. This failure is due not to cussedness but to ignorance of what Parliament intended by the obscure words of the legislation. The courts should not deny themselves the light which parliamentary materials may shed on the meaning of the words Parliament has used and thereby risk subjecting the individual to a law which Parliament never intended to enact.

Is there, then, any constitutional objection to a relaxation of the rule? The main constitutional ground urged by the Attorney General is that the use of such material will infringe s 1, art 9 of the Bill of Rights as being a questioning in any court of freedom of speech and debates in Parliament. As I understand the submission, the Attorney General was not contending that the use of parliamentary material by the courts for the purposes of construction would constitute an 'impeachment' of freedom of speech since impeachment is limited to cases where a member of Parliament is sought to be made liable, either in criminal or civil proceedings, for what he has said in Parliament, *e.g.* by criminal prosecution, by action for libel or by seeking to prove malice on the basis of such words. The submission was that the use of Hansard for the purpose of construing an Act would constitute a 'questioning' of the freedom of speech or debate. The process, it is said, would involve an investigation of what the minister meant by the words he used and would inhibit the minister in what he says by attaching legislative effect to his words. This, it was submitted, constituted 'questioning' the freedom of speech or debate.

Article 9 is a provision of the highest constitutional importance and should not be narrowly construed. It ensures the ability of democratically elected members of Parliament to discuss what they will (freedom of debate) and to say what they will (freedom of speech). But, even given a generous approach to this construction, I find it impossible to attach the breadth of meaning to the word 'question' which the Attorney General urges. It must be remembered that art 9 prohibits questioning not only 'in any court' but also in any 'place out of Parliament'. If the Attorney General's submission is correct, any comment in the media or elsewhere on what is said in Parliament would constitute 'questioning' since all members of Parliament must speak and act taking into account what political commentators and others will say. Plainly art 9 cannot have effect so as to stifle the freedom of all to comment on what is said in Parliament, even though such comment may influence members in what they say.

In my judgment, the plain meaning of art 9, viewed against the historical background in which it was enacted, was to ensure that members of Parliament were not subjected to any penalty, civil or criminal, for what they said and were able, contrary to the previous assertions of the Stuart monarchy, to discuss what they, as opposed to the monarch, chose to have discussed. Relaxation of the rule will not involve the courts in criticising what is said in Parliament. The purpose of looking at Hansard will not be to construe the words used by the minister but to give effect to the words used so long as they are clear. Far from questioning the independence of Parliament and its debates, the courts would be giving effect to what is said and done there. . . .

According to my judgment the use of clear ministerial statements by the court as a guide to the construction of ambiguous legislation would not contravene art 9. No doubt all judges will be astute to ensure that counsel does not in any way impugn or criticise the minister's statement or his reasoning.

The Attorney General raised a further constitutional point, namely that for the court to use parliamentary material in construing legislation would be to confuse the respective roles of Parliament as the maker of law and the courts as the interpreter. I am not impressed by this argument. The law, as I have said, is to be found in the words in which Parliament has enacted. It is for the courts to interpret those words so as to give effect to that purpose. The question is whether, in addition to other aids to the construction of statutory words, the courts should have regard to a further source. Recourse is already had to white papers and official reports not because they determine the meaning of the statutory words but because they assist the court to make its own determination. I can see no constitutional impropriety in this.

Finally, on this aspect of the case, the Attorney General relied on considerations of comity: the relaxation of the rule would have a direct effect on the rights and privileges of Parliament. To the extent that such rights and privileges are to be found in the Bill of Rights, in my judgment they will not be infringed for the reasons which I have given. . . .

I therefore reach the conclusion . . . that the exclusionary rule should be relaxed so as to permit reference to parliamentary materials where: (a) legislation is ambiguous or obscure, or leads to an absurdity; (b) the material relied on consists of one or more statements by a minister or other promoter of the Bill together if necessary with such other parliamentary material as is necessary to understand such statements and their effect; (c) the statements relied on are clear. Further than this, I would not at present go. . . ."

[Lord Keith of Kinkel, Lord Bridge of Harwich, Lord Griffiths, Lord Ackner, Lord Oliver of Aylmerton all concurred in their reasons with Lord Browne-Wilkinson on the admissibility of Hansard in judicial proceedings. The appeal was allowed with costs.]

The decision in *Pepper v. Hart* undoubtedly will be of significance for statutory interpretation in the years to come. The reasons why the House of Lords decided to alter its historical approach to Parliamentary materials are varied.

Gordon Bale, "Parliamentary Debates and Statutory Interpretation: Switching on the Light or Rummaging in the Ashcans of the Legislative Process" (1995) 74 Canadian Bar Review 1 at 17:

"A number of reasons combined to bring about the demise of the exclusionary rule. Perhaps the most important is the move toward a purposive approach to statutory interpretation that has gained momentum in Britain in the last four decades. Also the volume and complexity of modern statutes has required the judiciary to seek greater knowledge of the legislative context in order to construe them properly. There has been growing realization that the canons of interpretation are simply a grab bag of conflicting presumptions that offer little guidance to the proper interpretation of statutes. The powerful European influence exerted through greater contact with decisions of the European Court of Justice and the European Court of Human Rights has reinforced the advantage of a purposive approach to legislation in place of literal interpretation. Commonwealth countries, particularly Australia and New Zealand, have thrown out the traditional exclusionary rule. That this has been achieved without adverse consequences has exerted an influence in Britain. Another factor is that in spite of the rule judges frequently do look to the debates for guidance or to check that their interpretation accords with the purpose of the statute. Many counsel regarded this surreptitious peek at Hansard to be unfair to litigants because the exclusionary rule prevented them from making any submissions about the relevance and weight to accord the parliamentary record. Finally courts do not focus solely on the statute but look to extrinsic aids such as Reports of Royal Commissions, Law Commission Reports and White Papers at least to perceive the problem with which the statute was intended to cope. Admitting these extrinsic aids while excluding the sometimes more relevant parliamentary debates became logically indefensible. In view of the purposive approach to statutory interpretation the highly artificial distinction between looking for the mischief and not the intent appeared increasingly technical and inappropriate. Finally, counsel by wisely arguing for only limited modification of the exclusionary rule finessed the rule of law requirement that the statute book must remain a reliable guide to the citizen. Hansard will only be consulted when legislation is ambiguous, obscure or leads to an absurdity. The courts as interpreters will still be confined *by* the text but in the case of ambiguity they will not be confined *to* it. The appropriate separation of powers between parliament and the courts will be preserved."

The impact of the House of Lords decision in *Pepper v. Hart* will be felt by practitioners, courts, and Parliament alike. The impact on the practitioner was explicitly recognised by the Law Lords, and will be significant, with a resulting impact on the users of legal services.

T.St.J.N. Bates, "The Contemporary Use of Legislative History in the United Kingdom" (1995) 54 C.L.J. 127 at 136:

"The majority of the Law Lords may have considered these various difficulties would have a limited practical effect because the relaxation of the exclusionary rule was thought to have been carefully circumscribed and would, in any event, be policed by orders for costs. . . . However that may be, the assessment of the majority of the Law Lords has not been shared by the experienced practitioner nor is it borne out by practice. For example James Goudie

Q.C. has observed that standing committee debates, where much relevant material is likely to be found, are not held at all by the (English) Law Society, by the Supreme Court Library, or by the libraries of three of the Inns of Court and only partially by the fourth; and a few other libraries in London have incomplete sets on closed access or in store requiring advance notice. He described the position outside London as 'dire almost to the point of being non-existent'. In times of economic stringency the position of academic law libraries may be even worse. On a visit to Cambridge, the writer was informed that in 1991, as an economy measure, the Squire Law Library ceased even to take the Hansard reports of proceedings on the floor of the Commons and the Lords, let alone of standing committee debates, although they are still held by the University Library. . . .

The concerns of the practitioner are further exacerbated by the possibility that if there is a failure to research the full parliamentary material in advising a client on a question of statutory interpretation the practitioner may be liable for a breach of professional duty. Indeed some members of the English Bar have adopted the practice in their opinion work, both to avoid liability and reduce costs for the client, of including a disclaimer that the opinion has not involved researching the parliamentary material which as a result of *Pepper v. Hart* may be relevant to a question of interpretation. The client, for a further fee, may then presumably request the research to be undertaken."

The impact of *Pepper v. Hart* will also be felt by Parliament.

David Miers, "Taxing Perks and Interpreting Statutes: *Pepper v. Hart*" (1993) 56 M.L.R. 695 at 706:

". . . But what are the longer term implications of *Pepper v. Hart* upon the preparation and interpretation of legislation? Consider first the impact of the House's decision on the function of parliamentary debate on Bills. As *Pepper v. Hart* gives the government the opportunity to say in other words what the legal effect of a clause is to be, there will be an incentive to use the opportunity whenever some particularly difficult piece of legislation is to be debated, as a way of increasing the chances that the courts will interpret the section as the government wishes. Are we therefore to see (like planted Parliamentary Questions) carefully framed amendments at the Committee stage (which will of course need to be selected by the Chairman) permitting Ministers to clarify what kinds of conduct fall within a given clause? But precisely because judicial reliance may be placed upon their remarks, Ministers will have to be careful not to deviate from the advice that has been prepared by their civil servants and by Parliamentary Counsel, as the following remarks made by Lord Henley, a Government Minister, at the Committee Stage of the Education Bill 1992 make abundantly clear:

> 'I very carefully said that I am advised that this is the case. In the light of the recent court case, *Pepper v. Hart* . . . it is very important that I know exactly what I am saying from the Dispatch Box.'

For the inexperienced Minister, the desirability of keeping to the brief will thus be the more powerful. This advice will apply as much when Ministers are moving new government amendments as when they are responding to probing amendments put by opposition parties. If their remarks are self-contradicting, then they will presumably fail to meet the new criteria, which include clarity: this suggests that Ministers will be discouraged from doing much more than repeating the advice they have been given. This, it may be argued, places too great a significance to sticking to the script at the cost of allowing worthwhile change to occur through debate. Merely nodding assent or dissent to assertions put by the other side, on the other hand, would presumably not count as a 'statement' and thus no reliance could be placed upon such indications. These considerations will also apply where amendments to private Members' Bills are debated, since the new rule includes remarks made by their sponsors. Since few private Members' Bills succeed that are not supported by the government (and indeed may be government Bills in all but name), departments will also have to consider what responses are likely to be made by the sponsor, and correct them if necessary. All this suggests more work for Parliamentary Counsel."

Finally, what will be the impact on statutory interpretation in the courts? Miers gives one hypothesis.

David Miers, "Taxing Perks and Interpreting Statutes: *Pepper v. Hart*" (1993) 56 M.L.R. 695 at 709:

"*Pepper v. Hart* accords primacy to ministerial statements in the event of absurdity, obscurity and ambiguity. To put it mildly, this is a significant break with tradition. Even recent statements on what has long been called the 'golden rule' of interpretation, that is, that the court may select a secondary meaning of a statutory word or phrase where its ordinary meaning in context yields an absurdity in this case, have emphasised that this secondary meaning must be one that can be linguistically sustained by the words in dispute. In short, *Pepper v. Hart* is of the first constitutional importance: it has brought about a reversal in the relative authority of two kinds of parliamentary statement. In formulating its relaxation of the exclusionary rule, the House said, in the person of Lord Browne-Wilkinson, 'Further than this, I would not at present go.' In Australia, where judicial access to 'any relevant report of a committee of the Parliament or of either House of the Parliament that was made to the Parliament or to that House of the parliament before the time when the provision was enacted' is a statutory permission, the courts have sought since its introduction in 1984 to limit the effect of the Minister's words. This is particularly so 'when the intention stated by the Minister but unexpressed in the law is restrictive of the liberty of the individual.' In such cases, however unfortunate it may be that the executive's intentions have been thwarted by statutory oversight or inadvertence, 'the function of the court is to give effect to the will of Parliament as expressed in the law.' What then will be the response of courts here? Will they give priority to the Minister's clear views (and irrespective of the quality of the Minister) over unclear legislation whether the effect is to the advantage or disadvantage of the citizen; or will they adopt the view that where the Minister's intentions benefit the citizen, those wishes will prevail; but that otherwise the executive is bound by the enacted law? *Yes, Minister* may yet prove to be an interpretive policy that does not receive unqualified approval."

The reaction to the decision in *Pepper v. Hart* was not, by any means, unqualified support. A critical analysis of the decision is provided by Baker.

J.H. Baker, "Statutory Interpretation and Parliamentary Intention" (1993) 52 C.L.J. 353 at 354:

"It is submitted that evidence of ministerial statements is not relevant evidence because, allowing that statutes should be interpreted according to the intention of Parliament, no individual member of Parliament is in a position to state what that intention is or to speak for the silent majority. Parliament acts as a corporate body and the only expression of its common intention is the text to which the Queen and both Houses have given their unqualified assent. What passes in one House is not formally known to the other, or to the sovereign. Even if it is thought that the intention of Parliament is the same thing as the common intention of the greatest number of its members, what one individual member says in debates cannot be cogent evidence of what every other member intends. His remarks may be based on a sound and impartial legal understanding of the issues, but they may not. They may persuade some, but they may not persuade others. There is no debate in which every member speaks, or even a majority of members, and so the prevailing view cannot be ascertained from the speeches. Nor does the fact that a Bill secured the necessary assents enhance the evidentiary value of previous statements. It is not uncommon to vote for motions even when one disagrees with some of the statements and arguments of the person proposing them, because one is satisfied with the wording and one is voting for the wording and its effect rather than for the sentiments expressed orally by its proposer. In other cases one may be persuaded to vote in favour by the different reasoning of a speaker following the first mover, though any consideration of such speeches is apparently excluded under the new rule. Certainly there is no procedure for members of Parliament to register assent to a Bill coupled with dissent from all or some of the reasons given by its promoters. Silence by members is therefore equivocal. . . .

It is remarkable that these well-known principles were not properly discussed in *Pepper v. Hart*. The nearest we find to an implied response is the argument that the courts now take a purposive rather than a literal approach to construction. . . . The question is not whether the approach to interpretation is or should be purposive, which is not disputed, but how the purpose behind a document may properly and logically be established. In the case of statutes, it is axiomatic that the purpose to be sought is that of Parliament, and not that of the government. A minister speaks for the government, but not for Queen, Lords and Commons all at once. If the words of a minister are to be considered as evidence of parliamentary intention, should the minister be called as a witness so that he may be cross-examined? Apparently not. Again and again in the Lordships' speeches, the intention of the minister is equated with the intention of Parliament and is not regarded as a matter of evidence: the minister's words are to be read as a source of law, attached as it were to the Act. The exclusionary rule is consequently treated merely as a form of blindfold which for purely technical reasons serves to conceal the truth from the court. Yet what is in fact being concealed from the court is not the intention of Parliament, which can only be expressed in written form, but rather the policy of the government, which should be of no concern to the courts. It is, of course, a notorious fact that while a government remains in power it may whip in a majority of members of the House of Commons to vote in favour of its Bills. . . . It does not follow from *de facto* recognition of our party system, and is not a fact, that members belonging to the party in power may be whipped in to support the legal reasoning of a government minister, or the interpretation which he places on a particular Bill. The whip drives members' bodies into the lobby but is not used to correct their states of mind or to teach them law. It is surely an unwarranted assumption that a minister's interpretation of an ambiguous Bill indicates the intention even of the House of Commons, let alone of Parliament.

The government-centred approach of the House of Lords is, with respect, rather chilling. It is true that in the instant case it operated in favour of the taxpayer, but it must obviously work either way. In future, when an Act is unclear, the intention of Parliament is apparently to be equated with the policy of the government or with what a minister chose to say about that policy in the House of Commons. It took many centuries of constitutional struggle to eliminate the notion that the policy of the government should have the force of law; now, it seems, something very like it is slipping through the back door."

NOTES

- For the perspective of a legislative drafter on *Pepper v. Hart*, see Francis Bennion, "Hansard—Help or Hindrance? A Draftsman's View of *Pepper v. Hart*" (1993) 14 Statute Law Review 149.

- For an analysis of the much more liberal American approach to legislative history in statutory interpretation, see Stephen D. Grivin, "Hansard and the Interpretation of Statutes" (1993) 22 Anglo-American Law Review 475; and, for a discussion of other jurisdictions, see Gordon Bale, "Parliamentary Debates and Statutory Interpretation: Switching on the Light or Rummaging in the Ashcans of the Legislative Process" (1995) 74 Canadian Bar Review 1.

- In *Pepper v. Hart*, Lord Browne-Wilkinson discusses the admissibility of other Parliamentary materials as extrinsic aids to statutory interpretation. The "leading" case on the admissibility of material such as Parliamentary committee reports, which may contain draft legislation, is *Black-Clawson International Ltd v. Papierwerke Waldhof Aschaffenburg A.G.* [1975] 1 All E.R. 81, HL. The decision in *Pepper v. Hart* might be thought to indicate a more liberal approach to the weight to be given to such material as an indicator of the intention of Parliament. But, for an example of a case where the majority of the House of Lords refused to accord such material any weight in interpretation, see *R. v. Gomez* [1993] 1 All E.R. 1, HL. Lord Keith of Kinkel for the majority, and Lord Lowry in dissent, differed sharply on the usefulness of the report of the Criminal Law Revision Committee in the interpretation of the Theft Act. Interestingly, the decision in *Gomez* was delivered only a week after *Pepper v. Hart*! The cases indicate the degree to which resort to extrinsic materials ultimately is in the discretion of the courts.

• *Pepper v. Hart* is sometimes explained as an example of the penetration of a European approach to interpretation. We consider approaches to interpretation in the particular context of European law in Chapter 9.

• In *Three Rivers District Council and others v. Bank of England* (No. 2) [1996] 2 All E.R. 363, Q.B., Clarke J. held that a more flexible approach to the introduction of parliamentary materials would be adopted in the context of the interpretation of legislation having an international or European dimension. As well, courts at times have taken a liberal approach to the preconditions to the introduction of parliamentary debates specified in *Pepper v. Hart*; see, *e.g. Steele Ford & Newton v. Crown Prosecution Service* [1994] A.C. 22, 37, HL; *R. v. Warwickshire County Council*, ex p. *Johnson* [1993] A.C. 583, HL.

• There are numerous other external aids to the interpretation of statutes which courts routinely draw upon in deciding cases, including academic textbooks. However, unlike the civilian tradition, common law judges tend not to rely on academic writing to a significant extent, although this may be changing somewhat.

• "Both the principled and the practical objections to the admissibility of Hansard in courts are more compelling than any benefits that might be derived therefrom." Do you agree?

LEGISLATIVE INTENTION AND SOCIAL CHANGE

Up to this point, we have assumed that the courts, in interpreting legislation, focus upon discerning the intention of the legislature. However, statutory language often must be interpreted over a long period. During that time, social conditions and mores may well have changed substantially, in such a way that the interpretation which will seem reasonable and, indeed, necessary to a majority of the population, may not have been that which would have been intended by those who voted for a statute in Parliament. To what extent, then, should courts adapt interpretation to meet the changing needs of a society? Should statutory interpretation be a *dynamic* or a *static* process? The issue has been confronted by courts on many occasions, some of them now legendary.

Henrietta Muir Edwards and others v. Attorney-General for Canada [1930] A.C. 124, PC.

Lord Sankey L.C.:

"By s 24 of the British North America Act, 1867, it is provided that 'The Governor General shall from time to time, in the Queen's name, by instrument under the Great Seal of Canada, summon qualified persons to the Senate; and, subject to the provisions of this Act, every person so summoned shall become and be a member of the Senate and a senator.'

The question at issue in this appeal is whether the words 'qualified persons' in that section include a woman, and consequently whether women are eligible to be summoned to and become members of the Senate of Canada.

Of the appellants, Henrietta Muir Edwards is the Vice-President for the province of Alberta of the National Council of Women for Canada; Nellie L. McClung and Louise C. McKinney were for several years members of the Legislative Assembly of the said Province; Emily F. Murphy is a police magistrate in and for the said Province; and Irene Parlby is a member of the Legislative Assembly of the said Province and a member of the Executive Council thereof.

On August 29, 1927, the appellants petititoned the Governor General in Council to refer to the Supreme Court certain questions touching the powers of the Governor General to summon female persons to the Senate, and upon October 19, 1927, the Governor General in Council referred to the Supreme Court the aforesaid question. The case was heard before Anglin C.J., Duff, Mignault, Lamont, and Smith J.J., and upon April 24, 1928, the Court answered the question in the negative; the question being understood to be 'Are women eligible for appointment to the Senate of Canada.'

The Chief Justice, whose judgment was concurred in by Lamont and Smith JJ, and substantially by Mignault J., came to this conclusion upon broad lines mainly because of the common law disability of women to hold public office and from a consideration of various cases which had been decided under different statutes as to their right to vote for a member of Parliament.

Duff J., on the other hand, did not agree with this view. He came to the conclusion that women are not eligible for appointment to the Senate upon the narrower ground that upon a close examination of the British North America Act, 1867, the word 'persons' in s 24 is restricted to members of the male sex. The result therefore of the decision was that the Supreme Court was unanimously of the opinion that the word 'persons' did not include female persons, and that women are not eligible to be summoned to the Senate.

Their Lordships are of opinion that the word 'persons' in s 24 does include women, and that women are eligible to be summoned to and become members of the Senate of Canada.

In coming to a determination as to the meaning of a particular word in a particular Act of Parliament it is permissible to consider two points—namely: (i) The external evidence derived from extraneous circumstances such as previous legislation and decided cases. (ii) The internal evidence derived from the Act itself. As the learned counsel on both sides have made great researches and invited their Lordships to consider the legal position of women from the earliest times, in justice to their argument they propose to do so and accordingly turn to the first of the above points—namely: (i) The external evidence derived from extraneous circumstances. . . ."

[Lord Sankey then reviewed the historical position of women in relation to the holding of public office.]

"No doubt in any code where women were expressly excluded from public office the problem would present no difficulty, but where instead of such exclusion those entitled to be summoned to or placed in public office are described under the word 'person' different considerations arise.

The word is ambiguous, and in its original meaning would undoubtedly embrace members of either sex. On the other hand, supposing in an Act of Parliament several centuries ago it had been enacted that any person should be entitled to be elected to a particular office it would have been understood that the word only referred to males, but the cause of this was not because the word 'person' could not include females but because at common law a woman was incapable of serving a public office. The fact that no woman had served or has claimed to serve such an office is not of great weight when it is remembered that custom would have prevented the claim being made or the point being contested.

Customs are apt to develop into traditions which are stronger than law and remain unchallenged long after the reason for them has disappeared.

The appeal to history therefore in this particular matter is not conclusive. . . .

Their Lordships now turn to the second point—namely, (ii) the internal evidence derived from the Act itself. . . .

The British North America Act planted in Canada a living tree capable of growth and expansion within its natural limits. The object of the Act was to grant a Constitution to Canada. 'Like all written constitutions it has been subject to development through usage and convention': Canadian Constitutional Studies, Sir Robert Borden (1922), p. 55.

Their Lordships do not conceive it to be the duty of this Board—it is certainly not their desire—to cut down the provisions of the Act by a narrow and technical construction, but rather to give it a large and liberal interpretation so that the Dominion to a great extent, but within certain fixed limits, may be mistress in her own house, as the provinces to a great extent, but within certain fixed limits, are mistresses in theirs. 'The Privy Council, indeed, has laid down that Courts of law must treat the provisions of the British North America Act by the same methods of construction and exposition which they apply to other statutes. But there are statutes and statutes; and the strict construction deemed proper in the case, for example, of a penal or taxing statute or one passed to regulate the affairs of an English parish, would be often subversive of Parliament's real intent if applied to an Act passed to ensure the peace, order and good government of a British Colony': see Clement's Canadian Constitution (3rd ed., p. 347). . . .

A heavy burden lies on an appellant who seeks to set aside a unanimous judgment of the Supreme Court, and this Board will only set aside such a decision after convincing argument and anxious consideration, but having regard: (1) To the object of the Act—namely, to provide a constitution for Canada, a responsible and developing State; (2) that the word 'person' is ambiguous, and may include members of either sex; (3) that there are sections in the Act above referred to which show that in some cases the word 'person' must include females; (4) that in some sections the words 'male persons' are expressly used when it is desired to confine the matter in issue to males; and (5) to the provisions of the Interpretation Act; their Lordships have come to the conclusion that the word 'persons' in s 24 includes members both of the male and female sex, and that, therefore, the question propounded by the Governor General should be answered in the affirmative, and that women are eligible to be summoned to and become members of the Senate of Canada, and they will humbly advise His Majesty accordingly."

NOTES AND QUESTIONS

- The Judicial Committee of the Privy Council, composed primarily of the Law Lords, was the final court of appeal against decisions of colonial courts. It still exists, although most former British colonies have abolished appeals to the Privy Council.

- The "Persons Case", as it is widely known, is also famous for Lord Sankey's description of the British North America Act as a "living tree". What does this imply for the way in which courts approach the task of statutory interpretation? In this regard, what does Lord Sankey's comment that "there are statutes, and then there are statutes" mean?

The "Persons Case" is not solely of historical interest. Mossman argues that it exemplifies the way in which legal method itself is gendered.

Mary Jane Mossman, "Feminism and Legal Method: The Difference it Makes", in *At the Boundaries of Law* (Martha Albertson Fineman and Nancy Sweet Thomadsen, eds., Routledge, New York, 1991), pp. 285–298:

"Just a few years before the nineteenth century drew to a close, Clara Brett Martin was admitted to the practice of law in Ontario, the first woman to become a lawyer in the British Commonwealth. Her petition for admission was initially denied by the Law Society on the basis that there were no precedents for the admission of women as lawyers. However, in 1892 a legislative amendment was passed permitting women to be admitted as solicitors; three years later, another legislative amendment similarly permitted women to be admitted as barristers. Clara Brett Martin herself was finally admitted in February 1897 as a barrister and solicitor.

Because of the admission arrangements in Ontario, it was the Law Society of Upper Canada, rather than a superior court, which reviewed the issue of Clara Brett Martin's entitlement to admission as a lawyer. By contrast, there was a court challenge in the Province of New Brunswick when Mabel Penury French sought admission as a lawyer there in 1905. When her application was presented to the court, the judges decided unanimously that there were no precedents for the admission of women, and denied her application. In the next year, however, after the enactment of a legislative amendment, French was admitted as a lawyer in New Brunswick. The same pattern (judicial denial of the application followed by legislative amendment) occurred again some years later when she applied for admission by transfer in British Columbia, and in a number of other Canadian provinces when women applied for admission as lawyers.

In contrast to the cases where women sought to enter the legal profession and were denied admission by the courts, the celebrated Privy Council decision in the Persons case determined that Canadian women were eligible to participate in public life. . . .

The decisions in these cases offer an interesting historical picture of legal process in the cultural milieu of the early twentieth century. In the cases about the admission of women to the legal profession, judges accepted the idea that there was a difference between men and women, a difference which 'explained' and 'justified' the exclusion of women from the legal profession. Yet, the Privy Council's decision in the Persons case completely discounted any such difference in relation to the participation of women in public life.

The issue is why there were these differing approaches: was it the nature of the claims, the courts in which they were presented, or the dates of the decisions? More significantly, what can we learn from the reasoning in these cases about the nature of legal method, especially in the context of challenges to 'deeply-held beliefs, vested interests, and the status quo'? In other words, what do these cases suggest about the potential impact of feminism on legal method?

French's case in New Brunswick provides a good illustration of judicial decision making on the issue of women in law. Her case was presented to the court for direction as to the admissibility of women by the president of the Barristers' Society of New Brunswick (as *amicus curiae*), and the court decided that women were not eligible for admission. Indeed, Mr Justice Tuck emphatically declared that he had no sympathy for women who wanted to compete with men; as he said: 'Better let them attend to their own legitimate business'. . . .

The stated reasons in these cases were consistent with well-established principles of legal method. The principles can be analyzed in terms of three aspects: (1) the characterization of the issues; (2) the choice of legal precedents to decide the validity of the women's claims; and (3) the process of statutory interpretation, especially in determining the effect of statutes to alter common law principles. Both the principles themselves and their application to these specific claims are important for an understanding of the potential impact of feminism on legal method.

Characterizing the issue

In both *French* and the Persons case, the judges consistently characterized the issues as narrowly as possible, eschewing their 'political' or 'social' significance, and explaining that the court was interested only in the law. . . .

Equally clearly, the women claimants never intended to bring to the court a 'neutral' legal issue for determination; they petitioned the court to achieve their goals, goals which were unabashedly political. In the face of such claims, however, the court maintained a view of its process as one of neutral interpretation. More significantly, the court's power to define the 'real issues' carried with it an inherent absence of responsibility on the part of the (male) judges for any negative outcome. It was the law, rather than the (male) person interpreting it, which was responsible for the decision. The result of such a characterization process, therefore, is to reinforce the law's detachment and neutrality rather than its involvement and responsibility; and to extend these characteristics beyond law itself to judges and lawyers.

Yet, how can we accommodate this characterization of detachment and neutrality with the opinions expressed, especially in *French*, about the role of women? The ideas about gender-based difference expressed forcefully by Mr Justice Barker in that case appear very close to an expression about the 'desirability' of women as lawyers and not merely a dispassionate and neutral application of legal precedents. Thus, at least in *French*, there is inconsistency between the legal method declared by the judges to be appropriate, and the legal method actually adopted in making their decisions. In this context, the expressed idea of detachment and neutrality both masks and legitimates judicial views about women's 'proper' sphere.

Using precedents in the Common Law tradition

The existence of women's common law disability was regularly cited in both these cases as the reason for denying their claims to be admitted to the legal profession and to take part in public life. The judges used numerous precedents for their conclusion. . . . Obviously, the Privy Council was less concerned with the absence of precedent in their decision making than the judges in *French*. Is this approach simply an early example of a court of highest jurisdiction deciding not to be bound by precedent in appropriate cases, or is there some other explanation?

In terms of the legal method described by the judges, of course, there is no answer to this question. Neither the judgments in the Supreme Court of Canada nor Lord Sankey's opinion in the Privy Council expressly consider the reality of women's experience at that time at all, and they specifically do not consider the reality of experience for the actual women claimants in the Persons case. Thus, even if the judges' perspectives on women's place were different in the two courts, there is virtually nothing in the judgments expressly reflecting them. For this reason, it is impossible to demonstrate that Lord Sankey's differing perspective was the reason for the different outcome in the Privy Council. At the same time, it is hard to find any other convincing explanation.

What does, of course, seem clear is the existence of judicial choice in the application of precedents. In the process of choosing earlier cases and deciding that they are binding precedents, judges make choices about which aspects of earlier cases are 'relevant' and 'similar,' choices which are not neutral but normative. In suggesting that the earlier decisions (relied on by the Supreme Court of Canada as binding precedents) were not determinative, Lord Sankey was declaring that the earlier decisions should not be regarded as exactly the same as the situation before the court in the Persons case. In this way, Lord Sankey's decision demonstrates the availability of choice in the selection of facts, in the categorization of principles and in the determination of relevance. At the same time, his opinion completely obscures the process and standards which guided the choice he actually made. To the myth of 'neutrality,' therefore, Lord Sankey added the 'mystery' of choice.

Interpreting statutes and Parliament's intent

Even in the statutes which used gender-neutral language, however, there were problems of statutory interpretation in relation to these cases. The legislation reviewed in the Persons case,

as well as that at issue in the admission of both Martin and French, used the word 'person' in describing the qualifications for being appointed to the Senate and called to the bar respectively. In the Persons case in the Supreme Court of Canada, Chief Justice Anglin expressed his surprise that such a monumental change in the position of women could be conferred by Parliament's use of such insignificant means; as he stated rhetorically: 'Such an extraordinary privilege is not conferred furtively'. Not surprisingly, he concluded that the women's claim must be dismissed because there was no evident express intent on the part of Parliament to effect the change advocated by them; the use of the word 'person' was not, by itself, sufficient.
. . .

Once again, however, the opinion of the Privy Council is different. After reviewing at some length the legislative provisions of the B.N.A. Act, Lord Sankey stated conclusively:

'The word "person" . . . may include members of both sexes, and to those who ask why the word should include females, the obvious answer is why should it not. In these circumstances the burden is upon those who deny that the word includes women to make out their case.'[5]

Lord Sankey cited no precedent to support this presumption in favour of the most extensive meaning of the statutory language, even though it expressly contradicted the principles of statutory interpretation adopted by all the judges in the decision of the Supreme Court of Canada.

In the end, just as the Privy Council decision was puzzling in relation to the effect of legal precedents about women's common law disabilities, it is also difficult to reconcile Lord Sankey's conclusions about the interpretation of the statute to the principles and precedents accepted in the Supreme Court of Canada. Clearly, the Privy Council departed from the Supreme Court's approach to legal method in reaching its conclusion to admit the women's claim. What remains unclear are Lord Sankey's reasons for doing so.

Feminism and legal method

In such a context, what conclusion is appropriate about feminism's potential for perspective transforming in the context of legal method?

The analysis of these cases illustrates the structure of inquiry identified as legal method. First of all, legal method defines its own boundaries: questions which are inside the defined boundaries can be addressed, but those outside the boundaries are not 'legal' issues, however important they may be for 'politics' or 'morals,' etc. Thus, the question of women becoming lawyers or Senators was simply a matter of interpreting the law; it did not require any consideration of utility or benefit to the women themselves or to society in general. The purpose and the result of the boundary-defining exercise is to confer 'neutrality' on the law and on its decision makers; in so doing, moreover, the process also relieves both the law and its decision makers of accountability for (unjust) decisions—('our whole duty is [only] to construe . . . the provisions of the [constitution]').

More serious is the potential for judicial attitudes to be expressed, and to be used in decision making (either explicitly or implicitly), when there is no 'objective' evidence to support them; because of the myth of neutrality which surrounds the process, such attitudes may acquire legitimacy in a way which strengthens and reinforces ideas in 'politics' and 'morals' which were supposed to be outside the law's boundary. After the decision in *French*, for example, women were different as a matter of law, and not just in the minds of people like Mr Justice Barker. Thus, the power to name the boundaries of the inquiry (and to change them, if necessary) makes legal method especially impervious to challenges from 'the outside.'

Second, legal method defines 'relevance' and accordingly excludes some ideas while admitting others. Some facts, such as inherent gender-based traits, were regarded as relevant in *French*, for example, while in both cases the actual conditions in which women lived their lives were not relevant at all. What was clearly relevant in both cases were earlier decisions about similar circumstances from which the judges could abstract principles of general application.

---

[5] This portion of the judgment has not been included in the excerpted case.

That all of the earlier cases had been decided by men, who were interpreting legislation drafted when women had no voting rights, was completely irrelevant to the decision making in the cases analyzed; even though the cases represented direct and significant challenges to the continuation of gender-exclusive roles and the circumstances of the historical context may seem quite significant to women now. The irony of solemn judicial reliance on precedent in the context of significant efforts by women to change the course of legal history underlines the significant role of legal method in preserving the status quo.

Finally, the case analysis demonstrates the opportunity for choice in legal method: choice as to which precedents are relevant and which approach to statutory interpretation is preferred; and choice as to whether the ideas of the mainstream or those of the margins are appropriate. The existence of choice in legal method offered some possibility of positive outcomes in the women's rights cases, at the same time as legal method's definitions of boundaries and concept of relevance ensured that positive outcomes would seldom occur. Lord Sankey's opinion in the Privy Council is an example of choice in legal method, however, which is as remarkable for its common sense as it is for its distinctiveness in legal method. Yet because Lord Sankey obscured the reasons for his choice, he also preserved the power and mystery of legal method even as he endowed women with the right to be summoned to the Senate. Thus, the opportunity for choice of outcome, positive as it appears, will not automatically lead to legal results which successfully challenge 'vested interests' or the 'status quo,' especially in relation to the law itself.

The conclusion that legal method is structured in such a way which makes it impervious to a feminist perspective is a sobering one. Within the women's movement, it has concrete consequences for the design of strategies for achieving legal equality: it suggests, for example, the general futility of court action for achieving significant change in women's rights, even though such action may be useful to monitor interpretation by courts or to focus attention on legal problems. For a feminist who is also a lawyer, however, the effort of 'double-think' may be both taxing and ultimately frustrating; the needs of clients require her to become highly proficient at legal method at the same time as her feminist commitment drives her to challenge the validity of its underlying rationale.

This dilemma also exists for feminist scholars. Feminist legal scholars are expected to think and write using the approaches of legal method: defining the issues, analyzing relevant precedents, and recommending conclusions according to defined and accepted standards of legal method. A feminist scholar who chooses instead to ask different questions or to conceptualize the problem in different ways risks a reputation for incompetence in her legal method as well as lack of recognition for her scholarly (feminist) accomplishments. Too often, it seems almost impossible to be both a good lawyer and a good feminist scholar.

This dilemma is similarly acute for feminist law teachers and students. With the advent of large numbers of women law students and increased numbers of women on law faculties, many have concluded that there is now a feminist perspective in the law school. Such a conclusion ignores the power of legal method to resist structural change. For example, discussions about whether feminist law teachers should create separate courses with feminist approaches and content, or whether we should use such approaches and content in 'malestream' courses, or whether we should do both at once, etc clearly confirm the 'reality' of the existing categories of legal knowledge, and reinforce the idea of the feminist perspective as 'Other'. While the separate course approach marginalizes the feminist perspective, the process of 'tacking on' feminist approaches to malestream courses only serves to emphasize what is really important in contrast to what has been 'tacked on.' Even efforts to give equal time to the feminist perspective and to reveal the essential maleness of the 'neutral' approach may underline that what is male is what really has significance. On this basis, adding women's experience to the law school curriculum cannot transform our perspective of law unless it also transforms legal method.

Taking this conclusion seriously, as I think we must, leads to some significant conclusions for women who are feminists and who are lawyers, law teachers and law students. It is simply not enough just to introduce women's experience into the curriculum or to examine the feminist approach to legal issues, although both of these activities are important. Yet, especially because there is so much resistance in legal method itself to ideas which challenge the status quo, there is no solution for the feminist who is a law teacher except to confront the reality that gender and power are inextricably linked in the legal method we use in our work, our discourse, and our study. Honestly confronting the barriers of our conceptual framework may at least permit us to begin to ask more searching and important questions."

NOTES AND QUESTIONS

- Why is the idea of precedent *inherently* conservative? As a consequence, why is Lord Sankey's judgment so significant—both for what it reveals and for what it conceals?

- Mossman mentions Clara Brett Martin, the first woman lawyer in the British Commonwealth. Martin became a powerful symbol for equality in the legal profession but, after Mossman's article was published, it became apparent from Martin's private writings that she was vehemently anti-Semitic. It is worth remembering that historically the legal profession was closed not only to women, but also discriminated (and still does) on the basis of race, religion, ethnicity, class, sexuality, and other relations of power, which intersect in various ways.

Another example of the contested relationship between legislative intention, precedent, and social change can be found in the definition of a "family" in law and "society". These cases deal with the situation of death of a "statutory tenant" in rent protected housing. Under the law, a member of the tenant's "family" living with them cannot be evicted.

Gammans v. Ekins [1950] 2 K.B. 328, CA.

[The plaintiff, David Gammans, the owner of number 177, Avery Lane, Gosport, a house within the Rent Restriction Acts, let it to a Mrs Smith who lived there until her death in 1949. The defendant, J.J. Ekins, had lived with her for a number of years, and had taken her name. In the neighbourhood they were thought to be man and wife.

On the tenant's death the defendant refused to quit the premises claiming to be a member of the tenant's "family" within the meaning of section 12(1)(g) of the Increase of Rent and Mortgage Interest (Restrictions) Act, 1920. The landlord in these proceedings claimed possession on the ground that the defendant was a trespasser.

The county court judge gave judgment for the defendant, finding him to be a member of the tenant's family. The landlord appealed.]

Asquith L.J. [after stating the facts]:
"It has been held that 'family' in s 12(1)(g) of the Act of 1920 should be given its popular meaning. Consanguinity is not a prerequisite of membership of the same family. On the authorities, not only are children members of their parents' family, but a husband is a member of his wife's, an adopted child a member of the adopter parents', and a husband, on unusual facts, has been held to be a member of the same family as his wife's niece. Mr Blundell, I think, was right in saying that the material decisions limit membership of the same 'family' to three relationships: first, that of children; secondly, those constituted by way of legitimate marriage, like that between a husband and wife; and thirdly, relationships whereby one person becomes *in loco parentis* to another. Beyond that point the law has not gone. I do not think that we

should be justified in saying that the defendant was a member of the tenant's family. Either the relationship was platonic or it was not. The judge has not found which, and says that it makes no difference; but if their relations were platonic, I can see no principle on which it could be said that these two were members of the same family, which would not require the court to predicate the same of two old cronies of the same sex innocently sharing a flat.

If, on the other hand, the relationship involves sexual relations, it seems to me anomalous that a person can acquire a 'status of irremovability' by living or having lived in sin, even if the liaison has not been a mere casual encounter but protracted in time and conclusive in character.

But I would decide the case on a simpler view. To say of two people masquerading, as these two were, as husband and wife (there being no children to complicate the picture) that they were members of the same family, seems to be an abuse of the English language, and I would accordingly allow the appeal."

Jenkins L.J.:
"I agree. If the matter were free from authority, speaking for myself I would have little hesitation in holding that the defendant was not a member of the tenant's family within any ordinary accepted use of that expression or within the meaning of s 12(1)(g). There has, however, been a series of decisions, each of them addressed to the particular facts of the case before the court, which taken together have so extended the meaning of the word 'family' for the purposes of the sub-section as to make it possible to argue with a considerable degree of plausibility that there is no reason why the benefit of the sub-section should not be extended also to the defendant. But when the cases are examined, it will, I think, be found that none of them goes so far as we are invited to go in the present case. The defendant was not in my view a member of the tenant's family in any reasonable sense whatever. The parties for reasons of convenience, had chosen to live together and the defendant, to avoid as he said gossip, had taken the tenant's name of Smith. The neighbours assumed that they were husband and wife and accepted them as such. I cannot regard this as giving the defendant the same claim to be considered a member of the tenant's family as if they had been lawfully man and wife. . . .

If the county court judge's decision were to stand, an alarming vista would, it seems to me, be opened up: if, for instance, brothers and sisters are members of the tenant's family, I see no reason why two friends should not set up house together, one changing his or her name to that of the other, and then give out that they were sisters or brother and sister as the case might be; in which case, provided that they were accepted as such in the neighbourhood, there would, by parity of reasoning, be no ground why, when one of them, being a statutory tenant of the house in which they both resided died, the other should not claim to be a member of the statutory tenant's family on account of the artificial relationship which they had chosen for their own purposes to adopt. I agree that the appeal should be allowed."

Evershed M.R. [Evershed M.R. delivered concurring reasons and concluded with the comment]:
"It may not be a bad thing that by this decision it is shown that, in the Christian society in which we live, one, at any rate, of the privileges which may be derived from marriage is not equally enjoyed by those who are living together as man and wife but who are not married."

Questions

- Why are all of the members of the Court of Appeal so troubled by the legal implications of a finding in favour of Ekins in this case? In their minds, what are the implications? Half a century later, do those implications seem unacceptable?

- What is the *purpose* of the statutory provision in issue in this case? In light of that *purpose*, how would you define "family", *for the purposes of this statutory provision*?

Times change, and sometimes, so does the interpretation of a statutory provision, as the following judgment demonstrates.

Dyson Holdings Ltd v. Fox [1975] 3 All E.R. 13, CA.

Lord Denning M.R.:
"So far as we know, Jack Wright was a bachelor and Olive Agnes Fox was a spinster, who met 4 years ago and lived happily ever after. They lived together as man and wife. She took his name and was known as Mrs Wright. In 1940 they were bombed out and went to live at 3 Old Road, Lewisham. The rent book was in the name of Mr J Wright. They both went out to work and used their earnings to run the house. In every respect they were man and wife save that they had not gone through a ceremony of marriage.

After 21 years in the house, on 28 August 1961 Mr Jack Wright died. She remained on in the house and paid the rent, using the name Mrs Wright. The rent book remained in the name of 'J Wright' and the records of the landlord still showed the tenant as 'J Wright'.

I expect that the ownership changed hands from time to time, but in March 1973 the owners were a property company, Dyson Holdings Ltd. By this time Mrs Wright (as she was known) was herself getting on in years. She was 73. She wrote to the landlord asking for a statement of the weekly rent. She signed herself 'OA Wright'. This put the property company on enquiry. They asked their agents to call at the house. She told them that Mr Jack Wright died on 28 August 1961 and that she was his widow. The property company asked their agents to check up on the electoral roll. They did so. They found that she had given her name there as 'Olive Fox'. The property company inferred that she was not really his widow. If she had been his widow, she could, of course, have had protection under the Rent Acts. But, if she was not his widow, they thought they were entitled in law to get her out. So on 27 March 1973 they wrote to her:

> 'We are addressing you as Mrs O Wright although we understand from the Electoral Register that the person in occupation is Olive Fox and perhaps you would explain this in your reply. Until this matter is clarified, we are unable to accept any rent . . .'

So after all those years, the truth was out. She was not his widow. She was only a woman who had lived with him as his wife for 21 years. The property company refused to receive any rent from her and brought proceedings against her for possession on the ground that she was not protected by the Rent Act 1968. She had, they said, no tenancy and was a trespasser. They had accepted the rent from her, not knowing that the tenant had died. As soon as they discovered it, and that she was not his widow, they were entitled to possession. The judge accepted their argument. He held that he was bound by the decision of this court in *Gammans v. Ekins*. It was sad, he said, to have to turn this lady of 74 out; but felt he had no alternative. He ordered her out in 28 days. She appeals to this court.

Ever since 1920 the Rent Acts have protected a 'member of the tenant's family' in these words:

> '. . . the expression 'tenant' includes a widow of a tenant . . . who was residing with him at the time of his death, or where a tenant . . . leaves no widow or is a woman, such member of the tenant's family so residing aforesaid as may be decided in default of agreement by the county court.'

So in the present case the lady is protected if she was a 'member of the tenant's family'; but not otherwise. Those words have often been considered by the courts. The cases collected are in Megarry on the Rent Acts. The word 'family' in the 1968 Act is not used in any technical sense, but in a popular sense. It is not used in the sense in which it would be used by a studious and unworldly lawyer, but in the sense in which it would be used by a man who is 'base, common and popular', to use Shakespeare's words . . . .

[Lord Denning then considered *Gammans v. Ekins*]. But is this court at liberty to reject the distinction? Are we bound by *Gammans v. Ekins*? That case can be distinguished on narrow grounds, such as that the woman was the tenant and not the man, or that their relationship might perhaps have been platonic. But I dislike the device of distinguishing a case on narrow grounds. I prefer to say, as I have often said, that this court is not absolutely bound by a previous decision when it is seen that it can no longer be supported. At any rate, it is not so bound when, owing to the lapse of time, and the change in social conditions, the previous decision is not in accord with modern thinking. . . . I am glad to find that we are all of one mind on this, but in case there are some who are doubtful, I can put the case on a conventional ground.

It has been decided by the House of Lords that, when an Act uses an ordinary English word in its popular meaning as distinct from its legal meaning, it is for the tribunal of fact to decide whether or not that popular meaning covers the case in hand. The tribunal of fact must use its own understanding of the word and apply it to the facts which have been proved. A Court of Appeal should not interfere with its decision unless it was unreasonable in the sense that no tribunal acquainted with the ordinary use of language could reasonably reach that decision. That was the very ground of the decision of the House of Lords in *Brutus v. Cozens*.[6] In the light of that decision, it appears to me that *Gammans v. Ekins* was wrongly decided. In that case, the tribunal of fact—the county court judge—gave judgment for the man, finding him to be a 'member of the tenant's family'. The Court of Appeal recognised that the words were to be given their ordinary and popular meaning, but nevertheless they reversed the county court judge. I do not think they should have done. To my mind the decision of the county court judge in that case was a perfectly reasonable decision, as Evershed M.R. recognised. And, on the authority of *Brutus v. Cozens*, the Court of Appeal ought not to have interfered with it. They went wrong just as the Divisional Court did in *Brutus v. Cozens*.[7] Their decision cannot stand with that subsequent decision of the House of Lords. We are not, therefore, bound by it: see *Young v. Bristol Aeroplane*.[8]

I would, however, add a word of caution about *Brutus v. Cozens*. When an ordinary word comes to be applied to similar facts, in one case after another, it is very important that the various tribunals of fact should each apply it in the same way. For instance, if the question comes up: is an unmarried woman (living for many years as a man's wife) a member of his family? Each tribunal of fact should give the same answer. It would be intolerable if half of the judges gave one answer; and the other half another. . . .

So here in the present case, I think this court should give a definite ruling. We should rule that in this case this lady was a member of the tenant's family residing with him at the time of his death. As such, she was entitled to the protection of the Rent Acts. The property company were not entitled to turn her out. I would allow the appeal accordingly."

James L.J. [James L.J. reviewed the decision in *Gammans v. Ekins* and continued]:
"It is not so easy to decide whether in 1961 the ordinary man would have regarded the appellant as a member of Mr Wright's family. The changes of attitude which have taken place cannot be ascribed to any particular year. Had we to consider the position as at 1955 I would not be satisfied that the attitude reflected in the words of Asquith L.J. in *Gammans v. Ekins* had changed. I am confident that by 1970 the changes had taken place. There is no magic in the date 1961. I think that, having regard to the radical change which has by 1975 taken place, it would be a harsh and somewhat ossified approach to the present case to hold that in 1961 the appellant was not in the popular sense a member of the family.

I turn to the issue whether there is any rule of law which precludes the appellant being a member of the family for the purposes of the Rent Acts. If there is, it is to be found only in the decision of this court in *Gammans v. Ekins*. I confess that I have been troubled in the course of argument as to how far the decision of this court in that case is conclusive of the present appeal. The court in *Gammans v. Ekins* reversed the trial judge. They could not have done so unless the issue was a question of law. It is not a decision which can be explained on the basis of a question of fact. The cases which are said to be inconsistent with the decision are in my judgment not shown to be inconsistent. They are based on the added fact of birth of a child or children to the illicit union. . . . I cannot take the view that *Gammans v. Ekins* was wrongly

---

6 [1972] 2 All E.R. 1297, [1973] A.C. 854.
7 [1972] 2 All E.R. 1, [1972] 1 W.L.R. 484.
8 [1944] 2 All E.R. 293 at 298, [1944] K.B. 718 at 725.

decided. The decision is binding on this court, but it is binding only on the meaning to be given to 'family' at that time. The point decided was that applying the popular meaning of the word 'family' as it was used and understood in 1949 the evidence of relationship could not support a finding that the defendant was a member of the tenant's family. The decision is not authority for the proposition that at some later time a person in a similar position to Mr Ekins could not in law be a member of the tenant's family within the meaning of the increase of Rent and Mortgage Interest (Restrictions) Act 1920 and the Rent Act 1968. The word 'family' must be given its popular meaning at the time relevant to the decision in the particular case.

To hold that *Gammans v. Ekins* precludes the appellant from bringing herself within the Act would be to apply a precedent slavishly in circumstances to which it is not appropriate having regard to reality.

I would therefore allow this appeal."

Bridge L.J. [Bridge L.J. considered *Gammans v. Ekins* and continued]:
"Can we give effect to this change in social attitude and consequent change in the scope of a common English word without doing violence to the doctrine of judicial precedent and notwithstanding that in this case the appellant's status must be considered at the date of the original tenant's death in 1961? I have felt some hesitation on both these points, but in the end have concluded that it would be unduly legalistic to allow either consideration to defeat the appellant's claim. On the first point, if language can change its meaning to accord with changing social attitudes, then a decision on the meaning of a word in a statute before such a change should not continue to bind thereafter, at all events in a case where the courts have consistently affirmed that the word is to be understood in its ordinary accepted meaning. On the second point, where the modern meaning is plain, we should, I think, be prepared to apply it retrospectively to any date, unless plainly satisfied that at that date the modern meaning would have been unacceptable.

Accordingly I agree that this appeal should be allowed."

Appeal allowed. Leave to appeal to the House of Lords refused.

NOTES AND QUESTIONS

- How do the members of the Court of Appeal in *Dyson Holdings v. Fox* avoid the impact of the rules of horizontal precedent? Are the reasons convincing?

- The law-fact distinction is used by Lord Denning to justify his departure from the precedent of *Gammon v. Ekins*. How? Is the distinction clearer to you after reading his reasons? (*hint*: probably not!).

Reading the case law on family members should make you think of other situations, some of which were raised by the judges themselves, that might come up in litigation. The following is a recent example, where the surviving partner, unfortunately, did not have the success that Ms Fox experienced before the Court of Appeal.

Fitzpatrick v. Sterling Housing Association Ltd [1997] 4 All E.R. 991, CA.

Waite L.J.:
"The short but difficult question raised by this appeal is whether the surviving partner in a stable and permanent homosexual relationship can claim succession rights under the Rent Acts in respect of premises of which the deceased partner was a protected tenant. The facts are not in dispute. Mr John Thompson became the statutory tenant of a flat, No 75 Ravenscourt Road,

London W6 (the flat), in 1972. The appellant, Mr Fitzpatrick, moved in to live with him there in 1976, and the two of them maintained from then onwards a close, loving and faithful homosexual relationship. Early in 1986 Mr Thompson suffered, as a result of a fall, head injuries which required surgery and then a stroke which left him a tetraplegic. From the summer of that year Mr Fitzpatrick nursed him at home, and dedicated himself to providing, with love and devotion, the constant care which he required. In 1994 Mr Thompson died.

The landlords are a charity providing families and individuals with accommodation at affordable rents. It is common ground that they do not qualify as a housing action trust within the terms of the Housing Act 1985 (as now amended), and that they accordingly fall to be treated as private landlords subject to the Rent Acts. Mr Fitzpatrick applied to take over the tenancy of the flat (which comprises four rooms plus kitchen and bathroom) but the landlords, though willing to rehouse him in smaller accommodation in another of their properties, were not prepared to agree.

Mr Fitzpatrick applied to the West London County Court for a determination that he was entitled to succeed to the tenancy of the flat. His application was given a careful and sympathetic hearing in the Central London Trials Centre by Judge Colin Smith Q.C., who on 19 April 1996 dismissed it with obvious reluctance, holding that he was constrained by law to treat him as being outside the statutory definitions of a person entitled to succeed on the death of a statutory tenant. From that decision Mr Fitzpatrick now appeals to this court. . . .

The Law

A degree of transmission on death was a feature of the Rent Acts since their inception in 1920. At first it was achieved by extending the definition of 'the tenant' to include a widow or qualifying member of his family. That was replaced by a legislative scheme (maintained to this day) of setting out the rights of succession in a schedule specifying in the first paragraph the primary successor and in the second a default category of qualifying successor. Originally the primary successor was the deceased tenant's widow. From 1968 the secondary or default category was defined as a person who was a member of the original tenant's family residing with him for six months immediately before his death. A provision was added in the 1977 Act that if there was more than one such person the right of succession should be determined in default of agreement by the court. The Housing Act 1980 substituted 'surviving spouse' for 'widow' in the primary class, which was thus extended to widowers. [Waite L.J. then reviewed the statutory regime and case law]. . . .

The approach of the judge in this case

It was common ground that the judge was required, when construing the phrase 'a member of the original tenant's family', to apply the general interpretive principle of *Dyson*—i.e. to construe the term 'family' in its popular modern meaning, taking into account changed social attitudes and the changed needs and views of society. . . . [H]e stated his conclusion in these terms:

> 'I fully accept that a cohabiting relationship between members of the same sex of a permanent and stable kind would properly be regarded nowadays, whether in 1996 or 1994, by the man in the street as just as lasting and socially valuable a relationship as that between husband and wife. But, in my judgment, for the reasons I have attempted to give, this does not entitle me, even in construing the word 'family' in a popular sense as required by *Dyson*, to find that such a relationship falls within such definition. In my judgment, such a decision falls to be made by Parliament and not by the courts. It will be for others to decide whether Parliament should look at this question . . . it might be appropriate for it to do so.'

The argument in this appeal

Member of the original tenant's family

The applicability of this phrase has provided the central issue in the appeal. Can a sexual partner of the same sex be described as a member of his or her family?

Mr Chapman for the landlord charity accepts, as he did before the judge, the interpretative principle of *Dyson*, namely that the court is bound to give to the term 'member of the family' whatever connotation it demands in current popular thought and speech. He submits, however, that the judge was right to regard himself as constrained by authority to hold that when a sexual relationship between strangers in blood is relied on as constituting a family relationship, the attachment must bear the hallmark of the familial nexus represented either by marriage or by unmarried cohabitation of the kind that occurs between husband and wife. . . . The requirement that the partners should be living as husband and wife necessarily imports a male and female relationship and precludes its application to relationships between persons of the same sex. Mr Chapman also submitted that the judge's decision has the advantage of harmonising the two regimes of statutory and secure tenancies. He reminded us, finally, that Rent Act legislation, though it fulfils a public interest in the social control of land for the benefit of those least able to afford accommodation, is nevertheless by its nature expropriatory in its interference with rights of ownership of land, and should therefore, he submitted, be construed restrictively by adopting an interpretation of 'family membership' which limits, rather than enlarges, the range of potential successor to a statutory tenant.

Mr Luba urges that, on the contrary, Parliament must be deemed to have known what it was about when the decision was taken, at the time of the 1988 amendments to Sch 1, to leave the expression 'member of . . . the family' to be interpreted broadly, in the sense approved in *Dyson*—a decision which formed an important part of the case law in operation when those changes were made. Such an interpretation, in the light of modern social attitudes and conditions, can lead, he submits, to only one result. If unmarried heterosexual partners in a permanent relationship are capable of being held . . . to be members of the former tenant's family, what reason can there be in logic or humanity for declining to accord the same status to a partner in a lesbian or gay relationship?

Conclusion

If endurance, stability, interdependence and devotion were the sole hallmarks of family membership, there could be no doubt about this case at all. Mr Fitzpatrick and Mr Thompson lived together for a longer period than many marriages endure these days. They were devoted and faithful, giving each other mutual help and support in a life which shared many of the highest qualities to be found in heterosexual attachments, married or unmarried. To adopt an interpretation of the statute that allowed all sexual partners, whether of the same or opposite sex, to enjoy the privilege of succession to tenancies protected by the Rent Acts would, moreover, be consistent not only with social justice but also with the respect accorded by modern society to those of the same sex who undertake a permanent commitment to a shared life.

The survey which I have undertaken in this judgment shows, however, that the law in England regarding succession to statutory tenancies is firmly rooted in the concept of the family as an entity bound together by ties of kinship (including adoptive status) or marriage. The only relaxation, first by court decisions and then by statute, has been a willingness to treat heterosexual cohabitants as if they were husband and wife. That was a restrictive extension, offensive to social justice and tolerance because it excludes lesbians and gays. It is out of tune with modern acceptance of the need to avoid any discrimination on the ground of sexual orientation. In that respect I wholly agree with the comments of Ward L.J. The question is: how is it to be put right?

Discrimination is not, unfortunately, the only arbitrary feature in this area of the law. Endemic within its system is a high risk of harsh and anomalous results—excluding from rights of succession many deserving instances of common households in which the survivor would have a strong moral case to succeed to the tenancy. Friends of long standing (widowers or spinsters for example) who share accommodation in old age without any sexual element in their relationship, but who often give and receive much the same kind of devoted care as we have admired in this case, are (and always have been) excluded. If succession rights are to be extended to couples of the same sex in a sexually based relationship, would it be right to continue to exclude friends? If friends are to be included, how is the stability and permanence of their household to be defined?

These questions have to be judged in the light of a further policy consideration—fairness to home-owners. Every enlargement of the class of potential successors to rent controlled tenancies involves a deeper invasion of rights of house-owners to possession of their own property. That there is a need to reconcile these competing social priorities is something on which it would be easy to find a broad consensus. The difficulty arises when it comes to finding ways and means. At that point opinions are bound to vary, and a political judgment may in the end become necessary. That is what makes the process of reconciliation a task better suited to the legislative function of Parliament than to the interpretative role of the courts.

The law of succession to Rent Act protected tenancies is, in short, arbitrary and discriminatory. No one today would attempt to defend the favour it accords, outside the marriage tie, to heterosexual relationships over same-sex households. Few would support the potential for unfairness involved in a law which gives automatic succession rights to wives (however faithless) and children (however feckless) and at the same time denies any hope of succession to friends, however devoted their loyalty to the joint household. The judge was nevertheless right, in my view, to resist the temptation to change a bad law by giving it a new linguistic twist. He correctly acknowledged that such changes could only be made by Parliament.

They are changes which will certainly need to be made, if Parliament is to fulfill its function of reflecting the spirit of our times—in particular the spirit which recognises the value of all abiding relationships, the heterosexual, the lesbian, the gay—or even those which are not sexually based at all. As the law now stands, however, I feel bound, notwithstanding the respect and sympathy to which Mr Fitzpatrick is entitled, to dismiss the appeal."

Ward L.J. [Ward L.J. began with a consideration of the statutory regime, and reviewed the relevant case law in the United Kingdom and abroad]:

My approach to the question of construction

"(1) I begin with the purpose of the 1977 Act, which is essentially to give tenants fair rents and a status of irremovability. In *Curl v. Angelo* [1948] 2 All ER 189 at 192 Lord Greene M.R. described 'the real fundamental object of the Act' to be 'protecting a tenant from being turned out of his home'. In *Lloyd v. Sadler* [1978] 2 All ER 529 at 537–538, [1978] QB 774 at 790 Lawton L.J. said:

'The object of the Rent Act 1968 was to give security of tenure to persons . . . The 1968 Act took away many of the landlord's rights at common law and was intended to do so for the benefit of tenants.'

As Lord Greene M.R. had said earlier in *Cumming v. Danson* [1942] 2 All ER 653 at 654, the Acts were 'for the protection of tenants and not Acts for the penalising of landlords'. The teleological interpretation supports the conclusion that there is no justification for limiting the class of persons entitled to the benefit of the 1977 Act on the basis that the interference with the landlord's right to possession should be curtailed because the Act has a penal effect: on the contrary, the broad purpose of the Act is to preserve the family home for tenants and their successors. Consequently, those who occupy the property as their home should wherever it is possible—but of course not beyond that—be given protection against eviction.

(2) As I have already explained, the words of this Act must be given their contemporary meaning. Professor Ronald Dworkin expressed the point well in *Law's Empire* (1986) p 348, when he said:

'[The judge] interprets not just the statute's text but its life, the process that begins before it becomes law and extends far beyond that moment . . . [the judge's] interpretation changes as the story develops.'

Since families are dynamic, the statutory interpretation must equally reflect the motive forces, physical or moral, affecting behaviour and change in domestic organisation. . . .

(3) Since the inception of the Rent Acts in or before 1920, the home of members of the tenant's family has been preserved for them. As the decided cases show, the meaning of

family has been progressively extended. The movement has been away from the confines of relationships by blood and by marriage to the reality of family life, and from *de jure* to *de facto* relationships. . . . The trend in the cases, as I see them, is to shift the focus, or the emphasis, from structure and components to function and appearance—what a family does rather than what it is, or putting it another way, a family is what a family does. I see this as a functionalist approach to construction as opposed to a formalist approach. . . .

(4) We do not have (or should I say we do not *yet* have?) the equivalent of the Canadian Charter of Rights and Freedoms which enables the judges to strike down offensive discriminatory legislation. I must, therefore, be faithful to Parliament's sovereign will. Nevertheless, I am entitled to presume that Parliament always intends to conform to the rule of law as a constitutional principle and accordingly to respect the constitutional rights of the individual to enjoy equality under the law. . . . If, therefore, there is doubt about the ordinary meaning of the words of the statute, I would strain to place upon them that construction which produces a dignified result consistent with the purpose of the Act.

(5) To exclude same-sex couples from the protection the 1977 Act proclaims the inevitable message that society judges their relationship to be less worthy of respect, concern and consideration than the relationship between members of the opposite sex. The fundamental human dignity of the homosexual couple is severely and palpably affected by the impugned distinction. The distinction is drawn on grounds relating to their personal characteristics, their sexual orientation. If the law is as my Lords state it to be, then it discriminates against a not insignificant proportion of the population who will justly complain that they have been denied their constitutional right to equal treatment under the law.

(6) There being no remedy to cure such injustice, my approach will, therefore, be to say that if I find the statute ambiguous, or even if I am left in doubt as to its meaning, then I should err on the side of preventing the discrimination. . . .

Was the appellant a member of the original tenants family?

(1) *The Oxford English Dictionary* (compact edn, 1979) defines family as:

'1. The servants of a house or establishment; the household; 2. The body of persons who live in one house or under one head, including parents, children, servants etc.; 3. The group of persons consisting of the parents and their children whether actually living together or not; in wider sense, the unity formed by those who are nearly connected by blood or affinity . . .'

Mr Chapman contends for the third meaning. This is the 'traditional' family. The moment one uses the adjective to qualify the noun, the clearer it is that the meaning is wide.

(2) Hoggett (Hale J.), Pearl (Judge Pearl), Cooke and Bates state in their work *The Family, Law and Society* (4th edn, 1996) p 1:

'In the England of the 1990s, we must not assume that the answer to the question "What is a family?" is necessarily going to produce a simple and straight forward response . . . The following extract comes from the Judicial Studies Board's *Handbook on Ethnic Minority Issues* (1994) . . . 'Despite the fact that these images may have some basis in reality, as rigid stereotypes they can be misleading and dangerous. They over-generalise certain tendencies, and conceal the existence of considerable diversity in family composition among Britain's minority ethnic communities. They also do nothing to help with understanding why there may be differences in family patterns between ethnic groups.' "

Should one not, therefore, also question the validity of a heterosexual stereotype for the family?

(3) The test has to be whether the relationship of the appellant to the deceased was one

where there is at least a broadly recognisable *de facto* familial nexus. I would not define that familial nexus in terms of its structures or components; I would rather focus on familial functions. The question is more what a family does rather than what a family is. A family unit is a social organisation which functions through its linking its members closely together. The functions may be procreative, sexual, sociable, economic, emotional. The list is not exhaustive. Not all families function in the same way. Save for the ability to procreate, these functions were present in the relationship between the deceased and the appellant.

(4) Whilst there clearly is no right to self-determination it cannot be immaterial to have regard to the view the parties have of their own relationship. If the officious commuter on the Clapham omnibus had paid a visit to the deceased's household, asked all the relevant questions about their relationship and asked the deceased finally, 'What is Mr Fitzpatrick to you? Is he one of the family?', it seems to me to be inconceivable that the deceased would not have testily suppressed him by replying, 'Of course he is'. I doubt whether the ordinary man would be surprised by the answer as he apparently would have been hearing Ms Simpson. I am quite certain that he would not treat the answer as an abuse of the English language. Indeed, I am satisfied that the ordinary man is liberated enough to accept in 1997, or even in 1994, looking broadly at the appellant's life and comparing it with the other rich patterns of family life he knows, that the bond between the appellant and the deceased was de facto familial.

(5) I would therefore conclude that if, which is my preferred view, they were not living as a husband and his wife would live, then at least they were living as members of a family.

Conclusions

Writing on 'Financial Rights in Relationships outside Marriage: a Decade of Reforms in Australia' [1995] IJLF 233 Professor Bailey-Harris says:

'A pluralistic society requires the law not merely to tolerate but rather to recognise and support diversity in family formation—in other words to authenticate a range of family forms.'

In my judgment, our society has shown itself to be tolerant enough to free itself from the burdens of stereotype and prejudice in all their subtle and ugly manifestations. The common man may be vaguely disapproving of the homosexual relationship which is not for him but, having shrugged his shoulders, he would recognise that the relationship was to all intents and purposes a marriage between those partners. They lived a life akin to that of any husband and wife. They were so bound together that they constituted a family. . . .

To conclude otherwise would be to stand like King Canute, ordering the tide to recede when the tide in favour of equality rolls relentlessly forward and shows no sign of ebbing. If I am to be criticised—and of course I will be—then I prefer to be criticised, on an issue like this, for being ahead of the times, rather than behind the times. My hope, to reflect the intent of this judgment, is that I am in step with the times. For my part, I would have allowed this appeal."

[Roch L.J. delivered separate reasons, concurring with the result reached by Waite L.J.].

Appeal dismissed. Leave to appeal to the House of Lords refused.

NOTES AND QUESTIONS

• The *Dyson* approach to statutory interpretation is quite unique to this particular statutory regime. Far more common is a judicial focus on the intention of the legislature at the time a statute was enacted. The focus on contemporary under-standings of the term "family", and the recognition that the term changes its meaning over time, is exceptional.

- Counsel for Mr Fitzpatrick sought to introduce expert evidence of social scien-tists on the changing character of families in the United Kingdom. Such evidence was held inadmissible in this case as an aid to interpretation. Is such a restrictive approach to discerning the social context of words justifiable? On what basis? For a discussion of an alternative approach in Canada, in which courts are more open to sociological evidence, see Didi Herman, "'Sociologically Speaking': Law, Sexuality and Social Change" (1991) 2.2 Journal of Human Justice 57.

- Waite L.J. notes that an expansive approach to the definition of "family" in the Rent Act will infringe upon the rights of the property owner. This discussion implicitly raises the presumption, long standing in common law reasoning, that in the case of ambiguity, legislation will be interpreted so as not to infringe rights of property. By contrast, Ward L.J. points to a presumption that legislation should be interpreted, in the case of ambiguity, in a non-discriminatory fashion. What does the fact that conflicting presumptions can be raised about the same legal issue in the same case suggest about the value of such presumptions? Do they seem to guide judges to the results, or help justify the conclusions they reach on other grounds? On the indeterminacy of presumptions and "canons" of interpretation, see Karl N. Llewellyn, "Remarks on the Theory of Appellate Decision and the Rules or Canons about how Statutes are to be Construed" (1950) 3 Vanderbilt Law Review 395.

- As for Ward L.J.'s presumption that courts should interpret legislation in favour of the constitutional right of the individual to enjoy equality under the law, no authority is cited for this statement. From where does it originate? What does its invocation suggest about the flexibility and adaptability of the "rule of law"?

- Ward L.J. presents a highly optimistic (perhaps utopian) view of social pluralism and acceptance. Why is it necessary for him to *construct* this perspective in order to make his judgment consistent with the principles of *Dyson*? This also raises the interesting question of the extent to which judicial decision making should *reflect* social change or help *shape* social change (if the two, in fact, can be sep-arated).

INTERPRETIVE POLICIES AND PRESUMPTIONS

In *Fitzpatrick v. Sterling Housing Association*, reference was made to presumptions of interpretation, such as Ward L.J.'s articulation of a presumption in favour of non-dis-crimination. Over the course of the history of statutory interpretation, numerous pre-sumptions—both linguistic and policy-based—have grown up in the law. A familiarity with their existence is necessary so that you can recognise their relevance should a set of facts come along to which one of them applies.

Peter Goodrich, *Reading the Law* (Blackwell, Oxford, 1986), pp. 57–59:

"Special rules prescribing how certain commonly used combinations of words are to be interpreted have arisen. For example, the *ejusdem generis* rule deals with the combination of specific and general terms. It requires that where three or more specific examples are followed by a general word, then the parameters of the general category are to be determined by the common characteristics of the specific words (*Palmer v. Snow* [1900] 1 QB 725, at 727). The *noscitur a sociis* rule prescribes that words are to take their meaning from their context (*Muir v. Keay* [1875] LR 10 QB 594). A further category of aids to interpretation are general principles by which the task of interpretation is to be assisted. Many of the principles are general guides describing the attributes of the activity of legislation. For example in *Morris v. Beardmore* [1980] 2 All ER 753, the court had to consider the legislative provisions relating to the taking of specimens of breath by the police. The dispute related to the power of the police to enter private premises to effect a breathalyser test. In interpreting the statutory provision, Lord Scarman made the following reference to a general principle:

> 'When for the detection, prevention or prosecution of crime Parliament confers on a constable a power or right which curtails the rights of others it is to be expected that Parliament intended the curtailment to extend no further than its express authorisation. A constable, who in purported execution of his duty has infringed rights which Parliament has not expressly curtailed, will not, therefore, be able to show that he has acted in execution of his duty, unless (and this will be rare) it can be shown by necessary implication that Parliament must have intended to authorise such infringement (763 b-c).'

The narrow construction of penal provisions is another example of a similar principle, as seen in *R. v. Cuthbertson* [1980] 2 All ER 41 where Lord Diplock applied a restrictive principle to the interpretation of the Misuse of Drugs Act 1971, s 23 in the following fashion: 'the fact that the section is a penal provision is in itself a reason for hesitating before ascribing to phrases used in it a meaning broader than they would normally bear' (404). The above selection of secondary techniques is not exhaustive; it is merely a selection to draw attention to various categories of method and technique.

A final matter which demands consideration again focuses upon the relationship between the judiciary and the legislature. As has already been noted, the act of interpretation through the ascription of meaning to the text may be viewed as a law-making function. Whilst reference has been made to strategies available to the courts which purport to deny the law-making nature of interpretation, such strategies are not completely successful; even in explicit practice, successive readings purporting to follow a literal interpretation, for example, may not be in total agreement as to the meaning of the text. In the event of such an outcome a question arises as to the status of the respective interpretations. Suggestions that one judicial interpretation may or must be privileged can be read to imply that the interpretation is a source of law superior to the actual words of the statutory text, which directly challenges the position of the text as the supreme source of law. In *Ogden Industries v. Lucas* [1970] AC 113, Lord Upjohn considered the matter and concluded:

> 'It is quite clear that judicial statements as to the construction and intention of an Act must never be allowed to supplant or supersede its proper construction and *courts must beware of falling into the error of treating the law to be laid down by the judge in construing the Act rather than found in the Act itself.* No doubt a decision on particular words binds inferior courts on the construction of those words on similar facts but beyond that the observations of the judges on the construction of statutes may be of the greatest help and guidance but are entitled to no more than respect and cannot absolve the court from its duty in exercising an independent judgment [emphasis added by Goodrich].'

His observations provide a striking illustration of the narrow political line formally espoused by the judiciary, one which in the last instance predictably asserts the superiority of the legal text over its interpreters and wittingly or unwittingly denies that the ritual claim to 'literal obedience' to the statutory text may mask any number of strategies of interpretation."

The presumptions of interpretation can be illustrated through examples.

Gregory v. Fearn [1953] 1 W.L.R. 974, CA.

"Appeal from Judge Caporn sitting at Nottingham County Court.

The plaintiff, A. R. Gregory, acting in the course of his normal business as an estate agent, on April 2, 1952, which was a Sunday, signed a contract of agency for the sale of a house, whereby the vendor, the defendant, George Fearn, agreed to pay to the plaintiff £100 when the property was sold, the property to be deemed to have been sold 'and the commission payable on the receipt of a deposit or a purchase agreement being entered into by a purchaser.' Subsequently, the estate agent brought proceedings to recover the commission, alleging that he had introduced a purchaser, one Owen, who had entered into a purchase agreement, but had subsequently refused to complete because he found that he would not be able to use the premises for business purposes. Owen alleged that the plaintiff had misrepresented to him that it could be so used.

Judge Caporn held that as the contract appointing the plaintiff agent for the vendor had been made on a Sunday and involved the doing by the plaintiff of his ordinary business as an estate agent, it offended against section 1 of the Sunday Observance Act, 1677, and, consequently, that the plaintiff could not rely on it. He further decided, on other grounds which are not material to this report, that the plaintiff would not have been able to establish his claim to the commission even if the contract had been valid.

The plaintiff appealed.

Evershed M.R., after referring to the facts: Judge Caporn concluded against the plaintiff on the ground among others, that the agreement fell within the prohibition of section 1 of the Sunday Observance Act, 1677, as having involved the doing on the Lord's Day of business or work by a tradesman, that is, an estate agent, in his ordinary calling.

On the view which I take, it is not strictly necessary to decide that point. But it seems to me, as at presently advised, that Mr Heald is right when he says that an estate agent is not a 'tradesman' within the contemplation of that section, even if the execution by him of a contract of this kind was the doing of business or work in his ordinary calling. At first sight, Mr Heald's argument appeared to be difficult, because the formula in section 1 of the Act of 1677 is 'no tradesman, artificer, workman, labourer, or other person whatsoever'; and assuming that an estate agent is not a tradesman, he would be, prima facie, within the formula 'other person whatsoever.' It has, however, long been established that those words 'other person whatsoever' are to be construed *ejusdem generis* with those which precede it: so that, for the defendant to succeed on this point, it must be shown that an estate agent is a tradesman or something sufficiently like a tradesman to be covered by the *ejusdem generis* rule. . . ."

[Evershed M.R. dismissed the appeal. Birkett L.J. and Romer L.J. concurred].

McBoyle v. United States 293 U.S. 25 (1930).

Mr Justice Holmes delivered the opinion of the U.S. Supreme Court:

"The petitioner was convicted of transporting from Ottawa, Illinois, to Guymon, Oklahoma, an airplane that he knew to have been stolen, and was sentenced to serve three years' imprisonment and to pay a fine of $2,000. The judgment was affirmed by the Circuit Court of Appeals for the Tenth Circuit 43 F (2d) 273. A writ of certiorari was granted by this Court on the question whether the National Motor Vehicle Theft Act applies to aircraft. . . . That Act provides: 'Sec 2. That when used in this Act:

(a) The term 'motor vehicle' shall include an automobile, automobile truck, automobile wagon, motor cycle, or any other self-propelled vehicle not designed for running on rails; . . . Sec 3. That whoever shall transport or cause to be transported in interstate or foreign commerce a motor vehicle, knowing the same to have been stolen, shall be punished by a fine of not more than \$5,000, or by imprisonment of not more than five years, or both.'

Section 2 defines the motor vehicles of which the transportation in interstate commerce is punished in section 3. The question is the meaning of the word 'vehicle' in the phrase 'any other self-propelled vehicle not designed for running on rails.' No doubt etymologically it is possible to use the word to signify a conveyance working on land, water or air, and sometimes legislation extends the use in that direction. . . . But in everyday speech 'vehicle' calls up the picture of a thing moving on land. . . . For after including automobile truck, automobile wagon and motor cycle, the words 'any other self-propelled vehicle not designed for running on rails' still indicate that a vehicle in the popular sense, that is a vehicle running on land, is the theme. It is a vehicle that runs, not something, not commonly called a vehicle, that flies. Airplanes were well known in 1919, when this statute was passed; but it is admitted that they were not mentioned in the reports or in the debates in Congress. It is impossible to read words that so carefully enumerate the different forms of motor vehicles and have no reference of any kind to aircraft, as including airplanes under a term that usage more and more precisely confines to a different class. . . .

Although it is not likely that a criminal will carefully consider the text of the law before he murders or steals, it is reasonable that a fair warning should be given to the world in language that the common world will understand, of what the law intends to do if a certain line is passed. To make the warning fair, so far as possible the line should be clear. When a rule of conduct is laid down in words that evoke in the common mind only the picture of vehicles moving on land, the statute should not be extended to aircraft, simply because it may seem to us that a similar policy applies, or upon the speculation that, if the legislature had thought of it, very likely broader words would have been used.

Judgment reversed."

Problem question

You are a junior solicitor in a law firm. A senior partner has come to you for your legal opinion so that he can advise a client named Anne Artiste. Anne is a painter of watercolours who owns a small piece of land outside Stoketon. She has pulled an old caravan on this land. The caravan is still "on wheels". Anne uses this caravan as her studio and retreat. When inspired, she will often spend several days at a time working long hours in the caravan (and eating and sleeping there). Lately, she has been spending even more time at the caravan because she is not getting along with her partner. Anne also sells her paintings to people who come from far and wide to buy them. She has built a small shed next to the caravan which has a sign on it—"Anne's Gallery"—where her works are displayed and sold. Last month, a stray spaniel showed up. Anne tried to chase the dog away without success. However, one day she felt sorry for the dog and gave it some food and water. She has repeated this practice on occasion. The dog often goes away for fairly long periods, but lately it has rather taken to Anne and sometimes sleeps immediately outside the shed. Anne also has been concerned with her safety while staying in the caravan. She is comforted by the spaniel's loud and vicious barking whenever strangers are in the area. Purely as a further security measure, Anne has displayed a sign on the shed which reads "Warning: Dangerous Guard Dog on Premises".

Last week, an earnest local authority dog warden from Stoketon came to view some of Anne's watercolours. He found the spaniel running loose on Anne's property and barking earnestly and aggressively. Seeing the warning sign, the warden immediately charged Anne with a violation of section 1 of the Guard Dogs Act 1975. Anne has now retained your firm to represent her.

Your senior partner has asked you to write a 1,500 word memorandum of law, in which you explain the bases upon which a legal argument can be made before the Magistrates' Court that Anne has not acted in violation of the relevant statute. You are also asked to assess the likely chances of success of such an argument.

In order to answer this assignment, you will need to undertake legal research. In particular, you should find a copy of the Guard Dogs Act 1975, any cases which are of assistance to the issues of interpretation raised by the problem, and the relevant debates in *Hansard*, portions of which *might be* admissible in court.

9

STATUTORY INTERPRETATION: THE IMPACT OF EUROPEAN LAW

In this, our final chapter on the interpretation of statutes, we focus on the implications of European law for the principles of statutory interpretation which we have examined in previous chapters. Our focus is two fold. First, we look at the law of the European Community and European Union, and we begin with an examination of the approaches to statutory interpretation adopted by the European Court of Justice. Our interest is in how the interpretation of European law by the ECJ differs from the "traditional" approaches to interpretation in a common law system. We then turn to the interpretation of European law in common law courts and look at how our own courts approach European law, as well as how *domestic* law must be interpreted in light of Britain's legal obligations as a member of the European Union. In the second part of the chapter, our focus shifts to European human rights law, in the form of the European Convention on Human Rights. We will see that the Convention has had an increasing importance within U.K. law, one which may grow significantly as a result of the planned incorporation of the Convention into domestic law.

STATUTORY INTERPRETATION IN THE EUROPEAN COURT OF JUSTICE

We looked at the constitutional implications of membership in the European Union in Chapter 4. In this chapter, we examine the implications of that membership for statutory interpretation. We begin with a consideration of the European Court of Justice, the judicial arm of the E.U.

Paul Craig and Gráinne de Búrca, *E.C. Law: Text, Cases & Materials* (Clarendon Press, Oxford, 1995), pp. 79–82:

Role and methodology of the court

"The specific tasks to be performed by the Court are described in the Treaties. Its jurisdiction is set out in various Articles of the Treaties, the main provisions being Articles 169 to 186 of the EC Treaty. The Treaty on European Union enhanced the jurisdiction of the Court under Article 171, by empowering it to impose a pecuniary penalty on a Member State which has failed to comply with a previous judgment, in which that state was found to be in breach of Treaty obligations. . . .

[I]t is Article 164, the provision which sets out its task in very general terms, which has perhaps figured most prominently in the Court's shaping of its own sphere of influence. The Court has used this provision—imaginatively described as a 'pregnant formula'—to define its role very broadly. Article 164 provides that 'the Court of Justice shall ensure that in the interpretation and application of this Treaty, the law is observed'. . . . [T]he Court has utilized this provision to extend its review jurisdiction to cover bodies which were not expressly subject to it, and to measures which were not listed in the Treaty. In the name of preserving 'the rule of law' in the Community, the Court has extended its functions beyond those expressly outlined in the Treaty under which it was established. Given the fact that the competence of the Community, and hence of its institutions, has always been accepted to be an attributed competence, limited to what was given by the Treaty, the question of an inherent jurisdiction of the Court is problematic. . . .

[I]n addition to extending its own review jurisdiction under Article 164, the 'gap filling' role of the Court has also extended to developing principles of a constitutional nature as part of Community law to which it then claims to hold both the institutions and the Member States bound, when they act within the Community sphere. It has also played a significant role in its interaction with the other institutions, reacting to action taken by them or prompting them to act as a result of its decisions. As interpreter of the Treaties and their limits, the Court has had to adjudicate not just among the institutions in disputes over their respective powers and competences, but also, and more contentiously still, in questions concerning the proper sphere of the Community as against that of the Member States. This sort of adjudication can arise in many guises—either in direct challenges to Community action by Member States, or in actions between the institutions, or in preliminary references which may relate to the scope of areas of substantive Community law.

In the years of so-called institutional malaise or stagnation, the Court can be seen to have played a 'political' role through law, by rendering the Treaty effective even when its provisions had not been implemented as required by the Community, and in rendering secondary legislation effective even when it has not been properly implemented by Member States. It adopted an active part in the creation of the internal market through the litigation which came before it, by the negative means of requiring the removal of national barriers to trade, at a time when progress towards completing the Single Market through positive legislative harmonization was hindered by institutional inaction.

The Court has achieved the 'hobbyhorse' status which it occupies amongst European lawyers as much on account of its reasoning and methodology as on account of the impact of its decisions. Its approach to interpretation is generally described as a purposive or teleological method, although not in the sense of seeking the purpose or aim of the authors of a text. The fact that the *travaux préparatoires* to the Treaties were deliberately never published means that these are not a source which can be used, and this is reflected in much of the Court's case law. In a case in which Belgium invoked an argument based on the intention of the states at the time the Treaty was drafted, the Commission argued that 'as historical interpretation plays hardly any part in Community law it would be futile to refer to the intentions of the authors of the Treaty'. In the case of secondary legislation, although the discussions at Council and Commission meetings are not published, declarations and extracts from the minutes have occasionally been supplied and have been argued by parties before the Court as an aid to interpretation. The Court has not been consistent in its approach to such material, occasionally referring to it for assistance, but in most cases denying its relevance if it does not appear in the text of the legislation itself.

Rather than adopting a narrower historical-purposive approach, the Court tends to examine the whole context in which a particular provision is situated—which often involves looking at the preamble to the Treaties or to legislation—and it gives the interpretation most likely to further what the Court considers that provision in its context was aimed to achieve. Often this is very far from a literal interpretation of the Treaty or of legislation in question, even to the extent of flying in the face of the express language, and this aspect of the Court's methodology has attracted sharp criticism."

A good example of the primacy of a broad, contextual approach to interpretation can be found in the ECJ's interpretation of the "free movement" provisions of the E.C. Treaty. The relevant Treaty provision is Article 48(3), which provides that the freedom of movement of workers shall entail the right "(a) to accept offers of employment actually made; (b) to move freely within the territory of the Member States for this purpose. . .". The question was whether the right of free movement included the right of a citizen of the E.C. to look for work in another member state.

The Queen v. Immigration Appeal Tribunal, ex parte Antonissen [1991] E.C.R. 1–745, ECJ.

European Court of Justice:

"1. By an order of 14 June 1989, which was received at the Court on 21 September 1989, the High Court of Justice, Queen's Bench Division, referred to the Court for a preliminary ruling under Article 177 of the EEC Treaty two questions on the interpretation of the provisions of Community law governing the free movement of workers as regards the scope of the right of residence of nationals of Member States seeking employment in another Member State.

2. The questions arose in proceedings between Mr Gustaff Desiderius Antonissen, a Belgian national, and the Secretary of State for Home Affairs, who on 27 November 1987 decided to deport him from the United Kingdom.

3. Mr Antonissen arrived in the United Kingdom in October 1984. He had not yet found work there when, on 3 March 1987, he was sentenced by the Liverpool Crown Court to two terms of imprisonment for unlawful possession of cocaine and possession of that drug with intent to supply. He was released on parole on 21 December 1987.

4. The decision to order Mr Antonissen's deportation was based on section 3(5)(b) of the Immigration Act 1971 ('the 1971 Act'), which authorizes the Secretary of State to deport foreign nationals if he considers that it would be 'conducive to the public good'.

5. Mr Antonissen lodged an appeal against the Secretary of State's decision with the Immigration Appeal Tribunal. Before the Tribunal Mr Antonissen argued that since he was a Community national he must qualify for the protection afforded by Council Directive 64/221/EEC of 25 February 1964 on the coordination of special measures concerning the movement and residence of foreign nationals which are justified on grounds of public policy, public security or public health. The Tribunal took the view that, since he had been seeking employment in the United Kingdom for more than six months, he could no longer be treated as a Community worker and claim that the directive should apply in his case. The Tribunal based this part of its decision on paragraph 143 of the Statement of Changes in Immigration Rules (HC169), adopted pursuant to the 1971 Act, under which a national of a Member State may be deported if, after six months from admission to the United Kingdom, he has not yet found employment or is not carrying on any other occupation.

6. His appeal being dismissed, Mr Antonissen made an application for judicial review to the High Court of Justice, Queen's Bench Division, which stayed the proceedings and referred the following questions to the Court of Justice for a preliminary ruling:

'1 For the purpose of determining whether a national of a Member State is to be treated as a 'worker' within the meaning of Article 48 of the EEC Treaty when seeking employment in the territory of another Member State so as to be immune from deportation save in accordance with Council Directive 64/221 of 25 February 1964, may the legislature of the second Member State provide that such a national may be required to leave the territory of that State (subject to appeal) if after six months from admission to that territory he has failed to enter employment?

2 In answering the foregoing question what weight if any is to be attached by a court or tribunal of a Member State to the declaration contained in the minutes of the meeting of the Council when the Council adopted Directive 68/36?'

7. Reference is made to the Report for the Hearing for a fuller account of the facts of the case before the national court, the applicable legislation and the written observations submitted to the Court, which are mentioned or discussed hereinafter only in so far as is necessary for the reasoning of the Court.

8. By means of the questions submitted to the Court for a preliminary ruling the national court essentially seeks to establish whether it is contrary to the provisions of Community law governing the free movement of workers for the legislation of a Member State to provide that a national of another Member State who entered the first State in order to seek employment may be required to leave the territory of that State (subject to appeal) if he has not found employment there after six months.

9. In that connection it has been argued that, according to the strict wording of Article 48 of the Treaty, Community nationals are given the right to move freely within the territory of the Member States for the purpose only of accepting offers of employment actually made (Article 48(3)(a) and (b)) whilst the right to stay in the territory of a Member State is stated to be for the purpose of employment (Article 48(3)(c)).

10. Such an interpretation would exclude the right of a national of a Member State to move freely and to stay in the territory of the other Member States in order to seek employment there, and cannot be upheld.

11. Indeed, as the Court has consistently held, freedom of movement for workers forms one of the foundations of the Community and, consequently, the provisions laying down that freedom must be given a broad interpretation.

12. Moreover, a strict interpretation of Article 48(3) would jeopardize the actual chances that a national of a Member State who is seeking employment will find it in another Member State, and would, as a result, make the provision ineffective.

13. It follows that Article 48(3) must be interpreted as enumerating, in a non-exhaustive way, certain rights benefiting nationals of Member States in the context of the free movement of workers and that that freedom also entails the right for nationals of Member States to move freely within the territory of the other Member States and to stay there for the purposes of seeking employment.

14. Moreover, this interpretation of the Treaty corresponds to that of the Community legislature, as appears from the provisions adopted in order to implement the principle of free movement, in particular Articles 1 and 5 of Regulation No 1612/68/EEC of the Council of 15 October 1968 on freedom of movement for workers within the Community, which presuppose that Community nationals are entitled to move in order to look for employment, and hence to stay, in another Member State.

15. It must therefore be ascertained whether the right, under Article 48 and the provisions of Regulation No 1612/68, to stay in a Member State for the purposes of seeking employment can be subjected to a temporal limitation.

16. In that regard, it must be pointed out in the first place that the effectiveness of Article 48 is secured in so far as Community legislation or, in its absence, the legislation of a Member State gives persons concerned a reasonable time in which to apprise themselves, in the territory of the Member State concerned, of offers of employment corresponding to their occupational qualifications and to take, where appropriate, the necessary steps in order to be engaged.

17. The national court referred to the declaration recorded in the Council minutes at the time of the adoption of the aforesaid Regulation No 1612/68 and of Council Directive 68/36/EEC (of the same date) on the abolition of restrictions on movement and residence within the Community for workers of Member States and their families. That declaration read as follows:

'Nationals of a Member State as referred to in Article 1 [of the directive] who move to another Member State in order to seek work there shall be allowed a minimum period of three months for the purpose; in the event of their not having found employment by the end of that period, their residence on the territory of this second State may be brought to an end.

However, if the above mentioned persons should be taken charge of by national assistance (social welfare) in the second State during the aforesaid period they may be invited to leave the territory of this second State.'

18. However, such a declaration cannot be used for the purpose of interpreting a provision of secondary legislation where, as in this case, no reference is made to the content of the declaration in the wording of the provision in question. The declaration therefore has no legal significance. . . .

21. In the absence of a Community provision prescribing the period during which Community nationals seeking employment in a Member State may stay there, a period of six months, such as that laid down in the national legislation at issue in the main proceedings, does not appear in principle to be insufficient to enable the persons concerned to apprise themselves, in the host Member State, of offers of employment corresponding to their occupational qualifications and to take, where appropriate, the necessary steps in order to be engaged and, therefore, does not jeopardize the effectiveness of the principle of free movement. However, if after the expiry of that period the person concerned provides evidence that he is continuing to seek employment and that he has genuine chances of being engaged, he cannot be required to leave the territory of the host Member State.

22. It must therefore be stated in reply to the questions submitted by the national court that it is not contrary to the provisions of Community law governing the free movement of workers for the legislation of a Member State to provide that a national of another Member State who entered the first State in order to seek employment may be required to leave the territory of that State (subject to appeal) if he has not found employment there after six months, unless the person concerned provides evidence that he is continuing to seek employment and that he has genuine chances of being engaged."

The judgment in *Antonissen* is interesting, not only for the method of interpretation —which is far from literal—but also for the style of the judgment, which is representative of ECJ judgments more generally. The method of interpretation adopted in *Antonissen* has been subject to criticism.

Trevor C. Hartley, "Five Forms of Uncertainty in European Community Law" (1996) 55 C.L.J. 265 at 278:

"As is well known, the European Court adopts a different method of interpretation from that usually followed by English courts. Where a provision is clear and unambiguous, English courts will usually follow the plain meaning of the words used; the European Court, on the other hand, gives much greater emphasis to ensuring that the objective of the measure is attained. In order to do so, it will sometimes depart from the plain meaning.

The objection to this from a constitutional point of view is that it involves the Court taking on a legislative role and revising the work of the legislator. From a more general point of view, it raises the question how the objective of a measure is to be determined. The Treaties express the will of the Member States; most EC legislation is adopted by the Council, which is made up of the representatives of the Member States. In either case, therefore, the objective of a provision must depend on the intention of the Member States. As was said previously, however, the Member States often have no common intention, and are united only in their agreement to adopt a certain form of words. In such a case, an objective cannot be ascribed to the measure beyond that implied by the words themselves.

This question has been discussed recently in another article, in which examples were given of cases in the constitutional sphere in which it was thought that the European Court had departed from the plain meaning of the words used. Here, a different example will be chosen, the *Antonissen* case. The provision in question in that case, Article 48(3) EC, is clear and unambiguous in so far as it concerns person migrating to find work: it does not cover them. The Court, however, refused to accept that this was the correct interpretation. It gave three reasons: first, that such an interpretation would exclude the right of a Community migrant to move freely to another Member State to seek employment; secondly, that the Court had previously held that provisions—such as Article 48—that lay down the right of free movement of workers must be given a broad interpretation, since such freedom constitutes one of the foundations of the Community; and finally, that a 'strict' interpretation of Article 48(3) 'would jeopardise the actual chances that a national of a Member State who is seeking employment will find it in another Member State, and would, as a result, make the provision ineffective.'

The argument may be set out as follows: first, it is assumed—reasonably enough—that the objective of Article 48 is to allow nationals of one Member State to obtain employment in another; secondly, it is assumed—again reasonably—that this will be more difficult if workers cannot travel to another Member State to look for employment on the spot: from these two assumptions the conclusion is drawn that the plain meaning of the words must be ignored so as to ensure that workers have this right.

The objection to this is that it fails to recognise the possibility that, though the authors of the Treaty may have wished to make it easier for Community nationals to work in another Member State, this might not have been the only consideration they had in mind. Law-making almost always involves balancing conflicting interests and objectives. The words of a provision express the way the balance is struck by the legislator. To assume that there is only one objective, or that one objective must be pursued irrespective of all other considerations, is both irresponsible and naïve.

In the case of Article 48 EC, another objective that the Member States presumably had in mind was to avoid an influx of unemployed migrants who might be unable to support themselves. The wording of Article 48(3) reflects the balance struck by the Member States when they signed the Treaty in 1957. No doubt the situation changed as the years passed, and by 1968 the Member States were willing to take a further step. They could have done this by granting a right of entry in the legislation they adopted that year. They did not do this. Instead, they made the 'secret' declaration. The purpose of this was apparently to ensure that the right was granted under national law, rather than under Community law, thus allowing the Member States to decide its precise extent. This may have represented a compromise between those Member States that wanted to give further rights to migrant workers and those that were concerned about the economic and social consequences.

Where the text of a provision is itself unclear, the European Court's method of interpretation may not lead to any greater uncertainty; in some cases, indeed, it may be a good solution. Where the words of the provision are clear, however, it produces uncertainty, since it is never possible to predict with accuracy what the Court will regard as the objectives of the provision, what it will consider necessary to ensure their attainment and how far it will be willing to go in departing from the words of the provision in order to achieve those objectives."

NOTES

• Another unique characteristic of European legislation is the fact that there are 12 official languages of the E.U. (Danish, Dutch, English, Finnish, French, Gaelic, German, Greek, Italian, Portugese, Swedish, and Spanish). With the exception of Gaelic, they are also all working languages of the E.U.! As Millett argues:

"Because all . . . language versions are authentic, the literal meaning of a Community legislative text in one language cannot be relied on as a conclusive guide to its meaning. It has to be compared with the other language versions, and in the practice of the Court of Justice—usually also checked against another criterion of interpretation, such as the purpose of the provision in question. Thus the multilingual nature of Community legislation necessarily reduces the importance of the literal method of interpretation, which contrasts with the predominant place it enjoys in the interpretation of British domestic legislation."[1]

THE IMPACT OF EUROPEAN COMMUNITY LAW ON INTERPRETATION IN DOMESTIC COURTS

As we saw in Chapter 4, the principle of the supremacy of Parliament has had to be modified by the courts in light of Britain's membership in the European Community and European Union. In Chapter 4, we looked at the decision of the European Court of Justice and House of Lords in *Factortame number 2* [1991] 1 All E.R. 70, in which it was held to be the duty of national courts to override rules of national law which were in conflict with directly enforceable rules of European Community law. Our focus in this section is on a distinct, but related, matter: the approaches which domestic courts take to the interpretation of European legislation. As we discussed in the previous section, the European Court of Justice, in keeping with its continental European roots, takes a rather different approach to statutory interpretation than is typical of a common law court. Thus, we can ask, to what extent should (and do) common law courts adapt their approach to statutory interpretation when dealing with E.C. legislation? Although national courts sometimes will refer questions concerning the interpretation of E.C. law to the ECJ pursuant to Article 177 of the E.C. Treaty, in some cases they will interpret legislation themselves in light of European law. An early, and at that time unorthodox approach, was advocated some years ago by Lord Denning:

"Seeing these differences, what are the English courts to do when they are faced with a problem of interpretation? They must follow the European pattern. No longer must they examine the words in meticulous detail. No longer must they argue about the precise grammatical sense. They must look to the purpose or intent. To quote the words of the European Court in the *Da Costa*[2] case: they must limit themselves to deducing from 'the wording and the spirit of the treaty the meaning of the Community rules . . .'. They must not confine themselves to the English text. They must consider, if need be, all the authentic texts, of which there are now eight. They must divine the spirit of the treaty and gain inspiration from it. If they find a gap, they must fill it as best they can. They must do what the framers of the instrument would have done if they had thought about it. So we must do the same. Those are the principles, as I understand it, on which the European Court acts."[3]

The cynic might argue that for Lord Denning, Britain's entry into the European Community provided a ready justification for a more liberal, "gap filling" approach to statutory interpretation; one which was more in keeping with his long preferred approach.

---

[1] Timothy Millett, "Rules of Interpretation of EEC Legislation" (1989) 10 Statute Law Review 163.
[2] [1963] C.M.L.R. 224 at 237.
[3] *H. P. Bulmer Ltd and another v. J. Bollinger SA and others* [1974] 2 All E.R. 1226 at 1237–1238, CA.

Some years later, Lord Diplock pointed to both similarities and differences between the approach of the European Court of Justice and English courts:

"The European court, in contrast to English courts, applies teleological rather than historical methods to the interpretation of the Treaties and other Community legislation. It seeks to give effect to what it conceives to be the spirit rather than the letter of the Treaties; sometimes, indeed, to an English judge, it may seem to the exclusion of the letter. It views the Communities as living and expanding organisms and the interpretation of the provisions of the Treaties as changing to match their growth. For these reasons the European Court does not apply the doctrine of precedent to its own decisions as rigidly as does an English court. Nevertheless, as any browsing in the Common Market Law Reports will show, the European Court too seeks to maintain consistency in its decision in the interest of legal certainty. Consequently in the opinions of the Advocates General and the judgments of the court itself, citations of previous judgments in the court are as frequent as citations of previous authority in judgments of English courts. Thus, when there is a *cursus curiae*, a series of decisions to the same effect, or what is described in the court's own rules (article 95) as 'an established body of case law' an English court if the case before it is one to which an established body of case law plainly applies, may properly take the view that no real question of interpretation is involved that makes reference under article 177 necessary in order to give judgment."[4]

In *Henn and Darby*, Lord Diplock also explicitly warned of the "danger of an English court applying English canons of statutory construction to the interpretation of the Treaty or, for that matter, of Regulations or Directives".[5]

The question of interpretive approaches is made more complex when domestic legislation is enacted in order to fulfil obligations under European Community law. In this situation, courts here may be faced with the task of interpreting law made in this country in order to comply with European law. How should our courts interpret in that situation? The following case represents a judicial response.

Litster and others v. Forth Dry Dock and Engineering Co. Ltd and another
[1989] 1 All E.R. 1134, HL.

Lord Oliver of Aylmerton:
"My Lords, this appeal raises, not for the first time, the broad question of the approach to be adopted by courts in the United Kingdom to domestic legislation enacted in order to give effect to this country's obligations under the EEC Treaty. The legislation with which the appeal is concerned is a statutory instrument made on 14 December 1981 pursuant to para 2(2) of Sch 2 to the European Communities Act 1972 and entitled the Transfer of Undertakings (Protection of Employment) Regulations 1981, SI 1981/1794. The regulations were made by the Secretary of State, and this is common ground, in order to give effect to EC Council Directive 77/187 adopted by the Council of the European Communities on 14 February 1977 to provide for the approximation of the laws of the member states relating to the safeguarding of employees' rights in the event of transfer of undertakings, businesses or parts of businesses. The question which arises is whether it has achieved this object.

---

[4] *Henn and Darby v. Director of Public Prosecutions* [1981] A.C. 850 at 905, HL.
[5] *ibid.* at 904.

The approach to the construction of primary and subordinate legislation enacted to give effect to the United Kingdom's obligations under the EEC Treaty have been the subject matter of recent authority in this House (see *Pickstone v. Freemans plc* [1988] 2 All ER 803, [1989] AC 66) and is not in doubt. If the legislation can reasonably be construed so as to conform with those obligations, obligations which are to be ascertained not only from the wording of the relevant directive but from the interpretation placed on it by the Court of Justice of the European Communities, such a purposive construction will be applied even though, perhaps, it may involve some departure from the strict and literal application of the words which the legislature has elected to use.

It will, I think, be convenient to consider the terms of the directive and the regulations before outlining the circumstances in which the instant appeal arises. The broad scope of the directive appears from the following two recitals:

'Whereas economic trends are bringing in their wake, at both national and Community level, changes in the structure of undertakings, through transfers of undertakings, businesses or parts of businesses to other employers as a result of legal transfers or mergers; Whereas it is necessary to provide for the protection of employees in the event of a change of employer, in particular, to ensure that their rights are safeguarded . . .'

By art 1 it is provided that the directive shall apply to the transfer of an undertaking, business or part of a business to another employer. Article 2 contains definitions, the relevant ones for present purposes being:

'(a) "transferor" means any natural or legal person who, by reason of a transfer within the meaning of Article 1(1), ceases to be the employer in respect of the undertaking, business or part of the business; (b) 'transferee' means any natural or legal person who, by reason of a transfer within the meaning of Article 1(1), becomes the employer in respect of the undertaking, business or part of the business . . .'

Section II is headed '*Safeguarding of employees' rights*' and contains three articles of which the relevant ones for present purposes are arts 3 and 4. Article 3 provides (so far as material):

'1. The transferor's rights and obligations arising from a contract of employment or from an employment relationship existing on the date of a transfer within the meaning of Article 1(1) shall, by reason of such transfer, be transferred to the transferee. . .' . . .

Article 4 is, so far as material, in the following terms:

'1. The transfer of an undertaking, business or part of a business shall not in itself constitute grounds for dismissal by the transferor or the transferee. This provision shall not stand in the way of dismissals that may take place for economic, technical or organisational reasons entailing changes in the workforce . . .
2. If the contract of employment or the employment relationship is terminated because the transfer within the meaning of Article 1(1) involves a substantial change in working conditions to the detriment of the employee, the employer shall be regarded as having been responsible for termination of the contract of employment or of the employment relationship.' . . .

Turning now to the 1981 regulations, which came into operation in 1982 and which represent the British government's perception at that time of its obligations under the directive, these provide for relevant purposes as follows: . . .

'5 (1) A relevant transfer shall not operate so as to terminate the contract of employment of any person employed by the transferor in the undertaking or part transferred but any such contract which would otherwise have been terminated by the transfer shall have effect after the transfer as if originally made between the person so employed and the transferee. (2) Without prejudice to paragraph (1) above, on the completion of a relevant transfer— (a) all the transferor's rights, powers, duties and liabilities under or in connection with any such contract, shall be transferred by virtue of this Regulation to the transferee; and (b) anything done before the transfer is completed by or in relation to the transferor in respect of that contract or a person employed in that undertaking or part shall be deemed to have been done by or in relation to the transferee.

(3) Any reference in paragraph (1) or (2) above to a person employed in an undertaking or part of one transferred by a relevant transfer is a reference to a person so employed immediately before the transfer, including, where the transfer is effected by a series of two or more transactions, a person so employed immediately before any of those transactions . . .

8 (1) Where either before or after a relevant transfer, any employee of the transferor or transferee is dismissed, that employee shall be treated for the purposes of art V of the 1978 Act and Articles 2 to 41 of the 1976 Order (unfair dismissal) as unfairly dismissed if the transfer or a reason connected with it is the reason or the principal reason for his dismissal. . . .'

It will be seen that, as is to be expected, the scope and purpose of both the directive and the regulations are the same, that is to ensure that on any transfer of an undertaking or part of an undertaking, the employment of the existing workers in the undertaking is preserved or, if their employment terminates solely by reason of the transfer, that their rights arising out of that determination are effectively safeguarded. It may, I think, be assumed that those who drafted both the directive and the regulations were sufficiently acquainted with the realities of life to appreciate that a frequent, indeed, possibly the most frequent, occasion on which a business or part of a business is transferred is when the original employer is insolvent, so that an employee whose employment is terminated on the transfer will have no effective remedy for unfair dismissal unless it is capable of being exerted against the transferee. It can hardly have been contemplated that, where the only reason for the determination of the employment is the transfer of the undertaking or the relevant part of it, the parties to the transfer would be at liberty to avoid the manifest purpose of the directive by the simple expedient of wrongfully dismissing the workforce a few minutes before the completion of the transfer. The European Court has expressed, in the clearest terms, the opinion that so transparent a device would not avoid the operation of the directive, and if the effect of the regulations is that under the law of the United Kingdom it has that effect, then your Lordships are compelled to conclude that the regulations are gravely defective and the government of the United Kingdom has failed to comply with its mandatory obligations under the directive. If your Lordships are in fact compelled to that conclusion, so be it; but it is not, I venture to think, a conclusion which any of your Lordships would willingly embrace in the absence of the most compulsive content rendering any other conclusion impossible.

My Lords, the circumstances in which the question has arisen for decision in the instant case are these. The first respondents, Forth Dry Dock and Engineering Co Ltd, carried on a business of ship repairers at the Edinburgh dry dock, premises which they held under a lease from the Forth Ports Authority. At the material time, the 12 appellants were tradesmen employed in that business. They were part of a permanent workforce of skilled shipworkers of various trades who had been continuously employed by the first respondents since 1981 or 1982. In the year 1983 the group of companies of which the first respondents formed part was in financial difficulties and the receiver of the various companies in the group (including the first respondents) was appointed by the debenture holder, Lloyd's Bank, on September 28, 1983. The workforce was then told by the receiver's representative, a Mr Page, that the intention was to sell the business as a going concern and that their jobs would be safe. That belief may have been genuinely entertained at the time, but it was falsified in the event.

On 23 November 1983 the second respondents, Forth Estuary Engineering Ltd (Forth Estuary) was incorporated. A few days before the transfer of the first respondents' assets, which took place on 6 February 1984, the capital of Forth Estuary was increased from £1,000 to £20,000: 85% of the issued capital became vested in a Mr Brooshooft, who had been a financial adviser to the first respondents' company, and 10% in a Mr Hughes, who had been a director of and had managed the business of the first respondents. On 6 February 1984 an agreement was entered into between the first respondents, the receivers and Forth Estuary under which (a) all the first respondents' business assets, consisting of plant, machinery, equipment, furniture and office equipment specified in a schedule, were acquired by Forth Estuary at a price of £33,500 payable on execution of the agreement, (b) the first respondents undertook to cease business at close of business on that day (at which time the sale and purchase was to be carried into effect) and (c) the first respondents undertook forthwith to relinquish their rights under the lease of the dry dock which they held from the ports authority. Before this, it is not clear exactly when, Forth Estuary had obtained from the Forth Ports Authority a new lease of the property previously let to the first respondents (with the exception of one shed). It is interesting to note that under cl 14 of this agreement, its construction, validity and performance were to be governed by English law and the courts of England were given exclusive jurisdiction. As a matter of English law, therefore, the ownership of the assets transferred passed in equity to Forth Estuary on the execution of the agreement and those assets were, assuming, as we must assume, that the consideration was then paid as provided by the agreement, then held by the transferor as a bare trustee for the transferee. Up to this point the appellants had continued to be employed by the first respondents. It had, however, clearly been determined by the receivers, and, one infers, by Forth Estuary, that that situation was not to be permitted to continue and it is difficult, if not impossible, to resist the inference that the reason why it was not to be permitted to continue was that both parties were well aware of the provisions of the regulations to which I have already referred. It can hardly have been merely a fortunate coincidence that officers from the redundancy payments section of the Department of Employment were already at the dock on that afternoon when Mr Hughes and Mr Page arrived at approximately 3 pm having come straight from the office of Messrs Brodies, where the agreement had been signed. They addressed the workforce and told them that the business was to close down at 4.30 pm that day and that they were dismissed 'with immediate effect'. Each of the appellants was given a letter from the receivers under the first respondents' letterhead which was dated 6 February 1984 and was, so far as material, in the following terms:

> 'We would advise you that no further funds can be made available to pay your wages with effect from the close of business today and accordingly we have to inform you that your employment with the company is terminated with immediate effect. No payments will be made in respect of your accrued holiday pay, or the failure to give you your statutory period of notice. Under the Insolvency provisions of the Employment Protection Act, any claim you may have for the above will, subject to certain limitations, be paid to you by the Department of Employment out of the Redundancy Fund . . . Your wages up to the date of dismissal will be paid in the normal way and you will be issued with a P45 from the company's head office.'

One of the less creditable aspects of the matter is that one of the appellants, Mr Walker, who was the union shop steward, asked specifically whether the business was being taken over by Forth Estuary, and was told by Mr Hughes that he knew nothing about a new company taking over, while Mr Page said that he knew nothing about a company called Forth Estuary Engineering. This indicates a calculated disregard for the obligations imposed by reg 10 of the 1981 regulations. Within 48 hours of their dismissal, the appellants learned, at the local job centre, that Forth Estuary was recruiting labour and a group of them went to fill in application forms for employment. None was successful and indeed only three former employees of the first respondents were taken on. Work which was in progress on the vessels on 6 February was subsequently continued and completed by Forth Estuary, which very soon had a workforce of similar size to that of the first respondents, embracing the same trade but recruited at lower rates of pay elsewhere than from the existing employees. . . .

Two questions then arise. First, was the time which elapsed between the dismissals and the transfer of so short a duration that, on the true construction of reg 5, the appellants were 'employed immediately before' the transfer, as required by para (3) of that regulation? Second, if the answer to that question is in the negative, what difference (if any) does it make that the reason, or the principal reason, for the dismissals was, as it clearly was, the imminent occurrence of the transfer so that the dismissals were, by reg 8(1), deemed to be unfair dismissals? . . .

Regulation 8(1) does not follow literally the wording of art 4(1). It provides only that if the reason for the dismissal of the employee is the transfer of the business, he has to be treated 'for the purposes of art V of the 1978 Act' as unfairly dismissed so as to confer on him the remedies provided by ss 69–79 of the Act (including, where it is considered appropriate, an order for reinstatement or re-engagement). If this provision fell to be construed by reference to the ordinary rules of construction applicable to a purely domestic statute and without reference to treaty obligations, it would, I think, be quite impermissible to regard it as having the same prohibitory effect as that attributed by the European Court to art 4 of the directive. But it has always to be borne in mind that the purpose of the directive and of the regulations was and is to 'safeguard' the rights of employees on a transfer and that there is a mandatory obligation to provide remedies which are effective and not merely symbolic to which the regulations were intended to give effect. The remedies provided by the 1978 Act in the case of an insolvent transferor are largely illusory unless they can be exerted against the transferee as the directive contemplates and I do not find it conceivable that, in framing regulations intending to give effect to the directive, the Secretary of State could have envisaged that its purpose should be capable of being avoided by the transparent device to which resort was had in the instant case. . . . Having regard to the manifest purpose of the regulations, I do not, for my part, feel inhibited from making such an implication in the instant case. The provision in reg 8(1) that a dismissal by reason of transfer is to be treated as an unfair dismissal, is merely a different way of saying that the transfer is not to 'constitute a ground for dismissal' as contemplated by art 4 of the directive and there is no good reason for denying to it the same effect as that attributed to that article. In effect this involves reading reg 5(3) as if there were inserted after the words 'immediately before the transfer' the words 'or would have been so employed if he had not been unfairly dismissed in the circumstances described in reg 8(1)'. For my part, I would make such an implication which is entirely consistent with the general scheme of the regulations and which is necessary if they are effectively to fulfil the purpose for which they were made of giving effect to the provisions of the directive. . . .

In the instant case it is quite clear that the reason for the dismissal of the appellants was the transfer of the business which had just been agreed and was going to take place almost at once. The effect of reg 5, construed as I have suggested that it should be, is that their employment continued with Forth Estuary. I would therefore allow the appeal. . . ."

[Lord Keith of Kinkel, Lord Brandon of Oakbrook, Lord Templeman, and Lord Jauncey of Tullichettle also allowed the appeal].

NOTES

- The Acquired Rights Directive has become a fairly controversial area of the regulation of employment relations; in particular, the decision of the ECJ that the "contracting out" of services could constitute a "legal transfer" within the meaning of the Directive.[6] This decision had enormous consequences within the U.K., involving "individuals and trade unions who had been adversely affected by the government's policies in relation to the compulsory competitive tendering of services by the National Health Service and by local authorities, or by the transfer of the provision of services from the public sector to the private or 'quasi-private' sector".[7] As More argues, the ECJ has been criticized for giving undue weight to employee rights in a series of cases involving the Acquired Rights Directive, to the detriment of employer "flexibility". As More concludes, however,

[6] *Rask v. ISS Kantineservice A/S* [1992] E.C.R. I-5755; *Schmidt v. Spar- und Leikhkasse der früheren Ämter Bordesholm, Kiel und Cronshagen* [1994] E.C.R. I-1311.
[7] Gillian More, "The Acquired Rights Directive: Frustrating or Facilitating Labour Market Flexibility" in *New Legal Dynamics of European Union* (J. Shaw, and G. More, eds., Clarendon Press, Oxford, 1995), pp. 129, 134.

"the Court's teleological interpretation of the Acquired Rights Directive has allowed it to be adapted to meet the needs of employment protection, albeit in a changed economic environment".[8] *Forth Dry Dock* is an example of such an interpretive approach in the *domestic* courts, when interpreting a *domestic* statutory instrument designed to implement *European* law.

THE INTERPRETATION OF EUROPEAN HUMAN RIGHTS LAW

In Chapter 4, we examined the impact of the European Convention on Human Rights on the principle of the supremacy of Parliament through the role of the European Court of Human Rights in Strasbourg. Courts in this country also operate under the presumption that Parliament in the legislation it enacts intended to comply with *international* law. As a consequence, courts have been prepared to examine international treaties, to which the United Kingdom is a signatory, as an aid in the interpretation of *ambiguous* legislation.[9]

This has been of importance with respect to the European Convention on Human Rights. Prior to incorporation into English law, the Convention has only been of assistance to domestic courts as an aid in interpreting ambiguous legislation.[10] The extent to which the Convention could be and should be turned to by domestic courts has been the subject of considerable academic comment.[11] With incorporation (or "semi-incorporation", as it is sometimes described) of the Convention into domestic law, its role in the interpretation of legislation may become clearer. The legislation to incorporate the Convention is the Human Rights Act.

Human Rights Act 1998

An Act to give further effect to rights and freedoms guaranteed under the European Convention on Human Rights; to make provision with respect to holders of certain judicial offices who become judges of the European Court of Human Rights; and for connected purposes.

Interpretation of legislation

3(1) So far as it is possible to do so, primary legislation and subordinate legislation must be read and given effect in a way which is compatible with the Convention rights.

(2) This section—

(a) applies to primary legislation and subordinate legislation whenever enacted;

---

[8] *ibid.* at 145.

[9] See *James Buchanan & Co. Ltd v. Babco Forwarding & Shipping (U.K.) Ltd* [1978] A.C. 141, HL; *Fothergill v. Monarch Airlines Ltd* [1981] A.C. 251, HL.

[10] See *e.g. Brind v. Secretary of State for the Home Department* [1991] 1 All E.R. 720, HL; *Derbyshire County Council v. Times Newspapers and others* [1992] 3 All E.R. 65, CA; *R. v. Secretary of State for the Home Department and Another* ex p. *Norney and Others* (1995) 7 Admin. L.R. 861, HC.

[11] See, *e.g.* Michael K. Addo, "The Role of English Courts in the Determination of the Place of the European Convention on Human Rights in English Law" (1995) 46 N.I.L.Q. 1; Brian Bix and Adam Tomkins, "Unconventional Uses of the Convention?" (1992) 55 M.L.R. 721; Nicholas Grief, "The Domestic Impact of the European Convention on Human Rights as Mediated Through Community Law" [1991] P.L. 555; Eric Barendt, "Libel and Freedom of Speech in English Law" [1993] P.L. 449.

(b) does not affect the validity, continuing operation or enforcement of any incompatible primary legislation; and

(c) does not affect the validity, continuing operation or enforcement of any incompatible subordinate legislation if (disregarding any possibility of revocation) primary legislation prevents removal of the incompatibility.

4(1) Subsection (2) applies in any proceedings in which a court determines whether a provision of primary legislation is compatible with a Convention right.

(2) If the court is satisfied that the provision is incompatible with a Convention right, it may make a declaration of that incompatibility.

(3) Subsection (4) applies in any proceedings in which a court determines whether a provision of subordinate legislation, made in the exercise of a power conferred by primary legislation, is compatible with a Convention right.

(4) If the court is satisfied —

(a) that the provision is incompatible with a Convention right, and

(b) that (disregarding any possibility of revocation) the primary legislation concerned prevents removal of the incompatibility, it may make a declaration of that incompatibility. . . .

Remedial action

10(1) This section applies if—

(a) a provision of legislation has been declared under section 4 to be incompatible with a Convention right and, if an appeal lies—

(i) all persons who may appeal have stated that they do not intend to do so;

(ii) the time for bringing an appeal has expired and no appeal has been brought within that time; or

(iii) an appeal brought within that time has been determined or abandoned; or

(b) it appears to a Minister of the Crown or Her Majesty in Council that, having regard to a finding of the European Court of Human Rights made after the coming into force of this section in proceedings against the United Kingdom, a provision of legislation is incompatible with an obligation of the United Kingdom arising from the Convention.

(2) If a Minister of the Crown considers that there are compelling reasons for a proceeding under this section, he may by order make such amendments to the legislation as he considers necessary to remove the incompatibility.

(3) If, in the case of subordinate legislation, a Minister of the Crown considers—

(a) that it is necessary to amend the primary legislation under which the subordinate legislation in question was made, in order to enable the incompatibility to be removed, and

(b) that there are compelling reasons for proceeding under this section, he may by order make such amendments to the primary legislation as he considers necessary.

(4) This section also applies where the provision in question is insubordinate legislation and has been quashed, or declared invalid, by reason of incompatibility with a Convention right and the Minister proposes to proceed under paragraph 2(b) of Schedule 2.

(5) If the legislation is an Order in Council, the power conferred by subsection ("2) or (3) is exercisable by Her Majesty in Council. . . ."

The interpretation of the Human Rights Act raises a number of interesting issues, with which the courts will need to grapple.

Geoffrey Marshall, "Interpreting Interpretation in the Human Rights Bill" [1998]
P.L. 167 at 167:

The meaning of "possible" in Clause 3

"In the first place it is not clear how the phrase 'so far as it is possible to do so' is to be understood. In some sense or other anything is possible if those who apply rules of interpretation are willing to stretch, change or apply them differently. Is Clause 3 intended to change the existing rules of interpretation whenever a question of Convention rights is an issue? The Government White Paper 'Rights Brought Home' implies that some change is intended. It says that the Bill 'goes far beyond the present rule which authorises the courts to take the Convention into account in resolving any ambiguity in a legislative provision'. What the authors of the White Paper mean by going beyond the present rule is uncertain. At the Committee stage of the Bill in the House of Lords, Lord Cooke of Thorndon suggested that what is prescribed by Clause 3 differs from the present rules in that 'it enjoins a search for possible meanings as distinct from the true meaning which has been the traditional approach'. But the disjunction between the meaning now to be sought and the true meaning is an odd one, particularly as Lord Cooke went on to say that the new kind of interpretation now enjoined 'is not a strained interpretation but one that is *fairly* possible'. Does that mean that the courts should be encouraged to disregard the true (or most obvious or likely) meaning in some degree, but not to strain or distort it too grossly? Another possibility as to the meaning of 'possible' is of course that it means that if, when the normal rules of construction are applied, it is possible fairly to say that a legislative provision has a particular meaning and if that meaning is compatible with the Convention it should be so interpreted and if not, not. But if that is what it means, Clause 3 is redundant. On the other hand, if Clause 3 is not redundant, then we do not know what it means.

Legislative ambiguity and convention rights

In introducing the Bill the Lord Chancellor explained the purpose of Clause 3 by saying that 'If it is possible to interpret a statute in two ways—one compatible with the Convention and one not—the courts will always choose the interpretation which is compatible'. But leaving aside the difficulty of knowing what it means to say that there is a possibility of such an interpretation what are we to understand by an interpretation that is 'compatible with Convention rights'? Is this the same as an ambiguity that is resolved by reference to Convention rights or (in the language of the White Paper) interpreting legislation 'so as to uphold Convention rights'? In what kinds of cases will Convention rights be relevant to the resolving of ambiguity in a statutory provision?

Issues of construction that arise in the application of the language of statutes generally raise a question as to whether particular persons or circumstances fall within the general terms of the statutes. *Harris v. DPP*[12] is a not untypical example. That involved the interpretation of section 139 of the Criminal Justice Act 1988. The guilt of the accused, who was charged with possession of a prohibited article, namely a sharply pointed blade, depended on the meaning of 'folding pocket knife' since such knives were excluded from the operation of the statute. It was held that a small bladed knife whose blade could only be folded by operating a locking button was a fixed blade knife, not a folding pocket knife. Here the statute could be said to be capable of being interpreted in two ways. But is this the kind of case in which the existence of the Human Rights Bill and its putatively new rule of interpretation is relevant? Can it be said that since the Convention protects the right to liberty of the person and the right to fair trials, it becomes relevant in every criminal proceeding on the grounds that criminal conviction involves a loss of liberty and that guilt has to be established in accordance with the provisions of the Convention? If so, which of the two interpretations of 'folding pocket knife' is more compatible with the Convention? Is either? There is already said to be a presumption enjoining in some degree strict construction of penal statutes so as to give the

---

[12] [1993] 1 W.L.R. 1294.

benefit of the doubt to an accused where there is genuine uncertainty as to the proper application of statutory language. The principle seems to have been somewhat submerged in recent times when public policy and purposive interpretation have appeared to suggest that the courts will only apply the presumption 'if there are no considerations indicating the desirability of a wider interpretation', and public policy together with the intention of Parliament may often suggest a wider interpretation.

But is it to be supposed that Clause 3 of the Human Rights Bill creates a new or extended version of that presumption, so that the courts are to lean towards the construction that will lead to acquittal whenever any possible construction of statutory language might lead to that result? It would be odd to suppose that the Convention could prescribe such a conclusion whenever anyone alleged its relevance, or that Clause 3 is intended to change the approach to such questions of construction throughout the criminal law. . . .

'Reading or giving effect'

Although Clause 3 is headed 'Interpretation of legislation' what it says is that primary and subordinate legislation should be 'read and given effect' in a way which is compatible with the Convention. 'Read and given effect' may be intended to be read as meaning 'interpreted', but it would seem that it must involve not merely the resolution of ambiguity in statutory provisions but also the question whether a provision of primary or secondary legislation can be treated as being compatible or incompatible with rights guaranteed in the Convention. This seems not so much a question of interpretation or construction of language but of assessment or characterisation or proper description of the relevant legislative provision when placed alongside the relevant right or rights in the Convention. It is only as a result of such assessment or reading of the statutory provision that the court can be in a position to make—when necessary—the determination of incompatibility which should lead to parliamentary remedial action under Clause 10 of the Bill. If a litigant establishes that the statutory provision in question is incompatible with, or infringes the Convention, his right under the Convention is upheld (though the legislation remains valid under the provisions of Clause 3(b)) and his only remedy is a declaration of incompatibility until remedial action is taken. If the court finds that the legislation is compatible with the Convention the litigant fails to establish that he is entitled to protection under the Convention over and above that provided by the United Kingdom legislation.

At this point a startling paradox suggests itself about the wording of Clause 3. What it commands is the opposite of what might be assumed from a reading of the White Paper and the parliamentary statements made in introducing Clause 3. The White Paper says that the courts will be required to uphold the Convention rights unless it is impossible to do so. So a hopeful litigant under the Human Rights Bill might assume that the courts would lean towards holding that the Convention right in issue should prevail over the legislative provision under attack, which it can only do if the legislation is inconsistent or incompatible with the Convention right. But what Clause 3 urges the court to do, wherever possible, is to find that the legislation is *compatible* with the Convention rights. If it is so compatible, the Convention has no bite on the legislation and the litigant seeking protection under the Convention not provided for by the legislation loses his case. The more faithfully the courts follow the injunction to read legislation as being compatible with the Convention the less effect the Convention will have. If it were to have the advertised effect of allowing the Convention more easily to trump legislation that threatens rights, Clause 3 should presumably have provided that, whenever the possibility arises, primary and secondary legislation should be treated as *incompatible* with the Convention rights unless such a finding is ruled out because the legislation is clearly compatible. But then the only remedy would be a declaration of incompatibility until (and if) remedial action is taken under Clause 10.

Many speakers in the debate on the Human Rights Bill praised its drafting as ingenious and subtle. Perhaps, as with the failure of Clauses 3 and 4 to implement the White Paper's commitment to incorporate the Convention rights in United Kingdom law, the so-called interpretation provision in Clause 3 is a further example of ingenuity gone wrong. What interpretation the courts will place on Clause 3 is impossible to know."

Not surprisingly, a more optimistic forecast of the impact of the Human Rights Act has been made by the Lord Chancellor.

Lord Irvine of Lairg, "The Development of Human Rights in Britain under an Incorporated Convention on Human Rights" [1998] P.L. 221 at 225:

"On October 23, I introduced the Human Rights Bill into Parliament. It will incorporate into the domestic law of the United Kingdom the rights and liberties guaranteed by the European Convention on Human Rights. It will mean that our citizens can secure their rights from our own United Kingdom courts. They will not have to take the long slow road to the Court in Strasbourg. It is one of the major constitutional changes which this Government is making. . . .

The implications of the change

What then are the practical implications of this change to a rights based system within the field of civil liberties?

Domestication of freedom

First, the Act will give to the courts the tools to uphold freedoms at the very time their infringement is threatened. Until now, the only remedy where a freedom guaranteed by the Convention is infringed and domestic law is deficient has been expensive and slow proceedings in Strasbourg. They could not even be commenced until after all the domestic avenues of complaint and appeal had been exhausted. The courts will now have the power to give effect to the Convention rights in the course of proceedings when they arise in this country and to grant relief against an unlawful act of a public authority (a necessarily widely drawn concept). The courts will not be able to strike down primary legislation. But they will be able to make a declaration of incompatibility where a piece of primary legislation conflicts with a Convention right. This will trigger the ability to use in Parliament a special fast-track procedure to bring the law into line with the Convention.

This innovative technique will provide the right balance between the judiciary and Parliament. Parliament is the democratically elected representative of the people and must remain sovereign. The judiciary will be able to exercise to the full the power to scrutinise legislation rigorously against the fundamental freedoms guaranteed by the Convention but without becoming politicised. The ultimate decision to amend legislation to bring it into line with the Convention, however, will rest with Parliament. The ultimate responsibility for compliance with the Convention must be Parliament's alone.

Prioritising rights

That point illustrates the second important effect of our new approach. If there are to be differences or departures from the principles of the Convention they should be conscious and reasoned departures, and not the product of rashness, muddle or ignorance. This will be guaranteed both by the powers given to the courts but also by other provisions which will be enacted. In particular, Ministers and administrators will be obliged to do all their work keeping clearly and directly in mind its impact on human rights, as expressed in the Convention and in the jurisprudence which attaches to it. For, where any Bill is introduced in either House, the Minister of the Crown, in whose charge it is, will be required to make a written statement that, either in his view, the provisions of the Bill are compatible with the Convention rights; or that he cannot make that statement but the Government nonetheless wishes the House to proceed with the Bill. . . .

Substantive rights

Thirdly, the Convention will enable the courts to reach results in cases which give full effect to the substantive rights guaranteed by the Convention. It would not be appropriate for me to deal with individual aspects of the law which may come up for decision in the courts in future, but some general observations are possible. . . .

It is moreover likely—although individual cases will be for the courts to determine and I should not attempt to prejudge them—that the position will in at least some cases be different from what it would have been under the pre-incorporation practice. The reason for this lies in the techniques to be followed once the Act is in force. Unlike the old Diceyan approach where the Court would go straight to what restriction had been imposed, the focus will first be on the positive right and then on the justifiability of the exception. Moreover, the Act will require the courts to read and give effect to the legislation in a way compatible with the Convention rights 'so far as it is possible to do so . . .'. This, as the White Paper makes clear, goes far beyond the present rule. It will not be necessary to find an ambiguity. On the contrary the courts will be required to interpret legislation so as to uphold the Convention rights unless the legislation itself is so clearly incompatible with the Convention that it is impossible to do so. Moreover, it should be clear from the Parliamentary history, and in particular the Ministerial statement of compatibility which will be required by the Act, that Parliament did not intend to cut across a Convention right. Ministerial statements of compatibility will inevitably be a strong spur to the courts to find means of construing statutes compatibly with the Convention.

Whilst this particular approach is innovative, there are some precedents which will assist the courts. In cases involving European Community law, decisions of our courts already show that interpretative techniques may be used to make the domestic legislation comply with the Community law, even where this requires straining the meaning of words or reading in words which are not there. An illustrative case is *Litster*[13] concerning the construction of the Transfer of Undertakings Regulations. The issue was whether protection in the Regulations, limited to those employed in the business 'immediately before' the time of the transfer, extended to employees unfairly dismissed very shortly before the transfer. The applicants had clearly not been employed in the business immediately before the transfer as those words would normally be interpreted. Nor were the words ambiguous. Yet the House of Lords interpreted the Regulations (so as to accord with the European Court's existing interpretation of the underlying Community obligation which the Regulations were intended to implement) by implying additional words 'or would have been so employed if they had not been unfairly dismissed [by reason of the transfer]'. . . .

Guidance may also be found in the jurisprudence of the New Zealand courts. Under the New Zealand Bill of Rights Act 1990 a meaning consistent with the rights and freedoms contained in the Bill of Rights is to be given in preference to any other meaning 'wherever an enactment can be given [such] a meaning'. The existing New Zealand decisions seem to show that the only cases where the legislation will *not* be interpreted consistently with the protected rights are those where a statutory provision contains a clear limitation of fundamental rights. The difference from the approach until now applied by the English courts will be this: the Court will interpret as consistent with the Convention not only those provisions which are ambiguous in the sense that the *language* used is capable of two different meanings, but also those provisions where there is *no* ambiguity in that sense, unless a *clear* limitation is expressed. In the latter category of case it will be 'possible' (to use the statutory language) to read the legislation in a conforming sense because there will be no clear indication that a limitation on the protected rights was intended so as to make it 'impossible' to read it as conforming.

Principled decision-making

The fourth point may be shortly stated but is of immense importance. The courts' decisions will be based on a more overtly principled, and perhaps moral, basis. The Court will look at the positive right. It will only accept an interference with that right where a justification, allowed under the Convention, is made out. The scrutiny will not be limited to seeing if the

---

[13] *Litster v. Forth Dry Dock and Forth Estuary Engineering* (1990) 1 A.C. 546, HL, which we examined earlier in this chapter.

words of an exception can be satisfied. The Court will need to be satisfied that the interference with the protected right *is* justified in the public interest in a free democratic society. Moreover, the courts will in this area have to apply the Convention principle of proportionality. This means the Court will be looking *substantively* at that question. It will not be limited to a secondary review of the decision making process but at the primary question of the merits of the decision itself.

In reaching its judgment, therefore, the Court will need to expand and explain its own view of whether the conduct is legitimate. It will produce in short a decision on the *morality* of the conduct and not simply its compliance with the bare letter of the law."

NOTES AND QUESTIONS

• Briefly explain the impact of incorporation of the European Convention in domestic law on (a) principles of statutory interpretation; and (b) the supremacy of Parliament.

• It has been argued that the incorporation of the Convention may also have an impact on *private* litigation; known as the *horizontal effect* of rights: see Murray Hunt, "The 'Horizontal Effect' of the Human Rights Act" [1998] P.L. 423.

10

JUDGE MADE LAW: AN INTRODUCTION TO COMMON LAW REASONING

In this chapter, our attention turns to "judge made law"; that is, the common law, described as the foundation of our legal system. We will examine the fundamentals of the common law method of reasoning. We begin with some definitions of key concepts, then we turn to the historical development of the common law tradition, and we look at the process of common law reasoning, including the impact of membership in the European Union. We then focus upon common law reasoning from a more theoretical perspective, and the key question of the extent to which judges in a common law system *make* the law.

KEY CONCEPTS AND TERMINOLOGY

T.A. Downes, *Textbook on Contract* (5th ed., Blackstone Press, London, 1997), pp. 2–4:

Three meanings of "Common Law"

Historical: common law and equity

"After the Norman conquest of England local laws gave way to a general law of the country, which became known as the common law. The king's courts became the most important forum for the resolution of disputes between citizens. An action could only be brought in these courts by obtaining (purchasing) a writ. Over time the forms of such writs became fixed, and only Parliament could approve a new type of writ designed to meet a claim which could not be accommodated within the existing writs and forms of action. This rigidity in the legal system was often the cause of hardship to individual litigants, and the practice grew of petitioning the king for justice in the individual case. The petitions were dealt with by the chancellor, who in this period was a man of the church and who was regarded as the 'conscience' of the king. In due course a formal procedure for such petitions evolved, culminating in a Court of Chancery, presided over by the Lord Chancellor, applying a system of rules known as 'equity' rather than the common law of the ordinary courts.

Although the Court of Chancery was effective in remedying injustices, the existence of parallel jurisdictions brought problems and injustices of its own. Chancery developed procedures separate from, but at least as complex as, those of the common law courts. A litigant had to be sure of the classification of the rule he sought to have applied, in order to commence his action in the right court. The equity of the Chancery Court became a set of rules almost as precise as those of the common law. In the case of conflict between the two systems, the rules of equity prevailed. Parliament sought to put an end to these divisions with the Judicature Acts 1873–1875, which established a unified system of courts which were charged with applying both the common law and equity.

To the non-lawyer 'equity' is probably synonymous with the idea of natural justice. Although that was the origin of the Chancery jurisdiction, it has long since disappeared from the rules of equity. The rules of equity are just as capable today as those of the common law of producing resolutions of disputes which may be viewed as just or unjust. Indeed, since the two types of rules are now applied by the same courts, there is little significance left in the distinction. Nevertheless, in two respects it has left a legacy which still has an impact on today's courts. In the first place, while common law rules are available to plaintiffs as of right, equitable remedies are discretionary in the sense that they are subject to some general conditions of availability. For example, there is no absolute right to specific performance of a contract. Secondly, the existence of parallel systems of rules, the one based on formal procedures, the other based originally on the idea of substantial justice, has allowed some judges to invoke the tension between the two systems as a source of judicial creativity in developing the law to meet new situations. For example, Lord Denning has used this device in relation to the enforceability of promises and in relation to contracts affected by mistake.

Common Law and statute

In another sense, the common law is the law applied by the courts developed through the system of precedent without reference to legislation passed by Parliament. Although statute has become the most prolific source of law in this country, this has only relatively recently been the case. Centuries ago, much of the law was applied by the courts independently of any statutory source. The constitutional fiction was that the judges merely declared what the law was, as though it was already there and merely had to be discovered. Today it is accepted that the courts *created* the law, although there is no reason to suppose they often acted arbitrarily in so doing. No doubt they acted in response to the values and needs of society, as they perceived them, in making law. This process created the body of the common law, which in this sense includes the law made by all the courts, including those of Chancery.

Common law as a 'family' of legal systems

A wider meaning still of 'common law' is a description of a group of related legal systems. The English legal system was exported around the world wherever British influence dominated. The legal systems of the USA, and of the 'old' Commonwealth countries, are all based on the English common law. In much the same way, the legal systems of continental European countries were exported around the world. They are usually described as the civil law systems, of which the most influential has been that of France, because by producing the Code Civil Napoleon gave to France the first modern European legal system, which was copied elsewhere.

Criminal law, civil law and public law

Criminal law

Most people have some understanding of what criminal law is. It deals with actions, or failures to act, which are contrary to the interests of society as a whole, and for which some penalty has been prescribed. Criminal law is a species of public law, in the sense that prosecutions of those accused of committing crimes are (except rarely) brought by public officials in the name of the state. It must be remembered that a crime which is contrary to society's general interest may also cause particular loss or injury to an individual. It would then also be a civil wrong (called a 'tort'), for which the individual would be able to claim compensation. Such compensation would normally be claimed by civil action in the civil courts, but in a criminal trial the courts have power to award compensation to persons injured, payable by a person convicted at trial (s 35, Powers of Criminal Courts Act 1973, as amended by the Criminal Justice Acts of 1982, 1988 and 1991).

Civil law

As well as denoting the continental European family of legal systems, civil law is the title of one category of English law. In one sense civil law is all law other than criminal law. . . . By civil law, today we often mean English *private* law.

Public law

The expression public law has existed for some time, but had little significance other than to indicate that the subject-matter in some way involved a public authority. Continental European legal systems, on the other hand, had developed the idea of public law into a separate and specialised body of rules applicable only to cases involving the administration. English law has not yet taken such a radical step, but in *O'Reilly v. Mackman* [1982] 3 All ER 1124 the House of Lords drew a distinction between private law and public law rights. The latter can be asserted only by means of a special procedure which provides certain safeguards for the administration which do not exist in ordinary actions for private law rights. The full impact of this development in English law is still to be seen, and recently there have been some indications that not all judges favour making the distinction stronger.

Substantive law and procedure

The distinction between substantive law and procedure is, in simple terms, the distinction between the rules applicable to the merits of a dispute and the rules governing the manner of resolution of a dispute. For those who practise law the rules of procedure are very important, but at the academic stage of legal studies the focus is on the substantive rules. It is nevertheless important to have some understanding of procedure, because procedure can affect the application of the substantive rules. In fact, the rules of procedure were in the past of great significance in shaping the substantive rules, since English law has, from the time of the need to frame one's action within the form of an existing writ, proceeded from the existence of a remedy to the establishment of a right. It might almost be said that procedure came before substantive rights."

We will consider many of the points which Downes raises throughout this chapter and the rest of this text. For our purposes, he provides a good introduction to many of the terms which we will be using in considering common law reasoning. Central to that method of reasoning are the ideas of "case law" and "precedent".

Rupert Cross and J.W. Harris, *Precedent in English Law* (4th ed., Clarendon Press, Oxford, 1991), pp. 3–5:

"The strongly coercive nature of the English doctrine of precedent is due to rules of practice, called 'rules of precedent', which are designed to give effect to the far more fundamental rule that English law is to a large extent based on case-law. 'Case-law' consists of the rules and principles stated and acted upon by judges in giving decisions. In a system based on case-law, a judge in a subsequent case *must* have regard to these matters; they are not, as in some other legal systems, merely material which he *may* take into consideration in coming to his decision. The fact that English law is largely a system of case-law means that the judge's decision in a particular case constitutes a 'precedent'. If we place ourselves in the position of a judge in a later case, there may be said to be many different kinds of precedent. The judge may simply be obliged to consider the former decision as part of the material on which his present decision could be based, or he may be obliged to decide the case before him in the same way as that in which the previous case was decided unless he can give a good reason for not doing so. Finally, the judge in the instant case may be obliged to decide it in the same way as that in which the previous case was decided, even if he can give a good reason for not doing so. In the last-mentioned situation the precedent is said to be 'binding' or of 'coercive effect' as contrasted with its merely 'persuasive' effect in the other situations in which the degree of persuasiveness may vary considerably.

Some branches of our law are almost entirely the product of the decisions of the judges whose reasoned judgments have been reported in various types of law report for close on 700 years. Other branches of our law are based on statutes, but, in many instances, case-law has played an important part in the interpretation of those statutes. As the sovereignty of Parliament is more complete in England than practically anywhere else in the world, it might be thought that the rigidity of the doctrine of precedent in this country is of no particular importance because any unsatisfactory results of case-law can be swept away by legislation, but the promotion of a statute on matters of this nature is often slow and difficult. There are many instances in which the recommendations of Royal Commissions and Law Revision Committees, designed to ameliorate the situation produced by case-law have been ignored, apparently for no other reason than pressure on parliamentary time.

Perhaps the number of such instances will be reduced in the future because there are now in existence several very important law-reforming agencies, notably the Law Reform Committee dealing with the reform of the civil law on matters referred to it by the Lord Chancellor, the Criminal Law Revision Committee dealing with the reform of the criminal law on matters referred to it by the Home Secretary, and, most important of all, the Law Commission. The Commission was set up by statute in 1965, and it is charged with the task of reviewing the law with a view to systematic development and reform, including, in particular, codification. When the work of the Law Commission results, as it probably will do, in codes of the more important branches of English law, the role of case-law will, *pro tanto*, be diminished."

Cross and Harris raise the issue of the relationship between statute and common law, and suggest that there has been a historical process in which the role of statutes has increased, at the expense of judge made common law. We have already examined extensively the role of statutes in our legal system, and the relationship between statutes and common law is an important element in understanding common law reasoning.

HISTORICAL DEVELOPMENT OF THE COMMON LAW

William Geldart, *Introduction to English Law* (11th ed., Oxford University Press, Oxford, 1995), pp. 2–6:

"1. In spite of the enormous and ever-growing bulk of the Statute Law—our statutes begin with the reissue of Magna Carta in 1225 in the reign of Henry III, and a large volume is now added every year—much of the fundamental part of our law is still Common Law. No statute, for instance, yet prescribes in general terms that a man must pay his debts or perform his contracts or pay damages for trespass or libel or slander. The statutes assume the existence of the Common Law. Except in so far as they restate in the form of a code some particular branch of the law, they are the addenda and errata of the book of the Common Law; and they would have no meaning except by reference to the Common Law. If all the statutes of the realm were repealed, we should still have a system of law, though, it may be, an unworkable one; if we could imagine the Common Law swept away and the Statute Law preserved, we should have only disjointed rules torn from their context, and no provision at all for many of the most important relations of life. The Law Commissions Act 1965, however, established a body of Commissioners whose task it is to prepare legislation which shall reform and simplify the law, and the Commissioners stated, in announcing their first programme of work, that they intended to prepare a codification of the laws of contract and of landlord and tenant. These major codes have not yet been completed (the Annual Report of the Law Commission for 1972–3 stated that work on the preparation of a code of the law of contract had been suspended, and so it is now doubtful whether it will ever be completed), but certain codes dealing with more restricted areas of law have been enacted in recent years, *e.g.* the Theft Act 1968, the Animals Act 1971, the Forgery and Counterfeiting Act 1981, and the Criminal Attempts Act 1981; and the Law Commission has more recently expressed the intention to work towards a complete code of criminal law. The work of the Law Commission has in recent years also led to much obsolete legislation being repealed. For example, much of the old Sunday Observance legislation was swept away by the Statute Law (Repeals) Act 1969.

2. Where Statute Law and Common Law come into competition, it is the former that prevails. Our law sets no limits to the power of Parliament. As the constitutionalist A.V. Dicey wrote a century ago, 'The sovereignty of Parliament is (from a legal point of view) the dominant characteristic of our political institutions.' No court or judge can refuse to enforce an Act of Parliament, though in the exercise of its duty to interpret an Act a court may sometimes alter considerably the effect that the legislators had intended the Act to have. No development of the Common Law can repeal an Act of Parliament, but large parts of the Common Law have from time to time been abolished by Act of Parliament, and their place has been taken by statutory rules. . . .

3. How do we know the law? Here there is a great difference between Statute and Common Law. A statute is drawn up in a definite form of words, and these words have been approved by Parliament and have received the Royal assent. In general there is no difficulty in ascertaining the words of a statute. At the present day two identical printed copies are made, each bearing a certificate of the Clerk of Parliaments that the Royal assent has been given, and in the last resort reference can be made to these copies for the purpose of ascertaining the true words of the statutes. For practical purposes any copy made by the Queen's printer is sufficient. In the case of some old statutes there is a possible doubt not only as to the exact words of a statute, but even whether such a statute was ever made; but in practice such doubts hardly ever arise. . . .

On the other hand we have no authoritative text of the Common Law. There is no one form of words in which it has as a whole been expressed at any time. Therefore in a sense one may speak of the Common Law as unwritten law in contrast with Statute Law, which is written law. Nevertheless the sources from which we derive our knowledge of the Common Law are in writing or print. First among these come the reported decisions of the judges of the English courts. Ever since the reign of Edward I there have been lawyers who have made it their business to report the discussions in court and the judgments given in cases which seemed of legal interest. The earliest of these reports are the Year-Books. They are reports of cases made by anonymous reporters from the time of Edward I to that of Henry VIII. These are followed by reports produced by lawyers reporting under their own names. They were at first published (like textbooks) only as and when the author, or the representatives of a deceased author, saw fit to do so. It was not until the end of the eighteenth century that reports began to be regularly published contemporaneously with the decisions of the cases reported. At the beginning these reports seem to have served mainly the purpose of instruction and information. The fact that a judge had stated that such and such was the law was evidence, but not more than evidence, that such was the law. He might have been mistaken; another judge might perhaps decide differently. But in course of time we find a change in the attitude of judges and lawyers towards reported decisions. The citation of decided cases becomes more frequent; greater and greater weight is attached to them as authorities. From the sixteenth century onwards we may say that decided cases are regarded as a definite authority, which, at least in the absence of special reasons to the contrary, must be followed for the future. For the last 35 years, at any rate, the decisions of judges of the higher courts have had a binding force for all similar cases which may arise in the future."

This historical development of the common-law, and the rules of precedent in particular, have been traced by Goodrich.

Peter Goodrich, *Reading the Law* (Blackwell, Oxford, 1986), pp. 66–72:

"Based in custom and in the 'natural reason' or will of the people, the common-law tradition is supposedly the unique product of the English people and their legal class and is supposedly vernacular in its form and democratic in its functioning. While there is some measure of historical truth in such a perception of the common law as a distinctive tradition, it both exaggerates the national quality of the common law and actively misleads the student of the contemporary legal order, which is effectively the product of much wider political and economic developments dating from the late seventeenth century to the present day. However politically pleasing or doctrinally desirable it might be to view the national legal system as a unique national product, we will argue here and subsequently that such a view is very far from being an accurate account of either the historical or contemporary workings of the common law. To the limited extent that the early common law was systematized into any coherent form of jurisprudence, the important intellectual influences upon it during its formative periods were those of Christianity and of Roman law, while as a body of disparate customary norms, the common law was distinctive primarily for its inaccessibility, obscurity and formality. Neither of such features supports the popular image of a native system of law emanating from the people or from below. They suggest rather the necessary complexity and, more specifically, the political and economic dependency of law upon other strata of the social whole. We shall look briefly at each of the two features mentioned, first at the formal or intellectual basis of the common law and secondly at the content and accessibility of the purportedly national customary law.

The conceptual source of the common law can be traced with considerable precision to the Anglo-Saxon monarchies of the period before the Norman conquest of 1066. In keeping with the general historical tradition which displays so close a relationship between law, power and writing, it is interesting to note that the earliest known law within the common-law tradition was both sacred and written. The tradition in question is one of a theocratic kind, rule being the rule of God as represented through the king, and the law of God was collected and promulgated in a codified, written form from a very early date, with major collections being associated with Aethelbert (602–3), Wihtred and most famously with King Cnut (1016–38). The single distinctive feature of these codes was that they were written in the vernacular, rather than in Latin, while their content was principally and fairly directly drawn from the Creed and other biblical passages. The model of law upon which these early codes were based was that of Rome: the codes were theocratic in their form and expressed fairly directly the political authority of government both in the elaboration of a relatively sophisticated body of penal norms but also in the growing use of charters as a means of conferring, 'by the grace of god', rights, duties and concessions upon individuals, groups, institutions and so on. The most famous example of such a charter is the very much later Great Charter (Magna Carta) of 1215, a concessionary charter extracted from King John, which commences, significantly and typically enough: 'First, we have granted to God, and by this our present charter have confirmed for us and our heirs for ever, that the English church shall be free and shall have all her rights and liberties, whole and inviolable. We have also given and granted to freemen of our realm, for us and our heirs for ever, these liberties underwritten, to have and to hold to them and their heirs, of us and our heirs for ever.' The early charters provided a formal expression of the king's will and were of greater practical importance, in all probability, than the general law promulgated by the king.

The influence of Christian law and the sacred status of the royal source of law tends to undermine more democratic conceptions of the origins of the common law. The other influence, of course, was Roman law and Roman ideas of government which played an increasing role throughout Europe. The early English legal tradition did not escape the latinization of European culture and by the time of the conquest Latin was the major legal language. More importantly, the centralization of the legal system which occurred soon after the Norman conquest was very much an exercise in developing and systematizing native law according to the precepts and principles of Roman law. The first centralized courts were royal courts and the first judges were royally appointed from amongst the clergy and legally trained in canon law and Roman law. It was precisely the king's courts, located at Westminster, and the king's judges, who first fashioned the 'general custom' of the land into a system of legal rules and provided, in a highly complex set of royal 'writs' governing the situations in which remedies were available from the courts, the rudiments of the centralized administration of justice or common law.

Remaining with 'general custom' and the early centralization of authority, the crucial period would appear to run from the late twelfth century through to the end of the thirteenth century. It was during this period that Henry II consolidated the central control of the king's courts and royal judges, both based in Westminster though increasingly peripatetic, and the early emergence of the legal profession based around the Inns of Court followed soon after. The theocratic tradition of law-making was supplemented by the influence of Roman law and the first literary expositions of the common law, most notably those of Glanvill (*De Legibus*) which appeared around 1187 and that of Bracton (*De Legibus et consuetudinibus Angliae*) which is dated 1256 and was praised by the historian Maitland as the 'crown and flower of English medieval jurisprudence'. Bracton was himself both a prominent cleric, eventually becoming chancellor of Exeter Cathedral, and also a royally appointed judge; his work on the law and customs of England draws extensively upon his experience as a judge and his knowledge of and access to earlier transcripts of pleadings before the royal courts. The form of systematization which Bracton brought to the common law was, however, that of the Roman law in which, as a cleric, he had originally been trained. . . .

The rapid development and stabilization of a system of common law during the thirteenth century was accompanied by the emergence of an early professional legal class, based at Westminster and skilled in oral pleading. Paradoxically the notions of oral pleading (narrators) and of an unwritten law were short-lived and the history of the common law is by and large a history of the recording and documentation of custom in a professional and extremely obscure language, that of law French, and hidden in technical and often verbose reports, initially of pleadings (plea rolls) and later of arguments and judgments (*Year Books*). In many senses it would be inaccurate to regard the common law as ever having been wholly unwritten in its character; it is simply unwritten in the technical sense of not being 'written law' (*ius scriptum*) or legislation. From a very early date, and certainly from the ninth century, the basic rules of general custom—of royally approved practices—were collected and recorded, most famously by King Alfred who compiled a dome-book or *liber judicialis* for use throughout the kingdom of Wessex. The book was lost but is known to have been a resource for information and knowledge of common law until the mid-fifteenth century and is said by Blackstone to have 'contained, we may probably suppose, the principal maxims of the common law, the penalties for the misdemeanours and the forms of judicial proceedings'. The substantive significance of the dome-book as a record of law and procedures is limited, however, by the subsequent Danish and Norman invasions and the separation of local and general customs.

At the level of particular custom, the Norman monarchy brought with it feudal law based upon the grant of land and the rights and duties which went with the land. It was feudal law which, in general, the common lawyers sought originally to systematize and record as common law. Originally the recording of the unwritten law was in the exclusive hands of the royal judges and emanated fairly directly from the monarch in the form of writs (the writ—originally referring to sacred writ or writings—means both command and writing) devised and issued by the king's secretariat, the Chancery. The system of writs was extremely formalistic from its earliest days and by 1258, by edict (*the Provisions of Oxford*), had congealed into a largely static and closed system of extremely complex pleadings. More general evidence of the common law was no less specialized. The plea rolls were written records of pleadings made at Westminster which frequently did not include the judgment in the case while the *Year Books*, which started reporting cases from 1292, report the oral arguments before the courts in law French and are, in terms of the legal knowledge they presuppose, extremely demanding upon the reader. The law administered as the common law from Westminster was already inaccessible, esoteric and extremely technical, an 'occult science' which needed to be extracted with great difficulty and skill from the lengthy and arcane books of the law. These reports of arguments and judgments were neither official nor necessarily accurate. As Plucknett describes them:

> 'The whole business of pleading orally . . . was an immensely skilful and recondite game, conducted with great virtuosity by the leaders of the bar, and keenly relished by all others who were sufficiently learned to understand what it was all about. After such a display, it was an anti-climax to think of a decision. Time after time the Year Books will give pages of subtle fencing until we get the words: "and so to judgment". What the judgment was, nobody knew and nobody cared; what interested the reader was not the substantive law involved in a case, but the technique of conducting the pleadings. . . .'

The *Year Books* were eventually superseded by the ad hoc development of law-reporting from the early sixteenth century, when named private reporters would recall and publish more or less detailed and more or less accurate accounts of cases; Plowden, Dyer and Coke were among the most significant of the early reporters. The quality and content of the reports produced by the named reporters between 1550 and 1790 varied greatly and while frequent reference was made to earlier decisions, the reporting was frequently 'casual and careless' and on occasions 'grossly inadequate'. Again we would observe that such a haphazard written record of the common law hardly indicates any great certainty, predictability or widespread knowledge of law and procedure. Nor could one view the system of common-law judgment as a coherent and complete system of legal rules or as, in its modern sense, a legal order. It is only in the late eighteenth and early nineteenth centuries, with the renewed influence of Roman-law doctrines and classifications, with the shift from law French to the vernacular and with the emergence of professional and later official law reports that it becomes possible even to contemplate referring to the common law as a coherent system of rules or as an order of precedent. . . .

The modern and purportedly highly distinctive conception of a common-law system of binding precedent, of *stare rationibus decidendi*, meaning to follow the reasoning of previous decisions (*stare decisis*), dates back to the early years of the nineteenth century, if not before. In broad terms, the conception of binding precedent refers to the following of the rules (*rationes decidendi*) laid down in previous decision and its logical form and entailment are classically set out by Justice Parke in *Mirehouse v. Rennell* [1833] 1 Cl and F 527, 546, in the following terms:

> 'Our common law system consists in the applying to new combinations of circumstances those rules which we derive from legal principles and judicial precedents; and for the sake of attaining uniformity, consistency and certainty, we must apply those rules, where they are not plainly unreasonable and inconvenient, to all cases which arise; and we are not at liberty to reject them, and to abandon all analogy to them, in those to which they have not yet been judicially applied. . . . It appears to me to be of great importance to keep this principle of decision steadily in view, not merely for the determination of a particular case, but for the interests of law as a science.'

In short, legal decisions are to be arrived at, where the dispute is governed by the unwritten or common law, by reference, either directly or by analogy, to the rules set down in previously decided cases. Such pre-existent rules or principles (reasonings) are to be followed, according to Justice Parke, even where the deciding judge does not view them to be necessarily the best means to deciding the disputed issue: predictability and consistency of legal decision-making are accorded greater value than particular justice.

This early view of precedent was developed during the nineteenth century into what is traditionally regarded as one of the strictest and most extreme systems of precedent known in the history of western legal systems. While the rest of Europe entered the age of codifications and the emergent nation-states placed their faith in publicly available written codes of national law, the English developed and refined an antiquated system of highly technical and highly particular legal decisions into the modern common law. The motives behind the development belong firmly in the European political and economic context of the nineteenth century. For the common-law system, the nineteenth century was also an age of statute law, of partial codifications and of consolidating Acts, the great upsurge coming in the 1830s and continuing unabated to the present day. Parallel to this development of what were seen as systematizing, simplifying and democratizing statute laws was the development of the common law as national law, it being the peculiar view of English lawyers that common law represented a unique and jealously guarded national legal achievement. It was, however, only with the aid of principles drawn from the academics and the civil law, that the common law could be developed into a coherent and largely self-sufficient system of legal decision-making. In 1861, in *Beamish v. Beamish* [1861] 9 H.L. Cases 274, the House of Lords decided that precedent decisions of the House were to be binding in future cases, even upon the House itself. Only Parliament could alter the decisions of the House of Lords, a view reiterated in *London Street Tramways Co. Ltd v. London County Council* [1898] A.C. 375, 38, by Lord Halsbury in a succinct statement that 'a decision of the House on a question of law is conclusive', a view which remained the law until 1966 when the House of Lords issued a Practice Statement declaring that, in a limited number of circumstances, the House would no longer be bound to follow its earlier decisions. The lower courts, the Court of Appeal in particular (see *Davis v. Johnson* [1979] AC 264), however, remain bound by their own earlier decisions and the system of precedent in general is still doctrinally stated to be one of binding or strict precedent. The strongest legal argument is one which cites the *ratio decidendi* of a relevant precedent case; the issue of the forms which a precedent may take and the manner of its discovery and application are still the central methodological issues within the common law, although, paradoxically, 'theorists have not been able to agree upon an answer to the question, what is a *ratio*? Nor is there agreement as to the test to be used to identify a *ratio*, once the basic meaning of the term has been defined'."

QUESTIONS

- Define the following terms:

  a) common law;

  b) precedent;

  c) *ratio decidendi*.

- Explain the relationship between common law and statutory law.

- What is meant by the claim that the common law is "unwritten"? In what way is that claim misleading?

THE PROCESS OF COMMON LAW REASONING: "THINKING LIKE A LAWYER"

As Goodrich's historical analysis of the common law demonstrated, the history of the common law has been a rather haphazard process, in which general rules emerged from remedies granted in particular disputes. This process of moving from specific disputes to the development of general rules, (*i.e.* precedents), which are then applicable to a wide range of cases, is central to common law reasoning. It is a method of reasoning known as inductive (moving from the specific to the general), and is fundamental to our legal method.

Kenneth J. Vandevelde, *Thinking Like a Lawyer* (Westview Press, Boulder, 1996), pp. 49–55:

"The lawyer synthesizes the new rule by a method similar to the logical process of induction. Induction is a method of reasoning that, in essence, proceeds from the particular to the general.

For example, after tasting several raisins and finding that each of them is sweet, one may reason by induction that all raisins taste sweet. Induction produces a conclusion that is probable, though not certain. No matter how many raisins one eats, the possibility always exists that the next one may taste different from the others.

Nevertheless, courts formulate rules of law by a process that is inductive in form. If a number of cases have been decided in which a particular right or duty was found to exist, then the court may conclude that the same right or duty exists in all similar cases. By studying several particular instances, the court formulates a general rule.

For example, assume that various courts decide a number of cases imposing a duty on landowners to warn guests about various conditions on the land, such as a concealed pit, quicksand, or an unstable slope. As the number of cases grows, it becomes possible to think of these cases as collectively establishing a rule that requires the landowner to warn guests about hazards. In this situation, a rule is formulated by a process of induction. The rule, however, is broader than any of the specific cases on which it was based. The whole thus becomes greater than the sum of the parts.

By creating a rule broader than any one prior case, the court creates a rule broad enough to apply to the novel case. The novel case, accordingly, can be decided by application of the newly synthesized rule.

As noted above, induction does not compel a particular conclusion but can only suggest that the conclusion is probable. In the same way, the court is not compelled to accept the new, broader rule. Just as tasting a few raisins does not force one to conclude that all raisins taste the same, the prior decisions in cases involving certain specific hazards do not require the court to decide that other hazards are subject to the same rule. The court may correctly note that the holdings in the prior cases did not reach beyond quicksand, a concealed pit, and an unstable slope and may decide not to extend the holdings beyond those situations. . . .

The problem of indeterminacy

The premise for using inductive reasoning is that several similar items have been identified about which a generalization can safely be made. Yet, the lawyer will find that the process of formulating a generalization is not a mechanical one. Rather, it is a process that requires the exercise of judgment and that can lead to more than one result.

The lawyer must make at least two decisions in synthesizing the rule. First, the lawyer must decide which facts to include in the factual predicate, thus determining how to characterize the prior cases. Each of the prior cases may be subject to multiple characterizations, depending upon which facts of those cases the lawyer chooses to emphasize. In deciding how to characterize the cases included in the rule, the lawyer in effect is choosing the elements of the rule.

For example, the lawyer may characterize the cases involving the quicksand, the concealed pit, and the unstable slope as cases involving abnormal conditions, provided that each condition was abnormal for that area. Or, the lawyer may characterize them as cases involving hazards, because each condition was dangerous. Alternatively, the lawyer may characterize them as cases involving concealed hazards, on the theory that none of the hazards was obvious to the casual observer. Or, the cases may be characterized as involving natural hazards, if they were not the result of human activity. Finally, the lawyer may choose to emphasize the especially dangerous nature of the hazards and characterize the cases as involving life-threatening hazards.

All of these characterizations may be equally accurate. No one characterization is the 'correct' one that must be chosen to the exclusion of the others. The process of characterizing the facts is indeterminate. The lawyer can reach a particular characterization only by the exercise of judgment.

A second decision the lawyer must make is to set the level of generality at which the new rule should be formulated. This means deciding whether the prior cases are to be described in broad, general terms or in narrow, specific terms.

In the case of the concealed pit, the unstable slope, and the quicksand, for example, the lawyer must decide at what level of generality to characterize the conditions on the land that give rise to a duty to warn. At one extreme, they could be characterized as hazards. In that case, the lawyer could conclude that the various cases identified by research establish a general rule that the landowner has a duty to warn guests about all hazards on the land.

At the other extreme, the lawyer could characterize the conditions as falling within the three narrow categories of quicksand, concealed pits, and unstable slopes. Each of these categories might be characterized even more narrowly so that, under the lawyer's characterization of the rule, a landowner has a duty to warn only of concealed pits of a certain depth, unstable slopes of a specified angle, and quicksand pools of a particular size.

Between these extremes is a range of possible rules of differing levels of generality. The term 'life-threatening hazards,' for example, is more specific than the term 'hazards.'

Each of these levels of generality may yield a rule that is equally accurate. No particular level of generality is correct to the exclusion of the others. The choice of the level of generality at which to state the rule is indeterminate. The lawyer's selection of a particular level of generality must therefore be based on the exercise of judgment. Different lawyers generalizing about the same group of cases will produce rules at different levels of generality.

The judgments concerning which facts to include in the factual predicate and the level of generality at which to state a rule are interrelated. The more general the rule, the fewer the facts that need to be specified. For example, if the rule is formulated as applying to all hazards, then whether the hazards are natural or life-threatening is irrelevant and would not be specified in the rule. Put another way, stating the rule at a high level of generality allows the lawyer to be agnostic about which of various specifics to include in the factual predicate. The corollary, of course, is that if the lawyer decides to include numerous detailed facts in the factual predicate, then, necessarily, the rule cannot be stated at a high level of generality.

Addressing indeterminacy through policy judgments

The lawyer may attempt to solve the indeterminacy involved in synthesizing a rule by referring to the policies underlying the cases. In this situation, the lawyer uses the underlying policies as a guide in selecting the facts to include in the factual predicate of the rule and in choosing the level of generality at which to state the rule. As will be seen, however, use of the underlying policies does not entirely solve the problem of indeterminacy.

The first decision the lawyer must make is to select the facts to include in the factual predicate of the rule. As an initial matter, some of the prior cases may have specified that certain facts were dispositive. For example, the case involving the pit may have specified that a duty to warn was imposed because the pit was a concealed hazard; that is, the case made clear that the holding imposing a duty was based on the presence of two facts—the fact that the condition was hazardous and the fact that it was concealed.

To the extent that the prior cases leave unclear which facts were dispositive, the lawyer selects for inclusion in the newly synthesized rule those facts in the prior cases that were relevant to accomplishing the underlying policies. For instance, if the policy was solely the protection of personal safety, then the fact that the conditions were natural probably should not matter, since a condition may be hazardous whether it is natural or not. Nor perhaps should it matter that the conditions were concealed, since even an obvious hazard can threaten safety. If the policy, however, was to encourage people to be responsible for their own safety, then the fact that the condition was concealed becomes more relevant. In such situations, the court may wish to deny recovery to guests who put themselves at risk by encountering an obvious hazard.

A second decision the lawyer must make is to select the level of generality at which to state the elements in the newly synthesized rule. As a practical matter, the lawyer must state the elements in terms general enough to include the facts of any prior case from which the rule is being synthesized. Thus, if the lawyer wishes to include the quicksand, the slope, and the pit cases, then a term at least as general as 'hazard' may have to be used. Any narrower term could arguably exclude some of the cases.

The lawyer must also state the elements in terms at least general enough to include the novel case to which the rule will be applied. For example, assume that the lawyer concluded that, in the prior cases, the quicksand, the pit, and the slope were all in some way concealed, and thus the term 'concealed hazard' would include all prior cases. The lawyer's client, however, was injured by a hazard that was not really concealed, although the client unfortunately did not notice it. If the lawyer characterizes the facts of the prior cases as involving concealed hazards, the very case for which a rule is being formulated will be excluded. Accordingly, the lawyer characterizes the facts of the prior cases in still more general terms—perhaps as 'hazards'— in order to include the case under consideration.

The lawyer, however, also has the choice of synthesizing a rule in terms broader than is absolutely necessary in order to include the prior cases and the current case. Assume for a moment that the term 'concealed hazard,' in fact, would embrace all of the cases, then so would the more general term 'hazards' and the even more general term 'potentially danger-ous conditions.' The lawyer must decide whether to use one of these more general character-izations or to be only as general as is absolutely necessary to include the current case.

In choosing the level of generality, the lawyer must avoid overreaching. In other words, the lawyer cannot formulate the rule in terms so broad that it includes new cases that make the policy judgments underlying the prior cases inapplicable. If the rule is too broad, application of the rule can yield undesirable results.

For example, assume that in the quicksand, pit, and slope cases the courts were attempting to strike a balance between, on the one hand, compensating injury and, on the other hand, encouraging safety by refusing to compensate the careless. In each case, the court held that because the hazard was concealed, the victim could not have avoided injury by exercising care. Thus, the policy of encouraging safety did not preclude imposing liability on the landowner.

The lawyer who characterizes these cases as imposing liability for all 'hazards' may well be overreaching, because the policy judgments in the prior cases would not apply to any case in which the hazard was obvious. In the case of an obvious hazard, the victim might well have avoided injury by exercising care, and thus the policy judgment made in the prior cases does not apply. In cases in which the hazard is obvious, the policy of encouraging safety could require leaving the careless plaintiff uncompensated by not imposing liability on the land-owner.

Thus, the lawyer must state the newly synthesized rule at a level of generality sufficient to include the prior cases and the client's case. At the same time, the rule must not be stated at a level of generality high enough to encompass new cases in which the policies underlying the prior cases would require a different result.

Between these extremes, however, the lawyer may well have some degree of choice. Thus, reference to the underlying policies may not eliminate all of the indeterminacy in synthesiz-ing a new rule.

Using rule synthesis as an advocate

The discussion in the previous section implicitly assumed to some extent that the lawyer, in synthesizing a new rule, was acting as a dispassionate observer, looking for the 'true' nature of the rule that would explain the prior cases as well as govern the new case.

Yet, the lawyer engaged in the synthesis of a new rule is very often acting as an advocate, with the purpose of either constructing a new rule that will compel the result the client seeks or opposing the creation of the new rule. Let us consider the tactical moves that a lawyer in either situation may make in support of a client's position.

Supporting the new rule

First, the lawyer attempting to create the rule probably wants to generalize from as many cases as possible. Recall that the lawyer would probably argue that the rule being advocated is not a new rule at all but rather a well-established rule perhaps not previously articulated in explicit terms. The more cases that have recognized the rule, the more the rule looks like a well-established rule of law that the court must apply and the less the courts feel that it has ventured onto new terrain.

Second, the lawyer obviously wants to include in the factual predicate of the rule only those facts that clearly have counterparts in the current case. At times, that may be difficult because the court in a prior case may have stated explicitly that a particular fact—say, the fact that the hazard was concealed—was dispositive. If the fact was dispositive in the prior case from which the new rule is to be synthesized, then the fact generally has to be included in the new rule as well.

There is at least one argument the lawyer can make for excluding the dispositive fact from the new rule, and this is to contend that the dispositive fact was a sufficient, but not a necessary, condition for the result reached in the prior case. Thus, the fact need not be an element of the rule. This argument is bolstered considerably if the dispositive fact was absent from some prior cases. Even if it was present in all of them, the lawyer can argue that it was only a sufficient fact. This is done by demonstrating that the policies underlying the rule do not dictate that it be present. The lawyer might argue, for example, that the only policy mentioned by the court in the prior case was protecting persons against avoidable injury and that policy would have required imposition of a duty to warn whether the hazard was concealed or not. The lawyer is arguing, in effect, that the fact of concealment was not truly necessary to the result and any statements about the necessity of the fact should be considered dictum. Further, because the policy underlying the rule does not require that the hazard be concealed, the prior court's dictum to the effect that a concealed condition was a necessary fact should not be followed.

Third, the lawyer probably wants to formulate the rule in the most general terms possible, without overreaching. A more general rule embraces more prior cases because the broad language used obscures the minor differences among the cases, thus allowing more cases to fall within the rule. As explained above, the more cases that seem to have embraced the rule, the more willing the court will be to apply it in the novel case. At the same time, the broader the rule, the more likely it is to encompass the lawyer's case.

Opposing the new rule

A lawyer opposing recognition of the new rule may also employ a set of standard tactical moves. First, the lawyer attempts to restrict the number of cases on which the generalized rule may be based. This is done by confining the prior cases to their facts. That is, the lawyer points out that the quicksand case addressed only quicksand; the concealed pit case, only concealed pits; the unstable slope case, only unstable slopes. Therefore, anything beyond quicksand, concealed pits, and unstable slopes is mere dictum that need not be followed. Ultimately, the argument is that no general rule exists; there are only several specific rules, none of which applies here. This argument, in essence, is an appeal to the reluctance of courts to make new law.

Second, the lawyer tries to identify dispositive facts in the prior cases that are not present in the novel situation, searching through the prior cases for as many details as can be found and arguing that all of these details were necessary to (not merely sufficient for) the decisions and thus belong in the factual predicate of any newly synthesized rule. Thus, for example, the lawyer may argue that the quicksand, pit, and slope are all concealed, life-threatening natural hazards and thus the rule should be limited to concealed, life-threatening natural hazards. Obviously, the strategy is to formulate a rule that excludes the current case.

Third, the lawyer tries to formulate the rule as narrowly as possible, again with the hope that it will exclude the current case. One way to do this is to characterize the facts narrowly —a concealed pit would be called a concealed pit, not a hazard or an abnormal condition. For this argument to be effective, the lawyer must be prepared to explain why the policy judgments that underlie the rule do not apply in the same way when the rule is formulated in more general terms; that is, the lawyer must explain why a rule formulated in more general terms would overreach."

QUESTION

Define inductive reasoning and explain its relevance to common law analysis.

Vandevelde's description of common law advocacy provides a good introduction to how lawyers deal with precedent in a common law system. From his explanation, it is clear that the process involves fitting the precedents together in such a way to form a general rule, that can then be applied (or not) to a new factual situation. It should also be clear to you now that there is no one way in which the cases can fit together; after all, a new factual situation is a legal dispute with parties (and legal representatives) on both sides trying to make the precedents fit together to reach the outcome they desire. Thus, when dealing with common law problem cases in your legal education, it is imperative that you realize that there is no one "right answer". Instead, there are good answers, which engage with the cases creatively, while not trying to construct rules from them which the facts of those cases cannot realistically support. Vandevelde mentions in the passage above that a lawyer may characterise a statement in a precedent as merely "dictum"; and, therefore, as not "binding" on a future court. We have already examined the court structure in Chapter 6, and you may want to review that material to refamiliarize yourself with the idea of decisions being binding or merely persuasive, under the principle of *stare decisis*. However, even if a precedent is binding according to the hierarchy of courts, there is a crucial distinction in common law reasoning between the *ratio decidendi* of a precedent, and those parts of a judgment which are merely *obiter dicta*. Understanding common law reasoning requires an appreciation of the often difficult distinction between those two elements of a common law precedent.

Rupert Cross and J.W. Harris, *Precedent in English Law* (4th ed., Clarendon Press, Oxford, 1991), pp. 39–43:

"[E]very court is bound to follow any case decided by a court above it in the hierarchy, and appellate courts (other than the House of Lords) are bound by their previous decisions. This statement is too concise because it does not indicate that the only part of a previous case which is binding is the *ratio decidendi* (reason for deciding). . . .

The *ratio decidendi* is best approached by a consideration of the structure of a typical judgment. . . . It consists of a review of facts and arguments and a discussion of relevant questions of law. Several opinions are frequently delivered in appellate courts because appeals are always heard by more than one judge.

It is not everything said by a judge when giving judgment that constitutes a precedent. In the first place, this status is reserved for his pronouncements on the law, and no disputed point of law is involved in the vast majority of cases that are tried in any year. The dispute is solely concerned with the facts. For example, the issue may be whether a particular motorist was driving carelessly by failing to keep a proper look-out or travelling at an excessive speed. No one doubts that a motorist owes a legal duty to drive carefully and, very frequently, the only question is whether he was in breach of that duty when he caused damage to a pedestrian or another motorist. Cases in which the only issues are questions of fact are usually not reported in any series of law reports, but it is not always easy to distinguish law from fact and the reasons which led a judge of first instance or an appellate court to come to a factual conclusion are sometimes reported at length. For example, an employer is under a legal duty to provide his employees with a reasonably safe system of working. The question whether that duty has been broken is essentially one of fact, but the law reports contain a number of cases in which judges have expressed their views concerning the precautions which an employer should have taken in particular instances. When an injury would not have occurred if a workman had been wearing protective clothing it has been said that his employer ought to have insisted that such clothing should have been worn instead of merely rendering it available for those who desired to wear it, but the House of Lords has insisted that observations of this nature are not general propositions of law necessarily applicable to future cases and the decisions based upon them do not constitute a precedent. There is no point in endeavouring to ascertain the *ratio decidendi* of such cases.

The second reason why it is not everything said by a judge in the course of his judgment that constitutes a precedent is that, among the propositions of law enunciated by him, only those which he appears to consider necessary for his decision are said to form part of the *ratio decidendi* and thus to amount to more than an *obiter dictum*. If the judge in a later case is bound by the precedent according to the English doctrine of *stare decisis*, he must apply the earlier *ratio decidendi* however much he disapproved of it, unless, to use the words of Lord Reid, he considers that the two cases are 'reasonably distinguishable'. Dicta in earlier cases are, of course, frequently followed or applied, but dicta are never of more than persuasive authority. There is no question of any judge being bound to follow them. Even when the *ratio decidendi* of a previous case is merely a persuasive authority, it must be followed in later cases unless the judge has good reason to disapprove of it. It constitutes a precedent, and the difference between a persuasive precedent and an *obiter dictum* is only slightly less significant than that between binding and persuasive precedents. If, for example, a High Court judge of first instance comes to the conclusion that a proposition of law contained in a previous opinion of another High Court judge of first instance is ratio, he will be a great deal more reluctant to differ from it than would be the case if he was satisfied that it was merely a *dictum*, although a judge of first instance is not bound to follow the decision of another judge of first instance.

The distinction between *ratio decidendi* and *obiter dictum* is an old one. As long ago as 1673 Vaughan C.J. said:

'An opinion given in court, if not necessary to the judgment given of record, but that it might have been as well given if no such, or a contrary had been broach'd, is no judicial opinion; but a mere gratis dictum. . . .'

There are undoubtedly good grounds for the importance attached to the distinction between *ratio decidendi* and *obiter dictum*. In this context an *obiter dictum* means a statement by the way, and the probabilities are that such a statement has received less serious consideration than that devoted to a proposition of law put forward as a reason for the decision. It is not even every proposition of this nature that forms part of the *ratio decidendi*. To quote Devlin J., as he then was:

'It is well established that if a judge gives two reasons for his decision, both are binding. It is not permissible to pick out one as being supposedly the better reason and ignore the other one; nor does it matter for this purpose which comes first and which comes second. But the practice of making judicial observations *obiter* is also well established. A judge may often give additional reasons for his decisions without wishing to make them part of the *ratio decidendi*; he may not be sufficiently convinced of their cogency as to want them to have the full authority of a precedent, and yet may wish to state them so that those who later may have the duty of investigating the same point will start with some guidance. This is a matter which the judge himself is alone capable of deciding, and any judge who comes after him must ascertain which course has been adopted from the language used and not by consulting his own preferences.'

One thing which a judge cannot do is to prevent his decision on a point of law from constituting a precedent.

The above remarks of Lord Devlin represent orthodox judicial theory, and, at first sight, the power they concede to those who decide a case may seem somewhat surprising. If a judge has this amount of freedom to determine which of his observations is *ratio decidendi* and which *obiter dictum*, is there not a grave danger that he will exercise an undue influence on the future development of the law? He only has to state twenty propositions and say that he bases his decision on each of them to have created twenty new legal rules. It is true that the majority of the judges of former times would have denied that they possessed any power to make new law, but we are primarily concerned with the contemporary situation in which the declaratory theory of judicial decision no longer holds sway. It is also true that the last thing any modern English judge would wish to do is to fetter his successors by laying down a multitude of superfluous rules. But just now we are concerned with legal theory. The answer to the question raised is that there are several considerations which may be said to redress the balance in favour of the judges who come afterwards. No doubt the *ratio decidendi* of a previous case has to be gathered from the language of the judge who decided that case, but it is trite learning that the interpreter has nearly as much to say as the speaker so far as the meaning of words is concerned. Of even greater significance is the existence of certain rules of judicial practice concerning the construction to be placed by a future judge upon past decisions. By stressing the necessity of having regard to the facts of the previous case and the language of prior or subsequent judgments, these rules greatly curtail the influence that can be exercised on legal development by means of the reasons which a particular judge sees fit to give for his decisions."

One of the primary ways in which judges in future cases can exercise a high degree of control over the meaning of a precedent is through the use of analogical reasoning. That is, judges can extend the scope of a precedent to cover new situations by drawing *analogies* between the facts of the case at hand, and the precedent. Alternatively, the judge may *distinguish* the immediate case from the precedent on the basis that there is a *material* difference between them; which means the precedent will not be applied to the facts at issue. The "art" of applying and distinguishing case law is one of the most important skills for the student of the common law to develop and, indeed, for any legal advocate.

Kenneth J. Vandevelde, *Thinking Like a Lawyer* (Westview Press, Boulder, 1996), pp. 91–98:

Arguments for following the precedent

"As an initial matter, the lawyer arguing that a prior case should be followed in a later case emphasizes the numerous factual similarities between the two cases. Strictly speaking, the only relevant facts are those whose existence would further or impede one of the underlying policies. The advocate arguing that a prior case should be followed, however, rarely limits the argument to those facts. Rather, the advocate includes in the recitation of similarities virtually any fact that is not a trivial coincidence.

Second, the advocate argues that the inevitable dissimilarities are irrelevant, the basic contention being that none of the facts that make the cases different is relevant to furthering or impeding any of the underlying policies. Obviously, for example, the fact that the parties' names differ is irrelevant to any legitimate policy. To the extent possible, the advocate makes a parallel argument with respect to any dissimilarity between the cases.

This argument may be difficult to make where the court in the prior case has stated explicitly that a particular fact, not present in the current case, is dispositive. The best argument for following the case in that situation is to point out that in light of the policies underlying the prior case, the prior case would have been decided the same way even without the so-called dispositive fact. The lawyer is arguing, in effect, that the fact was not truly necessary to the result. Since it was not actually necessary to the result, any discussion of that fact should be considered dictum and need not be followed. It may be difficult to prevail in this argument because it requires the court to disregard how another court characterized its own decision.

A third technique for arguing that a precedent should be followed is to state the factual predicate of the precedent at a higher level of generality. For example, if the prior case held that the presence of a concealed pit on the land gives rise to a duty on the part of the land-owner to warn a guest, but the current case involves a guest who fell down a slope, the lawyer for the injured guest may characterize the prior case as involving a 'hazard' rather than a con-cealed pit. As the language becomes more general, it will tend to encompass the facts of the current situation. . . .

A fourth technique is to characterize the prior case, not in terms of its facts but in terms of the underlying policy judgments, which the lawyer argues should be followed. For example, the lawyer seeking to impose on a landowner a duty to warn customers about concealed hazards on the land may rely on cases holding that a manufacturer has a duty to warn consu-mers of product defects. The lawyer would then argue that the prior cases adopted a policy of protecting the unwary against physical injury and that such policy should prevail in the current case as well. This technique may require manipulating the level of generality at which the policy underlying the precedent is stated. The product defect cases, for example, may have described the underlying policy as protecting the stream of commerce against unsafe instru-mentalities. By restating the policy more generally as protecting the unwary, the lawyer makes the policy seem applicable to the subsequent case. That is, the impression is created that the result the lawyer seeks in the later case would further the policies articulated in the earlier case.

Arguments for distinguishing the precedent

The arguments for distinguishing a prior case mirror those for following it. First, the lawyer emphasizes every possible difference between the two cases, being especially alert to facts that the court in the prior case regarded as dispositive. Even if the facts were only sufficient for the holding and not necessary, the lawyer notes that the dispositive facts are not present in this case. If the later case differs concerning some such dispositive fact, then it is likely the court will distinguish the two cases. Assuming that the cases do not differ concerning any fact expli-citly considered dispositive in the earlier case, the lawyer attempting to distinguish the prece-dent may nevertheless point to differences in other facts in an effort to make the cases appear as different as possible.

Second, the lawyer attempts to dismiss similarities between the cases as irrelevant. If pos-sible, the lawyer argues that particular facts in the precedent that are similar to those in the later case were not explicitly found to be dispositive and are therefore irrelevant coincidences. If the facts were held to be dispositive, the lawyer can attempt to argue that the facts were not relevant to accomplishing the underlying policy, although this can obviously be a difficult argument to make.

Third, the lawyer attempting to distinguish the cases characterizes the precedent in the nar-rowest possible terms. The lawyer states the facts and the legal consequence with great spec-ificity, noting that any broader reading would constitute dictum, which the court need not follow. By stating the facts at very specific levels, the lawyer produces new dissimilarities. Thus, a pit is not merely a pit, but a concealed, life-threatening, 20-foot-deep pit.

Fourth, the lawyer may contend that the policy judgments underlying the prior case do not apply to the current case. This argument may follow any of several different approaches.

One approach is to argue that the policies that prevailed in the prior case require a differ-ent result in this case than was reached in the prior case. For example, assume that the prior case held that the government has the power to prohibit the use of offensive language on a television broadcast because the danger that a youngster might be injured by hearing the lan-guage outweighed the broadcaster's right to use it. In a later case, a television station broad-casts a documentary that realistically portrays the lives of young drug users in an effort to persuade juveniles that drug use could ruin their lives. To make the documentary more realis-tic and thus more credible, the station broadcasts film of drug users engaged in conversation with the police, their families, and each other—conversation involving the use of the same offensive language. The lawyer might argue that, in this case, the policy of protecting children actually would be *furthered* by permitting the offensive language to be broadcast. Thus, to further the policy that prevailed in the prior case the court should distinguish the prior case and void, rather than uphold, the ban on offensive language. . . .

Finally, the lawyer can argue that if the precedent is applied to this case, *stare decisis* would require that it also be applied to other cases in which it would produce a clearly undesirable result. This, again, is the parade of horribles or the slippery slope argument. The lawyer demonstrates that this case is indistinguishable from other hypothetical cases in which application of the precedent would lead to undesirable results. As with legal reasoning in the deductive form, this argument is distinguished by not requiring a demonstration that following the precedent would lead to a bad result in this case, only that it would entail application of the precedent to other cases in which it would produce an undesirable result. . . .

The problem of competing analogies

The prior discussion has assumed that the lawyer was attempting to determine whether one precedent should be followed or distinguished in deciding a current dispute. The precedent must be followed if it is like the current case.

Often, however, the lawyer encounters a situation where there are two or more precedents, each of which is like the current case in some respects. The problem is that the two precedents reached opposite results and thus both cannot be followed. In other words, the lawyer must choose between competing analogies. . . .

The lawyer nevertheless chooses between the competing analogies using the same techniques that are used to decide whether to follow or distinguish a single precedent. The correct analogy is the one that seems most like the current case, taking into account all similarities and dissimilarities."

EXERCISE

Consider the following problem. Construct arguments for the plaintiff and defendant, and then consider how, as a judge, you would decide the case and prepare reasons. You should draw upon the material on precedent which we have examined thus far as a guide for discerning the *ratio decidendi* of your precedent, and how to apply or distinguish it.

Edmund M.A. Kwaw, *The Guide to Legal Analysis, Legal Methodology and Legal Writing* (Emond Montgomery, Toronto, 1992), p. 198:

"You are a judge in a case in which Jason, a truck driver, and Louis, a pedestrian, are suing a day nursery. You learn from the evidence that as Jason was driving, he saw a little girl dart through the gate of the day nursery onto the road. He swerved to avoid hitting her. In doing so, he knocked down Louis, who happened to be walking on the sidewalk at that moment, and his truck also struck a lamp post. Jason suffered shock and Louis sustained bruises and a fractured leg. You learn from the evidence that the gate of the day nursery should not have been opened without a teacher or other adult being present. No one can explain how the gate got open. The only precedent is the (hypothetical) case that follows.

Samson v. Dunlop

Dunlop was a local farmer who had a flock of sheep. He was assisted in his work by three sheep dogs, Wolfie, Blackie, and Spotty. The three dogs were regarded as the best sheep dogs in the county. One day something peculiar happened. Instead of rounding up the sheep as they were supposed to, the three dogs began attacking the sheep. There was a stampede and the fence that kept the sheep in was broken. As the sheep rushed out, Samson the letter carrier, who happened to be riding along on his bicycle, swerved to avoid colliding with the sheep.

Samson lost control of the bicycle and smashed into a tree. In an action brought by Samson against Dunlop, the court held that farmers who were in control of livestock owed a legal duty to ensure that the livestock did not injure other people."

The implications of membership in the European Union on Common Law reasoning

As we have seen in previous chapters, membership in the European Union legal order is now a central element of our legal system. Consequently, an understanding of how precedent works within a common law system must be supplemented by a recognition that "classic" common law reasoning must now take into consideration the impact of the E.U. After all, the European Union emerged from the *civilian* rather than the *common law* tradition, in which precedent does not hold the same power. We will examine the differences between the two legal traditions in greater detail in Chapter 14. For now, our interest is in how the role of precedent must be modified to take European law into account. We have already considered the basic structure of that legal order in Chapter 4. We begin here with the status of cases decided by the European Court of Justice (ECJ), when they are considered by domestic courts.

Colin Manchester, David Salter, Peter Moodie, and Bernadette Lynch, *Exploring the Law: The Dynamics of Precedent and Statutory Interpretation* (Sweet and Maxwell, London, 1996), pp. 106–110:

"Although sections 2 and 3 [of the European Communities Act 1972] leave a number of matters unclear, the ECJ has nevertheless provided some indication of its views, where a case has been referred to it under Article 177, of how its ruling in that case should be regarded on return of the case to the (English or other national) court which referred it. The ECJ stated in *Milchkontor v. Haupzollamt Saarbrucken* Case 29/68 [1969] ECR 165 (*Milchkontor*) that a ruling given by it is binding on the court receiving it. To this extent, the notion of one court binding another court is introduced into the EC legal order. This is not, however, a departure from the principle of *res judicata*, *i.e.* that the decision in a case is generally final and binding only as between the parties to that case, since the ruling given by the ECJ on an Article 177 reference is confined to the particular case in question. This ruling consists of an interpretation or exposition of EC law, formulated in the abstract as a proposition of law rather than one which is dependent upon the material facts of the case, although the proposition will be formulated by reference to those facts. Although binding only on the parties to the case, the ruling is, however, one which the ECJ (presumably) expects English courts in future to follow, although it would (presumably) be a matter for the English courts to determine in what way that should be achieved. Not only might the ECJ expect English courts to follow rulings under Article 177 following references from English courts, but it may also expect any of its other decisions (including rulings under Article 177 following references from courts in other Member States) to be followed, although again it would (presumably) be a matter for the English courts to determine how those decisions should be followed. However, it is clear that, as a matter of EC law, it would be open to an English court in any future case to refer the case before it to the ECJ under Article 177 for a ruling on EC law, notwithstanding the existence of a previous ruling or any other ECJ decision on the particular point.

On receipt of a ruling under Article 177 from the ECJ, it will be for the English court to apply the ruling to the facts of the case before it. When a ruling is so applied, it may, from a traditional English perspective, become part of the *ratio* of that case and thus become part of a proposition of law based on the material facts of that case. As such, the ruling, as part of the *ratio* of the case, would therefore (presumably) be capable of forming a binding precedent, in the English sense, for application in future cases, although, of course, it would be open to a subsequent court to limit the scope of such *ratio* (and thus ruling) by distinguishing it on the ground that the case before it had materially different facts.

Whilst a ruling by the ECJ returned to an English court may become part of the *ratio* of a case in the manner indicated above, it is less clear how any ruling returned to a national court of another Member State or any other decision of the ECJ may do so. In any event, to the extent that any ECJ ruling or decision *has* become part of the *ratio* of a case, this may be seen as being inconsistent with the view that it must always remain open to a court in any future case to make a reference to the ECJ under Article 177.

It is clear from the above that ECJ cases may have a number of implications for the English doctrine of precedent. The extent of such implications, as will be seen below, may vary depending upon whether a court, when considering a point of EC law, decides to refer the case to the ECJ under Article 177 or decides itself to interpret that point.

(i) Implications of a decision to refer to the ECJ under Article 177

When cases have been referred to the ECJ and rulings on points of EC law have been received by the courts which referred the cases, those courts invariably seem to have accepted the rulings as binding on them (in accordance with the ECJ's stated view in *Milchkontor*). On receipt of such rulings, it is necessary for English courts to decide how the interpretations or expositions of EC law contained therein should be applied to the facts of the case. This may involve a consideration of the impact of the ruling on the provision in question in the English legislation and, as seen, different approaches have been adopted on this matter. In some cases, courts have regarded rulings as setting out a proposition of EC law which should be applied in preference to a provision in English legislation deemed to be inconsistent with that proposition (Priority Approach), an approach adopted, for instance, by the Court of Appeal in *Macarthys*, in which Lord Denning M.R. stated (at [1981] 1 All ER 111, 120):

> 'We have now been provided with the decision of that court [the ECJ]. It is important now to declare, and it must be made plain, that the provisions of article 119 of the EEC Treaty [as interpreted by the ECJ on an Article 177 reference from the present case] take priority over anything in our English statute on equal pay which is inconsistent with art 119.'

In other cases, courts have regarded the rulings as an aid to interpretation of a provision in English legislation. Thus courts have, on some occasions, used the ruling as an aid to resolving an ambiguity (Ambiguity Interpretation Approach) and, on other occasions, to interpret a provision in English legislation (not regarded as containing any ambiguity) in whatever manner is necessary to secure compliance with EC law (General Interpretation Approach). An instance of a court using a ruling as an aid to interpretation can be seen in *Garland*, where the House of Lords used a ruling to resolve an ambiguity in section 6(4) of the Sex Discrimination Act 1975 and where Lord Diplock stated (at [1982] 2 All ER 402, 416) that it was necessary to obtain a ruling from the ECJ 'so as to provide the House with material necessary to aid it in construing s 6(4) of the Sex Discrimination Act 1975.'

On occasions, courts receiving rulings have also expressed views (*obiter*) as to the status that such rulings will have in future cases. Thus, when the Court of Appeal in *Macarthys* received a ruling from the ECJ that article 119 of the EC Treaty required equal pay for men and women even where they were not employed at the same time, Lord Denning M.R. stated (at [1981] 1 All ER 111, 120): 'That interpretation must now be given by all the courts in England. It will apply in this case and in any such case hereafter.' Similarly, Lord Diplock in the House of Lords in *Garland*, reflecting on the decision in that case to make a reference to the ECJ under Article 177, stated (at [1982] 2 All ER 402, 415) that 'it was desirable to obtain a ruling of the European Court that would be binding on all courts in England, including this House.'

This means that the interpretation or exposition of EC law will be of general application, *i.e.* not limited in scope to future cases in which the *ratio* of the particular case in question might be considered applicable in view of the materially similar facts, and will apply irrespective of the position in the court hierarchy of either the court receiving the ruling or of any later court applying it. By regarding rulings returned to English courts as being generally binding in this way (subject to exercise of the right to refer under Article 177), the above statements appear to regard these rulings in much the same way as any other decisions of the ECJ (including rulings under Article 177 following references from courts in other Member States), a matter which is considered immediately below.

(ii) Implications of a decision by an English court to interpret EC law

. . . English courts may have regard to ECJ cases. These cases may include previous rulings under Article 177 following references from English courts or from courts in other Member States, as well as any other decisions of the ECJ. English courts appear to regard ECJ cases in each instance as being binding generally. As a consequence, interpretations of EC law contained in such ECJ cases may be binding on an English court in a particular case, irrespective of the presence or absence of similar material facts between the ECJ case(s) and the case in question and irrespective of the position of the English court in the court hierarchy.

Instances of where English courts have had regard to ECJ case law when interpreting EC law have included the decision of the Court of Appeal in *Pickstone* and the decision of the House of Lords in *Henn*. The Court of Appeal in *Pickstone* was concerned with interpreting two points of EC law, determining the scope of the principle of equal pay based on Article 119 and determining whether that principle had direct effect as regards work of equal value. On the first point, two of the three members of the Court of Appeal, Nicholls and Purchas L.JJ. found guidance on the interpretation of Article 119 in different decisions of the ECJ, notwithstanding material differences in the facts of those cases from the case in question. Nicholls L.J. referred to the case of *Macarthys*, an earlier ECJ case in which a ruling had been given under Article 177 following a reference from the English Court of Appeal, whilst Purchas L.J., found guidance on the interpretation of Article 119 in *Defrenne*, an earlier case in which a ruling had been given under Article 177 following a reference from a Belgian court. On the second point, Nicholls and Purchas L.JJ. referred to two ECJ decisions, *Jenkins v. Kingsgate (Clothing Productions) Ltd*, Case 96/8 [1981] 1 ECR 911 and *Worringham*, in which rulings had been given under Article 177 following references from English courts. These cases provided interpretations on the direct effectiveness of the principle of equal pay based on Article 119 and were considered to have application in preference to an earlier Court of Appeal decision on direct effectiveness, *O'Brien v. Sim-Chem Ltd.* [1980] 2 All ER 37. In *Henn*, the House of Lords had regard to a 'well- established body of case law of the European court' (*per* Lord Diplock at [1981] AC 850, 905), that provided guidance on the interpretation of Article 3 of the EC Treaty, under which quantitative restrictions on importation of goods as between Member States were prohibited, when determining the scope of that article."

THEORETICAL PERSPECTIVES ON COMMON LAW REASONING

In this section, our emphasis shifts to a more reflective mode, and we look at the broader, more theoretical implications of the common law system of precedent. Central to that inquiry, first of all, is the question of the extent to which we can say that judges are "makers" of law; rather than simply engaged in the task of "declaring" a common law that is already "there". Although it may seem obvious to us, at the end of the twentieth century, that judges are lawmakers, this viewpoint at one time would have been considered very radical. The common law was assumed to be already "there", and had always been there, just waiting to be declared by judges in the interpretation of cases. Cotterrell describes this as a "paradox" of the common law.

Roger Cotterrell, *The Politics of Jurisprudence* (Butterworths, London, 1989), pp. 26–30:

"A paradox seems to lie at the heart of classical common law thought. Common law as the embodiment of ancient wisdom is revealed by judges, not created by them. It is, therefore, always already existent. Yet obviously it develops with the accumulation, reinterpretation and restatement of precedents and the adjustment of legal doctrine to new circumstances reflected in the never-ending succession of cases brought before courts. How is the evolution of law explained in this conception? And why is it not possible to assert openly that judges *make* law, even if only within strict limits which would fix them as clearly subordinate to recognised legislators, such as (in the context of English history) a parliament or the monarch?

The formal answer to this last question is that law embodies an ancient wisdom which may, according to some conceptions of common law, be considered timeless or, according to others, be seen as continually evolving through collective experience. On either view judges can only reflect this wisdom and not change it. In some classical common law thought the claim of timelessness is taken to fantastic lengths. Influential seventeenth century lawyers, such as Sir Edward Coke, 'argued on the flimsiest of evidence that the common laws, including their most detailed procedural provisions, dated from the earliest times'. Even Magna Carta was treated as declaring ancient law, confirming and making enforceable rights which had long existed. Coke claimed that in all its major parts the law and constitution had remained unchanged since the Saxon era and even before. These strange views were always controversial but the reason for asserting them at times when the authority of common law was seriously challenged (as in the early seventeenth century) is not hard to see. This authority was traditional in nature. Rooting it in a distant or even mythical past emphasised that it was certainly not derived from the present power of any monarch or other political authority.

The authority or legitimacy of common law as a legal order entitled to the highest respect was seen as residing not in the political system but in the community. If a judge *made* law this could only be as an exercise of political power. The deliberate making of law would be a political act. But according to common law theory, the authority of the judge is not as a political decision-maker (certainly not as delegate of the king or parliament) but as representative of the community. Hence he has authority only to *state* the community's law, not to impose law upon the community as if he were a political ruler or the servant of one. And the community is to be thought of here as something uniting past and present, extending back through innumerable past generations as well as encompassing the present one. Clearly, if the term 'community' were to be defined rigorously in this context it would be necessary to ask who exactly is within this community and what is its nature. It would also be necessary to consider the compatibility of this communitarian conception of law with the fact that the judges referred to here are judges of the *royal* courts, the instruments of a centralised justice promoted by kings. But such issues are typically absent from classical common law thought. Thus, common law is, for Coke, simply 'the most ancient and best inheritance that the subjects of this realm have'.

The usual way of conceptualising this apparently unchanging inheritance in classical common law thought is as *custom*. As Brian Simpson remarks, it is odd nowadays to think of law in this way because lawyers are used to treating this law as posited by the judges. But this is another example of the tendency to impose alien modern theoretical conceptions on common law. Just as common law is not strictly to be thought of, in the classical conception, as rules, neither is it to be thought of as decisions. To term it 'a residue of immutable custom' is more accurate, but does not confront the fact that common law thought embraces complex notions explaining and justifying past practices (not just stating them as custom) and providing guidance for future conduct. Equally common law thought allows the development of new doctrines and ideas, so has a dynamism which custom may lack. Because of these characteristics Simpson prefers to term common law customary law, rather than custom. But this hardly seems to solve the theoretical problem of its development. Customary law still has the character of custom, looking back to the past rather than guiding the future. It is concerned with stating established practice rather than with means of developing legal doctrine to meet changing times.

The problem here is not that custom is changeless. There is no reason why it cannot be considered to change over time. Law as an expression of custom can, therefore, also change. The problem is that common law thought itself cannot really address this change or explain it as a *legal* process. The mechanisms of change are in society (or the community). Law changes solely through the mysterious processes by which custom changes. To explain or even recognise explicitly processes of legal change, classical common law thought would require some kind of sociological or anthropological insight. But the common lawyers were hardly sociologists. Common law thought predated any modern social science and, in any event, its practical case-by-case view of legal development would have found little room for any explicit general theory of social or cultural change. So classical common law thought emphasised continuity (which it could interpret legally in terms of precedents and fundamental principles), rather than change (for which it could find no specifically legal criteria of evaluation).

Historically, the conundrum of law as changeless yet always changing was avoided by devices made possible by cultural conditions. Common law was considered to be unwritten. Blackstone, following Hale, distinguished 'the common law, or *lex non scripta* of this kingdom' from the written law of Acts of Parliament. Even though this unwritten law was eventually reported in written form, the fact that the law itself was still considered unwritten presumably allowed individual innovation to be forgotten, subsumed in the image of a changeless collective legal knowledge. As the anthropologist Jack Goody has noted about societies lacking writing, it is not that the creative element is absent in them or that 'a mysterious collective authorship, closely in touch with the collective consciousness, does what individuals do in literate cultures. It is rather that the individual signature is always getting rubbed out in the process of generative transmission'. Certainly common law's unwritten character was seen as one of its strengths, making possible 'a flexible system which had developed along with the English people itself'.

In the early ages of common law the lack of writing allowed a convenient amnesia. Blackstone wrote in the eighteenth century that 'in our law the goodness of a custom depends upon its having been used time out of mind; or, in the solemnity of our legal phrase, time whereof the memory of man runneth not to the contrary. This it is that gives its weight and authority'. The traditional authority of common law required that its customs be shrouded in antiquity. But in the Middle Ages two or three lifetimes would be enough to make a principle of common law immemorial; 'in ten or twenty years a custom was of long standing; in forty years it was "age-old"'. Later the flexibility of memory was less satisfactory. When, in the seventeenth century, lawyers such as Coke found it necessary to assert with the greatest possible force the traditional authority of common law against the king, the 'idea of the immemorial . . . took on an absolute colouring . . . It ceased to be a convenient fiction and was heatedly asserted as literal historical truth'. It can easily be seen, therefore, that common law thought eventually backed itself into a corner. First, the idea that the law was unwritten eventually became a mere fiction as the common law was recorded—preserved, explained and digested in written form in public records, law reports and 'the authoritative writings of the venerable sages of the law'. Secondly, the purely traditional authority of the law eventually demanded an utterly unrealistic claim of unbroken continuity from ancient times. And, finally, the declaratory theory of common law judging had to be maintained in the face of abundant evidence of conscious judicial innovation in legal doctrine.

Three responses to this situation were possible. One was to declare that common law possessed no authority by which it could develop further. Legal innovation could only come through Acts of Parliament, or other legislative acts. Thus, as one judge put the matter, 'It is in my opinion impossible for us now to create any new doctrine of common law'. A second response was to embrace openly the idea that judges sometimes make law, discard all fictions and go on to ask serious questions as to *how* and under what conditions they should make it. But this pragmatic approach also involved discarding all the standard assumptions underpinning the authority and legitimacy of common law. Traditional authority would need to be replaced with something else—perhaps the charismatic authority of individual wise judges, a conception of delegated political power or, as in the United States, the authority of a specific constitutional document providing the ultimate foundation of legal and judicial systems. In any event such a new foundation of judicial authority, if it could be found, would be something different from that presupposed in classical common law thought.

A third solution was to discard the notion of common law as custom and the formal idea of an unchanging ancient law, and to emphasise instead the complex conception of the judge as spokesman of the community—neither individual creator of law nor mere restator of ancient truths, but representative of an evolving collective consciousness."

QUESTION

Explain the paradox of common law thought.

The issue of whether judges merely "declare" a common law which is already "there", and the degree to which precedent operates as an effective constraint upon judicial decision making, have long been the subject of vigourous debate. Beginning in the 1930s, for example, a school of legal thought known as "American legal realism" drew into question these established "truths". One of the members of this school, Jerome Frank, was particularly skeptical of the constraints which the common law mode of thought claimed to impose upon judges. It has been argued that most lawyers today are realists in one form or another, but Frank was particularly radical in his claim that there was a great divergence between what judges say in their decisions, (*i.e.* what they claim is the basis for their decisions, such as precedent), and what *really* is operating on judges in the process of decision making (which Frank viewed as an emotional response to the particular facts of the case). Thus, for legal realists, the gap between the rhetoric of common law judging, and its reality, was potentially vast.

Jerome Frank, *Law and the Modern Mind* (Peter Smith, Gloucester, MA, 1970), pp. 159–162:

"Lawyers and judges purport to make large use of precedents; that is, they purport to rely on the conduct of judges in past cases as a means of procuring analogies for action in new cases. But since what was actually decided in the earlier cases is seldom revealed, it is impossible, in a real sense, to rely on these precedents. What the courts in fact do is to manipulate the language of former decisions. They could approximate a system of real precedents only if the judges, in rendering those former decisions, had reported with fidelity the precise steps by which they arrived at their decisions. The paradox of the situation is that, granting there is value in a system of precedents, our present use of illusory precedents makes the employment of real precedents impossible.

The decision of a judge after trying a case is the product of a unique experience. 'Of the many things which have been said of the mystery of the judicial process,' writes Yntema, 'the most salient is that *decision is reached after an emotive experience in which principles and logic play a secondary part*. The function of juristic logic and the principles which it employs seem to be like that of language, to describe the event which has already transpired. These considerations must reveal to us the impotence of general principle to control decision. Vague because of their generality, they mean nothing save what they suggested in the organized experience of one who thinks them, and, because of their vagueness, they only remotely compel the organization of that experience. The important problem . . . is not the formulation of the rule but the ascertainment of the cases to which, and the extent to which, it applies. And this, even if we are seeking uniformity in the administration of justice, will lead us again to the circumstances of the concrete case . . . The reason why the general principle cannot control is because it does not inform . . . It should be obvious that when we have observed a recurrent phenomenon in the decisions of the courts, we may appropriately express the classification in a rule. But the rule will be only a mnemonic device, a useful but hollow diagram of what has been. It will be intelligible only if we *relive again the experience of the classifier'*.

The rules a judge announces when publishing his decision are, therefore, intelligible only if one can relive the judge's unique experience while he was trying the case—which, of course, cannot be done. One cannot even approximate that experience as long as opinions take the form of abstract rules applied to facts formally described. Even if it were desirable that, despite its uniqueness, the judge's decision should be followed, as an analogy, by other judges while trying other cases, this is impossible when the manner in which the judge reached his judgment in the earlier case is most inaccurately reported, as it now is. You are not really applying his decision as a precedent in another case unless you can say, in effect, that, having relived his experience in the earlier case, you believe that he would have thought his decision applicable to the facts of the latter case. And as opinions are now written, it is impossible to guess what the judge did experience in trying a case. The facts of all but the simplest controversies are complicated and unlike those of any other controversy; in the absence of a highly detailed account by the judge of how he reacted to the evidence, no other person is capable of reproducing his actual reactions. The rules announced in his opinions are therefore often insufficient to tell the reader why the judge reached his decision.

Dickinson admits that the 'personal bent of the judge' to some extent affects his decisions. But this 'personal bent,' he insists, is a factor only in the selection of new rules for unprovided cases. However, *in a profound sense the unique circumstances of almost any case make it an 'unprovided case' where no well-established rule 'authoritatively' compels a given result*. The uniqueness of the facts and of the judge's reaction thereto is often concealed because the judge so states the facts that they appear to call for the application of a settled rule. But that concealment does not mean that the judge's personal bent has been inoperative or that his emotive experience is simple and reducible."

NOTES AND QUESTIONS

- Frank's views were radical in his time and, to some extent, would still be considered unorthodox in many legal circles. Although they may accord with many "common sense" assumptions about human nature, why would they be threatening to common law judges, and those who place great "faith" in the common law?

- Having read some of his ideas, why do you think Frank was described as a "realist"?

- If you subscribe to Frank's views, what does that suggest about the sort of skills that are important for legal advocacy? In other words, in order to achieve a "good" result for your client, is an intricate knowledge of the relevant precedents of prime importance, or are other skills at least as crucial? What might be those skills?

Frank's skepticism, which was directed to the traditional understanding of precedent, seems less radical today. In part, this is because many writers and commentators on the law recognise quite openly that the process of deciding whether cases are analogous or distinguishable is itself laden with political and social values, and is not a "neutral", formalistic process.

Fiona Cownie and Anthony Bradney, *English Legal System in Context* (Butterworths, London, 1996), pp. 102–104:

"We can see an alternative to the traditional approach to precedent if we return to one of the essential features of any theory of precedent; the desire to treat similar cases in the same fashion and thus bring both certainty and consistency to the law. Here the basic question is how do we decide that two cases are or are not alike? Traditional theories approach this question on the basis that it is simply a matter of close reasoning to see what are and what are not the significant and trivial aspects of the two cases in issue. However, we have seen that, in law, as in other disciplines, what makes something trivial or significant does not depend solely on linguistic features. Nothing is essentially significant or essentially trivial. Meaning is socially defined by the small community of English lawyers. Thinking like a lawyer means not arguing more rigorously than others but, literally, thinking in the way that a lawyer would. . . . Prediction is achieved not just because the same rules are followed but because of an ability to empathise with those whose thought processes are being considered. One seeks to use words and judgments in the way other English lawyers would use them.

Several writers have argued that in considering how this social effect of language occurs we need to consider the influence of what they have called the legal canon in legal reasoning. . . . A canon is an accepted body of literature which it is said one should know if one is to be knowledgeable about a particular area. But a canon is more than simply a certain set of books (or in the case of a legal system, judgments). The works that constitute the canon are chosen for their alleged value. This value is moral or political. Works in the canon say something about the spirit of the system. However, since the canon reflects values in the system the selection of what is and what is not in the canon is in itself a value-laden act. The canon reflects and reinforces the politics of those who constitute the community for whom it operates. In the context of law this means that the influence of the canon on legal argument is itself not a value-free act. Arguments which are not reflective of the values of the canon will find it harder to find a purchase within the system.

The notion of the canon provides a framework within which the more traditional accounts of ratio and obiter can work. It allows us to understand how legal arguments can be acceptable even if they are not logical. The idea of a canon helps to explain how, on the one hand, there can be irresolvable problems in traditional accounts of precedent and yet, on the other hand, there can still be a reasonable degree of consistency and certainty in English legal reasoning. Social pressures supplement the principles of English legal reasoning to produce comparatively predictable outcomes to legal arguments. This explanation, though, has consequences for our understanding of the nature of legal reasoning. If reasoning is in part social, in part about values, who does the reasoning matters. The social background of judges and lawyers will affect how they respond to, and help construct, the atmosphere which in turn creates the canon."

Cownie and Bradney make an important point that one of the tasks of a legal method course must be to teach students how "to use words and judgments in the way other English lawyers would use them". Thus, even if judges decide cases on a basis other than formal legal reasoning, it remains important for the lawyer to be able to speak within that "traditional" legal discourse—since that is what is expected of him or her. In that sense, law (unfortunately, many would argue) remains a conservative enterprise, in the sense that one must use a language expected of you. It remains difficult to alter and broaden the scope of legal reasoning, so as to encompass, for example, more perspectives on the law. However, that is not to say that legal method and discourse forecloses innovation. Instead, it suggests that for the critical or radical lawyer, the task becomes particularly great. He or she must be able to converse in traditional legal discourse *at least as well* as his or her adversaries, but at the same time, must try to expand its scope and achieve outcomes more in keeping with his or her view of what "social justice" demands. At the same time, the barrister may need to convince a judge that what he or she is asking the judge to do is not too dramatic, by couching it within a language with which he (and it probably will be a "he") is most comfortable. It is no small task!

The job is not helped for the lawyer (and, indeed, for the law student) by the traditional differentiation between "law" (supposedly neutral, apolitical, and value-free) and "policy" (which is assumed to be something other than law). As Sugarman argues, the categories of common law thought, which have been entrenched through traditional legal education, have served to create this law/policy dichotomy, which conveniently serves to disguise the politics of law.

David Sugarman, "'A Hatred of Disorder': Legal Science, Liberalism and Imperialism" in *Dangerous Supplements* (Peter Fitzpatrick, ed., Pluto Press, London, 1991), pp. 34–35:

"The 'black letter' tradition continues to overshadow the way we teach, write and think about law. Its categories and assumptions are still the standard diet of most first-year law students and they continue to organise law textbooks and casebooks. Stated baldly it assumes that although law may appear to be irrational, chaotic and particularistic, if one digs deep enough and knows what one is looking for, then it will soon become evident that the law is an internally coherent and unified body of rules. This coherence and unity stems from the fact that law is grounded in, and logically derived from, a handful of general principles, and that whole subject areas such as contract and torts are distinguished by some common principles or elements which fix the boundaries of the subject. The exposition and systematisation of these general principles and the techniques required to find and to apply both them and the rules that they underpin, are largely what legal education and scholarship are all about.

The claim that law is unified and coherent is also sustained by a battery of dualisms: common law/statute law, law/politics, law/state, law/morality, legal/empirical, technique/substance, form/substance, means/ends, private law/public law, law/history, law/theory, which make it more tenable to regard law as 'pure' and 'scientific'.

Despite the variety of producers and consumers of legal discourse, it is what the judges say and the supposed needs of the legal profession as narrowly defined, that have had the greatest magnetic pull over the nature and form of legal education and scholarship. Other aspects that are equally important to understanding law, such as legislation, the operation of law in practice, as well as the history, theory, morality and politics of law, are ignored or marginalised.

The 'black letter' tradition is also the bearer of an important political message. The message is that the law (primarily through case law) and the legal profession (centrally, the judiciary) play a major role in protecting individual freedom; and that the rules of contract, torts and constitutional law, for example, confer the maximum freedom on individuals to act as they wish without interference from other individuals or the state. Policing the boundaries within, and between, legal subject areas constitutes a major foundation of the rule of law. In this way, the form as well as the content of the law become synonymous with our very definitions of individual freedom and liberty, and thereby acquire an additional patina of reverance and universality. The world, as pictured within the conceptual categories of legal thought, is basically sound. It is more or less the best that is realisable. In so far as a better world is possible, it would not fundamentally differ from the present.

Like any closed model of rationality, the 'black letter' tradition is shot through with contradictions, omissions and absurdities, which generations of judges and jurists have sought to repress. For instance, the notion of law as resting upon an objective body of principle founders when we consider that the quest for underlying principles must involve a selection from the sum of principles available and, therefore, has a strong evaluative element. Principles are thus inseparable from interpretation and theory which, in turn, are determined by values. Thus, the schizophrenia of the first-year law student: when is it that s/he is supposed to talk about 'law', and when is it that s/he can talk about 'policy'? We are heirs of this schizophrenia."

Because, as Sugarman argues, the common law is founded upon a set of legal categories and principles, it becomes necessary for people to "translate" social disputes and problems into those legal categories; *i.e.* to "fit" the issue into an existing category, no matter how inappropriate it might be. This is a process of *abstraction*, and it is central to common law reasoning. However, one of the key problems with such a form of reasoning is that "common sense" is frequently lost sight of as analogies are drawn between factual situations and legal disputes which seem to bear little resemblance to each other, as Mansell, Meteyard, and Thomson illustrate through three cases.

Wade Mansell, Belinda Meteyard, and Alan Thompson, *A Critical Introduction to Law* (Cavendish, London, 1995), pp. 56–59:

"The first, *Ashford v. Thornton* is very much a case which marks the transition, albeit a late one, from the explicit avoidance of issues to the new format which decides hard cases by reference not to social facts but to structured legal categories and technicalities. *Ashford v. Thornton* is a case decided in 1818 in which it was held that under some circumstances trial by battle was still available to an accused. The Chief Justice Lord Ellenborough held, in words which take us back very explicitly to rule magic, as follows:

'The general law of the land is in favour of the wager of battles, and it is our duty to pronounce the law as it is, and not as we may wish it to be. Whatever prejudices therefore may justly exist against this mode of trial, still as it is the law of the land, the Court must pronounce judgment for it.'

Incidentally, but as a matter of interest, the authorities considered, in reaching that decision, went all the way back to the law of Normandy before the Norman Conquest of 1066.

Ashford v. Thornton also provides us with an (admittedly) extreme example of the translation process used by law to put questions into a resolvable form. The application against Abraham Thornton at the behest of William Ashford, the deceased woman's brother was put in the following terms:

'. . . For that he the said Abraham Thornton not having the fear of God before his eyes, but being moved and seduced by the instigation of the devil, on the 27th day of May, in the 57th year of the reign of our Sovereign Lord George the Third by the Grace of God, &c with force of arms at the parish of Sutton-Coldfield in the county of Warwick, in and upon the said Mary Ashford spinster, in the peace of God and our said lord the King, then and there being feloniously, wilfully, and of his malice aforethought, did make an assault, and that the said did take the said Mary Ashford into both his hands, and did then and there feloniously, wilfully, violently, and of his malice aforethought, case, throw, and push the said Mary Ashford into a certain pit of water, wherein there was a great quantity of water, situation in the parish of Sutton-Coldfield aforesaid in the county aforesaid, by means of which said casting, throwing, and pushing of the said Mary Ashford into the pit of water aforesaid by the said A Thornton in form aforesaid, she, the said M Ashford in the pit of water aforesaid with the water aforesaid, was then and there choaked, suffocated, and drowned, of which said choking, suffocating, and drowning she, the said M Ashford, then and there instantly died. And so the said A Thornton, her the said Mary Ashford in manner and form aforesaid feloniously and wilfully, and of his malice aforethought, did kill and murder against the peace of our said lord the King his Crown and dignity.' (*Ashford v. Thornton* (1818) 106 ER 149).

While we would not now expect to see charges framed in such a way this *reductio ad absurdum* does make manifest the legal method of translating social events into legal format.

The second English case which we can use to illustrate both the sidestepping of the issues and the way law justifies decisions by referring to pre-existing rules is the case of *Thompson v. London and Midland Railway* [1930] 1 KB 41 which, although over 60 years old seems almost contemporaneous to lawyers.

The facts of that case as heard by the court were that the tragic Mrs Thompson had wished to travel for a day's outing from Manchester to Darwin on the London and Midland Railway. Mrs Thompson could neither read nor write and she requested her niece to purchase her rail ticket for her. When the niece bought the ticket she might have seen on the front of the ticket the word: 'excursion. For conditions see back.' Had Mrs Thompson's niece then turned the ticket over she would have seen a notice to the effect that the ticket was issued subject to the conditions in the rail company's timetables. The timetables were on sale at the ticket office and one of the conditions attaching to the issue of excursion tickets, according to the timetable was that all liability for injury to excursion passengers, however caused, was excluded.

Without being aware of these conditions Mrs Thompson set off for Darwin. Unfortunately, when the train arrived at Darwin and its arrival was announced to passengers, Mrs Thompson stepped out only to discover that there was no platform outside her door as the train in which she was a passenger was longer in length than the Darwin station platform. Mrs Thompson was injured in the fall and sought compensation from the railway company. The *legal* issue of the case did not concern itself with Mrs Thompson's injuries except extraordinarily indirectly. Mrs Thompson must have been amazed to discover what the question of her compensation turned upon. The legal question to be answered by the court was: 'was the clause excluding liability for injury, to be found in the timetable which was available at the ticket office, a part of the contract of carriage entered into by Mrs Thompson via her niece as agent and the railway company?'.

The court held that Mrs Thompson was unable to recover. They did so by referring to previous cases and the rules that they had laid down. The questions they asked were not concerned with what seemed the most socially relevant facts—the injury to Mrs Thompson and her need for compensation—but rather to the rules and circumstances under which it would be held that a party to a contract had had 'constructive' notice of the existence of a clause which purported to limit liability. Having said that it must be conceded, that, to many law students, the legal question will seem the obvious one. So commonsensical has contract become that many on hearing the facts of Mrs Thompson's case will want to know immediately the terms which governed the transaction. . . .

For a more modern and equally striking example of the 'translation' process at work readers may wish to turn to the decision of the European Court of Justice in *SPUC v. Grogan* [1991] 3 CMLR 689. The case arose out of a decision of the Irish Supreme Court to grant an injunction to restrain a student organisation from publishing and distributing guides to abortion clinics in the UK. It appeared to raise fundamental questions relating to the protection of human rights and to necessitate a balancing of the 'right to life' contained in the Irish Constitution on the one hand, and freedom of expression protected by Community law, on the other. Translated into a form susceptible to adjudication by a reluctant European Court, however, the case was deemed to hinge rather upon the meaning of 'services' within the European Community Treaty and the capacity of the Irish restriction upon the provision of information to interfere with the cross-border supply of services in the Community's internal market. Ultimately the decision of the Court was predicated upon the fact that the students responsible for the distribution of the information were not financially rewarded for their activities and hence not economically tied to the clinics in the UK whose services they were advertising. For the European Court, 'buying' an abortion was seen in the same light as the purchase of an insurance policy."

QUESTION

Compare the "common sense" and "legal" construction of the issues in the three cases. To what extent do you think that "translation" of the issues into legal discourse distorted what was really going on in the cases?

ESSAY QUESTION

Do judges merely "declare" the common law which is already in existence, or do they "make" the common law? Consider the wider *political* implications of your answer.

11

JUDGE MADE LAW: A CASE STUDY ON THE LAW OF NEGLIGENCE

In this chapter, we apply the material on case law which we examined in Chapter 10 to the development of a particular area of law: the general duty of care in tort. The focus is on the historical development of this area of judge made common law, in order to help make more concrete some of the theory which we have looked at thus far. This material is designed to help you to get a better "feel" for the central common law concepts of precedent, *ratio decidendi*, *obiter dictum*, and the application and distinguishing of cases. It is also designed to give you practice reading common law judgments, and we conclude this chapter with an exercise to test your ability to work with precedents and to engage in common law analysis.

HISTORICAL BACKGROUND TO THE LAW OF TORTS

We begin with some historical background to help you understand from where our modern conception of the duty of care principle—which will be the central focus of this chapter—emerged.

Carol Harlow, *Understanding Tort Law* (Fontana, London, 1987), pp. 15–22:

"'Crime' is a word in everyday use and reports of criminal cases fill the pages of the newspapers; to many people indeed, 'the law' is synonymous with criminal law. We all know roughly what a contract is, though its precise legal elements may elude us. In contrast, tort law is something of a puzzle. 'Tort' possesses no obvious meaning in modern English and is not a word in common use. In fact 'tort' is simply the French word for 'wrong' and the word points back through the centuries to the Norman-French which used to be the language of English law courts. Tort is the law of 'wrongs'.

To rechristen tort law as 'the law of wrongs' would get us very little further, however. Moreover, it would not get over the difficulty that it is the criminal law which is generally regarded as the law of wrongdoing. And to describe tort law as the 'civil law of wrongs' is still only half the truth. Contract law is also part of the civil law and breach of a contract could be described both as a 'wrong' and 'wrong'. Contract is generally said to be distinguishable from tort law in that the obligations imposed by contract law all result from the fact that the parties have entered into the contract in the first place. To this extent they can be said to be voluntarily undertaken. Tort law may involve liability to people with whom one has had no previous contact and the obligations are imposed by the common law and not pre-selected by the parties. Contract law revolves around the concept of a bargain, while tort law is much less cohesive. . . .

The tort law which we have today has its roots in medieval England when the distinction between civil and criminal proceedings which we now take for granted was far from clear. A lawyer's precedent as vivid as any to figure in the pages of the Sun illustrates the common stock from which crime and tort have developed. It comes from a collection of thirteenth-century cases which is known as Bracton's Notebook. A wishes to brings an 'appeal of peace and imprisonment'. The precedent describes him as being blameless; he was 'in the peace of our Lord the King' when B, the wrongdoer, 'came with his force against the peace, put him in chains and in irons in the stocks and kept him in prison for a long time and wounded and maimed him'. Today we associate the phrase 'breach of the peace' with criminal proceedings; modern magistrates still possess powers to bind people over to keep the peace if they seem likely to behave in a disorderly fashion. If we were to come across events like these in the pages of the Sun we should expect to find that B had been arrested by the police, charged with serious criminal offences, tried at the Old Bailey before a jury, and sentenced to a long term of imprisonment. A's role in the proceedings would be as a witness only. If the newspaper report went on to tell us that A was suing B for damages in a civil court we would be rather surprised. Yet in terms of the civil law, A's cause of action is much the same as it was when the precedent first appeared in Bracton's Notebook. A has committed an assault by causing B to fear the infliction of immediate unlawful force; by translating his threat into action and inflicting unlawful force he has committed a battery; and by his other actions he has made himself liable for false imprisonment. All three are forms of the tort known as 'trespass to the person', the word 'trespass' being merely another antique word for wrong . . . .

Not only do many of the 'wrongs' with which tort law deals overlap with criminal offences but many of the causes of action date back as far or nearly as far as Bracton. The continuity of tort law is one of its key characteristics. Let us look at another simple example. It is, as we have said, possible in principle to sue a burglar caught creeping about one's house at night. Once again, the cause of action has changed very little since Bracton's day. The principal cause of action would be trespass to land. Indeed, when the law of theft was codified by the Theft Act in 1968, it actually incorporated the ancient notion of trespass by defining burglary in terms of 'entry as a trespasser'. Despite the common warning, trespassers cannot always be prosecuted, especially where they do no damage, but they can be sued even if no damage, not even nervous shock, results. Once again we are dealing with a legacy of early law. Land was of central importance to feudal society and invasions of interests in land were treated with severity, partly because they might so easily result in the same sort of 'breach of the King's peace' as Bracton recorded.

Now assume that we are asking for the return of objects stolen by a burglar. Once again there is a trespass, this time trespass to goods, a tort which covers any deliberate taking or direct interference with property. To sell goods, or otherwise deal with them in a manner inconsistent with the owner's title is a conversion. Theft is generally a conversion and often a trespass to goods and land as well. But there is no absolute rule that criminal and civil law will coincide; some thefts are trespasses, others conversions and some neither.

The medieval court system in which our common law started its life differed greatly from our modern centralized system of courts, all subordinate to the High Court, the Court of Appeal and ultimately the House of Lords. There were many local courts in medieval England and the King's Courts established their jurisdiction only slowly. The King's Courts dispensed justice through 'writs' which came into existence and were added to over a long period of time. Even today a civil action is started by the issue of a writ, but in those days each writ provided a remedy for a specific wrong. The writs could be compared to the children's toy in which plastic shapes have to be posted through exactly corresponding slots. A medieval plaintiff could succeed only if he could find a writ which exactly corresponded to his cause of action. If he chose incorrectly, all he could do was start again. It is these writs or causes of action from which our modern torts are derived and whose curious and often archaic names survive in the pages of our textbooks. The priorities of this feudal and predominantly rural society were very different from our own and this had obvious consequences for the law. The absence of factories and fast cars, for example, made accident compensation less urgent than the preservation of 'the King's peace'. Indeed, the emphasis on 'force' in Bracton's precedent suggests this very necessary preoccupation with what we usually call 'law and order'. We can still see traces of this emphasis in all three of the trespass torts. Trespass is always intentional wrongdoing, and damage or loss need not be proved. It was not the mythical A's hardships which interested the King's Courts but the forcible interference with his person and property rights and the consequent possibility of retaliation by himself and his friends—in other words, the threat to 'the King's peace'. Once again, we are moving on to the territory of modern criminal law. . . .

We are beginning to assemble a picture of tort law as a collection of disparate wrongs without any connecting thread. To a certain extent this is an accurate picture. One of tort law's great scholars, Sir John Salmond, maintained to his dying day that the law of torts was no more than 'a body of rules establishing specific injuries' uncoordinated by general principles, a statement preserved in the latest edition of his classic book. At the end of the eighteenth century, when tort law had not yet been acknowledged as a subject in its own right and one single collection of cases had been published, the statement would have seemed uncontrovertible. Yet the common law in fact contained a mechanism which could fill the gaps between the specific, or 'nominate' torts and which would eventually be used to fashion a general principle of liability. This was the 'action on the case', a variant of the writ of trespass which allowed a plaintiff who could not fit the facts within an existing cause of action to issue a special writ appropriate to the facts of his case.

Technical terms like 'trespass' and 'case' make the law of torts seem more complicated than it really is. The student can understand how the action on the case worked without revisiting Bracton but by using the facts of a well-known nineteenth-century case, *Wilkinson v. Downton* (1897). Quite untruthfully and for a joke, the defendant (D) told the plaintiff (P) that her husband had been smashed up in an accident and that she was to fetch him home in a cab. The effect of this not very funny prank was to make P seriously ill from nervous shock. If you think about it, you will see that these facts do not amount to a trespass to the person: there is neither force nor threat of any force. To complicate the matter, nervous shock is a form of borderline physical injury which the common law was slow to accommodate, perhaps because, until psychology taught us otherwise, nervous illness was seen as hysteria or even malingering. Yet although the judge could not point to a precedent for the case, he felt able to award the plaintiff £100 in damages for nervous shock (together which 'special damages' of 1s 10 1/2 d for the railway fares which had been incurred). Taken at one level, this is like an 'action on the special case'; the plaintiff cannot fit her facts into trespass but the court feels that they deserve a remedy. At a second level, this 'action on the case' now provides a precedent for the more general proposition that someone who wilfully does some act which is calculated to cause harm without lawful justification is liable if the act does in fact cause harm. (It is incidentally also the start of a line of cases which hold that nervous shock is a form of damage for which the law will, in a proper case, allow compensation.) This was how the action on the case allowed the old writ system to spawn new torts. At first where physical injury was caused by an action which was neither intentional nor forcible nor aimed directly at the plaintiff, he could not recover. Then he could recover on the facts of his 'special case'. Then the courts began to acknowledge that all plaintiffs in this situation could recover and their action was called 'the action on the case'. At this stage, the wrong choice was fatal; the plaintiff had to start again.

By the late eighteenth century the distinction between the writs of trespass and case was becoming blurred. The causes of action had served their purpose and needed to be laid to rest. Several events converged during the nineteenth century to bring 'case' to the forefront of tort law and to foster its development into the new modern tort of negligence, which became the major vehicle for accident cases where the damage is neither immediate (direct) nor deliberately caused. First, the rapid development of railways and the Industrial Revolution created accidents and the need for a system of accident compensation. Secondly, during the early nineteenth century the rusty machinery of the English legal system was at last overhauled. In two stages, the forms of action were finally done to death. The Common Law Procedure Act of 1852 provided that no 'form or cause of action' need be mentioned by the plaintiff in the writ by which his action was started. The Judicature Act of 1873 finally interred the medieval writ system by providing that pleadings should 'contain and contain only, a statement in summary form of the material facts on which the party pleading relies'. The modern system of civil procedure in which the plaintiff outlines the general nature of his case and the facts on which he will rely, was born. Thirdly, came the birth in the late nineteenth century of the new profession of academic law.

The new professors saw their vocation as being 'to set forth the law as a coherent whole— to analyse and define legal conceptions—to reduce the mass of legal rules to an orderly series of principles and to aid, stimulate and guide the reform or renovation of legal literature' (Dicey, 1883). They set out to classify the law, choosing to create a sharp division between contract and tort. The new tort textbooks exemplified their objectives. The authors searched in the mass of common law cases for principles which they could use to replace the scaffolding previously supplied by the forms of action. Suddenly the intellectual climate was right for the emergence of a tort law based firmly on fault. The nineteenth century stood firmly on the principle that nobody should be held liable to compensate if he was not at fault. It was, in the words of a celebrated American judge, 'only just to give a man a fair chance to avoid doing the harm before he is held responsible for it' (Holmes). In time, the movement led to what I have described . . . as 'the rise and rise of negligence'. Even today, however, the consolidation of tort law around the fault concept is not complete. Many authors prefer, like Salmond, to talk of a 'law of torts' rather than of 'tort law'.

It is pertinent to ask at this point why all this feverish intellectual activity was necessary. The easiest way to have put the bones back into the flesh of the common law would have been for Parliament in 1873 to have codified it. If we want to see what the English law might have looked like had it been codified at this date we might look to the French Civil Code of 1806, introduced at the behest of Napolean, more methodical and more autocratic than our English Parliaments. The whole of the French law of 'delict' (another generic word for wrong) is compressed into five articles of the Code which are extremely general in character and leave ample room for judicial handiwork. The two key articles, numbers 1382 and 1383, simply provide:

'Art 1382
"Every act which causes damage to another person obliges the person by whose fault the damage has been caused to provide reparation."

Art 1383
"A person is responsible for the damage which has been caused not only by his own acts, but also through his negligence or imprudence."'

In many ways it is surprising that English law escaped codification in the nineteenth century. The idea was certainly fashionable amongst the intellectuals. Jeremy Bentham believed that the law ought to be codified, partly to lessen the grip which the judges had over it. In 1877, Sir James Stephen actually drafted a Criminal Code but it was never enacted as law. We simply have to accept that a great opportunity was missed and that an entirely different relationship was to develop between Parliament and the judges."

Notes and questions

- Not everyone would agree with Harlow that codification of the common law necessarily is an improvement. Can you think of advantages and disadvantages of each system?

- Note that the early law professor quoted by Harlow is A.V. Dicey, who we encountered in Chapter 2! Law professors such as Dicey to a considerable extent are responsible for the way in which the categories of common law are disseminated across the generations of lawyers. Critics of the common law would say they have a great deal to answer for.

The development of a general law of negligence in English common law did not come about easily or quickly. There were particular obstacles faced by those who advocated such a view.

David Howarth, *Textbook on Tort* (Butterworths, London, 1995), pp. 26–27:

"Negligence originally meant in English law what it means in everyday speech, not a wrong in itself but a way of committing wrongs. Negligence is to be contrasted with maliciousness or wickedness as a state of mind that people who do harm to others may have. By the end of the nineteenth century, a study of negligence in the English law of torts would have been about the various torts that could be committed without malice (or, in more modern terms, intentionality) but by wrongful inattention, for example the actions 'on the case' arising from collisions on the street and at sea and from various accidents that result in personal injuries. Furthermore, 'negligence' would have been a sufficient condition of liability when certain legal relationships went wrong—that between an innkeeper and a customer, for example, or between a bailor and a bailee (that is, a person who deposits a thing with somebody else and that somebody else).

But there were various obstacles to the creation of a general principle along the lines of articles 1382 and 1383 [of the French Civil Code]. One was that in the accident cases, the action 'on the case' alleging negligence had a rival in the action 'for trespass'—that is for the direct application of unlawful force. Confusion reigned as the courts appeared to say that for road accidents the proper action in a collision case was 'trespass', but that, exceptionally, the plaintiff had to prove fault, whether intention or negligence, but in other accident cases where there was a 'direct' application of force, there could be a 'trespass' action in which it was up to the defendant to disprove fault.

A second obstacle to the creation of a general principle was the notorious 'privity fallacy'. Many nineteenth century judges were impressed by the idea of the 'bargain', the idea . . . that for economists the only sure ground for saying that people want something is that they are prepared to exchange something for it. This idea was expanded into the notion of 'privity of contract', according to which people who had not taken part in making a bargain had no legal right to sue if the bargain was not fulfilled. But it also expanded in another direction, namely that bargain and exchange should be the only basis of civil liability either in all novel cases or in all cases in which the plaintiff could have formed a bargain with the defendant but did not do so.

The effect of the privity doctrine was that, for example, the ultimate consumer of a product had no legal recourse against the manufacturer of a product if it caused injury. The victim would be told either that he or she should sue the retailer in contract, or, if the victim had received the product as a gift, that since there was no contractual link or bargain between the plaintiff and anyone, there was no legal liability at all. It also meant that the wife of a tenant could not sue if she was injured by the fault of the landlord. The husband had a contract with the landlord in the form of the lease, but the wife had not contracted and therefore had no rights at all."

The undermining of the privity of contract fallacy is closely related to the development of a general principle of liability for negligence at common law. The development of that principle can best be understood through an examination of a series of cases. Our story begins in the late nineteenth century.

Heaven v. Pender (1883) 11 QBD 503, CA.

Brett, M.R.:
"In this case the plaintiff was a workman in the employ of Gray, a ship painter. Gray entered into a contract with a shipowner whose ship was in the defendant's dock to paint the outside of his ship. The defendant, the dock owner, supplied, under a contract with the shipowner, an

ordinary stage to be slung in the ordinary way outside the ship for the purpose of painting her. It must have been known to the defendant's servants, if they had considered the matter at all, that the stage would be put to immediate use, that it would not be used by the shipowner, but that it would be used by such a person as the plaintiff, a working ship painter. The ropes by which the stage was slung, and which were supplied as a part of the instrument by the defendant, had been scorched and were unfit for use and were supplied without reasonably careful attention to their condition. When the plaintiff began to use the stage the ropes broke, the stage fell, and the plaintiff was injured. The Divisional Court held that the plaintiff could not recover against the defendant. The plaintiff appealed. The action is in form and substance an action for negligence. That the stage was, through want of attention of the defendant's servants, supplied in a state unsafe for use is not denied. But want of attention amounting to a want of ordinary care is not a good cause of action, although injury ensue from such want, unless the person charged with such want of ordinary care had a duty to the person complaining to use ordinary care in respect of the matter called in question. Actionable negligence consists in the neglect of the use of ordinary care or skill towards a person to whom the defendant owes the duty of observing ordinary care and skill, by which neglect the plaintiff, without contributory negligence on his part, has suffered injury to his person or property. The question in this case is whether the defendant owed such a duty to the plaintiff.

If a person contracts with another to use ordinary care or skill towards him or his property the obligation need not be considered in the light of a duty; it is an obligation of contract. It is undoubted, however, that there may be the obligation of such a duty from one person to another although there is no contract between them with regard to such duty. Two drivers meeting have no contract with each other, but under certain circumstances they have a reciprocal duty towards each other. So two ships navigating the sea. So a railway company which has contracted with one person to carry another has no contract with the person carried but has a duty towards that person. So the owner or occupier of house or land who permits a person or persons to come to his house or land has no contract with such person or persons, but has a duty towards him or them. It should be observed that the existence of a contract between two persons does not prevent the existence of the suggested duty between them also being raised by law independently of the contract, by the facts with regard to which the contract is made and to which it applies an exactly similar but a contract duty. We have not in this case to consider the circumstances in which an implied contract may arise to use ordinary care and skill to avoid danger to the safety of person or property. We have not in this case to consider the question of a fraudulent misrepresentation express or implied, which is a well recognised head of law. The questions which we have to solve in this case are — what is the proper definition of the relation between two persons other than the relation established by contract, or fraud, which imposes on the one of them a duty towards the other to observe, with regard to the person or property of such other, such ordinary care or skill as may be necessary to prevent injury to his person or property; and whether the present case falls within such definitions. When two drivers or two ships are approaching each other, such a relation arises between them when they are approaching each other in such a manner that, unless they use ordinary care and skill to avoid it, there will be a danger of an injurious collision between them. This relation is established in such circumstances between them, not only if it be proved that they actually know and think of this danger, but whether such proof be made or not. It is established, as it seems to me, because any one of ordinary sense who did think would at once recognise that if he did not use ordinary care and skill under such circumstances there would be such danger. And every one ought by the universally recognised rules of right and wrong, to think so much with regard to the safety of others who may be jeopardised by his conduct; and if, being in such circumstances, he does not think, and in consequence neglects, or if he neglects to use ordinary care or skill, and injury ensue, the law, which takes cognisance of and enforces the rules of right and wrong, will force him to give an indemnity for the injury. In the case of a railway company carrying a passenger with whom it has not entered into the contract of carriage the law implies the duty, because it must be obvious that unless ordinary care and skill be used the personal safety of the passenger must be endangered. With regard to the condition in which an owner or occupier leaves his house or property other phraseology has been used, which it is necessary to consider. If a man opens his shop or warehouse to customers it is said that he invites them to enter, and that this invitation raises the relation between them which imposes on the inviter the duty of using reasonable care so to keep his house or warehouse that it may not endanger the person or property of the person invited. This is in a sense an accurate phrase, and as applied to the circumstances a sufficiently accurate phrase. Yet it is not accurate if the word 'invitation' be used in its ordinary sense. By opening a shop you do not really invite, you do not ask A. B. to come in to buy; you intimate to him that if it pleases him to come in he will find things which you are willing to sell. So, in the case of shop, warehouse, road, or premises, the phrase has been used that if you permit a person to enter them you impose on yourself a duty not to lay a trap for him. This, again, is in a sense a true statement of the duty arising from the relation constituted by the permission to enter. It is not a statement of what causes the relation which raises the duty. What causes the relation is the permission to enter and the entry. But it is not a strictly accurate statement of the duty. To lay a trap means in ordinary language to do something with an invitation. Yet it is clear that the duty extends to a danger the result of negligence without intention. And with regard to both these phrases, though each covers the circumstances to which it is particularly applied, yet it does not cover the other set of circumstances from which an exactly similar legal liability is inferred. It follows, as it seems to me, that there must be some larger proposition which involves and covers both sets of circumstances. The logic of inductive reasoning requires that where two major propositions lead to exactly similar minor premisses there must be a more remote and larger premiss which embraces both of the major propositions. That, in the present consideration, is, as it seems to me, the same proposition which will cover the similar legal liability inferred in the cases of collision and carriage. The proposition which these recognised cases suggest, and which is, therefore, to be deduced from them, is that whenever one person is by circumstances placed in such a position with regard to another that every one of ordinary sense who did think would at once recognise that if he did not use ordinary care and skill in his own conduct with regard to those circumstances he would cause danger of injury to the person or property of the other, a duty arises to use ordinary care and skill to avoid such danger. Without displacing the other propositions to which allusion has been made as applicable to the particular circumstances in respect of which they have been enunciated, this proposition includes, I think, all the recognised cases of liability. It is the only proposition which covers them all. It may, therefore, safely be affirmed to be a true proposition, unless some obvious case can be stated in which the liability must be admitted to exist, and which yet is not within this proposition. There is no such case. Let us apply this proposition to the case of one person supplying goods or machinery, or instruments or utensils, or the like, for the purpose of their being used by another person, but with whom there is no contract as to the supply. The proposition will stand thus: whenever one person supplies goods, or machinery, or the like, for the purpose of their being used by another person under such circumstances that every one of ordinary sense would, if he thought, recognise at once that unless he used ordinary care and skill with regard to the condition of the thing supplied or the mode of supplying it, there will be danger of injury to the person or property of him for whose use the thing is supplied, and who is to use it, a duty arises to use ordinary care and skill as to the condition or manner of supplying such thing. And for a neglect of such ordinary care or skill whereby injury happens a legal liability arises to be enforced by an action for negligence. This includes the case of goods, &c., supplied to be used immediately by a particular person or persons or one of a class of persons, where it would be obvious to the person supplying, if he thought, that the goods would in all probability be used at once by such persons before a reasonable opportunity for discovering any defect which might exist, and where the thing supplied would be of such a nature that a neglect of ordinary care or skill as to its condition or the manner of supplying it would probably cause danger to the person or property of the person for whose use it was supplied, and who was about to use it. It would exclude a case in which the goods are supplied under circumstances in which it would be a chance by whom they would be used or whether they would be used or not, or whether they would be used before there would probably be means of observing any defect, or where the goods would be of such a nature that a want of care or skill as to their condition or the manner of supplying them would not probably produce danger of injury to person or property. The cases of vendor and purchaser and lender and hirer under contract need not be considered, as the liability arises under the contract, and nor merely as a duty imposed by law, though it may not be useless to observe that it seems difficult to import the implied obligation into the contract except in cases in which if there were no contract between the parties the law would according to the rule above stated imply the duty. . . .

I cannot conceive that if the facts were proved which would make out the proposition I have enunciated, the law can be that there would be no liability. Unless that be true, the proposition must be true. If it be the rule the present case is clearly within it. This case is also, I agree, within that which seems to me to be a minor proposition—namely, the proposition which has been often acted upon, that there was in a sense, an invitation of the plaintiff by the defendant, to use the stage. The appeal must, in my opinion, be allowed, and judgment must be entered for the plaintiff.

Cotton, L.J.:

Bowen, L.J., concurs in the judgment I am about to read. In this case the defendant was the owner of a dock for the repair of ships, and provided for use in the dock the stages necessary to enable the outside of the ship to be painted while in the dock, and the stages which were to be used only in the dock were appliances provided by the dock owner as appurtenant to the dock and its use. After the stage was handed over to the shipowner it no longer remained under the control of the dock owner. But when ships were received into the dock for repair and provided with stages for the work on the ships which was to be executed there, all those who came to the vessels for the purpose of painting and otherwise repairing them were there for business in which the dock owner was interested, and they, in my opinion, must be considered as invited by the dock owner to use the dock and all appliances provided by the dock owner as incident to the use of the dock. To these persons, in my opinion, the dock owner was under an obligation to take reasonable care that at the time the appliances provided for immediate use in the dock were provided by him they were in a fit state to be used—that is, in such a state as not to expose those who might use them for the repair of the ship to any danger or risk not necessarily incident to the service in which they are employed. . . . I think that the same duty must exist as to things supplied by the dock owner for immediate use in the dock, of which the control is not retained by the dockowner, to the extent of using reasonable care as to the state of the articles when delivered by him to the ship under repair for immediate use in relation to the repairs. For any neglect of those having control of the ship and the appliances he would not be liable, and to establish his liability it must be proved that the defect which caused the accident existed at the time when the article was supplied by the dockowner. . . .

This decides this appeal in favour of the plaintiff, and I am unwilling to concur with the Master of the Rolls in laying down unnecessarily the larger principle which he entertains, inasmuch as there are many cases in which the principle was impliedly negatived. . . .

In declining to concur in laying down the principle enunciated by the Master of the Rolls, I in no way intimate any doubt as to the principle that anyone who leaves a dangerous instrument, as a gun, in such a way as to cause danger, or who without due warning supplies to others for use an instrument or thing which to his knowledge, from its construction or otherwise, is in such a condition as to cause danger, not necessarily incident to the use of such an instrument or thing, is liable for injury caused to others by reason of his negligent act.

For the reasons stated I agree that the plaintiff is entitled to judgment, though I do not entirely concur with the reasoning of the Master of the Rolls."

NOTES AND QUESTIONS

- What are the material facts of *Heaven v. Pender*?

- How does the judgment of Brett M.R. differ from that of Cotton L.J.? What rule for determining liability is formulated by Brett M.R.? By contrast, on what basis does Cotton L.J. find the defendants liable? Which is the broader rule (that is, of wider application)?

- What is the *ratio decidendi* of *Heaven v. Pender*?

- The contrasting approaches in *Heaven v. Pender* underscore a tension at the heart of the historical development of the law of negligence. As Howarth has explained:

> "The English legal system has never quite decided whether it is a general principle system or a specific interest or circumstance system. In the nineteenth century, the English judges leant heavily towards the specific interest or circumstance view, although discontent with that approach produced a few notable counterblasts, most famously that of Brett M.R. in *Heaven v. Pender*. The view appeared to be that to allow legal liability to extend beyond the bounds of contract, that is beyond the bounds of what people had subjected themselves to voluntarily, would be to impose an intolerable burden of state interference upon them. In consequence, the presumption had to be against liability, a presumption displaced only by established rules of custom and practice."[1]

- The reluctance to develop a general duty-imposing principle outside of the realm of contract, apparent in the judgment of Cotton L.J., is also exemplified by the decision of the House of Lords a few years later in *Derry v. Peek* (1889) 14 App. Case 337, HL. In *Derry v. Peek*, the material facts were as follows. The promoters of a company were sued for a false statement written in a document designed to invite the public to purchase shares in a company. The statement, although false, was made honestly but the promoters may have been careless in determining whether it was true or not. If Brett M.R.'s test had been widely accepted and applied to these facts, might the promoters have been liable for damages? In fact, in *Derry v. Peek* the promoters were found not to be liable in damages. Lord Herschell explained:

> "I have arrived with some reluctance at the conclusion to which I have felt myself compelled, for I think those who put before the public a prospectus to induce them to embark their money in a commercial enterprise ought to be vigilant to see that it contains such representations only as are in strict accordance with fact, and I should be very unwilling to give any countenance to the contrary idea. I think there is much to be said for the view that this moral duty ought to some extent to be converted into a legal obligation, and that the want of reasonable care to see that statements, made under such circumstances, are true, should be made an actionable wrong. But this is not a matter fit for discussion on the present occasion. If it is to be done the legislature must intervene and expressly give a right of action in respect of such a departure from duty."[2]

This passage demonstrates a judicial mindset, which you will encounter frequently in your legal studies, whereby a judge refuses to take a course of action, but encourages

[1] David Howarth, *Textbook on Tort* (Butterworths, London, 1995), pp. 162–163.
[2] *Derry v. Peek* (1889) 14 App. Cas. 337 at 376, HL.

the legislature to embark on it instead. Why do you think Lord Herschell felt unable to create (or "find") a duty of care whereby the promoters of the company could be held responsible for their statements of encouragement to investors? In fact, the legislature did intervene with the Directors' Liability Act 1890.

In the years following *Heaven v. Pender*, Brett M.R. became Lord Esher. He figures prominently in another famous negligence case, *Le Lievre and Dennes v. Gould*.[3] The case concerned the liability of a surveyor to a mortgagee for statements made as to the progress of a building. There was no contractual relationship between the parties (a vitally important point in all of these cases). The Court of Appeal found no liability, and Lord Esher goes on at some length to interpret the earlier decision of the Court of Appeal in *Heaven v. Pender*. The passage usefully demonstrates the way in which the *ratio* of a common law case can only be determined definitively in light of the way in which courts subsequently interpret it.

Le Lievre and Dennes v. Gould [1893] 1 Q.B. 491, CA.

Lord Esher, M.R.:

". . . No doubt the defendant did give untrue certificates; it was negligent on his part to do so, and it may even be called gross negligence. But can the plaintiffs rely upon negligence in the absence of fraud? The question of liability for negligence cannot arise at all until it is established that the man who has been negligent owed some duty to the person who seeks to make him liable for his negligence. What duty is there when there is no relation between the parties by contract? A man is entitled to be as negligent as he pleases towards the whole world if he owes no duty to them. The case of *Heaven v. Pender* has no bearing upon the present question. That case established that, under certain circumstances, one man may owe a duty to another, even though there is no contract between them. If one man is near to another, or is near to the property of another, a duty lies upon him not to do that which may cause a personal injury to that other, or may injure his property. For instance, if a man is driving along a road, it is his duty not to do that which may injure another person whom he meets on the road, or to his horse or his carriage. In the same way it is the duty of a man not to do that which will injure the house of another to which he is near. If a man is driving on Salisbury Plain, and no other person is near him, he is at liberty to drive as fast and as recklessly as he pleases. But if he sees another carriage coming near to him, immediately a duty arises not to drive in such a way as is likely to cause an injury to that other carriage. So, too, if a man is driving along a street in a town, a similar duty not to drive carelessly arises out of contiguity or neighbourhood. That is the effect of the decision in *Heaven v. Pender*, but it has no application to the present case. . . . A charge of fraud is such a terrible thing to bring against a man that it cannot be maintained in any Court unless it is shewn that he had a wicked mind. That is the effect of *Derry v. Peek*. What is meant by a wicked mind? If a man tells a wilful falsehood, with the intention that it shall be acted upon by the person to whom he tells it, his mind is plainly wicked, and he must be said to be acting fraudulently. Again, a man must also be said to have a fraudulent mind if he recklessly makes a statement intending it to be acted upon, and not caring whether it be true or false. I do not hesitate to say that a man who thus acts must have a wicked mind. But negligence, however great, does not of itself constitute fraud. The official referee who tried this case and heard the evidence came to the conclusion that the defendant, though he had acted negligently, had not wilfully made any false statement, or been guilty of any fraud. All that he had done was to give untrue certificates negligently. Such negligence, in the absence of contract with the plaintiffs, can give no right of action at law or in equity. All the grounds urged on behalf of the plaintiffs fail, and the appeal must be dismissed."

---

[3] [1893] 1 Q.B. 491, CA.

NOTES AND QUESTIONS

- How does Lord Esher reformulate *Heaven v. Pender* in light of the judgment of the House of Lords in *Derry v. Peek*? How does Lord Esher distinguish the case of *Heaven v. Pender*? How would you frame the *ratio* of Lord Esher's judgment in *Le Lievre v. Gould*?

- The distinction between negligence and fraud is an important one. Fraud is a state of mind which is not easy to prove in court. Negligence, also a state of mind, implies carelessness (as opposed to "wickedness") and therefore is easier to establish.

- You may well have noticed an important feature of both *Derry v. Peek* and *Le Lievre v. Gould*. Unlike *Heaven v. Pender*, the facts of these cases do not involve plaintiffs who have been physically injured, nor has the property of the plaintiffs been physically damaged. As a consequence, we say that these plaintiffs have suffered "economic loss" rather than "physical damage". This is a vitally important distinction in the law of torts, one which you no doubt will spend a great deal of time grappling with in your tort law courses! For our purpose, the important point is that courts have been very reluctant to allow recovery for "pure" economic loss in its various forms, for a number of reasons. The cases of *Derry v. Peek* and *Le Lievre v. Gould* provide early examples of that unwillingness.

THE DEVELOPMENT OF A GENERAL DUTY OF CARE

The development of a general duty of care—which as noted above courts were reluctant to recognise—finally appeared to be accepted in what is widely viewed as the most famous and important negligence case in the common law world. It is a Scottish case and, as a consequence, some of the procedural terminology appears "foreign" to English lawyers. However, its importance in the development of a general duty of care in negligence transcends its Scottish roots.

M'Alister (or Donoghue) (Pauper) v. Stevenson [1932] A.C. 562, HL.

[By an action brought in the Court of Session the appellant, who was a shop assistant, sought to recover damages from the respondent, who was a manufacturer of aerated waters, for injuries she suffered as a result of consuming part of the contents of a bottle of ginger-beer which had been manufactured by the respondent, and which contained the decomposed remains of a snail. The appellant by her condescendence averred that the bottle of ginger-beer was purchased for the appellant by a friend in a café at Paisley, which was occupied by one Minchella; that the bottle was made of dark opaque glass and that the appellant had no reason to suspect that it contained anything but pure ginger-beer; that the said Minchella poured some of the ginger-beer out into a tumbler, and that the appellant drank some of the contents of the tumbler; that her friend was then proceeding to pour the remainder of the contents of the bottle into the tumbler when a snail, which was in a state of decomposition, floated out of the bottle; that as a result of the nauseating sight of the snail in such circumstances, and in consequence of the impurities in the ginger-beer which she had already consumed, the appellant suffered from shock and severe gastro-enteritis. The appellant further averred that the ginger-beer was manufactured by the respondent to be sold as a drink to the public (including the appellant); that it was bottled by the respondent and labelled by him with a label bearing his name; and that the bottles were thereafter sealed with a metal cap by the respondent. She further averred that it was the duty of the respondent to provide a system of working his business which would not allow snails to get into his ginger-beer bottles, and that it was also his duty to provide an efficient system of inspection of the bottles before the ginger-beer was filled into them, and that he had failed in both these duties and had so caused the accident.

The respondent objected that these averments were irrelevant and insufficient to support the conclusions of the summons.

The Lord Ordinary held that the averments disclosed a good cause of action and allowed a proof.

The Second Division by a majority (the Lord Justice-Clerk, Lord Ormidale, and Lord Anderson; Lord Hunter (dissenting) recalled the interlocutor of the Lord Ordinary and dismissed the action].

Lord Buckmaster (dissenting):
". . . In my view, therefore, the authorities are against the appellant's contention and apart from authority it is difficult to see how any common law proposition can be formulated to support her claim.

The principle contended for must be this—that the manufacturer, or, indeed, the repairer, of any article, apart entirely from contract, owes a duty to any person by whom the article is lawfully used to see that it has been carefully constructed. All rights in contract must be excluded from consideration of this principle, for such rights undoubtedly exist in successive steps from the original manufacturer down to the ultimate purchaser, embraced in the general rule that an article is warranted as reasonably fit for the purpose for which it is sold. Nor can the doctrine be confined to cases where inspection is difficult or impossible to introduce. This conception is simply to misapply to tort doctrines applicable to sale and purchase.

The principle of tort lies completely outside the region where such considerations apply, and the duty, if it exists, must extend to every person who, in lawful circumstances, uses the article made. There can be no special duty attaching to the manufacture of food, apart from those implied by contract or imposed by statute. If such a duty exists it seems to me it must cover the construction of every article, and I cannot see any reason why it should not apply to the construction of a house. If one step, why not 50? Yet if a house be, as it sometimes is, negligently built, and in consequence of that negligence the ceiling falls and injures the occupier or anyone else, no action against the builder exists according to English law, although I believe such a right did exist according to the laws of Babylon. Were such a principle known and recognised, it seems to me impossible, having regard to the numerous cases that must have arisen to persons injured by its disregard, that with the exception of *George v. Skivington*[4] no case directly involving the principle has ever succeeded in the courts, and were it well known and accepted much of the discussion of the earlier cases would have been waste of time. . . ."

Lord Atkin:
"My Lords, the sole question for determination in this case is legal: Do the averments made by the pursuer in her pleading, if true, disclose a cause of action? I need not restate the particular facts. The question is whether the manufacturer of an article of drink sold by him to a distributor, in circumstances which prevent the distributor or the ultimate purchaser or consumer from discovering by inspection any defect, is under any legal duty to the ultimate pur-

[4] (1869) L.R. 5 Exch. 1.

chaser or consumer to take reasonable care that the article is free from defect likely to cause injury to health. I do not think a more important problem has occupied your Lordships in your judicial capacity: important both because of its bearing on public health and because of the practical test which it applies to the system under which it arises. The case has to be determined in accordance with Scots law; but it has been a matter of agreement between the experienced counsel who argued this case, and it appears to be the basis of the judgments of the learned judges of the Court of Session, that for the purposes of determining this problem the laws of Scotland and of England are the same. I speak with little authority on this point, but my own research, such as it is, satisfies me that the principles of the law of Scotland on such a question as the present are identical with those of English law; and I discuss the issue on that footing. The law of both countries appears to be that in order to support an action for damages for negligence the complainant has to show that he has been injured by the breach of a duty owed to him in the circumstances by the defendant to take reasonable care to avoid such injury. In the present case we are not concerned with the breach of the duty; if a duty exists, that would be a question of fact which is sufficiently averred and for present purposes must be assumed. We are solely concerned with the question whether, as a matter of law in the circumstances alleged, the defender owed any duty to the pursuer to take care.

It is remarkable how difficult it is to find in the English authorities statements of general application defining the relations between parties that give rise to the duty. The Courts are concerned with the particular relations which come before them in actual litigation, and it is sufficient to say whether the duty exists in those circumstances. The result is that the Courts have been engaged upon an elaborate classification of duties as they exist in respect of property, whether real or personal, with further divisions as to ownership, occupation or control, and distinctions based on the particular relations of the one side or the other, whether manufacturer, salesman or landlord, customer, tenant, stranger, and so on. In this way it can be ascertained at any time whether the law recognizes a duty, but only where the case can be referred to some particular species which has been examined and classified. And yet the duty which is common to all the cases where liability is established must logically be based upon some element common to the cases where it is found to exist. To seek a complete logical definition of the general principle is probably to go beyond the function of the judge, for the more general the definition the more likely it is to omit essentials or to introduce non-essentials. The attempt was made by Brett M.R. in *Heaven v. Pender*, in a definition to which I will later refer. As framed, it was demonstrably too wide, although it appears to me, if properly limited, to be capable of affording a valuable practical guide.

At present I content myself with pointing out that in English law there must be, and is, some general conception of relations giving rise to a duty of care, of which the particular cases found in the books are but instances. The liability for negligence, whether you style it such or treat it as in other systems as a species of 'culpa,' is no doubt based upon a general public sentiment of moral wrongdoing for which the offender must pay. But acts or omissions which any moral code would censure cannot in a practical world be treated so as to give a right to every person injured by them to demand relief. In this way rules of law arise which limit the range of complainants and the extent of their remedy. The rule that you are to love your neighbour becomes in law, you must not injure your neighbour; and the lawyer's question, Who is my neighbour? Receives a restricted reply. You must take reasonable care to avoid acts or omissions which you can reasonably foresee would be likely to injure your neighbour. Who, then, in law is my neighbour? The answer seems to be—persons who are so closely and directly affected by my act that I ought reasonably to have them in contemplation as being so affected when I am directing my mind to the acts or omissions which are called in question. This appears to me to be the doctrine of *Heaven v. Pender*, as laid down by Lord Esher (then Brett M.R.) when it is limited by the notion of proximity introduced by Lord Esher himself and A.L. Smith L.J. in *Le Lievre v. Gould*. Lord Esher says: 'That case established that, under certain circumstances, one man may owe a duty to another, even though there is no contract between them. If one man is near to another, or is near to the property of another, a duty lies upon him not to do that which may cause a personal injury to that other, or may injure his property.' So A.L. Smith L.J.: 'The decision of *Heaven v. Pender* was founded upon the principle, that a duty to take due care did arise when the person or property of one was in such proximity to the person or property of another that, if due care was not taken, damage might be done by the one to the other.' I think that this sufficiently states the truth if proximity be not confined to mere physical proximity, but be used, as I think it was intended, to extend to such close and direct relations that the act complained of directly affects a person whom the person alleged to be bound to take care would know would be directly affected by his careless act. That this is the sense in which nearness or 'proximity' was intended by Lord Esher is obvious from his own illustration in *Heaven v. Pender* of the application of his doctrine to the sale of goods. 'This' (*i.e.* the rule he has just formulated) 'includes the case of goods, etc., supplied to be used immediately by a particular person or persons, or one of a class of persons, where it would be obvious to the person supplying, if he thought, that the goods would in all probability be used at once by such persons before a reasonable opportunity for discovering any defect which might exist, and where the thing supplied would be of such a nature that a neglect of ordinary care or skill as to its condition or the manner of supplying it would probably cause danger to the person or property of the person for whose use it was supplied, and who was about to use it. It would exclude a case in which the goods are supplied under circumstances in which it would be a chance by whom they would be used or whether they would be used or not, or whether they would be used before there would probably be means of observing any defect, or where the goods would be of such a nature that a want of care or skill as to their condition or the manner of supplying them would not probably produce danger of injury to person or property.' I draw particular attention to the fact that Lord Esher emphasizes the necessity of goods having to be 'used immediately' and 'used at once before a reasonable opportunity of inspection.' This is obviously to exclude the possibility of goods having their condition altered by lapse of time, and to call attention to the proximate relationship, which may be too remote where inspection even of the person using, certainly of an intermediate person, may reasonably be interposed. With this necessary qualification of proximate relationship as explained in *Le Lievre v. Gould*, I think the judgment of Lord Esher expresses the law of England; without the qualification, I think the majority of the Court in *Heaven v. Pender* were justified in thinking the principle was expressed in too general terms. There will no doubt arise cases where it will be difficult to determine whether the contemplated relationship is so close that the duty arises. But in the class of case now before the Court I cannot conceive any difficulty to arise. A manufacturer puts up an article of food in a container which he knows will be opened by the actual consumer. There can be no inspection by any purchaser and no reasonable preliminary inspection by the consumer. Negligently, in the course of preparation, he allows the contents to be mixed with poison. It is said that the law of England and Scotland is that the poisoned consumer has no remedy against the negligent manufacturer. If this were the result of the authorities, I should consider the result a grave defect in the law, and so contrary to principle that I should hesitate long before following any decision to that effect which had not the authority of this House. I would point out that, in the assumed state of the authorities, not only would the consumer have no remedy against the manufacturer, he would have none against any one else, for in the circumstances alleged there would be no evidence of negligence against any one other than the manufacturer; and, except in the case of a consumer who was also a purchaser, no contract and no warranty of fitness, and in the case of the purchase of a specific article under its patent or trade name, which might well be the case in the purchase of some articles of food or drink, no warranty protecting even the purchaser-consumer. There are other instances than of articles of food and drink where goods are sold intended to be used immediately by the consumer, such as many forms of goods sold for cleaning purposes, where the same liability must exist. The doctrine supported by the decision below would not only deny a remedy to the consumer who was injured by consuming bottled beer or chocolates poisoned by the negligence of the manufacturer, but also to the user of what should be a harmless proprietary medicine, an ointment, a soap, a cleaning fluid or cleaning powder. I confine myself to articles of common household use, where every one, including the manufacturer, knows that the articles will be used by other persons than the actual ultimate purchaser—namely, by members of his family and his servants, and in some cases his guests. I do not think so ill of our jurisprudence as to suppose that its principles are so remote from the ordinary needs of civilized society and the ordinary claims it makes upon its members as to deny a legal remedy where there is so obviously a social wrong. . . .

If your Lordships accept the view that the appellant's pleading discloses a relevant cause of action, you will be affirming the proposition that by Scots and English law alike a manufacturer of products which he sells in such a form as to show that he intends them to reach the ultimate consumer in the form in which they left him, with no reasonable possibility of intermediate examination, and with the knowledge that the absence of reasonable care in the preparation or putting up of the products will result in injury to the consumer's life or property, owes a duty to the consumer to take that reasonable care.

It is a proposition that I venture to say no one in Scotland or England who was not a lawyer would for one moment doubt. It will be an advantage to make it clear that the law in this matter, as in most others, is in accordance with sound common sense. I think that this appeal should be allowed."

Lord Thankerton:

". . . We are not dealing here with a case of what is called an article *per se* dangerous or one which was known by the defender to be dangerous, in which cases a special duty of protection or adequate warning is placed upon the person who uses or distributes it. The present case is that of a manufacturer and a consumer, with whom he has no contractual relation, of an article which the manufacturer did not know to be dangerous, and, unless the consumer can establish a special relationship with the manufacturer, it is clear, in my opinion, that neither the law of Scotland nor the law of England will hold that the manufacturer has any duty towards the consumer to exercise diligence. In such a case the remedy of the consumer, if any, will lie against the intervening party from whom he has procured the article. . . .

The special circumstances, from which the appellant claims that such a relationship of duty should be inferred, may, I think, be stated thus, namely, that the respondent, in placing his manufactured article of drink upon the market, has intentionally so excluded interference with, or examination of, the article by any intermediate handler of the goods between himself and the consumer that he has, of his own accord, brought himself into direct relationship with the consumer, with the result that the consumer is entitled to rely upon the exercise of diligence by the manufacturer to secure that the article shall not be harmful to the consumer. If that contention be sound, the consumer, on her showing that the article has reached her intact, and that she has been injured by the harmful nature of the article owing to the failure of the manufacturer to take reasonable care in its preparation before its enclosure in the sealed vessel, will be entitled to reparation from the manufacturer.

In my opinion, the existence of a legal duty in such circumstances is in conformity with the principles of both the law of Scotland and the law of England. The English cases demonstrate how impossible it is finally to catalogue, amid the ever-varying types of human relationships, those relationships in which a duty to exercise care arises apart from contract, and each of these cases relates to its own set of circumstances, out of which it was claimed that the duty had arisen. In none of these cases were the circumstances identical with the present case as regards that which I regard as the essential element in this case, namely, the manufacturer's own action in bringing himself into direct relationship with the party injured."

[Lord Thankerton would allow the appeal.]

Lord Macmillan:

". . . The law takes no cognizance of carelessness in the abstract. It concerns itself with carelessness only where there is a duty to take care and where failure in that duty has caused damage. In such circumstances carelessness assumes the legal quality of negligence and entails the consequences in law of negligence. What then are the circumstances which give rise to this duty to take care? In the daily contacts of social and business life human beings are thrown into or place themselves in an infinite variety of relationships with their fellows, and the law can refer only to the standards of the reasonable man in order to determine whether any particular relationship gives rise to a duty to take care as between those who stand in that relationship to each other. The grounds of action may be as various and manifold as human errancy, and the conception of legal responsibility may develop in adaptation to altering social conditions and standards. The criterion of judgment must adjust and adapt itself to the changing circumstances of life. The categories of negligence are never closed. The cardinal principle of liability is that the party complained of should owe to the party complaining a duty to take care and that the party complaining should be able to prove that he has suffered damage in consequence of a breach of that duty. Where there is room for diversity of view is in determining what circumstances will establish such a relationship between the parties as to give rise on the one side to a duty to take care and on the other side to a right to have care taken.

To descend from these generalities to the circumstances of the present case I do not think that any reasonable man or any twelve reasonable men would hesitate to hold that if the appellant establishes her allegations the respondent has exhibited carelessness in the conduct of his business. For a manufacturer of aerated water to store his empty bottles in a place where snails can get access to them and to fill his bottles without taking any adequate precautions by inspection or otherwise to ensure that they contain no deleterious foreign matter may reasonably be characterised as carelessness without applying too exacting a standard. But, as I have pointed out, it is not enough to prove the respondent to be careless in his process of manufacture. The question is: Does he owe a duty to take care, and to whom does he owe that duty? I have no hesitation in affirming that a person who for gain engages in the business of manufacturing articles of food and drink intended for consumption by members of the public in the form in which he issues them is under a duty to take care in the manufacture of these articles. That duty, in my opinion, he owes to those whom he intends to consume his products. He manufactures his commodities for human consumption; he intends and contemplates that they shall be consumed. By reason of that very fact he places himself in a relationship with all the potential consumers of his commodities, and that relationship, which he assumes and desires for his own ends, imposes upon him a duty to take care to avoid injuring them. He owes them a duty not to convert by his own carelessness an article which he issues to them as wholesome and innocent into an article which is dangerous to life and health.

It is sometimes said that liability can arise only where a reasonable man would have foreseen and could have avoided the consequences of his act or omission. In the present case the respondent, when he manufactured his ginger-beer, had directly in contemplation that it would be consumed by members of the public. Can it be said that he could not be expected as a reasonable man to foresee that if he conducted his process of manufacture carelessly he might injure those whom he expected and desired to consume his ginger-beer? The possibility of injury so arising seems to me in no sense so remote as to excuse him from foreseeing it. Suppose that a baker through carelessness allows a large quantity of arsenic to be mixed with a batch of his bread, with the result that those who subsequently eat it are poisoned, could he be heard to say that he owed no duty to the consumers of his bread to take care that it was free from poison, and that, as he did not know that any poison had got into it, his only liability was for breach of warranty under his contract of sale to those who actually bought the poisoned bread from him? Observe that I have said 'through carelessness' and thus excluded the cases of a pure accident such as may happen where every care is taken. I cannot believe, and I do not believe, that neither in the law of England nor in the law of Scotland is there redress for such a case. The state of facts I have figured might well give rise to a criminal charge, and the civil consequences of such carelessness can scarcely be less wide than its criminal consequences. Yet the principle of the decision appealed from is that the manufacturer of food products intended by him for human consumption does not owe to the consumers whom he has in view any duty of care, not even the duty to take care that he does not poison them.

. . . It must always be a question of circumstances whether the carelessness amounts to negligence and whether the injury is not too remote from the carelessness. I can readily conceive that where a manufacturer has parted with his product and it has passed into other hands it may well be exposed to vicissitudes which may render it defective or noxious and for which the manufacturer could not in any view be held to be to blame. It may be a good general rule to regard responsibility as ceasing when control ceases. So also where between the manufacturer and the user there is interposed a party who has the means and opportunity of examining the manufacturer's product before he reissues it to the actual user. But where, as in the present case, the article of consumption is so prepared as to be intended to reach the consumer in the condition in which it leaves the manufacturer and the manufacturer takes steps to ensure this by sealing or otherwise closing the container, so that the contents cannot be tampered with, I regard his control as remaining effective until the article reaches the consumer and the container is opened by him.

The intervention of any exterior agency is intended to be excluded, and was in fact in the present case excluded. It is doubtful whether in such a case there is any redress against the retailer."

[Lord Macmillan would allow the appeal.]

[Lord Tomlin (dissenting) delivered reasons for dismissing the appeal.]

NOTES AND QUESTIONS

- What are the material facts of *Donoghue v. Stevenson*? What is the legal issue?

- Note that the factual question—whether *in fact* there was a snail in the ginger beer—was never considered, as the case did not go to trial. The judgment deals with the prior question whether, even if the facts are true, there is any cause of action. Thus, the Law Lords, for the purposes of argument on this point, assumed the facts as alleged by the plaintiff to be true. Had the case then gone to trial, those factual allegations would have had to be proven.

- The majority consisted of three Law Lords. How would you state the *ratio decidendi* of the case? Are there a variety of ways in which it can be stated? List a series of different possible *ratios*, in order of their breadth of scope. Do Lords Atkin, Macmillan and Thankerton seem to be in agreement as to what their ruling in this case stands for?

- Does Lord Atkin's formulation of the duty of care in negligence differ from Lord Esher's formulation in *Le Lievre v. Gould*? If so, how?

- The judgments in *Donoghue v. Stevenson* again exemplify the point made earlier in this chapter: that the history of negligence in this country is a story of tension between the imposition of a general duty of care, and a number of discrete duties applicable to different situations. Try to find specific references to this tension in the various judgments in *Donoghue v. Stevenson*.

- For further reading on the history of negligence law, see P.H. Winfield, "The History of Negligence in the Law of Torts" (1926) 42 L.Q.R. 184; and, for a critical analysis of the impact of *Donoghue v. Stevenson*, see J.C. Smith and P. Burns, "Donoghue v. Stevenson—The Not so Golden Anniversary" (1983) 46 M.L.R. 147.

Although you were asked to state the *ratio decidendi* of *Donoghue v. Stevenson*, you should not be concerned if you found no easy answer to the question! In fact, it was pointed out by Heuston, on the twenty-fifth anniversary of the decision, that the determination of the *ratio* of *Donoghue v. Stevenson* is a far from straightforward task.

R.F.V. Heuston, "*Donoghue v. Stevenson* in Retrospect" (1957) 20 M.L.R. 1 at 5:

The ratio decidendi *of the case*

"The ascertainment of the *ratio decidendi* of any decision given by an appellate court in the course of which several judgments have been delivered is notoriously a difficult task. One problem may be disposed of at once. It was agreed between counsel and stated by the judges in all the courts that the relevant principles of Scots and English law were identical. Now it has always been assumed that in such a case a decision of the House of Lords on an appeal from the Court of Session is binding on all courts in the English hierarchy. Those who adhere to a mechanical test for distinguishing *ratio decidendi* from *obiter dictum* would no doubt be obliged to deny this, for in a Scots appeal the only issue in the case is Scots law, and any statement as to the meaning or effect of English law must necessarily be *obiter*. It seems safer to say that the principles stated in *Donoghue v. Stevenson* have been universally recognised to be authoritative in England as well as in Scotland, and to turn to the more difficult task of discovering what those principles are. Lord Wright has appropriately referred to the decision to illustrate the proposition that 'Notwithstanding all the apparatus of authority, the judge has nearly always some degree of choice. . . . The higher the court, the less is the decisive weight of authority and the freer the choice.' On the assumption that it is possible to draw from a given decision as many general propositions as there are possible combinations of distinguishable facts, Professor Stone has observed that the decision could be restricted to mean that there is a duty not to sell opaque bottles of beverage containing dead snails to Scots widows, or expanded to mean that there is a duty not to distribute defective objects of any kind whatsoever which cause damage of any kind to any person into whose hands the object may come.

Now as between the parties themselves there can be no doubt that the case decided that if the pursuer could prove that which she averred she would have a good cause of action. So the case decided at least something to do with the duty owed by a supplier of chattels. There are some authorities who would deny that the case decided any more. This appears to have been the view taken by the experienced reporter who framed the 'somewhat conservatively worded headnote,' and in several later cases we find clear statements that the *ratio decidendi* is so confined. Nevertheless there has been a persistent belief that the case is authority for something more. Lord Normand has put this most clearly. 'The argument for the defender was that there were certain relationships, such as physical proximity or contract, which alone give rise to duties in the law of quasi-delict or tort, and that the relationship between the pursuer and defender was not one of them.' The decision was that the categories of negligence are not closed and that duties of care are owed, not only to physical neighbours, but to anyone who is 'my neighbour' in the wider sense, as stated by Lord Atkin, 'of a person . . . "so closely and directly affected by my act that I ought reasonably to have (him) in contemplation as being so affected when I am directing my mind to the acts or omissions which are called in question."' This is the neighbour principle so familiar to us all. Our inquiry at the moment is limited to discovering how far this principle can fairly be said to form a, or part of the, *ratio decidendi* of the judgment of (i) Lord Atkin himself, (ii) the majority of the House of Lords.

(i) A fair reading of the whole judgment in its context, not concentrating on this or that passage to the exclusion of others, makes it plain that Lord Atkin intended to show (a) that the liability of a supplier of chattels is not limited to cases in which the parties are in physical proximity to each other: a duty of care may exist even in the absence of spatial or temporal 'proximity' if there is a probability of harm inherent in the relationship of the parties, and the facts of the case before him provided a model for such a relationship; (b) that 'there must be, and is, some general conception of relations giving rise to a duty of care, of which the particular cases found in the books are but instances.' He then states the 'neighbour principle' in the term which we have already cited, and concludes that this 'appears to me to be the doctrine of *Heaven v. Pender* as laid down by Lord Esher when it is limited by the notion of proximity introduced by Lord Esher himself and A.L. Smith L.J. in *Le Lievre v. Gould.*' It is impracticable to draw a clear line anywhere between the two parts of the judgment. The reasoning is everywhere dovetailed and interlocked. The neighbour principle is part of the *ratio decidendi* of Lord Atkin's judgment, for it is a step in the argument, a vital link in the chain of reasoning which led to the formulation of the principle about manufacturers' liability. The significance to be attached to the neighbour principle will be discussed in detail later: it is enough to say here that it has been accepted by many as showing that *Donoghue v. Stevenson* provides a general criterion of liability—at least in the tort of negligence, and possibly throughout the whole field of tort. So that when Dean Wright tells us that 'Whether that decision will be expanded into a broad revolutionary principle or confined to a narrow category is one of the most important decisions that modern courts must make' it seems clear that he is not referring only to the part of the decision which deals with manufacturers' liability. Even those who, like Mr Landon, say that 'all that *Donoghue v. Stevenson* has done is to add a new category of negligence to our law' have been obliged to meet the argument that at least one law lord attempted to state the principle upon which such an addition had been made.

(ii) Whatever the status of the 'neighbour principle' in Lord Atkin's own judgment, it hardly seems possible to say that it forms part of the *ratio decidendi* of the decision, for the two other members of the majority seem to have been careful to avoid expressing their concurrence with it. Lord Thankerton said that he agreed with Lord Atkin's speech, but it is the proper inference from the context of this remark that his agreement was confined to that part of the speech which analyses the English cases on manufacturers' liability. In any case, he expressly said that it was impossible to catalogue finally the circumstances in which a duty of care might arise. Lord Macmillan recognised that new duties might be created—'the categories of negligence are never closed'—but maintained a cautious silence about the principle or principles upon which this might be done.

Two further points may be made. First, it is preferable to refer to this particular part of the judgment as enshrining a 'principle' and not a 'rule.' The former word connotes a degree of flexibility and adaptability which the latter does not. 'A principle is the broad reason which lies at the base of a rule of law: it has not exhausted itself in giving birth to that particular rule but is still fertile.' If, as is generally believed, Lord Atkin's judgment forms a guide for the future as well as an appraisal of the past, it is best to describe it in a way which will enable us to use its potentialities to the utmost. Secondly, there seems to be little profit in an attempt to discover the sources of the ideas expounded in the neighbour principle. Lord Atkin himself expressly refers to Lord Esher and indirectly to the lawyer's question to Jesus which inspired the story of the Good Samaritan. . . .

The conclusion is that there are four propositions for which the case commonly is (or can be) cited as authority: (1) that negligence is a distinct tort; (2) that the absence of privity of contract between plaintiff and defendant does not preclude liability in tort; (3) that manufacturers of products owe a duty of care to the ultimate consumer or user; and (4) that the criterion of the existence of a duty in the law of negligence (or perhaps in any part of the law of tort) is whether the defendant ought reasonably to have foreseen that his acts or omissions would be likely to result in damage to the plaintiff. Of these, only the second and third, and possibly the first, can truly be said to form part of the *ratio decidendi* of the decision. The fourth proposition, although perhaps the most commonly cited and in many ways the most significant, cannot properly be regarded a part of the *ratio decidendi* of the decision. No amount of posthumous citation can of itself transfer with retrospective effect a proposition from the status of *obiter dictum* to that of *ratio decidendi*; no doubt it will serve to magnify greatly the interest and importance of the case, but that is another matter."

Given the variety of propositions for which the case of *Donoghue v. Stevenson* might stand, it should seem increasingly clear to you that the *ratio* of a case is a fairly flexible concept. In fact, it could be argued that we can only approach a definitive *ratio* in light of how a case is interpreted by courts. The idea that there is necessarily a single, clear, and uncontentious *ratio* to any given case thus becomes unsustainable, as MacCormick illustrates using the example of *Donoghue v. Stevenson*.

Neil MacCormick, *Legal Reasoning and Legal Theory* (Clarendon Press, Oxford, 1978), pp. 84–86:

"[T]here is a possibility that some precedents contain relatively clear rulings on fairly sharply defined points of law, and that others contain implicit rulings of similar, but perhaps less, relative clarity. Yet others because of judicial disagreement or simply confusion contain none. It is only a dogmatic fiction that the third class has anything which could reasonably be called a *ratio* at all, and the truth is that in relation to that type of case even the most rigid doctrine of binding precedent cannot in practice obligate the judge in a later case to do more than find some 'explanatory' proposition which is consistent with the actual decision of the precedent case and also relevant to the instant case; all the better if his 'explanatory' proposition squares in some degree with some at least of what was said in the confused or conflicting opinion or opinions given in the precedent.

It should be remarked also that even where an express ruling is given encapsulating the kind of 'proposition' wherewith Lord Atkin concluded his speech in *Donoghue*, the doctrine of precedent even in its English form leaves the subsequent court with a significant 'explanative' discretion: it is at best the proposition, not the particular words in which it was couched, that is binding. Therefore the later Court is free to re-express the proposition, together with further conditions or qualifications which may be deemed appropriate to novel types of circumstance as revealed by the later case. That the norms of the system leave its operators with that discretion gives interpreters of the system a problem which has sometimes been mistakenly supposed to be more than a problem of words: in *Donoghue v. Stevenson* a certain 'proposition' was laid down about the manufacturer's duty to consumers of his products; in *Haseldine v. Daw* ([1941] 2 KB 343; [1941] 3 All ER 156) for example, the negligent repair of a defective lift was brought within the doctrine and the repairers held liable to those injured in its collapse (observe that the dissents of Lords Tomlin and Buckmaster had dealt with the case of repairers, though none of the affirming majority did); is the 'ratio' of *Donoghue v. Stevenson* the explicit ruling as given by the judges in *Donoghue* itself, or that ruling as re-expressed and extended in *Haseldine*?

The only observation I wish to make is that answering that question does not add to our knowledge of the real world at all. All that it does is to stipulate a particular usage for the technical term *ratio*, which is in fact somewhat ambiguous in its ordinary use, precisely because it is variably used in practice. Sometimes it is used as referring to the proposition as actually laid down in the original decision of a case, sometimes to that proposition as explained reinterpreted qualified or whatever in later cases.

There is not the least probability of any stipulation by me determining usage, so I offer none; I only observe that among judges and practitioners the predominant operational usage of the term *ratio* seems to be as referring to express statements of propositions of law made by judges in their justifying opinion in recorded cases, and (if my opinion matters) that seems to be the least confusing usage available for the term."

MacCormick makes the important point that often the *ratio* of a case can only be determined in light of what judges subsequently make of it. That is particularly apt in the case of *Donoghue v. Stevenson*. The central question of whether the majority of the Lords sought to establish a general duty of care in negligence only can be answered by examining how other courts then applied their reasoning. Four years after *Donoghue v. Stevenson*, an indication of its scope—as applying more broadly than, for example, common household goods or food and beverage—was apparent in a judgment of the Judicial Committee of the Privy Council.

Grant v. Australian Knitting Mills, Ltd [1936] A.C. 85, PC.

Lord Wright:
"The appellant is a fully qualified medical man practising at Adelaide in South Australia. He brought his action against the respondents, claiming damages on the ground that he had contracted dermatitis by reason of the improper condition of underwear purchased by him from the respondents, John Martin & Co., Ld, and manufactured by the respondents, the Australian Knitting Mills, Ld. The case was tried by Sir George Murray, Chief Justice of South Australia, who, after a trial lasting for twenty days, gave judgment for the appellant against

both respondents for 245*l* and costs. On appeal the High Court of Australia set aside that judgment by a majority. Evatt J. dissented, and agreed in the result with the Chief Justice though he differed in regard to the Sale of Goods Act, 1895. Of the majority, the reasoning of Dixon J., with whom McTiernan J. concurred, was in effect that the evidence was not sufficient to make it safe to find for the appellant. Starke J., who accepted substantially all the detailed findings of the Chief Justice, differed from him on his general conclusions of liability based on these findings.

The appellant's claim was that the disease was caused by the presence, in the cuffs or ankle ends of the underpants which he purchased and wore, of an irritating chemical, namely, free sulphite, the presence of which was due to negligence in manufacture, and also involved on the part of the respondents, John Martin & Co., Ld, a breach of the relevant implied conditions under the Sale of Goods Act.

The underwear, consisting of two pairs of underpants and two singlets, was bought by the appellant at the shop of the respondents, John Martin & Co., Ld, who dealt in such goods, and who will be hereafter referred to as 'the retailers,' on June 3, 1931. The retailers had in ordinary course at some previous date purchased them with other stock from the respondents, the Australian Kntting Mills, Ld, who will be referred to as the manufacturers; the garments were of that class of the manufacturers' make known as Golden Fleece. The appellant put on one suit on the morning of Sunday, June 28, 1931; by the evening of that day he felt itching on the ankles but no objective symptoms appeared until the next day, when a redness appeared on each ankle in front of an area of about two and a half inches by one and a half inches. The appellant treated himself with calomine lotion, but the irritation was such that he scratched the places till he bled. On Sunday, July 5, he changed his underwear and put on the other set which he had purchased from the retailers; the first set was washed and when the appellant changed his garments again on the following Sunday he put on the washed set and sent the others to the wash; he changed again on July 12. Though his skin trouble was getting worse, he did not attribute it to the underwear, but on July 13 he consulted a dermatologist, Dr Upton, who advised him to discard the underwear, which he did, returning the garments to the retailers with the intimation that they had given him dermatitis; by that time one set had been washed twice and the other set once. The appellant's condition got worse and worse; he was confined to bed from July 21 for seventeen weeks; the rash became generalized and very acute. In November he became convalescent and went to New Zealand to recuperate. He returned in the following February, and felt sufficiently recovered to resume his practice, but soon had a relapse, and by March his condition was so serious that he went in April into hospital, where he remained until July. Meantime, in April, 1932, he commenced this action, which was tried in and after November of that year. Dr Upton was his medical attendant throughout and explained in detail at the trial the course of the illness and the treatment he adopted. Dr de Crespigny also attended the appellant from and after July 22, 1931, and gave evidence at the trial. The illness was most severe, involving acute suffering, and at times Dr Upton feared that his patient might die.

It is impossible here to examine in detail the minute and conflicting evidence of fact and of expert opinion given at the trial: all that evidence was meticulously discussed at the hearing of the appeal before the Board. It is only possible to state briefly the conclusions at which the Lordships, after careful consideration, have arrived. [Lord Wright reviewed the evidence and concluded that the Chief Justice's findings of fact at trial should be upheld]. . . .

That conclusion means that the disease contracted, and the damage suffered by the appellant, were caused by the defective condition of the garments which the retailers sold to him, and which the manufacturers made and put forth for retail and indiscriminate sale. The Chief Justice gave judgments against both respondents, against the retailers on the contract of sale, and against the manufacturers in tort, on the basis of the decision in the House of Lords in *Donoghue v. Stevenson*. The liability of each respondent depends on a different cause of action, though it is for the same damage. It is not claimed that the appellant should recover his damage twice over; no objection is raised on the part of the respondents to the form of the judgment, which was against both respondents for a single amount.

So far as concerns the retailers, Mr Greene conceded that if it were held that the garments contained improper chemicals and caused the disease, the retailers were liable for breach of implied warranty, or rather condition, under s 14 of the South Australia Sale of Goods Act, 1895, which is identical with s 14 of the English Sale of Goods Act, 1893. . . .

The retailers, accordingly, in their Lordships' judgment are liable in contract: so far as they are concerned, no question of negligence is relevant to the liability in contract. But when the position of the manufacturers is considered, different questions arise: there is no privity of contract between the appellant and the manufacturers: between them the liability, if any, must be in tort, and the gist of the cause of action is negligence. The facts set out in the foregoing show, in their Lordships' judgment, negligence in manufacture. According to the evidence, the method of manufacture was correct: the danger of excess sulphites being left was recognized and was guarded against: the process was intended to be fool proof. If excess sulphites were left in the garment, that could only be because some one was at fault. The appellant is not required to lay his finger on the exact person in all the chain who was responsible, or to specify what he did wrong. Negligence is found as a matter of inference from the existence of the defects taken in connection with all the known circumstances: even if the manufacturers could by apt evidence have rebutted that inference they have not done so [Lord Wright went on to consider the relevance of *Donoghue v. Stevenson*]. . . .

It is clear that the decision treats negligence, where there is a duty to take care, as a specific tort in itself, and not simply as an element in some more complex relationship or in some specialized breach of duty, and still less as having any dependence on contract. All that is necessary as a step to establish the tort of actionable negligence is to define the precise relationship from which the duty to take care is to be deduced. It is, however, essential in English law that the duty should be established: the mere fact that a man is injured by another's act gives in itself no cause of action: if the act is deliberate, the party injured will have no claim in law even though the injury is intentional, so long as the other party is merely exercising a legal right: if the act involves lack of due care, again no case of actionable negligence will arise unless the duty to be careful exists. In *Donoghue's* case the duty was deduced simply from the facts relied on—namely, that the injured party was one of a class for whose use, in the contemplation and intention of the makers, the article was issued to the world, and the article was used by that party in the state in which it was prepared and issued without it being changed in any way and without there being any warning of, or means of detecting, the hidden danger: there was, it is true, no personal intercourse between the maker and the user; but though the duty is personal, because it is *inter partes,* it needs no interchange of words, spoken or written, or signs of offer or assent; it is thus different in character from any contractual relationship; no question of consideration between the parties is relevant: for these reasons the use of the word 'privity' in this connection is apt to mislead, because of the suggestion of some overt relationship like that in contract, and the word 'proximity' is open to the same objection; if the term 'proximity' is to be applied at all, it can only be in the sense that the want of care and the injury are in essence directly and intimately connected; though there may be intervening transactions of sale and purchase, and intervening handling between these two events, the events are themselves unaffected by what happened between them: 'proximity' can only properly be used to exclude any element of remoteness, or of some interfering complication between the want of care and the injury, and like 'privity' may mislead by introducing alien ideas. Equally also may the word 'control' embarass, though it is conveniently used in the opinions in *Donoghue's* case to emphasize the essential factor that the consumer must use the article exactly as it left the maker, that is in all material features, and use it as it was intended to be used. In that sense the maker may be said to control the thing until it is used. But that again is an artificial use, because, in the natural sense of the word, the makers parted with all control when they sold the article and divested themselves of possession and property. An argument used in the present case based on the word 'control' will be noticed later.

It is obvious that the principles thus laid down involve a duty based on the simple facts detailed above, a duty quite unaffected by any contracts dealing with the thing, for instance, of sale by maker to retailer, and again by retailer to consumer or to the consumer's friend.

It may be said that the duty is difficult to define, because when the act of negligence in manufacture occurs there was no specific person towards whom the duty could be said to exist: the thing might never be used: it might be destroyed by accident, or it might be scrapped, or in many ways fails to come into use in the normal way: in other words the duty cannot at the time of manufacture be other than potential or contingent, and only can become vested by the fact of actual use by a particular person. But the same theoretical difficulty has been disregarded in cases like *Heaven v. Pender*, or in the case of things dangerous *per se* or known to be dangerous . . . . In *Donoghue's* case the thing was dangerous in fact, though the danger was hidden, and the thing was dangerous only because of want of care in making it; as Lord Atkin points out in *Donoghue's* case, the distinction between things inherently dangerous and things only dangerous because of negligent manufacture cannot be regarded as significant for the purpose of the questions here involved.

One further point may be noted. The principle of *Donoghue's* case can only be applied where the defect is hidden and unknown to the consumer, otherwise the directness of cause and effect is absent: the man who consumes or uses a thing which he knows to be noxious cannot complain in respect of whatever mischief follows, because it follows from his own conscious volition in choosing to incur the risk or certainty of mischance.

If the foregoing are the essential features of *Donoghue's* case, they are also to be found, in their Lordships' judgment, in the present case. The presence of the deleterious chemical in the pants, due to negligence in manufacture, was a hidden and latent defect, just as much as were the remains of the snail in the opaque bottle: it could not be detected by any examination that could reasonably be made. Nothing happened between the making of the garments and their being worn to change their condition. The garments were made by the manufacturers for the purpose of being worn exactly as they were worn in fact by the appellant: it was not contemplated that they should be first washed. It is immaterial that the appellant had a claim in contract against the retailers, because that is a quite independent cause of action, based on different considerations, even though the damage may be the same. Equally irrelevant is any question of liability between the retailers and the manufacturers on the contract of sale between them. The tort liability is independent of any question of contract.

It was argued, but not perhaps very strongly, that *Donoghue's* case was a case of food or drink to be consumed internally, whereas the pants here were to be worn externally. No distinction, however, can be logically drawn for this purpose between a noxious thing taken internally and a noxious thing applied externally: the garments were made to be worn next the skin: indeed Lord Atkin specifically puts as examples of what is covered by the principle he is enunciating things operating externally, such as 'an ointment, a soap, a cleaning fluid or cleaning powder.'

Mr Greene, however, sought to distinguish *Donoghue's* case from the present on the ground that in the former the makers of the ginger-beer had retained 'control' over it in the sense that they had placed it in stoppered and sealed bottles, so that it would not be tampered with until it was opened to be drunk, whereas the garments in question were merely put into paper packets, each containing six sets, which in ordinary course would be taken down by the shopkeeper and opened, and the contents handled and disposed of separately, so that they would be exposed to the air. He contended that though there was no reason to think that the garments when sold to the appellant were in any other condition, least of all as regards sulphur contents, than when sold to the retailers by the manufacturers, still the mere possibility and not the fact of their condition having been changed was sufficient to distinguish *Donoghue's* case: there was no 'control' because nothing was done by the manufacturers to exclude the possibility of any tampering while the goods were on their way to the user. Their Lordships do not accept that contention. The decision in *Donoghue's* case did not depend on the bottle being stoppered and sealed: the essential point in this regard was that the article should reach the consumer or user subject to the same defect as it had when it left the manufacturer. That this was true of the garment is in their Lordships' opinion beyond question. At most there might in other cases be a greater difficulty of proof of the fact.

Mr Greene further contended on behalf of the manufacturers that if the decision in *Donoghue's* case were extended even a hair's-breadth, no line could be drawn, and a manufacturer's liability would be extended indefinitely. He put as an illustration the case of a foundry which had cast a rudder to be fitted on a liner: he assumed that it was fitted and the steamer sailed the seas for some years: but the rudder had a latent defect due to faulty and negligent casting, and one day it broke, with the result that the vessel was wrecked, with great loss of life and damage to property. He argued that if *Donoghue's* case were extended beyond its precise facts, the maker of the rudder would be held liable for damages of an indefinite amount, after an indefinite time, and to claimants indeterminate until the event. But it is clear that such a state of things would involve many considerations far removed from the simple facts of this case. So many contingencies must have intervened between the lack of care on the part of the makers and the casualty that it may be that the law would apply, as it does in proper cases, not always according to strict logic, the rule that cause and effect must not be too remote: in any case the element of directness would obviously be lacking. . . .

In their Lordships' opinion it is enough for them to decide this case on its actual facts. No doubt many difficult problems will arise before the precise limits of the principle are defined: many qualifying conditions and many complications of fact may in the future come before the Courts for decision. It is enough now to say that their Lordships hold the present case to come within the principle of *Donoghue's* case, and they think that the judgment of the Chief Justice was right in the result and should be restored as against both respondents, and that the appeal should be allowed, with costs here and in the Courts below, and that the appellant's petition for leave to adduce further evidence should be dismissed, without costs."

Notes and questions

- The case of *Grant v. Australian Knitting Mills* usefully illustrates how the breadth of *Donoghue v. Stevenson* was a live issue at that time. In what ways (sometimes imaginatively) did counsel for Australian Knitting Mills try to convince the Law Lords that the *ratio decidendi* should be read narrowly, so that the facts of *Grant* could be distinguished from *Donoghue v. Stevenson*? What responses to those arguments were made by Lord Wright? Note in particular the "floodgates argument" made by counsel (that is, if this case is decided in favour of the appellant, the floodgate of claims will be opened). How did Lord Wright respond?

- To what extent does it appear, on reading *Grant v. Australian Knitting Mills*, that a general principle of liability was emerging within English law?

- The tension between a general principle of liability and specific duties giving rise to liability continued. For example, in *Deyong v. Shenburn* [1946] 1 K.B. 227, CA, a case which concerned stolen garments and a pantomime dame, Du Parcq, L.J. held:

> "There are well-known words of Lord Atkin in *Donoghue v. Stevenson* as to the duty towards one's neighbour. It has been pointed out (and this only shows the difficulty of stating a general proposition which is not too wide) that unless one somewhat narrows the term of the proposition as it has been stated, one would be including in it something which the law does not support. It is not true to say that wherever a man finds himself in such a position that unless he does a certain act another person may suffer, or that if he does something another person will suffer, then it is his duty in the one case to be careful to do the act and in the other case to be careful not to do the act. Any such proposition is much too wide. There has to be a breach of a duty which the law recognizes, and to ascertain what the law recognizes regard must be had to the decisions of the courts. There has never been a decision that a master must, merely because of the relationship which exists between master and servant, take reasonable care for the safety of his servant's belongings in the sense that he must take steps to ensure,

so far as he can, that no wicked person shall have an opportunity of stealing the servant's goods. That is the duty contended for here, and there is not a shred of authority to suggest that any such duty exists or ever has existed (p. 233)."

You will recall that in the cases of *Derry v. Peek* and *Le Lievre v. Gould*, the Courts were not prepared to find a duty of care in the case of economic loss, as opposed to physical damage to person and property. In the wake of *Donoghue v. Stevenson*, the question remained of interest: does *Donoghue v. Stevenson* apply only to physical injury to person or property, or does its logic extend to economic loss? After all, economic loss is a form of injury to property: it is an injury to the plaintiff's wallet! This issue became tied up with the distinction between negligent words and negligent acts, and whether one could be held liable for negligent words. That distinction, as you will discover in your tort law course, is a rather confused one, and has not been a particularly helpful way in which to analyse these issues. In any event, the extent to which *Donoghue v. Stevenson* could be read as establishing a general principle applicable to economic loss—which would allow courts to revisit the issue raised in cases such as *Derry v. Peek* and *Le Lievre v. Gould*—came before the Court of Appeal.

Candler v. Crane, Christmas & Co. [1951] 2 K.B. 164, CA.

[The plaintiff was considering the possibility of his investing 2,000*l* in a limited liability company, but, before deciding to do so, desired to see the accounts of the company. The managing director of the company accordingly instructed the defendants, the accountants of the company, who were getting out the accounts, to press on and complete them, informing a clerk of the accountants, who had been requested by them to prepare the accounts, that they were required to be shown to the plaintiff who to his knowledge was a potential investor in the company. The clerk accordingly prepared the accounts and at the request of the managing director showed them to and discussed them with the plaintiff who took a copy of them and submitted them to his own accountant for advice. As a result the plaintiff invested his money in the company. The accounts were carelessly prepared, contained numerous false statements and gave a wholly misleading picture of the state of the company, which was wound up within a year, the plaintiff losing the whole of his investment. In an action brought by the plaintiff against the defendants, Lloyd-Jacob, J., found that the clerk was not guilty of fraud, but had been "extremely careless in the preparation of the accounts", and that the resulting damage to the plaintiff was plain. He held that the clerk had acted within the course of his employment, but dismissed the action on the ground that the defendants owed no duty of care to the plaintiff. The plaintiff appealed.]

Denning L.J. [who was asked to read his judgment first]:
". . . This case raises a point of law of much importance; because Mr Lawson on behalf of the plaintiff submitted that, although there was no contract between the plaintiff and the accountants, nevertheless the relationship between them was so close and direct that the accountants did owe a duty of care to him within the principles stated in *Donoghue v. Stevenson*; whereas Mr Foster on behalf of the accountants submitted that the duty owed by the accountants was purely a contractual duty owed by them to the company, and therefore they were not liable for negligence to a person to whom they were under no contractual duty.
. . . The only defences raised by the accountants at the hearing of the appeal were: (1) that Fraser was not acting in the course of his employment; and (2) that, even if he were, they owed

no duty of care to the plaintiff [Lord Denning then considered the first issue, and found that Fraser was acting in the course of his employment]. . . .

Now I come to the great question in the case: did the accountants owe a duty of care to the plaintiff? If the matter were free from authority, I should have said that they clearly did owe a duty of care to him. They were professional accountants who prepared and put before him these accounts, knowing that he was going to be guided by them in making an investment in the company. On the faith of those accounts he did make the investment, whereas if the accounts had been carefully prepared, he would not have made the investment at all. The result is that he has lost his money. In the circumstances, had he not every right to rely on the accounts being prepared with proper care; and is he not entitled to redress from the accountants on whom he relied? I say that he is, and I would apply to this case the words of Knight Bruce, L.J. in an analogous case ninety years ago: 'A country whose administration of justice did not afford redress in a case of the present description would not be in a state of civilization'.

Turning now to authority, I can point to many general statements of principle which cover the case made by some of the great names in the law . . . [b]ut it is said that effect cannot be given to these statements of principle, because there is an actual decision of this court in 1893 which is to the contrary, namely *Le Lievre v. Gould*.

Before I consider the decision in *Le Lievre v. Gould* itself, I wish to say that, in my opinion, at the time it was decided current legal thought was infected by two cardinal errors. The first error was one which appears time and time again in nineteenth century thought, namely, that no one who is not a party to a contract can sue on it or on anything arising out of it. This error has had unfortunate consequences both in the law of contract and in the law of tort. So far as contract is concerned, I have said something about it in *Smith v. River Douglas Catchment Board.*[5] So far as tort is concerned, it led the lawyers of that day to suppose that, if one of the parties to a contract was negligent in carrying it out, no third person who was injured by that negligence could sue for damages on account of it . . ., except in the case of things danagerous in themselves, like guns. This error lies at the root of the reasoning of Bowen, L.J., in *Le Lievre v. Gould*, when he said that the law of England 'does not consider that what a man writes on paper is like a gun or other dangerous instrument', meaning thereby that, unless it was a thing which was dangerous in itself, no action lay. This error was exploded by the great case of *Donoghue v. Stevenson*, which decided that the presence of a contract did not defeat an action for negligence by a third person, provided that the circumstances disclosed a duty by the contracting party to him.

The second error was an error as to the effect of *Derry v. Peek*, an error which persisted for thirty-five years at least after the decision, namely, that no action ever lies for a negligent statement even though it is intended to be acted on by the plaintiff and is in fact acted on by him to his loss. . . .

Let me now be constructive and suggest the circumstances in which I say that a duty to use care in statement does exist apart from a contract in that behalf. First, what persons are under such duty? My answer is those persons such as accountants, surveyors, valuers and analysts, whose profession and occupation it is to examine books, accounts, and other things, and to make reports on which other people—other than their clients—rely in the ordinary course of business. Their duty is not merely a duty to use care in their reports. They have also a duty to use care in their work which results in their reports. Herein lies the difference between these professional men and other persons who have been held to be under no duty to use care in their statements, such as promoters who issue a prospectus: *Derry v. Peek* (now altered by statute), and trustees who answer inquiries about trust funds: *Low v. Bouverie.*[6] Those parties do not bring, and are not expected to bring, any professional knowledge or skill into the preparation of their statements: they can only be made responsible by the law affecting persons generally, such as contract, estoppel, innocent misrepresentation or fraud. But it is very different with persons who engage in a calling which requires special knowledge and skill. From very early times it has been held that they owe a duty of care to those who are closely and directly affected by their work. . . .

---

[5] [1949] 2 K.B. 500, 514–17.
[6] [1891] 3 Ch. 82.

Secondly, to whom do these professional people owe this duty? I will take accountants, but the same reasoning applies to the others. They owe the duty, of course, to their employer or client; and also I think to any third person to whom they themselves show the accounts, or to whom they know their employer is going to show the accounts, so as to induce him to invest money or take some other action on them. But I do not think the duty can be extended still further so as to include strangers of whom they have heard nothing and to whom their employer without their knowledge may choose to show their accounts. Once the accountants have handed their accounts to their employer they are not, as a rule, responsible for what he does with them without their knowledge or consent. . . .

Thirdly, to what transactions does the duty of care extend? It extends, I think, only to those transactions for which the accountants knew their accounts were required. For instance, in the present case it extends to the original investment of 2,000*l* which the plaintiff made in reliance on the accounts, because the accountants knew that the accounts were required for his guidance in making that investment; but it does not extend to the subsequent 200*l* which he made after he had been two months with the company. This distinction, that the duty only extends to the very transaction in mind at the time, is implicit in the decided cases. . . .

My conclusion is that a duty to use care in statement is recognized in English law, and that its recognition does not create any dangerous precedent when it is remembered that it is limited in respect of the persons by whom and to whom it is owed and the transactions to which it applies.

One final word: I think that the law would fail to serve the best interests of the community if it should hold that accountants and auditors owe a duty to no one but their client. Its influence would be most marked in cases where their client is a company or firm controlled by one man. It would encourage accountants to accept the information which the one man gives them, without verifying it; and to prepare and present the accounts rather as a lawyer prepares and presents a case, putting the best appearance on the accounts they can, without expressing their personal opinion of them. This is, to my way of thinking, an entirely wrong approach. There is a great difference between the lawyer and the accountant. The lawyer is never called on to express his personal belief in the truth of his client's case; whereas the accountant, who certifies the accounts of his client, is always called on to express his personal opinion as to whether the accounts exhibit a true and correct view of his client's affairs; and he is required to do this, not so much for the satisfaction of his own client, but more for the guidance of shareholders, investors, revenue authorities, and others who may have to rely on the accounts in serious matters of business. If we should decide this case in favour of the accountants there will be no reason why accountants should ever verify the word of the one man in a one-man company, because there will be no one to complain about it. The one man who gives them wrong information will not complain if they do not verify it. He wants their backing for the misleading information he gives them, and he can only get it if they accept his word without verification. It is just what he wants so as to gain his own ends. And the persons who are misled cannot complain because the accountants owe no duty to them. If such be the law, I think it is to be regretted, for it means that the accountants' certificate, which should be a safeguard, becomes a snare for those who rely on it. I do not myself think that it is the law. In my opinion accountants owe a duty of care not only to their own clients, but also to all those whom they know will rely on their accounts in the transactions for which those accounts are prepared.

I would therefore be in favour of allowing the appeal and entering judgment for the plaintiff for damages in the sum of 2,000*l*."

Asquith, L.J.:

"On two points I entirely agree with the judgment delivered by Denning, L.J. I agree that the cause of action based on an alleged breach of duty occurring after the plaintiff became a shareholder cannot be made out if only because the damage relied on preceded the breach. I also agree, for the reasons he has given, that Fraser was clearly acting within the scope of his employment by the defendant firm in showing the draft accounts and giving certain other information to the plaintiff.

But I have the misfortune to differ from my brother on the more important point raised in this case. [Asquith, L.J. then considered the case law, culminating with *Donoghue v. Stevenson*]. . . .

Apart, however, from any limitation which should be read into Lord Atkin's language by reference to the facts of the case before him—the '*subjecta materies*'—it seems to me incredible that if he thought his formula was inconsistent with *Gould's* case he would not have said so. This case, now nearly sixty years old, had at that time stood for nearly forty years. He must have considered it closely. Yet his only reference to it is as annexing a valid and essential qualification to Lord Esher's formula in *Heaven v. Pender*. Not a word of disapproval of the decision on its merits. The inference seems to me to be that Lord Atkin continued to accept the distinction between liability in tort for careless (but non-fraudulent) misstatements and liability in tort for some other forms of carelessness, and that his formula defining 'who is my neighbour' must be read subject to his acceptance of this overriding distinction. . . .

In what has gone before it has been assumed that the two Law Lords who agreed with Lord Atkin's opinion or result accepted the broad formula about 'my duty to my neighbour' which he laid down, as well as in the narrow proposition limited to the liability of the negligent manufacturer of a chattel which reaches the consumer, without an opportunity of intermediate examination, and injures him. This assumption seems to me more than questionable. Lord Thankerton, though he says that he entirely agreed with Lord Atkin's discussion of the authorities, is clearly considering the authorities in their application to the narrow ambit of a manufacturer's liability, chattels and physical injury. His judgment does not travel outside these limits. Nor do I read Lord Macmillan's judgment as indorsing the wider proposition. There is a passage in which he lays down certain general propositions. It would have been easy for him to have adopted Lord Atkin's formula in terms if he had thought so broad a proposition justified. But when he says in an oft-quoted phrase, 'the categories of negligence are never closed' he is not, in my view, accepting an acid test of liability valid in all circumstances—he does not mention the word 'neighbour'; he is merely saying that in accordance with changing social needs and standards new classes of persons legally bound or entitled to the exercise of care may from time to time emerge—in this case by the addition of a careless manufacturer or circulator of a chattel—as parties bound, *vis-à-vis* consumers, or users, as parties entitled. In other words, what Lord Macmillan envisaged was the addition of another slab to the existing edifice, not a systematic reconstruction of the edifice on a single logical plan.

For these reasons I am of the opinion that *Donoghue's* case neither reverses nor qualifies the principle laid down in *Gould's* case. . . .

In the present state of our law different rules still seem to apply to the negligent misstatement on the one hand and to the negligent circulation or repair of chattels on the other; and *Donoghue's* case does not seem to me to have abolished these differences. I am not concerned with defending the existing state of the law or contending that it is strictly logical—it clearly is not. I am merely recording what I think it is.

If this relegates me to the company of 'timorous souls', I must face that consequence with such fortitude as I can command. I am of opinion that the appeal should be dismissed."

Cohen, L.J. [Cohen, L.J. delivered a judgment in substantial agreement with Asquith, L.J. He reasoned the decision in *Le Lievre v. Gould* was binding upon him]:

"The principle of that decision seems to me directly in point in the present case. It is binding on us unless it can be said to be inconsistent with some other decision of this court or of the House of Lords. I am unable to find any such decision. Mr Lawson asked us to say that it is inconsistent with the principle laid down by Lord Atkin in *Donoghue v. Stevenson*. It is to be observed that in *Donoghue v. Stevenson* Lord Atkin himself cited with approval some passages from the judgments of Lord Esher, M.R. and A.L. Smith, L.J. in *Le Lievre v. Gould*, and I am unable to believe that if he had thought the *ratio decidendi* in that case was wrong he would have cited those passage without making it clear that he was not approving the decision. I think, therefore, that although the relevant passages in Lord Atkin's speech are couched in such general terms that they might possibly cover the case of negligent misstatement, that question was not present to Lord Atkin's mind or intended to be covered by his statement. . . .

I would only add that despite the observations of my brother Denning, I do not think the conclusion I have reached will encourage accountants to fall short of the high standard of conduct which the Institutes to which they belong have laid down for their members.

In the result this appeal will be dismissed."

NOTES AND QUESTIONS

- The judgment in *Candler v. Crane, Christmas & Co.* is of particular interest for the way in which it demonstrates how judges engage in the process of applying and distinguishing precedents which are binding, and which may not be easy to reconcile. In this case, at issue was the impact of *Le Lievre v. Gould*, in light of the subsequent decision of the House of Lords in *Donoghue v. Stevenson*. How does the interpretation placed on these two decisions by Denning, L.J. differ from that of Asquith and Cohen L.JJ.? Which did you find more convincing and why?

- Denning, L.J. justifies his approach through an appeal to "policy". What policy arguments are deployed by him? How does Cohen L.J. seek to respond to them?

- The judgment of Asquith, L.J. might be described as an example of judicial conservatism in the development of the common law (something Denning, L.J. would never be accused of!). Which portion of his judgment explicitly adopts a conservative approach to the role of a Court of Appeal judge in the development of the common law? Did you find this approach satisfying? Why or why not?

Given the hierarchy of courts in the United Kingdom, and the nature of a system of binding precedent, it was ultimately up to the House of Lords to consider the impact of *Derry v. Peek* and *Le Lievre v. Gould* in light of *Donoghue v. Stevenson*. The question of the extent of a duty of care owed in the making of negligent misstatements was finally resolved by the House of Lords in 1963.

Hedley Byrne & Co. Ltd v. Heller & Partners Ltd [1964] A.C. 465, HL.

Lord Reid:

"My Lords, this case raises the important question whether and in what circumstances a person can recover damages for loss suffered by reason of his having relied on an innocent but negligent misrepresentation. I cannot do better than adopt the following statement of the case from the judgment of McNair J.: 'This case raised certain interesting questions of law as to the liability of bankers giving references as to the credit-worthiness of their customers. The plaintiffs are a firm of advertising agents. The defendants are merchant bankers. In outline, the plaintiffs' case against the defendants is that, having placed on behalf of a client, Easipower Ltd, on credit terms substantial orders for advertising time on television programmes and for advertising space in certain newspapers on terms under which they, the plaintiffs, became personally liable to the television and newspaper companies, they caused inquiries to be made through their own bank of the defendants as to the credit-worthiness of Easipower Ltd who were customers of the defendants and were given by the defendants satisfactory references. These references turned out not to be justified, and the plaintiffs claim that in reliance on the references, which they had no reason to question, they refrained from cancelling the orders so as to relieve themselves of their current liabilities. . . . [His Lordship stated the facts and continued:] The appellants now seek to recover this loss from the respondents as damages on the ground that these replies were given negligently and in breach of the respondents' duty to exercise care in giving them. In the judgment McNair J. said: 'On the assumption stated above as to the existence of the duty, I have no hesitation in holding (1) that Mr Heller was guilty of negligence in giving such a reference without making plain—as he did not—that it was intended to be a very guarded reference, and (2) that properly understood according to its ordinary and natural meaning the reference was not justified by facts known to Mr Heller.

Before your Lordships the respondents were anxious to contest this finding, but your Lordships found it unnecessary to hear argument on this matter, being of opinion that the appeal must fail even if Mr Heller was negligent. Accordingly I cannot and do not express any opinion on the question whether Mr Heller was in fact negligent. But I should make it plain that the appellants' complaint is not that Mr Heller gave his reply without adequate knowledge of the position, nor that he intended to create a false impression, but that what he said was in fact calculated to create a false impression and that he ought to have realised that. And the same applies to the respondents' letter of November 11.

McNair J. gave judgment for the respondents on the ground that they owed no duty of care to the appellants. He said: 'I am accordingly driven to the conclusion by authority binding upon me that no such action lies in the absence of contract or fiduciary relationship. On the facts before me there is clearly no contract, nor can I find a fiduciary relationship. It was urged on behalf of the plaintiff that the fact that Easipower Ltd were heavily indebted to the defendants and that the defendants might benefit from the advertising campaign financed by the plaintiffs, were facts from which a special duty to exercise care might be inferred. In my judgment, however, these facts, though clearly relevant on the question of honesty if this had been in issue, are not sufficient to establish any special relationship involving a duty of care even if it was open to me to extend the sphere of special relationship beyond that of contract and fiduciary relationship.'

The judgment was affirmed by the Court of Appeal both because they were bound by authority and because they were not satisfied that it would be reasonable to impose upon a banker the obligations suggested. . . .

The appellants' first argument was based on *Donoghue v. Stevenson*. That is a very important decision, but I do not think that it has any direct bearing on this case. That decision may encourage us to develop existing lines of authority, but it cannot entitle us to disregard them. Apart altogether from authority, I would think that the law must treat negligent words differently from negligent acts. The law ought so far as possible to reflect the standards of the reasonable man, and that is what *Donoghue v. Stevenson* sets out to do. The most obvious difference between negligent words and negligent acts is this. Quite careful people often express definite opinions on social or informal occasions even when they see that others are likely to be influenced by them; and they often do that without taking that care which they would take if asked for their opinion professionally or in a business connection. The appellant agrees that there can be no duty of care on such occasions, and we were referred to American and South African authorities where that is recognised, although their law appears to have gone much further than ours has yet done. But it is at least unusual casually to put into circulation negligently made articles which are dangerous. A man might give a friend a negligently-prepared bottle of home-made wine and his friend's guests might drink it with dire results. But it is by no means clear that those guests would have no action against the negligent manufacturer.

Another obvious difference is that a negligently made article will only cause one accident, and so it is not very difficult to find the necessary degree of proximity or neighbourhood between the negligent manufacturer and the person injured. But words can be broadcast with or without the consent or the foresight of the speaker or writer. It would be one thing to say that the speaker owes a duty to a limited class, but it would be going very far to say that he owes a duty to every ultimate 'consumer' who acts on those words to his detriment. It would be no use to say that a speaker or writer owes a duty but can disclaim responsibility if he wants to. He, like the manufacturer, could make it part of a contract that he is not to be liable for his negligence: but that contract would not protect him in a question with a third party, at least if the third party was unaware of it.

So it seems to me that there is good sense behind our present law that in general an innocent but negligent misrepresentation gives no cause of action. There must be something more than the mere misstatement. I therefore turn to the authorities to see what more is required.

The most natural requirement would be that expressly or by implication from the circumstances the speaker or writer has undertaken some responsibility, and that appears to me not to conflict with any authority which is binding on this House. . . .

A reasonable man, knowing that he was being trusted or that his skill and judgment were being relied on, would, I think, have three courses open to him. He could keep silent or decline to give the information or advice sought: or he could give an answer with a clear qualification that he accepted no responsibility for it or that it was given without that reflection or inquiry which a careful answer would require: or he could simply answer without any such qualification. If he chooses to adopt the last course he must, I think, be held to have accepted some responsibility for his answer being given carefully, or to have accepted a relationship with the inquirer which requires him to exercise such care as the circumstances require.

If that is right, then it must follow that *Candler v. Crane, Christmas & Co.* was wrongly decided. . . . This seems to me to be a typical case of agreeing to assume a responsibility: they knew why the plaintiff wanted to see the accounts and why their employers, the company, wanted them to be shown to him, and agreed to show them to him without even a suggestion that he should not rely on them.

The majority of the Court of Appeal held that they were bound by *Le Lievre v. Gould* and that *Donoghue v. Stevenson* had no application. In so holding I think that they were right. The Court of Appeal have bound themselves to follow all *rationes decidendi* of previous Court of Appeal decisions, and, in face of that rule, it would have been very difficult to say that the ratio of *Le Lievre v. Gould* did not cover *Candler's* case. Denning L.J., who dissented, distinguished *Le Lievre v. Gould* on its facts, but, as I understand the rule which the Court of Appeal have adopted, that is not sufficient if the ratio applies; and this is not an appropriate occasion to consider whether the Court of Appeal's rule is a good one. So the question which we now have to consider is whether the ratio of *Le Lievre v. Gould* can be supported. . . . [Lord Reid went on to conclude that the ratio in *Le Lievre v. Gould* was 'wrong'.]

Now I must try to apply these principles to the present case. What the appellants complain of is not negligence in the ordinary sense of carelessness, but rather misjudgment, in that Mr Heller, while honestly seeking to give a fair assessment, in fact made a statement which gave false and misleading impression of his customer's credit. It appears that bankers now commonly give references with regard to their customers as part of their business. I do not know how far their customers generally permit them to disclose their affairs, but, even with permission, it cannot always be easy for a banker to reconcile his duty to his customer with his desire to give a fairly balanced reply to an inquiry. And inquirers can hardly expect a full and objective statement of opinion or accurate factual information such as skilled men would be expected to give in reply to other kinds of inquiry. So it seems to me to be unusually difficult to determine just what duty beyond a duty to be honest a banker would be held to have undertaken if he gave a reply without an adequate disclaimer of responsibility or other warning. . . . [H]ere the appellants' bank, who were their agents in making the inquiry, began by saying that 'they wanted to know in confidence and without responsibility on our part,' that is, on the part of the respondents. So I cannot see how the appellants can now be entitled to disregard that and maintain that the respondents did incur a responsibility to them. . . .

I am therefore of opinion that it is clear that the respondents never undertook any duty to exercise care in giving their replies. The appellants cannot succeed unless there was such a duty and therefore in my judgment this appeal must be dismissed."

[Lord Morris of Borth-y-Gest, Lord Hodson, Lord Devlin and Lord Pearce agreed that the appeal should be dismissed.]

NOTES AND QUESTIONS

- It is important to realise that while *Hedley Byrne* is significant for its recognition of the possibility that a negligent misstatement can give rise to a duty of care, on the facts of this case liability had been excluded by contract. If you were giving legal advice to a bank, the day after *Hedley Byrne* was decided, what would you advise they do to protect themselves?

• Note the comments about *stare decisis* delivered by Lord Reid. You will recall from Chapter 6 the rule that the Court of Appeal is bound by its own decisions. How convinced is Lord Reid by Denning L.J.'s attempt in *Crane Christmas* to distinguish *Le Lievre v. Gould*? Given that Lord Reid disagreed with the approach taken by the majority in *Crane Christmas* and with the decision in *Le Lievre v. Gould*, why do you think he was not more positive about Denning L.J.'s dissent in *Crane Christmas*?

The reasoning of the House of Lords in *Hedley Byrne* was part of a move towards the general principle of liability approach which, it might be argued, began with Lord Atkin's judgment in *Donoghue v. Stevenson*. The tension between the specific duty versus general duty approaches has continued in tort law to the present day.

David Howarth, *Textbook on Tort* (Butterworths, London, 1995), pp. 164–165:

"[I]n the 1960s and 1970s, the general principle view came to the fore. In *Hedley Byrne v. Heller* [1964] AC 465, *Home Office v. Dorset Yacht* [1970] AC 1004 and ultimately in *Anns v. Merton London Borough Council* [1978] AC 728 the House of Lords came to the conclusion that there ought to be a presumption in favour of liability for harm caused by carelessness. The *Anns* 'two-stage' test, as formulated by Lord Wilberforce, was simply that there ought to be liability for harm caused by fault (stage 1) unless there were good reasons why not (stage 2). *Anns* inspired judges such as Lord Scarman to say in *McLoughlin v. O'Brian* [1983] 1 AC 410 that principle required the application of *Donoghue* 'untrammelled by spatial, physical or temporal limits'.

But a reaction set in after *Anns* and *McLoughlin*, led by Lord Keith of Kinkel. . . . Lord Keith's favourite text in cases such as *Yuen Kun Yeu v. A-G (Hong Kong)* [1988] AC 175 and *Murphy v. Brentwood District Council* [1991] 1 AC 398 and Lord Bridge's favourite text in *Caparo v. Dickman* [1990] 2 AC 605 and *Curran v. Northern Ireland Co-ownership Housing Association* [1987] AC 718 was a passage from the judgment of the Australian judge Brennan J. in *Sutherland Shire Council v. Heyman* (1985) 6 ALR 1. Brennan J. had said that:

'It is preferable, in my view, that the law should develop novel categories incrementally and by analogy with established categories, rather than by a massive extension of a prima facie duty of care restrained only by indefinable "considerations which ought to negative, or to reduce or limit the scope of the duty or the class of person to whom it is owed"'.

Ultimately, Lord Bridge went the whole way back to the pre-*Donoghue* circumstances and interests approach and declared in *Caparo* that:

'I think the law has now moved in the direction of attaching greater significance to the more traditional categorisation of distinct and recognisable situations as guides to the existence, scope and the limits of the varied duties of care which the law imposes.'

It seems, however, that just as *Anns* and *McLoughlin v. O'Brian* marked the high point of the last upswing of the general principles approach, *Caparo* may mark the high point of the swing in the opposite direction. Cases such as *Spring v. Guardian Assurance* [1994] 3 All ER 129 and *Henderson v. Merrett Syndicates Ltd* [1994] 3 All ER 506 seem to point to the construction of general principles of liability that cut across the traditional categories of tort and contract and if they do not point to the return to the *Anns* approach or, even more, to a French approach, at least there is again a consciousness that it is possible to construct principles and rules that go beyond mere analogies with the existing case law."

THE POLITICS OF COMMON LAW REASONING

You will learn more about the tensions in the development of the general duty of care in your tort law courses. For our purposes, one of the important points is that all of these developments have occurred through judicial reasoning, rather than legislative intervention. The development of a general duty of care—as well as attempts by courts to avoid its implications and to return to a series of specific duties to which analogies must be drawn in order to found a duty—is a prime example of how common law reasoning is an ongoing process engaged in by judges. After reading the series of cases on the development of negligence, it would be difficult to say that judges were merely "declaring" a common law which was already "there". The conclusion, rather, seems clearly to be that judges have been engaged in the "making" of law. The politics of the common law is an obvious issue to consider once we have reached the conclusion that judges are engaged in a process of law "making".

Edmund M.A. Kwaw, *The Guide to Legal Analysis, Legal Methodology and Legal Writing* (Emond Montgomery, Toronto, 1992), pp. 89–90:

Criticism of traditional Common Law analysis

"Traditional common law legal analysis has been criticized, especially by scholars of the critical legal studies school. These scholars argue that common law legal analysis paints an incomplete and unrealistic picture of the process of adjudication. According to their criticism, the principles of common law legal analysis—the doctrines of precedent, *stare decisis*, and *ratio decidendi*—are based on the misconception that there is a separate and distinct form of legal reasoning and analysis, which ultimately leads to the correct decision. The reality, the critics argue, is that, first, the above principles are so vague that they do not always lead to a logical conclusion or rationale in difficult cases, and some precedents are followed while others are not. Second, the nature of common law legal analysis is such that there are many different interpretations, distinctions, and justifications, which bestow on judges a significant amount of discretion. The principles of common law legal analysis therefore serve only to mask the values, ideology, preferences, and priorities of judges, which ultimately have an effect on the outcome of a case. . . .

The critics argue that the crucial questions always left unanswered are how do judges decide which precedent to follow and what approach do judges adopt in determining the significance of an ambiguous precedent? The answers, it is contended, lies in the values and priorities of different judges; these are the result of a mix of political, social, institutional, and experiential factors. This is clearly shown in the development of the law with regard to negligent misstatements discussed above.

In 1889, the English House of Lords decided in *Derry v. Peek* that unless fraud was established, a plaintiff could not bring an action for a statement that was made negligently but in good faith. In 1914, however, this precedent was not followed in *Nocton v. Ashburton*. The court said that the decision in *Derry v. Peek* had not precluded actions for statements where there existed a fiduciary relationship between the parties. Why the court had not taken into account the relationship between those who issued and prepared the company prospectus and the plaintiff in *Derry*, was not explained. This was followed in 1951 in *Candler v. Crane, Christmas & Co*, which also involved the preparation of company accounts. The House of Lords held that no fiduciary relationship existed. Subsequently, however, in *Hedley Byrne & Co Ltd v. Heller & Partners Ltd* decided in 1964, the law lords held that *Nocton* did not refer only to fiduciary relationships, but to all special relationships where one party trusted another to do something on his or her behalf. The court offered no explanation for not finding such a special relationship in *Candler*. All that the House of Lords said was that *Candler* had been wrongly decided.

In all these cases the House of Lords never provided any explanation of how it determined if it was bound by a precedent. There was no indication that the majority in the House were not, in reality, deciding the various cases on the basis of what they wished the law to be. Thus, although it was not stated in the discussion of all the precedents, the above cases could not have been decided without some ultimate reference to the values and choices of the judges concerned.

What the above suggests is that the doctrines of precedent and *stare decisis* cannot lead to a specific result or rationale in certain cases. Neither do these doctrines ensure continuity, predictability, rationality, or objectivity. Instead of determining the principles and outcomes of cases, they seem to support such outcomes."

QUESTION

Do you agree with Kwaw's assessment of common law reasoning? Defend your position.

Kwaw's focus is on how *stare decisis* in the common law system masks the underlying political and social choices which are made by judges. A further aspect of the development of the duty of care in negligence has also been subject to critique. If you review the judgments which have been excerpted in this chapter, you will notice that frequently judges have referred to the standard of the "reasonable man" as the basis for determining whether a duty of care was breached. Within judicial reasoning, this "reasonable man" standard is assumed, somehow, to operate objectively, neutrally, apolitically, and uncontroversially. Presumably, the question of what standard of behaviour a "reasonable man" would engage in, is obvious—at least to judges. Of course, if you think about it, there is no one, universal "reasonable man" standard. The determination of reasonableness inevitably involves social, cultural and political choices, and the standard of reasonableness will vary depending upon one's ideological position. Yet, common law reasoning tends to mask such choices within the language of reasonableness. Feminist tort theory in particular has usefully interrogated the gendering of the "reasonable man".

Joanne Conaghan, "Feminist Perspectives on the Law of Tort" in *The Critical Lawyers' Handbook 2* (Paddy Ireland and Per Laleng, eds., Pluto Press, London, 1997), pp. 127–128:

"The feminist critique of negligence's 'reasonable man' raises issues of form as well as substance. In other words, it is not just the content of the standard being applied which is under scrutiny, it is also the application of a single and allegedly objective, universal standard to human behaviour at all. What feminist legal theory reveals (in the company of critical legal theory in general) is that law is neither politically nor morally neutral but is value-laden: it is an expression of particular values and assumptions about the distribution of resources in society (and individual access to them) which has blatantly political consequences. Thus judges when assessing reasonable behaviour, whether they are articulating their own subjective opinions or whether they are engaged in a genuine attempt to give expression to what they believe are prevailing social standards of proper behaviour, are making, in effect, policy-based decisions, that is, decisions which appeal to particular values and moral preferences governing individual relationships with each other and with the state. These are values about which reasonable people may well disagree.

Thus the conventional understanding of the reasonable man as an objective measure of human behaviour is a legal fiction: he is in fact merely a particular expression of appropriate human behaviour inevitably reflecting the values and assumptions, experience and understanding of those responsible for his birth and subsequent upbringing. For this reason it is not enough to simply replace the 'reasonable man' standard with an appeal to the 'reasonable person' as is the practice in some of the more 'politically correct' textbooks. The reasonable person is no more objective than the reasonable man. Indeed the claim to objectivity is itself contentiously male: objectivity, it is alleged, is the method by which men's point of view is privileged and women's silenced."

CASE LAW EXERCISE

Your client, Albert, is a regular patron of a pub. One evening he consumed five pints of lager there, all of which were served to him by Barbara, the proprietor. Albert normally only drinks lemonade, but was upset because of an argument he had earlier with his wife, Carol. He became extremely intoxicated and then began to abuse other patrons in the pub. He was promptly asked to leave the establishment by Barbara. It was obvious to everyone at that point that Albert was very unsteady on his feet. Because of her long acquaintance with Albert, Barbara was aware that the location of Albert's house required him to cross a very busy road after leaving the pub. In fact, the road has a reputation in the neighbourhood for being dangerous for pedestrians, even when they are sober. Upon leaving the pub, Albert stumbled down the street, into the busy road, was hit by a passing motorist and badly injured. He now wishes to sue Barbara in negligence. The only relevant authorities in this case are *Barrett v. Ministry of Defence* [1995] 3 All E.R. 87, CA; and *Crocker v. Sundance Northwest Resorts* [1988] 1 S.C.R. 1186, a decision of the Supreme Court of Canada. The relevant portions of *Barrett* are set out below, and *Crocker* is sufficiently discussed, for our purposes, within the judgment in *Barrett*. Read the judgment as excerpted, and answer questions which follow it.

Barrett v. Ministry of Defence [1995] 3 All E.R. 87, CA.

Beldam L.J.:
"In these proceedings Mrs Dawn Barrett, widow of Terrence Barrett, claims damages for herself and her son Liam under the Fatal Accidents Act 1976 and for the benefit of the estate of her deceased husband under the Law Reform (Miscellaneous Provisions) Act 1934. She blames the appellant, the Ministry of Defence, for the death of her husband who was serving in the Royal Navy. On 12 May 1993 Judge Phelan, sitting as a deputy judge of the High Court, gave judgment for the plaintiff for £160, 651.16. . . . The appellant in this appeal challenges one of the two grounds on which the judge found it to have been in breach of duty to the deceased. . . .

At the time of his death Terence Barrett, the deceased, was thirty years of age and a naval airman serving at a shore based establishment of the Royal Navy at Barduffos in northern Norway. The naval base is somewhat isolated and the shore facilities are uninviting. It was used for a series of training exercises known as 'Exercise Clockwork'. On 6 January 1988 detachments of marine commandos, together with No 845 Helicopter Squadron from Royal Naval Air Station, Yeovilton arrived to take part in one of these training exercises. The deceased was attached to the squadron.

Because the recreational facilities ashore were limited, the appellant had installed several video rooms, computer equipment, a gymnasium, a sauna and other recreational and educational facilities. Within the base there were three bars: the ward room, the senior rates' bar and the junior rates' bar, at which duty free drink could be obtained. Drinking in these bars when off duty was one of the main recreations of personnel attached to the base. In January 1988 the senior naval officer at Barduffos was Lt Cdr Lomax. The evidence was to show that his attitude to the enforcement of the Queen's Regulations for the Royal Navy 1967 (BR 31) and of standing orders, in particular to excessive drinking and drunkenness, was unusually lax. As a consequence of the death of the deceased he was charged with and pleaded guilty to a breach of art 181 of the Queen's Regulations, which provides: 'It is the particular duty of all officers, Fleet Chief Petty Officers, Chief Petty Officers and leading ratings actively to discourage drunkenness, over-indulgence in alcohol and drug abuse by naval personnel both on board and ashore. . . .' His plea of guilty acknowledged that he had negligently performed the duty of actively discouraging drunkenness and over-indulgence in alcohol. . . .

The facts leading up to the death of the deceased were not in dispute. He died in his bunk between 2 am and 2.30 am on the morning of Saturday, 23 January 1988. Friday, 22 January was the deceased's thirtieth birthday. He had recently learned that after some ten years' service he was to be promoted leading hand and so had additional reason to celebrate. Friday evening was customarily an evening for heavy drinking. On this Friday a Hawaiian party event had been organised in the senior rates' bar. A number of the senior rates attending the party decided they would compete to see who could drink the most. Very substantial quantities of duty free spirits were consumed.

The deceased went to the junior rates' bar at about 9.15 pm to begin his celebrations. Having placed money behind the bar to treat his mess mates, the judge found he himself consumed there three cans of cider and two double Bacardis. At about 10.30 pm he was invited to the senior rates' bar where he was bought six Bacardis, each of which was a double measure. By about 11 pm he had consumed a minimum of four ciders and nine double Bacardis. It was not, however, suggested that the barmen in charge of either bar had served him personally with this number of drinks. Most of the drinks were bought for him. At about 11.30 pm he returned to the junior rates' bar to get fuel for his cigarette lighter and then went back to the senior rates' bar where, shortly afterwards, he became unconscious. He was carried back to the junior rates' bar where he was placed on a chair in the lobby. He was seen there by Lt Cdr Parker who had just returned from sledging. The deceased was then in a collapsed state and insensible. Petty Officer Wells, the duty senior rate whose office was nearby, organised a stretcher and the deceased was taken to his cabin where he was placed in his bunk in the recovery position. He was in a coma but tossing and turning. He was visited on about three occasions by the duty ratings. When his cabin mate went to turn in at about 2.30 am, he found that the deceased had vomited, had inhaled his vomit and was apparently asphyxiated. Attempts were made to revive him but without success. A board of inquiry was held and a ship's inquiry and many statements were taken from witnesses. Based on these statements and the evidence which he had heard, the judge found that at this isolated base cases of drunkenness, especially at the weekends, were commonplace and that disciplinary action that might lead to punishment was not taken.

The judge also found there was a much more relaxed attitude to drinking tolerated at this base than there would be in the United Kingdom. Drunkenness was common at the weekends when the men were off duty and especially on Friday nights. The judge summarised the situation disclosed by the evidence as 'a perfectly deplorable situation'.

The appellant does not challenge this assessment of the discipline at Barduffos. Of the deceased the judge found that he was quite a heavy drinker and this was widely known. There was little inducement for anyone to go ashore for recreation for alcohol prices were remarkably high in Norway and astonishingly low in the base. A good range of recreational facilities existed but boredom was inevitable and foreseeable. He was under the appellant's codes of discipline and it controlled all facilities. Disciplinary codes existed which, if implemented, would have greatly reduced drunkenness. He said that the deceased was a heavy drinker introduced to a potentially dangerous situation. In these circumstances the judge held that it was foreseeable in this particular environment that the deceased would succumb to heavy intoxication. Although it was only in exceptional circumstances that a defendant could be fixed with a duty to take positive steps to protect a person of full age and capacity from his own weakness, he considered in the exceptional circumstances that arose in this case it was just and reasonable to impose a duty to take care on the appellant. He also held that the appellant was in breach of that duty because it failed to enforce the standards it itself set in matters of discipline. . . .

The appellant does not challenge the judge's findings that it was in breach of duty to take care of the deceased once he had collapsed and it had assumed responsibility for him.

The appellant's principal ground of appeal is that the judge was wrong to hold that it was under any duty to take care to see that the deceased, a mature man thirty years of age, did not consume so much alcohol that he became unconscious. If the deceased himself was to be treated as a responsible adult, he alone was to blame for his collapse. . . .

The purpose of Queen's Regulations and standing orders is to preserve good order and discipline in the service and to ensure that personnel remain fit for duty and while on duty obey commands and off duty do not misbehave bringing the service into disrepute. All regulations which encourage self-discipline, if obeyed, will incidentally encourage service personnel to take greater pride in their own behaviour but in no sense are the regulations and orders intended to lay down standards or to give advice in the exercise of reasonable care for the safety of the men when off duty drinking in the bars.

The judge placed reliance on the fact that it was foreseeable that if the regulations and standing orders were not properly enforced in this particular environment the deceased would succumb to heavy intoxication. He also said it was just and reasonable to impose a duty in these circumstances. . . .

In the present case the judge posed the question whether there was a duty at law to take reasonable steps to prevent the deceased becoming unconscious through alcohol abuse. He said his conclusion that there was such a duty was founded on the fact that: 'It was foreseeable in the environment in which the defendant grossly failed to enforce their regulations and standing orders that the deceased would succumb to heavy intoxication.' And in these circumstances that it was just and reasonable to impose a duty.

The respondent argued for the extension of a duty to take care for the safety of the deceased from analogous categories of relationship in which an obligation to use reasonable care already existed. For example employer and employee, pupil and schoolmaster and occupier and visitor. It was said that the appellant's control over the environment in which the deceased was serving and the provision of duty free liquor, coupled with the failure to enforce disciplinary rules and orders were sufficient factors to render it fair, just and reasonable to extend the duty to take reasonable care found in the analogous circumstances. The characteristic which distinguishes those relationships is reliance expressed or implied in the relationship which the party to whom the duty is owed is entitled to place on the other party to make provision for his safety. I can see no reason why it should not be fair, just and reasonable for the law to leave a responsible adult to assume responsibility for his own actions in consuming alcoholic drink. No one is better placed to judge the amount that he can safely consume or to exercise control in his own interest as well as in the interest of others. To dilute self-responsibility and to blame one adult for another's lack of self-control is neither just nor reasonable and in the development of the law of negligence an increment too far. . . .

The respondent placed reliance on *Crocker v. Sundance Northwest Resorts Ltd* [1988] 1 SCR 1186, a decision of the Supreme Court of Canada. . . . In [*Crocker*] . . . the defendant was held liable to an intoxicated plaintiff for permitting him to take part in a dangerous ski hill race which caused him to be injured. The defendant had taken the positive step of providing him with the equipment needed for the race knowing that he was in no fit state to take part. The plaintiff had consumed alcohol in the defendant's bars. Liability was based not on permitting him to drink in the bars but in permitting him to take part in the race. . . . [T]he court founded the imposition of a duty on factors additional to the mere provision of alcohol and the failure strictly to enforce provisions against drunkenness.

In the present case I would reverse the judge's finding that the appellant was under a duty to take reasonable care to prevent the deceased from abusing alcohol to the extent he did. Until he collapsed I would hold that the deceased was in law alone responsible for his condition. Thereafter, when the appellant assumed responsibility for him, it accepts that the measures taken fell short of the standard reasonably to be expected. It did not summon medical assistance and its supervision of him was inadequate. . . .

The deceased involved the appellant in a situation in which it had to assume responsibility for his care and I would not regard it as just and equitable in such circumstances to be unduly critical of the appellant's fault. I consider a greater share of blame should rest upon the deceased than on the appellant and I would reduce the amount of the damages recoverable by the respondent by two-thirds holding the appellant one third to blame. . . .

Saville L.J. I agree.

Neill L.J. I also agree."

Questions

• What were the material facts of *Barrett*?

• What was the *ratio decidendi* of *Barrett*?

• In *Barrett*, the trial judge found the appellant in breach of a duty to the deceased on two grounds. Which ground was conceded by the appellant to be a breach of its duty?

• How would you describe the political ideology which underpins the judgment in *Barrett*? individualist? welfarist? Why?

• Construct a brief argument on the law in favour of your client Albert, which you could use in civil proceedings launched against Barbara.

Essay question

"The descriptive question that lawyers debate is whether in fact courts resolve issues primarily by the application of rules or by the application of policies. The orthodox view is that judges apply rules through the logical processes of deduction and analogy, turning to policies only in the occasional hard case. The competing theory is that judges in reality intuit the best result, that is, the result that is most satisfactory to them as a matter of policy, and only then do they turn to the rules to explain and justify the result they have reached on other grounds. In this view, the judge may even have the sensation of following the rules, but the interpretation of those rules as the judge applies them is guided by prior intuition about the most desirable resolution. In this way, the rules can seem to produce the correct result."

(Kenneth J. Vandevelde, *Thinking Like a Lawyer* (Westview Press, Boulder, 1996), p. 66).

Comment on the above quotation, using the cases discussed in this chapter as the basis for your answer. Describe the "values and assumptions" which have informed the development of a general duty of care in negligence.

12

PROCEDURAL ASPECTS OF LEGAL METHOD: INTRODUCTION TO THE CIVIL JUSTICE SYSTEM

In this chapter, our attention turns to issues of legal procedure. There is no attempt to present a comprehensive explanation of the rules of procedure. Instead, we focus on a number of current areas of controversy which centre on procedure in *civil* (as opposed to criminal) litigation. Issues of criminal procedure are beyond the scope of this chapter, and are normally covered in criminal law courses. We begin with a basic overview of the civil justice system, followed by attempts to respond to perceptions of a growing "crisis" in that system, culminating in the Woolf Report on Access to Justice. We look at the significance and implications of that report, and at criticisms of some of its recommendations. We then turn to some specific areas which are of importance to the current law reform agenda, including the possibility of "group actions", and the reform of legal aid and the increasing importance of a system of "conditional fees" for civil suits.

OVERVIEW OF THE CIVIL JUSTICE SYSTEM

Catherine Elliott and Frances Quinn, *English Legal System* (Longman, London and New York, 1996), pp. 267–276:

"The civil justice system is designed to sort out disputes between individuals, rather than between citizens and the state, as the criminal system does—though in legal terms an 'individual' may be a company or other organization, as well as one person. One party, known as the plaintiff, sues the other, called the defendant, usually for money they claim is owed, or because they claim the other party has done some harm to their interests (a civil wrong like this is called a tort). Typical examples might be the victim of a car accident suing the driver of the car for compensation, or one business suing another for payment for goods supplied.

Major changes have been made to the civil justice system in recent years, as a result of recommendations made by the Civil Justice Review and implemented in the Courts and Legal Services Act 1990.

History

The civil justice system developed in a rather piecemeal fashion, responding to different needs at different times, with the result that at the end of the eighteenth century, civil matters were being dealt with by several different series of courts. Three common law courts, supplemented by the Court of Chancery, did most of the work, but there was also a Court of Admiralty and the ecclesiastical (church) courts. They had different but often overlapping jurisdictions, and between them administered three different 'systems' of law: civilian law (based on Roman law), common law and equity. The courts were also largely centralized in London, making access difficult for those in the provinces.

With no coordination of the increasingly complex court system, inefficiency, incompetence and delays were common, and the courts acquired a reputation for binding themselves up in cumbersome procedural rules. Until well into the nineteenth century, litigation in the higher courts was an extravagance which could be afforded only by the very rich, and in many respects the system benefited the judges and the legal profession far more than litigants.

Reform began in 1846, with the creation of a nationwide system of county courts, designed to provide cheaper, quicker justice at local levels for local businessmen, and was followed in the early 1870s, by the creation of one Supreme Court, consisting of the High Court, the Court of Appeal and the Crown Court, although the High Court was still divided into five divisions. In 1881, these were reduced to three: Queen's Bench; Chancery; and what is now known as the Family Division.

The civil courts today

Today there are around 300 county courts, concerned exclusively with civil work. About 170 of them are designated as divorce county courts and thereby have jurisdiction to hear undefended divorces and cases concerning adoption and guardianship.

In the High Court, the three divisions mentioned above remain today—they act as separate courts, with judges usually working within one division only. Lord Woolf has recently recommended that these divisions should remain.[1] The Family Division hears cases concerning marriage, children and the family, such as divorce, adoption and wills. The Chancery Division deals with matters of finance and property, such as tax and bankruptcy. The Queen's Bench Division is the biggest of the three, with the most varied jurisdiction. The major part of its work is handling those contract and tort cases which are unsuitable for the county courts. Sitting as the Divisional Court of the Queen's Bench, its judges also hear certain criminal appeals originating in the magistrates' courts, and applications for judicial review. High Court judges usually sit alone, but the Divisional Court is so important that two or three judges sit together.

High Court trials happen either in London or in one of the 26 provincial trial centres. In theory, they are all presided over by High Court judges, but in fact there are not enough High Court judges to cope with the case load. Some cases therefore have to be dealt with by circuit judges, others by barristers sitting as part-time, temporary, deputy judges. In 1987, only half of all High Court sitting days were taken by High Court judges.

Although most civil cases are dealt with by either the county courts or the High Court, magistrates' courts have a limited civil jurisdiction, and some types of case are tried by tribunals.

Jurisdiction of the High Court and County Courts

The Civil Justice Review in 1985, was set up by the Lord Chancellor in response to public criticism of the delay, cost and complexity of the civil court system. Unusually, it was chaired by a non-lawyer, Maurice Hodgson, the Chairman of Bhs, and only a minority of its members were lawyers. They therefore tended to be less pro-lawyer than previous committees that had been dominated by judges and barristers, which may explain why many of the Review's more innovative suggestions were ignored or only partially implemented. Important changes were made to the division of work between the county courts and High Court by the Courts and Legal Services Act 1990, in response to some of the proposals of the 1985 Review. The Review's report described its purpose as being to 'improve the machinery of civil justice in England and Wales by means of reforms in jurisdiction, procedure and court administration and in particular to reduce delay, cost and complexity.'

One of its main findings was that too many cases were being heard in the High Court rather

---

[1] We consider Lord Woolf's recommendations later in this chapter.

than the cheaper and quicker county courts, often for relatively small amounts of money: in 1987, half of all money claims started in the Queen's Bench Division were for less than £3,000. Consequently it aimed to increase the number of cases heard in the county courts, thereby freeing High Court time for public law cases, specialist cases and cases considered to be of importance, complexity and substance.

The position now is that claims worth under £3,000 are automatically dealt with by the Small Claims procedure of the county court, the amount having been increased at the beginning of 1996 from £1,000. All personal injury cases worth less than £50,000 should be brought in the county court. Both the county court and the High Court have jurisdiction over any other tort or contract case. There is no longer a fixed maximum limit for cases heard in the county court, nor a minimum one for the High Court. In general though, cases worth less than £25,000 should be commenced in the county court, and cases worth more than £50,000 in the High Court; for actions falling between £25,000 and £50,000, the proper court will depend on the complexity and importance of the case. . . .

Civil procedure

Which court?

In many cases the choice of court will be straightforward, given the jurisdiction rules discussed above and the fact that the courts are increasingly willing to transfer cases if the 'wrong' court is chosen. Still there are clearly cases where a plaintiff will potentially have a choice between High Court and county court, and even though the core procedural rules are being harmonized, there are still differences between them.

The county court procedure tends to be simpler, especially for the represented litigant; if representation is felt to be needed, it can be performed by the solicitor alone, rather than the more expensive solicitor and barrister combination still considered prudent for High Court work; the courts are local, so probably more convenient; and the case is likely to be dealt with more quickly. The danger of cost sanctions must also be taken into account.

On the other hand, there is still a feeling that a High Court writ will have a greater threatening effect than a county court summons, which is especially important given the high number of civil cases settled out of court. Although the 1990 reforms have made the same remedies available in both courts, the idea that damages awarded in the High Court are likely to be higher may linger, and judgment enforcement procedures are thought to be more effective.

As far as lawyers are concerned, a further important difference between the courts is that the county courts do much of the pre-trial work for the parties, issuing the various documents needed during the course of the action, whereas when an action is brought in the High Court, solicitors take responsibility for preparing and serving most of the court documents. Such a degree of direct control gives a great strategic advantage to the plaintiff, enabling them to co-ordinate the timing of different stages of an action with the arduous, time-consuming task of gathering witness statements and medical evidence.

Pre-trial procedures

This is perhaps the most important area of civil process, since few civil cases actually come to trial. Usually an out-of-court settlement is negotiated before they ever reach the trial stage. For every 9,000 personal injury cases commenced only 300 are submitted for judgment. Outside personal injuries, for every 100,000 writs fewer than 300 actually come for trial.

Civil procedure is governed by the Rules of the Supreme Court, found in documents called the 'White Book' (for the High Court) and the 'Green Book' (for the county courts). The purpose of these rules is supposed to be to ensure that the case comes to court with the issue or issues clearly defined, and with what is agreed or disagreed clearly spelt out so that the trial can be conducted as quickly and efficiently as possible.

High Court actions start with a writ, county court ones by a summons. These are documents served informing the defendants that a case is being brought against them; they must acknowledge service. The plaintiff serves a statement of claim if bringing an action in the High Court, or the particulars of a claim in the county court. Both are formal documents outlining the facts and legal basis of the claim, and the remedy sought. The defendant responds with a defence. Either party may request more details from the other, in a document known as 'a request for further and better particulars'. These will then be supplied. Each party then provides the other with a list of the documents which they have in relation to the action. The parties can then ask to see some or all of these documents. This process is known as discovery.

Out of court settlements

The case may be settled out of court at any of these points—around a third of such settlements happen almost literally at the door of the court. The obvious advantage of this is a quicker end to the dispute, and a reduction in costs, although these start to build up from the time each side consults a lawyer, the trial itself is by far the most expensive part.

For the plaintiff, a settlement means they are sure of getting something, and do not have to risk losing the case altogether and probably having to pay the other side's costs as well as their own, but they must weight this up against the chances of being awarded a better settlement if the case goes to trial and they win. The defendant risks the possibility that they might have won and therefore had to pay nothing, or that they may be paying more than the judge would have awarded if the plaintiff had won the case, against the chance that the plaintiff wins and is awarded more than the settlement would have cost.

A further complication is that the defendant may, at any time during the process, make a payment into court, which the plaintiff may accept as settlement of the claim. If not, the process continues as before, but if the case continues to trial and the plaintiff wins but is awarded less than the sum paid in, they must pay the defendant's costs from the time of the payment in—which can result in the winner of the case being worse off than the loser. Although the judge knows that a payment into court has been made, the amount is not revealed, so that there is no way of ensuring that the award matches the payment in.

The trial

Civil trials are usually presided over by a single judge, with juries used in only a handful of cases. The burden of proof is usually on the plaintiff, who must prove their case on a balance of probabilities—that it is more likely than not. Obviously this is a lower standard of proof than the 'beyond reasonable doubt' of the criminal courts, and for this reason it is possible to be acquitted of a criminal charge yet still found negligent with regard to the same action— for example, one might be found not guilty of dangerous driving, yet still successfully sued for negligence by the person knocked down.

The trial is conducted along adversarial lines, with each side calling its own witnesses and cross-examining those of the other. As in a criminal trial, judges rely on the parties to present the evidence, rather than making their own investigations. However, unlike the judges in a criminal trial, since they do not usually need to ensure that everything has been explained so that a jury can understand it, they can read the papers beforehand, and direct the parties or their representatives that they need only cover unclear or disputed points in court.

In 1995 the Lord Chief Justice issued guidelines to the High Court in his Practice Direction ('Civil Litigation: Case Management'). The Practice Direction was aimed to streamline civil litigation and reduce costs in the High Court. It stated that judges should assume tighter control over the preparation and conduct of hearings and should penalize lawyers who failed to conduct cases economically. Judges were to exercise their discretion to limit discovery and the time spent giving oral evidence and reading aloud from documents in open court. Where possible witness statements could stand as the evidence-in-chief of the witness.

Costs

The cost of bringing or defending a civil action can be very high. Legal aid may be available; in many cases, especially those involving personal injury, the defendant's, and sometimes the plaintiff's, costs will be paid by insurance companies—when car accidents are involved, for example, one or both parties are likely to have been insured, and professionals such as doctors are insured against claims of negligence against them. As Hazel Genn's 1987 study showed, where only one party is insured, this can place great pressure on the other, unless they have been granted legal aid. The insured side may try to drag out the proceedings as long as possible, in the hope of exhausting the other party's financial reserves and forcing a low settlement.

If the case comes to trial, the winner is usually awarded costs; the loser must pay the legal costs of both parties, as well as any damages ordered. . . .

The small claims court

This is not actually a separate court, but a procedure used by county courts to deal with claims worth under £3,000. It was introduced in response to a report from the Consumers Association in 1967, claiming that county courts were being used primarily as a debt collection agency for businesses: 89.2 per cent of the summonses were taken out by firms and only 9 per cent by individuals, who were put off by costs and complexity.

The special procedure known as the Small Claims Court was introduced in 1973, with the aim of providing a cheap, simple mechanism for resolving small-scale consumer disputes. It is now mandatory for claims of under £3,000. Actions for possession and actions for damages for personal injuries in which the amount claimed exceeds £1,000 are exempted from automatic reference. The court also has a discretion to allow a case that would ordinarily be heard by the small claims procedure to be heard by the main county court where a complex factual issue is involved. In *Afzal v. Ford Motor Co. Ltd* (1994) the Court of Appeal commented that it would be an abuse of court procedure to overstate the amounts involved in a claim simply to avoid the small claims procedure.

Claimants start proceedings in the normal way by taking out a summons—county court officials can help with form filling—and have to pay a small sum, based on the amount claimed. Once the summons is served, the defendant has fourteen days to send back a defence; if none is returned, the court may simply rule in the claimant's favour.

These days the courts aim to sort out small claims in a single hearing, but the procedure does also allow for a pre-trial hearing, at which the judge—usually the district judge of the court—attempts to conciliate the parties, and if this is not possible, to at least isolate the issues in the case, and give directions on how to prepare and conduct the case.

If the case comes to court, the hearing is usually held in private rather than in open court, and the procedure is simple and informal, with few rules about the admissibility or presentation of evidence. The arbitrator plays a more interventionist role than most judges, asking questions and examining evidence as necessary, and must give both parties a fair and equal opportunity to present their case. It is usually a fairly quick process, with 60 per cent of cases taking less than 30 minutes.

The procedure is designed to make it easy for parties to represent themselves, without the aid of a lawyer, and legal aid for representation is not available. Litigants who do choose to be professionally represented have to pay the costs themselves, win or lose, as the judge may only award minor costs against a losing party. Under the Lay Representatives (Rights of Audience) Order 1992 made under s 11 of the Courts and Legal Services Act 1990, a party can choose to be represented by a lay person, who will have a right of audience in the Small Claims Court, though the party must also attend.

There is little right of appeal from the Small Claims Court: the judge's decision can be set aside but only on the ground that he or she acted contrary to the rules of natural justice in not granting the parties a fair hearing, or that the record of the proceedings showed that an error of law was made. As the court records of arbitrations are concise and do not usually state the reason for the award, the proceedings rarely give rise to an appeal."

NOTES AND QUESTIONS

- List advantages and disadvantages of the simplified small claims procedure. Do the advantages outweigh the disadvantages?

- Were you surprised by the number of cases which settle out of court? What are the advantages and disadvantages—from the perspective both of parties and of the civil justice system—of the existence of such a high percentage of settled claims?

After judgment in a civil case has been issued, there remains the possibility of appeal.

Penny Darbyshire, *Eddey on the English Legal System* (6th ed., Sweet and Maxwell, London, 1996), pp. 106–107:

"Appeal lies from the county court to the Court of Appeal (Civil Division) without leave unless the amount at issue falls below £5,000 in tort, contract, etc., or below £15,000 in equity and probate cases, etc. Leave is not necessary where the appeal is the result of an application for an injunction or concerns the upbringing of a child.

From the three Divisions of the High Court of Justice, and from Divisional Courts in civil matters, appeals also go to the Court of Appeal (Civil Division). In 1994, 2,260 such appeals were disposed of. The hearing in the Court of Appeal is not a complete retrial since witnesses are not normally heard again. The appellant, in furnishing notice of appeal, must specify precisely the grounds for appeal and will be limited to arguing these before the court. The parties have six weeks from the judge's judgment to give notice of appeal. The appeal will be heard by three Lord Justices of Appeal in about six months from the time when the appeal was set down for hearing.

A further appeal to the House of Lords is possible, but only if the Court of Appeal gives leave, or the House of Lords, by its Appeal Committee, itself gives leave. Only cases that raise points of law of general public importance reach the House of Lords. Appeals from the Court of Appeal (Civil Division) numbered 42 in 1994. For a hearing, five Lords of Appeal in Ordinary form a court.

Under the Administration of Justice Act 1969, it is possible for an appeal to go direct from the High Court to the House of Lords and so 'leapfrog' the Court of Appeal."

REFORM OF THE CIVIL JUSTICE SYSTEM: WOOLF AND BEYOND

The civil justice system has long been perceived to be in need of reform, and that process has intensified in recent years, culminating with the release of the Woolf Report on Access to Justice. The background to it is described by Darbyshire.

Penny Darbyshire, *Eddey on the English Legal System* (6th ed., Sweet and Maxwell, London, 1996), pp. 107–108:

"The problems of English civil procedure have been the subject of constant scrutiny throughout this century and much of the last. Prior to the Lord Chancellor's establishment of the Civil Justice Review in 1985, there had been no fewer than 63 reports, since the turn of the century on the same subject. With tedious and frustrating repetition, they all identify the same core problems so that the opening words of Chapter two of Lord Woolf's interim report, in 1995, give those of us who have been watching the legal system for some years more than a frisson of *dé-jà vu*:

'The process is too expensive, too slow and too complex.'

His Lordship quotes a number of famous judicial critics of the civil process who have all drawn attention to the fact that these problems militate against the provision of an accessible system of civil courts which is necessary if people are to be enabled to enforce their rights in civil law. Indeed, the very title of his Lordship's report, *Access to Justice*, seems like an ironic cliché, after years of concern over the lack of it.

The Civil Justice Review body reported in 1988. The review was remarkable for the breadth and depth of its scrutiny of the system, its radical approach and its success rate, in that many of its recommendations were soon translated into law, in the Courts and Legal Services Act 1990 and subsequent delegated legislation. Yet, despite the fact that its reforms were potentially the most radical since the Judicature Acts of 1893–95, they apparently did not solve those fundamental problems. No sooner had the dust settled on the new legislation than the two sides of the legal profession had established the Heilbron Committee, to produce a 1993 report on the continuing problems of civil justice and their proposals for dealing with them. The Lord Chancellor responded by commissioning Lord Woolf, when a Law Lord, to carry out yet another scrutiny of the system and suggest yet another list of proposed reforms."

Lord Woolf presented his report in two stages: an Interim Report in June 1995, and his Final Report in July 1996. The Overview to the Final Report summarizes the recommendations of his Interim Report, and moves on to consider his further recommendations.

Lord Woolf, *Access to Justice: Final Report to the Lord Chancellor on the Civil Justice System in England and Wales* (The Stationery Office, London, 1996), pp. 2–12:

The principles

1. In my interim report I identified a number of principles which the civil justice system should meet in order to ensure access to justice. The system should:

   (a) be *just* in the results it delivers;
   (b) be *fair* in the way it treats litigants;
   (c) offer appropriate procedures at a reasonable *cost*;
   (d) deal with cases with reasonable *speed*;
   (e) be *understandable* to those who use it;
   (f) be *responsive* to the needs of those who use it;
   (g) provide as much *certainty* as the nature of particular cases allows; and
   (h) be *effective*: adequately resourced and organised.

2. The defects I identified in our present system were that it is too expensive in that the costs often exceed the value of the claim; too slow in bringing cases to a conclusion and too unequal: there is a lack of equality between the powerful, wealthy litigant and the under-resourced litigant. It is too uncertain: the difficulty of forecasting what litigation will cost and how long it will last induces the fear of the unknown; and it is incomprehensible to many litigants. Above all it is too fragmented in the way it is organised since there is no-one with clear overall responsibility for the administration of civil justice; and too adversarial as cases are run by the parties, not by the courts and the rules of court, all too often, are ignored by the parties and not enforced by the court.

3. The interim report set out a blueprint for reform based on a system where the courts with the assistance of litigants would be responsible for the management of cases. I recommended that the courts should have the final responsibility for determining what procedures were suitable for each case; setting realistic timetables; and ensuring that the procedures and timetables were complied with. Defended cases would be allocated to one of three tracks:

   (a) an expanded small claims jurisdiction with a financial limit of £3,000;
   (b) a new fast track for straightforward cases up to £10,000, with strictly limited procedures, fixed timetables (20–30 weeks to trial), and fixed costs; and

(c) a new multi-track for cases above £10,000, providing individual hands-on management by judicial teams for the heaviest cases, and standard or tailor-made directions where these are appropriate.

4. My general analysis of the problems in the present system, and the broad agenda for reform which I proposed in the interim report, have provided the foundation for the more detailed work I have carried out in the second stage of the Inquiry. This has concentrated on particular areas of litigation where, in my view, the civil justice system is failing most conspicuously to meet the needs of litigants. These areas are medical negligence, housing and multi-party litigation. I have also developed more detailed proposals on procedure and costs for the new fast track. Another focus of special attention was the Crown Office List, which has a particularly important function in enabling individual citizens to challenge decisions of public bodies including central and local government.

5. In all these areas a particular concern has been to improve access to justice for individuals and small businesses. I am also concerned about the level of public expenditure on litigation, particularly in medical negligence and housing. In both of these areas substantial amounts of public money are absorbed in legal costs which could be better spent, in the one case on improving medical care and in the other on improving standards of social housing. An efficient and cost-effective justice system is also of vital importance to the commercial, financial and industrial life of this country and I was anxious to improve this, especially because of the evidence I received that there was a substantial risk of the existing system changing our competitive position in relation to other jurisdictions. Finally I was anxious to ensure that the judiciary and the resources of the Court Service were deployed to the best effect.

6. All the work I have carried out in the second stage of the Inquiry has confirmed the conclusions I reached in the interim report about the defects in the present system. This report therefore builds on the contents and recommendations of the interim report by:

(a) providing greater details as to the principal recommendations in the interim report;
(b) identifying the problems in those areas which have received special attention during the second stage of the Inquiry and the solutions I am recommending to those problems;
(c) describing the new rules; and
(d) making clear any change in my approach since the interim report.

7. An important part of my task in the Inquiry was to produce a single, simpler procedural code to apply to civil litigation in the High Court and county courts. This report is accompanied by a draft of the general rules which will form the core of the new code. In the second part of the Inquiry I have looked in detail at the specialist jurisdictions of the High Court with a view to accommodating them so far as possible within the general procedural framework embodied in the core rules. As a result of the work done by the Inquiry, it is apparent that a great many of the existing specialist rules are no longer required. Work is continuing on the more limited body of special rules which are still considered essential. Here I await with interest the views of those engaged in the specialist jurisdictions who could not express a formal opinion as to what extra rules are still needed until they had seen the general rules which have been prepared by the Inquiry.

8. If my recommendations are implemented the landscape of civil litigation will be fundamentally different from what it is now. It will be underpinned by Rule 1 of the new procedural code, which imposes an obligation on the courts and the parties to further the overriding objective of the rules so as to deal with cases justly. The rule provides a definition of 'dealing with a case justly', embodying the principles of equality, economy, proportionality and expedition which are fundamental to an effective contemporary system of justice. These requirements of procedural justice, operating in the traditional adversarial context, will give effect to a system which is substantially just in the results it delivers as well as in the way in which it does so.

9. The new landscape will have the following features.

Litigation will be avoided wherever possible.

(a) People will be encouraged to start court proceedings to resolve disputes only as a last resort, and after using other more appropriate means when these are available.

(b) Information on sources of alternative dispute resolution (ADR) will be provided at all civil courts.[2]

(c) Legal aid funding will be available for pre-litigation resolution and ADR.

(d) Protocols in relation to medical negligence, housing and personal injury, and additional powers for the court in relation to pre-litigation disclosure, will enable parties to obtain information earlier and promote settlement.

(e) Before commencing litigation both parties will be able to make offers to settle the whole or part of a dispute supported by a special regime as to costs and higher rates of interest if not accepted.

Litigation will be less adversarial and more co-operative.

(a) There will be an expectation of openness and co-operation between parties from the outset, supported by pre-litigation protocols on disclosure and experts. The courts will be able to give effect to their disapproval of a lack of co-operation prior to litigation.

(b) The court will encourage the use of ADR at case management conferences and pre-trial reviews, and will take into account whether the parties have unreasonably refused to try ADR or behaved unreasonably in the course of ADR.

(c) The duty of experts to the courts will be emphasised. Single experts, instructed by the parties, will be used when practicable. Opposing experts will be encouraged to meet or communicate as early as possible to narrow the issues between them. The court will have a power to appoint an expert.

Litigation will be less complex.

(a) There will be a single set of rules applying to the High Court and the county courts. The rules will be simpler, and special rules for specific types of litigation will be reduced to a minimum.

(b) All proceedings will be commenced in the same way by a claim.

(c) The claim and defence will not be technical documents. The claim will set out the facts alleged by the claimant, the remedy the claimant seeks, the grounds on which the remedy is sought and any relevant points of law. The defence will set out the defendant's detailed response to the claim and make clear the real issues between the parties. Both 'statements of case' will have to include certificates by the parties verifying their contents so tactical allegations will no longer be possible.

(d) During the course of proceedings the court on its own initiative, or on the application of either party, will be able to dispose of individual issues or the litigation as a whole where there is no real prospect of success.

(e) Claimants will be able to start proceedings in any court. It will be the court's responsibility to direct parties or to transfer the case, if necessary, to the appropriate part of the system.

(f) Discovery will be controlled; in a minority of cases the present scale of discovery will be possible but in the majority of cases there will be a new standard test for more restricted disclosure.

(g) There will be special procedures, involving active judicial case management, to deal with multi-party actions expeditiously and fairly.

(h) Instead of an irrational kaleidoscope of different ways of appealing or applying to the High Court against the decisions of other bodies, there will be a unified code.

---

[2] We consider alternative dispute resolution in detail in Chapter 13.

The timescale of litigation will be shorter and more certain.

    (a) All cases will progress to trial in accordance with a timetable set and monitored by the court.

    (b) For fast track cases there will be fixed timetables of no more than 30 weeks.

    (c) The court will apply strict sanctions to parties who do not comply with the procedures or timetables.

    (d) Appeals from case management decisions will be kept to the minimum, and will be dealt with expeditiously.

    (e) The court will determine the length of the trial and what is to happen at the trial.

The cost of litigation will be more affordable, more predictable, and more proportionate to the value and complexity of individual cases.

    (a) There will be fixed costs for cases on the fast track.

    (b) Estimates of costs for multi-track cases will be published by the court or agreed by the parties and approved by the court.

    (c) There will be a special 'streamlined' track for lower value or less complex multi-track cases, where the procedure will be as simple as possible with appropriate budgets for costs.

    (d) For classes of litigation where the procedure is uncomplicated and predictable the court will issue guideline costs with the assistance of users.

    (e) There will be a new test for the taxation of costs to further the overriding objective. It will be that there should be allowed 'such sum as is reasonable taking account of the interests of both parties to the taxation.'

Parties of limited financial means will be able to conduct litigation on a more equal footing.

    (a) Litigants who are not legally represented will be able to get more help from advice services and from the courts.

    (b) Procedural judges will take account of the parties' financial circumstances in allocating cases to the fast track or to the small claims jurisdiction.

    (c) Limited procedures and tight timetables on the fast track, and judicial case management on the multi-track, will make it more difficult for wealthier parties to gain a tactical advantage over their opponents by additional expenditure.

    (d) When deciding upon the procedure which is to be adopted the court will, if the parties' means are unequal, be entitled to make an order for a more elaborate procedure, conditional upon the other side agreeing to meet, in any event, the difference in the cost of the two possible procedures.

    (e) The new approach will be supported by more effective sanctions, including orders for costs in a fixed sum which are to be paid forthwith.

There will be clear lines of judicial and administrative responsibility for the civil justice system.

    (a) The Head of Civil Justice will have overall responsibility for the civil justice system in England and Wales.

    (b) The Presiding Judges on each Circuit will exercise their responsibility for civil work in conjunction with the two Chancery judges who will also oversee the business and mercantile lists.

    (c) A nominated Circuit judge will be responsible for the effective organisation of each civil trial centre and its satellite courts.

    (d) The new administrative structure will establish a partnership between the judiciary and the Court Service.

The structure of the courts and the deployment of judges will be designed to meet the needs of litigants.

    (a) Heavier and more complex civil cases will be concentrated at trial centres which have the resources needed, including specialist judges, to ensure that the work is dealt with effectively.

    (b) Smaller local courts will continue to play a vital role in providing easy access to the civil justice system. Housing claims, small claims, debt cases and cases allocated to the fast track will be dealt with there, as well as case management of the less complex multi-track cases.

    (c) Better ways of providing access to justice in rural areas will be maintained and developed.

    (d) There will be a more straightforward system of appeals. Appeals with no real prospect of success will be eliminated at an early stage.

    (e) The courts will have access to the technology needed to monitor the progress of litigation.

    (f) Litigants will be able to communicate with the courts electronically and through video and telephone conferencing facilities.

    (g) Trials will take place on the date assigned.

Judges will be deployed effectively so that they can manage litigation in accordance with the new rules and protocols.

    (a) Judges will be given the training they need to manage cases.

    (b) Judges will be encouraged to specialise in such areas as housing and medical negligence, and will be given the appropriate training to ensure that they understand the legal and technical issues fully.

    (c) Cases will be dealt with by the part of the system which is most appropriate. The distinctions between the county courts and High Court and between the divisions of the High Court will be of reduced significance.

    (d) Judges will have the administrative and technological support which is required for the effective management of cases.

The civil justice system will be responsive to the needs of litigants.

    (a) Courts will provide advice and assistance to litigants through court-based or duty advice and assistance schemes, especially in courts with substantial levels of debt and housing work.

    (b) Courts will provide more information to litigants through leaflets, videos, telephone helplines and information technology.

    (c) Court staff will provide information and help to litigants on how to progress their case.

    (d) There will be ongoing monitoring and research on litigants' needs.

10. My inquiry is concerned with the procedure of the civil courts. I have not dealt directly with the funding of litigation, but there are other developments in this area which will affect the new landscape I have just described. The most significant recent development in the funding of civil litigation is the current review of legal aid, on which there has been close co-operation between my Inquiry Team and the Legal Aid Reform Team.[3]

11. It is essential that the reforms of legal aid should take into account and support the recommendations I am making. The reform of civil procedure which I am proposing will be more effective if:

---

[3] We consider legal aid reform later in this chapter.

    (a) legal aid funding is available for pre-litigation resolution and ADR (including the costs of an expert conducting expert adjudication of small claims and cases on the fast track);

    (b) public funding is available for in-court advice services, especially on housing issues;

    (c) legal aid is available for solicitors and barristers providing 'unbundled' legal services to parties conducting their own cases on the fast track;

    (d) the Legal Aid Board's decisions take into account the court's allocation of a case to the appropriate track, and any directions of the court as to the future management of the case; in all cases but especially in multi-party actions;

    (e) the legal aid reforms recognise the importance of ensuring the survival of efficient small firms of solicitors, particularly in remote areas.

12. In addition there is the availability of conditional fee agreements and the growth in legal expenses insurance.[4] Both of these can help to make litigation more affordable, but they cannot in themselves deal with the underlying problems of excessive and unpredictable costs. Both conditional fees and insurance are, at present, available only in limited classes of cases. They will only become more generally available if costs are firmly controlled in the ways that I am proposing.

13. The Lord Chancellor welcomed my interim report and has made plain his commitment to reform. Having accepted the thrust of my recommendations, he has established an implementation team and embarked on a programme of phased implementation.

14. In January 1996 the Lord Chancellor appointed the Vice-Chancellor, Sir Richard Scott, to take on the duties envisaged for a Head of Civil Justice. The appointment is in itself a very important step. Sir Richard will be able to take charge of implementing many of the other recommendations. He will be able to provide the hands-on leadership for civil litigation which it has lacked in the past. He will be able to have an input into the selection of judges to be responsible for the handling of civil work at trial centres. He will be in a position to oversee the implementation of the other recommendations.

15. The Court Service, in consultation with the judiciary, has started to put into place the supporting structure which will be needed to introduce the new system of case management by the courts. This includes identifying the appropriate number and location of trial centres on each Circuit, and setting up a new arrangement for a partnership between the judiciary and administrative staff. The Judicial Studies Board is preparing for an intensive programme of training for judges involved in case management, based on a survey which the Board wishes to conduct to identify the special interests and needs of judges.

16. Some of my other recommendations which did not need to await this final report have already been implemented. The small claims jurisdiction has been increased to £3,000, except for personal injury claims, as from January 8, 1996. At the same time the test applied by district judges in considering transfer out of the small claims jurisdiction was modified, so that cases qualify for transfer if they are considered 'complex' rather than 'exceptionally complex'. The Judicial Studies Board is making arrangements to provide additional training for district judges in connection with their small claims work and has developed a protocol or best practice guide to promote the consistency of approach which I recommended. The option of paper adjudication, which I recommended, as of benefit in particular to small businesses and the self employed, is being considered by the Lord Chancellor's Department.

17. The effects of the increased jurisdiction are being monitored and research is being considered. I hope that the results of any monitoring or research will be published so that the effects of the increase in jurisdiction can be considered by all those involved, before any further increase is contemplated.

---

[4] We consider the role of conditional fee agreements in the provision of legal services later in this chapter.

18. I outlined my proposals for an enhanced role for ADR in the interim report and the past year has seen further developments, including a pilot mediation scheme at Central London County Court and plans for pilot mediation and arbitration schemes at the Patents County Court. I also understand that the Lord Chancellor is considering providing assistance with the ADR pilot scheme being conducted by Bristol Law Society and researching the effects of this. I welcome the recent publication by the Lord Chancellor's Department of a plain English guide on ADR entitled *Resolving Disputes Without Going to Court*, designed to make members of the public more aware of methods of resolving disputes which do not involve litigation. The new procedures I propose will emphasise the importance of ADR through the court's ability to take into account whether parties have unreasonably rejected the possibility of ADR or have behaved unreasonably in the course of ADR.

19. The interim report emphasised the importance of providing effective information, advice and assistance to all litigants and recommended that all the Civil Justice Review's recommendations in this respect should be implemented. Provision of such assistance until now has been very much a matter of local initiative and it says much for such local action that about one third of all county courts now host advice schemes. The creation of the Court Service as an agency, with its emphasis on customer service, and in particular the new management structure, now provides an opportunity to take a more strategic approach. The provision of information and advice directs people to appropriate means of resolving disputes, enables them to understand how to progress their cases and contributes to the effective disposal of court business. Just as case management involves spending time to save time, so the provision of appropriate help to litigants will result in a better use of court and legal aid resources. It will also ensure that access to justice is a reality rather than a slogan.

20. In the course of the Inquiry there has been unprecedented consultation with all involved in the civil justice system. Over the last year, judges, practitioners and consumers have worked together to hammer out new ways of tackling problems and to contribute to what is proposed in this final report. I see a continuing need for such involvement in the process of implementation. Much has been done. But much more remains to be done. The continuing involvement of all those who use the civil justice system will be given coherence and leadership by the Civil Justice Council which I recommended in the interim report. Local user committees, a specialist IT sub-committee and working groups developing further detail for the new fast track would all come under its aegis. The Council would continue and develop the process of co-operation and creativity that the Inquiry has benefited from.

21. The civil justice system in this country urgently needs reform. The time is right for change. The public and businesses want change, and the majority of the legal profession agree. The judiciary has strongly supported my Inquiry. I have been given a unique opportunity to help achieve the change which is needed.

22. My recommendations, together with the new code of rules, form a comprehensive and coherent package for the reform of civil justice. Each contributes to and underpins the others. Their overall effectiveness could be seriously undermined by piecemeal implementation. Their implementation as a whole will ensure that all the supporting elements of the civil justice system are directed towards the fundamental reform that is required.

23. Nevertheless, there should be a degree of flexibility in the approach to implementation. All the recommendations I have made, both in the interim report and in this report, are designed to meet the objectives for the civil justice system which I set out at the beginning of this overview. My detailed recommendations are based on a thorough review of the present system, including the wide consultation I have mentioned, but the objectives are of primary importance. The individual proposals should not be too rigidly applied if it is found that there are better ways of achieving the objectives. My overriding concern is to ensure that we have a civil justice system which will meet the needs of the public in the twenty-first century."

- What are the main problems with the civil justice system which are identified by Lord Woolf?

- Summarize the main recommendations of Lord Woolf which are designed to address the problems of the civil justice system. How would you describe the overall approach and philosophy behind his recommendations?

One important element of Lord Woolf's Interim Report was his recommendation for greater "case management" by the judiciary, which would signal a move away from the traditional *adversarial* approach to litigation:

> "Under the Woolf system the role of the judge prior to trial would be to be responsible for managing the case and seeing that the timetables . . . were adhered to. At present the litigants are responsible for choosing the venue for the trial and are responsible for pressing the proceedings. Under the Woolf system judges would be responsible for choosing the appropriate track for the individual case and for seeing that the case kept to its allocated timetable. Moreover, prior to trial, there would be an attempt to eliminate as many potential issues as possible and to see whether it was possible to settle the dispute wholly outside the bounds of the civil justice system. Judges would be responsible for trying to encourage a spirit of co-operation between the parties in order to facilitate the quickest and cheapest settlement of the case. In the case of fast track and multi-track cases, case management conferences, involving judges, litigants and their legal advisers would be held as well as pre-trial reviews enabling judges to keep a constant eye on the development of a case."[5]

The recommendation for an enhanced role for the judiciary in case management has been subject to criticism.

Michael Zander, "Are there any clothes for the Emperor to wear?" (February 3, 1995) New Law Journal, 154 at 538, 542, 545:

> ". . . My purpose is to call into question the main thrust of the Woolf Inquiry enterprise. I believe that implementation of many of Lord Woolf's likely main recommendations could make the system worse rather than better and could add to rather than reduce cost and delay. The terms of reference of the inquiry are very wide:
>
> > 'to improve access to justice and reduce the cost of litigation, to reduce the complexity of the rules and modernise terminology; and to remove unnecessary distinctions of practice and procedure.' . . .
>
> The starting point for any inquiry into what needs to be done about civil litigation must be to appreciate the nature of the terrain. This was sharply identified by the Cantley Report in 1979:

---

[5] Fiona Cownie and Anthony Bradney, *English Legal System in Context* (Butterworths, London, 1996), p. 188. On case management, see also I.R. Scott, "Caseflow Management in the Trial Court", in A.A.S. Zuckerman and Ross Cranston, *Reform of Civil Procedure: Essays on "Access to Justice"* (Clarendon Press, Oxford, 1995), p. 1.

'Most accidents which lead to claims do not lead to writs and most writs do not lead to trial and judgment. These cases are settled and settlement is an essential ingredient in our system of disposing of actions. In round figures, for every 9,000 personal injury writs issued in London there are no more than about 300 judgments (3.3 per cent). Outside the personal injuries field, for every 100,000 writs issued in London there are fewer than 300 judgments after trial (0.3 per cent). The figures for District Registries are not dissimilar. Any solution which concentrates on speeding cases to trial, but which makes settlement less likely or more expensive, might be bought at an unduly high price.'

In other words, the overwhelming majority of cases settle or fall away of their own accord at some point short of trial—without any intervention from the system. If that is so, why do we need new systems, new machinery? The answer given is to reduce cost and to reduce delay—and there are plenty of true horror stories of excessive cost and delay to back this understandable view.

Since the period identified as the Thatcher era it has become official dogma to be concerned about cost and delay and improvements in efficiency. Efficiency scrutinies and their progeny have proliferated all over the place. The Woolf Inquiry is only the latest manifestation of this pervasive modern tendency.

Obviously, there is nothing intrinsically wrong with reducing cost and delay or increasing efficiency. On the contrary. If it can be done without undue adverse consequences, I am wholly in favour. My concern is only to ask whether that is what is in fact likely to be achieved—and to direct attention to what may sometimes be lost in the process.

Plainly it is foolish to create new reform systems unless there is some reasonable expectation that the new systems will improve matters. The trouble is that, at least at present, there is no solid basis for making reform proposals in this field.

The first problem is that most relevant facts are not known. We have virtually no information about either delays or costs and the little information we have is more or less useless. So, for instance, we do not know what proportion of cases suffer delay in the sense of a passage of time beyond what is reasonable. Is it a large proportion or a tiny one? We have virtually no information about the causes of delay, nor how delay is perceived by litigants. We do not know what proportion of cases settle at different stages of the process. There is not even any agreed definition of delay for civil causes (In the US they look at our levels of delay with envy.)

The same ignorance exists with regard to the costs of litigation. Unfortunately, the Woolf Inquiry will produce little new information on these matters.

Lord Woolf has taken the point that the means adopted to move cases forward must be proportionate to the nature of the case. He will certainly propose various levels of pre-trial case management based on allocation of cases to different categories.

But, so far as I am aware, there is no way of identifying which cases might benefit from heavy, medium or light judicial case management—and which cases require none at all since they will settle anyway at a quite early stage. In the absence of such a method the system of allocation of cases is necessarily hit-and-miss.

Even if we had a way of assessing which cases 'need' case management, we would not be much further ahead since there is no sound knowledge anywhere as to what new systems to put in place to cure the perceived problems of cost and delay. In the US they have been working energetically on the problem for the past twenty or more years. The results, to say the least, have been disappointing. . . .

The climate for such reform here is much less favourable. It is clear from what he has said publicly that the main change Lord Woolf envisages is that the pre-trial progress of litigation would be driven by the judges and the system rather than the parties.

Cases would be assigned pre-trial to judges who, depending on the case category, would to varying degrees become responsible for overseeing and directing the progress of the case toward trial—fixing timetables (including the date of trial), dealing with pre-trial motions, holding a robust summons for directions and pre-trial hearings etc.

But English judges have no familiarity with case management as a concept. Their whole professional experience has been with a system that leaves the pace of litigation to the parties. It is difficult to imagine them taking easily to the demands of the new approach required by the Woolf reforms—for example in penalising failure to comply with time-limits. (Not to mention the very considerable administrative hassle and cost for the system of chasing compliance with time-limits and timetables—which may even require more judges.)

Moreover, in England, making judges take responsibility for case-load processing runs up against the major practical difficulty that judges travel on circuit and that so many cases are heard by part-timers. Lord Woolf's solution apparently is to have *teams* of judges responsible for case progressing—a concept likely to boggle the mind of anyone in the LCD [Lord Chancellor's Department] trying to organise the movements of judges. Teams of judges to deal with case management looks to me like a recipe for lowering rather than raising the efficiency of the system.

In my view the only way of being reasonably confident that proposed reforms will reduce delay and costs and increase efficiency is if they do not include significant *additional* procedures. The provisions in last week's important Practice Direction issued by the Lord Chief Justice mainly pass this test. The Practice Direction exhorts judges to place restrictions, inter alia, on discovery, on the length of oral submissions, on the time allowed for examination and cross-examination of witnesses, and on reading aloud to the court. . . .

Even, however, if we knew how to increase efficiency, it is by no means certain that this is what litigants most want. A study by the Rand Corporation investigated litigant satisfaction with different procedural systems for handling ordinary, mainly motor car related, tort actions in Virginia, Pennsylvania and Maryland. The study consisted of interviews with 286 litigants—145 plaintiffs and 141 defendants—almost all of whom had been represented by lawyers. The study suggests that litigants are less concerned about cost and delay and even the result of the case than is often supposed.

Winning or losing did correlate with satisfaction with the process. But the amount of money recovered or lost had only a slight impact on litigant satisfaction. The authors concluded, 'it is clearly a mistake to think that litigant evaluations of the tort system and its procedures are driven by how much they win or lose'.

Neither plaintiffs nor defendants registered any significant correlation between delay and their satisfaction with procedural fairness or the overall system. The authors concluded that procedural innovations which cut down delay 'cannot be counted on to enhance tort litigants' satisfaction or perceived fairness'.

Judgments of fairness and satisfaction with the system were equally unrelated to the costs. It made no difference whether the litigant was plaintiff or defendant and whether he paid the whole or part of the cost himself. 'Economic concerns of all sorts seemed to play at most a minor role in determining litigants' attitudes'.

Litigants' satisfaction was, however, very significantly related to their *expectations*. If they did better than they had anticipated in terms of money won or lost, delay and cost, it affected their satisfaction with the system. Most thought their cases had gone on too long—whether in the view of the researchers they had or not. Similarly, there was no correlation between actual costs and the litigants' evaluation of whether the lawyers' fees were justified.

But what seemed to affect litigant satisfaction most was whether the procedure was dignified, careful and unbiased. Impressions of the litigation process were the most powerful determinants of judgments about procedural fairness and about dignity. 'Litigants want procedures with which they can feel comfortable, but this does not mean that they want less formal procedures—informality does not make litigants either more or less comfortable'.

The Rand study certainly does not mean that we should ignore considerations of efficiency. It does suggest however that they are perhaps less important than is often supposed and that there are other considerations that are even more important.

So in regard to the likely Woolf proposals it may signify that, save for obvious and serious delay, it might be better to leave the pace of litigation to the parties than to require them to proceed at a pace determined by the court which may not be right for the parties.

One reason is that because only a small proportion of cases actually need stage management, a court-imposed system would be extremely wasteful of resources of both the system and the litigants. Another reason is that the court-imposed system would probably not deliver greater efficiency anyway. But the third is that the system may be doing more 'justice', actual and perceived, if it normally leaves it to the parties and interferes only when they are clearly behaving unreasonably.

Whichever of Lord Woolf's proposals are in the end implemented, it is vital that there is effective monitoring of the results by proper research. Ideally, changes should be implemented experimentally in a few courts. It is only if the impact of innovation is evaluated by before-and-after studies that we can learn from our mistakes."

NOTES AND QUESTIONS

- Do you find Zander's critique of the philosophy behind the Woolf Report compelling?

- To what extent should efficiency be the central goal of the civil justice system?

- To what extent should judges, rather than the parties themselves, control the litigation process?

- For an argument that judicial case management undermines the adversarial tradition and "English cultural values", see Neil Andrews, "The Adversarial Principle: Fairness and Efficiency: Reflections on the Recommendations of the Woolf Report", in A.A.S. Zuckerman and Ross Cranston, *Reform of Civil Procedure: Essays on Access to Justice* (Clarendon Press, Oxford, 1995), p. 169.

- On Lord Woolf's recommendations regarding small claims court procedures, see John Baldwin, "Raising the Small Claims Limit", in A.A.S. Zuckerman and Ross Cranston, *Reform of Civil Procedure: Essays on Access to Justice* (Clarendon Press, Oxford, 1995), p. 185. Baldwin makes a key point regarding the tension in Lord Woolf's recommendations in this area; a tension which is apparent in much of the report:

  "It is not clear whether the expansion of the small claims jurisdiction is intended merely to mop up the present overflow of cases from other parts of the civil justice system or whether it represents a genuine effort to enhance access to justice by inducing many people who are at present put off from using the courts to activate the small claims procedure in the future. If the objective is the latter (and there are many indications in the report that Lord Woolf is genuinely concerned about limited access), it is difficult to see how it is to be achieved without substantial corresponding increases in resources—something that Lord Woolf explicitly states in his report will not be needed to implement his proposals in their entirety (p. 190)."

The proposed "fast track" procedure has also been criticised on the grounds that it will compromise the pursuit of "truth" itself.

Conrad Dehn, Q.C., "The Woolf Report: Against the Public Interest?" in *Reform of Civil Procedure: Essays on "Access to Justice"* (A.A.S. Zuckerman and Ross Cranston, eds., Clarendon Press, Oxford, 1995), p. 149:

"The principal objective of the English civil justice system up to now has always been justice, to get at the truth as to what happened, who said and did what and why. Until now all proposals to reform the system have been designed to further this objective, by for example reducing the importance of technicalities and avoiding surprise. This Report is I think the first to recommend proposals calculated to make the achievement of this objective less likely.

The Report recognises the conflict between achieving this objective and the expenditure of time and money but in recommending that the achievement of this objective should no longer be put first, it does not in my view give sufficient weight to the fact that there are many parties and witnesses who give false evidence to serve their own interests, or because they are prejudiced, or because they are forgetful of matters inconsistent with their own interests, that it is intolerable and likely to be so regarded by the other party and possibly also by the public if such people can not be properly challenged and can therefore get away with their false evidence, and that it is only by the expenditure of time and money on the two instruments of discovery of documents and cross-examination, fashioned for that purpose, that they can be properly challenged.

It follows therefore that if these minor claims are to be determined in the manner suggested by the Report the chance of the truth being arrived at, of the result being one that accords with justice, must be materially reduced."

In a somewhat different vein, Zuckerman suggests that the problem with the civil justice system lies in the cost system for lawyers in this country, and contrasts it with the German system.

A.A.S. Zuckerman, "Lord Woolf's Access to Justice: *Plus ça change . . .*" (1996) 59 M.L.R. 773 at 795:

"It is widely accepted there there is something wrong with a system of civil justice in which the cost of taking a dispute to court is unpredictable, disproportionate and unlimited. Lord Woolf has sought to bring about a cultural change. He has proposed measures for reducing the cost and duration of litigation and for achieving a measure of reasonable proportionality between the value of the subject-matter in dispute and the cost of the legal resolution. His primary aim is to reduce the amount of work involved in litigation, and thereby costs. He proposes to achieve this by judicial case management, which will pass the control over the intensity and pace of the litigious process from lawyers to judges. He also envisages greater standardisation of procedure, whereby straightforward cases will be litigated by a fast simplified process.

Admirable as these proposals are, they do not directly address the cause of high costs. The high level of costs is the natural outcome of the economic incentives possessed by lawyers, whose remuneration rises as litigation becomes more complicated and lengthy. The history of law reform shows that a simplification of procedure is not enough to produce savings as long as there are incentives to devise new complications. Even judicial controls are vulnerable to being subverted by those with an economic interest to do so.

The German system proves the effectiveness of the strategy of reversing the economic incentives. In Germany, lawyers are paid a fixed litigation fee, which represents a small and reasonable proportion of the value of the dispute. As a result, they have no reason to complicate litigation unnecessarily. Access to justice in Germany is affordable by large sections of the public because costs are low. The predictability of costs has led to a thriving litigation cost insurance which places litigation within the reach of even citizens of modest means. Consequently, there is a greater volume of litigation in Germany which, in turn, enables lawyers to generate high incomes without subvention by the public purse.

Lord Woolf felt, presumably, that it was politically impractical to recommend even a mild form of fixed costs litigation due to implacable resistance by the legal profession to any limitation on the fees that lawyers may charge. His suggestions of fixed fees in the fast-track procedure represent a valiant effort to introduce some kind of a fixed cost system. Unfortunately, the fees under this system are neither fixed nor cheap.

Indeed, by comparison to costs in Germany, they are huge. In Germany, the costs in respect of a claim for £8,850 would be as follows. The lawyer will receive £1,260, which is about half of what Lord Woolf envisages as solicitor's fees alone (assuming the top band), and a mere quarter of the combined figure of £5,000 in respect of solicitor's fee and advocacy fee. German law allows only a fixed disbursement fee of £18, whereas there is no limit on the English comparable expenses. However, in Germany there will be a court fee payable of £510, which is considerably higher than the English court fee. Let us assume that some additional disbursements would be incurred in Germany in respect of expert witnesses and that they are of the same level as in England. The total cost in Germany will therefore be £2,288. This is still only about half the £5,500 English figure, which makes no allowance for court fees and which excludes any interlocutory applications.

The history of procedural reform, both recent and remote, shows the ineptness of the indirect approach. Attempts to cut down costs by simplifying procedure, by judicial pressure or by enouraging clients to resist rising costs have all been tried and found wanting. There is no alternative to a direct attack on the economic incentives to complicate and protract the litigation process. But a serious challenge to the vested interests of the legal profession cannot come just from a lone reformer, however bold and exalted. It must involve determined intervention at government level. Until this happens, experience will continue to dispel our hopes of improvement and litigation costs will remain as exorbitant as they have been for a very long time."

NEW DEVELOPMENTS IN THE CIVIL JUSTICE SYSTEM

In this section, we consider some new developments in the civil justice system which are ongoing. However, we should also look at these procedural innovations, and, indeed, at Lord Woolf's proposals, in a broader context. Cappelletti explains how we can understand civil justice reform in terms of the broader access-to-justice *movement*.

Mauro Cappelletti, "Alternative Dispute Resolution Processes within the Framework of the World-Wide Access-to-Justice Movement" (1993) 56 M.L.R. 282 at 283:

"The access-to-justice movement, as a theoretical approach, while certainly rooted in the realistic criticism of formalism and legal dogmatics, tends toward a vision more faithful to the complexity of human society. While the normative component of the law is not denied, it is seen as *one* element, and quite often not even the principal one of the law. The primary element is the *people, with all their cultural, economic and psychological features*. Moreover, the institutions and processes are prominent in this realistic vision. The result of the access-to-justice approach is a 'contextual' conception of the law. . . .

The idea of access is the historic response to criticism of liberalism and the *rule of law*. Such criticism, in its extreme expressions, maintains that the traditional civil and political liberties are a futile promise, indeed a deception for those who, because of economic, social and cultural reasons *de facto*, have no capacity to accede to and to benefit from those liberties. The access movement then undertakes to analyse and to search for the ways to overcome the *difficulties* or *obstacles* which make civil and political liberties non-accessible to so many people. With specific regard to civil procedure, there are three basic *obstacles* to overcome.

First is the *economic obstacle*, that is, the *poverty* of many people who, for economic reasons, have no or little access either to *information* or to *adequate representation*. Here the access movement, in its 'first wave,' has become the proponent of, and has focused its research interests on, such devices as legal aid and advice . . . . In addition to legal aid and advice, an alternative has been emerging, 'legal expenses insurance,' the growth of which in Europe has been documented for a number of years . . . .

The second obstacle (the 'second wave' in the access-to-justice movement) . . . is the one I used to call the *organisational* obstacle . . . which reflects some of the most important features of our epoch. These features are expressed by the so-called 'diffuse' or collective (group) rights and interests, which represent a phenomenon typical of, and of growing importance in, modern societies. One of the fundamental characteristics of contemporary societies is reflected in the transformation of the economy from one based primarily on individual relationships—one-to-one relationships—to one in which production, distribution and consumption have become *mass phenomena*. Similarly, 'social rights' have emerged as most important. Now, social rights typically bring about, or tend to bring about, benefits for broad categories of formerly discriminated or weak persons: children, women, old people, racial or linguistic minorities, those affected by a handicap, etc. In all these cases, the individual alone is usually incapable of vindicating effectively the rights involved; since these are collective or 'diffuse' rights, the only really effective protection is one which reflects the 'collective' or 'class' character of the right. The most obvious illustration is that of the isolated consumer of a good produced *à la chaine* and distributed in large quantities; another example is the case of the individual damaged by mass pollution. The isolated individual inevitably lacks sufficient motivation, information and power to initiate and pursue litigation against the powerful producer or the mass polluter. Even if such an unlikely event should occur, the result would be wholly inadequate to discourage the mass-wrongdoer from continuing the profitable damaging activities; the individual plaintiff would be the 'owner' of an insignificant *fragment* of the damage involved. Hence, it has become clear that there is here a newer kind of 'poverty,' let us call it *organisational poverty*, which makes judicial protection totally inefficient, unless such poverty is overcome. . . .

Moreover, we should keep in mind that the interests involved are primarily *private*, not public in nature, even though they belong to groups or classes of people. Governmental agencies are not always sensitive to such collective, yet private interests. Thus different devices have been developed, which better reflect the hybrid but essentially private nature of the 'diffuse' rights. These devices include the 'class action,' which is especially important in the United States. . . . As is well known, typical of the class action is that one or a few member(s) of the class—a class that might extend to thousands, even millions of persons—has standing to represent the entire class, if the court recognises him or her (or them) as an adequate representative of the entire class."

GROUP ACTIONS

We now consider a development in the civil justice system in this country—the group action—which seeks to resolve some of the organisational obstacles identified by Cappelletti. The group action—which is somewhat similar to the American "class action suit"—is a departure from the traditional adversarial format in civil litigation. It involves a large group of plaintiffs, with the action arising out of an event or circumstance which affected them all. Traditionally, there was little scope for the group action in English law, but this is a circumstance which appears to be changing. Zander's description of the group action is included here as an introduction to what may become an increasingly important aspect of the English civil justice system.

Michael Zander, *Cases and Materials on the English Legal System* (7th ed., Butterworths, London, 1996), pp. 44–47:

"English law has not in the past given much scope for what are called representative or class actions but in recent years there has been a considerable development of something similar, the group action. What is in issue here is an action involving several and often many persons either as plaintiff or defendant. Sometimes such an action arises out of a sudden disaster—a plane crash is an obvious example. Sometimes it arises out of the sale to many persons over a period of time of some consumer product such as a drug.

In the United States, class actions are used on a significant scale under the terms of Rule 23 of the Federal Rules of Civil Procedure which permits such actions where:

(1) the class is so numerous that joinder of all members is impracticable;
(2) there are questions of law or fact common to the class;
(3) the claims or defences of the representative are typical of the claims or defences of the class; and
(4) the representative parties will fairly and adequately protect the interests of the class. The equivalent English rule is Rules of the Supreme Court Ord 15, r 12, which states that 'Where numerous persons have the same interest in any proceedings—the proceedings may be begun and, unless the court otherwise orders, continued, by or against any one or more of them as representing all or as representing all except any one or more.'

The English rule would appear about as hospitable as the American to a liberal view of the representative action, but in practice it was viewed much more restrictively. Notably in *Markt & Co Ltd v. Knight SS Co Ltd* [1910] 2 KB 1021, it was held that damages could not be awarded to a representative plaintiff on behalf of a whole class. ('Damages are personal only. To my mind no representative action can lie where the sole relief is damages because they have to be proved separately in the case of each plaintiff and therefore the possibility of representation ceases', p. 1040).

The courts have also ruled that the members of the class must all have the same interest and the same grievance (*Duke of Bedford v. Ellis* [1901] AC 1).

But the restrictive aspects of the English approach appear to be giving way to a new and more open interpretation—see the decision of Vinelott J. in *Prudential Assurance Co Ltd v. Newman Industries Ltd* [1981] Ch 229; [1979] 3 All ER 507. The judge upheld representative proceedings brought by minority shareholders in Newman claiming a declaration and damages on behalf of themselves and all other shareholders. The defendants sought to persuade the judge to apply the statement in the *Supreme Court Practice* (the 'White Book'), that 'No representative action will lie to establish the right of numerous persons to recover damages each in his own several right where the only relief claimed is damages'. The judge held that the White Book was wrong. A representative action could be employed even when each plaintiff had a separate cause of action, subject to certain conditions. First, the court could not make an order which would give a member of the class a right which he could not have claimed in a separate action. Secondly, there must be a common element in the claim of all members of the class. Thirdly, the action must be for a declaration and for damages, and the individual members of the class would then have to come separately and prove their own individual damages.

The *Prudential* case was followed in *EMI Records Ltd v. Riley* [1981] 1 WLR 923 where an injunction was granted to a representative plaintiff on behalf of an association of record manufacturers. The concept was also endorsed in *M. Michaels (Furriers) Ltd v. Askew* (1983) 127 Sol Jo 597 (CA) where an injunction was granted against a representative defendant, thus binding members of the class he represented without their being parties to the litigation. But in 1986 it was held that three members of a branch of the union SOGAT could not be sued on behalf of or as representatives of all members of that branch.

The first massive group action for damages along American lines in the English courts was the claim of some 1,500 plaintiffs against Eli Lilly, the manufacturer of the drug Opren. The actions were coordinated by a consortium of a small number of solicitors' firms. Instead of separate statements of claim, plaintiffs were using two-page schedules which referred to a master statement of the claim running to over a hundred pages. In July 1986 Hirst J. ruled that a number of 'lead cases' should be chosen to be litigated on the different issues of liability. The remaining actions would then be stayed pending the result in these cases."

A number of procedural issues raised by the Opren case were litigated. One, concerning the issue of costs, is particularly useful for demonstrating how the judiciary sometimes has been prepared to be innovative with the rules of procedure in order to achieve what it perceives to be a "fair" and "just" result. The judgment of Sir John Donaldson is also important for his explanation of how the legal aid system operates, which is considered in more detail later in this chapter.

Davies (Joseph Owen) v. Eli Lilly & Co. and others [1987] 3 All E.R. 94, CA.

Sir John Donaldson M.R.:
"The Opren cases need no introduction, but some features need to be emphasised since it is said, probably rightly, that taken together they give this dispute a character which is unique in English legal history.

1. *The number of plaintiffs.* There are already some 1,500 plaintiffs, although due to the time limits governing claims this number is unlikely to rise appreciably.
2. *The average age of the plaintiffs.* Opren was prescribed in cases of arthritis, which is more usually encountered by the elderly rather than the young, and accordingly the average age of the plaintiffs is higher than would otherwise be the case. By contrast, as we were told, the main Thalidomide claimants were all children. This has the three following consequences.

   (a) *The need for speed.* If elderly plaintiffs are to be compensated by an award of damages, they need to receive that money at a time when they can still make use of it.
   (b) *The size of individual claims.* The same continuing disability suffered by two people, one older and one younger, will necessarily cause a greater loss, and give rise to a larger award of damages, in the case of the younger claimant, who will have to endure it for longer. Other things being equal, the Opren claimants cannot expect to receive awards which are very large as compared with awards in other cases primarily involving children.
   (c) *The availability of legal aid.* Older claimants are more likely to have disposal capital or income which will take them outside the scope of the legal aid scheme or, if this does not happen, will lead to their having to make a significant contribution to their own costs and, if they fail, to those incurred by the defendants. By contrast we are told that in the Thalidomide cases every major claimant, being a child, was legally aided, mostly with a nil contribution.

3. *The cost of the litigation.* This will be extremely high both for the plaintiffs and for the defendants. No individual plaintiff going it alone, even if successful, could expect to derive any benefit because the irrecoverable costs would exceed the amount of the damages which he would be awarded. There is of course another side to this coin in that the defendants, even if successful, could never expect even to begin to recover the costs which they had incurred in defending an isolated claim.
4. *The diversity of the side effects.* Although the plaintiffs do not allege 1,500 different side effects, there is a considerable diversity in the complaints and each will require some degree of separate investigation. Furthermore, even where two or more plaintiffs allege the same symptoms, each might, and being elderly probably will, have had significantly different medical histories. Accordingly, in theory at least, despite similar symptoms one might and one might not have a valid claim.
5. *The concept of the 'class action' is as yet unknown to the English courts.* In some jurisdictions, notably in the United States, where large numbers of plaintiffs are making related claims against the same defendants, there are special procedures laid down enabling all the claims to be disposed of in a single action. Clearly this is something which should be looked at by the appropriate authorities with a view to seeing whether it has anything to offer and, if so, introducing the necessary procedural rules. Meanwhile, the courts must be as flexible and adaptable as possible in the application of existing procedures with a view to reaching decisions quickly and economically.

At an early stage it was realised that one essential requirement for achieving this result was that a nominated judge should take charge of all the interlocutory applications which are necessary before the actions can be tried, and Hirst J. was nominated for this purpose. With his assistance and under his guidance considerable progress has been made. Thus, for example, a system of 'master pleadings' has been evolved, as a result of which individual plaintiffs do not have to incur the expense of pleading those aspects of their claim which are common to others. Again arrangements have been made for 'lead actions' to be selected which raise common issues and for these actions to be heard first, thus settling those issues for the benefit of all.

It was in the course of dealing with such matters that the problem arose with which this appeal is concerned. Very naturally no individual plaintiff wanted to undertake the burden, including the costs, of a lead action. So unfair would this burden be that consideration was given to how, within the powers and procedures of the court, the costs of the lead actions could be taken off the shoulders of the plaintiffs in whose names they were being brought.

One thought, which seems to have occurred to many people, including commentators who are not directly involved, was that the lead action should be chosen with an eye to the plaintiffs concerned being those who not only had the advantage of legal aid, but whose means were such that they had not been required to make any contribution. In this way it was thought that the whole cost of the lead actions, which might well be a very significant part of the cost of the whole proceedings, could be transferred to the broad shoulders of the state in the form of the legal aid fund. Such an approach has very considerable merit, at least from the point of view of the plaintiffs, and I do not criticise those who have espoused it. Unfortunately it betrays a woeful misunderstanding of how the legal aid scheme works. This is a point of general importance and the basis of the scheme deserves to be better known.

Put simply, but for present purposes wholly accurately, legal aid helps those who lose cases, not those who win them. Legal aid makes 'out and out' grants to those who lose cases. It only makes loans to those who win them. This is the way it works. Mr X has a claim which, looked at from his point of view, looks reasonable. He applies for legal aid. His means are assessed, and if they are sufficiently small he will be given legal aid. According to how small his means are, he may have to make some contribution to the legal aid fund, although there are many whose contributions are assessed as nil. Subject to his paying those contributions, which are never very large, the legal aid fund pays the whole of his costs of the litigation.

If at the end of the case he loses, he may be ordered to pay a small sum to the successful defendant, but, unless there has been a dramatic change in his circumstances (he has had a major win on the pools or something of that sort), this is the extent of his liability. His own costs of fighting the action will be borne by the legal aid fund and the defendant will be left to pay all the costs incurred by him in successfully defending the claim. In other words, the unsuccessful plaintiff has received an out and out grant from the state.

But suppose the plaintiff wins, as the legal aid fund claims that he does more often than not. Then a very different picture emerges. As the successful party, he does not have to pay the defendant's costs and usually the defendant will be ordered to pay his. Let him not celebrate too soon. He may find that the defendant has no money or the legal aid fund may have to incur further expense in making the defendant pay. Furthermore, and this is very important, the defendant will, at best, only be ordered to pay the plaintiff's 'taxed costs', and this is almost always less than the costs which have been incurred by the plaintiff in prosecuting his case to a successful conclusion. So there will always be a shortfall, which may be very large if the defendant cannot meet the order for costs or if the plaintiff failed on some subsidiary issue and has been ordered to pay the defendant's costs in fighting that issue.

'Why worry?' says the successful plaintiff to himself. 'I have my damages. I have paid my contribution to the legal aid fund and that fund has met all the costs which I have incurred.' Unfortunately for the temporarily happy plaintiff, Parliament has required the defendant to pay the damages not to him but to the legal aid fund. That fund is required to use his damages to pay itself back every penny of the costs which it has incurred in assisting him to fight his case. It is only if after this has been done that anything which is left will be paid to him. It may be that nothing will be left or it may only be relatively small change.

In other words, for the successful plaintiff the legal aid fund provides a loan, not a grant, at least to the extent that his damages are sufficient to repay the loan. Put slightly differently, every legally-aided plaintiff should realise that if he succeeds in recovering more by way of damages, costs and interest than it has cost to recover them, if the money actually paid by the defendant in respect of damages, costs and interest exceeds his own costs, which after all is what he expected, he will be in no better position than an unassisted litigant.

So let us look again at the scheme whereby the plaintiffs involved in the lead actions should be chosen from those who are legally assisted with nil contributions. None of them would ever get a penny piece by way of compensation. Anything which the defendants were ordered to pay in respect of damages, costs and interest would be totally absorbed in paying their own costs. This would be a grossly unfair situation and the judge rightly refused to agree to it. . . .

In these circumstances the judge decided to make a wholly novel order. In its detail it is of some complexity, but for present purposes it is only necessary to summarise its general effect. This was that, as from 8 June 1987, where particular plaintiffs incurred costs either personally or through the legal aid fund in pursuing lead actions, or thereby became liable to pay costs to the defendants, every other plaintiff should contribute rateably on a per capita basis. . . . And here we come to the nub of this appeal. . . .

Such an order would have been impossible before 1986, when the law was changed by a decision of the House of Lords in *Aiden Shipping Co Ltd v. Interbulk Ltd, The Vimeira* [1986] 2 All ER 409, [1986] AC 965, to the effect that s 51 of the Supreme Court Act 1981 gave the court the widest possible discretion to order anyone to pay costs incurred in proceedings, even if they were not themselves parties to those proceedings.

This was subject to two provisos. The first proviso was that the order was fair and could be justified as an exercise of judicial discretion. This is not challenged in this case. The second was that there was nothing in the Rules of the Supreme Court which prevented such an order being made. It is on this second proviso that counsel for the plaintiff relies. It is no obstacle in his way, since the House of Lords was not concerned with the precise point on which he relies, that Lord Goff, giving the leading opinion, said ([1986] 2 All ER 409 at 416, [1986] AC 965 at 980):

> 'If two separate sets of proceedings are heard together, because they have common features, it may be a matter of pure chance whether the expense of presenting an argument or evidence relevant to the common feature falls within one or other of the two sets of proceedings. Sometimes, indeed, it may be very difficult to attribute costs to one set of proceedings rather than the other. It is surely consistent with the interests of justice that, in such a case, the court's jurisdiction to make a global order for costs relating to both sets of proceedings should not be fettered by the imposition of an implied limitation on that jurisdiction.'

Substituting 1,500 sets of proceedings for two sets, that is virtually this case, and it was no doubt for that reason that before Hirst J. the judge's jurisdiction to make the order was not challenged. . . .

In my judgment not only can the order of the judge not be faulted, but he is to be congratulated on producing a very fair and workable order in a novel and highly complex situation. If he had given no indication of his thinking on costs and had refused to make any order at this stage, no plaintiff could have made any assessment of his potential liability in respect of costs. If he had merely given an indication of his thinking, the plaintiffs would have been in much the same position as they are under the order, save that they would have had no order which they could appeal. As it is, they have been able to appeal his order and know where they stand. Furthermore, if circumstances change, they can go back to the judge.

The real problem here is that in relation to any claim it can happen that it will cost too much to enforce it: the costs will be out of proportion to any benefit which is likely to be obtained. Maybe the perfect legal system would get over this problem, but our system has not yet done so. Trying 1,500 cases together is much cheaper than trying 1,500 cases separately, so the plaintiffs as a group can spend more before they reach the economic limit. But however you arrange things and whether there are 1,500 plaintiffs or only one, there is always some economic limit.

That is the long and the short of the problem. Whether the limit will be reached in the present cases is not for me to say, but I see no grounds for thinking that these cases are an exception to the general rule that settling genuine disputes by agreement between the parties is almost always in the interests of *all* parties.[6]

Accordingly I would dismiss the appeal."

[Lloyd L.J. and Balcombe L.J. delivered concurring reasons].

NOTES AND QUESTIONS

- The Opren case is interesting for the way in which Hirst J. was prepared to adapt the rules of civil procedure to meet the needs of a large group of plaintiffs. For other examples of judicially led procedural innovation, designed to meet social needs, see Sir Leonard Hoffmann, "Changing Perspectives on Civil Litigation" (1993) 56 M.L.R. 297.

- As Zander points out, the Opren solution is not the same as a "class action" in the American sense:

    "Technically, the position is different from that in an American class action. Under the American procedure, the result binds all members of the class. In the English system this is not so. Any Opren litigant could in theory have continued to fight his own case after the conclusion of the "test cases". But this is pure theory. In reality, the members of the class in the English situation are just as much bound by the result. Those on legal aid would not be allowed to continue the case and those not on legal aid would not be able to afford to do so. Various preliminary matters in this litigation reached the courts."[7]

- Should the English civil justice system adopt American-style class action procedures? What are the advantages and disadvantages of the class action?

- To what extent does the group action meet the concerns about organisational obstacles identified by Cappelletti?

- For further reading, see J.A. Jolowicz, "Protection of Diffuse, Fragmented and Collective Interests in Civil Litigation: English Law" (1983) C.L.J. 222; and, on the American system, see A. Miller, "Of Frankenstein Monsters and Shining Knights: Myth, Reality and 'The Class of Action Problem'" (1979) Harvard Law Review 664; L.S. Bush, "My Brother's Keeper—Some Observations on Federal Rule 23 and Mass Tort Class Action in the United States" (1986) C.J.Q. 109 and 201.

---

[6] We will consider the virtues of settlement of disputes, and alternative methods of dispute resolution more generally, in Chapter 13.

[7] Michael Zander, *Cases and Materials on the English Legal System* (Butterworths, London, 1996), p. 45.

THE LEGAL AID SYSTEM AND CONDITIONAL FEES

While the group action is an evolving change to the civil justice system, reform of the legal aid system, and the expansion of a system of conditional fees, is a product of direct, governmental attention. It is an area which has been a priority for both Conservative and Labour administrations in recent years, driven largely by concerns about the perceived spiralling cost of legal aid. The reform which is currently high on the government's agenda is a system of conditional fees which, like the class action, is widespread in the American civil justice system. You have read about the operation of the current system in the reasons of Sir John Donaldson in *Davies v. Eli Lilly*, and it is further explained by Cownie and Bradney.

Fiona Cownie and Anthony Bradney, *English Legal System in Context* (Butterworths, London, 1996), pp. 178–179:

"One feature that will affect people's willingness to use lawyers is the cost of the service. Legal costs are high. A study of personal injury cases for the Civil Justice Review showed that in 85% of successful cases in the county court and nearly 50% of cases in the High Court the plaintiffs' costs for the case amounted to 50% or more of the compensation recovered.

The government has said that '[i]t is one of the marks of a civilised society that it provides support for its citizens in gaining access to their rights within the rule of law'. Those who are unable to pay for a lawyer can resort to either state-funded legal advice or legal aid or both. The general distinction between legal advice and assistance and legal aid is that legal advice means all those things that a lawyer might do prior to commencing or defending proceedings in court. This includes not only giving advice but also drafting letters, negotiating and obtaining opinions from barristers. This is covered by the Green Form Scheme. Legal aid covers the lawyer's work in taking proceedings. However, individuals can also receive legal assistance by way of representation (ABWOR) for civil domestic proceedings in the magistrates' court, the Mental Health Review Tribunal and a board of prison visitors.

Civil legal aid exists for casees in the House of Lords, Court of Appeal, High Court, county court, magistrates' court, Employment Appeal Tribunal, Land Tribunal, a Commons Commissioner, and for proceedings in the Restrictive Practices Court under Part III of the Fair Trading Act 1973. It is not, however, available for every type of legal proceeding in these courts and tribunals. Most notably it is not available for either defamation cases or for undefended divorce proceedings.

Eligibility for civil legal aid or legal advice and assistance depends upon a person being able to show that they fall within the appropriate financial criteria, which look both to disposable income and disposable capital held. In the case of civil legal aid the person must also show that they have reasonable grounds for taking part in proceedings and that the case is one which is suitable for civil legal aid. Depending on their financial circumstances individuals who are granted legal advice or legal aid may be required to make a contribution to its cost.

Studies done over the past two decades have consistently noted the large and increasing number of people who fall outside the eligibility rules for legal aid. In 1993 Cousins estimated that only 37% of the population were eligible for legal advice and assistance whilst between 50 and 60% were eligible for civil legal aid. At the same time governments have expressed concern about the amount of public money spent on legal aid. The last government Green Paper on legal aid estimated that there would be 3.9 million instances of help under the legal aid schemes in 1995 to 1996 and that the bill for help in 1993 to 1994, £1,200 million, was five times the size of the bill ten years previously.

Most personal injury cases do not involve the use of legal aid. One survey showed that only 11% of accident victims applied for legal aid. This low figure is not just due to the statutory limits on eligibility described above. Solicitors are sometimes reluctant to suggest that their clients apply for legal aid even when these clients are eligible. Solicitors may feel that applying for legal aid will unnecessarily delay bringing the substantive proceedings, mean that they have to undertake administrative duties because they have to keep the legal aid authorities abreast of developments in the case or they may be concerned about the reduced rates that they have to charge for legally-aided clients. This means that a substantial number of litigants must either bear the costs themselves or find some source of funding other than the state."

Genn, in her analysis of out of court settlements in personal injury actions, considered the ways in which the legal aid system works "in practice". Her work is an example of socio-legal scholarship; that is, it examines the impact of law in a social context through interviews with those engaged with the legal process. Socio-legal scholarship is an important means by which to understand how law on the books functions *in practice*.

Hazel Genn, *Hard Bargaining: Out of Court Settlement in Personal Injury Actions* (Clarendon Press, Oxford, 1987), pp. 113–119:

"[W]here a plaintiff has obtained legal aid, the situation is completely transformed. The plaintiff bears no risk *vis-à-vis* his own solicitor or the insurance company since if the case is lost the legal aid fund will pay the plaintiff's solicitor (on a common fund basis and with an automatic reduction of 10 per cent). The insurance company, on the other hand, will not, in normal circumstances, be able to obtain their costs from the legal aid fund even if they successfully defeat the plaintiff's claim. That the position of legally aided clients was very strong was confirmed by every insurance company claims negotiator and defendants' lawyer interviewed. Indeed, many of those interviewed were quite indignant about the strength of the position in which legal aid placed plaintiffs and were critical of what was perceived as the ease with which plaintiffs were granted legal aid:

'Legal aid is a very big plus for a plaintiff. This is an absolute scandal to my mind, that plaintiffs can get legal aid in hopeless cases. I think they can get legal aid in absolutely ridiculous cases, and they can then go on and fight that case to trial, and if the defendants win they don't get their costs . . . I am afraid that there are unscrupulous plaintiffs' firms and unscrupulous counsel . . . Counsel will advise that it's a runner because they know that the insurers will pay something in legal aid cases and the insurers do pay because they know they are on a hiding to nothing. (Defendants' counsel.)

It does affect my expectation of what the case might be worth as to whether it will be worth some offer or no offer, because I think most defendants faced with a legally aided plaintiff . . . will probably want to make some sort of offer: in most cases, not always. This is simply because as far as costs are concerned they are on a hiding to nothing. They are never going to get their costs out of a legally aided plaintiff. So I suppose it does affect the strategy in that sense. (Plaintiffs' counsel.)'

These extracts indicate that the harsh philosophies expressed by insurers are compromised during settlement negotiations in certain cases where the balance of power is shifted by means of the legal aid rules. This modification of the balance between the parties results in the relatively widespread practice of making 'nuisance' payments to plaintiffs when it appears to be economically prudent to do so.

The tension between principle and economics in insurance company strategy was colourfully expressed by one chief claims inspector:

'Q: *You wouldn't want to feel that you were paying on an unworthy case?*
A: I certainly would not. But I do. Yes, I do. We all do. Our business is money and economically it is prudent . . . A cause of action is a splendid thing. It's got a very substantial nuisance value, there's no doubt about that . . . I must prefer to pay my friends to defeat my

enemies than to pay my enemies to placate them—and that's a little philosophy that we certainly do indulge in. But it can be very expensive. It can be very expensive to go to court and win and to throw out a plaintiff on a legal aid certificate and to recover nothing, whereas in fact a premium would have consoled that man in the early stages and sent him home with something, with no hard feeling.'

Another quotation described the extent to which insurance companies feel themselves to be at a disadvantage in this respect and how their response may not always be in keeping with strict economic sense:

'There's always a nuisance value to a claim. Now, in a way, as a plaintiff one can play on that, and particularly so, I think, and it's probably naughty to do it, but if one is legally aided, as of course so many plaintiffs are, then even if the defendant wins, they are not going to be able to recover their costs, which means there is a nuisance value to the extent of their costs, and in a small claim that's quite a large proportion of what the claim is, so it shouldn't be too difficult to get something out of the defendant. As a defendant, particularly as an insurance company on a claim like that, well, one says one can't be taken to the cleaners all the time and every so often one has to crucify somebody just to show that it can't be done (Counsel for plaintiffs and defendants.)'

The quotation also illustrates the perception of many barristers, based on their experience of the cases that are brought to them for advice, that the majority of personal injury claims being pressed are funded by legal aid. . . . [I]n fact about half the plaintiffs who bring claims for damages have neither the benefit of legal aid nor trade union backing.

Rather surprisingly, perhaps, the attitude of plaintiffs' solicitors appeared to be substantially at odds with defendants' perceptions of the impact of legal aid on a plaintiff's bargaining position. Many of those interviewed were opposed to applying for legal aid for their clients unless forced by the need to commence proceedings and, when questioned, did not regard legal aid as a particular bonus for clients. This may be a result of the perception of many solicitors that applications for legal aid tended to introduce additional delay in the processing of claims. It may also be evidence of another potential conflict of interest between solicitor and client . . . Although obtaining legal aid is in the interest of an eligible plaintiff, it may mean that his solicitor has to accept a reduced level of costs as a result of the 10 per cent reduction rule.

In a questionnaire completed by solicitors, almost two-thirds of respondents (61 per cent) agreed with the statement, 'Applying for legal aid delays proceedings'. Further, some 15 per cent of solicitors answering the postal questionnaire *disagreed* with the statement, 'legal aid encourages defendants to make offers'.

In interviews solicitors frequently stated that they would not always advise an eligible client to apply for legal aid. The usual reasons for this related to the delay it might introduce, the administrative burden of keeping the authorities informed, and the potential impact on their costs. . . .

On the evidence of the interviews with solicitors, there is clearly a problem in the financing of personal injury litigation. The only solicitors who found personal injury work particularly profitable were those who did a large amount, had an efficient system, and concluded claims quickly: for example, those firms who specialized in personal injury work on behalf of trade unions. Civil litigation is not as profitable in this country as other legal work. It is, as we have seen, time consuming. Bills of costs are based on the amount of work done, not on the size of the claim, but there is none the less a relationship between the amount of damages at stake and the size of the bill that can reasonably be submitted at the conclusion of the case. . . . Thus a solicitor cannot build up disproportionate costs without running the risk that the costs will be questioned. If a claim is settled but the costs disputed, it will involve more delay before the solicitor can recoup his costs. . . .

The influence of resources thus has an effect at all stages of the claims process. If there is a practical limit to the amount of costs that can be recovered, solicitors may tend to economize on investigation research and the accumulation of evidence. This determines the quality of information available upon which to base bargaining strategy. It may impede the ability of the solicitor to progress the claim quickly in order to push defendants into making early offers of settlement. Where the plaintiff is privately funded there may be a natural reluctance to plunge the plaintiff into proceedings. . . . The question of finance also adds a further dimension to the uncertainty about success, in the sense that failure involves not only the loss of potential damages, but the risk of having to pay legal costs:

> 'Very largely, you're giving advice on inadequate information, but for the reasons I've said, that solicitors haven't had the money or the time to go and see these people . . . It's not so much that the work is not lucrative, it's that the paymasters won't pay what it would cost to have a Rolls-Royce service. The money you get from legal aid is appalling—plus the deduction for some reason which I don't understand; in civil cases, we all have to take 10 per cent off to help pay for it, which seems to me monstrous. The criminal people don't have to. And the unions only have limited coffers . . . The plaintiff who is neither legally aided nor union aided is in a hopeless position. How is he going to be able to afford to pay for doctors and experts? It's impossible. (plaintiffs' counsel.)'"

As Genn's interviews suggest, the legal aid system is perceived as having problems. For those who do not qualify for legal aid, financing legal proceedings can be prohibitively expensive. And the costs of the legal aid system are perceived to be becoming prohibitive. The impact of legal aid on the relative bargaining power of plaintiffs and defendants also might be perceived by some to be a problematic aspect of the system (although it could be said that the relatively strong bargaining position of defendants *vis-à-vis* non-legally aided plaintiffs is more problematic!). In any event, the legal aid system is in the midst of reform and "modernisation". Zander explains some of the changes, and offers a critical commentary.

Michael Zander, "The Government's Plans on Legal Aid and Conditional Fees" (1998) 61 M.L.R. 538 at 546:

Reform of Legal Aid

"Radical proposals for the reform of legal aid were brought forward by Lord Mackay, Lord Chancellor in the then Conservative Government, in a Green Paper published in May 1995 and then a White Paper published in June 1996. Lord Mackay's proposals were subjected to fierce criticism by lawyers and non-lawyers alike. Lord Irvine of Lairg, writing as Shadow Lord Chancellor, castigated them. In particular, he rejected Lord Mackay's proposed cap on legal aid expenditure, though on the other hand, he said that there would be no more money for legal aid under a future Labour Government. He did not explain how this circle would be squared. Lord Irvine's first pronouncement as Lord Chancellor on his policy with regard to legal aid was in his speech to the Law Society's annual conference in Cardiff on 18 October 1997. It appeared from his speech that his plans for legal aid were even more radical and controversial than anything proposed by Lord Mackay. He said that conditional fee agreements (CFAs) would be extended to all money and damages actions and that legal aid for all such claims would be abolished. This proposal produced consternation and a storm of criticism. . . .

    This battering had some result. On 5 March 1998 Lord Irvine published a consultation paper—*Access to Justice with Conditional Fees*—in which the Government outlined those of its proposals on legal aid that it thought could be implemented swiftly without primary legislation. The Consultation Paper confirmed that, subject to the consultation exercise, CFAs would be extended to all money and damages claims. Legal aid would be abolished for personal injury litigation, other than non-medical negligence cases. Legal aid would also be withdrawn from disputes about inheritance; matters affecting the administration of a trust or relating to the position of directors of companies or the interests of minority shareholders; partnerships disputes; boundary disputes; and 'cases pursued in the course of business'. All such cases should be financed through CFAs. 'In competition for the use of taxpayers' money, the Government does not believe that these categories can command sufficient priority to warrant continued coverage within legal aid'. According to the Consultation Paper, these changes would lead to some 60 per cent of money or damages claims being removed from the scope of the legal aid scheme. The remaining 40 per cent of cases would be dealt with after it had been shown that CFAs worked and that the insurance industry had sensible answers to the issues posed. . . .

The storm of criticism provoked by Lord Irvine's legal aid plans had therefore persuaded the Government to moderate its views. Legal aid would continue to be available—at least for the time being—for housing cases; and for money and damages claims where the assisted person is the defendant. In regard to those categories the Consultation Paper stated that the Government believed that, once conditional fees were extended, the necessary insurance products and experience would become available 'reasonably quickly to allow it to remove the remaining categories from the scope of legal aid'. But it wanted to give both lawyers and the insurance industry the time needed to get experience to be able to handle such cases. . . .

The resources available for legal aid, the Lord Chancellor said, were finite. The days of 'free-flowing legal aid' were gone forever. 'No Government could tolerate an ever-growing, demand-led budget that just cannot be controlled.' The fact is that every Government since the inception of the scheme in 1949 has tolerated an ever growing, demand-led budget for legal aid. This, it might be said, has been one of the chief glories of the English system—that the use of the scheme was determined by the numbers of eligible citizens with proper cases who came forward to use it. Lord Mackay was the first Lord Chancellor to adopt the Treasury view that this was no longer to be tolerated. . . .

In his speech in Cardiff Lord Irvine went on to say that legal aid would in time be restricted to providers who had a contract with the Legal Aid Board. Providers would be franchised by the Board. Franchising would be broadened by the addition of a new dimension to permit monitoring of quality of the work done. One way of measuring quality would be to test firms' success in predicting the outcome of cases! The restriction of legal aid to franchised providers with contracts will drastically reduce the number of access points for members of the public seeking legally aided services. . . .

Another change announced by the Lord Chancellor in his Cardiff speech was that the merits test for civil legal aid would be tightened. Lawyers advising that legal aid should be granted would be required to give predictions in the form of precise percentages as to the chances of success. Unless the litigation concerned something vital such as keeping a roof over one's head, at least a 75 per cent prospect of success would be required. 'No prudent person would run the risk of litigating out of his own resources with less than a 75 per cent likelihood of success.' If this were implemented it could have a serious dampening effect on the grant of legal aid—which, no doubt, is why it is being proposed. . . .

Potentially the most positive part of Lord Irvine's plan for legal aid is the plan for a Community Legal Service. This had already been trailed in the Labour Party's Election Manifesto: 'We will develop local, regional and national plans for the development of Legal Aid according to the needs and priorities of regions and areas'. In his Cardiff speech Lord Irvine said that the principal aim of a Community Legal Service would be to help people decide if their problem is really a legal one and to point them in the right direction. This would involve the coordination of Citizens' Advice Bureaux and other information and advice centres into a coherent scheme. 'Local communities should have a strong say in the development of information and advice services which meet their needs.' But in the House of Lords debate Lord Irvine painted a broader and more exciting role for the proposed Community Legal Service: 'The service could provide telephone helplines; education in rights and obligations; legal advice on the Internet; referrals to alternative dispute resolution; legal representation in tribunals; even interactive kiosks in every high street or supermarket dispensing basic information about the law and the legal system.' . . . But Lord Irvine warned in Cardiff that there would be no new money for all of this. 'The resources needed [for the Community Legal Service] will come from the re-focusing of the legal aid scheme . . . The re-focusing will be achieved by a combination of better prioritisation, contracting and the use of conditional fees for money claims.' For the time being it is probably prudent to reserve judgment on the project until it becomes clear whether and to what extent these ideas fructify. That will largely depend on the overall cost-savings flowing from the Government's plan to abolish legal aid for personal injury cases on the basis that it will be replaced by conditional fee agreements."

The Government is pressing ahead with the plan for extending the availability of conditional fee agreements in civil proceedings: sometimes known as "no-win, no-fee" agreements. According to the Lord Chancellor:

"These agreements will result in a huge expansion of access to justice. Today only the very rich or the very poor can afford to litigate. In future everyone with a really strong case will be able to secure his rights free of the fear of ruin if he loses. They will bring the majority of our people into access to justice. Conditional fees have been the means by which at least 45,000 personal injury cases have been brought. Many, in all likelihood, would not have been brought but for the existence of conditional fees."[8]

Zander outlines the government's plans for conditional fee agreements.

Michael Zander, "The Government's Plans on Legal Aid and Conditional Fees" (1998) 61 M.L.R. 538 at 538:

"Conditional fees have only been permitted since 1995. Under a conditional fee agreement (CFA) the client agrees to pay a success fee of up to 100 per cent of the solicitor's normal bill if the case is won, but pays nothing (or sometimes, just disbursements) if it is lost. The Law Society recommended that solicitors should not agree to a success fee that would take more than 25 per cent of the damages. CFAs have so far only been permitted for personal injury (PI) claims, for insolvency cases and for claims under the European Convention on Human Rights. Research by the Policy Studies Institute (PSI) suggests that so far they are basically used only for PI cases, in respect of which the Law Society negotiated a very attractive insurance arrangement under which for a modest premium the client is protected against the risk of losing. It seems that new policies through Accident Line Protect are running at the rate of some 1,500 a month. . . .

In his Cardiff speech the Lord Chancellor said that his officials would be consulting 'on the maximum possible extension of conditional fee agreements to all civil proceedings, other than family cases'. CFAs had been working well in the personal injury field. ' "No win-no fee" ' agreements', he said, 'are for the great majority of people the only practicable way of pursuing their rights'. Legal aid would continue for all civil cases not claiming damages or other money—such as matrimonial and other family law work, care of children, judicial review and the threat of homelessness, plus the whole of criminal legal aid. But in damages actions and money claims those who previously would have been eligible for legal aid would be in the same position as those on middle or higher incomes. 'Taking forward a civil case will depend on whether or not it has the merit to persuade a lawyer to handle it on a "no win, no fee" basis. The decision whether or not to go ahead with any particular case will depend on its strength, not on the financial resources of the client.' The chief justification given by Lord Irvine in Cardiff for this radical approach was equality between the poor and the rest of the population."

NOTES AND QUESTIONS

- Why are conditional fee agreements such an attractive policy option as a partial replacement for the legal aid system?

[8] Press Release: Lord Chancellor's Department (July 29, 1998).

- Do you agree with the legal aid reform package? Discuss.

- To what extent do the proposed reforms correct problems which were identified in Genn's research?

- For further reading on reform of legal aid, see Richard Moorhead, "Legal Aid in the Eye of a Storm: Rationing, Contracting, and a New Institutionalism" (1998) 25 Journal of Law and Society 365.

ENFORCEMENT OF JUDGMENTS

It is easily forgotten that obtaining a positive result in civil proceedings frequently is not the end of the plaintiff's story. In order to actually recover damages, the plaintiff must seek *enforcement* of the judgment. That is, the plaintiff must somehow *get* the damages from a defendant who, not surprisingly, will be reluctant to part with his or her money. This is another area of the civil justice system which the government is keen to reform.

The Lord Chancellor Lord Irvine, "And justice for everyone", *The Guardian*, April 4, 1998, p. 14:

"Having spent a working lifetime in the courts, I have to be honest and say that they often fail to provide the service which they should to those seeking justice. I am committed to changing this—simplifying procedures, speeding up processes, and opening up access to the courts to millions of ordinary people and not just those who are very rich or very poor.

Going to court is rarely a pleasant business, even for those with a strong case. The system is unfamiliar, it can often take a long time, and it can be expensive. But having won your case, does the defendant do what the court has ordered? Too often he or she does not. Too often the defendant evades efforts to force compliance with the judgment. Too often the system is failing people just when they thought their ordeal was over.

That is why I have launched a major review of the enforcement of civil court judgments as part of our wider reforms of the justice system. Many people find that they have to go back to court after judgment to issue further proceedings for enforcement—and even then they are unsuccessful in obtaining what is due to them.

Consumer groups, Citizens' Advice Bureaux and the National Audit Office have criticised the effectiveness of the current arrangements. I have to agree with them. Research conducted by Professor John Baldwin of the University of Birmingham suggests that, six months after the court's decision, more than one-third of successful litigants have been unable to secure payment of all of what the court had ordered should be paid.

Worse, almost one in seven never obtains satisfaction. This is a state of affairs which cannot be allowed to continue.

That is why this review is so important. I believe it is essential in providing this country with real access to justice and an effective civil justice system.

First, the mechanisms for enforcement need to be looked at. The main enforcement methods are obtaining an order requiring deductions from the defendant's salary, or from money held by a third party on his or her behalf, commonly a bank or building society, and authorising the bailiffs or the sheriff to recover money, seize goods or repossess property. We need to know how effective these methods are and how they could be improved.

One way might be to provide better guidance for claimants on the suitability of the various methods. Another might be to find better ways of accessing more detailed information about defendants' financial circumstances. Both of these would help people to target enforcement in a way most likely to bring success.

We will be looking at all types of ownership to see if there are assets not accessible to existing enforcement mechanisms. We will also examine the powers of bailiffs to determine whether they need to be changed.

We will also consider whether some form of agency should be responsible for carrying out these enforcement procedures.

Part of the problem is that cynical defendants can play the system to try to spin out the time before they pay up. They hope that claimants will give up altogether. We want to make it much harder for those with the ability to pay their debts to avoid payment. Of course, we will look to protect the position of those in genuine financial hardship.

Enforcement of civil court judgments, like most parts of the justice system, is a complex area. Nevertheless, I want the review to move as quickly as it can, so that we can have reforms in place during this Parliament.

I want to reform our court system and rebuild public confidence. Nothing could undermine that confidence more than the idea that people could be unable to obtain the justice that satisfaction of a judgment represents. This review sets us on a course to reform this and to make the courts work better for all."

REFORM OF APPEALS PROCEDURES

The process of reform also extends to the appeals procedures. Once again, the focus is on increased efficiency.

Press Release: Lord Chancellor's Department, "Lord Chancellor Set to Announce Reforms to Civil Appeal System" (July 22, 1998):

"Judges were told this evening that plans for major reform of appeals procedures in the civil courts are about to be published. The Lord Chancellor, Lord Irvine, said he will be issuing two consultation papers on Friday detailing changes to modernise the civil appeal system.

He said: 'I believe these changes will ensure that appeals are dealt with at the right level; that only cases of sufficient importance, value and complexity will find their way to the Court of Appeal; and that the end result will be significant savings for individuals and the taxpayer.'

Speaking at the annual Lord Mayor's judges' dinner at the Mansion House, Lord Irvine said the proposals would help the Government meet its promise to modernise civil justice from top to bottom.

The Lord Chancellor's proposals are based on recommendations made by Sir Jeffrey Bowman's review of the civil division of the Court of Appeal, published in September 1997. The proposals include:

- allowing the Court of Appeal Civil Division, (CA) to exercise jurisdiction in courts of one, two or three judges depending on the nature of the case;
- certain appeals which now reach the CA would be heard at a lower level - the largest category of such cases being appeals against decisions in fast track cases;
- it would still be possible for appeals which would normally be heard in a lower court to reach the CA in certain circumstances. In particular, an appeal could be considered if it raises an important point of principle or practice or one which for some other special reason should be considered by the CA;
- the requirement for leave to appeal would be extended to nearly all cases coming to the CA;
- there would be an increasing role for appropriate judicial case management;

- there is a need for much focused procedures. Cases would be better prepared at a much earlier stage in the process and realistic timetables should be set, which must be strictly observed;
- the CA would impose appropriate time limits on oral argument on appeals;
- the balance of judicial time would lean more towards reading and less towards sitting in court;
- there is a need to develop the use of information technology to support the proposals;
- information for litigants in person about the appeal process and what it can deliver must be available at an early stage. The information must be easily understandable and delivered in a range of different ways; and
- the Civil Appeals Office would be headed by a single administrative head, accountable to the Chief Executive of the Court Service and have line management responsibility for every member of staff in the Civil Appeals Office."

ESSAY QUESTION

What are the major problems with the civil justice system in this country today? Devise a reform agenda.

13

PROCEDURAL ASPECTS OF LEGAL METHOD: THE ADVERSARIAL SYSTEM AND ALTERNATIVES

In this chapter, we continue our focus on procedural issues and the civil justice system. Our attention turns more broadly to the adversarial system and the philosophy behind it, as we examine approaches to dispute resolution. We begin with "alternative dispute resolution" (ADR) which, as we saw in Chapter 12, has assumed an important place in the reforms advocated by Lord Woolf in his report *Access to Justice*. We then look at the tribunal system as an alternative to formalised judicial proceedings.

OVERVIEW OF THE ADVERSARIAL SYSTEM

John D. Farrar and Anthony M. Dugdale, *Introduction to Legal Method* (3rd ed., Sweet and Maxwell, London, 1990), pp. 62–73:

"It might seem obvious that to solve a dispute you must first discover the true facts, but we should remember that this has not always been the case in our legal system and neither is it entirely the case today. For much of the Middle Ages our courts did not find the facts at all, rather they presided over an ordeal. If the disputant survived the ordeal, *e.g.* his hand had not festered after being burnt by a hot iron, then God had intervened in his favour and that proved his allegations. This method of resolving disputes is often referred to as that of 'Proof' as opposed to 'Trial.' It worked because it was acceptable to the parties. Today it would seem irrational and hence unacceptable but we still accept other methods which do not involve finding the facts, *e.g.* mediation of industrial disputes. To understand why this is so we should perhaps remember one further point; there is often no absolute, irrefutable way of determining what facts are true. Truth is as elusive in this as in other contexts. Consequently the question is not how we should find the truth but rather what are the acceptable means of dealing with a dispute as to the facts. In this chapter we shall examine the two main approaches taken by adjudicators, the adversarial and inquisitorial methods, and then after comparing the merits of these methods, examine briefly the other approaches adopted in our society.

The adversarial method

The adversarial method is one which gives the parties and their lawyers a great deal of control over the way in which facts are collected and presented. Each party to the dispute will collect its own evidence in the form of witnesses, expert opinions, etc, and will present that evidence to the court in the way most favourable to its own version of the facts and adverse to that of the other party. The role of the judge is limited to that of an umpire, ensuring that the evidence is presented in accordance with certain ground rules such as the rule that a lawyer must not ask his own party's witnesses questions which 'lead' them to a particular answer, *e.g*, 'You did see X, didn't you?' The judge must not intervene to question a witness himself save to clarify an ambiguity in the witness's answers. When all the evidence has been presented he must decide which version of the facts he prefers. He may very well feel that some important evidence is missing, that the lawyers have failed to ask the right questions or call all the relevant witnesses but there is nothing he can do about that. He must make up his mind on the basis of the evidence presented by the two adversaries.

It is perhaps easier to understand the adversarial method by looking at a particular case, and we will take as our example *Whitehouse v. Jordan*[1] . . . . Mrs Whitehouse . . . had alleged that Mr Jordan, the obstetrician, had negligently pulled too hard with the forceps when attempting to deliver her baby. Her evidence consisted of her own story that she had been lifted *up off* the delivery bed by the pulling and the evidence of two expert witnesses, retired obstetricians, who having read the hospital notes and heard her story concluded that she had been pulled *down off* the bed and that Mr Jordan must therefore have been acting negligently. For Mr Jordan there was his own evidence. He could not remember the facts in any detail but on the basis of his notes concerning the delivery and his usual practice he was certain that he could not have pulled so hard. In his support was the evidence of his junior colleague present at the delivery, that of his superior to whom he reported the events and that of four consultant obstetricians who concluded from the hospital notes that he had not acted negligently. The evidence of the two midwives present at the delivery was not presented by either side seemingly because they could not be traced, a pity as they might have appeared to have been more neutral observers of the facts than either of the parties.

At the trial Mrs Whitehouse's barrister questioned her and her witnesses so as to bring out their story and opinions. This process is known as the *examination in chief*. After he had questioned each witness, Mr. Jordan's barrister cross questioned them, trying to shake their evidence, probing the conflicts as between being pulled *up* or *down* off the bed. This process is called the *cross-examination*. The same method was then applied to Mr Jordan's witnesses. . . .

On the basis of all this conflicting, and in some respects incomplete evidence the judge had to make up his mind and he concluded that on the balance of probabilities Mr Jordan had pulled too hard and was liable. . . . [T]he Court of Appeal and the House of Lords held that the evidence did not justify this conclusion. The conflict of judicial opinion illustrates more clearly than the conflict of the witnesses, the difficulties of finding the facts.

Civil litigation like that in *Whitehouse* is the classic illustration of the adversarial method. The process involves neutrality between the parties. Neither side is forced to disclose more of its evidence before the trial than the other. At the trial although the plaintiff bears the burden of proof, *i.e.* in the absence of any evidence he loses, the standard or extent to which he must prove his case is simply 'on the balance of probabilities' a standard which favours neither party. . . .

The inquisitorial method

The characteristic of this method lies in the fact that the adjudicating body has considerable control over the way in which the evidence is collected and presented. Just as there are varieties of adversarial method, there are also varieties of inquisitorial method. We can illustrate two such by reference to the system for determining disputes about Industrial Injury Benefit. A person is entitled to benefit if he satisfies a number of conditions including (1) that he is an employee rather than being self-employed and (2) that his injury was caused by an accident at work. Disputes as to the first issue are determined by a government minister, the Secretary of State. In practice this usually means that a civil service lawyer will conduct an inquiry and report to the minister who will then make his decision. If the decision goes against the claimant he can appeal to the ordinary courts and have the decision overturned if it was supported by no evidence. Subject to this check, the process is a good illustration of purely inquisitorial method, with the decision maker or his investigator in absolute control of the

[1] [1981] 1 W.L.R. 246, (1980) 125 S.J. 167, [1981] 1 All E.R. 267, HL.

collection of evidence. Disputes as to the second issue are resolved by a tribunal. At first sight the proceedings before the tribunal may appear adversarial in nature; the claimant will present his case and then the social security officer will present the administration's view of the facts. But appearance deceives; the officer is regarded more as an investigator providing information for the tribunal than as an adversary of the claimant; similarly the claimant's role is to provide information and answer questions. The tribunal controls the proceedings: indeed, it may appoint its own expert assessor. The method is modified inquisitorial: the tribunal does not investigate itself but adopts an inquisitorial attitude whilst relying on the information and investigation of others.

As with the adversarial method, it is easier to appreciate the nature of the inquisitorial method by taking an example, and ours is ex p. *Moore*[2], a case concerning . . . causation of injury. Ms Moore had suffered from a form of slipped disc which she claimed was due to her bending at work in her job as a crane driver. The tribunal held against her and she took her case to an appeal tribunal. Before this tribunal a consultant surgeon gave evidence on her behalf. Government medical officers gave evidence suggesting that the disc problem was caused by a pre-existing condition and not the bending. The tribunal also heard reports of the opinions of two other doctors given in previous cases as to the likely causes of disc problems. These doctors did not appear before the tribunal and could not therefore be questioned in an adversarial way by Ms Moore. Nevertheless, the tribunal relied on their opinions and those of the government doctors in concluding that the weight of evidence was against Ms Moore. Ms Moore then asked the ordinary courts to overturn the decision on grounds that by taking account of the reports of the doctors who had not been questioned, the tribunal acted against the principles of natural justice which required a fair hearing. The Court of Appeal dismissed her claim. . . .

Non-adjudicatory methods

. . . It is obvious that some types of disputes are rarely subject to adjudication by either adversarial or inquisitorial methods. Most industrial disputes are resolved by bargaining between the parties or possibly by mediation, *i.e.* a process under which a third party suggests a possible settlement but the two parties are left to decide whether to accept it. . . .

Mediation is being used in the United States, Australia and New Zealand to deal with a range of criminal as well as civil cases involving parties who have some form of continuing relationship with each other, whether as neighbours, fellow workers or members of the same household or organisation. In many such cases, as in labour disputes, the 'win-lose' outcomes of adjudication may work against future harmony between the parties. Moreover, the incident which triggers the legal system intervention, for example an assault, often seems to be only a symptom of underlying tensions. Unlike a court which gives judgment with respect to the particular claim or charge before it, mediators assist the disputants to explore their differences and to develop a mutually acceptable formula for future co-existence.

It should also be realised that most civil disputes are settled before trial. In the commercial context the parties will often bargain rather than even start the pre-trial process. In the personal injury context, they will often start the pre-trial process of collecting evidence, but they frequently do this and devise their pre-trial tactics with the aim of forcing a good settlement rather than having the case adjudicated. In recent years American Courts have encouraged parties to use various forms of Alternative Dispute Resolution (ADR) systems in an effort to produce cheaper, faster settlements. The Lord Chancellor's Department has suggested that ADR systems might also have a role to play in the English system. In the context of criminal cases, bargaining is again important. There is considerable evidence to suggest that the practice of plea bargaining, under which the accused pleads guilty in return for a lighter sentence, is rife. Many would see this as undermining criminal justice and the presumption of innocence, trial by jury, etc. But it appears to be acceptable to the participants. It avoids the time, expense and uncertainty of a trial. It enables the parties to control their own fates rather than relinquishing the power to an adjudicator. What it ignores is the wider interest of society in seeing the innocent acquitted and the guilty properly sentenced.

---

[2] [1965] 1 Q.B. 456, CA.

One final comment: there are perhaps some disputes which can be avoided entirely. Lord Justice Lawton suggested in the *Whitehouse* case that the victims of medical mishaps such as the Whitehouse baby 'should be cared for by the community rather than by the hazards of litigation'. This could be achieved by a system of state compensation paid not on proof of negligence but simply on proof of injury. Such a scheme has been introduced in New Zealand. Similarly, it has been suggested that some criminal offences should be de-criminalised, *i.e.* either disregarded or treated as contraventions subject to an on-the-spot fine. Clearly this approach would reduce the number of disputes requiring resolution. These questions obviously raise issues of social policy, but this is true of all methods."

NOTES AND QUESTIONS

- The excerpt from Farrar and Dugdale provides a good introduction to the themes of this chapter. Note that our legal system employs both adversarial and inquisitorial methods. The latter are associated with tribunals, which we will look at in detail. Note also that the adversarial system assumes a *competitive* relationship between opposing sides, with a neutral judge in the middle. In this chapter, we will look at dispute resolution methods which emphasise the value of constructing more *cooperative* and *conciliatory* relationships between parties. You should keep these two relationship models in mind as you read this chapter.

- The *Whitehouse* case, not surprisingly, has been the subject of some controversy. For further reading, see Sally Sheldon, "'A Responsible Body of Medical Men Skilled in that Particular Art . . .': Rethinking the *Bolam* Test" in *Feminist Perspectives on Health Care Law* (Sally Sheldon and Michael Thomson, eds., Cavendish, London, 1998), p. 15.

- Can you think of types of cases that are particularly ill suited for the adversarial system?

SETTLEMENT WITHIN THE ADVERSARIAL PROCESS

The most common method for the resolution of disputes *within* the adversarial process is settlement. In a sense, this is ironic, since the character of the adversarial process demands that parties must prepare for litigation, in which they will state their positions in the extreme, rather than from a standpoint of compromise. The Woolf Report, despite its focus on early settlement, may not necessarily result in changes to the litigation mindset.

Hazel Genn, "Access to Just Settlements: The Case of Medical Negligence" in
***Reform of Civil Procedure: Essays on "Access to Justice"*, (A.A.S. Zuckerman**
and Ross Cranston, eds., Clarendon Press, Oxford, 1995), pp. 393–397:

". . . The assumption of the proposed reforms is that through the twin principles of judicial case control and simplification of the procedures that facilitate adversarialism, problems of cost and delay will resolve themselves—settlements will occur earlier. One of the themes of the report is that 'the philosophy of litigation should be primarily to encourage early settlement of disputes.' The problem, however, resides in the means of promoting settlements.

Attacking parties and their lawyers for the legitimate use of adversarial litigation tactics highlights the difficulty of achieving *just* settlements by means of court procedures. The rules of litigation are geared toward preparation for win or lose adjudication. They have not been designed to facilitate an efficient and relatively bloodless compromise between diametrically opposed positions. Will the new litigation 'tracks' and judicial managers adopt radically different rules designed primarily to promote settlement through bureaucratic case processing? Or might the new system simply represent a cut-down and speeded-up adversarial process which may exacerbate resource inequalities between the parties to the settlement process?

There is great variety in civil litigation: different types of disputes, different types of parties, and different configurations of parties. As a result it is not easy to generalise about the dynamics of litigation or to propose a litigation system appropriate to all. An instructive snippet of information which reinforces this point comes from a small survey of satisfaction with the civil justice system among corporate clients. Somewhat buried among the reported data showing widespread criticism of the length and complexity of the litigation process, frustration at delays and its implications for management time, there is one statistic which reveals that 77% of insurance defendants, expressed satisfaction with the current litigation system. This, up to a point, speaks for itself. It suggests that the current system is operating to the satisfaction of at least some defendants with deep-pockets. What represents a problem or barrier to one party presents an opportunity to another. . . .

The vast majority of civil claims are settled without trial and in personal injury and medical negligence cases settlement is clearly the norm. The Oxford study found that 97% of successful personal injury cases settled out of court. In the recent Law Commission study of damages payments in personal injury (including medical negligence) cases it was found that 94% of plaintiffs receiving between £5,000 and £20,000 in damages had settled their claims out of court, and among those who received over £20,000, some 91% had settled their claims out of court.

Settlement is so pervasive that it has been argued that in civil litigation those cases that result in contested hearings are to be considered as deviant. Therefore, when we talk about refining litigation procedures we are considering the procedures by which the parties move toward settlement rather than trial. The conduct of negotiations and the path to settlement are largely dictated by court procedures. There is no separate settlement procedure. Settlement is achieved by preparing for trial—going through the ritualistic procedures determined appropriate for adversarial contest in open court. Parties who want peace and want it on good terms have no alternative, within the context of adversarial court procedures, but to prepare for war. 'There are not two distinct processes, negotiation and litigation; there is a single process of disputing in the vicinity of official tribunals that we might call litigotiation, that is, the strategic pursuit of a settlement through mobilizing the court process.' Once the parties are committed to litigation, there are no procedures that might facilitate creative outcomes or that might minimise conflict. Negotiation within the litigation context is 'fundamentally different from the negotiations that might occur over the purchase of a house or in the context of developing a political agreement'. Indeed, if one were to devise a system in which disputes could be rapidly negotiated to a compromise leaving both parties reasonably content with the outcome, one would be highly unlikely to start with anything resembling the rules of court."

Given that in so many respects, litigation seems an inappropriate basis upon which to encourage parties to settle cases, there have developed various "alternatives" to the adversarial process, designed to facilitate dispute resolution. It is to these alternatives that we now turn.

ALTERNATIVES TO THE ADVERSARIAL PROCESS: "ADR"

As we saw in Chapter 12, "alternative dispute resolution" or "ADR" is very much on the law reform agenda. Lord Woolf strongly recommended ADR as a means of solving some of the problems he identified in the civil justice system. Similarly, Lord Mackay, when he was Lord Chancellor in the Conservative administration, advocated ADR as a means to relieve some of the pressures on the civil justice system, which he identified as:

> "first, the demand for more provision; second, concern about the rate at which the cost of justice has grown; third, questions about the appropriateness of traditional legal procedures and remedies; fourth, opposition to promoting more litigation."[3]

ADR takes many forms, and we will look at some of them in this chapter. What the different forms share is an underlying attempt to construct a more cooperative, less contentious—less *adversarial*—relationship between parties. The focus, for the most part, is on coming to an agreement that everyone can live with; rather than the "winner take all" mentality associated with the adversarial system. ADR is a means to take disputes out of the civil justice system, although as we will see, increasingly ADR is becoming something of a supplement to that system. A useful definition of ADR has been supplied by Naughton:

> "'Any method of resolving an issue susceptible to normal legal process without resorting to that process. It includes mediation and other non-binding procedures. It excludes litigation and arbitration.' A more user friendly definition might be: 'Dispute resolution without coercion.' In this country ADR is likely to describe either mediation or a formalised settlement conference although arguably it could extend to traditional negotiation."[4]

A more expansive introduction to ADR follows.

John Howard Society of Alberta, "Briefing Paper on Alternative Dispute Resolution" (online publication: <http://www.acjnet.org/docs/alterjhs.html>):

"The development of alternative dispute resolution mechanisms and programs requires the articulation of clear goals. In the United States, the formal goals of alternative dispute resolution include relieving court congestion, costs and delays, enhancing community involvement, facilitating access to justice and providing more 'effective' dispute resolution. . . .

Dispute resolution can include arbitration, negotiation, adjudication, conciliation, ombudsperson, mediation or some combination of these methods. These methods may differ from each other on seven dimensions or characteristics: whether the program is voluntary or nonvoluntary, whether the program is binding or non-binding, whether there is third party involvement, the degree of formality, the nature of the proceedings, the outcome and whether the dispute is public or private. . . .

Conciliation is a method of dispute resolution that brings disputants together with a third party so that they can negotiate with each other. In conciliation, the third party may persuade the disputants to meet face-to-face or the third party may simply convey information between the disputants. The ombudsperson approach to dispute resolution involves a third party who acts as a fact-finder to investigate grievances. The ombudsperson uncovers information in order to make a judgement about the merits of the dispute, there is little contact between the ombudsperson and the disputants and the ombudsperson arrives at an independent, advisory decision.

Adjudication involves a third party, usually a judge or jury, to hear the facts of a dispute and determine guilt or innocence or civil liability. Disputants present arguments and proof

---

[3] Lord Mackay of Clashferm, "Access to Justice—the Price" (1991) 25 The Law Teacher.
[4] Philip Naughton, "ADR Comes in From the Cold" (1995) 145 N.L.J. 383.

according to established procedures to a neutral third party who has the power to hand down a binding decision based upon objective standards.

Arbitration involves an independent third party who hears both sides of the problem and decides what the solution ought to be. Arbitration is usually entered into by agreement by the two parties that they would do so in the event of a dispute. The parties themselves decide the identity and number of arbitrators, the procedure to be followed in the process, upon what factors the decision is to be based and the extent to which the decision can be challenged. The arbitration is 'binding' if the third party can apply sanctions for failure to accept or abide by the determination; the arbitration is 'non-binding' if the arbitrator does not have any powers of enforcement. Two advantages of arbitration are that it allows the dispute to remain private and provides the disputants with control over the process of the dispute resolution.

Negotiation as a method of dispute resolution is any form of direct or indirect verbal communication in which disputing parties attempt to arrive at a settlement. Each party communicates their perceptions in an effort to develop a settlement that is satisfactory to both parties. Compromise is the essence of negotiation and there is no third party involved in the negotiations.

The final form of dispute resolution is mediation. Mediation involves an independent third party who acts as a facilitator in resolving a dispute. The mediator provides a forum within which the disputants construct their own mutual agreement. The mediator is an impartial, neutral third party who has no decision-making power and who controls and structures the negotiations, defuses emotional tensions and keeps the channels of communication open.

While there is no definitive method of knowing which dispute resolution process is best for a particular conflict, there are some factors which can guide such a decision. First, one must consider the nature of the dispute. Some disputes require a definitive solution (such as a court decision); other disputes may have recurring applications (such as the amount of damages awarded to different disputants resulting from similar harms). For example, a conflict in which no clear guidelines for resolution are available and in which any particular solution will have multiple ramifications is not well suited for adjudication.

A second factor to be considered when selecting a dispute resolution mechanism is the nature of the relationship between the disputants. If the disputants have a long-term relationship, negotiation or mediation would be preferable because these methods probe the underlying relationship rather than simply dealing with surface symptoms. If a conflict is an isolated event, the dispute may be more amenable to adjudication or arbitration.

The amount at stake in the dispute can also be a factor in determining which dispute resolution mechanism to use in a given case. While the determination about the amount at stake may appear to be a simple thing, there is not always a rational connection between the amount in dispute and the appropriate process; a small case may be complex and a large case may be simple. As such, it has been suggested that there should be a preliminary, investigative, conciliative stage which would screen out cases that do not need to take a court's time.

Speed and cost must also be taken into consideration in any decision about dispute resolution processes. For example, arbitration using agreed-upon, simplified rules may be speedier and less costly than adjudication. However, the data regarding the speed and cost of the various processes is far from sophisticated and does not include intangible costs such as inadequate dispute resolution.

The final consideration when deciding upon a dispute resolution mechanism is the power relationship between the parties. If one person has substantially less bargaining power than the other, adjudication in which principle rather than power will determine the outcome may be preferable."

You should keep all of the above factors in mind as we consider the merits of ADR. Our primary focus will be mediation, but it is important to recognise that the term ADR encompasses an array of different dispute resolution mechanisms, and different methods may be suitable to different cases.

The increasing importance of ADR in this country was demonstrated by the Lord Chief Justice's Practice Direction, which applies to cases in the Queen's Bench and Chancery Divisions, delivered on January 25, 1995. The Practice Direction includes a pre-trial

"Check List" which solicitors are to lodge with the court. Included in the check list is the question: "have you or counsel discussed with your client(s) the possibility of attempting to resolve this dispute (or particular issues) by alternative dispute resolution (ADR)?"[5]

While the attractiveness of ADR from a policy standpoint can be traced back to the pressures on the civil justice system, from the point of view of "access to justice", Cappelletti sees it as providing possible solutions to the "procedural obstacles" of the civil justice system.

Mauro Cappelletti, "Alternative Dispute Resolution Processes within the Framework of the World-Wide Access-to-Justice Movement" (1993) 56 M.L.R. 282 at 283:

"This idea [of ADR] is not new of course: conciliation, arbitration, mediation have always been important elements of the means of dispute settlement. However, there is a new *element* in that modern societies have developed *new reasons* to prefer such alternatives. It is important to stress the fact that such new reasons include the very essence of the access movement, that is the fact that the judicial process now is, or should be, open to larger and larger segments of the population, indeed in theory at least to the entire population. This is, of course, the cost of access to justice, which is the cost of democracy itself; a cost that advanced societies must be ready and happy to bear.

Alternative dispute process is an area in which the Ford Foundation developed a pioneer programme as early as 1978, which launched a broad search for what was called 'new approaches to conflict resolution,' dealing particularly with 'complex public policy disputes,' 'regulatory disputes,' 'disputes arising out of social welfare programmes,' all of which were intended to 'find ways to handle disputes outside the formal system.' . . .

[T]he search for alternatives has represented what Professor Bryant Garth and I happened to call 'the third wave' in the access-to-justice movement. Needless to say, there are here many hard questions and difficulties—perhaps contradictions, as was emphasised by Professor Abel in a well-known and often cited article ten years ago.[6] Among the hard questions to be faced, two stand out. First, what are the best kinds of institutions to be promoted? Possibilities include arbitration, mediation, conciliation and, of course, an array of simplified procedures as well as small claims courts. Second, which are the best kinds of persons to staff such institutions? These may include lay persons and, quite often . . . persons involved with and personally aware of the same kinds of interests and problems as the parties in the case. . . . Another hard question concerns the minimum standards and guarantees to be maintained even in these alternative kinds of adjudicatory organs and procedures. The risk, of course, is that the alternative will provide only a *second class justice* because, almost inevitably, the adjudicators in these alternative courts and procedures would lack, in part at least, those safeguards of independence and training that are present in respect of ordinary judges. And the procedures themselves might often lack, in part at least, those formal guarantees of procedural fairness which are typical of ordinary litigation. . . .

[However], there are situations in which *conciliatory* (or 'co-existential') justice is able to produce results which, far from being 'second class,' are better, *even qualitatively*, than the results of contentious litigation. The best illustration is provided by those cases in which litigation is but an episode in a complex and continuing relationship; here, conciliatory justice or, as one might call it, 'mending justice,' has the potential to preserve the relationship treating the litigious episode as a provisional disruption, rather than a final break of the relationship. Further, such a procedure is usually more accessible, more rapid, informal and less expensive, and the adjudicators themselves might be better aware of the environment in which such an episode has arisen and more capable and eager to understand the parties' plight. This might explain the extraordinary success of arbitration in commercial matters. . . .

---

[5] [1994] 1 All E.R. 34.
[6] Richard L. Abel, "The Contradictions of Informal Justice", in *The Politics of Informal Justice*, volume 1 (R.L. Abel, ed., Academic Press, New York, 1982), p. 287.

This country also presents most interesting developments in the area of alternative dispute processes . . . . I must mention two reports, one prepared by Henry Brown for the Courts and Legal Services Committee of the Law Society, the other by a Committee under the chairmanship of Lord Justice Beldam for the General Council of the Bar. Apart from some brief references to other countries, the Brown Report focuses on developments in England and Wales, and includes 'adjudicatory ADR processes' (arbitration and expert determination), 'non-adjudicatory and hybrid processes' (including mediation, mini trials, court annexed arbitration, neutral fact-finding experts and med-arb, that is, the amalgam of mediation and arbitration), plus other 'hybrid forms' (such as the 'moderated settlement conference'). The report also includes a valuable discussion of the 'ethical implications' of ADR. The Brown Report is concluded by a 'five-year action plan' which foresees a further and pervasive growth. The prospect for special teaching and training in ADR is also mentioned and forcefully recommended.

The Beldam Report begins with a rapid survey of some contemporary ADR initiatives in Britain and overseas, and a commentary on submissions received from official bodies. It then concludes that 'court-based alternative dispute resolution' would be of value across a wide field of civil disputes. It approves mediated negotiations as the most appropriate form for ADR to take, proposes lawyers as the mediators and visualises the process located firmly within the courts' system. The Report concludes with a proposal for pilot schemes in some county courts and at least one division of the High Court. . . ."

NOTES AND QUESTIONS

- What is meant by the fear that ADR will bring about "second class justice"? Do you think those fears are justified?

- Why might ADR be particularly suited to situations where the parties have an ongoing relationship which needs to be maintained? Give examples of such situations.

- The Brown Report proposes court based ADR. What are the advantages and disadvantages of ADR being formally tied to the court structure, as opposed to being completely removed from it?

ADR is not without its critics. A central issue is whether participation in ADR should be mandatory, as opposed to voluntary. This issue is closely connected to whether ADR should be an integral part of the civil justice system, or removed from it. Ingleby states the case against mandatory participation.

Richard Ingleby, "Court Sponsored Mediation: The Case Against Mandatory Participation" (1993) 56 M.L.R. 441 at 441, 445, 449:

"One response to the perception of a crisis in contemporary legal systems has been the promotion of mediation as an alternative form of dispute resolution. Although informal modes of dispute resolution have been under critical examination for some time, the debate has been given fresh life by the converging interest in sponsoring mediation of court administrators, or more precisely, court budget and legal aid administrators, and mediation interest groups. This is not to suggest any formal alliance or joint strategy, but rather that the two groups have a common interest and interdependency in cases being diverted from the legal system to mediators. Court administrators have too many cases and mediators too few. For these two groups the merit of mediation is an article of faith. They argue that, in relation to litigation, mediation is quicker and cheaper, more accessible, more flexible, produces solutions which are more durable and preserves continuing relationships.

The uncritical sponsorship of mediation is problematic from two angles. First, is 'settlement' always desirable? Should we necessarily assume that failure to settle or achieve settlement is a negative, dissonant feature in an otherwise well-ordered and satisfactorily functioning world? On the contrary, some conflict may be constructive and the submersion of at least some types of conflict harmful. Second, even if these goals are deemed desirable, is there any evidence that mediation, and in particular, mandated mediation, can meet them? The assumptions underlying this paper are that arguments in favour of voluntary mediation should be treated with caution. Much of the research about voluntary mediation is carried out on self-selecting samples, where there are reasons for settlement beyond the elements of the mediation process. More broadly-based studies have been cautious about the alleged benefits of mediation in relation to costs, the preservation of continuing relationships, and the impact on court backlogs. Indeed, there seems to be wide agreement with the proposition that ADR programmes have unanticipated effects, and may indeed increase the costs and formality of dispute processing. It should also trouble the advocates of mediation that the public has so far shown a limited demand for such services.

Mandation in relation to mediation may take a number of forms. The clearest is a requirement that parties attend mediation before they are entitled to a court hearing. Less directly, it may be the financial compulsion constituted by the withholding of legal aid if mediation is not attempted; or the inability to afford any other form of dispute resolution. But what of a judicial question as to the possibility of parties attempting mediation? Parties, or more particularly their counsel, might feel constrained to respond positively so as to maintain the support of the court.

In this paper, I discuss three sets of arguments against compulsory participation in mediation:

- Definitional arguments—mediation loses its defining characteristics if the parties do not enter of their own volition or the process is institutionalised.
- Lack of justification - the arguments in favour of compulsory mediation are based on unwarranted extrapolations from data about voluntary mediation. Indeed, compulsory mediation may increase the costs and formality of dispute processing.
- The rule of law—compulsory mediation represents a challenge to many of the ideas comprehended by the rule of law. . . .

Although some features of mediation, such as proceedings being held in private, may remain if the parties are compelled to participate, does mediation remain the sort of process comprehended by the descriptions offered in the introduction if participation in the process is compulsory? There has always been some ambivalence as to the justifiability of coercion into ADR. Although some would go no further than education or encouragement, others have seen coercion as unproblematic, especially if the parties maintain the right to reject whatever solution emerges from the process. The right not to settle in mediation stems from the legal inability of the mediator to impose a settlement on the parties, one of the features which distinguishes mediation from, and therefore constitutes it as an alternative to, adjudication. The importance of the term 'alternative' in the ADR label is to create a dichotomy between litigation and mediation. The writer's observations suggest that the dichotomy may be a false one, and that the practice is some way from the ideal-type. . . .

The second set of arguments against mandated mediation is based on the lack of authoritative evidence to support the claims made in favour of mediation. General reservations about such claims were made in the Introduction. In this section I expand on those themes, using data based on observation of such processes to argue that compulsory mediation may actually increase the costs and formality of processing disputes. Where mediation is institutionalised within legal settings, the process has to be described and its relationship with other proceedings clarified. If settlement results, this has to be formalised and if there is no settlement the parties have to be redirected into the preparations for a court hearing. In other words, the observed conferences revealed a less informal process than that which the mediation professionals might have envisaged and a less easily organised world than court managers might desire. Parties do not always attend conferences. Whether the reason for non-attendance is a deliberate refusal to negotiate or a genuine misunderstanding as to the date or purpose of the conference, the party who does attend has incurred the costs of so doing and received no benefit. A party might attend the conference but without the authority to settle. The lack of authority may be a legal impediment, or may result from the need to take into account the decisions of third parties, such as family members or company partners. Parties might attend the conference but not have made the required disclosure beforehand. The party who has made disclosure will have incurred those costs and will incur further costs if the pre-conference preparation has to be repeated at trial. One party may deliberately obstruct the settlement process to prolong the relationship. There is scope for practitioners to exploit the 'without prejudice' aspects of the conference by making strategic use of its procedures.

One way of overcoming such obstacles to settlement would be to create and enforce obli-gations to attend the conference and pursue settlement. But the definition of what consti-tutes 'bona fides' is not an easy question. Once the obligation to make reasonable attempts at settlement was enforced, it would be only a matter of time before it was litigated, creat-ing the paradox of sattelite litigation, where court time would be used to decide issues about a process which was designed to save court time. These obligations to settle would be situ-ated in a context where there is already considerable formality, despite the aim of informal-ity in ADR.

The matching argument, that cases be allocated to the most appropriate mechanism, is an attempt to retrieve ADR from arguments about the unsuitability of particular processes to particular cases. Yet there is no satisfactory theory of 'rational allocation' whereby ADR mechanisms could be directed to those cases which might be resolved more cheaply as a result of their use. The notion of matching processes to disputes is based on two unsustainable notions: that it is possible to create a categorisation of ADR mechanisms; and that a dispute is a single entity. What constitutes a dispute is the perceptions of at least two parties. What is appropriate for one may be more or less appropriate for another. To mandate referral to a process which does not treat the parties' legal entitle-ments as the most important consideration is to officially privilege one party. The legiti-macy of litigation is its relationship with the rule of law. The alternatives . . . have no such claims.

In this section, the argument is that compulsory mediation represents a challenge to the ideas comprehended by the rule of law. The contention is not that formal adjudication is ideal, but the more modest claim that 'professionalised justice' is preferable to the 'incorporated justice' which is represented by the increasing institutionalisation of ADR. For the present dis-cussion the most important distinctions are between: the objective rules and the acknowledge-ment of opposing interests of professionalised justice; and the absence of publicly stated rules and denial of opposition in incorporated justice.

Two ideas comprehended by the rule of law are that 'the law should conform to standards designed to enable it effectively to guide action' and 'the legal machinery of enforcing the law should not deprive it of its ability to guide through distorted enforcement.' The challenge which mediation and other forms of alternative dispute resolution pose to these ideas has already been the subject of extended discussion, which has concentrated on the publicity of adversary proceedings, the diversion of cutting-edge cases from the formal justice system, the protection of disputants and third party interests, and the separation of powers. In addition to these considerations, the data raise a third rule of law argument, an attitudinal one, that the effect of compulsory mediation is to create rules against litigation, to replace the habit of settlement in 'professionalised justice' with a rule in favour of settlement in 'incorporated justice.' That habit of settlement is converted into a rule in favour of settlement when indi-viduals are no longer constituted as bearers of rights but as components of a problem, when litigation is deviant rather than different behaviour. The danger in compulsory mediation is that this particular 'interplay or even interpenetration of law and discipline' will lead to 'dis-ciplinary power' being exercised without judicial restraint. Although, in institutionalised ADR proceedings, settlement is purveyed as a pragmatic response to the prohibitive costs of litigation, those who choose not to be pragmatic are punished (with costs rather than incar-ceration) for the deviance constituted by standing on their rights, their 'wasting' of public resources, comparably with defendants in criminal trials who are given heavier (or not lighter) sentences for disputing their guilt by a plea of not guilty.

Lest this prognosis be dismissed as fanciful, it is worth remembering that even in the 'pure' mediation process observed in the Federal Court [of Australia], it was possible to detect quasi-adjudicative features. The habit of settlement in professionalised justice exists because of the costs, delays and trauma of the court, and the rules protecting without prejudice discussions and payments into court. Its existence does not depend on being reiterated by court officials. It is difficult to see how much more promotion of settlement can or should be brought to bear, especially when such moves take place under the guise of voluntary processes. The implications of court officials or court-sanctioned mediators warning disputants against the financial and emotional costs of insisting upon their rights seem to have past unnoticed. If it really is the case that 'there's no point in looking for justice, you should just settle for what's on offer,' then why have courts at all?"

NOTES AND QUESTIONS

- Assume that the government is considering a mandatory programme for mediation in order to solve some of the problems of the civil justice system. As an advisor to the government, you have been asked to assess the implications of this strategy. Write a short brief explaining the advantages and pitfalls of mandatory ADR.

- Note that we have returned, again, to the concept of the "rule of law". Explain the implications of mandatory ADR for the "rule of law". In what sense is Ingleby using the term "rule of law" when he expresses concerns about ADR's impact upon it?

A more broad based critique of ADR, focused not just on the concerns about making ADR mandatory, has been expressed by Fiss.

Owen M. Fiss, "Against Settlement" (1984) 93 Yale Law Journal 1073 at 1075, 1076, 1078, 1085:

"The advocates of ADR are led to support such measures and to exalt the idea of settlement more generally because they view adjudication as a process to resolve disputes. They act as though courts arose to resolve quarrels between neighbors who had reached an impasse and turned to a stranger for help. Courts are seen as an institutionalization of the stranger and adjudication is viewed as the process by which the stranger exercises power. The very fact that the neighbors have turned to someone else to resolve their dispute signifies a breakdown in their social relations; the advocates of ADR acknowledge this, but nonetheless hope that the neighbors will be able to reach agreement before the stranger renders judgment. Settlement is that agreement. It is a truce more than a true reconciliation, but it seems preferable to judgment because it rests on the consent of both parties and avoids the cost of a lengthy trial.

In my view, however, this account of adjudication and the case for settlement rests on questionable premises. I do not believe that settlement as a generic practice is preferable to judgment or should be institutionalized on a wholesale and indiscriminate basis. It should be treated instead as a highly problematic technique for streamlining dockets. Settlement is for me the civil analogue of plea bargaining: Consent is often coerced; the bargain may be struck by someone without authority; the absence of a trial and judgment renders subsequent judicial involvement troublesome; and although dockets are trimmed, justice may not be done. Like plea bargaining, settlement is a capitulation to the conditions of mass society and should be neither encouraged nor praised.

The imbalance of power

By viewing the lawsuit as a quarrel between two neighbors, the dispute-resolution story that underlies ADR implicitly asks us to assume a rough equality between the contending parties. It treats settlement as the anticipation of the outcome of trial and assumes that the terms of settlement are simply a product of the parties' predictions of that outcome. In truth, however, settlement is also a function of the resources available to each party to finance the litigation, and those resources are frequently distributed unequally. Many lawsuits do not involve a property dispute between two neighbors, or between AT&T and the government (to update the story), but rather concern a struggle between a member of a racial minority and a municipal police department over alleged brutality, or a claim by a worker against a large corporation over work-related injuries. In these cases, the distribution of financial resources, or the ability of one party to pass along its costs, will invariably infect the bargaining process, and the settlement will be at odds with a conception of justice that seeks to make the wealth of the parties irrelevant.

The disparities in resources between the parties can influence the settlement in three ways. First, the poorer party may be less able to amass and analyze the information needed to predict the outcome of the litigation, and thus be disadvantaged in the bargaining process. Second, he may need the damages he seeks immediately and thus be induced to settle as a way of accelerating payment, even though he realizes he would get less now than he might if he awaited judgment. All plaintiffs want their damages immediately, but an indigent plaintiff may be exploited by a rich defendant because his need is so great that the defendant can force him to accept a sum that is less than the ordinary present value of the judgment. Third, the poorer party might be forced to settle because he does not have the resources to finance the litigation, to cover either his own projected expenses, such as his lawyer's time, or the expenses his opponent can impose through the manipulation of procedural mechanisms such as discovery. It might seem that settlement benefits the plaintiff by allowing him to avoid the costs of litigation, but this is not so. The defendant can anticipate the plaintiff's costs if the case were to be tried fully and decrease his offer by that amount. The indigent plaintiff is a victim of the costs of litigation even if he settles. . . .

The absence of authoritative consent

The argument for settlement presupposes that the contestants are individuals. These individuals speak for themselves and should be bound by the rules they generate. In many situations, however, individuals are ensnared in contractual relationships that impair their autonomy: Lawyers or insurance companies might, for example, agree to settlements that are in their interests but are not in the best interests of their clients, and to which their clients would not agree if the choice were still theirs. But a deeper and more intractable problem arises from the fact that many parties are not individuals but rather organizations or groups. We do not know who is entitled to speak for these entities and to give the consent upon which so much of the appeal of settlement depends.

Some organizations, such as corporations or unions, have formal procedures for identifying the persons who are authorized to speak for them. But these procedures are imperfect: They are designed to facilitate transactions between the organization and outsiders, rather than to insure that the members of the organization in fact agree with a particular decision. Nor do they eliminate conflicts of interests. The chief executive officer of a corporation may settle a suit to prevent embarassing disclosures about his managerial policies, but such disclosures might well be in the interest of the shareholders. The president of a union may agree to a settlement as a way of preserving his power within the organization; for that very reason, he may not risk the dangers entailed in consulting the rank and file or in subjecting the settlement to ratification by the membership. . . .

Justice rather than peace

The dispute-resolution story makes settlement appear as a perfect substitute for judgment, as we just saw, by trivializing the remedial dimensions of a lawsuit, and also by reducing the social function of the lawsuit to one of resolving private disputes: In that story, settlement appears to achieve exactly the same purpose as judgment—peace between the parties—but at considerably less expense to society. The two quarreling neighbors turn to a court in order to resolve their dispute, and society makes courts available because it wants to aid in the achievement of their private ends or to secure the peace.

In my view, however, the purpose of adjudication should be understood in broader terms. Adjudication uses public resources, and employs not strangers chosen by the parties but public officials chosen by a process in which the public participates. These officials, like members of the legislative and executive branches, possess a power that has been defined and conferred by public law, not by private agreement. Their job is not to maximize the ends of private parties, nor simply to secure the peace, but to explicate and give force to the values embedded in authoritative texts such as . . . statutes: to interpret those values and to bring reality into accord with them. This duty is not discharged when the parties settle.

In our political system, courts are reactive institutions. They do not search out interpretive occasions, but instead wait for others to bring matters to their attention. They also rely for the most part on others to investigate and present the law and facts. A settlement will thereby deprive a court of the occasion, and perhaps even the ability, to render an interpretation. A court cannot proceed (or not proceed very far) in the face of a settlement. To be against settlement is not to urge that parties be 'forced' to litigate, since that would interfere with their autonomy and distort the adjudicative process; the parties will be inclined to make the court believe that their bargain is justice. To be against settlement is only to suggest that when the parties settle, society gets less than what appears, and for a price it does not know it is paying. Parties might settle while leaving justice undone."

Armstrong explains the tension which Fiss describes, as stemming from two competing models of the civil justice process.

Nick Armstrong, "Making Tracks" in *Reform of Civil Procedure: Essays on "Access to Justice"* (A.A.S. Zuckerman and Ross Cranston, eds., Clarendon Press, Oxford, 1995), p. 97:

"The debate over the function of a civil justice system revolves around a tension between two different models of civil process: the 'dispute resolution' model and the 'policy implementation' model. Under the former, adjudication is understood simply as a method for peacefully resolving a conflict between private parties. The private interests are sovereign, and the state or public interest is limited to maximising the satisfaction of those interests in order to avoid forcible self-help. In other words, the interests of the parties must be realised, and the civil justice system must preserve its reputation of being capable of realising those interests, in order to create the incentives for disputants to use the court system: 'the rules of procedure should contain some carrots as well as sticks.' The provision of courts and legal services, or 'access to justice', may therefore be explained as 'civilisation's substitute for vengeance'.

The policy implementation model, by contrast, recognises a wider public interest. As well as observing the need to resolve the immediate dispute, this model also takes account of its potential effect on the future conduct of others. The existence of the private conflict becomes an opportunity to clarify and determine the standards by which society governs itself. Those standards include the Rule of Law, the maintenance of which transcends the interests of the private parties in order to achieve justice for those who are never involved in actual proceedings.

The difference between the two models, therefore, is one of emphasis between private and public interests. Under the dispute resolution model, the private interests of the parties take precedence; under the policy implementation model, they must sometimes yield to the wider public interest."

NOTES AND QUESTIONS

- In the case arising out of the Opren litigation which we considered in Chapter 12, *Davies v. Eli Lilly*, the Master of the Rolls, Sir John Donaldson, concluded that, "settling genuine disputes by agreement between the parties is almost always in the interests of *all* parties". Having read the excerpt from Fiss' article, do you agree with the sentiments expressed by the Master of the Rolls? Why or why not?

- Can you think of examples of types of cases which support Fiss' views against the virtues of settlement?

- Some evidence suggests that one deterrent to ADR settlements is the legal profession, which might well share some of Fiss' views. According to one study:

  "[A]s many as 84 per cent of cases where both parties were legally represented ended in both parties rejecting an offer of mediation. This compared to just 67 per cent where neither party was represented. Lawyers also appeared to have a negative influence on the success rate of mediations. Only 55 per cent of mediations were settled where both parties had solicitors advising them compared with 76 per cent of cases where no lawyers were involved."[7]

Why do you think the presence of lawyers appears to lessen the chances of a successful ADR settlement? What do these findings suggest about legal culture?

- In response to the critics of ADR, Menkel-Meadow has replied:

  "[M]ost of these critiques ignore the fact that ours is a party-initiated system —one in which the parties may choose to remove their disputes from the formal legal system at any time should they choose to negotiate privately. Thus, the key to understanding the appropriateness of any negotiation process is whether justice is ill-served by the processes the parties choose, be they public litigation or private negotiation. Difficulties abound here—what are the appropriate baseline measures of what is a good settlement or fair process? Can the parties or their lawyers make an intelligent choice of process? Do they understand enough about the differences between and among processes? Are the lawyers sufficiently skilled at either negotiation or advocative activities or both to choose the process that will work most effectively for their clients? Most significantly, which processes will produce the 'best' solution?"[8]

---

[7] Robert Verkaik, "Report: Solicitors Stem Growth of ADR", *Solicitors' Gazette*, July 29, 1998, p. 1.
[8] Carrie Menkel-Meadow, "Lawyer Negotiations: Theories and Realities—What we Learn from Mediation" (1993) 56 M.L.R., 361 at 369–370.

Menkel-Meadow's point is that it will require a more sophisticated analysis of particular cases to determine the merits (or not) of ADR as opposed to litigation. She suggests that there are no simple answers. This point is one to bear in mind as you examine the various perspectives on ADR which are the focus of this section.

FEMINIST PERSPECTIVES ON MEDIATION

Feminist lawyers and legal scholars have long considered the promise and perils of ADR. In particular, mediation has been the subject of considerable debate, especially in the family law context. The following two excerpts underscore both the possibilities and also the pitfalls of mediation; in terms of advancing an alternative approach to law and dispute resolution. We start with the case *for* mediation.

Janet Rifkin, "Mediation from a Feminist Perspective: Promise and Problems" (1984) 2 Law and Inequality 21 at 21, 25:

"The interest in alternative dispute resolution is intensifying in this country and others as well. Programs offering mediation, arbitration, negotiation and conciliation services are proliferating throughout the United States, Canada, Australia and Western Europe. These programs may be court-related or community-based. In either case, the overt justifications for mediation programs are similar. Mediating conflict as a substitute for litigating disputes has been justified by two basic rationales: First, the formal court system is not suited to handle the range and number of disputes being brought to it. Second, the adversary process itself is not suited to resolve interpersonal disputes.

While mediation is flourishing, concern about the theory and practice of 'informal' justice is also increasing. Most of the criticisms focus on the manipulative potential of informal systems such as mediation. For example, critics suggest the bureaucratic logic that supports state legality is as much a part of the process in informal and non-bureaucratic settings as it is in the formal court of law. Critics also suggest that the state, faced with fiscal crisis, achieves spending cuts by resorting to informalization, accompanied by appeals to popular participation, consensual social life, and the struggle against bureaucracy. Others argue that mediation fosters the privatization of life—the cult of the personal—and denies the existence of irreconcilable structural conflicts between classes or between citizen and state. Finally, critics claim that mediation is detrimental to the interests of women, who, being less empowered, need both the formal legal system and aggressive legal representation to protect existing rights and pursue new legal safeguards.

Although these criticisms remain, the debate about mediation lacks a careful questioning of law and alternative dispute programs from a feminist perspective. For the most part, mediation's critics predicate their questions on the traditional view of law that litigation leads to social change and that the 'lawsuit' is *the* appropriate and most effective vehicle for challenging unfair social practices, for protecting individuals, and for delineating new areas of guaranteed 'rights.'

This dominant view leaves unchallenged the patriarchal paradigm of law as hierarchy, combat, and adversarialness; and, therefore, generates only a certain kind of questioning of mediation. This viewpoint has not asked whether and in what way alternative dispute resolution reflects a feminist analysis of law and conflict resolution, and whether in theory and practice mediation challenges or reinforces gender inequality in contemporary society.

My intention in this discussion is to articulate some of the questions basic to an understanding of the relationship between law, mediation and feminist inquiry. . . . What is not yet clearly developed is how mediation in theory reflects 'a new jurisprudence, a new relation between life and law.' Further, what is not yet known is whether in practice, mediating disputes reflects feminist jurisprudential differences from the male ideology of law or whether mediating simply reinforces the 'objective epistemology' of law. . . .

Mediation in practice operates as a process of discussion, clarification, and compromise aided by third party facilitators. It is a process in which the third party has no state-enforced power. A third party's power lies in the ability to persuade the parties to reach a voluntary settlement. It involves the creation of consensus betwen the parties in which the parties are brought together in an atmosphere of confidentiality to discover shared social and moral values as a means of coming to an agreement.

In mediation, the focus is not on formal and substantive rights. The emphasis is on the process by which the individual parties are encouraged to work out their own solution in a spirit of compromise. The intervention of a mediator turns the initial dyad of a dispute into a triadic interaction of some kind. However, the disputing parties retain their ability to decide whether or not to agree and accept proposals for an outcome irrespective of the source of the proposals.

The following chart highlights some of the main contrasts between adjudication and the practice of mediation.

Adjudication	Mediation
public	private
formal	informal
strict evidentiary rules	no formal parameters—conversationalist
coercive	voluntary
emphasis on conflict of interest, value dissensus	emphasis on areas of agreement, points in common
win/lose—combative	compromise—conciliatory
decision oriented	agreement oriented
rule oriented	person oriented
professional decision maker	community lay volunteers
representation by lawyer	direct participation

Although the mediator is a neutral intervenor with no self-interest, a mediator does become a negotiator. In that role the mediator inevitably brings to the process, deliberately or not, certain ideas, knowledge and assumptions. What a mediator can do is also affected by the particular context and the parties' expectations of mediation. . . .

The rhetoric of mediation rejects the 'objectivist epistemology' of the law. Theoretically, in mediation precedents, rules, and a legalized conception of facts are not only irrelevant but constrain the mediator's job of helping the parties to reorient their perception of the problem to the extent that an agreement can be reached. The legal rights of the parties are not central to the discussion which takes place in mediation. Again, in theory, the lack of focus in mediation on abstract legal rights contrasts with the emphasis on them in legal proceedings.

These differences, however, are clearer in theory than in practice. The following two case studies reflect this. . . .

Case study 1: separation and divorce

The participants in this study were a man and a woman who wanted to separate after fifteen years of marriage. They had three children aged six, eight, and ten. They had each retained separate counsel but after legal negotiations had broken down they decided to try mediation.

The woman came to the office first. The couple had agreed to separate ten months before but still occupied the same house. Relations were hostile and communication strained. The woman said that her children were not speaking to her and she felt that her husband was turning them against her. At the initial interview the woman said that the atmosphere among them—the lawyers, the children, and she and her husband—was so hostile that resolution of their marital dispute appeared impossible. She also indicated that she thought he needed 'help.'

The husband's interview verified her description. His anger and frustration were compounded because he had lost his job and was moving out of town within a month. He wanted to resolve the dispute before he moved. He also commented that she needed 'help.'

The following is a *summary* of their concerns:

Custody:　　　　*He* wanted custody of the children.
　　　　　　　　She supported his having custody, but feared that she might never see them again. During the mediation she agreed to give him full custody of the children once assured of ample visitation rights.
Child Support:　*He* would 'take care of his kids.'
　　　　　　　　She was not in a position to support the children.
Alimony:　　　　*He* wasn't willing to give her alimony.
　　　　　　　　She was uncertain of her financial needs but said that she wanted some financial help while looking for a job. She agreed to no alimony.
Property:　　　　The financial settlement involved an extensive and complex division of property. The main asset was their house. She agreed to accept a lump sum of money and twenty-five per cent of the net sale of the house over $80,000 in lieu of alimony.

Their attitudes and relationship with their lawyers became one of the most difficult and perhaps interesting aspects of this case. Both of their attorneys initially agreed that mediation might be useful. The man stated that he planned to drop his lawyer and represent himself in court if the mediation went well. His lawyer offered to put any final mediation agreement into legal language for presentation to the court. In the end, the man represented himself with his attorney's approval.

The woman came to the project with conflicting feelings about her lawyer. Although aware that she might gain financially with a formal, contested divorce, she feared the process could irreparably damage her relationship with her children. The case coordinator initially advised her to talk with her attorney about using mediation. She did so and her attorney agreed, with some reservations about her ability to protect her own interests. As the mediation proceeded, she was advised several times to consult with her attorney but the case coordinator suspected that she was not doing so.

In the end, her attorney rejected the final mediation agreement and told her it was impossible for him to represent her if she insisted on keeping the agreement as the divorce settlement. She chose to discontinue the relationship with her attorney and she, like her husband, represented herself in court proceedings. Her attorney was very upset and told the judge in her presence that he objected to her mediated settlement. The judge accepted the agreement after speaking with her at length.

Case study 2: sexual harassment

A twenty-five year old undergraduate woman was very troubled about what she described as sexual harassment by one of her professors. She claimed that he had made many inappropriate inquiries in class about the backgrounds of the women students, wanting to know about their boyfriends, their parties, and other similar matters. During a conversation with him regarding a research assistantship, he offered to drive her home. She consented to this and on the way, they stopped for a drink. During their conversation she learned the position would involve working closely with him. The conversation led to a discussion of personal matters and he told her of his unhappy marriage. Later on he mentioned that he was very attracted to her and would like to go to bed with her. She felt extremely uneasy and said that she would have to think about it.

The next day she went to his office and rejected his sexual proposal. He said that he was disappointed. Two weeks passed without any mention of the job. When she finally approached him, he told her the position was no longer available. She was upset and went to the department chair, who recommended that she consider mediation. She also spoke to the school's dean, who initially reacted with disbelief, but later believed the student after speaking to the professor. The dean told them both that he wanted the dispute worked out in mediation, but indicated that if he received another complaint he would dismiss the faculty member.

In a lengthy meeting with the mediation staff, the student learned that she could arrange for a more formal, potentially punitive process by requesting the administration to form an ad hoc hearing committee. She considered this alternative but requested mediation, claiming she did not want the professor fired. The professor also agreed to mediation.

During a four hour mediation session with the two parties, the student explained why the incident was so upsetting. The professor responded with tears and an apology. At the end of the mediation, they shook hands and both expressed satisfaction to the mediator. She said she mostly wanted the opportunity to make him hear her point of view. He said he understood and expressed appreciation at being spared the humiliation of a more public proceeding. She also expressed her relief at being able to avoid the pain of a public and more formalized hearing where her credibility might be subject to review and cross-examination. At the end of the mediation he apologized and offered her a job, which she rejected. He also promised not to penalize her by lowering her grade.

Summary

Although critics of mediation charge that it may keep the less powerful party from achieving equality and equal bargaining power, it is not so clear from these case studies how this operates in practice. These objections to mediation are inextricably tied to the view that the formal legal system offers both a better alternative and a greater possibility of achieving a fair and just resolution to the conflict. The general assumption that the lawyer can 'help' the client more meaningfully than a mediator is part of the problem with this view. In many instances, although new substantive rights or legal protections are realized, patterns of domination are reinforced by the lawyer-client relationship, in which the client is a passive recipient of the lawyer's expertise. This is particularly true for women clients, for whom patterns of domination are at the heart of the problem.

In both case studies, it can be argued that the pattern of *dominance* was affected. 'Dominance produces hierarchical arrangement of the partners, which is reflected in differences in such aspects of the relationship as freedom of movement, the utilization of resources, and rights and responsibilities.' In these situations, the women felt that the relationship of dominance had been altered and the hierarchy in the relationship had to some extent been altered. A transformation of the pattern of dominance will affect the power relationships as well.

Although mediation programs are proliferating, many questions remain. Why is the interest in alternatives intensifying? What kinds of disputes are best suited to mediation? Who should be mediators—lay persons, lawyers, or other professionals? What kind of training should mediators receive? Can mediation in practice alter the patterns of gender inequality in our society more effectively than formal law? Can the teaching of mediation begin to change and challenge the traditional approach to legal study? The answers to these questions may remain unclear, but if these issues are not addressed, mediation will simply become another popular 'technique' marketed as a panacea for a range of complex social problems."

NOTES AND QUESTIONS

- According to Rifkin, in what ways does mediation exemplify a "new way of thinking about law"? In other words, how does the process of mediation differ from more formal and legalised methods of resolving disputes?

- Consider the two case studies discussed in the extract. Did you find the outcomes to be satisfactory or problematic? Was the mediation process able to cope adequately with the power relationships that existed as between the parties?

- Do you think that mediation *necessarily* provides a preferable way of resolving disputes, as opposed to a more formal and binding legal process, in cases involving domestic violence or abusive relationships? Are there advantages in these (and other) cases provided by the legal system and the "rule of law"? For further reading on the subject, see Hilary Astor, "The Weight of Silence; Talking About Violence in Family Mediation", in *Public and Private: Feminist Legal Debates* (Margaret Thornton, ed., Oxford University Press, Melbourne, 1995).

As a contrast to Rifkin's advocacy of mediation, examine Grillo's concerns (below). Although she is particularly concerned about *mandatory* mediation processes, which we have already considered, she has reservations about mediation in general, and the dangers for women in dispute situations.

Trina Grillo, "The Mediation Alternative: Process Dangers for Women" (1991) 100 Yale Law Journal 1545 at 1547, 1601, 1607:

"The western concept of law is based on a patriarchal paradigm characterized by hierarchy, linear reasoning, the resolution of disputes through the application of abstract principles, and the idea of the reasonable person. Its fundamental aspiration is objectivity, and to that end it separates public from private, form from substance, and process from policy. This objectivist paradigm is problematic in many circumstances, but never more so than in connection with a marital dissolution in which the custody of children is at issue, where the essential question for the court is what is to happen next in the family. The family court system, aspiring to the idea of objectivity and operating as an adversary system, can be relied on neither to produce just results nor to treat those subject to it respectfully and humanely.

There is little doubt that divorce procedure needs to be reformed, but reformed how? Presumably, any alternative should be at least as just, and at least as humane, as the current system, particularly for those who are least powerful in society. Mediation has been put forward, with much fanfare, as such an alternative. The impetus of the mediation movement has been so strong that in some states couples disputing custody are required by statute or local rule to undergo a mandatory mediation process if they are unable to reach an agreement on their own. Mediation has been embraced for a number of reasons. First, it rejects an objectivist approach to conflict resolution, and promises to consider disputes in terms of relationships and responsibility. Second, the mediation process is, at least in theory, cooperative and voluntary, not coercive. The mediator does not make a decision; rather, each party speaks for himself. Together they reach an agreement that meets the parties' mutual needs. In this manner, the process is said to enable the parties to exercise self-determination and eliminate the hierarchy of dominance that characterizes the judge/litigant and lawyer/client relationships. Third, since in mediation there are no rules of evidence or legalistic notions of relevancy, decisions supposedly may be informed by context rather than by abstract principle. Finally, in theory at least, emotions are recognized and incorporated into the mediation process. This conception of mediation has led some commentators to characterize it as a feminist alternative to the patriarchally inspired adversary system.

Whether mandatory mediation, required as part of court proceedings, fulfills these aspirations, or instead substitutes another objectivist, patriarchal, and even more damaging form of conflict resolution for its adversarial counterpart, is the subject of this Article. Many divorcing couples seem pleased with their mediation experiences. Indeed, studies have shown that mediation clients are more satisfied with their divorce outcomes than persons using the adversary system. Although there are significant methodological problems with each of these studies, the existence of substantial client satisfaction with some models of mediation cannot be completely discounted.

Nonetheless, I conclude that mandatory mediation provides neither a more just nor a more humane alternative to the adversarial system of adjudication of custody, and, therefore, does not fulfill its promises. In particular, quite apart from whether an acceptable result is reached, mandatory mediation can be destructive to many women and some men because it requires them to speak in a setting they have not chosen and often imposes a rigid orthodoxy as to how they should speak, make decisions, and be. This orthodoxy is imposed through subtle and not-so-subtle messages about appropriate conduct and about what may be said in mediation. It is an orthodoxy that often excludes the possibiltiy of the parties' speaking with their authentic voices.

Moreover, people vary greatly in the extent to which their sense of self is 'relational'—that is, defined in terms of connection to others. If two parties are forced to engage with one another, and one has a more relational sense of self than the other, that party may feel compelled to maintain her connection with the other, even to her own detriment. For this reason, the party with the more relational sense of self will be at a disadvantage in a mediated negotiation. Several prominent researchers have suggested that, as a general rule, women have a more relational sense of self than do men, although there is little agreement on what the origin of this difference might be. Thus, rather than being a feminist alternative to the adversary system, mediation has the potential actively to harm women.

Some of the dangers of mandatory mediation apply to voluntary mediation as well. Voluntary mediation should not be abandoned, but should be recognized as a powerful process which should be used carefully and thoughtfully. Entering into such a process with one who has known you intimately and who now seems to threaten your whole life and being has great creative, but also enormous destructive, power. Nonetheless, it should be recognized that when two people themselves decide to mediate and then physically appear at the mediation sessions, that decision and their continued presence serve as a rough indication that it is not too painful or too dangerous for one or both of them to go on. . . .

As discussed earlier, several feminist scholars have suggested that women have a more 'relational' sense of self than do men. The most influential of these researchers, Carol Gilligan, describes two different, gendered modes of thought. The female mode is characterized by an 'ethic of care' which emphasizes nurturance, connection with others, and contextual thinking. The male mode is characterized by an 'ethic of justice' which emphasizes individualism, the use of rules to resolve moral dilemmas, and equality. Under Gilligan's view, the male mode leads one to strive for individualism and autonomy, while the female mode leads one to strive for connection with and caring for others. Some writers, seeing a positive virtue in the ethic of care, have applied Gilligan's work to the legal system. But her work has been criticized by others for its methodology, its conflation of biological sex with gender, and its failure to include race and class differences in its analysis. (Indeed, it is not likely that the male/female differences Gilligan notes are consistent across racial and class lines.) The 'ethic of care' has also been viewed as the manifestation of a system of gender domination. Nevertheless, it is clear that those who operate in a 'female mode'—whether biologically male or female—will respond more 'selflessly' to the demands of mediation.

Whether the ethic of care is to be enshrined as a positive virtue, or criticized as a characteristic not belonging to all women and contributing to their oppression, one truth emerges: many women see themselves, and judge their own worth, primarily in terms of relationships. This perspective on themselves has consequences for how they function in mediation.

Carrie Menkel-Meadow has suggested that the ethic of care can and should be brought into the practice of law—that the world of lawyering would look very different from the perspective of that ethic. Some commentators have identified mediation as a way to incorporate the ethic of care into the legal system and thereby modify the harshness of the adversary process. And, indeed, at first glance, mediation in the context of divorce might be seen as a way of bringing the woman-identified values of intimacy, nurturance, and care into a legal system that is concerned with the most fundamental aspects of women's and men's lives.

If mediation does not successfully introduce an ethic of care, however, but instead merely sells itself on that promise while delivering something coercive in its place, the consequences will be disastrous for a woman who embraces a relational sense of self. If she is easily persuaded to be cooperative, but her partner is not, she can only lose. If it is indeed her disposition to be caring and focused on relationships, and she has been rewarded for that focus and characterized as 'unfeminine' when she departs from it, the language of relationship, caring, and cooperation will be appealing to her and make her vulnerable. Moreover, the intimation that she is not being cooperative and caring or that she is thinking of herself instead of thinking selflessly of the children can shatter her self-esteem and make her lose faith in herself. In short, in mediation, such a woman may be encouraged to repeat exactly those behaviors that have proven hazardous to her in the past. . . .

It has been said that '[d]isputes are cultural events, evolving within a framework of rules about what is worth fighting for, what is the normal or moral way to fight, what kinds of wrongs warrant action, and what kinds of remedies are acceptable.' The process by which a society resolves conflict is closely related to its social structure. Implicit in this choice is a message about what is respectable to do or want or say, what the obligations are of being a member of the society or of a particular group within it, and what it takes to be thought of as a good person leading a virtuous life. In the adversary system, it is acceptable to want to win. It is not only acceptable, but expected, that one will rely on a lawyer and advocate for oneself without looking out for the adversary. The judge, a third party obligated to be neutral and bound by certain formalities, bears the ultimate responsibility for deciding the outcome. To the extent that women are more likely than men to believe in communication as a mode of conflict resolution and to appreciate the importance of an adversary's interests, this system does not always suit their needs.

On the other hand, under a scheme of mediation, the standards of acceptable behavior and desires change fundamentally. Parties are to meet with each other, generally without their lawyers. They are encouraged to look at each other's needs and to reach a cooperative resolution based on compromise. Although there are few restrictions on her role in the process, the mediator bears no ultimate, formal responsibility for the outcome of the mediation. In sum, when mediation is the prototype for dispute resolution, the societal message is that a good person—a person following the rules—cooperates, communicates, and compromises.

The glories of cooperation, however, are easily exaggerated. If one party appreciates cooperation more than the other, the parties might compromise unequally. Moreover, the self-disclosure that cooperation requires, when imposed and not sought by the parties, may feel and be invasive. Thus, rather than representing a change in the system to accommodate the 'feminine voice,' cooperation might, at least for the time being, be detrimental to their lives and the lives of their children. Under a system of forced mediation, women are made to feel selfish for wanting to assert their own interests based on their need to survive."

NOTES AND QUESTIONS

- Explain the difference between an "ethic of care" and an "ethic of justice". To what extent do you think those ethics are gendered? Are there political dangers to women implicit in the ascription of an "ethic of care" and to men?

- Grillo's article raises a point which we have already considered: is compromise always a good thing? Can you think of circumstances where it clearly is not? In those cases, is mediation a poor substitute for more formalised legal proceedings?

- Which argument do you find more convincing—Rifkin's or Grillo's? Does it all depend upon the particular context of the dispute? Should we avoid "grand theories" about the promise and dangers of mediation in favour of context-specific analysis?

The alternative of administrative tribunals

We now change focus, and turn to a further alternative to the adversarial, civil justice system which we have focused on in this book. In Chapter 3 we examined judicial review, the means by which courts oversee and supervise the exercise of powers by administrative tribunals. In this section, we look at the tribunal system itself, and how the operation of tribunals differs from courts. We examine how tribunals operate in practice, and the extent to which tribunals should be "court like", specifically in terms of whether individuals should have the right to be represented by legal counsel. As you read this material you might think about the concerns about tribunals expressed by Dicey, which we looked at in Chapter 2, namely, to what extent is a system of tribunals compatible with the "rule of law" and, on the other hand, to what extent are the virtues of the tribunal lost if it comes to replicate the ordinary courts?

The tribunal system is clearly the most important method for resolving disputes. Numerous areas of life—from social security benefits to unfair dismissal to landlord and tenant disputes—are now handled by tribunals. You may be surprised to learn that tribunals handle several times the number of disputes which are decided by courts of law. Moreover, while tribunals are often characterised in terms of providing speedy, relatively inexpensive resolution of disputes, the areas with which they deal are no less important than those dealt with by courts. For example, Mental Health Review Tribunals consider the compulsory detention of the mentally ill; and Immigration Appeal Tribunals consider whether people can remain in this country. These are clearly issues of the greatest importance for the individual, and they are entrusted to tribunals. We thus might start by asking, what is the difference, if any, between courts of law and administrative tribunals?

Tribunals and courts compared

We begin with two "classic" excerpts on the similarities and differences between courts and tribunals.

Harry Street, *Justice in the Welfare State* (Stevens & Sons, London, 1975), pp. 2–9:

The Welfare State

"We have the main clue once we see that this trend [towards administrative tribunals] started when Lloyd George pioneered his National Health Insurance Act of 1911. It is the extension of the Welfare State which leads to matters being taken away from the courts. When the State provides benefits for citizens it has to devise machinery for ascertaining who has a good claim. When the State imposes controls there has to be a procedure which ensures that the citizen's freedom is not interfered with in an arbitrary manner. The 1911 Act set up special tribunals to handle contested claims for unemployment benefit. These tribunals worked exceptionally well, so much so that the sceptical became convinced that the judges were not the only ones who could do justice in disputes between the government and the public. These unemployment tribunals became the pattern for many others.

We usually call all these bodies administrative tribunals. The name is a good one. It distinguishes them from the ordinary courts. It also reminds us that it is a question of policy to be resolved by the Administration what arrangements are appropriate for deciding a particular set of claims. For instance, the Government decides to introduce a State scheme of unemployment benefits. It works out how the money is to be raised and prescribes the qualification for benefit, and the manner of making payments. It has to meet the situation where a citizen claims benefit and a government official does not accept this claim. It is purely an administrative matter how the Act is going to handle those contested issues. That matter will be resolved, not by laying it down that because there is a dispute it is a judicial question for a judge, but by asking what in the circumstances is the most efficient manner of performing this administrative task.

Links with government

We can readily see how decisions like that are closely linked with the Administration. Plainly the Administration is going to be responsible for the routine day to day payment of benefits. It will be less than say one case in ten thousand where there is an unresolved doubt about a claim to benefit. The Administration will be inclined to regard that one in ten thousand cases as just another administrative problem—calling for a special solution, yes—but it would be natural for it to think of recourse to some institution connected with the responsible department, rather than for it to say: 'This is a judicial issue, which must obviously be decided by one of Her Majesty's judges.' What I have just said about benefits is also true of granting a licence to do something or other, or of other ways in which the State now regulates our activities.

What is needed above all else is a cheap and speedy settlement of disputes. For these cases we do not want a Rolls-Royce system of justice. Some would say that there is too much of the Rolls and not enough of the Mini even in much of our trials in the law courts. If the average claim to benefit is less than £10 we do not want a judge on a pensionable salary of over £12,000 a year[9] with all the trappings (so often foisted on unwilling judges) of special judges' lodgings, private butler, police escort, ushers and marshal, to decide the claim. Nor do we want to wait for years to elapse between the making of the claim and the arrival at a final decision.

We can compile a very long list of matters of ths kind which have arisen under the Welfare State for decision by administrative tribunals. Claims for unemployment benefit, family allowances, maternity benefits, death grants, industrial injury benefits, sickness benefits, supplementary benefits (the old National Assistance) and all other social security benefits are settled in this way. The Government decides to regulate rents of houses—and so we have rent assessment committees and rent tribunals. We have a nationalised health service; therefore we need tribunals to investigate complaints against doctors, dentists, opticians and chemists within the service. We interfere with the freedom of businesses to carry goods and passengers on the road where they will; tribunals supervise this regulation of road transport. The right of the Englishman to do as he likes with his land is taken away from him because we recognise the superior claims of public bodies to acquire it on payment of compensation—disputes about compensation go to the Lands Tribunal. We protect the employee by giving him certain rights to compensation if he is made redundant; we interfere with the employer's freedom to dismiss him—industrial tribunals are there to apply these new laws. Injured servicemen may be entitled to a pension—pensions appeal tribunals will decide. When there is compulsory national service, claims for postponement of service and for eventual reinstatement in civilian employment are heard by special tribunals. Regional Health Authorities find it necessary to detain under the Mental Health Act 1959 those who suffer from mental illness or disorder; we have mental health review tribunals to review, on the application of the Secretary of State for Social Services, the patient or his nearest relatives, the case of anyone liable to be detained.

The quest for speed, cheapness and efficiency

There are many other explanations for this movement away from the ordinary courts. Ministers and their top civil servant advisers have in this century frequently come to doubt whether the courts are the appropriate body to decide many of these new cases. They see

---

[9] Note the effect of inflation since 1975!

rightly that many of these disputes are not merely about private rights: the public good on the one hand and the interest of the particular citizen on the other must be weighed in the balance. They look at many decisions in the courts, even at the level of the House of Lords, and find them wanting in that they appear to disregard the social element of a problem. For example, the courts have chosen to hold that there is no law against letting a tumble-down house; even though the landlord knew of the defects, he is held by them not to be liable to anybody injured on the premises because of their defective condition. Again, the courts held that traders who were determined to obtain a monopoly were free to combine together in order to drive a rival trader out of business. Administrators asked themselves whether judges who arrived at such decisions could be relied on to show a proper regard for the public interest, which would often be paramount or decisive in cases referred to them.

There was also a lack of confidence in the way in which courts interpreted Acts of Parliament. This was important because the new kinds of decisions were almost always ones where the meaning of a section of an Act had to be found.... Politicians feared that the courts might frustrate the social purposes of their Acts if they approached cases in this constricted literal fashion. A more serious charge has been levelled at the judges; that they brought to statutory interpretation nineteenth-century notions of the inviolability of property; that they woud lean over backwards to find that a statute had not taken away an individual's property rights, even if expropriation for public purposes on payment of compensation was the cardinal aim of the Act. Of course it does not matter whether these suspicions and attitudes of our politicians and civil servants were well-founded; I am looking for the reasons why they diverted topics away from the judges. I am not saying that all their reasons were valid.

Whatever his other faults, the politician or civil servant is sometimes prepared to admit that he might have been wrong, and to change his mind. Flexibility is seen as a key attribute in a decision-maker. Yet the courts have long had a different approach: that once a decision has been reached in a case, it should be a binding precedent for other judges to follow in similar future cases. If the new class of cases had been tried by the courts, principles would have become rigid; courts would have to do for evermore what their predecessors had done, even though they were convinced that the earlier decisions were wrong. It was thought that this judicial inflexibility was inappropriate for many of the new kinds of decision.

The ordinary judge has to be a jack of all trades. This week he may try a murderer, and next week he may hear successively running-down claims, industrial accidents, claims by a deceived house buyer for recovery of his purchase price, and actions for breach of contract to deliver goods. Many of the new State schemes are extraordinarily complex; mastery of the laws can be obtained only by intense specialisation. Governments therefore thought it wise to set up tribunals specially to handle cases under any one particular item of social legislation; they felt that judges who were general practitioners could not be expected to have the necessary expertise and ready familiarity with these detailed new provisions. Sometimes it was considered that the necessary consistency of decision could be attained only if all cases were decided by the same person. Rent tribunals are an obvious example. Nobody would pretend that the reasonable rent of a furnished house or flat can be determined with mathematical precision. Public confidence would be lost if, say, comparable flats in the same block were given markedly different rent ceilings—we know how magistrates are criticised for having different ideas about fines for road traffic offences such as speeding. Continuity and consistency of decision should ensue if the same personnel make decisions in a given area.

There is another less obvious but equally important reason for the development of administrative tribunals. The High Court judge and the lawyer who practises before him have an instinctive yearning for certainty; they like their law to be cut and dried, to have it settled once and for all so that lawyers and their clients know exactly where they stand. There is a lot to be said for this view. We are all entitled to know, for instance (or to have our solicitor tell us), whether what we propose to do is a crime. If we buy a house, we do not want to be told that in the present state of the law it is uncertain whether we shall acquire a good title to it. But the administrators maintain that they cannot run the modern State like that. They talk of the formulation of standards. They see a stage between a fixed rule and anarchy. They find it impossible to legislate in advance for every specific instance. For them decision-making is not then some mechanical process; one cannot use a slot machine or even a computer in order to obtain the answer. In their statutes they use words like 'fair,' 'adequate' and 'reasonable,' intending that these standards shall be applied to particular cases in the light of experience. They doubt whether judges will find it congenial to work in this way. They also observe that when judges have in the past had to handle such concepts they have been prone to crystallise what should have been merely instances of the standard into rigid legal rules from which they would depart only with reluctance. For instance, courts which had to decide whether a motorist was driving with reasonable care would be tempted to say, once it had been held that a motorist was liable for not being able to pull up within the range of his lights, that a new rule of law had emerged for all circumstances—that it was always careless not to be able to pull up within the limits of one's vision.

Whitehall did not want this to happen to their administrative standards. They see them as flexible. Take some examples from modern administrative schemes. Are premises education- ally suitable? Is a building of special architectural interest? Has a man capacity for work? Is employment available in a district? We see that not only must these standards be developed in the light of experience; technical experts must assist in applying them. The working out of these from case to case is not for lawyers-judges alone; the educationist, the architect, the town planner, the valuer, the industrialist and the trade union official have to participate in this task. Neither politicians nor the judges themselves regarded the courts as ideally equipped for duties of this kind.

The judging process in many of these areas demands an adaptability which judges are not accustomed to display. A local valuation court is not content to sit back and listen to what the house owner and rating officer tell them about the rateable value of the house; its members go and see for themselves. A social security tribunal dealing with a claim for industrial injuries can interrupt the hearing for half an hour to go and visit the scene of the accident. Judges do not do this kind of thing (at least publicly); those who decide these new kinds of dispute must.

A related point is the traditional passiveness of courts—they act only when someone takes the initiative in bringing matters before them. If supervision is to be effective, then sometimes representatives of the administrative agency must unearth wrongdoers and bring them before the agency for a hearing. This approach is commonplace in America in such matters, for example, as monopolies, restrictive practices and false advertising, and there are signs that we may follow in some spheres of administrative control.

Unless a litigant engages a lawyer he is never at ease in court. The judge is aloof, the proce- dure is formal, there is an atmosphere of uncomfortable dignity. A man likes to be able to have his say in his own way, unrestrained by the niceties of the rule against hearsay evidence and the rest. He often does not want to be reprimanded every time—and it will be often—that he fails to distinguish between cross-examining a witness and making a point in his own favour. Administrative tribunals are sufficiently informal to permit these liberties; courts never are."

In contrast to Street, Abel-Smith and Stevens, in another "classic" text, do not see a clear distinction between courts and tribunals.

Brian Abel-Smith and Robert Stevens, *In Search of Justice: Society and the Legal System* (Penguin, London, 1968), pp. 224–228:

The difference between courts and tribunals

"A foreign non-lawyer who was unaware of the prestige of the British judiciary and of tradi- tional concepts such as the separation of powers, which have come to be associated with courts rather than tribunals, might well ask what the difference really is between a court and a tribunal. What does it matter if some particular adversary procedures have come to be called courts while others are described as tribunals? Both are normally established under statutes. Both interpret laws made by or under statute as well as their own case law, although the latter may be more flexible under administrative tribunals. Both are normally chaired by persons appointed by the Lord Chancellor, although in the case of most courts there are no other members of the bench.

We would argue that such differences as there are between them are not in any sense fundamental but at most differences in degree. Tribunals tend to include a much wider range of skills on the bench; and the most significant hallmark of policy-oriented tribunals is specialization. The most cursory examination of the courts shows that the decision-makers consist of lawyers or laymen or both. Trusted laymen (JPs) staff the majority of magistrates' courts. They also sit with legally qualified chairmen at county quarter sessions. . . .

Tribunals, on the other hand, normally use as decision-takers and not just as witnesses, persons with specialized experience (employers or trade unionists) and persons with professional skills other than legal skills. Thus doctors sit on tribunals which assess the degree of disability in National Insurance claims. Those with expertise in housing problems and land prices sit on Rent Assessment Committees and on the Lands Tribunal. Employers and trade unionists sit on social security tribunals because their knowledge of labour practices is considered valuable. Tribunals are developed ad hoc, and their composition is decided to suit the precise function each is intended to serve. Specialization is therefore one of the most obvious aspects of tribunals, and it is the main distinguishing feature between the ordinary courts and the policy-oriented type of tribunal such as the Patents Appeal Tribunal, the Industrial Court, the Lands Tribunal or the Air Transport Licensing Board. Specialization is also a mark of the 'court-substitute' type of tribunal, such as the Rent Tribunals, the Rent Assessment Committees, Industrial Tribunals and the various social security tribunals. But again it is a question of degree rather than basic difference—the Companies Court and the Commercial Court are specialized lists within the court structure.

With respect to the court-substitute type of tribunals we would argue that the chief features which distinguish them from the regular courts are their cheapness, their speed and efficiency, their privacy and their informality. Civil courts, with the exception of Magistrates' courts in certain types of case, charge fees. Tribunals do not. Thus, Rent Tribunals, National Insurance Tribunals and the like emphasize lack of expense. Those appearing before such tribunals can be represented by persons other than lawyers, and this also helps to keep costs down—particularly where parties are represented by trade unionists. Persons must have the permission of the court to be represented by a non-lawyer in a county court or a magistrate's court, and there is no precedent for such representation before the High Court. At the same time, and even bearing in mind the dangers of excessive legalism, we think it dangerous that any form of legal aid is unknown before most tribunals. . . .

Tribunals are as informal as is consistent with an orderly conduct of their affairs. The attempt is usually made to create an atmosphere in which people who appear in person will not feel ill at ease or nervous. While the magistrates' courts, particularly in juvenile cases, go some way in the same direction, the physical layout of courts, the robes and modes of address are forbidding even for persons with considerable poise and self-confidence in any other setting. Moreover, as we have seen, the attitude of some judges and occasionally their remarks can be such as to humiliate litigants. But this difference must not be overestimated. In particular, the increase in legal chairmen and legal representation since 1958 has often eradicated this difference.

Another articulated difference between courts and tribunals as a whole lies in the more restricted rights of appeal found in many of the latter (although the Franks Report, which led to the Tribunal and Enquiries Act, 1958, was in many senses a victory for the lawyers and so led to a wider right of appeal from tribunals). . . .

Some lawyers would argue that there was a further fundamental difference between the two streams. Courts are said to be administering rules of law while tribunals are thought to be administering both law and policy. We would maintain that no such clear line can or should be drawn. Indeed it was the evolution of this myth which helped establish the tribunal system by convincing the judges of the ordinary courts that they were concerned with legal but not with policy questions. But continued insistence on this unsatisfactory distinction makes it increasingly difficult to entrust new matters to the courts or to merge courts and tribunals. Properly understood, tribunals are a more modern form of court. In some cases they may have more discretion than the courts, and this is particularly true of the policy-oriented tribunals. But certainly they have no more discretion than the Chancery Division has in handling trusts, wards or companies. Conversely the court-substitute tribunals are often as precedent-conscious as, and may even exercise a much narrower discretion than, the ordinary courts.

But we would reaffirm our position that there is no fundamental difference between courts and tribunals. We would argue, therefore, that every effort should be made to merge the two. A well-structured court system, with reform and flexible procedures based on the county court or Civil Tribunal, with specialized 'lists', might then offer a general adjudicatory system, with a spectrum of judges specialized in the many fields in which a potential litigant might be interested."

NOTES AND QUESTIONS

- Why are Abel-Smith and Stevens skeptical of the distinction between law and policy?

- Having read the excerpts from Street and Abel-Smith and Stevens, do you think that tribunals and courts are roughly the same, or quite different from each other? Why?

- The adjudication of disputes before tribunals usually involves three persons: the chairperson, who is usually legally qualified, and two non-lawyers, who will likely be expert in the particular field in which the tribunal works.

- Abel-Smith and Stevens mention the year 1958, an important date in the history of the tribunal system. In 1957 the government set up a committee to consider reform of the tribunal system: the Franks Committee. It produced the Report of the Committee on Administrative Tribunals, which was followed in 1958 by the Tribunals and Inquiries Act. The Franks Committee stated that tribunals should be characterised by openness, fairness, and impartiality, and that those who chaired tribunals should be legally qualified. It also recommended a Council on Tribunals, to keep under review the workings of tribunals. Also recommended, and implemented, was the principle that representation should be possible before tribunals and, if necessary, representation by a qualified lawyer. Moreover, tribunals in general should give reasons for decisions if requested to do so.

A recent discussion of the tribunal system by Genn underscores a high degree of continuity in the years since Street and Abel-Smith and Stevens wrote their analyses.

Hazel Genn, "Tribunals and Informal Justice" (1993) 56 M.L.R. 393 at 393:

Tribunals and informal justice

"Informal tribunals that review administrative decisions and adjudicate on disputes between individuals have been part of the British system of civil justice for some time. Their popularity with policy-makers, at least, has led to a remarkable proliferation in the last 50 years, and currently in the UK hear over a quarter of a million cases annually, representing some six times the number of contested civil cases disposed of at trial before the High Court and County Courts together. New tribunals are being created all the time. Such tribunals have historically been viewed as cheap, non-technical substitutes for the ordinary courts for a wide range of grievances and disputes, in which parties can initiate actions without cost or fuss."

Tribunals in the UK have been largely overlooked by scholars concerned with developments in informal justice, who have tended to focus on small claims procedures, conciliation, mediation and arbitration. This omission may be because the history of tribunals predates the contemporary trend towards informalism, and because tribunals do not represent 'alternatives' to courts, unlike, for example, some small claims procedures and arbitration hearings. Tribunals are the only mechanism provided by Parliament for the resolution of certain grievances against the State, and for some specific disputes between individuals. They are the result of deliberate choice, and in the early days of the Welfare State, at least, it has been argued that this choice was underpinned by philosophical as well as practical considerations. Tribunals ought, however, to be of interest to those who study alternative dispute resolution mechanisms. They display many of the characteristics welcomed by proponents of informalism, and some of the historical and modern justifications for the creation of tribunals rest on presumed advantages over ordinary courts which echo the claims made for ADR and criticisms of conventional court adjudication.

Defining tribunals

In the UK there are about 50 different types of tribunals and some 2000 tribunals altogether. Tribunals are supervised on a general basis by the Council on Tribunals, but there is no common procedure followed by these bodies, no general appeal process or appellate body. Some tribunals have lay members, others have specialist qualifications. Some tribunals act in a strictly judicial fashion, while others look more broadly at policy considerations. It is, in fact, impossible to provide a simple definition of a tribunal. The label is given to many different kinds of bodies with widely differing functions, and covering a vast range of subject areas including private as well as public law issues.

The four tribunals included in the study from which this paper has developed are, in effect, court-substitutes.[10] They do not have responsibility for making regulations or devising policy, but are required to act as informal courts, reviewing administrative decisions or adjudicating between disputing parties. There are great differences between tribunals in the degree of informality to be found in proceedings, and in their function. SSATs [social security appeal tribunals] and hearings before immigration adjudicators, for example, provide a first tier of appeal from administrative decisions. Industrial tribunals, on the other hand, adjudicate at first instance on disputes between employers and employees. They are not concerned with administrative decision-making, but with disputes between private parties. There are also many differences in the composition of tribunals. SSATs and industrial tribunals are composed of a legal chairman and two lay members. Immigration cases, on the other hand, are heard before a single legally trained Adjudicator. Although in each of the four tribunals the right to apply for a hearing before a tribunal without incurring cost is virtually automatic, the procedures in each tribunal thereafter are very different. Procedures in SSATs are very informal and defined inaccurately as being 'inquisitorial' with proceedings being conducted around a large table. Immigration hearings and industrial tribunals are considerably more formal and more obviously adversarial, with raised platforms and evidence often given on oath.

Such similarities as there are between tribunals tend to reside in the *absence* of certain features of courts. For example, the absence of strict rules of evidence; the absence of court robes; the frequent absence of representatives appearing for applicants, etc. Indeed, it might be argued that the *only* common, unifying aspects of adjudicative institutions that bear the label 'tribunal' concern their superficially distinctive procedures and personnel. Since it is in the presumed *procedural* advantages over conventional courts that the most compelling arguments for establishing tribunals have been made, it seems appropriate that an analysis of the activities of tribunals should concentrate on the benefit conferred by this procedural innovation on those whose cases are decided by tribunals.

---

[10] Genn's study focused on tribunals dealing with welfare benefits, immigration disputes, employment disputes and detention under mental health legislation.

Procedural advantages: tribunals and the 'preferred option'

The arguments for establishing tribunals to deal with certain categories of dispute rather than giving jurisdiction to the ordinary courts have variously been based on constitutional arguments; allegations of class bias in the courts; practical arguments concerning lack of resources in the courts to handle new and potentially huge caseloads; and finally, the positive benefits of tribunals over ordinary courts in terms of their speed, cheapness, informality and expertise. . . .

In the early days of the modern tribunal system, the intention was that tribunals should provide easy access to specialist adjudicators at no cost to applicants. There was no charge for the initiation of applications to tribunals and no cost for applicants if they lost. The hearings were to be 'informal' and there was an assumption that the informality of proceedings would make it possible for applicants to represent themselves at hearings. Tribunal chairmen would take a relatively active role in hearings and adopt flexible procedures. The process was intended to be swift, not bogged down in 'technicality' and not bound by strict rules of evidence. Since there was perceived to be no need for highly trained judges, the system could be operated relatively inexpensively. Although tribunal chairmen would not be of the same calibre as judges, their concentration on specific subject areas would lead to expertise and, presumably, good quality decision-making. Tribunals were therefore presented as being 'good' for applicants who would often be from among the most disadvantaged groups in society and who, it was assumed, would be overawed and dismayed at the prospect of bringing their case to a court.

These attributes of tribunals had evidently already been sufficiently established by 1957 for the Franks Committee to set them out as descriptive characteristics rather than as a set of objectives to be attained by tribunals:

> 'tribunals have certain characteristics which often give them advantages over the courts. These are cheapness, accessibility, freedom from technicality, expedition and expert knowledge of their particular subject.'

This well-worn formulation has been repeated countless times throughout the literature on tribunals since the publication of the Franks Report. The confident assertions about the advantages of tribunals have not always been borne out by empirical studies of the operation of tribunals in practice. Nonetheless, some of the most up-to-date analyses of tribunals by public lawyers continue to repeat the description. For example:

> 'The[se] differences between tribunals and courts are usually seen as being advantages of tribunals, and as reasons for establishing a tribunal rather than a court; both because cheapness, speed, and so on, are good in themselves; and because, in some areas at least, many applicants before tribunals are poor and ill-educated, and so would find a traditional court very intimidating. Tribunals can be seen, therefore, as having both technical and social advantages over courts.'

Other writers, however, argue that decisions to establish rights of appeal to tribunals rather than courts have been based primarily on political and cost considerations, not in the belief that tribunals will provide greater access to justice:

> 'The tribunals were not established to make up for defects in the judicial system. The choice was never between appeal to tribunals and appeal to the courts, but between appeal to tribunals and no appeal. Their introduction did not represent an incorporation of the idea of legality into new areas of society for its own sake. The provision of a formal right of appeal . . . was introduced as a counter-measure to political protest and as a means of making oppressive changes in the relief of poverty more palatable by giving a symbolic appearance of legality whilst ensuring that this had no real effect.'

The doubts expressed about the political objectives driving the growth of tribunals in the UK during the twentieth century are also to be found in modern criticisms of small claims procedures in this country and other forms of ADR abroad. Theoretical and empirical studies of tribunals, small claims courts, mediation and arbitration contain consistent themes questioning the stimulus for their creation and the extent to which they achieve the benefits claimed for them.

The most commonly stated reasons for establishing informal dispute mechanisms outside of the administrative law field have been either that the courts are overburdened, or that the ordinary courts are in some way inappropriate for dealing with certain classes of dispute because their procedures and the cost of bringing cases before them represent an obstacle to free access to justice. There is, however, a critical strand in the literature on informal justice sceptical of these explanations. Abel has argued that in the civil justice field at least, the modern trend towards informalism, based on efficiency arguments, represents a 'downgrading' of the problems of the poor and a relegation of their disputes to second-class forms of justice. In Abel's analysis, 'informal' tends to be synonymous with 'inferior.' Similar arguments have been made more recently in this country in relation to changes in court jurisdiction designed to reallocate cases down the court hierarchy. Sedley argues that the recent reorganisation has been driven by a desire to free the courts for the resolution of international commercial disputes and in so doing individual rights have been trivialised and diverted to courts of 'poorer' quality.

The suggestion that the problems of the poor have been relegated to inferior adjudicative institutions in order to free the courts for the problems of businessmen may be true. It must be acknowledged, however, that the business community has itself criticised the cost, paraphenalia and lack of speed involved in court litigation. Business is experimenting with alternative methods of settling commercial disputes. In recent years, the rapid growth of arbitration and other innovative forms of ADR in the commercial field in this country and abroad represents a reaction against the disadvantages of attempting to resolve business disputes through the courts. The value of ADR for businesses in long-term relationships has been recognised, in this country, by the establishment of a Centre for Dispute Resolution which provides a mechanism that will spare businesses 'the expensive, time consuming and costly process of litigation.'

The *desire* to establish simplified methods of resolving disputes, and to improve access to justice for *all* sections of society, is a rational response to the perceived shortcomings of the civil courts. However, although there may be a common desire to search for court-alternatives for the problems of the poor and for the problems of commercial men alike, it is highly improbable that the solution for one group will necessarily be appropriate for another. In order to devise court-alternatives which serve the legal needs of the poor and disadvantaged, it is necessary to have a clear understanding of the nature of those needs, and second to appreciate how formal and informal legal institutions operate in practice, rather than in theory. It is possible that some of the shortcomings identified by critics of informal courts and tribunals may lie less in the *principle* than in the *practice* of informal justice."

NOTES AND QUESTIONS

- Assess the argument that the growth of tribunals represents a "downgrading" of the claims of the poor. Could the courts provide a better alternative for such claims?

- List the advantages and disadvantages of tribunals as dispute resolution bodies. For what types of disputes do you think tribunals are best suited (if any)?

To what extent do tribunals *in practice* achieve the objectives which we have now examined? Baldwin has studied the Social Security Appeal Tribunals, and he finds the process to be full of tensions regarding tribunal procedure and the role of the chairperson.

**John Baldwin, "The adjudication of claims" (June 5, 1992) New Law Journal 794
at 795:**

"In the wake of the series of damaging criticisms made of supplementary benefit appeal tribunals in the 1970s—criticisms that directly led to the reforms of the 1980s—a determined
attempt is nowadays made by the chairmen and members of social security appeal tribunals
to facilitate the presentation of cases by ordinary citizens. Lay chairmen have been replaced
by qualified lawyers, and a responsibility is placed upon chairmen to enter the arena of dispute
to assist unrepresented claimants. 'It makes a mockery of the tribunal system,' as the former
President of SSATs explained, 'to leave [the claimant] totally to his own devices to argue his
appeal as best he may.'

The tribunals are expected to adopt an inquisitorial approach and take the initiative in
questioning both parties in an attempt to elicit all the evidence. In addition, departmental presenting officers are instructed to play the role of *amicus curiae* and not to assume prosecuto-
rial stances. In 45 per cent of the hearings we observed, no appellant turned up, and, even
where an appellant was present, only about a third were represented. In such circumstances,
the contest between the presenting officer and the appellant would be a most unequal one if
the tribunal operated on strictly adversarial lines.

But have these developments improved the position of appellants appearing before tribunals? The idea that life will be made easier for them if the chairmen and members offer assistance and that any imbalance between the parties will be redressed by discouraging presenting
officers from acting as advocates for the Department is certainly seductive. It seems almost
self-evident that a tribunal that strives to be informal in its approach should lend a helping
hand to any appellant who is floundering. Yet our observations of hearings indicated that the
chairmen of social security appeal tribunals who seek to play a full inquisitorial role and to
assist an appellant who is struggling to present a coherent case are likely to run into difficulty.
Nor is it as easy as it might first appear for presenting officers to play a full *amicus* role.

Turning first to the chairman's inquisitorial function, we found two factors in particular
limited the extent to which the role could be played. First, because of the removal of discretion from large areas of the social security system, the tribunals often have little or no room
for manoeuvre in reviewing an adjudication officer's decision.

Secondly, in almost a half of the cases coming before the tribunal, no appellant is present
to be offered assistance. We were frequently told by tribunal chairmen and members that cases
in which appellants failed to attend received a more cursory examination than those in which
the appellant appeared in person. This was also borne out in our own observations of the
hearings themselves.

It soon becomes clear to anyone who attends tribunal hearings that some chairmen play the
inquisitorial role much more naturally and effectively than do others. Some chairmen are able
to adopt it in a sensitive and expert manner, skilfully eliciting information from claimants and
encouraging them to participate fully in the discussion. Others experience evident unease in
descending into the fray in this way and revert to adversarial type at the first opportunity. Still
others do not strive to play an inquisitorial role at all. On a more general level, the way chairmen run hearings varies enormously. Some are patient and sympathetic, facilitating the difficult task that appellants and other parties face in getting across the essentials of their case.
Other chairmen perform these tasks much less satisfactorily.

We looked closely at the way that hearings were conducted, and we assessed the chairman's
handling of a case as good or excellent in 57 per cent of the hearings we attended, and as adequate in a further quarter of the hearings. In about one in every six hearings, however, the
chairman's conduct of the case was in our view open to serious criticism.

It is not difficult to understand why some chairmen find that adopting a traditional, adversarial approach comes more naturally to them. The body of law with which these tribunals
deal is both technical and complex, and it was perhaps remarkable how far chairmen were
prepared to allow arguments to be developed which could only cloud the legal issues.
Claimants often rely on a commonsense or intuitive notion of what is right or just, in ignorance of the legal merits of their appeal. This means that many cases are in a strict legal sense
flimsy, indeed often doomed from the outset.

Many appellants leave the tribunal dissatisfied with decisions which they see as having been based upon the application of objectionable legal rules, and several chairmen conceded to us in interview that they often shared appellants' views about the law. All the chairmen to whom we spoke, however, said that they had no alternative but to apply the regulations regardless of their personal feelings about a case. One appellant in the Midlands made her objection forcefully as follows:

> 'They just go by the law, and that's it. There's no flexibility in the law, it's rigid. There's no compassion built in. They were all sorry; they were genuinely sorry. The form they give you tells you that you can appeal. This seems to me a bit stupid when there's no chance of you winning the appeal. It's like putting you in a race that you can never win. They slightly raise your hopes, then dash them again. It makes it seem like a sham.'

The tension between the tribunal's sympathy for many claimants and its obligation to apply the law dispassionately runs through the whole of social security adjudication, and chairmen have to find a way in the hearing of allowing appellants to have their say while at the same time steering proceedings along the course that the present law requires. So there is a limit to how far a chairman can be expected to maintain an inquisitorial approach, once the tribunal has satisfied itself that the appeal is based on arguments which have no merit in law."

NOTES AND QUESTIONS

- Note the tension which Baldwin identifies between flexibility and the application of strict legal rules. From reading his analysis, do you think the present approach has the balance right?

- What is meant by a tribunal taking an "inquisitorial" approach to a hearing? How does an inquisitorial approach differ from an adversarial approach?

- Devise a set of guidelines for chairpersons of tribunals concerning their role in the hearing process. Focus on the extent to which an inquisitorial role should be adopted.

LEGAL REPRESENTATION BEFORE TRIBUNALS

From Baldwin's analysis it is apparent that the appearance of an individual before a tribunal in person makes a significant difference to the outcome. A related issue is whether that individual should be allowed legal representation before the tribunal. Intuitively, our assumption probably is that representation might make a difference to the result. After all, isn't that what lawyers are supposed to do? On the other hand, we know that tribunals are intended to be informal, relatively inexpensive and speedy. If lawyers get involved, will those values be undermined? Will the tribunal process inevitably become more "court like" if the tribunal is open to lawyers arguing cases? The issue of legal representation thus goes to the heart of the values which inform the tribunal system, and the question of whether tribunals are "different" (and in what ways) from courts. In this country, legal representation is generally allowed to individuals who appear before tribunals, but that right in practice is undermined for many by the fact that legal aid is not available! Genn has analysed the impact of legal representation on tribunal *outcomes*.

Hazel Genn, "Tribunals and Informal Justice" (1993) 56 M.L.R. 393 at 398:

"Despite the frequent absence of representatives from informal court and tribunal hearings, evidence from empirical research carried out in some tribunals and small claims courts consistently indicates that when present, representation can give an advantage to the represented party. Empirical studies in the UK on the contribution of representation to tribunals generally suggests that represented tribunal applicants are more likely to achieve a favourable outcome to their hearing than unrepresented applicants. However, some of the findings have been criticised for failing to take account of the possibility that representatives select the strongest cases. . . .

One of the chief results of the official view of tribunals in this country is their virtual exclusion from the Legal Aid scheme, although legal or lay representation is permitted in all tribunals.[11] The absence of legal aid is generally explained or defended on the ground that tribunal procedures have been so designed that applicants should be able to bring their cases in person and without legal representation. Tribunal procedures are generally flexible; strict rules of evidence do not apply; applicants are permitted to tell their story in their own words; and tribunal chairs are free to take a more interventionist role than judges in court. Indeed, it is argued not only that legal representation is unnecessary in tribunals, but that the presence of lawyers might undermine the speed and informality that are the hallmarks of tribunal procedures. Despite the absence of legal aid for representation, however, some of those who bring their case before tribunals pay for legal representation or obtain free representation from law centres, tribunal representation units, the Free Representation Unit and a host of specialist advice agencies across the country who provide a limited representation service. Repeated calls for the extension of legal aid to tribunals have fallen on deaf ears, although the research upon which this paper is based was commissioned specifically by the Lord Chancellor's Department to address some of the arguments made about the need for representation to be available to tribunal applicants. . . .

An analysis of the effect of representation on the outcome of hearings established that, in all four tribunals, the presence of a skilled representative significantly and independently increased the probability that a case would succeed. In social security appeals tribunals, the presence of a skilled representative increased the likelihood of success from 30 to 48 per cent. In hearings before immigration adjudicators, the overall likelihood of success was increased by the presence of a representative from 20 to 38 per cent. In mental health review tribunals, the likelihood of a favourable change in conditions rose from 20 to 35 per cent as a result of representation. The effect of representation on the outcome of industrial tribunal hearings is more complicated to state since both parties to hearings are able to appear with a representative. If the respondent was not represented and the applicant was represented by a lawyer, the applicant's success figure was increased from 30 to 48 per cent. Where the respondent was legally represented and the applicant was unrepresented, the applicant's probability of success fell to 10 per cent.

The research indicated clearly that the presence of a representative influences the *substantive* outcome of hearings, irrespective of the process value that representation may provide. It also showed that the type of representation used by appellants was very important, and that specialist representatives exerted the greatest influence on the outcome of hearings. . . ."

QUESTION FOR DEBATE

Given Genn's findings on the impact of legal representation on tribunal outcomes, should legal aid be available for cases which come before administrative tribunals?

---

[11] Exceptions are the ABWOR scheme for Mental Health Review Tribunals, the Employment Appeal Tribunal (but not Industrial Tribunals) and the Lands Tribunal.

Genn concludes that the tradeoff for the value of informality in the tribunal system is inaccuracy in decision making, and she concludes with a proposal for the design of ADR mechanisms.

Hazel Genn, "Tribunals and Informal Justice" (1993) 56 M.L.R. 393 at 411:

"The potential loss of protection that may accompany informal procedures has been robustly articulated by other writers. Cane, for example, suggests that the 'price' of informality in tribunals 'is a certain amount of legal inaccuracy' and that efforts have to be made to avoid insisting on 'strict legal niceties' if such informality is to be preserved. The problem, however, is in establishing the nature and level of inaccuracy that might represent an acceptable cost of informality. Many of the matters heard by tribunals, for example, constitute win or lose situations because there is no other feasible outcome. The right to remain in the country, or to be released from a mental hospital, or the right to a social security benefit are all or nothing situations in which an 'accurate' decision means the loss of an important right. It is clear, however, that the degree of inaccuracy suffered in informal proceedings could be reduced if knowledge about the operation of informal procedures were used to inform decisions about when such procedures should be adopted and how they should be designed. This is important in the current climate. Continuing dissatisfaction with the cost and delay of pursuing civil claims through the courts, together with a dramatic decrease in the availability of legal aid for civil claims, is increasing the pressure to find satisfactory alternatives to the court-resolution of civil disputes. This pressure provides the conditions within which the claims made for ADR, by ADR 'suppliers' to those who can choose to purchase their own alternative to court adjudication, may find a receptive audience, especially within the LCD [Lord Chancellor's Department]. There remain questions, however, about how ordinary and disadvantaged litigants are to achieve just and fair outcomes within informal procedures. They have different needs and competencies from those of commercial litigants keen to maintain relationships and get on with their business.

In order to design appropriate court alternatives outside of the commercial field, consideration must be given to: the nature of the dispute or grievance at issue and the range of possible outcomes; the balance of resources between the parties in terms of finance, experience and competence; and the complexity of the relevant law. Consideration must also be given to the training of those who preside over informal proceedings. This study has indicated that, in the absence of representation, informal court judges and tribunal chairs have a difficult task. It has also shown that they hold the key to procedural fairness and have an important influence on the outcome of hearings."

Although the trade-offs that informal dispute resolution mechanisms involve may seem problematic, the problem should also be kept in perspective.

Michael Sayers and Adrian Webb, "Franks Revisited: A Model of the Ideal Tribunal" (1990) 9 C.J.Q. 36 at 49:

"Perhaps there should be wider recognition of the importance of tribunals and of the decisions they make, often of far greater consequence than those in the courts because—quite apart from the significance of a case to an individual party—there are such large numbers of cases, some are very important in themselves and some create vital precedents. To take an extreme example in recent times, supplementary benefit, the number of recipients increased between 1948, when there were 1 million, and 1983, when there were 4.3 million plus dependents, so totalling 7.2 million—about ⅛th of the population; and we must then remember the low take-up rate, estimated recently at less than three quarters. If one takes the whole social security field the figures are even more dramatic: over 20 million people receive benefits. These benefits cost over £48 billion, apart from £2 billion on administration—that is fully 10 per cent of gross domestic product—which is reflected in the size of the appeal system.

The social security field is the exception rather than the rule, but even so it is difficult to see how many areas of interaction—especially between state and citizens—could operate without the tribunal system. Tribunals are by no means perfect and the principles and guidelines outlined above (which are in themselves imperfect) underline the fact that important improvements remain to be made. Nonetheless, tribunals are an essential, generally effective and increasingly key element in the pursuit of justice and redress in our society. The main alternatives, to have no independent appeal system or to rely solely upon the courts, seem unthinkable or impractical. Tribunals are particularly suitable for dealing with the vulnerable in society. Tribunals can make an important contribution to keeping the wheels of justice and administration turning as swiftly and as smoothly as possible."

Sainsbury and Genn have suggested that many of the values which underpin the Woolf Report could be forwarded by transferring some types of disputes out of the courts and into tribunals.

Roy Sainsbury and Hazel Genn, "Access to Justice: Lessons from Tribunals" in *Reform of Civil Procedure: Essays on "Access to Justice"* (A.A.S. Zuckerman and Ross Cranston, eds., Clarendon Press, Oxford, 1995), p. 413:

"In many ways, the Woolf Report is a bold and imaginative attempt to improve access to justice. However, most of its recommendations are for changes within the existing structures and jurisdictions of a court system which has proved itself somehow impervious to many of the efforts to improve it. It is for this reason that we feel that, alongside the proposals that Woolf suggests, there is scope for a more radical experiment in improving access to justice through greater use of the tribunal system.

In proposing that tribunals could undertake some of the current jurisdictions of the civil courts, we are not suggesting that they are invariably superior to courts nor that courts are fatally flawed. There is clearly a need for a variety of institutional forums in which to hear disputes and challenges between private citizens, and between citizens and the state. However, within our jurisprudence there are no principles which guide or dictate the allocation of decision-making powers between the various arms of the executive and judiciary. Hence, divisions of labour between the courts and tribunals have essentially been ad hoc and pragmatic. . . .

Changing the culture of any enterprise is difficult and often slow, if it can be achieved at all. People attracted to, and proficient within, an adversarial culture may well find it difficult to adapt to a new culture, even if they are minded to. It is puzzling, therefore, that Woolf does not consider more fully the form of dispute resolution that seems to offer exactly the kind of culture that he wishes to see, that is, the tribunal system. Although we recognise that there will always be a need for a variety of appropriate means of resolving disputes, including courts and tribunals, we also see scope for a new role for tribunals in specific areas based on pragmatism or their particular expertise.

There are a number of important reasons why tribunals are a credible alternative to the ordinary courts. In addition to the greater accessibility of tribunals in terms of cost, speed and simplicity of procedures, tribunals are also distinct from most courts in another crucial respect: specialist expertise. Tribunals benefit from specialist expertise in two ways. First, full-time legal Chairs of tribunals are specialists in the subject-matter of the tribunal simply because they hear only the cases within that jurisdiction. The second way in which tribunals benefit from specialist expertise comes from the inclusion in many three-person tribunals of a member with special professional knowledge of the field in question. . . .

Those who are unfamiliar with the work of tribunals sometimes wrongly assume that tribunals' decision making has more in common with routine administrative decision making than with individualistic judicial evaluations of fact and law. In fact tribunal decision making conforms to the traditional model involving hearing, evaluating and weighing evidence, assessing the credibility of witnesses, and reaching accurate decisions in accordance with the relevant body of law and regulations. Procedures must conform with principles of natural justice and tribunal decisions are subject to appeal. . . .

It would be hard to argue against a counsel of caution in devolving responsibilities from the courts to tribunals. But in light of the crisis in the civil justice system, it appears to make sense to consider seriously any opportunity for reducing the pressures on hard-pressed courts. It might not have been the intention in the Woolf Report to foreclose debate about expanding the role of tribunals, but that could be the effect of failing to consider the advantages and disadvantages of such a course of action. The Woolf inquiry may not be the forum to pursue the debate further, but to anyone concerned with improving access to justice for ordinary citizens disadvantaged by lack of detailed knowledge of the courts and by limited resources, we suggest that the tribunal model could form part of a wider strategy in pursuit of that laudable objective."

ESSAY QUESTIONS

- Discuss the relationship between the values which underpin the tribunal system and those of the "rule of law". Does the existence of tribunals enhance or undermine the rule of law?

- Assess Sainsbury and Genn's recommendation for the transfer of disputes from courts to tribunals. What are the advantages and disadvantages of such a programme?

14

COMPARATIVE LEGAL METHOD: THE CIVILIAN TRADITION

This final chapter provides an introductory glimpse at comparative law. The aim is for you to gain a better understanding of common law reasoning through a comparative approach, in which we examine another legal tradition: the civilian system. Of course, there are many legal traditions in the world, and the development of many of them was curtailed brutally by the colonial legacy. Should you take a course in comparative law you will gain a much better appreciation of the subject. For our purposes, this introduction hopefully will whet your appetite. A basic knowledge of the civilian tradition and its legal method is also of increasing importance when dealing with the law of the European Union. After all, the E.U. is a product of the civilian tradition, and although increasingly informed by the common law approach, its legal method remains indebted to the civil law.

In this chapter, we begin with some background on these two legal systems, and then we look in more detail at a particular example of the civil law system through an examination of French law. We then focus upon the different "styles" of the two approaches, and we also look at how the "problem" of judicial law making, which we examined earlier in the context of the common law system, is dealt with in civilian countries. Finally, our focus broadens to consider comparative law in the context of differences between legal *cultures*, and how a consideration of comparative legal culture drives our inquiries back to the question with which we started this text, "what is law"?

INTRODUCTION TO COMPARATIVE LEGAL CULTURES AND METHOD

We begin with some introductory material on legal traditions and cultures, with the aim of better understanding the common law tradition and legal method.

John D. Farrar and Anthony M. Dugdale, *Introduction to Legal Method* (3rd ed., Sweet and Maxwell, London, 1990), pp. 247–250:

The civilian tradition

"This is the oldest of the surviving traditions and can perhaps be traced to 450 BC, the date of the XII Tables in Rome which were a priestly codification of early Roman law.
It is the tradition of the original six member states of the EEC and Spain and Portugal

together with their former colonies. It is the background to much of the early development of the EEC and indeed it has had a strong influence on the development of both public and private international law.

Roman law developed from a priestly system to a highly developed secular system through the influence of jurists (jurisconsults) who did not actually perform the function of a modern lawyer but wrote systematic treatises on particular branches of law. The law itself consisted of the *jus civile*, which only applied to citizens of the Roman empire, and the more flexible *jus gentium* which applied to non citizens. Both systems underwent considerable modification over centuries. In the sixth century AD the emperor Justinian arranged for the production of a Digest and codification of the law which assimilated the laws and doctrinal writings, eliminating conflict. Institutes were also prepared as a primer for law students. This mammoth work of rationalisation enabled Roman law to survive the decline and ultimate destruction of the Roman Empire. The Roman law tradition survived the Dark Ages and was studied in the medieval universities as the basis of rational principles of law.

However, it not only survived as a scholarly tradition, but also as a source of common law of nations at a time when Europe was subject to a multiplicity of local customs and laws. Voltaire reckoned that one changed one's laws as often as one changed one's horse in riding through eighteenth century France. In arriving at a just solution of mercantile disputes Roman law was often resorted to on the Continent. It also influenced the development of the canon law of the Christian Church and the movement towards the early conceptions of international law.

So, therefore, an important ingredient in the civilian tradition is the common inheritance of Roman law. However, a combination of the enlightenment of the eighteenth century and revolution created an impetus to modern codification. This was achieved in the Napoleonic period in France at the beginning of the nineteenth century, although Frederick the Great had attempted a less successful codification of parts of Prussian law in the eighteenth century. The Code Napoléon was a masterly codification of French customary law and Roman law as it stood at 1804. Directly and indirectly it was the blueprint for much European codification. Its basis was simple clear statements of law which left much unsaid. A different approach was adopted in the German codification measures of the end of the nineteenth century. Here the emphasis was on detail and a self contained code—every answer was to be found in the code itself. Most modern Civilian systems opt for one of these two models of codification although each system has areas of law which are not completely codified.

A further characteristic of Civilian systems is the high status accorded to doctrinal writings. While not a source of law as such they rank as high as or of higher status than judicial precedent as a guide to the interpretation of the codes. Where the law is codified the code is the definitive source. The status of judicial precedent is naturally less than in common law systems. It is not that precedent is unimportant in practice but that in theory its validity derives from the words of the code itself. Individual precedents are not binding. A body of precedent is regarded as good evidence of the true meaning of the code. . . .

Last, the Civilian tradition tends to employ more inquisitorial procedures with regard to fact finding than the common law and the whole of its procedure is administered by a career judiciary.

The Common Law tradition

. . . First, the common law, while slightly influenced by the form, did not receive the substance of the Roman law inheritance. It steadfastly resisted it for reasons which were partly political and partly professional. Roman law was linked with Catholicism and later with Stuart autocracy. England, unlike Scotland, developed its own professional structure and tradition from an early date. This was until remarkably recently outside the university framework. English law was not taught at the universities until the eighteenth century, but was the province of the Inns of Court and the profession. The history of legal education in the seventeenth and eighteenth century is rather appalling. Small parts of Roman law did influence some aspects of the common law, but this is mainly as a result of nineteenth century rationalisation.

Secondly, in spite of Bentham and the codification movement in the nineteenth century, the only area of codification has been in commercial law. . . .

Thirdly, as we have seen, although text books by living authors are now cited there is still less status accorded to doctrinal writing in the common law tradition. The status seems to depend *ad hominem* to a greater extent than in the civilian system and reflects perhaps the closed social world of the English judiciary.

Fourthly, the status of judicial precedent is much higher and it is an actual source of law. The standard of the judiciary in the common law world has been high and the process of ratiocination is more obvious in a common law judgment than in the bleak arrested style of a French judgment. As a continuing source, however, with the multiplication of reports the form of the law remains irrational and almost uncontrollable.

Fifthly, the terminology, but not necessarily the practice of interpretation, differs from the civilian tradition as we have seen.[1]

Last, the common law tradition shows a marked preference for adversarial procedure before judges with forensic experience. The emphasis is perhaps more on justice than on truth."

QUESTIONS

- According to Farrar and Dugdale, what are the principal points of divergence between the common law and civilian tradition? What are the similarities?

- What do Farrar and Dugdale mean by their statement that, in the common law tradition, "the emphasis is perhaps more on justice than on truth"?

THE CIVILIAN APPROACH IN PRACTICE: THE EXAMPLE OF FRENCH LAW

With the introductory comments of Farrar and Dugdale in mind, we can now attempt to contextualise the discussion by looking at a particular example of the civil law in practice drawn from a text on the French law of contract. You should attempt to read this extract with a view to understanding the similarities and differences between common law, as it has evolved in this country, and the civilian approach, as it is practiced in France.

Barry Nicholas, *The French Law of Contract* (Oxford University Press, London, 1982), pp. 1–23:

Common Law and Civil Law

"French law belongs to that family of legal systems to which we attached the name of 'Civil law'. This family embraces the systems of continental Europe (or at least western Europe), and also of Latin America and many other countries which derive their legal systems from continental Europe. The name is often criticized, especially by Civil lawyers themselves, because it refers to only one element in the tradition which unites those systems, and also because it ignores the differences which distinguish one from another. (In much the same way in ordinary life a stranger sees the resemblances between members of a family, while they themselves are more aware of their individuality.) But the usage is inveterate among Common lawyers, and the name, if properly understood, does point to some important

---

[1] We will look more closely at practices of interpretation later in this chapter.

characteristics which the systems have in common and which are foreign to the Common law.

The origin of the name is clear. To the Romans the term *ius civile* had meant, at its widest, the law of a particular state, or, more narrowly, the law of Rome herself. It was in accordance with this usage that Justinian's compilation of Roman law came to be known, after its redis-covery in the eleventh century, as the *Corpus Iuris Civilis*. And 'Civil law' thereafter meant the rediscovered Roman law. As this law was 'received' by the emergent states and cities of conti-nental Europe as a *ius commune*, or common law, which was applied in default of, or to a varying extent in substitution for, the local law, it was natural that the English, whose courts had stood apart from this reception, should see in this common factor the identifying mark of the legal systems of the Continent. Nor did they habitually make any distinction between this contemporary Civil law and the historical law of Rome. Blackstone, for example, calls it 'the imperial law.'

During the last two hundred years, however, the justification for thus seeing the laws of the Continent as predominantly Roman law in a modern context has diminished. The most important influence in this dwindling of the Roman element has been the movement for cod-ification, the first great achievement of which was the enactment of Napolean's *Code civil* in 1804. The codes which thereafter spread over Europe were important (in this context) in two ways. First, they cut the law off from its Roman roots: the *Corpus Iuris Civilis* could no longer be cited as direct authority. If Roman rules were still applied, this was because they were embodied in the relevant code, and not (except as a matter of history) because they were to be found in the *Corpus Iuris*. Moreover, as Roman law disappeared from the courts, it took on a different appearance in the lecture room. The interest shifted from the task of interpret-ing the *Corpus Iuris* as a practical system to that of unearthing the classical law. For that law lay buried beneath both the editorial work of Justinian and the heavy layer of interpretation and harmonization which had been elaborated by centuries of activity in the universities of Europe. 'Civil law' (or *ius commune*) was now seen to be not the same as Roman law.

This does not mean that there are no common elements in, say, French and German law which justify our still speaking of them as 'Civil law systems', but they are Civil law in a dif-ferent sense. They belong to the Civil law because their methods of thought, their attitudes to law and its sources, derive from the centuries in which the *ius commune*, Romanistic but not Roman, was created out of the materials in the *Corpus Iuris*. And those methods and atti-tudes are different, as we shall see, from those of the English Common law, which was nur-tured in a quite other environment.

The Roman element, therefore, has dwindled since the coming of the codes. Its importance was indeed never as exclusive as the English use of the name 'Civil law' suggested. Apart from Canon law (which was Roman in spirit and, like Roman law, universal), there were everywhere two other elements: customary law and legislation. But these varied from one legal system to another, or even, in the case of customary law, from one local area to another, and it was natural for the Common lawyer to emphasize the universal element. Moreover, the non-Roman elements were mainly to be found in those areas of the law (the law of the family and of inheritance) which are everywhere most likely to be affected by differences of culture and of what one now calls 'policy'. The contribution of Roman law, on the other hand, was strong-est in the parts which have, at least until recently, been most exclusively the handiwork of lawyers: the law of obligations . . ., the law of property, and the general conceptual frame-work of the whole system. The advent of the codes, however (and this was the second way in which they diminished the Roman character of the systems to which they applied), unified and systematized the customary element, while the spirit of the times and the complexity of modern life has everywhere produced an ever-swelling volume of legislation only loosely related to the traditional Roman framework.

It is this framework which provides a link between the Common lawyer's use of 'Civil law' and the meaning which French lawyers give to *droit civil*. In its widest sense this denotes the whole of private law. In practice, however, as a glance at any of the many works published under this title will show, the term refers primarily and usually to the contents of the *Code civil*. And the *Code civil* is concerned with the central and traditional parts of the private law: the law of persons (or family law), the law of property and of succession, and the law of obligations. This is the heart of the private law, the trunk of the tree from which grow the more particular branches. All other parts (and, as has just been said, they are now both extensive and important) pre-suppose the *droit civil*. And the *droit civil* in this sense goes back to Justinian's Institutes, which provide the framework of the *Corpus Iuris* and therefore of the 'Civil law' in the Common lawyer's sense, even though (it must be said again) the substance which is now attached to some parts of this framework is anything but Roman. The framework, however, though it is to be found in varying forms in all 'Civil law' systems, is not, from the point of view of the common lawyer, the most important of the differentiating characteristics of those systems. We should now look more closely at those differences of method and atittude to which reference has already been made.

Characteristics of French Law

The differences of method and attitude which has now to be identified derive, we have said, from the *ius commune*. For though important elements of French law come, as we have seen, from canon law, customary law, and legislation, the Common lawyer finds the principal differentiating characteristics of the system in the inheritance from this *ius commune*.

The heart of the matter is that the *ius commune* is a law of the book, elaborated in the universities, whereas the Common law is a law of the case, created by the courts. The *ius commune*, in theory at least, sprang fully formed from the *Corpus Iuris Civilis*, the function of the universities being that of interpretation. The Common law, on the other hand, is in a state of continuous creation and by its nature is never complete. Again, the *ius commune* was seen as universally valid, regardless of time or place. It was a set of rules for the conduct of life in society—rules which might or might not be applied in any particular court or jurisdiction. (Hence it is still true today that in the universities of the Continent law is studied by large numbers who will never go into practice.) The Common law, by contrast, is concerned to provide solutions to individual disputes, not to propound universal precepts; and it is expressed, in its traditional form, in terms of actions or remedies rather than of substantive rules. Insofar as nowadays it does think in terms of rules, those rules are seen as a generalization from the solutions of individual disputes, whereas for the Civil lawyers the rules logically precede the solutions. In short, for the Common law the beginning is the case, whereas for the *ius commune* the beginning is the book.

With the advent of the codes the character of the book changes, but the conception of law remains the same. The beginning is now the code or codes, not the *Corpus Iuris*, but the primacy of the written law remains. Law is still seen as a system, complete and intellectually coherent, composed of substantive rules. And the creative function is still that of interpretation, a function exercised in the first place by the universities. The decisions of the courts are, in conventional theory, merely an application of the enacted law. Some of these features need further examination in the particular context of French law.

Primacy of legislation

In the conventional French analysis there are only two sources of law: legislation and custom. The latter is only interstitial and in the present context can be ignored. Law is primarily and characteristically a body of rules enacted by the state, to be found in the codes and, in an ever-increasing measure, in legislation supplementary to the codes. Indeed, just as a Common lawyer will derive a general principle from particular cases, a French lawyer may, by what has been called 'amplifying induction', find in individual enactments evidence of a wide legislative intent which can be applied outside the area covered by the individual enactments. The Common lawyer's approach is quite different. For him law has characteristically been the unwritten law found in the decisions of the courts. It is true, of course, that legislation is the primary source in the sense that in case of conflict it will prevail, but it has traditionally been regarded as an inroad on or suspension of the Common law, which will revive when the legislation is repealed. Particular enactments will therefore be restrictively interpreted. So far from inferring a more general legislative intent, the Common lawyer will argue that if Parliament had intended to lay down a more general principle, it would have done so expressly.

This difference is reflected in a difference in the approach of the two systems to the interpretation of legislation (and, as a corollary, a difference in the style of drafting). The English courts, seeing legislation as an inroad on the basic unwritten law, interpret it restrictively, so as to minimize the inroad. This attitude would make no sense for the French lawyer for whom the basic law is itself legislation. In the period of the *ius commune*, when lawyers had to adapt the unchanging texts of the *Corpus Iuris* to the changing needs of society and to find a harmony in the rich disordance of these texts, they necessarily adopted a very free and creative method of interpretation. The method remains, and it is indeed in accord with the relatively subordinate position which is allotted to the judiciary by the French version of the separation of powers. Legislation is a manifestation of the will of the state and the function of the judiciary as an organ of the state is to give effect to that will.

This function is pre-supposed by the simplicity and brevity of French legislative drafting. The English draftsman tries to make his text 'judge-proof' by anticipating every eventuality, and he often in consequence produces a complex and technical formulation which only a lawyer can interpret. The French draftsman, by contrast, can rely on the collaboration of the courts, and his text is therefore often limited to quite broad propositions. That this is true of the *Code civil* is well known (and it is a source of pride and confidence to the Frenchman that his law is presented in a simple and intelligible form) but even the necessarily more complex legislation of modern times may leave much to be filled in by interpretation.

Character of the codes

If legislation is the characteristic form of law in France and the codes are the characteristic form of legislation, the *Code civil* is the characteristic code. The Napoleonic codification consisted of five codes, but the term *Code Napoléon* was reserved for the *Code civil* alone. And with justice. For the *Code civil* is the centre-piece to which the great influence of the whole codification is attributable.

A code in the strict sense is a systematic and complete statement of a body of law. In this sense the *Corpus Iuris Civilis* of Justinian is not a code. For though it is complete, it is not in any recognizable way systematic. The *Code civil* is systematic, though its system (which echoes, without entirely reproducing, that if the Institutes of Gaius and Justinian) is, as a piece of analysis, easily criticized; and it is a complete statement of the law governing relations between individuals (except insofar as these are governed by the *Code de commerce*) as that law was understood in 1804. We have seen, however, that even then the simplicity and brevity of its drafting left much to be supplied by interpretation, and it is now not complete in any sense. For the increasing complexity of modern life has called forth a large body of additional legislation. Some of this can be said merely to amplify the provisions of the Code, but by far the greater part is concerned with matters quite outside the area of the traditional *droit civil*. Codification, moreover, creates an expectation that all law will be presented in a systematic form, and a good deal of the additional legislation has itself been reduced to the form of subordinate codes. In England, by contrast, even in those areas of the law which are largely the creation of legislation, a systematic statement of the whole body of the law is not undertaken. At most, as in the Companies Act 1985, a consolidation of existing legislation is found, but this leaves the essential Common law foundations unstated; and when such a consolidation comes to be amended, as in the Companies Act 1989, no attempt is made to build the new legislation into the old. A codifying statute is a rarity, and the few which have been enacted deal in fact with areas of the law which were almost entirely judge-made. . . .

Authority of case law

The courts of the *ancien régime* (the *parlements*) were one of the main objects of the hostility of the Revolutions, not least because of their pretensions to a law-making function. The Constituent Assembly of 1790 took care that the new courts should be confined to the narrowly judicial function of applying the law in suits between private individuals (or, in criminal matters, between the state and the individual). They were to have no jurisdiction over the administration, and in exercising their proper function they were not to lay down general rules. They were even required to refer any matter of interpretation to the legislature. This was of course quite impracticable and remained a dead letter, but the prohibition against laying down general rules when deciding individual cases was repeated in article 5 of the *Code civil*.

This attempt to prevent the growth of case law was undermined, however, by another requirement laid down by the Assembly. The *parlements* had not given reasons for their decisions, but now, in order to ensure that the courts did not exceed their powers, every decision was to be 'motivated'. The form of judgment which the courts adopted to meet this requirement (and which survives without significant change today) does not set out, as an English judgment does, the process of argument by which the decision was reached—this would have been inconsistent with the ruling mechanistic view of the judicial process; but equally it does not simply state the legislative text on which the decision was based—the generality of many provisions in the Codes would have defeated the original purpose of the requirement of 'motivation'. Typically the form adopted states the facts, the grounds of the *pourvoi* (in the case of the *Cour de cassation*), and a principle from which, by syllogistic reasoning applied to the facts, the decision can be logically derived. In every case the judgment, however long, is framed as a single sentence, of which the subject ('The Court . . .') is placed at the beginning and the main verb, stating the decision ('quashes', 'rejects', etc.), at the end, everything else being incorporated in subordinate clauses beginning with 'whereas' (*attendu* or in some courts *considérant*). The judgments of lower courts are usually fuller than those of the *Cour de cassation* and, since those courts are judges of both fact and law, they state the facts at greater length, but the form is in all essentials the same. The principle is presented as self-evident and is in theory, in the normal case, derived from a text or texts which are cited at the beginning of the judgment. But it is of course in the act of derivation that the creative power of the judiciary resides, and the result of requiring that act to be recorded was inevitably the evolution of what is in substance a vast body of judge-made law.

It was not, however, until late in the nineteenth century that the literature of the law began seriously to take cognizance of this development. This delay reflects the dominance in the thought of the period of the positivist view of law as the expression of the will of the state (a view which accords, as we have seen, with the doctrine of the separation of powers and which is still to be found in French textbooks). The persistence of the mechanistic view of the role of the courts was also, however, encouraged by the form of the judgment, which, by making no reference to the arguments which have led the court to adopt the governing principle (even when the court is in fact reversing a previously established principle), conceals the creative process.

No-one, in any event, now disputes that the decisions of the courts (*la jurisprudence*) must play a large part in any attempt to state the law. To go no further, what we should call the law of torts, which is stated in the *Code civil* in only five articles, is very largely a creation of the courts, and the law of unjustified enrichment derives from a decision of the *Cour de cassation* in 1892 which did not even purport to be based on a text. The writers regularly, and increasingly, take account of *jurisprudence*; no practitioner would fail to deal with it in presenting a case; and though the judgments (with some exceptions in the lower courts) continue to make no reference to it, it is fully examined in the *conclusions* of the representative of the *ministère public* and in the *rapport*.

The constitutional theory that *jurisprudence* cannot be a legal source is, however, normally maintained. Theory and practice may be reconciled by drawing a distinction between a source (in law) and an authority (in fact). It is an obvious and important fact that courts do follow previous decisions, and statements of what the law is necessarily take account of this fact. But it is nevertheless a fact and not a rule; no court is legally required to follow any previous decision. There is no system of binding precedent, though there is a practice which produces similar results. This may look like splitting hairs to preserve a principle, but the distinction between rule and fact does have practical consequences, and the results, though similar, are not identical.

The practical consequences lie partly in the way in which judgments are formulated and partly in the attitude of the judges. The former is indeed something of a technicality. A court may not cite as the justification for its decision a previous decision, or line of decisions, even of the *Cour de cassation*. If it does so, the decision will be quashed for lack of legal foundation. Conversely, if the *Cour de cassation* wishes to quash a decision as being in conflict with its own *jurisprudence*, and every lawyer knows this is what it is doing, it will nonetheless state as the foundation for its decision not the *jurisprudence*, but the text or legal principle of which the *jurisprudence* is ostensibly an interpretation.

As far as the attitude of judges is concerned, the consequences of the distinction between rule and fact are not merely technical. To say that an English judge of first instance is bound by decisions of the Court of Appeal is not merely to say that he will in fact follow those decisions, or that even if he does not, his decision will be overturned on appeal; it is an assertion both that the judge accepts that he must follow those decisions and that, if he were not to do so, even on good grounds, he would be subject to criticism by the profession. The French judges accept that they ought usually to follow decisions of the *Cour de cassation*, if only because stability and predictability are important in the law, but their legal duty is to apply the law and if they are convinced that a decision of the *Cour de cassation* does not represent the law, they will ignore it; and they will not incur the same criticism as would an English judge. Resistance of this kind to decisions of the *Cour de cassation* is not very uncommon and may, if maintained, particularly by several *Cours d'appel*, presage a change (*revirement*). For what is true of the lower courts is true also of the *Cour de cassation*, and there has never been any suggestion that that court is bound by its own decisions. It is usually said, however, that there is one court—the *Assemblée plénière*—which has such authority that no other court would think of going against it.

There is, then, no rule of binding precedent, but there is a well-established practice that lower courts will normally follow the *jurisprudence* of the *Cour de cassation*. This leaves open, of course, the question of what constitutes a *jurisprudence*. It has often been said that the important difference in practice between the English and the French systems of precedent is that in England a single decision is sufficient, whereas in France authority attaches to what is called a *jurisprudence constante*, *i.e.* to a concordant series of decisions. But it is easy to point to single decisions which marked a new departure—and were immediately recognized as doing so. The significant distinction is rather between an *arrêt de principe* and an *arrêt d'espèce*, *i.e.* between a judgment which is intended to establish a principle (either because the case law has been uncertain or conflicting or because the court has decided to alter its previous jurisprudence) and one which, as an English lawyer might say, is to be confined to its own facts. This is not to suggest that all decisions are capable of being labelled as one or the other. The great majority of the vast number of *arrêts* rendered each year by the *Cour de cassation* are unremarkable decisions which merely augment an already well-established *jurisprudence constante* on the matter in issue. It is to the small residue of cases which do not fit into this category that the distinction applies. It is not, of course, a distinction which declares itself on the face of the *arrêt*, and its application is a matter of art as much as of science, but the reader of the French reports will acquire a part of the skill if he remembers that in a literary form as laconic as that of the French judgment, particularly as it is practised in the *Cour de cassation*, no word is wasted and none is unconsidered. For example, the formulation of the principle which constitutes the major premise of the judgments may be repeated unaltered through dozens or hundreds of cases, while the critical reader wonders at the increasingly forced interpretation of either the principle or the facts which is necessary in order to complete the syllogism, until finally a small alteration is made which so adjusts the principle that the forced interpretation is no longer necessary. Again, when the *jurisprudence* is uncertain or in disarray, a categorical statement of a general principle, particularly if it is placed at the beginning of the *arrêt* as what is called a *chapeau*, will be seen as the mark of an *arrêt de principe*.

There remains a very considerable difference in the methods by which in the two systems the principle established by a decision is identified. In the first example given above the alert reader will notice the change in formulation, but may well be left in doubt as to what it portends. The judgment itself will give him no assistance. If he is fortunate, this may be one of the rare cases in which the *conclusions* or the *rapport* are published. Otherwise he must interpret the change in the light of the *doctrine* on the subject, which will have discussed the difficulties presented by the previous cases. An attempt at such an interpretation will often be appended as a *note* to the report.

In an English judgment, on the other hand, the principle of the case is not encapsulated in a single carefully pruned and polished sentence. The decision of the case typically evolves from an examination of the previous cases and a discussion of how far the pattern set by those cases needs to be adapted to accommodate the new fact situation. The characteristic English intellectual device of 'distinguishing' is unknown in France, both because the form of the judgment provides no opportunity for it and because, at least in the *Cour de cassation*, the facts play a subordinate role, and may indeed be so elliptically stated as to be unintelligible without a reference to the decision of the court below. The reason for this is in part that the *Cour de cassation* is, as we have seen, concerned only with an examination of the proposition of law relied on by the court below, and in part that the courts as a whole still think of the judicial process as one of applying to the facts before them a rule established a priori. The cases are illustrations of principles rather than the material from which principles are drawn.

This attitude to facts lends considerable importance to the distinction between fact and law. Findings of fact are within the uncontrolled discretion of the court which tries the case (and this, on the French view of the nature of an appeal, includes the relevant *cour d'appel*). The *Cour de cassation* cannot interfere with this *pourvoir souverain du juge du fond* unless the interpretation of the primary facts is so unreasonable that it can be said to have 'denatured' them. From this it follows that the wider the area of what is categorized as fact, the more restricted will be the unifying power of the *Cour de cassation*. The view of cases as illustrations, which is an aspect of the tendency of a 'law of the book' to formulate broad rules, leaves a large area to fact. In the Common law, by contrast, since the law evolves from the cases, there is a constant tendency for fact to harden into law. Case-made rules are by their nature narrow. From time to time an act of judicial generalization, or perhaps the intervention of the legislature, will produce a broad rule or principle, but the process of producing small rules out of facts will then resume.

In general therefore the area of fact is wider in French law than in English. This means, of course, that the operation of the law is less predictable, that the discretion of the court is more extensive. . . . To put the matter in another way, in many areas French law is less detailed than English, even though the number of reported decisions is much larger. An English book on contract will be re-edited every four or five years and each new edition will embody many changes. Its French counterpart will probably be re-edited less often and the changes will be much less numerous.

Functions of doctrine

By *doctrine* is meant the whole body of writing about the law by those learned in it. As its name indicates, it originated in the teaching of the universities and it is still to a very large extent the work of academic writers. As we have seen, the *ius commune* was created in the universities out of the materials in the *Corpus Iuris*, and it was to the universities that the courts looked for an authoritative interpretation of that law. Any system of law, if it is to be capable of growth and adaptation, must have, in addition to a body of rules, a web of principles from which those rules derive. These principles can never be exhaustively defined or finally fixed. They derive from a continuing debate. In classical Roman law this debate was conducted by the jurists; in medieval England it was to be heard in the courts (and its content was much more technical). In Europe of the *ius commune* the debate was conducted in the universities and in the literature which emanated from them. If one is to find its equivalent in the Common law, at any rate before the beginnings of academic writing in the last two decades of the nineteenth century, one must look in the judgments of the courts. The argumentative form of the English judgment provides, in the hands of the great judges, something of that web of principles to which we have referred. The English judgment fulfils in fact two functions. In its *ratio decidendi* it constitutes a source of law; in its discursive element it provides a part of what is supplied in French law by *doctrine*. The part which it cannot provide is large-scale systematic exposition, and it is only in the course of the last 100 years that this gap has gradually been filled, as it always has been in France, by academic writing. There remains a marked, though diminishing, difference in the authority which is attached to such writing in the two systems. In France *doctrine* has inherited the authority enjoyed by the universities in the period of the *ius commune*, an authority which is augmented by the relatively subordinate position which is, as we have seen, accorded to the judiciary in the constitutional scheme. The positions are reversed in England, though the standing accorded to academic writing by the courts (and its influence on their decisions) has risen considerably in recent decades.

The typical product of French *doctrine* is the large-scale treatise or the student's manual. It is in accord with the French conception of law as a system that these works usually embrace the entire *droit civil*, or the entire *droit commercial*, or at least a large and coherent part of it, such as the law of obligations. . . . In addition to the treatises and manuals, there are also specialized monographs (often academic theses) and articles, but the peculiar contribution of French *doctrine* has been the *note* appended to a case and providing an explanation of and commentary on it. This has provided a bridge between traditional *doctrine* and the courts. On the one hand, it has brought into the mainstream of the law the rich contribution of *jurisprudence* which would otherwise have been locked up in the cramped clauses of the judgments, and, on the other hand, it has brought the courts into touch with the critical and creative debate of which we have already spoken.

It should be said that not all *notes* are the work of academic writers. They may also be contributed by practitioners or by judges—even on occasion, as we have already remarked, by a judge who took part in the decision.

Conceptualism and pragmatism

It is sometimes said that the Civil law is excessively conceptual or 'logical' or 'formalist', whereas the Common law is pragmatic and concrete. (A similar contrast is made, within the Common law between English law and American law.) This observation seems to bear two different meanings.

1. It can mean that the Civil law will apply a given principle or concept 'logically' even though the practical consequences are unjust or inconvenient, whereas the Common law will abandon a principle if its consequences are unacceptable. More precisely this is a contrast not between logic and the lack of it, but between an approach which treats principles as having an immutable meaning (or at least is unwilling to re-examine the established interpretation in the light of its consequences), and one which acknowledges that meanings and interpretations change with circumstances. In other words, it is a contrast between an approach which speculates as to the correct conceptual analysis of a situation or relationship without adverting to the consequences which flow from that analysis (or without considering what policy may account for the attribution of those consequences to that analysis) and an approach which acknowledges that principles and concepts are shorthand for practical consequences. For the realist or antiformalist cannot dispense with concepts without abandoning the element in law which ensures that like is treated alike; he can only insist that concepts be seen in the context of their consequences.

    As far as French *jurisprudence* is concerned, this Common lawyer's view is encouraged by the form of the judgment, which gives no place to a consideration of practical consequences or of questions of 'policy'. It appears to treat principles as frozen in a single interpretation, whereas the English judgment makes plain the process by which convenience prevails over 'logic', or, more precisely, by which the previously accepted principle or interpretation is distinguished from one which can accommodate the argument from convenience. We have seen, however, that the form of the judgment does not correctly record the process by which the decision is reached.

    As far as *doctrine* is concerned, the criticism was certainly well-founded in the nineteenth century, when the survival of eighteenth century natural law ideas, combined with an exclusive concentration on deriving the law from an examination of the words of the Code, did produce an attitude like that characterized above. Nor was this attitude confined to France. It was to be found even more markedly in German writing. And this in turn dominated the work of the contemporary English analytical jurists and the early English academic textbooks. It probably survived longest in Italy, where an isolation of doctrinal writing from the decisions of the courts and a general lack of interest in the application of principles to facts is still noticeable.

Present-day *doctrine*, particularly the most recent works, is much more practically orientated than it used to be and devotes a great deal of attention to the decisions of the *Cour de cassation*, but it can still sometimes appear to the English lawyer to be examining a closed system. To some extent this is a mistaken impression, attributable to the different status of case law. As we have seen, the English lawyer, because he is constantly returning to the cases, is visibly rooting his principles and concepts in practical situations, whereas the French lawyer derives his principles and concepts primarily from the Code and legislation. That these principles and concepts are not reconcilable with *jurisprudence* is not, as it would be in England, a reason for abandoning them outright, though it is one ground for criticizing them. And to say that a principle is not rooted in the cases does not mean that it takes no account of practical considerations. What is true is that the emphasis in doctrinal writings is placed more on rational coherence and less on practical consequences than it is either in Common law writing or, usually, in the *rapports* or *conclusions* presented to the courts.

2. This brings us to the second sense which can be borne by the observation which we are discussing. In this second sense the observation refers to the fact, which we have already noted, that the French *droit civil* is, ostensibly at least, a complete and coherent system, each part of which is capable of being related to every other part. As we can see from the many cross-references which editions of the *Code civil* provide, a French lawyer takes it for granted that one article can be interpreted in the light of another in a quite different part of the Code or in some subsequent legislation. This view of the law as a single, intellectually coherent system is common to all Civil law systems (it is carried to a far higher degree of generality by German law than by French) but it does not come readily to the mind of the Common lawyer. This is not, however, a matter of the presence or absence of logic or concepts, but of the scale on which each system thinks. English law thinks in pigeon-holes and rarely seeks to relate one pigeon-hole to another. This is the reason for its unease when it has to deal, for example, with the borderland between contract and tort. This relative lack of large-scale concepts reflects, of course, the primacy of the judge over the academic lawyer in the development of English law."

QUESTIONS

- It is sometimes claimed that common law lawyers start from the "specific", whereas civilians begin from the "general". What does this mean?

- What is the role of judicial precedent in the civil law system? How does it differ from its role in the common law system?

- How would a French judgment differ in style and content from an English judgment?

- Explain what is meant by the characterisation of French civil law as "conceptual" and English common law as "pragmatic".

CODIFICATION AND LEGITIMACY

In earlier chapters, we examined how judges engage in a process of "law making" within the common law system and we saw how that role as law maker was "masked" by a judiciary which attempted to construct its task as one of "finding" a common law which was already "there". In that way, judges sought to avoid opening themselves up to claims of illegitimacy. The question of legitimacy is also important within the civilian tradition. In this case, resort to the codes is the means through which the judiciary has legitimised its decisions.

Peter Goodrich, *Reading the Law* (Blackwell, Oxford, 1986), pp. 37–40:

"The contemporary civilian legal traditions embody and express the principles and presuppositions outlined above in terms of the tradition of written law as the primary source of law. In form, codification dominates written law. It provides the fundamental law in both the public (law relating to the powers of the State and the State/individual relationship) and the private (law relating to relationships between individuals) domains. Codification is also supplemented by written laws of a secondary status (statutes, decrees) which may be used to add detail to the basic rules contained within the codes. The style of codified law throughout Europe has generally been influenced by one of the earliest modern examples of a code of private law, the *Code Napoléon*, which attempted to use simple, general statements of principle as the basis for legal regulation. The other end of the spectrum is reflected in the Code of Frederick the Great of Prussia who attempted to provide detailed rules to meet every eventuality; for example, the code contained clauses dealing with rules for deciding upon the sexuality of hermaphrodites and provisions relating to the practice of breast-feeding. Both approaches to the drafting of codes pose their respective sets of problems for the relationship between the primacy of the code and the task of interpretation. The demand that the code should at all times be *the* source of law and that this position should not be undermined, together with the political principle of the separation of powers, influential from the eighteenth century onwards in most European states, which demands that the law-making power be located in the legislature, are the main legal and political factors that influence the dilemma arising from the task of interpretation.

In practice the judiciary are involved in interpreting words and phrases whose meaning is unclear, dealing with lacunae within a text which purports to be a complete exposition of the law and applying the code to situations which could not have been foreseen by the legislature. Civilian systems have experimented with various mechanisms to resolve the problem of law-making through interpretation. As the legislature is the ultimate source of law, ideally it should resolve the problems of interpretation returning the definition to the judiciary for application. Such a mechanism was used after the French Revolution but was found to be impossible to operate in practice. A second technique is to provide a provision within the code which prescribes how the judges are to deal with the task of interpretation. For example in the Italian Civil Code (1942) the code provides that:

> 'In interpreting the statute, no other meaning can be attributed to it than that made clear by the actual significance of the words according to the connections between them, and by the intention of the legislature.
>
> If a controversy cannot be decided by a precise provision, consideration is given to provisions that regulate similar cases or analogous matters; if the case still remains in doubt it is to be decided according to general principles of the legal order of the State.'

In practice neither the objective that the code be *the* source of law nor the complete separation of law-making from law-application is realized. In the French legal system, for example, judicial interpretations have, even in legal doctrine, over time become accepted as a source of law known as jurisprudence. This jurisprudence has been responsible for developing areas of law, as for example with Article 1384 of the *Code Napoléon* which states, in paragraph 1, that: 'A person is responsible not only for the damage caused by his own actions, but also for that which is caused by the actions of persons for whom he must answer *or that caused by things under his care.*' The jurisprudence of the French courts developed the words emphasized to fill a gap in the law (concerning the relevant standard of care owed) which had not been met by the legislature, and succeeded in providing for liability without fault for damage caused by things under one's care. The use of general statements of law creates the need for the judiciary to define the detailed application of the principles. The use of specific rules may raise the need for a creative style of interpretation to meet the demands of novel factual situations.

To meet the needs generated by the legal, political and practical contexts of law-application, the judiciary within civilian legal systems have developed a range of approaches to the task of interpretation. As most judges wish to be seen to be supporters of the prevailing legal and political ideology, preference is given to approaches to interpretation that follow the letter of the law, adopting and applying a grammatical construction of the text and a literal sense to the meaning of the words used. When the dispute before the courts cannot satisfactorily be resolved in this literal manner the courts depart from the technique. Numerous alternative styles have been developed and practised in the various civilian legal systems. An example from France is contained in a speech made on the occasion of the centenary celebrations of the French *Code Civil* by Ballot-Beaupré (1836–1917), president of the French Supreme Court (*Cour de Cassation*). He delivered a speech which confirmed his support for the literal approach to interpretation where the text is unambiguous, clear and precise in its application. However, when ambiguity or doubts arise, then the judge should have the widest powers of interpretation. The judge should not be confined by the historical context of the document to be interpreted. The judge must operate as if the clause were being drafted today. Having regard to contemporary ideas, social manners, institutions, economic and social conditions he must say 'justice and reason require that the text be literally interpreted and humanely adapted to the realities and requirements of modern life'. Another technique found operating in the German courts involves the use of general clauses to neutralize or adapt specific provisions. For example the German Supreme Court (Reichsgerict) has used clause 826 ('Whoever intentionally causes injury to another in a manner violating good morals is bound to repair the injury') to alter the apparent meaning of other clauses. Clause 823, for example, was interpreted by reference to clause 826 to facilitate the award of damages as compensation which appeared to be excluded by the wording of clause 823, a more specific provision.

The status of jurisprudence as law is informally recognized in that reference to previous decisions containing interpretations of the law is made during the course of legal argument, and may be found in notes and commentaries made about the code. The politically and doctrinally important claim that the judiciary is not making law is maintained to varying degrees within the various civilian legal systems. For example, in the *Cour de Cassation*, the French Supreme Court, judgments handed down do not contain references to interpretations provided in the court's previous decisions but refer only to clauses within the code, thereby supporting the fiction that the code is complete, providing all that is necessary to resolve the issues before the court. Similarly, the reports of the decisions of the Italian courts omit references to sources other than the code, it being the view of Italian jurists that 'the work of the legal [scientists] is like the work of other scientists, not concerned so much with the resolution of practical problems as with the search for scientific truth, for ultimates and fundamentals; not concerned so much with individual cases as with generic problems, the perfection of learning and understanding, not, in a word, with engineering, but with pure science'. The practices referred to are fictional in the very concrete sense that annual series of annotated case reports are published listing the decisions relevant to each section of the code and these are used both academically and in relevant legal argument.

Whilst it is possible to observe from the behaviour of the courts that the codified law is not the sole source of law, codified law still plays a central role within the civilian legal culture as the ultimate source of legitimacy to which all other activities must relate. It is in this sense that it retains its primacy within the legal system. The secondary sources and techniques of law-interpretation more generally must all relate back to the codified law and claim their origin in it."

COMPARATIVE LAW AND EUROPEAN INTEGRATION

Some understanding of comparative methodology will be of increasing importance with greater legal integration within the European Union. The following two extracts, the last in this text, illustrate two different perspectives on the potential of comparative methodology in the context of European Union. The first, by Markesinis, argues that it is through universities that a greater convergence and understanding between civilians and common law lawyers will be achieved. The second, by Legrand, argues that in order to engage in comparative analysis, we need to take a broader approach, one which engages with legal *cultures*, rather than simply with legal doctrine.

B.S. Markesinis, "A Matter of Style" (1994) 110 L.Q.R. 607 at 625:

"In this lecture a number of differences have been noted between the style and contents of the English and German cases which can, ultimately, be traced to fundamental and interrelated decisions taken by these systems in the distant past. The English ones, of course, are well-known: a preference for procedure over principles of substantive law; a neglect of the academic component of the law; the appointment of judges from a small group of leading practitioners; and the adoption of the jury system with all the consequences this has had on procedure and presentation of legal argument. Known though these are, they may well be repeated here since two new developments are seriously affecting the second of the above-named factors and, indirectly, the law that is handed down by our courts. The developments to which I am referring are the greater interaction between English and continental European universities and the fact that nowadays in England a university training has become an essential ingredient of a legal (including judicial) career. These two developments are, I believe, to determine what we will 'take' in future years from continental systems and, also, what we might be able to 'give' them in exchange. . . .

If this development is now seen in the context of the even newer 'European' perspective— and by that I mean the growing significance for municipal law of the decisions of the European Courts in Luxembourg and Strasbourg *and* the growing contacts under Erasmus-type programmes—it can lead to the conclusion that it is no longer fanciful to predict a steady growth in the impact that European law and doctrine will have on ours. This may not affect the style of judgments—a main theme of this paper—indeed, I hope it does not! But it is bound to strengthen their doctrinal content—the second theme of this paper—combatting the idea that because the tasks of judge and jurist are (in *some* respects) different *they must also be carried out in complete isolation from each other*. In this sense, too, the tide of European ideas will prove difficult to contain. The student of today, who will be the judge of tomorrow, will be unlikely to resist this influence since it will not be alien to him but, on the contrary, will have played a part in his formation and training.

But will the influence be one-sided? I think not and I hope not. If we do not remain in our shells we, too, can and will influence developments elsewhere. Moreover, I believe our *main* contribution may well be something of a paradox since it will come from our universities (which in historical terms were the junior partners in the development of our law) exporting the teaching techniques they have developed relying on the work of our judges. For, though statutory law is increasing in size and complexity, case law is still at the base of common law education. This and the tutorial system (to varying but, by comparison to continental universities, small numbers of students) are the distinctive features of our legal education. The political tradition of the European universities makes the second feature enviable but totally inimitable. But the first feature, coupled with the emergence of English as the new *lingua franca* of the western world, gives the common law a powerful instrument with which to make its own contribution to the transnational set of legal rules which many refer to as the new *jus commune*. Let me say just a few more words as to how this could come about.

Though certain features of the common law judgment may come to be imitated by foreign judges (and others rightly avoided), it would be foolish to predict any wholesale European importation of the model. But the study of English judgments *is* growing as more and more young lawyers from the continent of Europe spend short or longer periods of time in common law universities (the Oxford *Magister Juris* being, perhaps, one of the best illustrations). Though particular solutions of our law may often appeal to foreign lawyers, none, I think, return to their countries believing that our doctrinal analyses or theoretical constructions can ever equal theirs. But I do believe that they return to their base impressed by the common law decision, by its grammatical clarity, by the way it has revealed and discussed the issues that in their country are hidden by legal jargon, and—most importantly—by the way it is used as a tool for imparting further legal know-how. Here, I believe, we score heavily over continental models. And, I hope, we will exploit this strength in the context of many current, private and semi-public schemes aiming to draw up a European law curriculum or, even, design a European law school by becoming involved in such projects rather than rejecting them out of hand. For, behind these projects is not utopian idealism but the growing need *somehow* to harmonise teaching materials and interrelate legal cultures for the world of tomorrow in which lawyers will find themselves being as mobile as their clients. (And this is not mentioning the former eastern European countries which are looking westward for ideas for their legal education and for new laws which they need in order to cope with the new kind of economies that they have adopted.)

The English judgment—and the learning of law through studying the judgment—is, in short, along with our language, one of the two major implements at our disposal in the struggle for shaping the European legal culture of the next century. If we wish to have some impact on this new world we must be prepared to use them."

QUESTIONS

• To what extent do you think Markesinis' belief in the influence of university legal education on a growing awareness of legal cultures and systems is realistic?

• Draft a list of compulsory courses for a European law degree in a European university.

• To what extent do you see your legal education as being "European"?

Pierre Legrand, "How to Compare Now" (1996) 16 L.S. 232 at 233:

"[O]ne can be forgiven for thinking that Europe has become a comparatist's paradise. There is now (if there had not been before) a prominent role for the comparatist to play—a role which is actually so meaningful that her work can help determine whether or not there will, one day, arise a common law of Europe with the obvious implications that can be imagined for every European citizen. In other words, the importance of comparative legal studies extends far beyond matters of theory, cardinal as they are, and raises salient political issues. Comparatists who care about their subject, who value the contribution it can make to the European legal order, should rejoice. But, here lies the paradox I propose to briefly explore: comparatists who care about their subject, who value the intellectual contribution it can make to today's and tomorrow's Europe, *cannot* rejoice because the fascinating opportunities presented within the European Union at this juncture have laid bare the poor quality of comparative work about law as practised over the last decades. The comparative moment has exposed comparative legal studies for what it is: 'obsessively repetitious and sterile', writes an American commentator; 'superficial', remarks a British observer; 'disappointing' notes another American colleague; 'extremely problematical, if not precarious', asserts yet another American critic; 'mediocre', argues a Belgian academic; and marred by 'theoretical poverty', insists a Romanian author. Two questions must inevitably be addressed at this stage. The first matter I wish to examine concerns what comparative legal studies is doing, or not doing, that warrants such fierce criticism. My other preoccupation lies with how, if at all, the situation can be redressed.

To turn to the first point—where has comparative legal studies gone wrong?—I venture to suggest that the principal difficulty lies with comparatists themselves or, more accurately, with *so-called* 'comparatists'. The problem is that comparative work suggests an expanded intellectual range, if not erudition. Moreover, comparative legal studies has an air of the exotic about it. On these accounts, it has, most regrettably, become fashionable. As a result, self-styled 'comparatists' who wish to appear savant and relish exoticism are mushrooming all over Europe. The difficulty is, however, that such 'comparatists' take a very narrow view of the comparative enterprise which they basically reduce to a dry juxtaposition of the rules of one legal culture (or what they regard as such) with those of another. They do not compare, they *contrast*. In the process, of course, they fail to ask the most fundamental questions about the act of comparison in law. . . .

Most reasonably, comparative legal studies is about law. But, who undertakes comparative work equipped with a theory of law? Who has a sense of where the law begins and where it ends? Who has reflected upon what counts as law and what counts as non-law? Where is the boundary to be drawn between the normal and the deviant, the normal and the pathological? For most 'comparatists', the matter is easily resolved. For them, there is no need for a theory. Indeed, some of my colleagues, as they have intimated to me, are plainly irritated by the mere *suggestion* of the need for theory. In short, the law is to be found in legislative texts and judicial decisions. And, it is *that* which 'comparatists' emphatically study. However, their conviction is not the outcome of deep reflection on the ontology of law. Rather, it is the mere extension of what these 'comparatists' were taught about the meaning of law, often by teachers who themselves were not comparatists or theoreticians but were simple technicians of the national law. Let me advocate that things are not so evident and that the meaning of law for comparative legal studies is rather more complex than is usually assumed.

I argue that there is much of the utmost relevance to a deep understanding of a legal order, of an experience of law, that is simply not to be found in legislative texts and in judicial decisions. Let us take a painting. Let us take, specifically, a painting from 1812 by the French painter, Jacques-Louis David, now to be found at the National Gallery of Art, in Washington, DC, depicting Napoleon in his study drafting the French civil code by candlelight. In my view, this painting offers the comparatist at least as much understanding of the French legal mind as any article of the French civil code. In the way this painting illustrates the historically-conditioned relationship between the legislative and judicial powers in France, it tells the comparatist at least as much about the notion of judicial restraint that governs judicial behaviour in France today as does article 5 of the French civil code prohibiting judges from engaging in overt law-making. I claim, in other words, that this painting is just as relevant to French law, is as much a genuine, useful, and intelligible part of French law as any provision of the civil code. This is because the David painting, and others like it, have helped to shape French minds within the legal community, and beyond, at least as much as what any provision of the civil code may have achieved, literally and symbolically. In my view, therefore, the notion of 'French law' *cannot* be reduced to that of 'binding law in France'. French law is much more than a compendium of rules and propositions. Accordingly, to say that the study of French law consists in the study of French legislative texts and judicial decisions is plainly inadequate.

French law is, first and foremost, a cultural phenomenon, not unlike singing or weaving. The reason why the French have the *chansonniers* they have lies somewhere in their history, in their Frenchness, in their identity. Similarly, the reason why the French have the legislative texts or the judicial decisions they have, say, on a matter of sales law, lies somewhere in their history, in their Frenchness, in their identity. And, this is what 'comparatists' do not (want to) see: they stop at the surface, looking merely to the rule or proposition—and they forget about the historical, social, economic, political, cultural, and psychological context which has made that rule or proposition what it is. They forget that law is an indissoluble amalgam of historical, social, economic, political, cultural, and psychological data, a compound, a hybrid, a 'monster', an 'outrageous and heterogeneous collag[e]'. A French statute is not an accident. When the French, or the Spanish, or the Italians, or the Dutch, or the Germans adopt a legislative text, they do something typically French, typically Spanish, typically Italian, typically Dutch, and typically German. The comparatist can make a valuable contribution to a 'deep' understanding of the rule or judicial decision as it is produced by a given legal culture because she can read beyond it and can see the whole in the part. The comparatist can make sense of why things are the way they are, for instance, by relating a given passage from the statute book —which will possibly vanish in a few years from now to be replaced by yet another text—to a socio-historical or socio-cultural context, thereby conferring upon it 'deep meaning'. In other words, to borrow Eörsi's metaphor, the comparatist knows that 'the small piece of steel which happens to be built into the Eiffel Tower could also have been build into Waterloo Bridge', but remains aware that 'in the former case it is *a component part of a tower and not of a bridge*'. Thus, the comparatist enjoys the power to explicate. However, little explication will be found in any survey of current literature in the field of comparative legal studies where the insistence remains firmly on the 'small piece of steel' rather than on the 'small piece of steel *as part of a tower*' or on the 'small piece of steel *as part of a bridge*'.

There is at least one very serious consequence following from this unwillingness or inability to practise what I call 'deep' comparative inquiries which is that of an *illusion* of understanding of the other legal tradition within the European Union. Many civilians, for example, sincerely believe that they understand the common law tradition. A Spanish lawyer, to take an illustration, will look at the Spanish solution to a complex issue of family law, will then consider the English solution to the problem as it arises in England, and, on that basis, will assume that she has an understanding of English law, of the common law way of thinking about the law. In fact, by thinking of law in ways that sever it from its life-world, the 'comparatist' deprives herself of insights of great importance for comparative thought. Specifically, because the 'comparatist' ignores the socio-historical or socio-cultural context, she does not realize that the common law of England operates on the basis of epistemological assumptions which are hidden behind the judicial decision or the statute and which determine them, and that these assumptions distinguish in a fundamental way the common law tradition from the civil law world."

NOTES AND QUESTIONS

- Note that Legrand is asking the question with which we started this book, "what is law?". His argument is that it is only through engaging with that question that we can begin to understand the comparative enterprise.

- Can you imagine gaining a better understanding of law from looking at a painting? What does your answer suggest about the relationship of legal discourse to other "socio-cultural" currents?

- What has this chapter on comparative law taught you about common law reasoning and English legal method?

INDEX

[All references in the index are to page number]